# DERIVATIVE PRODUCTS & PRICING

**The Swaps & Financial Derivatives Library**

**Third Edition Revised**

# DERIVATIVE PRODUCTS & PRICING

## The Swaps & Financial Derivatives Library

## Third Edition Revised

*Satyajit Das*

John Wiley & Sons (Asia) Pte Ltd

Published in 2006 by John Wiley & Sons (Asia) Pte Ltd
2 Clementi Loop, #02-01, Singapore 129809

*Other Wiley Editorial Offices*

John Wiley & Sons, Inc., 111 River Street, Hoboken, NJ 07030, USA
John Wiley & Sons Ltd, The Atrium, Southern Gate, Chichester, PO19 8SQ, England
John Wiley & Sons (Canada) Ltd, 22 Worcester Road, Rexdale, Ontario M9W 1L1, Canada
John Wiley & Sons Australia Ltd, PO Box 174, North Ryde, NSW 2113, Australia
Wiley-VCH, Boschstrasse 12, 69469 Weinheim, Germany

*Library of Congress Cataloging-in-Publication Data*
ISBN-13    978-0-470-82164-0
ISBN-10    0-470-82164-7

Typeset in 10/13 points, Times by Cepha Imaging Pvt, Ltd
Printed in Singapore by Saik Wah Press Pte Ltd
10 9 8 7 6 5 4 3 2 1

# Contents

# Profile

Satyajit Das is an international specialist in the area of financial derivatives, risk management, and capital markets. He presents seminars on financial derivatives/risk management and capital markets in Europe, North America, Asia and Australia. He acts as a consultant to financial institutions and corporations on derivatives and financial products, risk management, and capital markets issues.

Between 1988 and 1994, Mr. Das was the Treasurer of the TNT Group, an Australian based international transport and logistics company with responsibility for the Global Treasury function, including liquidity management, corporate finance, funding/capital markets and financial risk management. Between 1977 and 1987, he worked in banking with the Commonwealth Bank of Australia, Citicorp Investment Bank and Merrill Lynch Capital Markets specialising in fund raising in domestic and international capital markets and risk management/derivative products.

In 1987, Mr. Das was a Visiting Fellow at the Centre for Studies in Money, Banking and Finance, Macquarie University.

Mr. Das is the author of *Swap Financing* (1989, IFR Publishing Limited/The Law Book Company Limited), *Swaps and Financial Derivatives: The Global Reference to Products, Pricing, Applications and Markets* (1994, IFR Publishing Limited/The Law Book Company Limited/McGraw-Hill), *Exotic Options* (1996, IFR Publishing/The Law Book Company), *Structured Notes and Derivative Embedded Securities* (1996, Euromoney Publications) and *Structured Products & Hybrid Securities – Second Edition* (2001, John Wiley & Sons). He is also the major contributor and editor of *The Global Swaps Market* (1991, IFR Publishing Limited), *Financial Derivatives & Risk Management: A Guide to the Mathematics* (1997, Law Book Company/McGraw-Hill/MacMillan Publishing), *Credit Derivatives* (1998, John Wiley & Sons) and *Credit Derivatives & Credit Linked Notes – Second Edition* (2001, John Wiley & Sons). He has published on financial derivatives, corporate finance, treasury and risk management issues in professional and applied finance journals (including Risk, Journal of International Securities Markets, Capital Market Strategies, Euromoney Corporate Finance, Futures & OTC World (FOW), Financial Products and Financial Derivatives & Risk Management).

Mr. Das holds Bachelors' degrees in Commerce (Accounting, Finance and Systems) and Law from the University of New South Wales and a Masters degree in Business Administration from the Australian Graduate School of Management.

# Introduction

## 1 Introduction

The development of derivative instruments has emerged as perhaps the most significant aspect of capital markets in the last 20 years. Exchange-traded and over-the-counter derivatives have radically altered the practice of borrowing, investment and risk management. The changes affect the fundamental nature of financial activities and the manner in which financial transactions are undertaken.

The availability of derivative instruments provides benefits to market participants. These benefits include the ability to manage the price exposure and create exposure synthetically to assets. There are additional benefits in terms of enhancing the liquidity of the underlying asset markets and in reducing the volatility of asset prices. The availability of these types of instruments enhances the attractiveness of investment (both direct and portfolio) in asset markets.

Derivative markets exhibit the following characteristics:

- Derivatives have rapidly expanded to cover a variety of asset classes. Derivatives are available in debt/interest rates, currency, equities and commodities (particularly energy, metal and agricultural markets). Derivatives have also expanded into other markets including previously non-tradeable assets. This includes credit risk, inflation risk, insurance, weather risk, property, bandwidth/telephone minutes, macro-economic indexes and emissions quotas.
- The product range has developed. Non-generic and structured products increasingly complement standard derivative product structures. For example, exotic/non-standard options have emerged as a powerful instrument for risk structuring and transformation.
- The range of market participants is broad. Participants include financial institutions, corporations, investors (both institutional and retail), supra-national entities and governments. A number of dealers (primarily banks and securities dealers) are active in trading in derivative products providing liquidity. Derivatives are used for a wide range of funding, investment and risk management applications. Derivative elements are frequently embedded in structured

investment products for a wide range of investors. Derivatives are available in developed markets and increasingly in emerging markets.

## 2   Background and Objectives of Book

*Derivative Products & Pricing (The Swaps & Financial Derivatives Library) Third Edition Revised* is the successor to *Swaps & Financial Derivatives – Third Edition*. This book was first published in 1989 (as *Swap Financing*). A second edition was published in 1994 (as *Swaps & Financial Derivatives – Second Edition* (in most of the world) and *Swaps & Derivative Financing – Second Edition* (in the USA)). The changes in the market since the publication of the second edition have necessitated this third edition.

*Derivative Products & Pricing – Third Edition Revised* is not an updated version of the previous edition. The book has been completely rewritten and reorganised. Extensive new material has been added to all sections to update existing areas of coverage. In addition, several new chapters covering areas of market development have been included. This has resulted in a significant expansion in the size of the text. *Derivative Products & Pricing – Third Edition Revised* is more than double the size of its predecessor.

*Derivative Products & Pricing – Third Edition Revised* is designed to bring together all aspects of derivative instruments within a cohesive and integrated framework in a single work. The text covers all aspects of derivatives including:
- Design of derivative instruments.
- Pricing, valuation and trading/hedging of derivatives.
- Management of market, credit and other risk associated with derivatives trading.
- Documentation, accounting, taxation and regulatory aspects of derivatives.
- Applications of derivatives.
- Different types of derivative structures including synthetic asset structures using derivatives, exotic options, interest rate/currency, equity, commodity, credit and new derivative markets.
- Impact of electronic trading markets on derivative markets.
- Evolution and prospects of derivative markets.

*Derivative Products & Pricing – Third Edition Revised* is designed to be a comprehensive reference work for practitioners and students of derivative instruments and markets. It covers all aspects of the market. The focus is global, with coverage of exchange-traded markets, over-the-counter markets and all asset classes (including emerging asset classes).

The approach taken is practical rather than theoretical. Derivatives are examined from the different perspective of the investor, the issuer and the dealers/traders in these instruments. The emphasis is on *actual* transactions that are stripped down to analyse and illustrate the dynamics of individual structures and to understand the types of products available.

The book is intended for bankers/dealers, investors and issuers seeking either an understanding of the market or a reference work on the market. The book will also appeal to regulators, analysts, accountants, lawyers and consultants active in advising market participants involved in or contemplating involvement in these products. It will be of use to academics and students interested in derivatives.

The text is structured either to be read through from start to finish or, for the more experienced user of these products, to be used as a reference source where individual sections are read as required.

# 3 Structure of Book

The book is structured as follows:
- **Part 1** describes the role and function of derivatives. It consists of a single chapter. **Chapter 1** sets out the basic building blocks of all derivatives (forward and option contracts).

- **Part 2** outlines the basic derivative instruments. There are two Chapters structured as follows:
  - **Chapter 2** sets out basic structure of exchange-traded products (futures and options on futures contracts).
  - **Chapter 3** sets out the basic structure of over-the-counter products (forwards, options and swaps).

- **Part 3** focuses on the pricing and valuation of derivative instruments. There are 8 chapters structured as follows:
  - **Chapter 4** sets out an overview of risk neutral/arbitrage free pricing approaches.
  - **Chapter 5** sets out a description of interest rates (including zero coupon rates) and yield curve modelling.
  - **Chapter 6** sets out the pricing of forwards and futures contracts.
  - **Chapter 7** sets out the pricing of options using the Black-Scholes-Merton framework and its variations.
  - **Chapter 8** sets out the pricing of interest rate options including interest rate term structure models.

- **Chapter 9** sets out the derivation of volatility and correlation estimates.
- **Chapter 10** sets out the pricing of interest rate and currency swaps.
- **Chapter 11** sets out the determination and behaviour of swap spreads.

- **Part 4** describes derivative trading and portfolio management. There are 5 chapters structured as follows:
  - **Chapter 12** sets out the general approach to derivative trading and portfolio management including the process of integration of risk.
  - **Chapter 13** sets out the hedging of/trading in individual instruments such as interest rate or currency swaps.
  - **Chapter 14** sets out the hedging of/trading in derivative portfolios such as an interest rate portfolio.
  - **Chapter 15** sets out the estimation of option risks such as delta, gamma, vega, theta and rho.
  - **Chapter 16** sets out the technique of dynamic hedging of option positions (delta hedging).

Each chapter includes selected references designed to allow readers to expand their knowledge of individual subjects as required. There is a detailed index to facilitate use of the work as a reference source.

## 4 Contributions

*Derivative Products & Pricing – Third Edition Revised* has a number of inclusions:
- There are Chapters on accounting and taxation aspects of derivatives contributed by PricewaterhouseCoopers. I would like to thank PricewaterhouseCoopers and the individual authors within the firm for contributing the chapters. In particular, I would like to thank John Masters for arranging the participation of PricewaterhouseCoopers. I would also like to thank Jacqui Fawcett/ Jane Docherty for coordinating the project.
- There is a Chapter on documentation of/ legal issues relating to derivatives contributed by Ben Bowden of Linklaters. I would like to thank Ben Bowden for his participation.
- A CD-ROM is included containing RiskMetrics Group's ("RMG") RiskMetrics and CreditMetrics technical documents. I would like to thank RMG, especially Chris Finger, Allan Malz and Lawrence Dunn, for arranging the inclusion of this material.

- A CD-ROM is included containing the analyst range of add-in pricing/valuation software manufactured by the TechHackers division of Unisys Corporation ("Unisys"). The software is available for a trial period for evaluation to readers. The reader must contact Unisys to activate the software. After expiry of the trial period, the reader may purchase the software from Unisys to continue access. I would like to thank Ross Dubin and Arup Khan for arranging Unisys' participation.
- Bloomberg agreed to allow a number of screen shots to be re-printed. I would like to thank Wendy de Cruz, Amanda Dobbie and Craig Davies for their assistance.
- Several authors and organisations agreed to make available material to be reproduced in the Work. The authors and organisations are acknowledged within the text itself.
- Several individuals read portions of the text and offered helpful comments. The individuals are acknowledged within the text itself.

## 5 Publisher

I would like to thank Law Book Company/IFR Publishing/McGraw-Hill for publishing the previous edition of this Book.

I would like to thank the Publishers of this Edition – John Wiley - for agreeing to publish the third edition of the Book. I would like to thank Nick Wallwork for agreeing to publish the work. I would like to thank Karen Noack who copy edited the book. I would also like to thank Hot Fusion for the cover design. I would particularly like to acknowledge the work of Selvamalar Manoharan who worked extremely hard to edit and co-ordinate the publication of the book.

## 6 Personal Acknowledgments

The first edition of *Swaps/Financial Derivatives* published in 1989 was the first book I wrote. Since that time, there have been 10 publishing projects including *Derivative Products & Pricing – Third Edition Revised*. Each of these books has only been possible because of the faith, support and understanding of three individuals – my parents (my father Sukumar Das and my mother Aparna Das) and my friend Jade Novakovic. I would like to thank my parents Sukumar and Aparna Das for their support and encouragement in my work. It is their sacrifices and efforts that made my life and work possible. I would like to thank my friend

Jade Novakovic. Her belief, support, patience and understanding made this Book, like the others before it, possible. My debt to these three people is immeasurable. I can never repay my debt to my mother, father and Jade. This book is dedicated to these three people.

Satyajit Das

This Book is dedicated to

My friend Jade Novakovic

My mother Aparna Das

My father Sukumar Das

# ROLE AND FUNCTION OF DERIVATIVES

# 1
# Financial Derivatives Building Blocks – Forward & Option Contracts

## 1 Overview

Financial derivatives have revolutionised global capital markets. The emergence of substantial markets in forward/futures, options, swaps and other derivative instruments has significantly altered the conduct of borrowing, investment and risk management activities. The significant economic benefits of financial derivatives include:
- Permitting the unbundling of and trading in risks.
- Ability to hedge price risks and synthesise investments with greater efficiency and lower costs.
- Increase liquidity of and trading in financial assets.

The current size of the global derivatives markets is significant. The markets continue to grow strongly. Current trends include the development of products to unbundle new types of risk such as credit and insurance to facilitate trading and hedging in these assets[1].

---

[1] See discussion in Das, Satyajit (2004) Structured Products Volume 2; John Wiley & Sons (Asia), Singapore at Chapter 21 focusing on the development, evolution and prospects for the market.

In this Chapter, the focus is on the concept of financial derivatives, the key features of the two building block derivative instruments (forward and option contracts), and the overall structure of the derivatives markets.

## 2 Financial Derivatives

### 2.1 Concept

Financial derivatives may be defined as a class of instruments the value of which depends upon the value of other assets. In essence, they are instruments that allow trading in the return or price fluctuations of other assets *without the necessity of trading in the assets themselves*. This is achieved by linking the payoffs to holders of derivative instruments to changes in values in the underlying assets.

Investment or trading in any financial institution entails two separate elements:
- Commitment of cash in the case of a purchase of a financial asset or receipt of cash in the case of the sale of a financial asset (referred to as cash or liquidity).
- Exposure to the returns on the asset covering the income paid by the asset and also any fluctuations in the capital price of the asset (referred to collectively as return).

Any financial asset entails a *fixed* combination of attributes. Trading in the asset entails trading the *combination* of the cash and the return profile of the underlying asset. Trading in derivatives on the asset entails trading in the pure return profile of the underlying asset. In effect, financial derivatives on any asset bifurcate the cash component from the return component of the underlying asset. This relationship is depicted in **Exhibit 1.1**.

The ability to separate the return characteristics of any underlying asset is the major driver of derivative activity and applications. The key features of financial derivatives that are based on this feature include:
- Ability to isolate and trade individual risks or return attributes of assets *independent of trading in the underlying asset itself.*
- Ability to construct synthetic assets and liabilities from combinations of cash assets and derivatives.
- Value of all financial derivatives must be based on and bounded by the traded value of the underlying assets on which the derivative is based.

The capacity to use derivatives to unbundle and trade risk attributes separately is illustrated below with an example of risk decomposition.

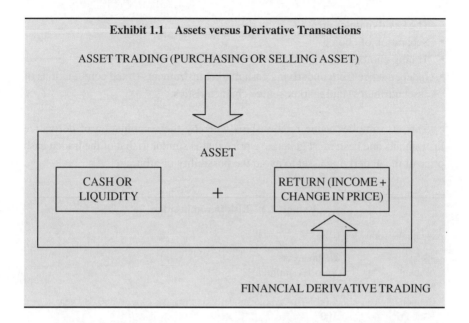

**Exhibit 1.1    Assets versus Derivative Transactions**

ASSET TRADING (PURCHASING OR SELLING ASSET)

ASSET

| CASH OR LIQUIDITY | + | RETURN (INCOME + CHANGE IN PRICE) |

FINANCIAL DERIVATIVE TRADING

## 2.2   Risk Decomposition with Financial Derivatives[2]

Financial derivatives are, in economic terms, contracts for differences. The key element of the contract is the concept of cash settlement of derivative positions with reference to changes in a nominated financial market rate or price. As already noted, from an economic perspective, derivatives allow the isolation of risks or attributes of assets. This allows:

• Separation of management and trading in the price risk of an asset from trading in the asset itself.
• Creation of desired combination of risks through synthetic asset and liability structures.

**Exhibit 1.2** sets out the inherent ability to de-construct conventional financial instruments into a cash investment combined with a series of derivative elements.

---

[2]   For an overview of this process, see Smithson, Charles W. "A LEGO® Approach to Financial Engineering: An Introduction to Forwards, Futures, Swaps and Options" (Winter 1987) Midland Corporate Finance Journal vol 4 no 4 16–28; Smith, Donald J, "The Arithmetic of Financial Engineering" (Winter 1989) Journal of Applied Corporate Finance vol 1 no 4 49–58; Bernasconi, Jean-Luc "Derivatives – Another Look at the Basics" in "Understanding Derivatives" (1994) Prospects Special Issue at 5–11.

The key dynamics are:

- Separation of choice.
- Timing choices.
- Independence from underlying cash market instruments (fixed combinations of asset attributes) and market source characteristics.

This also implies value relationships whereby the combination of derivative instruments and cash must generate a price that is similar to that of the traded cash price of the underlying asset to avoid the possibility of arbitrage.

---

**Exhibit 1.2    Risk Decomposition**

Assume the following bond:

| | |
|---|---|
| Issuer | Company A |
| Amount | Euro 100 million |
| Maturity | 10 Years |
| Coupon | 6.00% pa payable annually on the basis of a 30/360 day year. |
| Issue Price | 100 |
| Yield To Maturity | 6.00% pa (equivalent to 100 bps over the equivalent German Risk Free Rate) |
| Call Option | The bond is redeemable at par after 5 years. |
| Rating | A |

The bond can be decomposed into and reconstructed from a number of distinct and separate transactions. The decomposition set out below is from the perspective of a US$ investor. The individual steps are as follows:

- Invest the US$ equivalent of Euro 100 million (US$110 million assuming a spot exchange rate of Euro 1 = US$1.10) in a risk free 10 year asset yielding floating rate US$ money market rates.
- Enter into a 10 year cross currency floating-to-floating (basis) swap where the investor receives Euro floating rates (Euro-IBOR) and pays US$ floating rates (funded by its US$ investment).
- Enter into a Euro interest rate swap where the investor receives fixed rate Euro for 10 years against payment of Euro floating rates (funded by the cross currency basis swap outlined in Step 2).

The above three steps create a Euro 10 year bond. To add the default risk aspect to the transaction, the following additional transaction is necessitated:

- The investor enters into a default risk swap where it assumes the default risk of Company A in return for receipt of an annual fee.

The effect of this step is to create a *corporate bond* whereby the investor suffers a loss of coupon and/or principal (subject to recovery in bankruptcy) upon the default of the issuer.

The spread over the equivalent risk free rate that derives from the fee received in exchange for entry into the default swap is designed to compensate for the credit risk assumed.

The call option can also be added by the investor entering into a final transaction:

- Enter into a sale of a European exercise receiver swaption whereby the counterparty has the right at its option to receive 6.00% pa I Euro against payment of Euro floating rate for a period of 5 years exercisable in 5 years time.

The individual steps are set out in a diagrammatic form below:

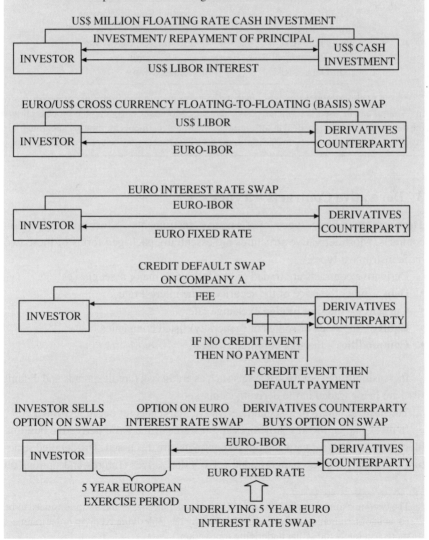

The pricing of the bond should equal the sum of the individual components. This ignores both the transaction costs and additional credit risks assumed in each of the different elements.

The decomposition illustrates the separate and distinct risks that exist in each transaction and the capacity to unbundle the risks and to trade these separately[3]. This is set out in the Table below:

| Risk | Source |
| --- | --- |
| Liquidity | Floating Rate Investment |
| Currency Risk | Cross Currency Basis Swap |
| Interest Rate Risk | Euro Interest Rate Swap |
| Call or Prepayment Risk | Euro Swaption |
| Credit/Default Risk | Default Swap |

The analysis is designed to highlight that derivative instruments in conjunction with a cash investment can be used to replicate physical assets. Moreover, reversing the process allows the de-construction of physical assets into the constituent elements facilitating separate trading in individual risk aspects, including credit risk. This process can be applied to other assets.

## 3   Derivative Contracts – Types

There are two basic types of derivative instruments – forward and option contracts. Most derivative structures are essentially packaged forms of these two basic instrument types.

Derivative contracts are traded on the following major asset classes:
- **Debt** – either the price of the security or the interest rate.
- **Currency** – the spot foreign exchange rate.
- **Equity** – the stock or shares of (generally) listed companies.
- **Commodities** – the spot commodity itself.

Increasingly, newer types of assets such as credit risk (credit spreads and default risk) are being traded in the derivatives markets.

The basic structure of asset and derivative markets is set out in **Exhibit 1.3**.

In this Chapter, the key structures and features of the basic derivative building block instruments (forward and option contracts) are discussed. The detailed structure and features of exchange-traded ("ET") derivatives (futures and options on

---

[3]   The decomposition is a simplification. For example, the swaps and swaptions need to be capable of termination in the event of default by the underlying credit in order to reflect more accurately the actual underlying transaction.

futures contracts) and over-the-counter ("OTC") instruments (such as swaps) are discussed in detail in Chapters 2 and 3.

Exhibit 1.3    Structure of Asset & Derivative Markets

## 4 Forward Contracts

### 4.1 Concept

A forward contract is an agreement under which the purchaser agrees to buy from the forward seller and the seller agrees to sell to the purchaser a specified asset on a specified date at a known price (the forward price). This forward price is specified at the time the contract is entered into.

The key elements of a forward contract are:

- A binding contractual agreement to buy or sell the agreed asset at an agreed future date.
- The agreement *at the time of entry into the forward contract* of the price of the purchase or sale of the asset.
- Deferral of any cash flows relating to the purchase or sale *until the agreed future date* when the buyer delivers cash in return for receipt of the asset. Forward contracts are also capable of being cash settled. Under this method of settlement, the parties to the contract make or receive a payment based on the difference between the actual market price of the underlying asset and the agreed forward price (see discussion below).

The key terms/terminology of forward contracts are summarised in **Exhibit 1.4**. The economic impact of entry into the forward contract is based on the price of the underlying asset at maturity. If at maturity the actual price is higher than the forward price, the forward purchaser will make a gain. If the price is lower, the forward purchaser suffers a loss. For the forward seller, the payoffs are clearly reversed. The mathematical payoffs under the forward contract are set out in **Exhibit 1.5**. The payoff (profit and loss profile) from a bought or sold forward contract is set out in graphic form in **Exhibit 1.6**.

| **Exhibit 1.4**   **Forward Contract – Terms and Terminology** | |
| --- | --- |
| **Term** | **Meaning** |
| Forward Contract | A legally binding agreement between two parties whereby the forward purchaser agrees to purchase or take delivery of and the forward seller agrees to sell or deliver an agreed quantity of a specific asset at an agreed date in the future in return for which the forward purchaser will pay to the forward seller a price per unit of the asset agreed by the parties at the time of entry into the forward contract. |
| Forward Purchaser | The party that agrees to purchase the asset at the forward date at the forward price from the forward seller. |
| Forward Seller | The party that agrees to sell the asset at the forward date at the forward price to the forward purchaser. |
| Long or Bought Position | The position entered into by the forward purchaser. |
| Short or Sold Position | The position entered into by the forward seller. |
| Forward or Maturity or Settlement Date | The maturity or expiry date of the forward contract on which the forward contract must be cash or physically settled. |
| Forward Price | The price for the purchase and sale agreed between the forward purchaser and seller at the time of entry into the forward contract. |
| Physical Settlement | The settlement of the forward contract by delivery of the underlying asset by the forward seller to the forward purchaser in return for receipt of the forward price. |
| Cash Settlement | The settlement of the forward contract between the forward purchaser and seller by payment of the net gain (if any) by the party suffering the loss to the other party to the contract. The net gain is calculated based on the difference between the forward price and the price of the asset at the forward or maturity date of the forward contract. |
| Settlement Price | The price of the asset at the forward or maturity date determined in accordance with an agreed method used to calculate the settlement amount for cash settlement. |

---

### Exhibit 1.5    Forward Contract – Economic Returns

For a forward purchaser, the return is:

$$S_m - F$$

For a forward seller, the return is:

$$F - S_m$$

Where:

$S_m$ = The price of the underlying asset at the maturity of the forward contract
$F$ = The contracted forward price under the forward agreement

---

### Exhibit 1.6    Forward Contract – Payoff Profile

The graph below sets out the payoff profile for a forward contract at maturity where the forward price is $100.

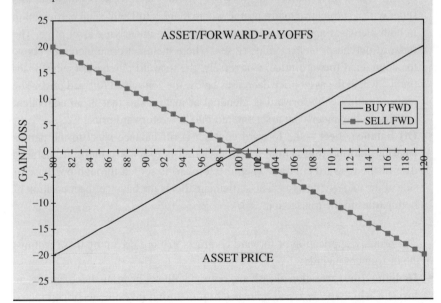

## 4.2   Forward Contracts – Key Features

Key features of forward contracts include:

- **Separation of liquidity from return exposure** – a key element of the forward contract is the ability for a party to acquire price exposure to the underlying asset without the necessity to purchase the asset itself. Payment for the asset is deferred until the maturity of the contract. For the seller, the key element is the ability to divest exposure to the asset price by using a sold forward position to offset a holding in the asset without the necessity of selling the asset itself.

- **Leverage** – the ability to defer case flows until maturity introduces the ability to leverage the price exposure. This is because unlike trading in the asset, trading in the forward contract requires *no immediate commitment of capital*. The leverage inherent in a forward purchase contract is similar to that achieved by purchasing the asset and financing the full (100%) purchase price. Similarly, the leverage inherent in a forward sold contract is similar to that achieved by selling the asset and investing the full (100%) selling price received. It is analogous to a repurchase (repo) contract[4] being used to finance a bought position and invest the proceeds of a short position.

- **Symmetric return profile** – the forward provides both forward purchaser and seller with a symmetric return profile where there is full and equal participation in both increases and decreases in the price of the underlying asset price. The forward purchaser (seller) gains (loses) where the asset price increases above the contracted forward price. Conversely, the forward purchaser (seller) loses (gains) where the asset price decreases below the contracted forward price. The return profile of the forward is identical at maturity to that of an equivalent position in the underlying asset entered into at the forward price.

- **Off balance sheet** – the forward contract is off balance sheet to the parties entering into the transaction. The transaction is executory until the maturity date of the forward contract when the forward is settled through purchase or sale of the underlying asset. The settlement affects the balance sheet position of both parties to the transaction.

The primary application of forward contracts that are driven by these features of the instrument include:

- **Hedging** – the separation of cash and return facilitates hedging. For example, an investor with expected cash inflows (from maturing investments or contracted

---

[4]   See discussion of repurchase contracts and securities borrowing and lending transactions in Chapter 6.

payment receipts) in the future could enter into a forward purchase of a bond to guarantee the return on that future investment. The investor does not require cash payment at the time of entry into the forward purchase but only at the maturity date of the forward contract. This perfectly matches the investor's underlying cash flow position and facilitates the hedge in this case. Similarly, an investor concerned about a short term increase in interest rates may sell forward the bond to neutralise any exposure to increases in interest rates to effectively lock in the selling rate on the bond. This transaction allows the investor to minimise exposure to movements in interest rates without the necessity to sell the bond. The investor might prefer not to sell the security for a number of reasons including regulatory reasons (the bond is required to be held as part of minimum liquidity requirements) or tax or accounting reasons (realisation of gains or losses).

- **Speculation** – the separation of cash and return also makes it highly efficient for traders to use forwards to take positions to benefit from expected price movements. The major benefits include creation of direct price exposure, minimum capital commitment, the off balance sheet nature of the transaction and absence of requirements to use funding lines. These benefits provide traders with enhanced returns from favourable changes in prices but also increases their risk of loss from unfavourable changes in prices[5].

## 4.3   Cash versus Physical Settlement

As noted above, forward contracts are capable of being settled either by physical delivery or by cash settlement. Under physical settlement, the forward seller delivers the asset to the forward purchaser in return for receipt of the agreed forward price. Under cash settlement, the forward purchaser or the forward seller makes payments to the other party to the transaction based on the economic value of the contract. The economic value of the contract is calculated as the difference between the agreed forward price and the actual price of the asset at the forward date. In both cases, the settlement takes place at the maturity date of the forward contract.

In economic terms, the two settlement mechanisms should yield identical results. This is illustrated in **Exhibit 1.7**.

The differences between physical and cash settlement can be summarised as follows:

- **Cash requirement or proceeds** – cash settlement will result in *net* gains and losses being paid between the counterparties to the transaction. In contrast,

---

[5]   The benefits and risk of derivatives in this regard are no different from the benefits of leverage (through borrowing) generally.

physical settlement will require *gross* payment flows equal to the face value of the contract. The net settlement mechanism reduces the credit risk on the transaction. It also increases the efficiency of the transaction from the viewpoint of speculators or traders seeking pure price exposure to price movements in the underlying assets.

---

**Exhibit 1.7   Forward Contract – Cash versus Physical Settlement**

**1.   Assumptions**
Assume that Company A ("A") enters into a forward with Company B ("B") on the following terms:

| | |
|---|---|
| Forward Purchaser | A |
| Forward Seller | B |
| Asset | 100 units of an Asset (S) |
| Forward Date | 1 year from date of entry |
| Forward Price | $100 |

Assume that in 1 year from the date of entry into the forward contract, the actual spot price is either $90 or $115. The mechanics and economic impact of physical and cash settlement are now set out.

**2.   Physical Settlement**
Under physical settlement, irrespective of the final price of the asset, the settlement of the forward contract would be as follows:
- A pays B $10,000 (calculated as $100 × 100 units).
- A receives delivery from B of 100 units of S.

The economic impact of the transaction will depend on the price of S at the time of physical settlement:
- If the price of S is $90 then:
  1. A has purchased 100 units of S at a price of $10,000 which is valued at the current market price ($90) at $9,000 ($90 × 100). This results in A incurring an economic loss of $1,000 (current value of assets ($9,000) minus value paid for assets under forward contract ($10,000)).
  2. B has sold 100 units of S at a price of $10,000 that are valued at the current market price ($90) at $9,000 ($90 × 100). This results in B incurring an economic gain of $1,000 (value received for assets under forward contracts ($10,000) minus current value of assets ($9,000)).
- If the price of S is $115 then:
  1. A has purchased 100 units of S at a price of $10,000 which is valued at the current market price ($115) at $11,500 ($115 × 100). This results in A incurring an economic gain of $1,500 (current value of assets ($11,500) minus value paid for assets under forward contract ($10,000)).
  2. B has sold 100 units of S at a price of $10,000 that are valued at the current market price ($115) at $11,500 ($115 × 100). This results in B incurring an economic loss

of $1,000 (value received for assets under forward contracts ($10,000) minus current value of assets ($11,500)).

It is important to note that the gain or loss in this case is *unrealised* (that is non-cash at the time of settlement of the forward contract). Closure of the position (sale of the assets acquired by A or repurchase of the assets sold by B) would result in realisation of the gain or loss.

### 3. Cash Settlement

Under cash settlement, a settlement amount must be calculated and then paid by the party suffering the loss to the other party to the contract. The settlement amount is determined as follows:

For a forward purchaser, the cash settlement is:     $(S_m - F) \times N$
For a forward seller, the cash settlement is:     $(F - S_m) \times N$

Where:

$S_m$ = The price of the underlying asset at the maturity of the forward contract
$F$ = The contracted forward price under the forward contract
$N$ = The number of units of the asset underlying the forward contract

Cash settlement in this case would be as follows:
- If the price of S is $90 then the settlement amount is $1,000 (calculated as [($100 − $90) × 100] and is payable by the forward purchaser to the forward seller.
- If the price of S is $115 then the settlement amount is $1,500 (calculated as [($100 − $115) × 100] and is payable by the forward seller to the forward purchaser.

The determination of the settlement amount requires the determination of a settlement price at the forward or maturity date. The mechanism for establishing this price will be agreed between the parties to the forward contract. Typically this will take the form of establishing the market price at the maturity date of the forward contract. It should be noted that the relevant date for setting the price will effectively be the pricing date for *value* at the maturity of the forward contracts. For example, where the asset market trades for value in two days (for example foreign exchange) then the settlement price will be determined two days prior to the maturity of the forward contract. The typical source for the settlement price will be:
- In more liquid asset markets, the closing market price or the price at an agreed time on the relevant day derived from a mutually acceptable screen/information service or industry publication.
- In less liquid asset markets, the price might be derived using a dealer poll mechanism where leading dealers in the relevant asset are sampled to provide quotes that are then averaged to establish the settlement price.

It is important to note that the gain or loss in this case is *realised* (that is, it is cash at the time of settlement of the forward contract). The position of both A and B as purchaser or seller in respect of the asset remains unaltered, with A not receiving ownership of and B not disposing of its position (if any) in the asset.

**4. Equivalency of Cash Versus Physical Settlement**

Despite their differences, the cash and physical settlement are economically equivalent. This can be shown as follows:

- In the case of physical settlement, if A sells the asset after acquisition or if B purchases the asset from the market to delivery into the forward, then the gains and losses generated would be identical to those under the cash settlement option. This is shown below:
  1. If the asset price is $90 then A could, following settlement of the forward contract, sell its position at the market price and would realise a loss of $1,000 [market price ($90) – price paid under forward ($100) × number of units of the asset (100)]. B would realise a gain of $1,000 if it bought the assets in the market to delivery into the forward contract [price received under forward ($100) – market price ($90) × number of units of the asset (100)]. An alternative manner of conceptualising B's position would look at the difference between sales proceeds received had it sold its position into the market ($9,000) and the proceeds received under the forward contract ($10,000).
  2. If the asset price is $115 then A could, following settlement of the forward contract, sell its position at the market price and would realise a gain of $1,500 [market price ($115) – price paid under forward ($100) × number of units of the asset (100)]. B would realise a loss of $1,500 if it bought the assets in the market to deliver into the forward contract [price received under forward ($100) – market price ($115) × number of units of the asset (100)]. An alternative manner of conceptualising B's position would look at the difference between sales proceeds received had it sold its position into the market ($11,500) and the proceeds received under the forward contract ($10,000).
- In the case of cash settlement, both A and B could by entering into transactions involving the underlying asset that would in combination with the cash settlement result in an economically identical position for both parties. This is shown below:
  1. If the market price is $90 then A would purchase the assets in the market for $9,000 ($90 × 100) which together with the cash settlement paid of $1,000 would result in A having ownership of 100 units of the asset for a total consideration of $10,000 ($9,000+$1,000) and an average price per asset of $100 ($10,000/100). B would sell its asset in the market for $9,000 ($90 × 100) which together with the cash settlement received of $1,000 would result in B having sold 100 units of the asset for a total consideration of $10,000 ($9,000 + $1,000) and an average price per asset of $100 ($10,000/100).
  2. If the market price is $115 then A would purchase the assets in the market for $11,500 ($115 × 100) which together with the cash settlement received of $1,500 would result in A having ownership of 100 units of the asset for a total consideration of $10,000 ($11,500 – $1,500) and an average price per asset of $100 ($10,000/100). B would sell its asset in the market for $11,500 ($115 × 100) which together with the cash settlement paid of $1,500 would result in B having sold 100 units of the asset for a total consideration of $10,000 ($11,500 – $1,500) and an average price per asset of $100 ($10,000/100).

- **Receipt or disposal of assets** – physical settlement entails both access to and disposal of the underlying asset (for the seller) and receipt of the asset (for the purchaser). Cash settlement does not entail either access to or transfer of the ownership of the underlying asset. This means that the physical settlement mechanism is problematic where either seller does not own or cannot acquire the asset and also where the purchaser cannot take delivery (for example because of legal restrictions on ownership). Physical settlement inherently places an implicit limit on the volume of trading in the forward contracts on the asset. It would not be possible to trade higher volumes than the amount that can be satisfied by physical assets available for delivery. Cash settlement in contrast does not assure either party of access to or ability to dispose of the underlying assets.
- **Basis risk** – physical settlement does not entail any basis risk as the transaction is concluded by the actual delivery or purchase of the underlying asset for the agreed price. However, cash settlement introduces basis risk into the transaction. This risk derives from the fact that the *settlement price* used to calculate the cash settlement amount and the actual price at which either purchaser or seller transacts to respectively buy and sell the asset may differ. These differences may be driven by a variety of factors including:
  1. *Liquidity* – the absence of sufficient liquidity or trading volumes in the cash market may mean that the actual price at which the transactions are completed differs significantly from those used to determine the cash settlement amount.
  2. *Price source* – the price source used to determine the cash settlement amount may be different to that used to transact the actual purchases and sale transactions.
  3. *Timing discrepancies* – the time at which the cash settlement price is derived may vary from that at which the actual transactions are undertaken.

  The presence of basis risk is significant in that it inherently reduces the efficiency of the use of the forward contract to either hedge or assume risk of market price changes.
- **Need for settlement price** – physical settlement does not require a price source to determine the settlement amount. However, cash settlement inherently requires a price source to enable calculation of the settlement amount. Determination of the settlement price does not create significant problems in developed and liquid markets. However, in less developed market or markets that lack sufficient liquidity to enable determination of a transparent and reliable market price, the determination of a settlement price is more difficult and creates additional complexity.

## 5  Option Contracts

### 5.1  Concept

A forward contract entails an obligation to buy or sell the stated asset. In contrast, an option contract gives the purchaser the *right* but not the *obligation* to purchase or sell an asset. A call option gives the purchaser the right to purchase an asset. A put option gives the purchaser the right to sell the asset. In both cases, the purchase price or selling price is specified at the time the option contract is originated. This price is usually referred to as the strike or exercise price.

The key elements of an option contract are:

- A binding agreement between the parties where the seller of the option agrees to sell to (call option) or buy from (put option) the option buyer at the buyer's option the relevant asset on a specified day in return for payment or receipt of an agreed sum (the strike price).
- The price for any purchase or sale is agreed *at the time of entry into the option contract*.
- The option is capable of being exercised by the buyer on a single date known as the expiry date in the case of a European option and on any date on or before the expiry date in the case of an American option.
- The option buyer pays a fee (the option premium) to the option seller in return for receiving the right to buy or sell the asset at the strike price on or by the exercise date.
- As with forward contracts (see discussion above), the option can be settled by physical delivery or cash settled. Settlement is only necessitated where the option is exercised by the buyer. Physical delivery entails the actual delivery of the asset in return for payment of the strike price. Cash settlement entails the payment by the seller of the difference between the market price of the asset at the time of exercise of the option and the strike price[6].

The key terms/terminology of option contracts are summarised in **Exhibit 1.8**.

The economic consequences of the option contract are based on the prevailing price of the underlying asset at the time of exercise of the option. The purchaser of a call option contract has the right to purchase the asset at the exercise price. If the price of the asset rises above the exercise price then the value of the option

---

[6]  As discussed in detail above in relation to forward contracts, there is little economic difference between the cash settlement and physical delivery settlement of an option. It is also feasible to replicate a cash settlement from a physical settlement and vice versa by trading in the underlying asset.

also increases. However, because the option contract does not obligate the purchaser to purchase the asset if the price falls, the value of the option does not fall by the same amount as the price declines. A similar but reverse logic applies in the case of put options.

The pay-off profile for the party that has sold (written or granted) the call or put option is different. In contrast to the purchaser of the option, the seller of the option has the obligation to perform. For example, if the holder of the option elects to exercise the option to purchase the asset then the seller of the option is obligated to sell the asset.

The option premium affects the outcomes. The payment of the premium reduces the gains to the buyer where the option is exercised and results in a loss equal to the option premium amount where the option is not exercised. The premium received by the option seller represents a gain where the option is not exercised and serves to reduce the loss sustained where the option is exercised against the seller.

The mathematical payoffs under option contracts are set out in **Exhibit 1.9**. The payoffs from a purchase or sale of a call and a put option are set out in **Exhibit 1.10**.

| Exhibit 1.8 | Option Contract – Terms And Terminology |
|---|---|
| **Term** | **Meaning** |
| Option Contract | A legally binding agreement between two parties where the option purchaser has the right but not the obligation to either purchase or sell and the option seller agrees to sell or purchase an agreed quantity of a specific asset at an agreed price (the strike price) on or by an agreed date in the future. |
| Call Option | An option contract that gives the option purchaser the right but not the obligation to purchase the asset from the option seller. |
| Put Option | An option contract that gives the option purchaser the right but not the obligation to sell the asset to the option seller. |
| Option Purchaser | The party which in exchange for the payment of the option premium obtains the right to purchase the asset from or sell the asset to the option seller. |
| Option Seller (Grantor or Writer) | The party that in exchange for receipt of the option premium provides the option purchaser with the right to purchase from or sell the asset to the option seller. |
| Strike (Exercise) Price | The agreed price at which any future purchase or sale of the asset is to take place. |

| Term | Meaning |
|------|---------|
| Exercise or Expiry Date | The agreed date on or before which the option purchaser will exercise the right to either purchase the asset from or sell the asset to the option seller. |
| European Exercise | An option that is only capable of exercise on the exercise date. |
| American Exercise | An option that is capable of exercise at any time on or before the exercise date. |
| Option Premium or Fee | The amount paid by the option purchaser to the option seller usually at the commencement of the transaction in return for entry into the option contract. |
| Physical Settlement | The settlement of the option contract by the option purchaser by purchase from or delivery to the option seller of the underlying asset in return for payment or receipt of the strike price. |
| Cash Settlement | The settlement of the option contract between the option purchaser and option seller by payment of the net gain (if any) by the option seller to the option purchaser. The net gain is calculated based on the difference between the strike price and the price of the asset at the exercise date of the option contract. |
| Settlement Price | The price of the asset at the exercise date determined in accordance with an agreed method used to calculate the settlement amount for cash settlement. |

---

**Exhibit 1.9    Option Contract – Economic Returns**

For a call option, the economic return is:
- For the call option purchaser:    Maximum of $[O - P; S_m - K - P]$
- For the call option seller:    Minimum of $[P; K - S_m + P]$

For a put option, the economic return is:
- For the put option purchaser:    Maximum of $[O - P; K - S_m - P]$
- For the put option seller:    Minimum of $[P; S_m - K + P]$

Where:

$S_m$ = The price of the underlying asset at the maturity of the option contract
$K$ = The strike price under the option contract
$P$ = The option premium

**Exhibit 1.10    Option Contract – Payoff Profile**

The graphs below set out the payoff for the buyer and seller of a call and put option respectively where the strike price of the underlying option is $100 and the option premium is $5.

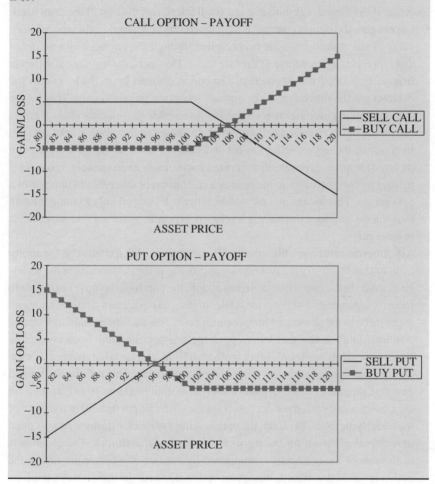

## 5.2    Option Contracts – Key Features

Key features of option contracts include:

- **Separation of liquidity from return exposure** – as with forward contracts, option contracts convey the ability for the option purchaser to acquire price exposure (through a call option) or shed exposure (through a put option) to the underlying asset without the necessity to purchase or sell the asset itself. In the case of a call option, payment for the asset (the strike price) is deferred until the maturity of the contract. In the case of a put option, the seller does not receive any proceeds until maturity. The only amount paid at commencement of the transaction is the option premium that is a small fraction of the cost of the asset itself.

- **Leverage** – the option contract is also inherently leveraged in that the full face value of the underlying asset is controlled through the payment of a premium that represents a percentage of the face value. However, the leverage is different from that under a forward contract. The option contract limits the loss under the contract for the purchaser to the amount of option premium paid. This means that the option purchaser is leveraged to *favourable* movements in asset prices (increases in the case of a call option or decreases in the case of a put option). In contrast, the option seller has limited gains (limited to the option premium received) but has exposure to unlimited losses from unfavourable movements in asset prices (increases in the case of a call option or decreases in the case of a put option). This means that the option seller is leveraged only to unfavourable movements but does not have a leveraged exposure to favourable movements in asset prices.

- **Asymmetric return profile** – the key element of the option contract is the ability of an option buyer to get *asymmetric* exposure to price fluctuations in the underlying asset. In the case of the call (put) option, the purchaser achieves exposure to increases (decreases) in the price while limiting exposure to a decline (increase) in the price to the amount of the premium paid. This facilitates hedging existing positions in a manner that leaves open the prospect of gains from favourable price movements while providing protection from adverse price changes. For the option seller, options create a more complex exposure. This reflects the limited gain (the premium received) against the risk of unlimited loss from increases (in the case of a call option) or decreases (in the case of a put option) in the price of the underlying asset. In effect, the option seller provides *insurance* against price movements in return for the payment of the option premium. The economics of the sale of the option are complicated by the fact of whether the sale of the option is naked or covered. Where the option is naked, the option seller is taking a position on expected future movements in the underlying asset price. Where the option is covered, the option seller has a position in the underlying asset that acts to hedge the option itself. For example, the seller of a call (put) option may have an existing holding (short position) in the asset. This means that in the case of exercise the seller delivers its existing asset in the case of a call (purchases the asset in the case of a put) effectively closing out its underlying asset position. This has the effect of limiting the opportunity of further gains from price increases (for the call) or decreases (for the put) on the underlying asset position. The above outcome is different to that under a forward contract where the exposure is *symmetric*. This means that the forward buyer or seller is exposed to *both* increases and decreases in the price of the underlying asset.

- **Off balance sheet** – the option contract, like the forward contract, is off balance sheet to the parties entering into the transaction. The transaction is executory until the exercise date of the option contract when the option is settled through purchase or sale of the underlying asset. The settlement affects the balance sheet position of both parties to the transaction at the time of exercise.

The applications of option contracts are driven by these features of the instrument and include:

- **Hedging** – the separation of cash and return facilitates hedging with option contracts. This is similar to forward contracts. However, the asymmetric nature of the contract payoffs creates different types of hedges. Hedges involving options provide protection to the party seeking to hedge from unfavourable asset price movements while allowing continued participation in favourable price movements. Option contracts therefore overcome an inherent problem of forward contract based hedges. The forward hedge always assures the hedger of a known price. This dictates that the party hedging benefits where asset prices change unfavourably but forgoes the opportunity to gain from the underlying position where asset prices change favourably. For example, an investor with expected cash inflows (from maturing investments or contracted payment receipts) in the future could enter into the purchase of a call option on a bond to guarantee the *minimum* return (maximum price) on that future investment. The investor is able to benefit from an increase in returns on the bond (higher rates). If the price of the bond falls then the call option would not be exercised and the bond purchased at the lower price in the market. The investor does not require cash payments at the time of entry into the option other than the payment of the option premium but only at the exercise date of the option contract. This perfectly matches the investor's underlying cash flow position and facilitates the hedge in this case. Similarly, an investor concerned about a short term increase in interest rates may buy a put option on the bond to neutralise any exposure to increases in interest rates to effectively lock in a maximum selling rate (minimum price) on the bond. The investor still has the potential to benefit from falls in interest rates (increases in bond prices). If the bond price increases then the investor would not exercise the option and would sell the bond at the higher market price. This transaction allows the investor to minimise exposure to movements in interest rates without the necessity to sell the bond.

- **Structured Protection** – the capacity to adjust the strike price of the option enables the exact nature of risk hedged or assumed to be structured in accordance with the price expectations of the party entering into the transaction. For example, out-of-the-money options (options where the strike price is either well above the current forward asset price in the case of a call or well below the current forward asset price in the case of a put) may be utilised to provide protection against large unexpected movements in the asset price. The lower cost of these options means that they provide low cost insurance or risk protection against large unexpected price changes. This capacity to structure the degree of protection against changes in asset prices is not available with forward contracts.
- **Speculation** – the separation of cash and return also makes it highly efficient for traders to use options to take positions to benefit expected price movements. As with forward contracts, the use of options to take positions provides traders with enhanced returns from the inherent leverage. However, unlike forwards, purchased options can be used to enable price exposure to be created with limited downside risk (the loss is limited to the option premium paid). Alternatively, the sale of options can be used to position against the lack of volatility in asset price. In this situation, the option premium received is kept with no requirement to make payments under the option contract as the asset price does not move significantly, thereby not triggering exercise. In this way, sales of options allow speculators to monetise the lack of volatility or price movement in an asset market.
- **Yield Enhancement** – the sale of options against an underlying asset position can be used to enhance the yield on the underlying holding of the asset. For example, an investor holding an asset can sell call options against the asset position. The premium received will increase the return. The risk assumed by the investor is that in case of an increase in the asset price, the bond will be called away by the option purchaser. This will have the impact of causing the investor to underperform the asset market. The investor may be willing to accept that risk on the basis that it would have sold the bond if the price increased in any case (a targeted sale) or it does not expect the price to rise above the option strike level.

# 6   Economic Relationship between Forwards & Options

Put-call parity[7] defines the relationship between the price of a European call option and a European put option with the same exercise price and time to expiration.

---

[7]  Put-call parity defines a fundamental pricing relationship of option contracts. For a detailed discussion, see Chapter 7.

Put-call parity can be stated as follows:

$$P_{ce} + PV(K) = P_{pe} + S$$

Where

$P_{ce}$ = Price of an European call option

$PV(K)$ = Present value of the Strike Price of the option (K)

$P_{pe}$ = Price of an European put option

$S$ = Price of the asset in the spot market

This implies that buying a call and investing PV of K is identical to buying a put and buying the asset[8].

The put-call parity condition can be restated as follows:

- Synthetic call (reversal)   $P_{ce} = P_{pe} + S - PV(K)$

  This implies that a call option position can be replicated by purchasing the asset, purchasing a put option and borrowing the present value of the strike price of the option.

- Synthetic put (conversion)   $P_{pe} = P_{ce} - S + PV(K)$

  This implies that a put option position can be replicated by short selling the asset, purchasing a call option and investing the present value of the strike price of the option.

- Bought or long asset/forward   $S = P_{ce} - P_{pe} + PV(K)$

  This implies that a bought forward can be replicated by purchasing a call option and selling a put option. A bought asset position can be created by combining the option positions with an investment of the present value of the strike price of the option.

- Sold or short asset/forward   $-S = P_{pe} - P_{ce} - PV(K)$

  This implies that a sold forward can be replicated by purchasing a put option and selling a call option. A sold asset position can be created by combining the option positions with a borrowing of the present value of the strike price of the option.

The put-call parity relationship and the synthetic asset and option positions can be illustrated diagrammatically as in **Exhibit 1.11**. The major implication of

---

[8]   Where the underlying asset pays out a cash flow of C, put-call parity can be restated as: $P_{ce} + PV(K + C) = P_{pe} + S$. It is important to note that the put-call parity theorem is only valid for European options. Synthetic positions for American options are not always pure. For example, if S decreases and an American put is exercised, then you would lose the difference between K and S immediately, not at the forward date. This means that put-call parity for American options can be stated as follows: $P_{ca} - S + PV(K) < P_{pa} < P_{ca} - S + K$.

**Exhibit 1.11    Put-Call Parity and Synthetic Positions**

The graphs below set out the payoffs of a synthetic call option, a synthetic put option and synthetic asset or forward positions. The positions are constructed using call and put options where the strike price of the underlying option is $100 and the option premium is $5.

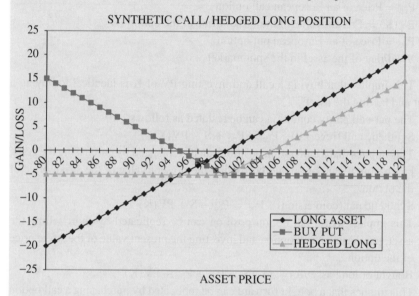

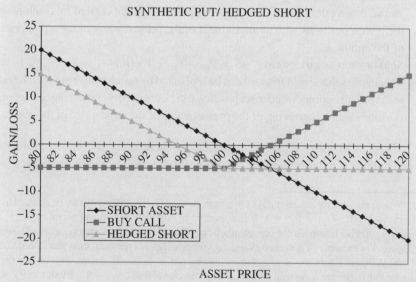

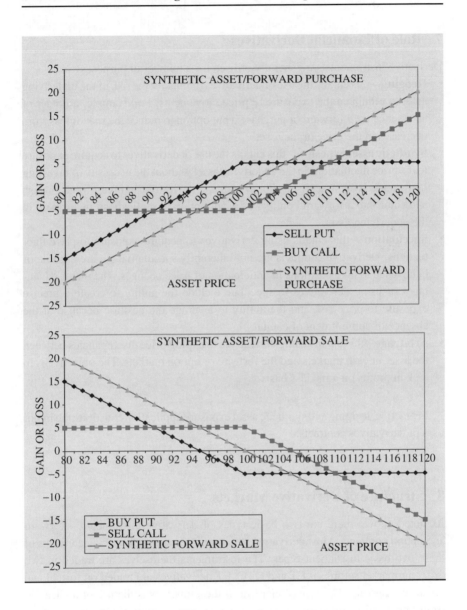

put-call parity is that it effectively allows the creation of assets from combinations of derivatives and synthetic construction of derivative positions. This means effectively that similar *economic* outcomes can be created from different combinations of instruments.

# 7   Role of Financial Derivatives

Derivative instruments are generally utilised for a number of purposes:

- **Hedging** – this entails the use of derivatives to transfer the risk of the underlying asset to eliminate the exposure to price movements. For example, a holder of an asset can sell forward or purchase a put option to reduce the risk of loss from decreases in the price of the asset.
- **Synthetic asset exposure** – this entails the use of derivatives to acquire exposure to the price fluctuations in the underlying asset without the necessity of investing in the underlying asset itself. For example, an investor can invest funds in cash and enter into a forward contract or a call option to replicate an investment in the underlying asset.
- **Speculation** – this entails using derivatives to acquire exposure to price fluctuations. Derivative contracts are not inherently speculative but are capable of being used to take positions in anticipation of price changes. The major advantages of using derivatives to speculate include the ability to create a precise exposure to price risk and the ability to leverage the position because of the absence of commitment of capital.
- **Arbitrage** – this entails using derivatives to exploit price discrepancies between the asset or cash markets and the forward or option markets. The objective is to lock in profits on a riskless basis.

In practice, hedging and synthetic asset exposure application constitute the major uses of derivatives contracts.

# 8   Structure of Derivative Markets

As noted above, there are two basic types of derivative instruments – forward and option contracts. Most derivative structures are essentially packaged forms of these two basic instrument types. The instruments themselves are traded in two different market settings – ET and OTC. ET derivatives are traded on formal and organised markets. The central element of these markets is the use of a Clearing House mechanism and cash-based collateral system to minimise the credit risk of participants. In contrast, OTC derivatives are traded as bilateral contracts between counterparties who assume full credit risk on each other in respect of performance under the terms of the contracts. The detailed structure of ET derivative markets is discussed in Chapter 2. The detailed structure of OTC derivatives markets is discussed in Chapter 3.

In practice, ET and OTC markets are complementary. **Exhibit 1.12** sets out a comparison of the key features and differences between the two markets. **Exhibit 1.13** sets out the overall structure of the markets and relationship between the ET and OTC market. The structure outlined highlights how derivative dealers often utilise the ET traded markets to hedge risks incurred in trading with clients (the OTC market) and/or other dealers (the inter-bank markets).

The range of derivatives available is summarised in **Exhibit 1.14**. Credit derivatives are not included in the Table as they are difficult to classify as purely forward and option contracts.

| Exhibit 1.12 | Comparison between Exchange-Traded and Over-the-Counter Markets | |
|---|---|---|
| **Dimension** | **Exchange-Traded Markets** | **Over-the-Counter Markets** |
| Underlying Asset | Standardised | Customised |
| Contract Maturity | Fixed | Customised |
| Credit Risk | Clearing house | Counterparty |
| Pricing | Transparent | Less transparent |
| Liquidity | Higher | Lower |
| Cash requirements | Uncertain | Deferred till maturity |
| Delivery | Restricted | Negotiated |

**Exhibit 1.13   Structural Relationship between Exchange-Traded and Over-the-Counter Derivatives Markets**

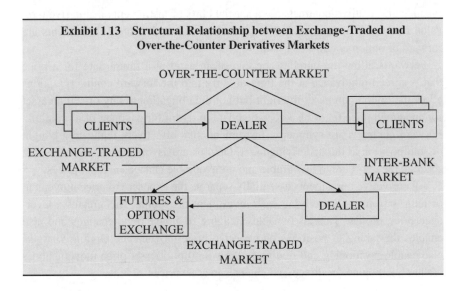

| Exhibit 1.14 | Range of Derivative Instruments | | | |
| --- | --- | --- | --- | --- |
| **Product Type** | **Interest Rates** | **Currency** | **Equity** | **Commodity** |
| **Forward Contract** | | | | |
| Exchange-Traded | • Interest Rate Futures | • Currency Futures | • Equity Index Futures<br>• Single Stock Futures | • Commodity Futures |
| Over-the-Counter | • FRAs<br>• Interest Rate Swaps | • Currency Forwards<br>• Currency Swaps | • Equity Forwards/ Swaps | • Commodity Forwards/ Swaps |
| **Option Contract** | | | | |
| Exchange-Traded | • Options on Interest Rate Futures | • Options on Currency Futures | • Options on Equity Index Futures<br>• Stock Options | • Options on Commodity Futures |
| Over-the-Counter | • Cap/Floors<br>• Options on Interest Rate Swaps/ Swaptions | • Currency Options | • Equity Options/ Equity Warrants | • Commodity Options |

## 9  Summary

Financial derivatives contracts are a special class of instruments that derive their value from other instruments. The primary forms of derivative instruments are forward or option contracts.

Forwards allow the purchase or sale of an asset at a future date for a price that is agreed in advance at the time of entry into the forward contract. Options allow the option purchaser the right but not the obligation to buy or sell an asset for an agreed price on or by a specified date in return for payment of a premium. Forward contracts are symmetric instruments that effectively replicate a bought or sold position in the underlying asset. Options are asymmetric instruments that separate the exposure to favourable and unfavourable changes in asset prices.

All derivative instruments essentially separate the exposure to price movement or returns from the underlying cash investment or receipt. This creates a leveraged price profile. This also enables hedging of future price changes and also enables the taking of positions on expected price movements. Option contracts also enable positioning and trading in the volatility of asset price movements as well as positioning for directional changes in asset prices.

# DERIVATIVE INSTRUMENTS

# 2
# Exchange-Traded Products – Futures & Options on Futures Contracts

## 1 Overview

Financial derivatives consist of two primary types of instruments – forward contracts and option contracts. These instruments constitute the building blocks or key elements of all derivative products. Derivative instruments are traded in two different market contexts – exchange traded ("ET") and over-the-counter ("OTC") markets. In this Chapter, ET traded products are discussed. OTC products are discussed in Chapter 3.

The structure of the Chapter is as follows:

- The two primary ET products (futures contracts and options on futures contracts) are described.
- The institutional structure of markets (trading mechanics, system of deposits and margins, settlement process including delivery) is considered.
- Individual ET products on interest rates, currency, equity and commodity are examined.
- ET product innovations (such as FLEX options, Rolling Spot contracts etc) are analysed.

# 2  Exchange-Traded Products[1]

## 2.1  Futures Contracts

A futures contract is defined as a binding obligation enforceable at law to buy or sell a stated quantity of a specified asset on a specified date in the future at a predetermined price.

From an *economic* perspective, a futures contract is identical to a forward contract in that a futures contract also obligates its owner to purchase or sell a specified asset at a specified forward price on the contract maturity date. The economic returns and payoffs on a futures position are identical to that under a forward contract.

Technically, a futures contract is a forward contract that is settled daily with a new forward contract being written simultaneously (this relates to the inherent mark-to-market mechanism utilised in ET markets in the form of the margining of positions).

The major difference between futures and forward contracts relates to the institutional structure of the two markets:

- Trading in futures contracts must be undertaken on an exchange through member firms in accordance with the rules established by the exchange itself.
- In the case of futures contracts, the underlying asset to be traded is specified by the exchange. The contract specifications will specify the details of the underlying asset (including quality), the value of the contract, the price quotation mechanism, the basis for settlement and the trading dates for the contract. This is intended to create a homogenous asset through a process of standardisation. This is designed to facilitate trading and enhance liquidity. Examples of the specification of futures contracts are discussed later in this Chapter.
- The use of a Clearing House that acts as a counterparty to each transaction. This is designed to reduce the credit or default risk.
- Contracts must be settled according to the rules of the exchange by either cash settlement (the usual settlement mechanism) or delivery (not permitted for some contracts and infrequently used when available).

---

[1]  For an overview of futures and options markets, see Fitzgerald, M. Desmond (with Lubochinsky, Catherine and Thomas, Patrick) (1993) Financial Futures – Second Edition; Euromoney Books, London; Hull, John C. (1995) Introduction to Futures and Options Markets; Prentice Hall, Englewood Cliffs; Powers, Mark J. and Vogel, David (1984) Inside the Financial Futures Market – Second Edition; John Wiley & Sons, New York; Schwarz, Edward W., Hill, Joanne M. and Schneeweis, Thomas (1986) Financial Futures: Fundamentals, Strategies and Applications; Irwin, Homewood, Illinois.

Futures contracts on interest rates (short term interest rates, (varying maturity) government bonds, swap rates), currencies, equity (primarily equity indexes) and commodities are available.

## 2.2   Options on Futures Contracts

Options in ET markets are generally options on the underlying futures contract. Exercise of the option results in the trader taking a purchased or sold position in the underlying futures contract.

Options on the asset and options on futures contracts can co-exist. However, one is usually sufficient. In the limiting case, an option on a futures contract (the specifications of which allow settlement by physical delivery) which expires on the day the futures contract is delivered allows settlement immediately, providing the actual physical asset. Consequently, no useful distinctions would exist between an option on the assets and an option on the futures.

The major features of options on futures contracts and futures contract include:

- The underlying commodity in futures options is standardised.
- The supply of futures options is not constrained by the deliverable supply of specific assets.
- The futures price is instantly available during trading hours and widely disseminated.
- Options on futures are traded at the same physical location as futures, facilitating both trading and exercise of the option (which is easily accomplished by book entry).
- The underlying asset is standardised, listed and traded at organised exchanges, enhancing trading and liquidity.
- Options on the futures contract are guaranteed by the Clearing House, which specifies deposit and variation margin requirements minimising counterparty risk.

## 3   Institutional Structure of Exchange-Traded Markets

### 3.1   Overview

The key differences between OTC forwards/options and ET futures/options on futures contracts relate to the institutional structure of futures markets. The most significant of these institutional arrangements include:

- The structure of trading and the role of the Clearing House.

- The system of initial margins/deposits and margin calls.
- The settlement of open contracts.

## 3.2  Futures and Option Exchanges

As noted above, ET traded products are traded exclusively on futures and options exchanges. Futures and options exchanges are established with the following objectives:
- Design and list specific futures and options contracts for trading.
- Allow traders to enter into transactions that must be entered into through member firms of the exchange.
- Enable the settlement and clearing of futures and options contracts entered into on the exchange.
- Control, supervise and regulate trading on the exchange to maintain an efficient and transparent market.
- Develop a secure and sound framework for trading futures and options contracts on the exchange.

Some of the major futures and options exchanges in the world are set out in **Exhibit 2.1**.

| Exhibit 2.1    Major Futures and Options Exchanges | | |
|---|---|---|
| **Exchange** | **Country** | **Major Contracts** |
| **North America** | | |
| Chicago Board of Trade ("CBOT") | USA | US Treasury Bond; 10 year Note; 5 year Treasury Note |
| Chicago Board Options Exchange ("CBOE") | USA | Equity options |
| Chicago Mercantile Exchange ("CME") | USA | 3 month Eurodollar; 90 day Treasury bill; S & P 500; Euro, yen etc currency contracts; Rolling Spot Currency |
| Montreal Exchange ("ME") | Canada | Canadian Government bond; Canadian Bankers Acceptance |
| New York Mercantile Exchange ("NYMEX") | USA | Light Sweet Crude; Heating Oil; Natural Gas |
| **South America** | | |
| Bolsa de Mercuradorias & Futuros ("BMF") | Brazil | Stock index; 1 day Interest Rate Futures |

**UK/Europe**

| | | |
|---|---|---|
| Eurex (joint venture between Deutsche Terminborse ("DTB") of Germany and Swiss Options & Financial Futures ("SOFFEX") of Switzerland) | Germany/ Switzerland | Euro-ibor; Euro Bund; Euro Bobl; Euro Schatz; DAX index; Swiss market index |
| European Options Exchange ("EOE") | Netherlands | Options on Dutch government bonds and EOE stock index |
| International Petroleum Exchange ("IPE") | UK | Brent crude; Gas oil |
| London International Financial Futures Exchange ("LIFFE") | UK | Euro-ibor; 3 month Sterling; Long Gilt; FTSE stock index futures |
| London Metals Exchange ("LME") | UK | Aluminium; Copper; Zinc; Tin; Nickel; Lead |
| Marche a Terme International de France ("Matif") | France | CAC stock index; Euro French (notionnel) bonds |
| Mercato Italiano Futures ("MIF") | Italy | Euro Italian government bonds (BTP) |
| Meff Renta Variable ("Meff RV") and Meff Renta Fija ("Meff RF") | Spain | Ibex stock index |
| Stockholm Options Market ("OM") | Sweden | OMX stock index; Swedish government bond |

**Asia-Pacific**

| | | |
|---|---|---|
| Hong Kong Futures Exchange ("HKFE") | Hong Kong | Hang Seng stock index; HIBOR |
| Korea Stock Exchange ("KSE") | Korea | Korean (KOSPI) stock index futures contracts; Korean Government bonds |
| Kuala Lumpur Options & Financial Futures Exchange ("KLOFFE") | Malaysia | Malaysian stock index; KLIBOR rate |
| Sydney Futures Exchange ("SFE") | Australia | 90 day bank bill interest rate; 3 and 10 year Commonwealth Treasury bonds; All Ordinaries share price index |
| Singapore International Monetary Exchange ("SIMEX") | Singapore | 3 month Eurodollar; 3 month Euroyen; Nikkei 225 stock index; SIBOR, S$ government bonds |
| Tokyo International Financial Futures Exchange ("TIFFE") | Japan | 3 month Euroyen rates |
| Tokyo Stock Exchange ("TSE") | Japan | 10 year and 20 year Japanese Government bond futures; TOPIX stock index |

**Africa**

| | | |
|---|---|---|
| South African Futures Exchange ("SAFEX") | South Africa | JSE stock index; South African government bonds |

The exchanges are experiencing a period of rapid change. This manifests itself in a number of ways including:

- A number of exchanges have merged with other exchanges or entered into joint ventures.
- Certain contracts can be traded, settled and cleared on exchanges other than the home exchange on which the contract is actually listed.
- International trading systems, that enable contracts to be traded after the home exchange has closed, allowing 24 hour trading.
- The emergence of electronic trading markets[2] that compete with traditional exchanges.

The changes to exchanges are driven primarily by economies of scale/scope in trading and exchange operation, increasing internationalisation of financial markets/trading activities and changes in trading/clearing technology.

Most futures exchanges are owned by the member futures broking firms who act as agents to execute transactions on the exchange. However, some exchanges have completed or are contemplating de-mutualisation of their ownership. This would entail public ownership with stock listed on established stock exchanges. Historically, the brokers who owned exchanges ranged from small operators to large multi-national operations. Over time, ownership of exchanges has generally become more concentrated among dealers (large banks and investment banks). These institutions, through their futures broking operations together with some large global broking houses, dominate trading on exchanges.

Membership of a futures and options exchange can usually be at various levels[3]:

- **Full membership** (also referred to as a floor/clearing member or a Futures Commission Merchant ("FCM")) – this allows both trading and clearing of contracts on the exchange.
- **Local membership** (also known as Floor Traders or Scalpers) – this allows a trader to trade on his or her own behalf or for members under the sponsorship of a full clearing member. The local member cannot clear his or her trades directly but must clear trades through a clearing member.
- **Associate membership** – this allows trading and clearing contracts through a full clearing member but at reduced commission rates in those markets to which their membership relates[4].

---

[2]  See Das, Satyajit (2004) Structured Products Volume 2; John Wiley & Sons (Asia), Singapore at Chapter 20.

[3]  The precise structure and arrangements vary between different exchanges.

[4]  Not all exchanges have an Associate Membership system.

The regulations, reporting and capital requirements vary significantly between the different types of membership. The most onerous requirements are applicable to full members.

Futures exchanges are regulated by specific legislation that is administered by an appointed administrative body. For example, in the US, the Commodity Futures Trading Commission ("CFTC") is responsible for the regulation of futures and options markets. There are equivalent bodies in each jurisdiction.

## 3.3   Mechanics of Trading

Trading in futures markets is conducted on the organised exchange. The process of trading is set out in **Exhibit 2.2**.

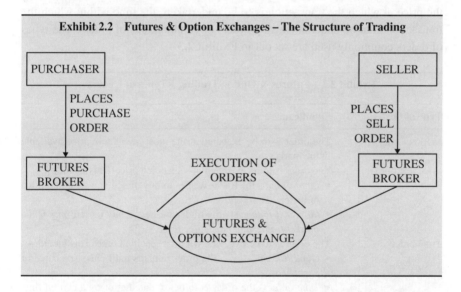

**Exhibit 2.2    Futures & Option Exchanges – The Structure of Trading**

The purchaser and the seller place their orders with their futures brokers. The futures brokers must be members of the exchange. The futures brokers execute the transaction using the trading mechanism in place at the relevant exchange. This can be either by open outcry or (increasingly) by electronic trading systems that automatically match buy and sell orders.

Various types of orders are commonly used to trade. While a relatively elementary aspect of futures and option trading, an understanding of the various elements is essential. The order will usually be given by the trader wishing to undertake a transaction with a futures broker. The order directs the broker to take certain actions on behalf of the trader. The instructions will cover several key elements including:

- Exchange.
- Contract involved.
- Delivery month relevant.
- Number of contracts to be traded.
- Nature of the transaction – buy or sell.
- Price at which the contracts are to be traded.
- Time in which the order will remain open for execution.
- Any conditionality (if appropriate) on the order.

The numerous dimensions dictate that a wide variety of orders are theoretically feasible. In practice, the major types of orders focus on specifically structuring the price at which the transaction is to be undertaken, the time within which the transaction is to be undertaken, stop orders or combinations of orders. The types of orders commonly used are set out in **Exhibit 2.3**[5].

| Exhibit 2.3 Futures & Option Trading – Types of Orders | |
| --- | --- |
| **Type of Order** | **Significance** |
| Market Order | The order is to be executed at the most favourable price available in the market. |
| Price limit orders | The order is to be executed at a specified price. This includes: <br> • *Limit order* – the trader wishes to buy or sell at a specified price or better. <br> • *Market if touched* – the trader wishes to buy or sell *only if the market trades at a particular price*. |
| Time order | The order is to be executed within a specified time. This includes: <br> • *Good till cancelled* – the order remains until either executed or cancelled. <br> • *Time order* – the order is to be executed at or by a certain time unless cancelled. <br> • *Market at open or close* – the order is to be executed during the official opening or closing of the market on the day the order is placed. <br> • *Fill or kill (or quick) order* – the order must be executed immediately at the price stated or is cancelled. |

[5] The list of order types is not meant to be comprehensive but provide an illustration of the major types of orders used.

| Stop order | The order is used to close out an existing position upon market moves to lock in gains or limit losses. |
| Spreads or Combinations | This entails a simultaneous purchase and sale of one contract on two different delivery months or two separate contracts. |

The role of the futures broker includes:

- Educate the trader regarding trading futures and options contracts, including the specifics of the contract, settlement and clearing of the contract and risks of trading.
- Providing advice to the trader regarding market conditions and also the intended trade (if required by the trader).
- Execute trading orders on behalf of the trader.
- Arrange to post required deposits and subsequent variation margins (see discussion below) required by the exchange.
- Liaise with the exchange (if required) in relation to positions entered into by the trader.

The futures broker is compensated for its activities by the payment of brokerage fees. These are charged on per contract traded basis (usually charged on a round turn (a combined buy and sale of a contract)). In addition, the trader pays clearing and exchange fees.

## 3.4   Role of the Clearing House[6]

Following execution of the futures transactions, the Clearing House of the futures exchange is interposed between the buyer and seller of the futures contract. This process is set out in **Exhibit 2.4**.

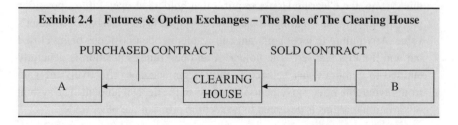

**Exhibit 2.4   Futures & Option Exchanges – The Role of The Clearing House**

PURCHASED CONTRACT      SOLD CONTRACT

A  ←  CLEARING HOUSE  ←  B

---

[6] For a discussion of current developments in Clearing Houses, see Saunderson, Emily "Future's in the Clearing" (July 1988) Risk 33–36; "The Clearing Houses" (July 1999) A Supplement to Futures & OTC World.

The role of the Clearing House is effectively to guarantee each contract. The mechanism utilised is for the Clearing House to assume the opposite side to each contract. Through this mechanism the Clearing House stands between the principal trading partners, although it does not itself engage in any floor trading activity. The Clearing House also ensures that both the purchaser and seller of a futures contract comply with the offset, margin and delivery procedures of the futures exchange.

The Clearing House is separate from the Exchange itself. It may be owned by the Exchange members or the clearing function performed by a specialised clearing company (such as ICCH or OCC). The Clearing House is structured with high credit quality[7]. This is achieved by a combination of capital/reserves, common bond/members' guarantee, insurance, compensation funds/deposits and credit lines.

## 3.5   System of Margins/Deposits

Central to the operation of a futures market is the credit enhancement function performed by the Clearing House that guarantees the settlement of the contract and the performance of the counterparties. The Clearing House operates a system of deposits (also known as initial margins) and variation margins to reduce its credit exposure to the purchaser or seller of the futures contract.

The process required is as follows:

- **Initial margin (deposit)** – every trader is required to pay an initial margin (an agreed % of contract value) when it enters into a transaction. The deposit is returned (with interest) upon settlement of the contract. The initial margin acts as a performance bond.
- **Variation margins** – the system of variation margins operates in addition to the initial margin. It requires that adverse price movements (that is unrealised losses) in the value of contracts must be covered daily by further deposits. Under this system, the Clearing House requires that holders of open futures positions place funds with the Clearing House each day equal to the change in a contract's value. Any failure to meet a margin call results in open positions being closed out and the loss realised. The holder of an open futures position is generally entitled to withdraw any balance in the margin account (effectively the gain from favourable price movements) in excess of the deposit amount. The system of variation margins is designed to protect the profit of the other trader.

---

[7]   For a discussion of the credit quality of Clearing Houses see (June 1995) Credit Risks of Clearing Houses at Futures and Options Exchanges; Moody's Investors Service, Global Credit Research, New York.

The system of initial and variation margins is designed to enhance the credit risk of each counterparty to the transaction and protect them from the risk of default by the counterparty to the transaction. This system of credit enhancement is predicated on two essential levels of protection:

- **Variation margins** – the requirement of daily variation margins means that at the commencement of trading, all open contracts are effectively marked to market. This means that there is no amount owing and therefore no credit exposure between the buyer and seller of the futures contracts. It is equivalent to the contract having been closed and reopened at the current market price.
- **Initial margin** – the initial margin is available to cover losses where a party to a contract fails to meet a variation margin call. The Clearing House as noted above will close out the position where a variation margin call is not met. In this case, the Clearing House will draw upon the initial margin to cover the loss incurred. In this way, the initial margin acts as a performance bond.

Minimum levels for initial and variation margin arrangements are prescribed by the Clearing House. These are subject to change based on the price volatility in the underlying asset markets[8]. Individual futures clearing brokers (through which individual purchasers and sellers must transact and clear positions) may require greater margins than the minimum levels specified by the Clearing House based on the credit standing of the counterparty. Initial and variation margins must be paid in cash or alternatively using high grade securities (usually government securities) as collateral.

The system of initial and variation margins creates a degree of cash flow uncertainty in trading in futures. However, it permits trading in significant volumes with minimal credit exposure.

The initial and variation margin system applicable to options on futures contracts is similar to that applicable to futures contracts. The major issue with options on futures contracts is that the premium is not paid to the option seller at the start of the transaction. The position is different from that in the OTC market where the premium is paid to the seller at the time of entry into the transaction. In an option on a futures contract, the parties post initial margins and option contracts are marked to market daily. The option writer may withdraw profits as they accrue as the premium on the option reduces. The full premium cannot be posted to the writer until the option position is closed out or until it expires unexercised.

---

[8]    For a discussion on the methodology of establishing margins using the SPAN and TIMS system, see Martin, John "Managing Risk: Exchange Style" (November 1995) Financial Derivatives & Risk Management Issue 3 64–74.

The operation of the system of deposits and margins is described in detail in **Exhibit 2.5**.

---

**Exhibit 2.5   Futures & Options Exchanges – Margining of Contracts**

**1.   Assumptions**

Assume that Counterparty A (A) enters into a futures contract on an Exchange on 15 January 2003. The underlying contract is trading at a price of 94.00 (for a contract value of $940,000). Each point on the futures contract (.01) is valued at $25. A enters into 1 bought contract. The process of initial and variation margins is illustrated below.

**2.   Initial Margin**

Assume the initial margin requirement is set at 2.00% of contract value. Initial margins bear interest at the overnight cash rate (currently 5.00% pa).

A will be required to lodge an initial deposit equivalent to $18,800 ($940,000 × 2%) with its clearing broker.

**3.   Variation Margin**

Assume that the contract closes on 15 January 2003 at 93.50. This means that on a mark-to-market basis A's position is registering a loss of $1,250 ($25 × 50 (94.00 – 93.50)). This means that in addition to the initial margin, A must lodge $1,250 (a total of $20,050) with its clearing broker.

Assume that the contract closes on 16 January 2003 at 93.25. This means that the position is registering a loss of $625 ($25 × 25 (93.50 – 93.25)). A must therefore lodge an additional $625 in variation margins with its clearing broker. This means that it has lodged margins totalling $20,675 with the exchange.

**4.   Contract Settlement**

Assume on 17 January 2003, A closes out its position by selling the contract for 93.40. This realised a loss of $1,500 on the position ($25 × 60 (94.00 – 93.40)). The Clearing House matches the bought and sold position and cancels the contracts. The Clearing House deducts the loss from A's margin account and pays the remainder to A through its clearing broker, together with interest on its initial margin. The amount paid back to A is $19,175 (the margin balance of $20,675 less the loss $1,500).

**5.   Failure to Make Variation Margin**

Assume that the position is open and the contract closes on 17 January 2003 at 92.60. This results in a margin call on A of $1,625 ($25 × 65 (93.25 – 92.60)). In the event that A fails to meet the margin call, the Clearing House would undertake the following actions:

1. Close out A's position realising a loss of $3,500 ($25 × 140 (94.00 – 92.60)). The Clearing House deducts the loss from A's margin account and pays the remainder to A through its clearing broker. The amount paid back to A is $17,175 (the margin balance of $20,675 less the loss $3,500).
2. The Clearing House acts on its own behalf to buy 1 sell contract at the market price of 92.60 to hedge its unhedged position resulting from the default of A. [In practice, the calculation of loss on A's position would be based on the price at which the Clearing House was able to re-establish its fully hedged position.]

In cases where the initial and variation margin system proves insufficient to cover losses, the Clearing House will resort to a variety of capital resources to cover the losses incurred. These will include:

- Insurance policies.
- Capital or reserves.
- Resort to members to cover losses (this is typically in the form of a common bond whereby every member firm guarantees other firms such that if a clearing firm fails, then the exchange has the ability to ask the remaining clearing members for any residual loss amount after liquidating all the defaulting firm's assets).

The interposition of the Clearing House has the effect of eliminating credit exposure to the counterparty to the futures/options contract. The clearing mechanism substitutes credit exposure to the Clearing House for credit exposure to the counterparty. The Clearing House seeks to manage its credit risk through the system of initial and variation margins.

## 3.6   Closing Positions

Open futures or options on futures position may be closed out both at or prior to maturity of the contract. Prior to maturity, a party may liquidate a position by entering into an offsetting contract; that is buying or selling the contract previously sold or bought. The Clearing House cancels the two contracts against each other with a cash settlement being effected equalling the difference between the bought and sold contract prices. This is feasible because of the interposition of the Clearing House and also the standardisation of the underlying asset. There is no necessity for a trader to locate the counterparty to the original transaction. The trader's position is with the Clearing House and entry into an equal but opposite position enables the contract to be effectively and contractually closed out. **Exhibit 2.6** sets out the process of closing out a position prior to maturity.

## 3.7   Settlement of Futures Positions

As noted above, open futures position may be closed out both at or prior to maturity of the contract. At maturity, the contract may be settled at maturity in one of two ways:

- **Cash settlement** – under this alternative the contract is cash settled against the closing price or final settlement price if it has not already been closed out by the trader.

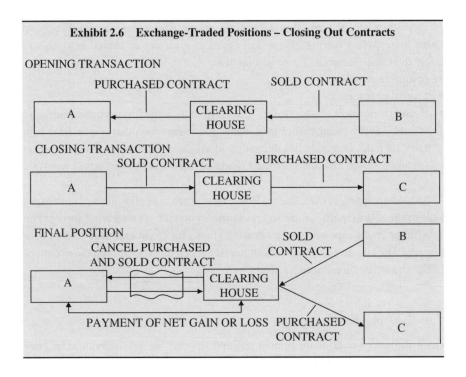

**Exhibit 2.6    Exchange-Traded Positions – Closing Out Contracts**

• **Delivery** – under this alternative the trader may close out its position by delivery (where the contract specifications permit).

Under the delivery option, a party may physically deliver (where he has sold) or take delivery of (where he has bought) the underlying asset at the contract expiry date. Delivery is at the option of seller and governed by the rules established by the Exchange and Clearing House.

As noted above, futures contracts are not usually closed out by delivery even when the contract specification permits settlement by delivery.

## 3.8    Exchange-for-Physical ("EFP") Transactions

An alternative approach to settlement is an Exchange for Physical ("EFP"). EFP settlement allows two parties to a futures contract to exchange a position in a futures contract for a position in a physical asset at an agreed date. The concept is designed to make a contract that is non-deliverable capable of settlement by delivery, or where the contract is deliverable, making non-deliverable assets (that is assets not consistent with the contract specifications) deliverable. The major application of

EFP transactions is the hedging of specific underlying assets, basis trading and the reduction/elimination of basis risk in hedging.

The basic structure of EFP transactions requires the rules of the exchange to allow exchange of a futures position in any market and in any delivery month for the actual underlying asset at any time up to the last delivery day in that commodity. The arrangement allows delivery of assets that vary from the asset specified by the contract subject to the rules of the exchange and the agreement of the buyer and seller.

The EFP transaction is subject to certain pre-requisites:

- The parties to the transaction must hold futures positions.
- The seller involved must be in possession of the actual asset and a simultaneous cash transaction for an amount equal to the contract unit must occur when a futures contract is traded through the EFP.

The typical process is as follows:

- The parties to the contract arrange a mutually satisfactory cash transaction to take place at a forward date. This is similar to a forward contract. However, the price at which the forward contract will take place is agreed to be at a premium or discount to the futures price in an agreed delivery month.
- The parties would then separately hedge their respective positions by entering into futures contracts.
- The parties must then inform the exchange through their futures broker of the specific terms of the transaction and the EFP nature of the trade. The exchange will then advise the market that the EFP trade has been entered into.
- The transaction will be cleared and settled in a manner consistent with the normal practice of the relevant Clearing House. Actual delivery will take place consistent with the terms of the original agreement between the parties.

# 4   Exchange-Traded Products – Types

ET products are available on all asset classes. The principal examples include:

- **Interest rates/debt prices** – this consists of futures contracts and options on futures contracts on either short term interest rates or on medium to long term bonds.
- **Currencies** – this consists of futures and options on futures contracts on foreign currencies.
- **Equity** – this consists of futures and options on futures contracts on primarily equity indexes.

- **Commodities** – this consists of futures and options on futures contracts on individual commodities (precious metals, other metals, energy/oil products and agricultural products ("softs")) and commodity indexes.

Certain innovations have also been introduced in recent years. These include FLEX (flexible) options, the Rolling Spot Currency Futures Contract and equity futures and options on futures contracts on individual stocks. In the following Sections, futures and options on futures contracts on interest rates/debt prices, currencies, equity and commodities are discussed. Contract specifications are subject to change. Potential users of any contract should contact the relevant exchange and/or their futures brokers to obtain up-to-date contract specifications.[9]

## 5 Interest Rate Products

### 5.1 Types

As noted above, the primary ET interest rate products consists of futures contracts and options on futures contracts on the following underlying assets:

- **Short term interest rates** – these are generally contracts on inter-bank indicator rates for a duration of usually around 3 months (although some shorter term contracts are available). Contracts on short term government or risk free rates are relatively rare though there are some examples of these types of contracts.
- **Bond prices** – these are generally contracts on bond prices (indirectly in term interest rates). Contracts are usually on government bonds. Contracts on non-government risk are relatively rare. Contracts are usually on medium to long maturity bonds (ranging from 3 to 30 years).
  Example of interest rate futures contracts are set out in **Exhibit 2.7**.

### 5.2 Short Term/Money Market Interest Rate Futures Contracts

#### 5.2.1 Structure of Short Term Interest Rate Futures Contracts

Short term or money market interest rate futures and options on futures contracts are generally contracts on inter-bank indicator rates for a duration of usually around 3 months. Examples of typical contract specifications are set out in **Exhibit 2.8**.

---

[9] In the following Sections, some futures/options on futures contract specifications are included. Contract specifications are subject to change. Potential users of any contract should contact the relevant exchange and/or their futures brokers to obtain up-to-date contract specifications.

**Exhibit 2.7    Interest Rate Futures & Options on Futures Contracts**

**1.   Short Term Interest Rates**

| Jurisdiction | Exchange | Contracts |
|---|---|---|
| USA | CBOT | 30 day Federal Funds US$5 million |
| | CME | 1 month Eurodollar US$3 million |
| | CME | 3 month Eurodollar US$1 million |
| Europe | LIFFE/EUREX/MATIF | 3 month Euro-ibor Euro 1 million |
| Japan | CME/TIFFE/SIMEX | 3 month Euro Yen 100 million |
| UK | LIFFE | Sterling LIBOR GBP 500,000 |
| Switzerland | LIFFE | 3 month Euro Swiss SFR 1 million |
| Australia | SFE | 3 month A$ Bank Bill Rate A$500,000 |
| Hong Kong | HIBOR | 3 month HK$ HIBOR HK$ [5,000,000] |
| Canada | ME | 3 month Canadian Bankers Acceptances C$1 million |
| Brazil | BMF | 1 day Interest Rate Real 100,000 |

**2.   Bond Price & Rates**

| Jurisdiction | Exchange | Contracts |
|---|---|---|
| USA | CBOT | 5 year Treasury Note US$100,000 |
| | CBOT | 10 year Treasury Note US$100,000 |
| | CBOT | Treasury Bonds US$100,000 |
| Europe | EUREX | 2 year German Euro Government Bonds Euro 100,000 (Euro Schatz) |
| | EUREX | 5 year German Euro Government Bonds Euro 100,000 (Euro BOBL) |
| | EUREX | 10 year German Euro Government Bonds Euro 100,000 (Euro Bund) |
| Japan | TSE | 10 year Japanese Government Bond Yen 100 million |
| UK | LIFFE | Long Gilt GBP 50,000 |
| Australia | SFE | 3 year Commonwealth Treasury Bonds A$ 100,000 |
| | SFE | 10 year Commonwealth Treasury Bonds A$ 100,000 |
| Canada | ME | 10 year Canadian Government Bond C$ 100,000 |
| Korea | Korea Futures Exchange | 3 year Korean Government Bond Won 1,000,000 |

**Exhibit 2.8    Short Term Interest Rate Futures & Options on Futures Contracts-Specifications**

**3 Month Eurodollar – Futures Contract**

| | |
|---|---|
| Unit Of Trading | $1,000,000 |
| Contract Maturity | March, June, September, December |
| Delivery/Exercise/Expiry Day | Last trading day – cash settled |
| Last Trading Day | 11.00 AM 2 London business days before the third Wednesday of the contract month |
| Quotation | 100.00 minus rate of interest |
| Minimum Price Movement | 0.0025 (0.25 bps or $6.25 per contract) for spot month contract; 0.05 (0.5 bps or $12.50 per contract) for all other contracts |
| Final Settlement Price | Based on the British Bankers' Association Interest Settlement Rate |

**3 Month Eurodollar – Option on Futures Contract**

| | |
|---|---|
| Unit Of Trading | 1 IMM 3 month Eurodollar futures contract |
| Strike Prices | 0.25 (25 bps) intervals e.g. 95.00, 95.25 |
| Contract Maturity | Quarterly option; the nearest 8 March quarterly expiration months |
| Delivery/Exercise/Expiry Day | An option may be exercised until 19:00 (Chicago time) on any business day the option is traded. |
| Last Trading Day | Immediately preceding the 3rd Wednesday of contract month. |
| Quotation/ Minimum Price Movement | Index points and basis points similar to the 3 Month Eurodollar contract |
| Minimum Price Movement | 0.01/0.005 respectively |

The primary features of short term interest rate contracts include:

- The underlying contract is usually an inter-bank rate. This reflects the predominant role of the inter-bank money market in channelling short term funds flows. It also reflects the importance of the 3 month inter-bank rate as a key money market benchmark rate. Important variations on this basic structure include:
    1. *Shorter underlying maturity* – the 1 month US$ Federal Funds rate and 1 month Eurodollar contract have both enjoyed success. The BMF's 1 day interest rate contract has also been successful.
    2. *Differential credit risk* – the major example of this is the 3 month US$ Treasury Bill contract.

- The value of an individual point (0.01) is fixed. However, a 1 bps movement in interest rates does *not* result in a $25 price change per $1,000,000 face value 3 month security *for all yield levels*. It creates significant problems in terms of convexity and efficiency of hedging[10]. While this format is common, it is not mandatory. For example, the Australian dollar 3 month Bank Bill Futures Contract and the option on that futures contract traded on the Sydney Futures Exchange specify a variable tick point value that is calculated as the actual basis point value *at the current interest rate level*[11].
- The contracts are typically cash settled. Settlement by delivery is difficult because of the difficulty of exercising into the underlying cash deposit. However, there are examples of deliverable short term interest rate futures products. For example, the Australian dollar 3 month Bank Bill Futures Contract and the option on that futures contract are both capable of settlement by delivery. The contracts require delivery of eligible short term bank securities (bankers' acceptance accepted by or certificates of deposit issued by designated banks).
- The final settlement price is determined by a dealer sampling or polling process.

### 5.2.2 Pricing/Quotations of Short Term Futures Contracts

Short term interest rate futures contracts are typically quoted in price terms as 100.00 minus rate of interest. For example, 6.75% is quoted as 93.25 (100 – 6.75).

**Exhibit 2.9** sets out sample quotations for short term futures contracts (the 3 month Eurodollar Contract is used as an example). The quotations provide a range of information including:

- **Contract month** – the maturity date for trading of the specific contract.
- **Open** – the opening price of the contract on the particular trading day.
- **High** – the highest trading price attained on the trading day.
- **Low** – the lowest trading price attained on the trading day.
- **Settlement Price & Change** – the settlement price of the contract on the particular trading day and the change in price from the previous trading day.
- **Settlement Yield & Change** – the settlement yield (calculated as 100.00 minus the settlement price) and the change in yield from the previous trading day.
- **Open Interest** – the number of contracts open for each contract month.

---

[10] See discussion in Chapters 5, 6 and 13.

[11] The 3 month Bank Bill Rate is the benchmark inter-bank rate in the Australian domestic market. The rate is for 3 month Bankers Acceptances (accepted by designated banks). For discussion of convexity, see discussion in Chapters 5, 6 and 13.

- **Estimated volume** – the estimated volume of contracts traded on the relevant trading day.
- **Open Interest** – the total number of contracts open as at the end of the trading day.

For options, the quotation displays the following additional information:
- **Strike Prices** – the strike price of the options (in price terms).
- **Premiums** – the premium for the options are displayed in price terms.

Key aspects of the structure of the short term markets are as follows:
- The concentration of liquidity at the shorter contract maturities is evident. The 3 month Eurodollar contract is exceptional in that it has significant liquidity at longer contract maturity dates. In contrast, most other short term interest rate futures contracts lack liquidity beyond 18–24 months from the spot month.
- The options traded are variable and appear to be concentrated at particular strike prices.

---

**Exhibit 2.9    Short Term Interest Rate Futures & Options on Futures Contract – Price Quotations**

**3 Month Eurodollar Futures Contract**

```
   Send        Help
 <HELP> for explanation.                                      DGT4 Govt   CTM
 Enter # <GO> to scroll contracts.    Run EXCH for realtime authorized exchanges
 Session:D                    Contract  Table
 90DAY  EURO$ FUTR                          Delayed monitoring enabled
 Exchange Web Page        Pricing Date:  1/ 8/02    Price Display: 2
 Chicago Mercantile Exchange     Delayed prices      ---LATEST AVAILABLE---        2
 Grey date = options trading                         4412118 857729 Previous
 ↓ Scroll     Last   1Change  Time High 2 Low    Tic OpenInt TotVol  Close
 1)EDF2 Jan02 98.1475s -.0075 Close 98.160 98.140  228   53288   5412 98.1550
 2)EDG2 Feb02 98.140s  unch  Close 98.145 98.130  250   27591   3715 98.140
 3)EDH2 Mar02 98.060s  -.010 Close 98.080 98.045  974  683930  97361 98.070
 4)EDJ2 Apr02 97.930s  -.010 Close 97.930 97.930   39    1816      5 97.940
 5)EDK2 May02 97.830s  -.010 Close 97.830 97.830   32     329      5 97.840
 6)EDM2 Jun02 97.665s  -.025 Close 97.710 97.630 1896  620571 148770 97.690
 7)EDU2 Sep02 97.155s  -.020 Close 97.200 97.115 2421  592715 208735 97.175
 8)EDZ2 Dec02 96.545s  -.010 Close 96.600 96.505 2332  579426 122030 96.555
 9)EDH3 Mar03 95.930s  unch  Close 95.990 95.890 1608  365918  70590 95.930
 10)EDM3 Jun03 95.325s  +.020 Close 95.390 95.270 1183  220889  51189 95.305
 11)EDU3 Sep03 94.830s  +.025 Close 94.890 94.780  886  195598  41911 94.805
 12)EDZ3 Dec03 94.450s  +.015 Close 94.520 94.410  592  143042  24156 94.435
 13)EDH4 Mar04 94.285s  +.010 Close 94.340 94.235  143  127696  12113 94.270
 14)EDM4 Jun04 94.120s  +.005 Close 94.175 94.080  119  110753  12167 94.115
 15)EDU4 Sep04 93.985s  unch  Close 94.055 93.935  117   99452  11065 93.985
 16)EDZ4 Dec04 93.815s  -.005 Close 93.885 93.770   94   63663   8731 93.820
 17)EDH5 Mar05 93.795s  -.010 Close 93.860 93.775   76   64279   7024 93.805
 Australia 61 2 9777 8600    Brazil 5511 3048 4500    Europe 44 20 7330 7500    Germany 49 69 920410
 Hong Kong 852 2977 6000 Japan 81 3 3201 8900 Singapore 65 212 1000 U.S. 1 212 318 2000  Copyright 2002 Bloomberg L.P.
                                                               I522-112-1 09-Jan-02  9:08:55
 Bloomberg
 PROFESSIONAL
```

```
  Send        Help   ▮
<HELP> for explanation.                        DGT4 Govt   CTM
Enter # <GO> to scroll contracts.   Run EXCH for realtime authorized exchanges
Session:▮            Contract Table
90DAY EURO$ FUTR                      Delayed monitoring enabled
Exchange Web Page         Pricing Date: ▮1/ 8/02▮  Price Display: ▮
Chicago Mercantile Exchange     Delayed prices      --LATEST AVAILABLE---        ▮
Grey date = options trading                        4412118 857725 Previous
↓ Scroll    Last  ▮Change  Time   Bid ▮ Ask    Tic OpenInt TotVol  Close
 1)EDM5 Jun05  93.705s  -.015 Close              86   68910   5715  93.720
 2)EDU5 Sep05  93.630s  -.015 Close              84   76955   5295  93.645
 3)EDZ5 Dec05  93.510s  -.020 Close              84   47878   5599  93.530
 4)EDH6 Mar06  93.520s  -.020 Close              55   42256   3028  93.540
 5)EDM6 Jun06  93.470s  -.020 Close              60   33803   2800  93.490
 6)EDU6 Sep06  93.425s  -.020 Close              63   39468   2737  93.445
 7)EDZ6 Dec06  93.320s  -.020 Close              65   27096   2704  93.340
 8)EDH7 Mar07  93.335s  -.020 Close 93.305       21   17581    501  93.355
 9)EDM7 Jun07  93.290s  -.020 Close 93.260       20   17355    460  93.310
10)EDU7 Sep07  93.250s  -.020 Close 93.220       20   13970    360  93.270
11)EDZ7 Dec07  93.140s  -.020 Close 93.110       19   12792    355  93.160
12)EDH8 Mar08  93.155s  -.020 Close 93.125       17   11765    295  93.175
13)EDM8 Jun08  93.110s  -.020 Close 93.080       16   11117    195  93.130
14)EDU8 Sep08  93.070s  -.020 Close 93.040       16    9536    195  93.090
15)EDZ8 Dec08  92.960s  -.020 Close 92.930       16    4849    195  92.980
16)EDH9 Mar09  92.975s  -.020 Close 92.945       17    2256    191  92.995
17)EDM9 Jun09  92.930s  -.020 Close 92.900       17    2056    191  92.950
Australia 61 2 9777 8600     Brazil 5511 3048 4500     Europe 44 20 7330 7500     Germany 49 69 920410
Hong Kong 852 2977 6000 Japan 81 3 3201 8900 Singapore 65 212 1000 U.S. 1 212 318 2000  Copyright 2002 Bloomberg L.P.
                                                                   I522-112-1 09-Jan-02  9:13:21
▮Bloomberg
 PROFESSIONAL
```

```
  Send        Help   ▮
<HELP> for explanation.                        DGT4 Govt   CTM
Enter # <GO> to scroll contracts.   Run EXCH for realtime authorized exchanges
Session:▮            Contract Table
90DAY EURO$ FUTR                      Delayed monitoring enabled
Exchange Web Page         Pricing Date: ▮1/ 8/02▮  Price Display: ▮
Chicago Mercantile Exchange     Delayed prices      --LATEST AVAILABLE---        ▮
Grey date = options trading                        4412118 857725 Previous
            Last  ▮Change  Time   Bid ▮ Ask    Tic OpenInt TotVol  Close
 1)EDU9 Sep09  92.890s  -.020 Close 92.860       17    2647    191  92.910
 2)EDZ9 Dec09  92.785s  -.020 Close 92.755       17    2033    191  92.805
 3)EDH0 Mar10  92.805s  -.020 Close 92.775       13    3035    191  92.825
 4)EDM0 Jun10  92.760s  -.020 Close              12    2698    211  92.780
 5)EDU0 Sep10  92.720s  -.020 Close 92.690       13    2087    191  92.740
 6)EDZ0 Dec10  92.620s  -.020 Close 92.590       13    1876    191  92.640
 7)EDH1 Mar11  92.645s  -.020 Close 92.615       13    3536    191  92.665
 8)EDM1 Jun11  92.605s  -.020 Close 92.575       13    1368    191  92.625
 9)EDU1 Sep11  92.570s  -.020 Close 92.540       13    1990    191  92.590
10)EDZ1 Dec11  92.470s  -.020 Close 92.440       13     249    191  92.490
Australia 61 2 9777 8600     Brazil 5511 3048 4500     Europe 44 20 7330 7500     Germany 49 69 920410
Hong Kong 852 2977 6000 Japan 81 3 3201 8900 Singapore 65 212 1000 U.S. 1 212 318 2000  Copyright 2002 Bloomberg L.P.
                                                                   I522-112-1 09-Jan-02  9:13:34
▮Bloomberg
 PROFESSIONAL
```

*Source:* Bloomberg

## 5.3    Bond Futures Contracts[12]

### 5.3.1    Structure of Bond Futures Contracts

Bond futures contracts are generally contracts on bond prices (indirectly in term interest rates). Contracts are usually on government bonds. Contracts on non-government risk are relatively rare. Contracts are usually on medium to long maturity bonds (ranging from 3 to 30 years). Examples of typical contract specifications are set out in **Exhibit 2.10**.

---

**Exhibit 2.10    Bond Futures & Options on Futures Contract-Specifications**

**US Treasury Bond – Futures Contract**

| | |
|---|---|
| Unit Of Trading | One U.S. Treasury Bond having a face value at maturity of $100,000 or multiple thereof |
| Contract Maturity | March, June, September, December |
| Last Delivery Day | Last business day of the delivery month |
| Last Trading Day | Seventh business day preceding the last business day of the delivery month |
| Quotation | Points ($1,000) and thirty-seconds of a point (e.g. 80–16 is equal to 80 16/32 or 80.50) |
| Minimum Price Movement; Tick Size & Value | 1/32 of a point ($31.25/ contract); par is on the basis of 100 points |
| Delivery method | Federal Reserve book-entry wire- transfer system |
| Deliverable grades | U.S. Treasury Bonds that, if callable, are not callable for at least 15 years from the first day of the delivery month or, if not callable, have a maturity of at least 15 years from the first business day of the delivery month. The invoice price equals the futures settlement price times a conversion factor plus accrued interest. The conversion factor is the price of the deliverable bond ($1 par value) to yield 6 percent. |

---

[12] See Parkhurst, Charles H. (March 1988) Government Bond Futures: Tools for Global Risk Management and Portfolio Enhancement; Salomon Brothers Inc. Bond Portfolio Analysis Group, New York; (1999) Practical Uses of Treasury Futures; Chicago Board of Trade, Chicago.

**Treasury Bond – Option on Futures Contract**

| | |
|---|---|
| Unit Of Trading | 1 CBOT U.S. T-Bond Futures contract (of a specified delivery month) having a face value at maturity of $100,000 or multiple thereof |
| Strike Prices | 1 point strikes ($1,000) for the nearby contract month in a band consisting of the at-the-money, 4 above and 4 below. 2-point ($2,000) strikes are listed outside this band. Back months are also listed in 2 point strike price intervals. |
| Contract Maturity | The front month of the current quarter plus the next 3 contracts of the regular quarterly cycle (March, June September and December). If the front month is a quarterly contract month, no monthly contract will be listed. |
| Expiration/ Last Trading Day | Last Friday preceding by at least 5 business days the last business day of the month preceding the option contract month |
| Minimum Price Movement; Tick Size & Value | 1/64 of a point ($15.625/contract) rounded up to the nearest cent/contract |

The primary features of bond contracts include:
- The underlying contract is usually a government bond. The contracts fall into two types:
    1. Contracts where the underlying is a specific or any one of a number of government bonds which satisfy certain criteria. These contracts are generally deliverable. As described below, contracts of this type will typically trade as a contract into the cheapest to delivery bond at any given time. The Treasury bond, Euro Bund and JGB contracts are examples of these types of contract.
    2. Contracts where the underlying is a *notional bond*. These contracts are generally non-deliverable and cash settled. In this case the notional bond will always have a known coupon and fixed maturity from the maturity date of the contract. The contract is priced using a market yield for a government bond determined by a dealer polling mechanism (such as that used for the Eurodollar contract). The SFE A$ 10 year Treasury Bond contract is an example of this type of contract.
- The contracts are typically deliverable. Contracts where the underlying is a notional bond are generally cash settled. The delivery process on bond futures is specialised and is discussed below.

### 5.3.2   Pricing/Quotations Bond Futures Contracts

Bond futures contracts are typically quoted in price terms. **Exhibit 2.11** sets out sample quotations for bond futures contracts (the Treasury Bond Contract is used as an example). However, the translation of the quoted price into a settlement price requires the use of conversion factors. This reflects the physically deliverable nature of the underlying bonds with different coupons and different maturities (see discussion below).

The quotations are very similar to those applicable to short term interest rate contracts. The major difference is the concept of contract lifetime highs and lows. It refers to the highest or lowest prices attained by the contract during the trading life of the contract.

Key aspects of trading of bond futures include:

* The concentration of trading in the near month contract. This contrasts with the interest in trading a greater range of contract maturities in the case of short term interest rate futures contracts.

---

**Exhibit 2.11   Bond Futures & Options on Futures Contract – Price Quotations**

**Treasury Bond – Futures and Options Contract**

```
   Send      Help
<HELP> for explanation.                              DGT4 Comdty CTM
Date reset to next business day.    Enter # <GO> to scroll contracts.
Session:D             Contract  Table
US  10YR  NOTE  FUT                       Monitoring enabled.
Exchange Web Page        Pricing Date: 1/ 8/02    Price Display: 2
Chicago Board of Trade                        --LATEST AVAILABLE---     2
Grey date = options trading                   [549177 115598 Previous
            Last   1Change  Time   Bid 1 Ask   Tic OpenInt TotVol]  Close
 1)TYH2 Mar02 105-09 s  - 01  Close              2552  541353 113418  105-10
 2)TYM2 Jun02 103-30+s  - 01  Close               114    7824   2178  103-31+
 3)TYU2 Sep02 102-21 s  - 01  Close                 6       0      0  102-22
 4)TYZ2 Dec02                                           0      0
 5)TYH3 Mar03                                           0      0




Australia 61 2 9777 8600     Brazil 5511 3048 4500    Europe 44 20 7330 7500      Germany 49 69 920410
Hong Kong 852 2977 6000 Japan 81 3 3201 8900 Singapore 65 212 1000 U.S. 1 212 318 2000 Copyright 2002 Bloomberg L.P.
                                                                     I522-112-1 09-Jan-02  9:25:05
■Bloomberg
 PROFESSIONAL
```

```
  Send      Help
TYH2  ↑105-09s  -  01                              Comdty OMON
At 07:00 Vol 113,418 Op 105-02 Hi 105-17+ Lo 105-01 OpInt 541,353
 TYH2 Comdty        Go    Security    Contract Months    Template         Edit
                Option Monitor:  US 10YR NOTE FUT  Mar02
 Center   105.27 Number of Strikes  18 -or-   % from Center    Exchange C
                                                              (Composite   )
```

| Symbol | Strike | Bid | Ask | Last | Volume | Symbol | Strike | Bid | Ask | Last | Volume |
|---|---|---|---|---|---|---|---|---|---|---|---|
| TYH2 FEB 02 | | (Contract Size: 100000.0 | | | | TYH2 FEB 02 | | (Contract Size: 100000.0 | | | |
| 1) | 97 | | | | | 19) | 97 | | | '01 s | |
| 2) | 98 | . | | | | 20) | 98 | | | '01 s | |
| 3) | 99 | | | | | 21) | 99 | | | '01 s | |
| 4) | 100 | | | | | 22) | 100 | | '01 | '01 s | |
| 5) | 101 | | | 4'19 s | | 23) | 101 | | | '01 s | 1221 |
| 6) | 102 | | | | | 24) | 102 | '02 | '03 | '02 s | 2259 |
| 7) | 103 | | | 2'24 s | | 25) | 103 | | | '06 s | 7682 |
| 8) | 104 | | | 1'34 s | | 26) | 104 | | '19 | '16 s | 7262 |
| 9) | 105 | '55 | | '55 s | 2679 | 27) | 105 | | | '37 s | 1189 |
| 10) | 106 | | | '26 s | 8946 | 28) | 106 | | | 1'08 s | 1 |
| 11) | 107 | | | '10 s | 3871 | 29) | 107 | | | 1'56 s | |
| 12) | 108 | | '05 | '03 s | 831 | 30) | 108 | | | | |
| 13) | 109 | '01 | '02 | '01 s | 25 | 31) | 109 | | | | |

```
Australia 61 2 9777 8600      Brazil 5511 3048 4500      Europe 44 20 7330 7500      Germany 49 69 920410
Hong Kong 852 2977 6000 Japan 81 3 3201 8900 Singapore 65 212 1000 U.S. 1 212 318 2000  Copyright 2002 Bloomberg L.P.
                                                                                        I522-112-1 09-Jan-02  9:25:35
Bloomberg
PROFESSIONAL
```

*Source:* Bloomberg

- The disparate liquidity in options on bond futures with trading concentrated on certain strike and maturities.

### 5.3.3   Bond Futures Contracts – Pricing & Quoting Issues

*Overview*

Bond futures contracts are typically deliverable. This means that the contract is capable of being satisfied by delivery of an *actual bond*. The standardisation inherent in the structure of the bond futures contract enables it to serve as a proxy for *a large number of bonds* (that are eligible for delivery). The contractual basis of the bond future contract means that the price of the futures contract will reflect the actual cash price of the underlying bond or bonds *most likely to be delivered*. The bond likely to be delivered may also change during the life of the contract as market conditions change. This dictates that the pricing of the bond futures contract must reflect the underlying cash market bond. This is the case despite the fact that bond futures are typically not settled by delivery. The fact that the contract enables delivery of the relevant bond or bonds ensures that the bond futures contract trades at a value that reflects the actual cash value of the underlying instrument.

This requires a number of adjustments to be made to the pricing of bond futures contracts. These are mainly in relation to:

- Invoice price.
- Conversion factors.
- Cheapest to deliver ("CTD") bond[13].

*Invoice Price & Conversion Factors*

Treasury bond futures are quoted in price terms (in US$ and $1/32^{nd}$ of a dollar). However, the quoted price must be adjusted for two factors:

- **Conversion factor** – the conversion factor system is used to equate the standardised futures contract (with a standardised coupon) to the actual prices of individual bonds eligible for delivery. A specific factor is assigned to each deliverable bond (based on its coupon and remaining maturity) to enable comparison of different bonds at a given point in time.
- **Accrued interest** – the actual bond at the time of delivery will have accrued interest and the cash settlement price of the contract is adjusted to reflect this fact.

In effect, the actual price paid and received is given by:

$$\text{Cash Price} = (\text{Quoted Futures Price} \times \text{Conversion Factor}) + \text{Accrued Interest}$$

**Exhibit 2.12** sets out an example of the calculation of the Conversion Factor for the Treasury Bond contract. **Exhibit 2.13** sets out an example of calculating the actual cash settlement price for a contract.

---

[13] In illustrating these concepts, the US Treasury Bond Contract traded on CBOT is used as an example. Other contracts utilise broadly similar approaches although there are specific differences between markets. For a good description of these aspects of bond futures, see (1999) Practical Uses of Treasury Futures; Chicago Board of Trade, Chicago; (1998) The Treasury Futures Delivery Process; Chicago Board of Trade, Chicago; see also Meisner, James F. and Labuszewski, John W. "Treasury Bond Futures Delivery Bias" (1984) Journal of Futures Markets vol 4 no 4 569–577.

---

### Exhibit 2.12     Treasury Bond Futures Contract – Conversion Factor

The Conversion Factor for a bond is calculated as follows:
- The value of the bond on the first day of the delivery month on the assumption that the interest rate for all maturities equals 6% pa compounded semi-annually[14].
- The bond maturity and coupon payments are rounded down to the nearest 3 months. If after rounding the bond has an exact number of six monthly or semi-annual periods then the first coupon is paid at the end of the first six month period. However, if after rounding the bond does not have an exact number of six month periods, which means there is a "stub" three month period (as a result of the rounding to the nearest three month period) then the first coupon is assumed to be paid after 3 months and accrued interest is subtracted.

The application of this approach can be illustrated with the following examples.

**1.   Example 1**

Assume a 12% coupon bond with 18 years and 1 month to maturity. Applying the rounding rules (round down to nearest 3 month), the bond is assumed to have a life of 18 years or 36 semi-annual periods and the first coupon is assumed to be paid at the end of the first six month period.

Using $100 as face value, the bond price is calculated using 36 payments of $6 coupon ($12/2) and a future value of $100 at the end of 36 semi-annual periods discounted at 3.00% per each semi-annual period (6.00% pa/2). This equates to a value of the bond of: $165.50. This gives a Conversion factor as follows:

$$\text{Conversion Factor} = \text{Value of Bond/Face Value} = 165.50/100 = 1.6550$$

**2.   Example 2**

Assume a 12% coupon bond with 18 years and 4 months to maturity. Applying the rounding rules (round down to nearest 3 month), the bond is assumed to have a life of 18 years 3 months or 36 semi-annual periods and a stub period of 3 months. The bond price is therefore calculated at *3 months from today*.

Using $100 as face value, the bond price is calculated using 36 payments of $6 coupon ($12/2) and a future value of $100 at the end of 36 semi-annual periods discounted at 3.00% per each semi-annual period (6.00% pa/2). This equates to a value of the bond of: $165.50. The coupon due at the beginning of the first period ($6.00) is now added to give a bond value of $171.50.

---

*Cheapest to Deliver*

The deliverable nature of the bond futures contract means that at any given time there may be a number of bonds that are eligible for delivery into the contract. The

---

[14]   This was originally 8.00% pa but was changed to reflect lower market yields.

The bond value is now discounted back for 3 months using a rate of 1.4889% pa (calculated as $\sqrt{1.03} - 1$). This equates to 168.98 (171.50/1.014889). The accrued interest for 3 months ($3.00 calculated as $6.00/2) is now deducted to give a bond value of $165.98.

This gives a Conversion factor as follows:

$$\text{Conversion Factor} = \text{Value of Bond/Face Value} = 165.98/100 = 1.6598$$

---

**Exhibit 2.13   Treasury Bond Futures Contract – Cash Settlement Price**

The cash settlement price is given by:

$$\text{Cash Price} = (\text{Quoted Futures Price} \times \text{Conversion Factor}) + \text{Accrued Interest}$$

Accrued interest is calculated on a simple interest basis using the actual number of days elapsed since the last coupon payment date. For example, assume a bond with a 12% coupon and maturity of 15 November 2020 and a pricing date of 27 September 2002. The number of days between the last coupon date (15 May 2002) and the pricing date (27 September 2002) is 135 days. The number of days in the current interest period (between the last coupon date of 15 May 2002 and the next coupon date of 15 November 2002) is 184 days.

The accrued interest per $100 face value of bonds is:

$$\$100 \times 6.00\% \ (12\%/2) \times 135/184 = \$4.4022$$

Assume the quoted futures price is 106 and $14/32^{nd}$ (106.4375), a conversion factor of 1.6550 and accrued interest of $4.4022. The cash price is:

$$\text{Cash Price} = 106.4375 \times 1.6550 + 4.4022 = 180.5563$$

This means that the buyer would pay and the seller would receive $180,556 per $100,000 face value of the bond futures contract.

---

seller of a bond futures contract has the option of delivering any of the eligible bonds. The seller has an economic interest to deliver the bond that is the cheapest *in cash price terms*. This is the cheapest to deliver ("CTD") bond. This means that the market at any given time tends to trade as a forward *on the cheapest to deliver bond*. The futures price is driven by the CTD bond. This requires identification of the current CTD bond. This is irrespective of whether or not the seller wishes to settle by delivery.

The seller will always seek to deliver the CTD bond and its relative cheapness is determined by comparing the invoice cost of the various bonds in the market with their corresponding futures market invoice amount. The CTD bond is one for which the following relationship is lowest:

[Quoted Price of the Bond + Accrued Interest] − [(Quoted Futures Price
   × Conversion Factor) + Accrued Interest]

which simplifies into

[Quoted Price of the Bond] − [Quoted Futures Price × Conversion Factor]

An alternative way in which the CTD bond can be identified is to use the implied repo rate. The bond with the highest implied repo rate will tend to be the cheapest to deliver bond.

In practice, each bond eligible for delivery is compared to determine the CTD. **Exhibit 2.14** sets out an example of this process.

There are a number of special institutional factors in delivery of a treasury bond futures contract. One of these is the "wild card play or option". The Treasury bond futures contract ceases to trade at 2.00 p.m. (Chicago time or Central Standard Time). The seller has until 8:00 p.m. (Central Standard Time) to issue the notice of intention to deliver to the Clearing House. The cash market in Treasury Bonds continues to trade till approximately 4:00 p.m. The daily closing price (calculated as at 2:00 p.m.) is used to calculate the invoice price in the event of delivery.

This timing discrepancy creates the wild card option where, if after futures close and the invoice price is set, bond prices decline, the seller of a Treasury bond futures

---

**Exhibit 2.14   Treasury Bond Futures Contract – Cheapest to Deliver Calculation**

Assume that the Treasury bond futures contract is trading at 94 and $16/32^{nd}$ (94.50). Assume that there are 4 bonds eligible for delivery currently being traded:

| | Market Price (Clean Price or Ex-Interest) | Conversion Factor |
|---|---|---|
| Bond A | 97.7500 | 1.0257 |
| Bond B | 99.6250 | 1.0364 |
| Bond C | 117.2500 | 1.2245 |
| Bond D | 139.4375 | 1.4667 |

The CTD calculates the bond that has the lowest [Quoted Price of the Bond] – [Quoted Futures Price × Conversion Factor]. This is set out below:

|  | Quoted Price of the Bond – [Quoted Futures Price × Conversion Factor] | Cost of Delivering Bond |
|---|---|---|
| Bond A | 97.75 – (94.50 × 1.0257) | 0.8214 |
| Bond B | 99.625 – (94.50 × 1.0364) | 1.6852 |
| Bond C | 117.25 – (94.50 × 1.2245) | 1.5348 |
| Bond D | 139.4375 – (94.50 × 1.4667) | 0.8344 |

Based on the above analysis, the CTD is Bond A.

contract could exploit the wild card option by choosing to buy eligible securities and initiate delivery into the relatively higher priced futures market.

This has a number of implications. The implied delivery option influences the convergence of cash and adjusted futures price at expiration. The two will rarely converge fully because the seller of a futures contract continues to have the benefit of the wild card option. In effect, the pricing of the futures contract incorporates the wild card option.

The CTD process exhibits certain characteristics. The conversion factor system introduces inevitable biases in the relationship between the bond futures contract and the underlying cash market. This is the result of the assumptions underlying the determination of the conversion factors.

The typical biases include:
• If yields exceed 6.00% then the conversion factor system may favour the delivery of lower coupon, longer maturity bonds. If yields exceed 6.00% then the conversion factor system may favour the delivery of higher coupon, shorter maturity bonds. The further yields are away from 6.00% the greater the biases.
• Where the yield curve is positively sloped, the system favours delivery of longer maturity bonds. A negatively sloped yield curve favours delivery of shorter bonds.
• The determination of the CTD is also affected by the behaviour of specific bonds in the cash market. Some bonds tend to trade at prices in excess of their theoretical value reflecting tax factors or the ability to strip the bonds. This price effect influences the likelihood of an individual bond being the CTD bond.

The CTD may change during the life of the contract due to movements in market parameters. This may create opportunities to enhance returns. Most dealers in the bond futures use proprietary models to identify the likelihood of a change in CTD under different market scenarios and identify cheap securities[15].

### 5.3.4   Interest Rate Contracts – Innovations

The major innovations in interest rate futures have focused in shorter maturity indexes or indexes of different credit quality. Two important innovations have been:

- **Spread products** – this entails futures and option contracts on the *spread* (difference) between two other listed contracts enabling trading of yield curve shape or credit value differences.
- **Flexible ("FLEX") Options** – this allows counterparties to list by agreement an option contract that is not currently listed on the exchange. An example of a FLEX contract on the U.S. Treasury Bond future is set out in **Exhibit 2.15**[16].

| **Exhibit 2.15   Flexible Options on Bond – CBOT Contract Specifications** | |
|---|---|
| Unit of Trading | The minimum size to initiate a Request for Quote ("RFQ") in an unopened Flexible Treasury Bond Options series is 200 contracts, each having a face value at maturity of $100,000. If an option series is opened, the minimum transaction is 100 lots. |
| Strike Prices | May be expressed: (1) in absolute levels, set to any 1/32 of a point; or, (2) in levels relative to the underlying futures contracts, set 8/32 of a point increments |
| Exercise Price | RFQ initiators can choose either an American or European exercise style |
| Delivery/Exercise/ Expiry Day | The buyer of an American-style Flexible Treasury Bond Option may exercise the option on any business day prior to expiration by giving notice to the Board of Trade Clearing Corp by 16:00 Chicago time. Options expiring in-the-money on the last day are automatically exercised. Expiration occurs on any Monday through Friday provided that: (1) it is not an exchange holiday; and (2) the date does not exceed the expiration date of the standard option whose underlying is the most deferred futures contract to have had trading activity. |

---

[15]  For example, see Koenigsberg, Mark (December 1990) The Salomon Brothers Delivery Option Model-Understanding Treasury Bond Futures II; Salomon Brothers Bond Portfolio Analysis Group, New York.

[16]  The FLEX concept is also available in relation to options on futures contracts on currencies and equity indexes on some exchanges. For example, see "A Promising Inaugural for Listed E-Flex Options" (December/January 1997) Derivatives Strategy 10–11.

| Last Trading Day | Unexercised Flexible T-bond Options expire on the last trading day. On the last trading/expiration day, trading ceases at noon and expiration occurs later that day at 16.30 Chicago time |
| Minimum Price Movement; Tick Size & Value | 1/64 of a point ($15.625/contract) rounded up to the nearest cent/contract |
| Daily Price Limit | 3 points ($3,000 per contract above or below the previous day's settlement price (expandable to 4 $1/_2$ points). Limits are lifted on the last trading day |

# 6   FX/Currency Products[17]

## 6.1   Overview

The primary feature of contracts on foreign exchange/currency is that the underlying is a foreign exchange rate. The major currency futures contracts are set out in **Exhibit 2.16**.

**Exhibit 2.16    Currency Futures & Options on Futures Contracts**

| Exchange | Contracts |
|---|---|
| CME | US$/Yen Yen 12.5 million |
| CME | US$/Euro Euro 125,000 |
| CME | US$/Canadian Dollar C$ 100,000 |
| CME | US$/Pound Sterling GBP 62,500 |
| CME | US$/Swiss Franc SFR 125,000 |
| CME | US$/Mexican Peso Peso 500,000 |
| BMF | US$/Brazilian Real US$ 50,000 |

## 6.2   Structure of Currency Futures

Currency futures and options on futures contracts are generally contracts on the exchange rate of a specific currency against the US$. An example of typical contract specifications is set out in **Exhibit 2.17**. The key aspect of the structure of currency

---

[17] See Chapula, Karel V. "Foreign Currency Futures: Reducing Foreign Exchange Risk" (Winter 1982) Economic Perspectives vol VI issue 3 3–11; Goldstein, Henry N. "Foreign Currency Futures: Some Further Aspects" (November-December 1983) Economic Perspectives vol VIII issue 6 3–13.

contracts is the necessity to close out position by physical delivery of the relevant currencies.

---

**Exhibit 2.17    Currency Futures & Options on Futures Contract-Specifications**

**Japanese Yen – Futures Contract**

| | |
|---|---|
| Unit Of Trading | Yen 12,500,000 |
| Contract Maturity | Six months in the March Quarterly cycle (March, June, September and December) |
| Delivery/Exercise/Expiry Day | Third Wednesday of the contract month |
| Quotation | US$ per yen |
| Minimum Price Movement | 0.0000005 |
| Tick Size & Value | $12.50 |
| Delivery | Physical delivery takes place on the third Wednesday of the contract month in the country of issuance at a bank designated by the Clearing House. |

**Japanese Yen – Option on Futures Contract**

| | |
|---|---|
| Unit Of Trading | One IMM Japanese Yen futures contract |
| Strike Prices | First contract months: $0.00005 intervals |
| Contract Maturity | Quarterly, Serial and Weekly Options; the nearest futures contract in the March quarterly cycle (March, June, September, December) whose termination follows the options's last day of trading by more that two Exchange business days |
| Expiration/ Last Trading Day | Two Fridays before the third Wednesday of the contract month. |
| Quotation | US$ per yen |
| Minimum Price Movement | 0.000001 |
| Tick Size & Value | $12.50 |

---

## 6.3    Pricing/Quotations of Currency Futures

Currency futures contracts are typically quoted in price terms (number of units of foreign currency per US$ or vice versa). The quotations are very similar to those applicable to bond contracts.

Key aspects of trading of currency futures prices include:

- The concentration of trading in the near month contract.

- The relative low volume in both futures and options relative to the OTC forward and option markets on currencies.

## 6.4   Currency Contracts – Innovations

Currency futures and options have never reached the volumes of interest rate and equity index contracts. A major factor underlying this is the existence of the OTC spot, forward and option markets in currencies that pre-dated the futures and option markets.

Currency futures innovations have focused on two primary areas:

- **Third currencies or cross rates** – a number of attempts (with limited success) has been made to introduce cross rate futures and options. The Financial Futures Exchange ("FINEX") introduced a number of these contracts such as Euro/Yen, Euro/Sterling, Euro/Swiss Franc and Euro/Swedish Kroner.
- **Rolling spot currency futures contract** – this was an interesting attempt to use futures to replicate the characteristics of the currency spot market. **Exhibit 2.18** sets out the specifications of the rolling spot contract. Options on the rolling spot contract are also available[18].

## 7   Equity Products[19]

### 7.1   Overview

The primary feature of equity contracts is that the underlying is an equity index. The major equity index futures contracts are set out in **Exhibit 2.19**.

### 7.2   Structure of Equity Futures

Equity futures and options on futures contracts are generally contracts on the specific equity index in the currency of the index. The contract value is determined by multiplying the index value by a monetary amount. An example of a typical contract specification is set out in **Exhibit 2.20**.

---

[18]   See Alldis, Robert and Cookson, Robert "Spot the Similarity" (July 1993) Risk 6.

[19]   See Fabozzi, Frank J. and Kipnis, Gregory M. (1989) The Handbook of Stock Index Futures and Options; Dow-Jones Irwin, Homewood, Illinois; Margolis, Louis I. and Hanson, H. Nicholas (November 1984) Stock Index Options & Futures; Salomon Brothers Inc., New York.

**Exhibit 2.18    Rolling Spot Currency Futures Contract – CME Contract Specifications**

| Currency | Pound Sterling | C$ | Euro | Yen | Swiss Franc |
|---|---|---|---|---|---|
| Unit of Trading | GBP 250,000 | US$250,000 | Euro 250,000 | US$250,000 | US$250,000 |
| Minimum Price Movement | 0.0001 | 0.0001 | 0.0001 | 0.0001 | 0.0001 |
| Tick Value | US$25.00 | C$25.00 | US$25.00 | Yen 2,500 | SFR 25.00 |

| | |
|---|---|
| Quotation | Prices are quoted in units of foreign currency per US$ (i.e. in European terms) for all currencies except Pound Sterling and Euros |
| Last Trading Day | Two business days prior to the third Wednesday of the contract month |
| Expiration/ settlement date | Listed at start of trading on Monday and expires at close of trading on Friday. Daily settlement. |
| Delivery prior to settlement | An EFP transaction can be arranged at any time in which the trader sells the Rolling Spot contract and simultaneously receives a spot foreign exchange position in return (or vice versa) |
| Delivery | CME currency contracts are settled by physical delivery. Clients who are long currency futures should establish an "order to pay" bank for each underlying currency prior to the delivery date |
| Settlement | The daily settlement for a Rolling Spot futures contract has two elements, the traditional mark-to-market and the daily adjustment for the "roll" via a cash debit/credit. At 11:00 Chicago time, the CME Clearing House surveys 8 foreign exchange dealers at random on spot/next prices and calculates the mid-points of the bid offer pairs of the midpoints is the second component of that day's settlement. The daily adjustment rate is posted at approximately 11:30 Chicago time. |

## 7.3  Pricing/Quotations of Equity Futures

Equity index futures contracts are typically quoted in index price terms. **Exhibit 2.21** sets out sample quotations for equity contracts (the S & P 500 Contract is used as an example). The quotations are very similar to those applicable to bond contracts.

Key aspects of trading of equity index futures include:

- The concentration of trading in the near month contract.
- The disparate liquidity in options with trading concentrated on certain strike and maturities.

**Exhibit 2.19    Equity Index Futures & Options on Futures Contracts**

| Jurisdiction | Exchange | Contracts |
|---|---|---|
| USA | CME | S & P 500 $250 × index |
| | CBOT | Dow Jones Industrial Average $10 × index |
| | CME | Mini S & P 500 $50 × index |
| | CME | Mid Cap 400 $500 × index |
| | CME | NASDAQ 100 $100 × index |
| | CME | Russell 2000 $500 × index |
| Europe | Eurex | DJ Euro STOXX 50 Index Euro 10 × index |
| Germany | Eurex | DAX 30 Euro 25 × index |
| France | MATIF | CAC-40 Stock Index Euro 10 × index |
| Italy | Idem | MIB 30 Euro 5 × Index |
| Spain | MeffRV | IBEX 35 Euro 10 × index |
| Netherlands | Amsterdam Exchange | AEX Index Euro 10 × index |
| Sweden | OM | OMX Index Skr 100 × index |
| Japan | SIMEX | Nikkei 225 Yen 500 × Index |
| Japan | Osaka Stock Exchange | Nikkei 225 Yen 1,000 × Index |
| UK | LIFFE | FTSE-100 GBP 10 × Index |
| Switzerland | Eurex | Swiss Market Index SFR 10 × Index |
| Australia | SFE | S & P Share Price Index A$25 × Index |
| Hong Kong | HKFE | Hang Seng Index HK$50 × index |
| Canada | TSE | TSE C$500 × Index |
| Brazil | BMF | Bovespa Real 3.00 × Index |
| Korea | Korean Stock Exchange | KOSPI 200 Korean Won 500,000 × Index |
| New Zealand | New Zealand Futures Exchange | Barclays 30 NZ$20 × Index |
| South Africa | Safex | JSE All Share Rand 10 × Index |

## 7.4   Equity Contracts – Innovations

The major equity contract innovations have focused upon:

- **New indexes and sub-indexes** – this has basically focused on providing investors with a variety of indexes that specifically match the underlying equity investment portfolios to facilitate hedging. The NASDAQ and Russell contracts are examples of these contracts.

- **Retail denomination** – this has basically focused on reducing the index values to enable retail investors to more easily trade the underlying index. The Mini S & P contract is an example of this type of contract.

**Exhibit 2.20    Equity Futures & Options on Futures Contract-Specifications**

**Standard & Poor's (S & P) 500 Stock Index – Futures Contract**

| | |
|---|---|
| Unit Of Trading | S & P 500 Index times $250 |
| Contract Maturity | March, June, September, December |
| Delivery/Exercise/Expiry Day | Third Friday of contract month – cash settled |
| Last Trading Day | The business day immediately preceding the day of determination of the Final Settlement Price (normally the Thursday prior to the third Friday of the contract month) |
| Quotation | Index points |
| Minimum Price Movement | 0.10 index points ($25 per contract) |
| Tick Size & Value | $5.00/ .01 point |
| Daily Price Limit | A system of price limits operate after large price movements |
| Final Settlement Price | All open positions at the close of the final trading day are settled in cash |

**Standard & Poor's (S & P) 500 Stock Index – Option on Futures Contract**

| | |
|---|---|
| Unit Of Trading | One S & P 500 stock index futures contract |
| Strike Prices | 5 point intervals for two nearest contracts; 10 point intervals for other contracts |
| Contract Maturity | All 12 calendar months |
| Delivery/Exercise/Expiry Day | For all contract months, an option may be exercised by the buyer up to and including the last day of trading |
| Last Trading Day | March, June, September, December - same day as underlying future |
| Other months - 3rd Friday of the contract month | |
| Quotation | Index points |
| Daily Price Limit | Same as S & P 500 contract |
| Minimum Price Movement; Tick Size & Value | 0.10 index points; US$25.00 per contract |

- **Individual equity contracts** – this has basically focused on introducing contracts where the underlying is *an individual stock* rather than an equity index[20].
- **Long Term Equity Anticipation Securities ("LEAPS")** – these are basically long dated options on individual equity securities or on indexes[21]. Equity LEAPS typically expire in approximately 2 to 3 years from the date of initial listing[22].
- **Ratio contracts** – this has focused on enabling the trader to trade the relative performance of an individual stock relative to the underlying index[23]. This was introduced by the Australian Stock Exchange on a number of large Australian stocks[24].
- **Low Exercise Price Options ("LEPOS")**[25] – these are low exercise price options that effectively behave like a forward on the underlying equity index or stock[26].

---

[20] See Das, Satyajit (2004) Structured Products Volume 2; John Wiley & Sons (Asia), Singapore at Chapter 1.

[21] See Das, Satyajit (2004) Structured Products Volume 2; John Wiley & Sons (Asia), Singapore at Chapter 1.

[22] See Hunter, Robert "Index LEAPS Pick Up Speed" (July-August 1997) Derivatives Strategy 8–11; Thackaray, John "The Discreet Charm of Long Dated Equity Options" (November 1995) Derivatives Strategy 54–55.

[23] See Das, Satyajit (2004) Structured Products Volume 2; John Wiley & Sons (Asia), Singapore at Chapter 1.

[24] See Irving, Richard "Simply the Best" (September 1994) Risk 13–14; Locke, Jane "Relative Values" (August 1995) Risk 21–22; Elms, David "Rationale of Ratios" (August 1995) Risk 24–28; Coultas, Jonothan and Considine, Matthew "Australian Share Ratios" (November 1995) Financial Derivatives and Risk Management Issue 3 45–50; Gillespie, Thomas "Share Ratios: Valuation and Uses" (November 1995) Financial Derivatives and Risk Management Issue 3 51–57; Cox, Rod "New Listed Products: LEPOS; Stock Futures; Endowment Warrants" (7 May 1996) Paper presented to ATAX Conference on Innovative Financial Products; Sydney, Australia; Hathaway, Neville "Ratios: Settling the Differences" (July-September 1996) JASSA 24–27.

[25] See Das, Satyajit (2004) Structured Products Volume 2; John Wiley & Sons (Asia), Singapore at Chapter 1.

[26] See Ho, Peter "LEPOs: A Giant Leap Forward with a Little Exercise Step" (Second Quarter 1995) ASX Perspectives 59–63; Hathaway, Neville "Pricing Low Exercise Options" (Second Quarter 1995 ) ASX Perspectives 57–59; Petzel, Todd E. "The Myth of the Zero-Strike Price Option" (Summer 1995) Derivatives Quarterly 33–37; Cox, Rod "New Listed Products: LEPOS; Stock Futures; Endowment Warrants" (7 May 1996) Paper presented to ATAX Conference on Innovative Financial Products; Sydney, Australia.

**Exhibit 2.21    Equity Index Futures & Options on Futures Contract – Price Quotations**

## S & P 500 – Futures Contract

| Send | Help |
| --- | --- |

```
<HELP> for explanation, <MENU> for similar functions.      DGT4 Index  CT
Enter # <GO> to scroll contracts.   Run EXCH for realtime authorized exchanges
Session:D              Contract Table
                                           Delayed monitoring enabled
```

Exchange Web Page          Pricing Date: 1/ 8/02
Chicago Mercantile Exchange       Delayed prices
Grey date = options trading

| | | Last | Change | Time | Bid | Ask | Tic | OpenInt | TotVol | Previous Close |
| --- | --- | --- | --- | --- | --- | --- | --- | --- | --- | --- |
| | | | | | | | | ---LATEST AVAILABLE--- | | 2 |
| | | | | | | | | 493290 | 64366 | Previous |
| 1)SPX | spot | 1160.71 | -4.18 | 8:59 | 1160.3 | 1161.0 | 5340 | 0 | 0 | 1164.89 |
| 2)SPH2 | Mar02 | 1163.30s | -3.50 | Close | | | 3198 | 469433 | 62432 | 1166.80 |
| 3)SPM2 | Jun02 | 1165.70s | -3.60 | Close | | | 112 | 14853 | 1086 | 1169.30 |
| 4)SPU2 | Sep02 | 1168.90s | -3.60 | Close | | | 47 | 7242 | 818 | 1172.50 |
| 5)SPZ2 | Dec02 | 1173.40s | -4.10 | Close | | | 47 | 1620 | 30 | 1177.50 |
| 6)SPH3 | Mar03 | 1179.40s | -4.60 | Close | | | 47 | 55 | 0 | 1184.00 |
| 7)SPM3 | Jun03 | 1186.90s | -5.10 | Close | | | 47 | 87 | 0 | 1192.00 |
| 8)SPU3 | Sep03 | 1196.40s | -4.60 | Close | | | 47 | 0 | 0 | 1201.00 |
| 9)SPZ3 | Dec03 | 1207.40s | -3.60 | Close | | | 46 | 0 | 0 | 1211.00 |

Australia 61 2 9777 8600      Brazil 5511 3048 4500      Europe 44 20 7330 7500      Germany 49 69 920410
Hong Kong 852 2977 6000 Japan 81 3 3201 8900 Singapore 65 212 1000 U.S. 1 212 318 2000  Copyright 2002 Bloomberg L.P.
                                                                                        1522-112-1 09-Jan-02  9:30:46

**Bloomberg** PROFESSIONAL

| Send | Help |
| --- | --- |

```
SPX  ↑1160.71  -4.18  1160.31/1161.03      Index  OMON
At 08:59  Op 1164.89 Hi 1167.60 Lo 1157.46
```

| SPX Index | GO | Security | Contract Months | Template | Edit |
| --- | --- | --- | --- | --- | --- |

```
            Option Monitor:  S&P 500 INDEX
Center  1160.71 Number of Strikes 18 -or-   % from Center   Exchange C
                                                            (Composite )
```

| | | | CALLS | | | | | | PUTS | | |
| --- | --- | --- | --- | --- | --- | --- | --- | --- | --- | --- | --- |
| Symbol | Strike | Bid | Ask | Last | Volume | Symbol | Strike | Bid | Ask | Last | Volume |
| SPX JAN 02 | | (Contract Size: 100.00) | | | | SPX JAN 02 | | (Contract Size: 100.00) | | | |
| 1) SP | 1025 | 137.10 | 139.10 | 147.00 y | | 19) SP | 1025 | .20 | .50 | .35 | 651 |
| 2) SP | 1050 | 112.40 | 114.40 | 120.50 y | | 20) SP | 1050 | .45 | .80 | .70 | 660 |
| 3) SP | 1075 | 87.80 | 89.80 | 86.00 | 25 | 21) SP | 1075 | 1.00 | 1.20 | 1.20 | 4431 |
| 4) SP | 1080 | 82.90 | 84.90 | | | 22) SP | 1080 | .85 | 1.30 | 1.40 | 260 |
| 5) SP | 1090 | 73.30 | 75.30 | 61.30 y | | 23) SP | 1090 | 1.20 | 1.65 | 1.65 | 206 |
| 6) SP | 1100 | 63.60 | 65.60 | 62.00 | 26 | 24) SP | 1100 | 2.00 | 2.05 | 2.25 | 2047 |
| 7) SP | 1115 | 49.60 | 51.60 | 50.10 y | | 25) SP | 1115 | 2.50 | 3.20 | 3.00 | 15 |
| 8) SP | 1125 | 40.70 | 42.70 | 44.00 y | | 26) SP | 1125 | 3.50 | 4.20 | 4.10 | 11630 |
| 9) SP | 1140 | 28.10 | 30.10 | 28.30 | 54 | 27) SP | 1140 | 6.50 | 6.80 | 6.50 | 655 |
| 10) SP | 1150 | 20.70 | 22.70 | 20.90 | 343 | 28) SP | 1150 | 8.40 | 9.40 | 9.20 | 1159 |
| 11) SP | 1160 | 14.40 | 15.90 | 14.00 | 475 | 29) SP | 1160 | 11.50 | 13.00 | 14.00 | 1299 |
| 12) SP | 1175 | 7.30 | 8.30 | 7.50 | 2011 | 30) SP | 1175 | 19.20 | 20.70 | 21.30 | 484 |
| 13) SP | 1180 | 5.50 | 6.50 | 5.20 | 456 | 31) SP | 1180 | 22.20 | 24.20 | 21.00 | 1 |

Australia 61 2 9777 8600      Brazil 5511 3048 4500      Europe 44 20 7330 7500      Germany 49 69 920410
Hong Kong 852 2977 6000 Japan 81 3 3201 8900 Singapore 65 212 1000 U.S. 1 212 318 2000  Copyright 2002 Bloomberg L.P.
                                                                                        1522-112-1 09-Jan-02  9:30:30

**Bloomberg** PROFESSIONAL

*Source:* Bloomberg

Despite continuing efforts of exchanges to introduce new products, innovations have met with limited success with many of the new products failing to attain the required liquidity and trading depth. The bulk of trading continues to focus on the large capitalisation equity index contracts[27].

# 8    Commodity Futures Products

## 8.1    Overview

Commodity contracts are among the oldest futures products traded on exchanges. Commodity contracts also cover a wide variety of futures and options on futures that are traded on many underlying commodities. **Exhibit 2.22** sets out the major commodity contracts available.

## 8.2    Structure of Commodity Futures

Commodity futures and options on futures contracts are generally contracts on a specific commodity. Examples of typical contract specifications are set out in **Exhibit 2.23**.

There are several features of the commodity futures contracts requiring consideration:

- The underlying commodity is generally defined with great specificity covering quantity, quality, delivery location (including terms of trade) and currency of price. This reflects the great diversity of commodity produced and traded within a particular type of commodity.
- Most commodity contracts are traded in US$ price terms although there are a number of exceptions to this rule.
- Most commodity contracts are able to be settled by delivery.

## 8.3    Pricing/Quotations of Commodity Futures

Commodity contracts are generally traded in price per unit terms. **Exhibit 2.24** sets out sample quotations for commodity contracts (the US$ WTI Contract and Copper Contract is used as an example).

---

[27] For a discussion of the use of equity indexes in portfolio management, see Das, Satyajit (2004) Structured Products Volume 2; John Wiley & Sons (Asia), Singapore at Chapters 1 and 5.

Exhibit 2.22    Commodity Futures & Option on Futures Contracts

| Type | Exchange | Contracts |
|---|---|---|
| Energy & Petroleum | Nymex | Crude Oil Light Sweet (WTI) 1,000 barrels |
| | IPE | Brent Crude 1,000 barrels |
| | Nymex | Heating Oil Number 2 42,000 gallons |
| | Nymex | Gasoline – NY Unleaded 42,000 gallons |
| | Nymex | Natural Gas 10,000 MMMBtu |
| | IPE | Gas Oil 100 metric tons |
| Precious Metals | Comex | Gold 100 troy ounces |
| | Comex | Silver 5,000 troy ounces |
| | Nymex | Platinum 50 troy ounces |
| | Nymex | Palladium 100 troy ounces |
| Metals | Comex | Copper 25,000 pounds |
| | LME | Copper 25 metric tons |
| | LME | Aluminium 25 metric tons |
| | LME | Tin 5 metric tons |
| | LME | Lead 25 metric tons |
| | LME | Nickel 6 metric tons |
| | LME | Zinc 25 metric tons |
| Grains & Oilseeds | CBOT | Corn 5,000 bushels |
| | CBOT | Oats 5,000 bushels |
| | CBOT | Soybeans 5,000 bushels |
| | CBOT | Soybean meal 5,000 bushels |
| | CBOT | Soybean oil 60,000 pounds |
| | CBOT | Wheat 5,000 bushels |
| | Kansas City Board of Trade | Red Wheat No. 2 5,000 bushels |
| Foods & Fibre | New York Board of Trade ("NYBOT") | Cocoa 10 metric tons (US$) |
| | LIFFE | Cocoa 10 metric tons (GBP) |
| | NYBOT | Coffee C 37,500 pounds |
| | LIFFE | Robusta Coffee 5 tons |
| | Tokyo Grain Exchange ("TGE") | Arabica Coffee 5,450 Kgs (50 bags) |
| | NYBOT | Sugar-World 112,000 pounds |
| | NYBOT | Sugar-Domestic 112,000 pounds |
| | London Commodity Exchange ("LCE") | Sugar 50 tons |
| | NYBOT | Orange Juice 15,000 pounds |
| | NYBOT | Cotton 50,000 pounds |
| | SFE | Wool |

| Livestock | CME | Cattle Feeder 50,000 pounds |
| | CME | Cattle Live 40,000 pounds |
| | CME | Hogs – Lean 40,000 pounds |
| | CME | Pork Bellies 40,000 pounds |
| Lumber & Pulp | CME | Lumber 80,000 board feet |
| | OMLX | Pulp 24 air dry tons |

---

**Exhibit 2.23    Commodity Futures & Options on Futures Contract-Specifications**

**Light Sweet Crude Oil – NYMEX Contract**
**Futures Contract**

| Unit of Trading | 1,000 US Barrels (42,000 gallons) |
| Contract Maturity | 30 consecutive months plus long dated futures initially listed for 36, 48, 60, 72 and 84 months prior to delivery |
| Last Trading Day | 3rd business day prior to the 25th calendar day of the month preceding the delivery month |
| Quotation | US dollars and cents per barrel |
| Minimum Price Movement/Tick Size & Value | 0.01 (1 cent) per barrel; US$10.00 per contract |
| Daily Price Limit | A system of price limits applies |
| Delivery | F.O.B. seller's facility, Cushing, Oklahoma, at any pipeline or storage facility with pipeline access to TEPPCO, Cushing Storage or Equilon Pipleline Co.., by in-tank transfer, in-line transfer, book-out or inter-facility transfer (pumpover) |
| Delivery Period | All deliveries are rateable over the course of the month and must be initiated on or after the first calendar day and completed by the last calendar day of the delivery month |
| Deliverable Grades | Specific grades with 0.42% sulphur by weight or less not less than 37° API gravity nor more than 42° API gravity. The following crude streams are deliverable. West Texas Intermediate, Low Sweet Mix, New Mexican Sweet, North Texas Sweet, Oklahoma sweet, South Texas Sweet. Specific foreign crudes are also deliverable. |
| Inspection | Inspection must be conducted in accordance with pipeline practices. A buyer or seller may appoint an inspector to inspect the quality of oil delivered. However, the buyer or seller who requests the inspection will bear its costs and will notify the other party that the inspection will occur. |

**Option on Futures Contract**

| | |
|---|---|
| Unit Of Trading | One NYMEX light sweet crude oil contract |
| Option Type | American style |
| Strike Prices | 20 strike prices in increments of $0.50 (50 cents) per barrel above and below the at-the-money strike price and the next ten strike prices in increments $2.50 above the highest and bleow the lowest strike prices for a total of at least 61 strike prices. |
| Contract Maturity | 12 consecutive months plus 3 long-dated options at 18, 24 and 36 month out on a June/ December cycle. |
| Expiration/ Last Trading Day | Trading ends 3 business days before the underlying futures contract. |
| Quotation | US$ dollars and cents per barrel |
| Daily Price Limit | None |
| Minimum Price Movement/ Tick Size & Value | 0.01 (1 cent) per barrel; US$10.00 per contract |

**Natural Gas – NYMEX Contract**
**Futures Contract**

| | |
|---|---|
| Unit of Trading | 10,000 million British Thermal Units (MMBtu) |
| Contract Maturity | 72 consecutive months commencing with the next calender month |
| Last Trading Day | 3 business days prior to the 1st calendar day of the delivery month |
| Quotation | US dollars and cents per MMBtu |
| Minimum Price Movement/ Tick Size & Value | 0.01 (1 cent) per MMBtu; US$10.00 per contract |
| Daily Price Limit | A system of price limits is applicable. |
| Delivery | Sabine Pipe Line Co.'s Henry Hub in Louisiana. Seller is responsible for the movement of the gas through the Hub; the buyer, from the Hub. The Hub fee will be paid by the seller. |
| Delivery Period | Delivery shall take place no earlier than the first calendar day of the delivery month and shall be no later than the last calendar day of the delivery month. All deliveries shall be made at, as uniform as possible, an hourly and daily rate of flow over the course of the delivery month |
| Deliverable Grades | Pipeline specifications in effect at time of delivery |

**Option on Futures Contract**

| | |
|---|---|
| Unit Of Trading | One NYMEX natural gas futures contract |
| Option Type | American style |
| Strike Prices | 20 strike prices in increments of $0.05 (5 cents) per mmBtu above and below the at-the-money strike price in all months, plus an additional 20 strike prices of $0.05 per mmBtu above the at-the-money price will be offered in the first 3 nearby months and the next 10 strike prices in increments of $0.25 (25 cents) per mmBtu above the highest and below the lowest strike prices in all months. |
| Contract Maturity | 12 consecutive months plus contracts initially listed 15, 18, 21, 24, 27, 30, 33, 36, 39, 42, 45, 48, 51, 54, 57, 60, 63, 66, 69 and 72 months out on a March, June, September, December cycle. |
| Delivery/Exercise/Expiry Day | Trading terminates on the business day immediately preceding the expiration of the underlying futures contract. |
| Quotation | US$ dollars and cents per barrel |
| Minimum Price Movement/ Tick Size & Value | 0.01 (1 cent) per barrel; US$10.00 per contract |

**Gold – COMEX Contract**
**Futures Contract**

| | |
|---|---|
| Unit of Trading | 100 troy ounces (5% more or less) of refined gold, assaying not less than .995 fineness, cast either in one bar or in three one kilogram bars, bearing a serial number and identifying stamp of a refiner approved and listed by COMEX |
| Contract Maturity | The current calendar month, the next two calendar months and any February, April, August and October thereafter falling within a 23 month period and any June and December falling within a 60 month period beginning with the current month |
| Delivery/Settlement Day | First notice day: the last business day of the month prior to the maturing delivery month. Last notice day: the second last business day of the maturing delivery month |
| Last Trading Day | 3rd last business day of the maturing delivery month |
| Minimum Price Movement/ Tick Size & Value | US$0.10; US$10 per contract |
| Daily Price Limit | Initial price limit based upon the preceding day's settlement price is US$75 |

**Option on Futures Contract**

| | |
|---|---|
| Unit Of Trading | One COMEX gold futures contract |
| Strike Prices | US$10/oz for strike prices below US$500 |
| | US$20/oz for strike prices between US$500 and US$1,000 |
| | US$50/oz for strike prices above US$1,000 |
| | On the first day of trading for any option contract month, there will be thirteen strike prices each for puts and calls |
| Contract Maturity | The nearest six of the following contract months: February, April, June, August, October and December. Additional contract months - January, March, May, July, September and November will be listed for a period of two months. A 24-month option is added on a June-December cycle. |
| Expiration/Last Trading Day | Second Friday of the month prior to the delivery month of the underlying futures contract |
| Daily Price Limit | Initial price limit based upon the preceding day's settlement price is US$75 |
| Minimum Price Movement/Tick Size & Value | Multiples of 10 cents; US$0.10 per troy ounce |

**Copper**
**LME Contract**

| | |
|---|---|
| Unit of Trading | 25 tonnes |
| Prompt Day | Daily for 3 months forward, then every Wednesday for the next three months and then every 3rd Wednesday of the month for the next 57 months (a total of 63 months forward) |
| Quotation | US$ per tonne |
| Minimum Price Movement/Tick Size & Value | US$0.50 per tonne; US$12.50 |
| Contract Standard | Grade A – Electrolytic Copper in the form of either Grade A cathodes or standard dimensions in the weight range of 110 Kgs to 125 Kgs at the seller's option. All copper delivered must be of brands listed in the LME approved list of Copper - Grade A brands and conform with the appropriate category of British Standard EN 1978:1998 (cathode grade designation Cu-CATH-1) |
| Delivery Points | At LME approved warehouses in the United Kingdom, Continental Europe and Far East |

**Option on Futures Contract**

| | |
|---|---|
| Unit Of Trading | One LME Grade A Electrolytic Copper futures contract |
| Strike Prices | Fixed gradations in each currency |
| Prompt Day | First Wednesday of each month or next business day |
| Last Delivery Day | Third Wednesday of each month or the next business day |
| Quotation | Traded in both US$, Sterling, Yen and Euro per tonne |

Trading in commodity contracts is characterised by the following:

- Large concentration of volume in the near month contract with absence of trading in more distant months. There are exceptions to this such as the WTI crude oil and natural gas contracts.
- There is significant seasonality in both trading and price behaviour.

**Exhibit 2.24    Commodity Futures & Options on Futures**
**Contract – Price Quotations**

**1.    Crude Oil**

```
┌──────────┬───────────┐
│   Send   │   Help    │
<HELP> for explanation.                              DGT4 Comdty CTM
Date reset to next business day.    Enter # <GO> to scroll contracts.
Session:D             Contract Table
CRUDE OIL FUTR                              Monitoring enabled.
Exchange Web Page         Pricing Date: 1/ 8/02
New York Mercantile Exchange                    ---LATEST AVAILABLE---    2
Grey date = options trading                     442745 177865 Previous
↓ Scroll    Last  1Change  Time   Bid 1 Ask   Tic OpenInt TotVol  Close
 1)CLG2 Feb02  21.25s  -.23 Close                1859 121248 64080  21.48
 2)CLH2 Mar02  21.57s  -.21 Close                 760  68423 57150  21.78
 3)CLJ2 Apr02  21.73s  -.21 Close                 127  34961 25008  21.94
 4)CLK2 May02  21.69s  -.21 Close        21.90     81  19454  7770  21.90
 5)CLM2 Jun02  21.63s  -.21 Close        21.77     75  30411 10818  21.84
 6)CLN2 Jul02  21.57s  -.21 Close  21.50           16  14360  3192  21.78
 7)CLQ2 Aug02  21.53s  -.21 Close  21.45            5  13971  1186  21.74
 8)CLU2 Sep02  21.50s  -.21 Close  21.41           12  13546   880  21.71
 9)CLV2 Oct02  21.47s  -.21 Close                   5  10821   493  21.68
10)CLX2 Nov02  21.44s  -.21 Close                   8   8125   400  21.65
11)CLZ2 Dec02  21.41s  -.21 Close                  23  23900  3337  21.62
12)CLF3 Jan03  21.40s  -.21 Close                   3  12066  1625  21.61
13)CLG3 Feb03  21.39s  -.21 Close                   8   5902    12  21.60
14)CLH3 Mar03  21.38s  -.21 Close                   3   4711    50  21.59
15)CLJ3 Apr03  21.37s  -.21 Close                   3   1679     0  21.58
16)CLK3 May03  21.37s  -.20 Close                   3   1960   100  21.57
17)CLM3 Jun03  21.37s  -.19 Close  21.30            5  11349   325  21.56
Australia 61 2 9777 8600      Brazil 5511 3048 4500      Europe 44 20 7330 7500      Germany 49 69 920410
Hong Kong 852 2977 6000 Japan 81 3 3201 8900 Singapore 65 212 1000 U.S. 1 212 318 2000  Copyright 2002 Bloomberg L.P.
                                                                  I522-112-1 09-Jan-02  9:34:32
Bloomberg
PROFESSIONAL
```

| Send | Help |
|---|---|

**CLG2 ↓21.25s – .23**      Comdty **OMON**

At 06:46 Vol 64,080 Op 21.20 Hi 21.50 Lo 21.03 OpInt 121,248

| CLG2 Comdty | Go | Security | Contract Months | Template | Edit |
|---|---|---|---|---|---|

Option Monitor:    CRUDE OIL FUTR    Feb02

Center    **21.28** Number of Strikes **18** -or- **■** % from Center    Exchange C
(Composite )

| | | CALLS | | | | | | PUTS | | | |
|---|---|---|---|---|---|---|---|---|---|---|---|
| Symbol | Strike | Bid | Ask | Last | Volume | Symbol | Strike | Bid | Ask | Last | Volume |
| CLG2 FEB 02 | (Contract Size: 1000.00) | | | | | CLG2 FEB 02 | (Contract Size: 1000.00) | | | | |
| 1) | 17.5 | | | 3.78 s | | 19) | 17.5 | | | .03 s | 200 |
| 2) | 18.0 | | | 3.30 s | | 20) | 18.0 | | | .05 s | |
| 3) | 18.5 | | | 2.82 s | | 21) | 18.5 | | | .07 s | 150 |
| 4) | 19.0 | | | 2.35 s | 101 | 22) | 19.0 | .07 | | .10 s | 403 |
| 5) | 19.5 | | | 1.91 s | 162 | 23) | 19.5 | | | .16 s | 510 |
| 6) | 20.0 | | | 1.50 s | 205 | 24) | 20.0 | | | .25 s | 868 |
| 7) | 20.5 | | | 1.15 s | 204 | 25) | 20.5 | | | .40 s | 165 |
| 8) | 21.0 | | | .85 s | 363 | 26) | 21.0 | | | .60 s | 1594 |
| 9) | 21.5 | | | .60 s | 694 | 27) | 21.5 | | | .85 s | 86 |
| 10) | 22.0 | .40 | .55 | .41 s | 542 | 28) | 22.0 | | | 1.16 s | |
| 11) | 22.5 | | | .28 s | 4 | 29) | 22.5 | | | 1.53 s | |
| 12) | 23.0 | | | .19 s | 840 | 30) | 23.0 | | | 1.94 s | |
| 13) | 23.5 | | | .12 s | 181 | 31) | 23.5 | | | 2.37 s | |

Australia 61 2 9777 8600   Brazil 5511 3048 4500   Europe 44 20 7330 7500   Germany 49 69 920410
Hong Kong 852 2977 6000 Japan 81 3 3201 8900 Singapore 65 212 1000 U.S. 1 212 318 2000 Copyright 2002 Bloomberg L.P.
I522-112-1 09-Jan-02 9:34:51

**Bloomberg**
PROFESSIONAL

## 2. Copper

| Send | Help |
|---|---|

. <HELP> for explanation.       DGT4 Comdty **CTM**

Date reset to next business day.    Enter # <GO> to scroll contracts.

Session:**D**      **Contract Table**

**COPPER FUTURE**        Monitoring enabled.

Exchange Web Page      Pricing Date: **1/ 8/02**

COMEX division of NYMEX       ---LATEST AVAILABLE---   **2**

Grey date = options trading

| ↓ Scroll | Last | **1**Change | Time | Bid **1** Ask | Tic | OpenInt | TotVol | Previous Close |
|---|---|---|---|---|---|---|---|---|
| 1)HGF2 Jan02 | 70.35s | -.60 | Close | | 11 | 1282 | 156 | 70.95 |
| 2)HGG2 Feb02 | 70.60s | -.65 | Close | | 9 | 2386 | 36 | 71.25 |
| 3)HGH2 Mar02 | 70.85s | -.65 | Close | | 1079 | 38121 | 18745 | 71.50 |
| 4)HGJ2 Apr02 | 71.15s | -.65 | Close | | 8 | 1191 | 6 | 71.80 |
| 5)HGK2 May02 | 71.40s | -.65 | Close | | 47 | 5503 | 133 | 72.05 |
| 6)HGM2 Jun02 | 71.70s | -.65 | Close | | 4 | 1172 | 3 | 72.35 |
| 7)HGN2 Jul02 | 71.95s | -.65 | Close | | 36 | 6833 | 137 | 72.60 |
| 8)HGQ2 Aug02 | 72.25s | -.65 | Close | | 3 | 953 | 3 | 72.90 |
| 9)HGU2 Sep02 | 72.50s | -.65 | Close | | 5 | 3762 | 75 | 73.15 |
| 10)HGV2 Oct02 | 72.75s | -.65 | Close | | 4 | 0 | 0 | 73.40 |
| 11)HGX2 Nov02 | 73.00s | -.65 | Close | | 3 | 0 | 0 | 73.65 |
| 12)HGZ2 Dec02 | 73.30s | -.65 | Close | | 10 | 5463 | 64 | 73.95 |
| 13)HGF3 Jan03 | 73.45s | -.65 | Close | | 3 | 0 | 0 | 74.10 |
| 14)HGG3 Feb03 | 73.65s | -.65 | Close | | 3 | 0 | 0 | 74.30 |
| 15)HGH3 Mar03 | 73.85s | -.65 | Close | | 3 | 402 | 10 | 74.50 |
| 16)HGJ3 Apr03 | 74.00s | -.65 | Close | | 3 | 0 | 0 | 74.65 |
| 17)HGK3 May03 | 74.20s | -.65 | Close | | 3 | 0 | 0 | 74.85 |

Australia 61 2 9777 8600   Brazil 5511 3048 4500   Europe 44 20 7330 7500   Germany 49 69 920410
Hong Kong 852 2977 6000 Japan 81 3 3201 8900 Singapore 65 212 1000 U.S. 1 212 318 2000 Copyright 2002 Bloomberg L.P.
I522-112-1 09-Jan-02 9:33:56

**Bloomberg**
PROFESSIONAL

*Source:* Bloomberg

## 8.4   Commodity Contracts – Innovations

The major innovations in commodity contracts have been focused upon:

- **New commodities** – this has been driven by the increase in trading interest in certain commodities. The new electricity contracts are examples of this trend.
- **Commodity indexes** – this has focused on trading contracts on indexes such as the Goldman Sachs Commodity Index ("GSCI") and Bridge Commodity Research Bureau Index ("CRB").

# 9   Summary

ET traded derivative products are a key component of the global derivatives market. Futures contracts and options on futures contracts are available on interest rates (short term benchmark rates and bond prices), currencies, equity indexes and a wide variety of commodities. These instruments play a significant role in the derivatives markets. ET derivatives allow hedgers and traders to assume and shed exposures to rate and price movements. ET derivatives allow traders at banks and financial institutions to hedge (either temporarily or on a long term basis) rate and price exposures assumed when trading with or providing risk management products *to their clients*. In this way, the ET derivatives markets acts as a mechanism for both primary and secondary risk transfer.

The key feature of the ET traded markets are their standardisation, which facilitates concentration of liquidity in a few contracts assisting in creating market depth, and the credit enhancement mechanisms embodied in the clearing mechanisms utilised in such markets. The major disadvantage of the ET markets is that the standardisation of the underlying required exposes hedgers and traders to *basis* risk (that is, the risk that the price changes in the contract do not track price changes in the underlying position as a result of differences between the two).

# 3

# Over-the-Counter Products – FRAs, Interest Rate Swaps, Caps/Floors, Currency Forwards, Currency Swaps, Currency Options

## 1  Overview

Financial derivatives consist of two primary types of instruments – forward contracts and option contracts. These instruments constitute the building blocks or key elements of all derivative products. Derivative instruments are traded in two different market contexts – exchange traded ("ET") and over-the-counter ("OTC") markets. In this Chapter, OTC traded products are discussed. ET products were discussed in Chapter 2.

The structure of the Chapter is as follows:

- The primary features of OTC markets are considered.
- The types of OTC products are outlined.
- Interest rate products and currency OTC products are described.

## 2  OTC Derivative Markets

The primary feature of OTC derivative products derives from the fact that transactions are bilateral contracts negotiated between the counterparties to the transaction.

This aspect of OTC derivatives has several consequences:

- **Customisation of instrument** – the terms of a specific transaction are capable of customisation (underlying asset, maturity, settlement mechanics) by negotiation between the counterparties. This has the effect, if required, of enabling the counterparties to minimise basis risk from the use of derivatives (in effect a close match to the underlying asset being hedged can be created).
- **Credit risk** – the bilateral nature of the transaction entails direct credit exposure on the counterparty. This reflects the fact that each party is directly dependent upon the performance of the other counterparty to the transaction. This exposure is different to the position in ET markets where credit enhancement mechanisms are used (Clearing House and margins). In practice, credit enhancement mechanisms are used increasingly in the OTC derivatives market[1]. However, OTC derivatives entail direct counterparty credit exposure[2].
- **Market structure** – the bilateral nature of OTC derivatives dictates that they are traded in a *virtual* market. There is no central market at which trading is undertaken. This is in marked contrast to ET markets where trading *must* take place through the relevant exchange. The majority of OTC derivative transactions are concluded by telephone or other electronic methods. Transactions are between counterparties that may be located in different jurisdictions. This market structure has several consequences, including liquidity and pricing. The customisation of contracts, lack of a clearing mechanism and lack of a central market means that liquidity of OTC markets may be lower than for ET products. The lack of a central market and public dissemination of prices means that pricing is less transparent and transacting more expensive in terms of transaction costs (compared to ET markets).

# 3 OTC Products – Types[3]

OTC derivatives consist primarily of repackaging of the basic building block derivative instruments – forwards and options. An important aspect of OTC products is the addition of swap contracts and option contracts entailing a package of options.

---

[1] See Das, Satyajit (2004) Risk Management; John Wiley & Sons (Asia), Singapore at Chapter 6.
[2] For a discussion of credit risk in derivative transactions, see Das, Satyajit (2004) Risk Management; John Wiley & Sons (Asia), Singapore at Chapters 5, 6 and 7.
[3] For discussion of types of OTC derivative products, see Schwartz, Robert J. and Smith, Jnr., Clifford W. (Editors) (1990) The Handbook of Currency and Interest Rate Risk Management; New York Institute of Finance, New York.

Swap contracts are essentially a package or portfolio of forward contracts that are combined into a single transaction. The primary drivers for swaps include the ability to match the cash flow profile of underlying transactions (debt and investments), the benefits of a single transaction (rather than a series of transactions) and the ability to transact at a single rate rather than a series of different rates. These factors may have significant accounting and taxation implications.

The multiple option packages include transactions such as cap and floors. The transactions entail entry into a series of separate (strip) of options in a single transaction. The drivers for these structures are similar to those for swaps.

The range of OTC derivatives available is summarised in **Exhibit 3.1**. In this Chapter, the primary focus is on certain basic building block OTC derivative instruments on interest rates (FRAs, caps/floors, interest rate swaps) and currencies (currency forwards, currency options and currency swaps). Non-generic/ non-standard structures on interest rates/currencies are dealt with in the context of non-generic products[4]. OTC derivatives on equity/commodities are dealt with in the context of derivative structures on the specific asset class[5].

The description of the products is set out as follows:

- FRAs and caps/floors are described.
- Currency forwards and currency options are outlined.
- Interest rate swaps and currency swaps are described.
- Some older structures such as back-to-back and parallel loans are also examined.

**Exhibit 3.1    Range of OTC Derivative Instruments**

| Product Type | Interest Rates | Currency | Equity | Commodity |
|---|---|---|---|---|
| **Over-the-Counter Forward Contract** | • FRAs<br>• Interest Rate Swaps | • Currency Forwards<br>• Currency Swaps | • Equity Forwards/ Swaps | • Commodity Forwards/ Swaps |
| **Over-the-Counter Option Contract** | • Cap/Floors<br>• Options on Interest Rate Swaps/ Swaptions | • Currency Options | • Equity Options/ Equity Warrants | • Commodity Options |

---

[4]    See Das, Satyajit (2004) Risk Management; John Wiley & Sons (Asia), Singapore at Chapters 4, 13, 14 and 15.

[5]    See Das, Satyajit (2004) Structured Products Volume 2; John Wiley & Sons (Asia), Singapore at Chapters 1 and 7.

# 4   Forward Rate Agreements ("FRAs")[6]

## 4.1   Structure

A FRA is an agreement in respect of forward interest rates between two parties that wish to protect themselves against a future movement in interest rates. The parties involved agree on an interest rate for a specific period of time from a specified future settlement date based on an agreed principal amount. Economically, a FRA is simply a forward contract on interest rates.

The buyer is the party to the FRA seeking to protect itself against a future rise in the relevant interest rate. The seller is the party to the FRA seeking to protect itself against a future fall in the relevant interest rate. No commitment is made by either party to lend or borrow the principal amount. The exposure to both parties is only the interest difference between the agreed rate and actual settlement rate (that is cash settlement).

**Exhibit 3.2** sets out the mechanism for cash settlement of a FRA. Key terms usually utilised in connection with FRAs are set out in **Exhibit 3.3**. A typical FRA confirmation (for a US$ FRA covering a period of three months commencing in 3 months time) is set out in **Exhibit 3.4**.

---

### Exhibit 3.2   FRA Settlement Mechanics

Cash settlement takes place on the settlement date. The settlement rate procedure is pre-agreed. For example, in the US$ FRA market, the settlement rate is based on market rates such as those displayed on Reuters screen page LIBO or its equivalent.

If the settlement rate is higher than the agreed rate, the borrower will receive the difference from the lender or vice versa:

Settlement amount = [(The difference between the Settlement Rate and Agreed Rate)

$\times$ Contract Run $\times$ Principal Amount]/[(36,000 or 36,500)

+ (Settlement Rate $\times$ Contract Period)]

For currencies or markets where the custom is to utilise discounted (that is net receipts less than par value) securities, the Principal Amount figure is the face value amount discounted at the agreed rate. 36,000 is used for currencies where the basis of calculation is actual/360 days; 36,500 is utilised for currencies where the basis for interest calculations is actual/365 days.

---

6   See Treves, Daniel "The Case for the FRA" (November 1984) Euromoney 196; Brown, Richard "FRAs Move into Market as Hedging Alternative" (January 1985) Euromoney Corporate Finance 24; (1986) Forward Rate Agreements Accounting, Tax and Control Considerations; Peat, Marwick, Mitchell and Co, Banking and Financial Services Group Briefing Notes, Sydney.

| Exhibit 3.3    FRA Terminology | |
|---|---|
| **FRA** | A forward (or future) rate agreement. |
| **Forward Rate** | A future rate of interest agreed between the parties at the outset (also called the agreed rate or the guaranteed rate). |
| **Buyer (Or Borrower)** | The party wishing to protect itself from a rise in interest rates. |
| **Seller (Or Lender)** | The party wishing to protect itself from a fall in interest rates. |
| **Settlement Date** | The start date of the loan or deposit upon which the FRA is based. |
| **Contract Period** | The period between the date the rate was agreed and the settlement date. |
| **Maturity Date** | The date on which the FRA contract period ends. |
| **Fixing Date** | For most currencies two business days before the settlement date. For same day value currencies, this will be on the settlement date. |
| **Settlement Rate** | The mean rate quoted by specified reference banks for the relevant period and currency. For most currencies LIBOR as shown on Bridge-Telerate Page 3750 or Reuters Page LIBO. |
| **Run** | Period or term of underlying investment or borrowing – normally 90 or 180 days, that is, a three or six month run. |

### Exhibit 3.4    FRA Confirmation

To [Party A]

The purpose of this letter agreement is to confirm the terms and conditions of the FRA Transaction entered into between us on the Trade date specified below (the "FRA Transaction"). This letter agreement constitutes a confirmation as referred to in the Interest Rate and Currency Exchange Agreement specified below.

The definitions and provisions contained in the 1991 ISDA Definitions (as published by the International Swap Dealers Association, Inc.) are incorporated into this Confirmation. In the event of any inconsistency between those definitions and provisions and this Confirmation, this Confirmation will govern.

This confirmation supplements, forms part of, and is subject to, the Interest Rate and Currency Exchange Agreement dated [ ], as amended and supplemented from time to time (the "Agreement") between you and us. All provisions contained in the Agreement govern this confirmation except as expressly modified below.

**General**

| | |
|---|---|
| Type | US$ FRA |
| Notional Amount | US$100 million |
| Trade Date | 15 May 2001 |
| Effective Date | 17 May 2001 |
| Settlement Date | 17 August 2001 subject to the [Following/Modified/ Preceding Business] day Convention |
| Maturity Date | 17 November 2001 |

**Parties**

| | |
|---|---|
| Seller (Lender) | Party A |
| Buyer (Borrower) | Party B |

**Rates**

| | |
|---|---|
| Fixed Rate | 5.75% pa payable semi-annually in accordance with the Fixed Rate Day Count Fraction |
| Floating Rate | US$ LIBOR of the Designated Maturity reset semi-annually plus the Spread payable semi-annually in accordance with the Floating Rate Day Count Fraction |
| Fixed Rate Day Count Fraction | Semi-annual money market basis calculated on an actual/360 day year |
| Designated Maturity | 3 Months |
| Spread | Nil |
| Rate Set Date | 15 August 2001 |
| Floating Rate Day Count Fraction | Semi-annual money market basis calculated on an actual/360 day year |
| FRA Discounting[7] | [Applicable/Not Applicable] |
| | If Applicable then, the following will be nominated: |
| | Discount Rate: |
| | Discount Rate Day Count Fraction: |

**Other Terms**

| | |
|---|---|
| Netting of Payments | Applicable |
| Documentation | Standard ISDA |
| Calculation Agent | Party B |
| Governing Law | London |

**Account Details**

Payments to Party A
Account for Payment
Payments to Party B
Account for payments

**Offices**

Party A
Party B

**Broker/Arranger (if applicable)**

Please confirm that the forgoing correctly sets forth the terms of our agreement by executing the copy of this Confirmation enclosed for that purpose and returning it to us or sending us a letter or telex substantially similar to this letter which letter or telex sets forth the material terms of the Swap Transaction to which this confirmation relates and indicates agreement to those terms.

Party B

---

[7]   For a consideration of this aspect of FRA structures, see the examples set out in **Exhibit 3.6**.

## 4.2 FRA – Quotations

FRAs are quoted in interest rate terms. **Exhibit 3.5** sets out the typical form of quotation of FRA contracts.

Key aspects of the quotation convention include:
- All FRAs are quoted in rate terms.
- The rate structure is as follows:
    1. The lower rate is the bid rate. This is the rate at which the dealer is prepared to buy a FRA and the rate at which the counterparty would sell a FRA effectively locking in a deposit rate.
    2. The higher rate is the offer (ask) rate. This is the rate at which the dealer is prepared to sell a FRA and the rate at which the counterparty would buy a FRA effectively locking in a borrowing rate.
- The FRAs are quoted in month combinations. For example, a $1 \times 4$ FRA refers to a contract on the 3 month rate in 1 month's time. The first number refers to the settlement date of the FRA in months from the effective date. The second number refers to the maturity date (that is the date on which the FRA contract period ends) in months from the effective date.
- FRAs are generally quoted for the standard runs matching the underlying money market dates in the relevant currency. Customised transactions to specific dates required to match a counterparty's underlying transactions are also feasible. In general terms, FRAs for standard runs and specifically matched to short term interest rate futures contract maturities in the relevant currencies trade at significantly lower rates and with lower transaction costs (bid-offer) than for other FRAs. This reflects the problems of hedging for the trader[8].

| Exhibit 3.5 US\$ FRA Quotations | |
|---|---|
| **Maturity (months)** | **Bid/Ask** |
| $1 \times 4$ | 1.87/89 |
| $2 \times 5$ | 1.92/94 |
| $3 \times 6$ | 2.02/04 |
| $4 \times 7$ | 2.16/18 |
| $5 \times 8$ | 2.28/30 |

---

[8]   See Chapter 13.

| Maturity (months) | Bid/Ask |
|:-----------------:|:-------:|
| 6 × 9             | 2.43/45 |
| 7 × 10            | 2.61/63 |
| 8 × 11            | 2.79/81 |
| 9 × 12            | 3.04/06 |
| 1 × 7             | 2.03/05 |
| 2 × 8             | 2.14/16 |
| 3 × 9             | 2.21/23 |
| 4 × 10            | 2.38/40 |
| 5 × 11            | 2.52/54 |
| 6 × 12            | 2.71/73 |
| 12 × 18           | 3.92/94 |
| 18 × 24           | 5.07/09 |
| 1 × 10            | 2.30/32 |
| 2 × 11            | 2.36/38 |
| 3 × 12            | 2.49/51 |
| 6 × 18            | 3.35/38 |
| 12 × 24           | 4.54/56 |

## 4.3   FRA – Applications

FRAs are typically used to hedge exposure to short term interest rates on deposits and borrowings. **Exhibit 3.6** sets out the role and application of FRAs.

---

### Exhibit 3.6   FRA Examples

**1.   Hedging Future Investment**

Assume a company will have $1 million to deposit in three months for a six month period. The company treasurer is concerned that interest rates will fall over the next few months and therefore wishes to secure today's implied interest rate. Assume 3 × 9 FRAs (that is the six month interest rate in three months from the present) are quoted 17.75–18.00% pa and that the client agrees to the forward rate of 17.75% pa. The relevant market uses discounted securities for short term interest rate transactions and interest calculations are on the basis of an actual/ 365 day basis.

To determine the FRA settlement it is necessary to calculate the discount sum:

$$[(\text{Face Value} \times 36{,}500)/((\text{Agreed Rate} \times \text{Days}) + 36{,}500)]$$

$$= [(1{,}000{,}000 \times 36{,}500)/((17.75 \times 182) + 36{,}500)] = \$918{,}689.67$$

The settlement under the FRA will be as follows:
- If in three months time the settlement rate is 15.00% then the FRA provider will settle the difference in favour of the company as follows:

$$[((17.75 - 15.00) \times 182 \times 918,689.67)/(36,500 + (15.00 \times 182))] = \$11,720.73$$

- If in three months time the rate is 19.75% then the company will settle the difference in favour of the FRA provider as follows:

$$[((19.75 - 17.75) \times 182 \times 918,689.67)/(36,500 + (19.75 \times 182))] = \$8,340.37$$

**2. Hedging Future Borrowing**

Assume a company will need to borrow $1 million in one month for a six month period. The company treasurer thinks that interest rates may rise by the time the company borrows the money and wishes to fix the borrowing cost today. Assume the company and the FRA provider agrees on a 1 × 7 FRA rate of 8.50% pa. The relevant market uses par value transactions for short term interest rate transactions and interest calculation are on the basis of an actual/360 day basis.

The settlement under the FRA will be as follows:
- If in one month the settlement rate is 10.00% pa then the FRA provider will settle the difference in favour of the company as follows:

$$[((10.00 - 8.50) \times 182 \times 1,000,000)/(36,000 + (10.00 \times 182))] = \$7,218.40$$

- If in one month the settlement rate is 7.00% pa then the company will settle the difference in favour of the TRA provider as follows:

$$[((8.50 - 7.00) \times 182 \times 1,000,000)/(36,000 + (7.00 \times 182))] = \$7,324.14$$

## 4.4 FRAs – Compared to Futures[9]

FRAs are functionally similar to futures contracts on short term interest rates. Counterparties can use the futures market to protect themselves against interest rate fluctuations affecting their borrowing or investments as an alternative to using FRAs. The futures strategy to hedge a borrowing consists of selling financial futures; that is contracting to sell US$ Eurodollar (LIBOR) contracts for delivery at a future date simultaneously or as close as possible to when the company expects to borrow. At that time, if interest rates increase, then the higher interest cost will be offset by gains on the sold futures contracts. If rates decrease, then

---

[9] The comparison between FRAs and short-term interest rate futures is very similar. It is presented in generic terms and is applicable to all OTC products relative to comparable products in the ET market.

the lower interest cost will offset the loss on the sold futures contract. The effect should be that the net interest cost (subject to basis risk) would be identical. In order to hedge the interest rate exposure on an investment, financial futures would be bought. The same effect can be achieved through the use of FRAs.

The principal advantages of FRAs over interest rate futures include:

- As FRAs are not transacted through a futures exchange there is no requirement for initial or variation margin calls. This means lower administration costs and no cost of financing deposit/margin calls.
- Futures contracts are standardised as to amount, settlement day, etc. FRAs can be negotiated to precisely match the identified hedging requirements.
- The counterparty's exposure to credit risk is limited to the interest variation based on the principal. It will be lower than the principal amount. The extent of the credit risk depends on the interest rate volatility.
- The FRA is settled by exchange of a cash sum. Consequently, it does not gross up the balance sheet. This is in contrast to a forward deposit transaction (an agreement to place or take a deposit for a specified period at a specified value date). In these transactions funds equal to the principal of the deposit will be exchanged on the value date. The deposit or borrowing will then be carried on the balance sheet throughout the hedge period.
- A FRA hedge can be closed out at any stage by entering into an equal and opposite FRA at a new price. This price will reflect the interest rate for the period at the time of closing the hedge.
- A counterparty's borrowing rate and futures rate do not necessarily move in parallel. This basis risk can diminish the value of the hedge. FRAs can lock in a specific floating interest rate index regardless of fluctuations in other prevailing rates.
- For long-term hedging contracts, especially those having delivery dates in the distant future, the futures market may be thin. It may be difficult to buy and sell in significant amounts. FRAs may eliminate some of the liquidity problem.

However, FRAs do have disadvantages relative to interest rate futures including:

- There is no formal market in which FRAs can be traded. Secondary market liquidity in FRAs may be limited.
- FRAs entail credit risk (although only for the settlement amount) on the counterparty. In futures contracts, this is covered by substitution of the Clearing House as the counterparty to a transaction protected by the deposit and margins.

The differences between FRAs and interest rate futures contracts highlight the difference between exchange-traded and OTC products generally.

## 4.5 FRA – Product Variations

There are a number of significant variations on the conventional FRA including:
- **FRA Strip** – this entails using a "strip" or a series of FRAs to lock in the interest rate over a series of interest rate reset dates. A strip of FRAs can be utilised to create a fixed rate loan or investment. The FRAs act as a hedge guaranteeing the interest rate on each rollover date allowing determination at the outset of the interest rate over the whole period. An example of this type of transaction is set out in **Exhibit 3.7**. A strip of FRAs is functionally identical to an interest rate swap for the term.
- **Synthetic FRA** – this entails using a combination of FRAs and foreign exchange forward contracts to create a synthetic FRA in a foreign currency. This is used where FRAs are not available in a currency. An example of this type of transaction is set out in **Exhibit 3.8**.

---

**Exhibit 3.7    FRA Strip Hedge**

**1.    FRA Strip Hedge for Investment**
An investor seeks to hedge exposure on $10 million of investments currently earning floating interest rates for a period of 18 months ending 15 October 2003. All calculations are based on an actual/360 day year.

| Maturity Dates | Numbers of Days | FRA Rates (%) | US$ LIBOR Rate on Rate Setting Dates | FRA Settlement (US$) |
|---|---|---|---|---|
| 15 April 2002 | | | 4.75 | |
| 15 October 2002 | 183 | 5.125 | 5.00 | 6,164 |
| 15 April 2003 | 182 | 5.375 | 5.125 | 12,386 |
| 15 October 2003 | 183 | | | |
| | | | **Total** | 18,550 |

The net result of the transaction is an effective 18 month investment yield of 5.08% pa compounded semi-annually calculated on an actual/360 year.

**2.    FRA Strip Hedge for Borrowing**
A borrower seeks to hedge an exposure on a $10 million floating rate borrowing for a period of 12 months ending 4 June 2002. All calculations are based on an actual/360 day year.

| Maturity Dates | Numbers of Days | FRA Rates (%) | US$ LIBOR Rate on Rate Setting Dates | FRA Settlement (US$) |
|---|---|---|---|---|
| 4 June 2001 | 91 | | 12.00 | |
| 3 September 2001 | 91 | 13.00 | 12.50 | −12,252 |
| 3 December 2001 | 91 | 12.50 | 13.00 | 12,237 |
| 4 March 2002 | 92 | 12.00 | 13.25 | 30,898 |
| 4 June 2002 | | | | |
| | | | Total | 30,883 |

The net result of the transaction is an effective 12 month borrowing cost of 12.37% pa compounded quarterly calculated on an actual/360 day year.

---

### Exhibit 3.8    Synthetic FRA Transaction

A borrower wishes to lock in a two month borrowing cost in NZ$ for NZ$10 million. Normally, the borrower would achieve this objective by buying a NZ$ 1 × 3 month FRA, that is a FRA on two month NZ$ interest rates in one month's time. However, assume that NZ$ FRAs are not directly available, although A$ FRAs for the required term as well as A$ and NZ$ currency forwards are available.

The current market rates are[10]:

| | |
|---|---|
| A$/NZ$ Spot: | A$1.00 = NZ$1.1660 |
| 1 month forward | A$1.00 = NZ$1.1710 (.0050 forward points) |
| 3 months forward | A$1.00 = NZ$1.1840 (.0180 forward points) |
| A$ FRAs 1 × 3 | 13.24% pa annual effective |

In these circumstances the borrower could synthesise a NZ$ FRA as follows:
- Buy NZ$10 million against a sale of A$8,539,710 for value in one month at the quoted rate of NZ$1.1710.
- Sell NZ$10,334,744 against a purchase of A$8,728,669 (calculated as A$ 8,539,710 × (1 + 0.1324 × 61/365) for value in three months at the quoted rate of NZ$1.1840.
- Enter into a two month A$ FRA commencing in one month at a rate of 13.24% pa.

This series of transactions would provide the borrower with a known fully hedged cost of NZ$ funds.

Under the transaction, the borrower would draw down A$ funding for two months in one month at a rate of 13.24% pa guaranteed under the FRA. The A$ would be converted into NZ$ through the A$ and NZ$ foreign exchange contract. The A$ amount drawn down

---

[10]  Bid-offer spreads are omitted for ease of exposition.

is determined by the need to generate NZ$10 million of funding. At maturity, the borrower would repay NZ$10,334,744 that would be converted into A$8,728,669 through the forward contract. The A$ amount at maturity corresponds to the amount required to meet the principal and interest commitment on the A$ liability.

The overall transaction results in a guaranteed borrowing cost for NZ$10 million for two months in one month's time of 21.78% pa annual effective.

# 5 Caps/Floors[11]

## 5.1 Structure

Caps and floors are different types of option transactions designed to hedge interest rate exposure.

An interest rate cap is an agreement between the seller or provider of the cap and a borrower to limit the borrower's floating interest rate to a specified level for a period of time. The borrower selects a reference rate to hedge (for example US$ LIBOR), a period of time to hedge (for example 12 months, two years, five years, ten years), and the level of protection desired (for example 6.00%, 8.00%, 10.00%). The seller or provider of the cap, for a fee, insures the buyer against the reference rate exceeding the specified ceiling rate during the terms of the agreement. If market rates exceed the maximum rate, then the cap provider will make payments to the buyer sufficient to bring its rate back to the maximum rate. When market rates are below the maximum rate, no payments are made and the borrower pays market rates. The buyer of a cap therefore enjoys a fixed rate when market rates are above the cap and floating rates when market rates are below the cap.

An interest rate floor is similar to an interest rate cap agreement. An interest rate floor is an agreement between the seller or provider of the floor and an investor which guarantees that the investor's floating rate of return on investments will not

---

[11] See Brodeur, Brian J "Rate Swaps or Caps" (May 1985) Intermarket 19–23; Lynn, Leslie and Hein, Michael "Interest Rate Caps and Collars" (December 1985) Euromoney Corporate Finance, Special Sponsored Section; Haghani, Victor J. and Stavis, Robert M. (1986) Interest Rate Caps and Floors: Tools for Asset Liability Management; Salomon Brothers Inc, Bond Portfolio Analysis Group, New York; Rowley, Ian and Neuhaus, Henrik "How Caps and Floors Can Influence Desired Cash Flow" (July 1986) (July) Euromoney Corporate Finance 37–42; Smith, Donald J "Putting the Cap on Options" (January 1987) Euromoney Corporate Finance 20–22; Fall, William, "Caps versus Swaps Versus Hybrids" (April 1988) Risk 21–24.

fall below a specified level over an agreed period of time. The investor selects a reference rate to hedge, the period of time to hedge and the level of protection desired. If market rates fall below the minimum or floor rate, then the floor provider will make payments to the buyer sufficient to bring its rate back up to the agreed floor. When market rates are above the floor, no payments are made and the investor enjoys market rates of return.

An interest rate collar is a variation on the cap agreement. The seller or provider of the collar agrees to limit the borrower's floating interest rate to a band limited by a specified cap rate and floor rate. The borrower selects a reference rate to hedge (for example US$ LIBOR), a period of time to hedge (for example 12 months, five years, ten years), and the upper and lower levels of interest rates that the entity is willing to accept (for example 5.00% and 8.00%, 6.00% and 11.00%). The seller or provider of the collar, for a fee, insures the borrower against the reference rate exceeding the specified cap rate or being below the specified floor rate during the term of the agreement. If market rates exceed the cap rate, then the collar provider will make payments to the buyer sufficient to bring its rate back to the cap. If market rates fall below the floor, then the borrower makes payments to the collar provider to bring its rate back to the floor. When market rates are between the floor and the cap, the borrower pays the market rate. The buyer of a collar therefore has its borrowing rate confined to a band or collar ranging from the floor to the cap. In economic terms, the buyer of the collar has simultaneously bought a cap and sold a floor. A collar for an investor combines a sold cap and a bought floor on the relevant interest rate index.

At the end of each settlement period (for example, monthly, quarterly or semi-annually as agreed depending on the type of index) during the term of a cap/floor agreement, the market rate is compared to the cap or floor rate. Cash settlement is effected between the counterparties based on the difference between the actual market rate for the relevant maturity and the agreed cap or floor strike rate. For example, if the market rate is higher than the cap rate, then the borrower will receive a cash payment equal to the difference between the market rate and the cap rate multiplied by the principal amount of the hedge. The settlement mechanics for floors and collars are similar.

Economically, a cap is effectively a series of put options on the price of a security pricing off short term interest rates or a call option on the relevant short term interest rates. A floor is effectively a series of call options on the price of a security pricing off short term interest rates or a put option on short term rates.

**Exhibit 3.9** sets out a confirmation for a cap transactions setting out details of the typical terms and conditions relevant to such transactions.

| Exhibit 3.9 Cap, Floor and Collar Confirmation |
|---|

To [Party A]

The purpose of this letter agreement is to confirm the terms and conditions of the Swap Transaction entered into between us on the Trade date specified below (the "Swap Transaction"). This letter agreement constitutes a confirmation as referred to in the Interest Rate and Currency Exchange Agreement specified below.

The definitions and provisions contained in the 1991 ISDA Definitions (as published by the International Swap Dealers Association, Inc.) are incorporated into this Confirmation. In the event of any inconsistency between those definitions and provisions and this Confirmation, this Confirmation will govern.

This confirmation supplements, forms part of, and is subject to, the Interest Rate and Currency Exchange Agreement dated [ ], as amended and supplemented from time to time (the "Agreement") between you and us. All provisions contained in the Agreement govern this confirmation except as expressly modified below.

| **General** | |
|---|---|
| Notional Amount | US$100 million |
| Trade Date | 15 May 2001 |
| Effective Date | 17 May 2001 |
| Termination Date | 17 May 2004 subject to the [Following/Modified/Preceding Business] day Convention |
| **Fixed Amounts** | |
| Fixed Rate Payer | Party A |
| Fixed Rate Payer Payment Dates | Every 17 November and 17 May commencing 17 November 2001 and terminating on 17 May 2004 subject to the [Following/Modified/Preceding Business] day Convention |
| Fixed Amount | |
| **Floating Amounts** | |
| Floating Rate Payer | Party B |
| Cap Rate | 6.00 % pa |
| Floating Rate Payer Payment Dates | Every 17 November and 17 May commencing 17 November 2001 and terminating on 17 May 2004 subject to the [Following/Modified/Preceding Business] day Convention |
| Floating Rate Option | US$ LIBOR of the Designated Maturity reset semi-annually plus the Spread payable semi-annually in accordance with the Floating Rate Day Count Fraction |
| Designated Maturity | 6 Months |
| Floating Rate Day Count Fraction | Semi-annual money market basis calculated on an actual/360 day year |

---

[12] For a rate collar transaction there would be no Fixed Amounts or Fixed Rate Payer. Instead, one party would pay a Floating Amount based on a cap rate and the other party would pay a Floating Amount based on a floor rate. Separate Floating Amount provisions would need to be included for each party.

| | |
|---|---|
| Reset Dates | Every 17 May and 17 November commencing 17 May 2001 and terminating on 17 November 2003 subject to the [Following/Modified/Preceding Business] day Convention |
| Rate Cut-Off Dates | |
| Method of Averaging | [Unweighted/ Weighted Average] |
| Comounding | |
| Compounding Date | |
| Discounting | |
| Discount Rate | |
| Discount Rate Day Count Fraction | |
| **Other Terms** | |
| Calculation Agent | Party B |
| Governing Law | London |
| **Account Details** | |
| Payments To Party A | |
| Account For Payment | |
| Payments To Party B | |
| Account For Payments | |
| **Offices** | |
| Party A | |
| Party B | |
| **Broker/Arranger (if applicable)** | |

Please confirm that the forgoing correctly sets forth the terms of our agreement by executing the copy of this Confirmation enclosed for that purpose and returning it to us or sending us a letter or telex substantially similar to this letter which letter or telex sets forth the material terms of the Swap Transaction to which this confirmation relates and indicates agreement to those terms.

Party B

## 5.2   Cap/Floor – Quotations

Cap and floors are quoted in premium terms. Key aspects of the quotation convention include:

- Cap and floor contracts are quoted in premium terms. Collars are also quoted in premium terms (netting the cap and floor premiums taking into account the bid-offer spreads as one option is sold and the other is purchased). The premium is quoted in percentage or basis points terms of the face value or notional principal of the transaction. The premium paid is calculated in dollar terms by applying the premium percentage to the face value/notional principal.

- The bid premium refers to the premium paid to a seller by the dealer for a cap or floor. The offer premium refers to the premium paid by the purchaser to the dealer for a cap or floor.
- Cap and floor contracts are quoted against either 3- or 6-month benchmark short-term rates in the relevant currency. Generally, a number of strike prices, based around the current swap rate for the relevant maturity, are quoted in the inter-bank market. The counterparty may customise the specific transaction to match underlying transactions.
- Dealers quote caps and floors to non-professional (client) counterparties in premium terms. In inter-bank dealings, dealers may deal and quote in volatility terms. Traders buy volatility (buy options including caps/floors) or sell volatility (sell options including caps/floors). Quotes are structured such that dealers bid for volatility at a level lower than the level where they offer to sell volatility. In the inter-bank market, quotes may be in terms of implied volatility, which are then converted into a premium based on an option pricing model[13].

## 5.3   Cap/Floor – Applications

Caps provide protection against rising short-term interest rates without fixing rates. With the hedge in place, the buyer of the cap continues to borrow at the short end of the yield curve. When the yield curve is upward sloping, borrowing short-term results in considerable cost savings compared to fixed rate alternatives such as bonds or interest rate swaps that are priced off the term yield curve. Locking in a fixed rate in a positive yield curve environment results in an immediate increase in interest cost. The per annum cost of a cap may be much less than this immediate increment. The fixed rate borrower has no additional risk if rates rise, but has a high cost if rates decline. If rates rise only moderately or decline, then the short-term borrower with a cap may achieve substantial savings without unlimited risk.

A similar logic is applicable to floors. Floors provide the buyer with protection against declines in short-term interest rates while allowing participation in rates above the nominated floor rate level.

Buyers of cap and floors agreements generally pay an upfront fee (the option premium) determined by the cap or floor level, the maturity of the agreement, the instrument being hedged and market conditions. The premium will depend upon how close to current forward rates the cap is set and the volatility of the short-term interest rate index.

---

[13]  See Chapters 7, 8 and 9.

Collars provide protection against rising interest rates without fixing rates. As in cap agreements, buyers of collars continue to borrow at the short-term end of the yield curve and may enjoy substantial cost savings compared to fixed rate alternatives with no risk of higher interest rates. The basic rationale of the collar is the use of the sold option to finance the purchased option. In the case of a normal collar structure for a borrower, the purchased cap is financed by a sold floor that limits the borrower's capacity to participate in interest rate declines below the level of the sold floor. For investors, the sold cap reduces participation in increases in interest rates while using the premium received to reduce the cost of a purchased floor that provides protection against interest rates declines. Common structures include zero cost collars where the cost of the purchased and sold option exactly offset to provide protective structures for borrowers and investors at no explicit premium cost.

**Exhibit 3.10** sets out an example of the application of a cap and floor transaction.

---

### Exhibit 3.10    Cap & Floor Transaction

**1.  Cap Transaction**

A borrower purchases a cap at a strike cap level of 8.00% pa on 3 month LIBOR for a period of 12 months (commencing 1 June 2001 and ending on 1 June 2002). The cap is designed to hedge exposure to increasing interest rates on a $10 million floating rate borrowing which prices off 3 month LIBOR.

The actual cash flows from the transaction are set out below:

| Dates | Number of Days in Interest Rate Period | Cap Rate (% pa) | 3 Month LIBOR (On Repricing Date) (% pa) | Net Settlement Amount ($) |
|---|---|---|---|---|
| 1 June 2001 | | | 6.25 | – |
| 1 September 2001 | 92 | 8.00 | 6.75 | – |
| 1 December 2001 | 91 | 8.00 | 8.35 | 8,750 |
| 1 March 2002 | 90 | 8.00 | 7.80 | – |
| 1 June 2002 | 92 | | | |

The net settlement amount is calculated as: $10 million $\times$ (8.35% $-$ 8.00%) $\times$ 90/360 = $8,750. The settlement amount assumes a constant face value borrowing as distinct from a discount instrument.

The effective borrowing cost over the full 12 month period is 7.39% pa on an annual effective basis, based on a 360 day year. The effective borrowing yield is calculated as the 3 month LIBOR rate (where it is below the cap rate) or the cap rate (where 3 month LIBOR is above the cap rate) compounded over the period[14].

---

[14]  Please note the premium cost is ignored in this calculations.

The cap is effectively a series of put options on the price of a security pricing off 3 month LIBOR or a call option on 3 month LIBOR.

## 2. Floor Transaction

An investor purchases a floor at a strike floor level of 8.50% pa on 3 Month Treasury Bills for a period of 12 months (commencing 1 June 2001 and ending 1 June 2002). The transaction is designed to protect its investment returns on $10 million of money market investment that is priced off 3 month Treasury Bills.

The actual cash flows from the transaction are set out below:

| Dates | Number of Days in Interest Rate Period | Floor Rate (% pa) | 3 Month Treasury Bills (On Repricing Date) (% pa) | Net Settlement Amount ($) |
|---|---|---|---|---|
| 1 June 2001 | | | 9.05 | – |
| 1 September 2001 | 92 | 8.50 | 8.60 | – |
| 1 December 2001 | 91 | 8.50 | 8.25 | 5,917 |
| 1 March 2002 | 90 | 8.50 | 8.00 | 12,095 |
| 1 June 2002 | 92 | | | |

The Net Settlement Amount is calculated as: $[(\$10,000,00)/(1 + (8.50\% \times 90/365)] - [(\$10,000,00)/(1 + (8.25\% \times 90/365)] = \$5,917$. This reflects the fact that the transaction is structured on the basis of a constant face value and varying present value reflecting the use of discounted instruments.

The effective investment rate over the full 12 month period is 8.95% pa on an annual effective basis based on a 365 day year. The effective investment return is calculated as the 3 month Treasury Bill rate (where it is above the floor rate) or the floor rate (where 3 month Treasury Bill rates are below the floor rate) compounded over the period[15].

The floor is effectively a series of call options on the price of a security pricing off 3 month Treasury Bill rate or a put option on 3 month Treasury Bill Rate.

# 6 Currency Forwards[16]

## 6.1 Structure

Currency forward agreements (also known as foreign exchange or FX forwards) are outright forward transactions where the terms of the underlying transaction requires

---

[15] Please note the premium cost is ignored in this calculations.

[16] See (1983) Foreign Exchange and Money Market Operations; Swiss Bank Corporation, Zurich; Kubarych, Roger M. (1983) F+oreign Exchange Markets in the United States – Revised Edition; Federal Reserve Bank of New York, New York; Riehl,

delivery of a fixed amount of one currency in exchange for a known amount of a second currency. As with all forwards, the forward price (the forward exchange rate) is known and fixed at the time of entry into the currency forward transaction.

Currency forwards are OTC forward contracts where the underlying asset is the spot exchange rate. Currency forward agreements normally call for a single specific exchange at a date ranging from a few days to several years in the future. Long dated currency forward contracts (maturity greater than 1 year) are often referred to as Long Term FX contracts ("LTFX")[17].

Currency forwards are used primarily for hedging existing or anticipated currency exposures arising from cash flows denominated in a foreign currency. This includes currency exposures arising from long-term borrowing or investment or future receivables or payables.

For example, a United States company with A$ liability decides that the currency exposure is unacceptable and decides to buy A$ forward. At the same time, an Australian company plans to purchase assets in the United States and wants to guarantee the A$ price of its investment. To satisfy the respective hedging needs of the two companies, a currency forward contract could be structured. The United States company sells US$ to and buys A$ from the Australian company. The Australian company on the other hand will use the acquired US$ to pay for its US$ denominated investments. The currency risk of the two companies has been eliminated at the cost of the forward premium or discount between the two currencies.

**Exhibit 3.11** sets out confirmations for a currency forward transaction setting out details of the typical terms and conditions relevant to such transactions.

## 6.2   Currency Forwards – Quotations

Currency forwards are quoted as a premium or discount to the current spot rate. The price on forward currency contracts (the premiums/discounts to spot rates) generally will reflect the prevailing market interest rates for the two currencies for the same maturity. The longer the maturity in general, the wider the bid/ask spread, reflecting the lower liquidity of the market in the longer maturity ranges.

---

Heinz and Rodriguez, Rita M. (1983) Foreign Exchange and Money Markets; McGraw-Hill, New York; Anthony, Steve (1989) Foreign Exchange in Practice; Law Book Company, Sydney; Exchange Markets.

[17]  See Hilley, J. L., Beidleman, C. R. and Greenleaf, J. A., "Why There is No Long Forward Market in Foreign Exchange" (January 1981) Euromoney 94–103; Beidleman, Carl R., Hilley, J. L. and Greenleaf, J. A. "Alternatives in Hedging Long-Date Contractual Foreign Exchange Exposure" (Summer 1983) Sloan Management Review 45–54.

---

**Exhibit 3.11   Currency Forward Confirmation**

The terms of the particular FX transaction to which this confirmation relates are as follows:

**General**

| | |
|---|---|
| Trade Date | 15 May 2001 |
| Value Date | 17 November 2001 subject to the [Following/ Modified/Preceding Business] day Convention |

**Payments**

| | |
|---|---|
| Amount and Currency Payable by Party A | US$10,000,000 |
| Amount and Currency Payable by Party B | Yen 1,146,500,000 |
| Exchange Rate | US$1: Yen 114.65 |

**Other Terms**

| | |
|---|---|
| Documentation | Standard ISDA |
| Governing Law | London |

**Account Details**
Payments to Party A
Account for Payment
Payments to Party B
Account for Payments

**Offices**
Party A
Party B

**Broker/Arranger (if applicable)**

This document constitutes a "Confirmation" as referred to in the [Master Agreement]. The definitions and provisions contained in the 1992 FX and Currency Option Definitions (as published by the International Swap Dealers Association, Inc.) are incorporated into this Confirmation. In the event of any inconsistency between those definitions and provisions and this Confirmation, this Confirmation will govern. This Confirmation supplements, forms part of, and is subject to the Master Agreement dated as of [date], as amended and supplemented from time to time (the "Agreement"), between you and us. All provisions contained in the Agreement govern this Confirmation except as expressly modified above.

Please confirm that the forgoing correctly sets forth the terms of our agreement by executing the copy of this Confirmation enclosed for that purpose and returning it to us or sending us a letter or telex substantially similar to this letter which letter or telex sets forth the material terms of the Transaction to which this confirmation relates and indicates agreement to those terms.

Party B

**Exhibit 3.12** sets out examples of currency forward quotes.

| Exhibit 3.12 | Currency Forward Quotations |
| --- | --- |

| Maturity | US$/Euro (Euro 1 = US$) |
| --- | --- |
| Spot | 0.9928/0.9938 |
| | **Forward Points** |
| Tom/Next | −1/−1 |
| 1 week | −2/−2 |
| 1 month | −12/−11 |
| 2 months | −22/−22 |
| 3 months | −34/−32 |
| 4 months | −44/−44 |
| 5 months | −53/−52 |
| 6 months | −62/−60 |
| 9 months | −81/−79 |
| 1 year | −94/−91 |
| 2 years | −64/−47 |
| 3 years | 33/ 66 |
| 4 years | 145/193 |
| 5 years | 290/ 318 |

Notes:
1. Forward points are in FX points (0.0001).

## 6.3   Currency Forward – Variations

### 6.3.1   Overview

There are several structures of the basic currency forward. In practice, there are two types of currency forwards used in foreign exchange markets. In the inter-bank market, dealers use currency or FX swaps. This consists of a simultaneous spot transaction that is reversed at a forward date. Dealers use currency or FX swaps to manage the risk of and fund trading positions. The structure eliminates spot exposure leaving only interest rate exposure. Non-professional counterparties generally use outright forwards (that is a forward transaction without the spot leg). Outright forwards are appropriate to hedging future cash flows and currency exposures. There are also a number of variations to the standard currency forward structure. Two variations (par forwards and non-deliverable forwards) are discussed below.

## 6.3.2   Par Forward Contract

A common variation to the basic currency forward structure is the par forward structure. The basic logic is the requirement to transact a whole series of forwards at a single rate rather than transact individual forwards at different rates reflecting the structure of premiums and discounts prevailing in the market. **Exhibit 3.13** sets out an example of a par forward contract. The cash flows generated by the two approaches are different, although the economics (at least on a net present value basis) are identical.

---

**Exhibit 3.13   Par Forward Contract**

**Scenario 1**

Assume a counterparty has the need to purchase US$1 million every month for four months. The following structure of currency rates prevails:

| | | |
|---|---|---|
| Spot rate | A$1 = US$0.6600 | |
| Forward points | 7 July 2001 | −50 |
| | 7 August 2001 | −100 |
| | 7 September 2001 | −150 |
| | 7 October 2001 | −200 |

The following Table compares the results under a normal currency forward and a par forward contract.

| | Normal Forward | | Par Forward | |
|---|---|---|---|---|
| **Dates** | **Forward Rate (A$1=)** | **A$ Deliverable (per US$ 1 million)** | **Forward Rate (A$1=)** | **A$ Deliverable (per US$ 1 million)** |
| 7 July 2001 | 0.6550 | 1,526,717 | 0.6476 | 1,544,163 |
| 7 August 2001 | 0.6500 | 1,538,461 | 0.6476 | 1,544,163 |
| 7 September 2001 | 0.6450 | 1,550,387 | 0.6476 | 1,544,163 |
| 7 October 2001 | 0.6400 | 1,562,500 | 0.6476 | 1,544,163 |

The par forward rate is calculated as the nominal rate adjusted for the funding cost. In effect, the net present value of both series of cash flows should be equal.

The calculations are as follows:
- Nominal rate = (0.6550 + 0.6500 + 0.6450 + 0.6400)/4 = 0.6475
- Funding cost = cost or benefit to the company due to different cash flows. The cost to the company in the current example is A$785 which is compensated for in a benefit of one foreign exchange point (0.6475 + 0.0001 = 0.6476).

**Scenario 2**
A purchase of a $1 million one year forward can be transacted in one of the following ways:
- A forward purchase of US$1 million for value in one year's time at A$1 = US$0.6200 reflecting a spot rate of A$1/US$0.6600 and the one year forward premium of 0.0400 (that is, approximately 7.00% pa).
- A par forward with the forward being transacted at the spot rate of US$0.6200 with deferred settlement at an interest cost of 7.00%.

## 6.3.3   Non-Deliverable Forwards ("NDFs")

A NDF contract is economically equivalent to a cash settled outright currency forward. A NDF contract is structurally identical to a currency forward. The only difference is the fact that the settlement at maturity of the contract is by net cash settlement, not physical delivery of currency amounts. The net settlement effected at maturity is calculated to reflect the difference, if any, between the contracted forward rate and the prevailing actual spot exchange rate on the settlement date. **Exhibit 3.14** sets out the structure of a NDF forward.

---

**Exhibit 3.14   NDF Forward Transaction**

Assume a counterparty wished to sell New Taiwanese dollars (NT$) forward. The transaction is to hedge an underlying investment exposure that is not eligible for currency forward coverage in the formal or official NT$ currency market. The counterparty enters into a NDF with a dealer for US$1 million for a 6 month maturity at rate of US$1 = NT$40.

The net outcome under the NDF contract for an increase or decrease in the exchange rate is summarised in the Table below.

|  | NT$ Appreciates | NT$ Depreciates |
|---|---|---|
| Spot Rate at Settlement Date | 35.00 | 45.00 |
| NT$ Amount at NDF Contracted Rate (NT$ 40) | 40,000,000 | 40,000,000 |
| NT$ Amount at NDF Settlement Rate | 35,000,000 | 45,000,000 |
| Net Settlement | Counterparty pays US$142,857 (calculated as NT$ 5,000,000 @ NT$35) | Counterparty receives US$111,111 (calculated as NT$ 5,000,000 @ NT$45) |

Where the NT$ at maturity is the same as the contracted NDF rate, there is no settlement between the counterparties under the NDF contract.

The overall result of the cash flows under the NDF is to provide a hedge to the counterparty. This reflects the fact that any gain or loss on the NDF contract is offset to the change in the value of the NT$ asset sought to be hedged.

The method for calculating the net settlement amount is prescribed at the time of entry into the transaction. The net settlement rate is set typically two days before the settlement (in effect for value at the settlement date) based on an acceptable screen source or a dealer poll mechanism (entailing dealer quotes from around 4 dealers). Settlement is effected in US$ or another freely convertible currency.

NDF transactions are used to hedge currency exposures or speculate on currency markets, in particular in emerging markets. The major drivers for NDFs include:

- The absence of any requirement to undertake any actual physical funds transfer in the local market, reduced counterparty credit risk and the (often high) transaction costs of trading in local currencies.
- The structure can be designed to be undertaken between two offshore counterparties and therefore avoid currency controls or restrictions. This is important in controlled markets as it enables participants with exposures not eligible for hedging under the controlled regime to hedge their price exposures.

A variation on the NDF concept is the synthetic or NDF linked currency deposit. The structure combines a deposit in US$ with a NDF forward. The objective is to allow foreign investors access to domestic money markets and (often high) local currency interest yields. This access may not be available directly and/or the credit risk of direct participation may discourage foreign investor participation. **Exhibit 3.15** sets out the structure of this type of NDF linked currency deposit transaction.

---

**Exhibit 3.15    NDF Linked Currency Deposit Transaction**

An investor wishing to synthesise a high yielding deposit in Philippine Pesos ("PHP") using NDF linked currency deposits would enter into the following transaction. The market rates are as follows:
- Spot currency rate is US$1 = PHP42.00
- PHP 6 month interest rate is 15.00% pa.
- US$ 6 month interest rate is 5.00% pa.

The investor deposits US$1 million. On a normal US$ deposit, the investor would receive US$1,025,000 at the end of 6 months (calculated as US$1,000,000 × 5.00% pa × 0.5 year).

In a NDF linked currency deposit transaction, the investor receives the following payment at maturity:

Principal redemption amount calculated as US$1,075,000 × (42.00/US$/PHP spot exchange rate at settlement). [The US$1,075,000 is calculated as the principal of US$1,000,000 plus interest return of 15% pa or US$75,000 (calculated as US$1,000,000 × 15% pa × 0.5 years)].

The return to the investor for different currency scenarios is set out below:

|                              | PHP Appreciates | PHP Unchanged | PHP Depreciates |
|------------------------------|-----------------|---------------|-----------------|
| US$/PHP spot rate at maturity| 39.00           | 42.00         | 45.00           |
| Redemption Amount (US$)      | 1,157,692       | 1,075,000     | 1,003,333       |
| Return (US$)                 | 157,692         | 75,000        | 3,333           |
| Return (% pa)                | 31.54           | 15.00         | 0.67            |

The investor has the same investment risk profile as if it had made a direct investment in PHP money market assets.

# 7  Currency Options[18]

## 7.1  Structure

A currency option follows the normal structure of an option. The major distinguishing feature of a currency option is the fact that the underlying asset is a spot foreign exchange transaction.

**Exhibit 3.16** sets out confirmations for a currency forward transaction setting out details of the typical terms and conditions relevant to such transactions.

## 7.2  Currency Option – Quotations

Currency option premiums are typically quoted either as a percentage of the strike price or as a fixed number of exchange points. The premium may be expressed in either currency. The dollar value of the currency is derived from either form of quotation. **Exhibit 3.17** sets out an example of a currency option quotation. Currency option quotes to clients are in terms of option premium. Inter-bank option dealings are in terms of implied volatility.

---

[18] See Giddy, Ian H. "The Foreign Exchange Option as a Hedging Tool" (Fall 1983) Midland Corporate Finance Journal vol 1 no 3 32–42; Giddy, Ian H. "Foreign Exchange Options" (1983) Journal of Futures Markets vol 3 no 2 143–166; Sutton, William (1988) The Currency Options Handbook; Woodhead-Faulkner, Cambridge; Giddy, Ian H. and Dufey, Gunter "Uses and Abuses of Currency Options" (Fall 1995) Journal of Applied Finance vol 8 no 3 49–57.

## Exhibit 3.16   Currency Option Confirmation

The terms of the particular FX transaction to which this confirmation relates are as follows:

**General**

| | |
|---|---|
| Trade Date | 15 May 2001 |
| Buyer | Party A |
| Seller | Party B |

**Currency Option Details**

| | |
|---|---|
| Currency Option Style | [American/European] |
| Currency Option Type | US$ Call/Yen Put |
| Call Currency & Amount | US$10,000,000 |
| Put Currency & Amount | Yen |
| Strike Price | US$1: Yen 120.00 |
| Expiration Date | 15 November 2001 subject to the [Following/Modified/Preceding Business] day Convention |
| Expiration Time | 3:00 p.m. Tokyo time |
| Settlement Date | 17 November 2001 subject to the [Following/Modified/Preceding Business] day Convention |
| Premium | 2.20% |
| Premium Payment Date | 17 May 2001 |
| In-the-money Amount | [Yes/No] |
| Settlement | If selected, then if the option is in-the-money, then the option will be automatically exercised. |
| | The parties must make an election for in-the-money settlement in the Confirmation or through other means. In the case where parties elect In-the-money Settlement, parties should also specify in the Confirmation or through another means the currency in which the Currency Option will settle. Parties may additionally specify the rate for conversion in the Confirmation if the currency for In-the-money Settlement is selected therein and such currency is a currency other than the call currency or put currency. If such rate is not specified in the Confirmation, market practice suggests that the rate used for conversion will likely be the relevant spot price, unless the parties otherwise agree. |

**Other Terms**

| | |
|---|---|
| Part Exercise of Option | [Permitted/not permitted] |
| Documentation | Standard ISDA |
| Governing Law | London |

**Account Details**

Payments to Party A
Account for Payment
Payments to Party B
Account for Payments

**Offices**
Party A
Party B

**Broker/ Arranger (if applicable)**

This document constitutes a "Confirmation" as referred to in the [Master Agreement]. The definitions and provisions contained in the 1992 FX and Currency Option Definitions (as published by the International Swap Dealers Association, Inc.) are incorporated into this Confirmation. In the event of any inconsistency between those definitions and provisions and this Confirmation, this Confirmation will govern. This Confirmation supplements, forms part of, and is subject to the Master Agreement dated as of [date], as amended and supplemented from time to time (the "Agreement"), between you and us. All provisions contained in the Agreement govern this Confirmation except as expressly modified above.

Please confirm that the forgoing correctly sets forth the terms of our agreement by executing the copy of this Confirmation enclosed for that purpose and returning it to us or sending us a letter or telex substantially similar to this letter which letter or telex sets forth the material terms of the Transaction to which this confirmation relates and indicates agreement to those terms.

Party B

---

**Exhibit 3.17    Currency Option Quotation**

Assume the following information regarding a US$ call/A$ put option for US$10 million:

| Spot Rate: | A$1: US$0.6850 | |
| Strike Price: | A$1: US$0.6900 | |

| Premium: | % of Strike | 1.25% |
| | US$ per A$ | 0.008625 |
| | A$ Per US$ | 0.018248 |

The actual dollar premium would be calculated as follows:
* **Percentage of strike** – premium is:

   US$10,000,000 × 1.25% = US$125,000

* **US$ per A$** – premium is:

   A$14,492,753.62 (calculated as US$10,000,000 at strike price of A$1 = US$0.6900) × 0.008625 = US$125,000

* **A$ per US$** – premium is:

   US$10,000,000 × 0.018248 = A$182,481.75 (which at current spot exchange rate of A$1: US$0.6850 equates to US$125,000).

## 7.3   Currency Option – Applications

Currency options are used to hedge currency exposures on an asymmetric basis. **Exhibit 3.18** sets out an example of the use of currency options. In both cases, purchased currency options are used to establish the maximum cost (in local currency terms) or minimum receipts (in local currency terms) without precluding the possibility of gains from favourable movements in exchange rate.

---

**Exhibit 3.18    Currency Options Applications**

**1.   Hedging Foreign Currency Payables**

Assume a US$ based importer is required to make a Yen payment in 3 months' time of Yen 100 million. The spot exchange rate is US$1 = Yen 120 and the 3 month forward rate is US$1 = Yen 116.50. The importer purchases a call option on Yen (put on US$) for value in 3 months at a strike of Yen 116.50 for payment of a premium of Yen 1.165 (1%).

In 3 months' time, the importer undertakes the following transactions:

* If the US$ is trading below Yen 116.50 then the importer exercises the option and purchases Yen at Yen 116.50. The effective cost of the Yen is 115.3350 (reflecting the option premium cost).
* If the US$ is trading above Yen 116.50 then the importer abandons the option and purchases yen in the spot market at a more favourable rate than under the option. The effective breakeven for the importer is Yen 117.6650 (the level of the strike price adjusted for the premium above which the importer gains).

The result of the hedging strategy is summarised in the table below:

**US$ Cost to Importer (per Yen 100 million)**

|                    | US$ Depreciates | US$ Appreciates |
|--------------------|-----------------|-----------------|
| US$/Yen            | 115.00          | 125.00          |
| Outright Forward   | 858,369         | 858,369         |
| Call Option on Yen | 867,039         | 807,526         |

**2.   Hedging Foreign Currency Receivables**

Assume a US$ based exporter is expecting a Yen payment in 3 months' time of Yen 120 million. The spot exchange rate is US$1 = Yen 120 and the 3 month forward rate is US$1 = Yen 116.50. The exporter purchases a put option on Yen (call on US$) for value in 3 months at a strike of Yen 116.50 for payment of a premium of Yen 1.165 (1%).

In 3 months' time, the exporter undertakes the following transactions:

* If the US$ is trading above Yen 116.50 then the exporter exercises the option and purchases US$ at Yen 116.50. The effective level of the Yen achieved is 117.6650 (reflecting the option premium cost).

- If the US$ is trading below Yen 116.50 then the exporter abandons the option and purchases US$ in the spot market at a more favourable rate than under the option, The effective breakeven for the exporter is Yen 115.3350 (the level of the strike price adjusted for the premium below which the exporter gains).

The result of the hedging strategy is summarised in the table below:

**US$ Receipts to Exporter (per Yen 100 million)**

|                   | US$ Depreciates | US$ Appreciates |
|-------------------|-----------------|-----------------|
| US$/Yen           | 115.00          | 125.00          |
| Outright Forward  | 858,369         | 858,369         |
| Put Option on Yen | 860,844         | 849,870         |

# 8   Interest Rate Swaps[19]

## 8.1   Structure

An interest rate swap is a transaction in which two parties agree to exchange streams of cash flows based on a hypothetical (or notional) principal amount where one

[19] See Price, John A. M., Keller, Jules and Neilson, Max "The Delicate Art of Swaps" (April 1983) Euromoney 118–125; Price, John, "Modern Currency Exchange Financing Techniques" (October 1983) The Chartered Accountant in Australia 30–34; Antl, Boris (Editor) (1983) Swap Financing Techniques; Euromoney Publications, London; Das, Satyajit Interest Rate Swaps (1983, No. 1, April) JASSA 10–13; Interest Rate Swaps (1983/84 Vol. 1) Bulletin of Money, Banking and Finance 1–40; Price, John and Henderson, Schuyler K. (1984) Currency and Interest Rate Swaps; Butterworths, London; Beidleman, Carl R. (1985) Financial Swaps; Dow Jones-Irwin, Homewood, Illinois; Antl, Boris (Editor) (1986) Swap Finance – Volumes 1 and 2; Euromoney Publications, London; Antl, Boris (Editor) (1987) Swap Finance Update Service; Euromoney Publications, London; Price, John and Henderson, Schuyler K. (1987) Currency and Interest Rate Swaps – 2nd Edition; Butterworths, London; Kopprasch, Robert W., Macfarlane, John, Ross, Daniel R. and Showers, Janet (1985) The Interest Rate Swap Market: Yield Mathematics, Terminology and Conventions; Salomon Brothers Inc., New York; Balducci, Vince, Doraiswami, Johnson, Cal and Showers, Janet (September 1990) Currency Swaps: Corporate Applications and Pricing Methodology; Salomon Brothers Inc., New York; Marshall, John F. and Kapner, Kenneth R. (1990) Understanding Swap Finance; South-Western Publishing Co., Cincinatti, Ohio; Daugaard, Daniel (1991) The Swaps Handbook; Financial Training and Analysis

stream is calculated with reference to a floating interest rate and the other stream is calculated based on a fixed interest rate. The payment to be made by one party is calculated using a benchmark floating rate of interest in the relevant currency (such as LIBOR) while the payment to be made by the other party is determined on the basis of a fixed rate of interest. An interest swap can be used to transform one type of interest obligation into another and thereby enable a swap participant to tailor its interest obligations to meet its needs in a given rate environment. Economically, an interest rate swap is a portfolio of forward contracts on interest rates in the relevant currency.

## 8.2   Interest Rate Swap – Example

In its most common form, an interest rate swap is undertaken between two counterparties. The first may be a borrower that wants to pay interest at a fixed rate but has already borrowed at a floating rate. The second may be a borrower that wants to pay interest at a floating rate but has already borrowed at a fixed rate. The borrower wanting to pay a fixed rate borrows the principal amount that it needs on a floating rate basis. The borrower wanting to pay a floating rate borrows an identical amount at fixed rates. If a borrower were entering into the swap with respect to an existing debt, it would not undertake a new borrowing.

The two counterparties then enter into an agreement in which each undertakes to make periodic payments to the other in amounts equal to or determined on the same basis as the other's interest cost. Only payments calculated in the form of interest are made. No principal payments are made by the counterparties. The net result of this exchange is that each party is able to obtain the type of interest rate (fixed or floating) that it wants and on acceptable terms.

**Exhibit 3.19** sets out in diagrammatic form the basic structure of an interest rate swap. **Exhibit 3.20** sets out the cash flows for a three year $ interest rate swap.

Services Pty Ltd., Sydney; Beidleman, Carl R. (Editor) (1991) Interest Rate Swaps; Business One Irwin, Homewood, Illinois; Flavell, Richard (1991) Swaps Training Manual; Euromoney Books, London; Beidleman, Carl R. (Editor) (1992) Cross Currency Swaps; Business One Irwin, Homewood, Illinois; (1992) Interest Rate Swaps – IFR Self Study Workbooks; IFR Publishing, London; (1993) Currency Swaps – IFR Self Study Workbooks; IFR Publishing, London; Dattatreya, Ravi E., Venkatesh, Raj E. S. (1994) Interest Rate & Currency Swaps; Probus Publishing, Chicago, Illinois; Marshall, John F. and Kapner, Kenneth R. (1993) Understanding Swaps; John Wiley & Sons, Inc., New York; Flavell, Richard (2002) Swaps and Other Derivatives; John Wiley & Sons, Chichester.

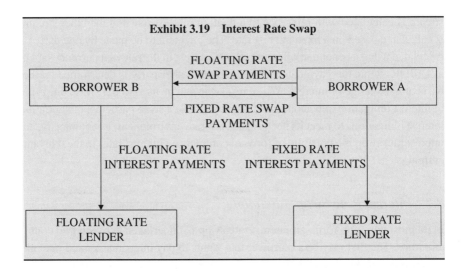

Exhibit 3.19    Interest Rate Swap

**Exhibit 3.21** sets out a typical transaction confirmation, confirming entry by a company into an interest rate swap detailing the typical terms and conditions of such transactions.

A number of essential features of the interest rate swap should be noted:

- The transaction amount is referred to as the notional principal/amount. It is notional in the sense that it is not usually exchanged as both participants do not obtain the underlying liquidity or funding through the swap. In any case, an exchange would be redundant as each counterparty would provide the other with the same amount in the same currency. The notional amount is used as the basis for interest calculations under the swap. For example, in **Exhibit 3.20** the 7.50% pa and the LIBOR interest flows are calculated on the notional principal amount ($100 million).
- The swap transaction is totally independent from any underlying borrowing transactions for either party. The swap affects only the interest or coupon flows of a separately undertaken liability.
- The original lenders are not parties to the swap. Each borrower continues to be obligated to its own lender for the payment of both principal and interest. The lenders would not necessarily be aware that the swap had been undertaken. Each swap party takes the risk that the other may not make its swap payments, which would leave the non-defaulting party with the interest cost of its own borrowing uncovered by the swap. The swap does not relieve either borrower from the obligation to pay both principal and interest on its own borrowing.

## Exhibit 3.20   Interest Rate Swap – Cash Flows

The following cash flows are for a 3-year interest rate swap. Company A borrows $100 million for 3 years at a rate of 7.50% pa and enters into a swap with Company B which borrows $100 million for 3 years on a floating rate basis at a cost of 6 month LIBOR plus a margin of 0.50% pa. The swap is undertaken on the following terms: Company B pays 7.50% pa in return for receiving 6 month LIBOR.

| | Company A Interest Rate Swap | | | | Company B Interest Rate Swap | | | |
| Year | Underlying Loan Cash Flows | Swap Receipts | Swap Payments | Net Cash Flows | Underlying Loan Cash Flows | Swap Receipts | Swap Payments | Net Cash Flows |
|---|---|---|---|---|---|---|---|---|
| 0 | +100.00 | – | – | +100 | +100 | – | – | +100 |
| 0.5 | −3.75 | +3.75 | −(LIBOR × $100 m × fraction of year) | −(LIBOR × $100 m × fraction of year) | −((LIBOR + 0.50 % pa) × $100 m × fraction of year) | +(LIBOR × $100 m × fraction of year) | −3.75 | −4.00 |
| 1.0 | −3.75 | +3.75 | −(LIBOR × $100 m × fraction of year) | −(LIBOR × $100 m × fraction of year) | −((LIBOR + 0.50 % pa) × $100 m × fraction of year) | +(LIBOR × $100 m × fraction of year) | −3.75 | −4.00 |
| 1.5 | −3.75 | +3.75 | −(LIBOR × $100 m × fraction of year) | −(LIBOR × $100 m × fraction of year) | −((LIBOR + 0.50 % pa) × $100 m × fraction of year) | +(LIBOR × $100 m × fraction of year) | −3.75 | −4.00 |
| 2.0 | −3.75 | +3.75 | −(LIBOR × $100 m × fraction of year) | −(LIBOR × $100 m × fraction of year) | −((LIBOR + 0.50 % pa) × $100 m × fraction of year) | +(LIBOR × $100 m × fraction of year) | −3.75 | −4.00 |
| 2.5 | −3.75 | +3.75 | −(LIBOR × $100 m × fraction of year) | −(LIBOR × $100 m × fraction of year) | −((LIBOR + 0.50 % pa) × $100 m × fraction of year) | +(LIBOR × $100 m × fraction of year) | −3.75 | −4.00 |
| 3.0 | −3.75 | +3.75 | −(LIBOR × $100 m × fraction of year) | −(LIBOR × $100 m × fraction of year) | −((LIBOR + 0.50 % pa) × $100 m × fraction of year) | +(LIBOR × $100 m × fraction of year) | −3.75 | −4.00 |
| 3.0 | −100.00 | – | – | −100 | −100 | – | – | −100 |

Notes:
1. (+) indicates a receipt, while (−) indicates a payment. All cash flows are in $ millions.
2. The accrual on the fixed rate payments assumes equal interest rate payments for simplicity.
3. LIBOR is equal to 6 month LIBOR set semi-annually calculated on the relevant fraction of a year (actual days/360 in the case of $ LIBOR or based on the applicable day count). It is also assumed LIBOR on the loan and the swap are the same; that is, rates (plus 0.50% pa in respect of the margin on the loan) are set on the same day by the same rate setting mechanism.

### Exhibit 3.21    Interest Rate Swap Confirmation

To [Party A]

The purpose of this letter agreement is to confirm the terms and conditions of the Swap Transaction entered into between us on the Trade date specified below (the "Swap Transaction"). This letter agreement constitutes a confirmation as referred to in the Interest Rate and Currency Exchange Agreement specified below.

The definitions and provisions contained in the 1991 ISDA Definitions (as published by the International Swap Dealers Association, Inc.) are incorporated into this Confirmation. In the event of any inconsistency between those definitions and provisions and this Confirmation, this Confirmation will govern.

This confirmation supplements, forms part of, and is subject to, the Interest Rate and Currency Exchange Agreement dated [ ], as amended and supplemented from time to time (the "Agreement") between you and us. All provisions contained in the Agreement govern this confirmation except as expressly modified below.

**General**

| | |
|---|---|
| Notional Amount | US$100 million |
| Trade Date | 15 May 2001 |
| Effective Date | 17 May 2001 |
| Termination Date | 17 May 2004 subject to the [Following/Modified/Preceding Business] day Convention |

**Fixed Amounts**

| | |
|---|---|
| Fixed Rate Payer | Party A |
| Fixed Rate Payment Dates | Every 17 November and 17 May commencing 17 November 2001 and terminating on 17 May 2004 subject to the [Following/Modified/Preceding Business] day Convention |
| Fixed Rate | 6.25% pa payable semi-annually in accordance with the Fixed Rate Day Count Fraction |
| Fixed Rate Day Count Fraction | Semi-annual bond equivalent basis calculated on an actual/ 365 day year |

**Floating Amounts**

| | |
|---|---|
| Floating Rate Payer | Party B |
| Floating Rate Payment Dates | Every 17 November and 17 May commencing 17 November 2001 and terminating on 17 May 2004 subject to the [Following/Modified/Preceding Business] day Convention |
| Floating Rate | US$ LIBOR of the Designated Maturity reset semi-annually plus the Spread payable semi-annually in accordance with the Floating Rate Day Count Fraction |
| Designated Maturity | 6 months |
| Spread | Nil |
| Floating Rate Day Count Fraction | Semi-annual money market basis calculated on an actual/ 360 day year |

**Other Terms**

| | |
|---|---|
| Netting of Payments | Applicable |
| Documentation | Standard ISDA |
| Calculation Agent | Party B |
| Governing Law | London |

**Account Details**
Payments to Party A
Account for Payment
Payments to Party B
Account for Payments

**Offices**
Party A
Party B

**Broker/Arranger (if applicable)**

Please confirm that the forgoing correctly sets forth the terms of our agreement by executing the copy of this Confirmation enclosed for that purpose and returning it to us or sending us a letter or telex substantially similar to this letter which letter or telex sets forth the material terms of the Swap Transaction to which this confirmation relates and indicates agreement to those terms.

Party B

## 8.3 Interest Rate Swap – Quotations

Interest rate swaps are quoted in interest rate terms on the fixed and floating interest payments. Interest rate swaps of a given maturity are quoted as a fixed rate (for example, 8.00% pa) against a floating rate index quoted flat (that is, with no margin over or under the index).

There are two basic quotation formats:

- **Spread Markets** – in certain markets the price on an interest rate swap is quoted as a spread over a fixed rate index against the floating rate index flat. The US$ swap market is quoted in spread terms. For example, in US$ interest rate swaps, a dealer quotes the price on a 5 year fixed rate US$ against LIBOR swap to a fixed rate payer as the 5 year Treasury rate plus 60 bps versus 6 month LIBOR. In markets other than the US$ swap market, the relationship of swap rates to the comparable government securities rate may be inconsistent and weak.
- **Absolute Rate Markets** – in most markets, the price on an interest rate swap is quoted as an absolute interest rate against the relevant floating rate index.

The linkage between swap rates and government or other benchmark bond rates merits additional comment. The relationship which developed originally in the US$ swap market appears to be based upon two factors:

- **Credit spread** – spreads over a risk-free rate such as the government bond rate act as a proxy for credit risk differentials. In developed capital markets such as the US$ market, the risk premiums embodied in spread differentials for borrowers of different credit quality are relatively well established. Although the risk premium changes over time, the fact that they are readily determinable means that they can form the basis for swap arbitrage analysis. A result of this is that swaps which function as a means of creating synthetic fixed and floating rate borrowings tend to be priced "off" a benchmark risk free rate in a manner similar to that of pricing direct borrowings. This thesis is confirmed to some degree by the fact that the relationship between swap prices and government bond rates is strongest in markets with well developed risk premium structures. In markets where certain types of securities issues are not readily possible, the linkage is significantly weaker[20].

- **Use of government bonds to hedge swap transactions** – swap rates are related to the cost of hedging swap transactions[21]. Before a swap is matched with an offsetting swap, it is generally hedged with a combination of securities, futures contracts and some form of floating rate investment or funding such as repurchase agreements. For example, if the intermediary is the fixed rate payer on the swap, the hedge usually involves the purchase of an appropriate amount of government securities with the same maturity as the swap. The purchase of securities is in turn financed by borrowing in an appropriate market (in practice, the money market or, if available, the short-term repurchase agreement market). The government security creates a hedge against capital loss if long-term interest rates change. It also generates fixed rate income that matches the fixed payments of the swap. The floating rate income from the swap covers the floating rate cost of funding the purchase. Swaps of shorter maturity (usually up to two to three years) are more likely to be hedged in the short term interest rate futures market.

A number of other quotation conventions should be noted:

- Under market convention, an offer (bid) swap price indicates the price at which the market is willing to receive (pay) the fixed rate under the swap. The dealer's

---

[20] See Chapter 11.
[21] See Chapters 12, 13 and 14.

spread representing dealer earnings is the difference between the offer and bid swap price.

- The term "trade date" refers to the date on which the counterparties commit themselves to the swap.
- The "effective date" on a swap is the date on which fixed and floating interest starts accruing. Normally, this is a period of up to two business days after the trade date depending upon market convention in the particular swap market. The "settlement date" is the date on which the transaction is priced for value. Normally in swap transactions this is the same as the effective date.
- Swap agreements are executed on an "as of" basis; that is, the agreement is prepared and executed some time after the effective date. This custom enhances the liquidity of the swap market.

**Exhibit 3.22** sets out the structure of interest rate swap quotations and terminology. **Exhibit 3.23** sets out examples of interest rate swap quotations.

It should be noted that the quotations available are for *generic* swap transactions (that is, standard structures). Inter-bank dealing among dealers is primarily in these types of instruments. The quotes listed are primarily applicable to these instruments. Transactions entered into with clients are more structured. These transactions incorporate a number of non-generic features. The prices for these transactions will usually entail some adjustment to the quotes for generic swaps[22].

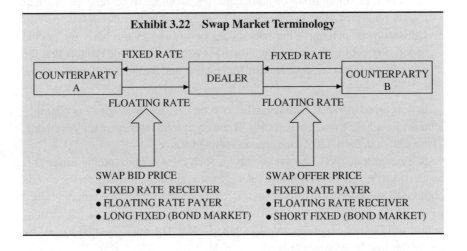

**Exhibit 3.22    Swap Market Terminology**

---

[22] See Chapter 10.

| Exhibit 3.23    US$ Interest Rate Swap Quotations | | |
|---|---|---|
| Maturity (years) | Absolute Swap Rates (% pa) | Swap Spreads (bps pa) |
| 2 | 3.44/3.46 | 42/44 |
| 3 | 4.24/4.26 | 64/67 |
| 5 | 5.08/5.11 | 58/60 |
| 7 | 5.42/5.45 | 60/63 |
| 10 | 5.76/5.80 | 63/67 |
| 15 | 6.05/6.07 | 67/71 |
| 20 | 6.16/6.21 | 74/79 |
| 25 | 6.16/6.21 | 66/71 |
| 30 | 6.19/6.24 | 55/60 |

## 8.4   Floating Rate Benchmark

An essential element in an interest rate swap is the benchmark floating interest rate utilised. It is also necessary in FRAs and currency swaps. The benchmark rate ideally should display the following characteristics:

- **Universal acceptance** – the rate should be acceptable to all counterparties to facilitate entry into the transaction.
- **Transparent determination** – the rate should be determined using transparent methods. It should not be capable of being easily manipulated or influenced by any single or small group of participants. It should also be reflective of *real* market rates prevailing in the market.
- **Utilisation in pricing** – the rate should be utilised as the basis for pricing underlying debt transactions by all market participants. This ensures that the rate will provide a reasonable basis for hedging and trading for all participants.

In developed markets, the availability of a benchmark floating rate is not problematic. Benchmark rates such as LIBOR and equivalent rates are readily available. These rates generally satisfy the criteria outlined above.

In emerging markets, the availability of such rates is more problematic. This results from the fact that benchmark rates are not available or do not meet the criteria outlined. This typically derives from the regulated structure or the less developed nature of the market. Under these conditions undertaking derivative transactions requires the use of an *acceptable* benchmark rate. The rates must be agreed by counterparties. Rates commonly used include:

- **Inter-bank rates** – these are inter-bank/certificate of deposit rates used or quoted by banks in money market transactions in the relevant currency.

- **Treasury bill rates** – these are rates on *government* short dated obligations.
- **Commercial paper rates** – these are rates on commercial paper issued by either banks or other issuers of an acceptable credit quality.
- **Implied swap rates** – these are implied interest rates in the relevant currencies calculated from available forward foreign exchange prices. Given spot and forward foreign exchange rates between the US$ and relevant currency and the US$ interest rate for the maturity of the forward, it is feasible to derive the implied interest rate in the currency[23].

In practice, in emerging markets one of these rates is used as the floating rate benchmark.

The use of these rates inevitably creates basis risk for participants. This arises from the fact that the transactions sought to be hedged may not move in an identical manner to the hedge itself because of differences in the rates used in the underlying transactions and that used to determine the swap settlement.

## 8.5   Interest Rate Swaps – Rationale

The decoupling of the interest rate characteristics of a transaction is essentially one of the key features of swaps generally. It essentially allows a number of aspects of financing transactions to be separated or unbundled including:
- Source of funding; that is, which market or lender.
- Form of funding; that is, fixed or floating rate.
- Timing of raising the required funding.

## 8.6   Interest Rate Swaps – Structural Variations

### 8.6.1   Overview

There are a number of common variations in interest rate swap structures including incorporation of a dealer as intermediary and use of net as distinct from gross settlements under the swap.

### 8.6.2   Intermediated Swap Structures[24]

In the basic structure both borrowers directly swap their obligations under their respective loans. Each borrower therefore takes the risk that the other may not

---

[23]   See discussion in Chapter 6.
[24]   The benefits etc noted here are equally applicable to currency swap transactions.

make its swap payments. However, in practice most interest rate swaps do not utilise this direct structure. In practice, a third party (generally a dealer) is interposed between the borrowers to create an intermediated swap. Borrowers on both sides generally deal solely with the dealer and have separate contracts with the intermediating dealer. **Exhibit 3.24** sets out the structure of an intermediated swap transaction.

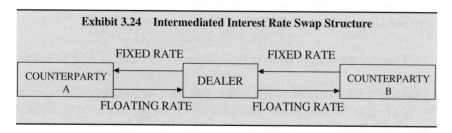

**Exhibit 3.24    Intermediated Interest Rate Swap Structure**

The use of an intermediary (generally a dealer) in financial products has a number of implications:

- **Anonymity** – the identity of both parties is only known to the dealer. This preserves the anonymity of both counterparties and also the confidentiality of the transaction.

- **Credit risk** – the interposition of an intermediary in a swap insulates each borrower from the other. The structure substitutes the credit risk of the dealer for the credit risk of the counterparty. The dealer, for a fee, guarantees that each borrower will receive the swap payment due from the other. The exact risk assumed by the dealer varies between transactions. In general, in the type of transaction considered to date, the intermediating dealer's guarantee is limited to the interest or coupon obligations swapped. If either party to the swap fails to make a swap payment due to the intermediary, then the dealer will not meet its corresponding payment under the swap. Consequently, the risk being assumed is limited to any excess that the dealer must pay to the other party over the payment to be received. Where the swap encompasses exchanges of principal as well as interest or coupon obligations (as in a currency swap), the dealer will guarantee the principal amount in addition to the net swap payments. The fee payable to the dealer is based on the principal amount of the borrowing covered by the swap and/or the amount of the interest swap payments received by it and reflects the extent of credit risk assumed[25].

---

[25]   For a discussion on swap credit risk, see Das, Satyajit (2004) Risk Management; John Wiley & Sons (Asia), Singapore at Chapter 5.

- **Cash flow mismatches** – the presence of an intermediary also eliminates the need for exact matching of the two legs of the swaps. At its simplest, the separation of contractual obligations would generally enable transactions involving different amounts and a number of parties with slightly different needs to be matched. For example, economies of scale and price advantages may be achieved by structuring a transaction using a large bond offering by a particularly creditworthy borrower and swapping the proceeds with a number of floating rate borrowers. Additional flexibility in respect of early termination may also be facilitated by the interposition of an intermediary. In addition, the two matching transactions do not need to be transacted simultaneously. This creates significant timing flexibility. These advantages generally favour the intermediated form of interest rate swap and most transactions utilise this structure[26].

## 8.6.3  Net Swap Settlements

Swap transactions generally are settled in net rather than gross terms. This is predicated on eliminating the flow of cash representing the full payment to be made by each swap counterparty to the other. Instead, a net amount is either paid or received representing the difference between the amount under the swap required to be paid to and the amount simultaneously due from the counterparty. **Exhibit 3.25** sets out an example of the operation of the net settlement process.

---

**Exhibit 3.25    Swap Settlement – Net Settlement Process**

Assume an interest rate swap at a rate of 7.50% pa payable semi-annually. The net settlement amounts under the swap (based on a notional principal amount of $100 million) would be as follows:

| Year | Days in Interest Period | Assumed 6 Month LIBOR (% pa) | Swap Cash Flows ($ million) | | Net Settlement Amount ($ million) |
|------|------|------|------|------|------|
| | | | Fixed (7.50% pa on Actual/365) | Floating (Actual/360) | |
| 0.5 | 183 | 4.350 | 3.760 | 2.211 | 1.549 |
| 1.0 | 182 | 4.875 | 3.740 | 2.465 | 1.275 |
| 1.5 | 184 | 7.980 | 3.781 | 4.079 | −0.298 |
| 2.0 | 181 | 6.563 | 3.719 | 3.299 | 0.420 |

---

[26]  See Chapter 13 and 14.

**Notes:**
1. The swap fixed rate is 7.50% pa payable semi-annually on an actual/365 day basis
2. The swap floating rate is calculated as the assumed floating rate index (LIBOR) × swap notional principal ($100 million) × number of days/360
3. The (+) indicates a receipt, while a (−) indicates a payment.

These settlement amounts achieve the following effective interest commitments for each party.

For the fixed rate receiver in the swap, assuming it had an underlying fixed rate obligation at an interest rate cost of 7.50% pa (payable semi-annually on an actual/365 day basis) the position after the swap would be as follows:

| Year | Interest Paid (Actual/365) ($ million) | Swap Settlement ($ million) | Total Payments ($ million) | Effective Interest Rate (% pa) |
|---|---|---|---|---|
| 0.5 | 3.760 | −1.549 | 2.211 | 4.350 |
| 1.0 | 3.740 | −1.275 | 2.465 | 4.875 |
| 1.5 | 3.781 | 0.298 | 4.079 | 7.980 |
| 2.0 | 3.719 | −0.420 | 3.299 | 6.563 |

For the fixed rate payer in the swap, assuming it had an underlying floating rate obligation at an interest rate cost of 6 month LIBOR plus 50 bps pa (payable semi-annually on an actual/360 day basis), the position after the swap would be as follows:

| Year | Interest Paid (Actual/365) ($ million) | Swap Settlement ($ million) | Total Payments ($ million) | Effective Interest Rate (% pa) |
|---|---|---|---|---|
| 0.5 | 2.465 | 1.549 | 4.014 | 8.007 |
| 1.0 | 2.717 | 1.275 | 3.993 | 7.963 |
| 1.5 | 4.334 | -0.298 | 4.036 | 8.051 |
| 2.0 | 3.551 | 0.420 | 3.971 | 7.919 |

As a result of the interest rate swap, the fixed rate payer ends up with an effective fixed interest rate of approximately 8.00% pa (made up as follows – 7.50% pa and margin of 50 bps pa). The fixed rate receiver ends up with an effective cost equivalent to the floating rate index.

### 8.6.4 Interest Rate Swap Using Discount Instruments

Another structural variation is the use of discount instruments as part of the underlying funding for a swap. The difficulty relates to the fact that the proceeds of discount instruments (such as banker's acceptances or commercial paper) are less than its face value or par. In order to allow exact cash flow matching under the swap, where a discount instrument is being used, it is necessary to structure the drawdown of for example commercial paper such that the face value is varied to provide net proceeds equal to the notional principal amount of the swap.

For example, in the example discussed in **Exhibit 3.20**, if the floating rate at commencement of the transaction was 8.00% then company B should have drawn down $104.25 million face value of 6 month discounted securities. The securities would provide B with proceeds of $100 million (the notional principal amount of the swap) if discounted at 8.50% pa ( LIBOR plus the margin of 1.00%). This procedure would be repeated every 6 months to maintain the underlying funding at the required level.

# 9 Currency Swaps

## 9.1 Structure

A currency swap entails a transaction in which two counterparties agree to exchange their respective currency and interest rate positions between an agreed pair of currency. In a currency swap, the counterparties exchange the two currencies with a concomitant agreement to reverse the exchange of currencies at a fixed date in the future.

The amount to be swapped is established in one currency. The prevailing spot exchange rate is used to establish the amount in the other currency. Currency swaps entail periodic payments between the counterparties in the relevant interest rates in the respective currencies. The rates can be either fixed or floating. All currency swaps involve exchange of different currency cash flows in the future, each respective payment being contingent upon the other. This is an important point as it distinguishes a currency swap from a loan. It is a forward conditional commitment making it a contingent obligation (an off-balance sheet item). Economically, currency swaps are equivalent to a portfolio of forward currency contracts.

## 9.2 Currency Swap – Example

Consider the following example. Company A borrows A$100 million for five years at 14.00% pa payable annually. Company B borrows the US$ equivalent of A$100 million being US$65 million for five years at LIBOR payable semi-annually (this assume a spot exchange rate of A$1: US$ 0.65).

The currency swap would operate in three distinct phases: initial principal exchange, periodic interest payments and a re-exchange of principal at maturity. At commencement of the transaction, Company A would pay the proceeds of its

A$ issue to Company B in return for Company B paying the proceeds of its US$ borrowing to company A. This exchange is effected at the prevailing spot exchange rate. Each party effectively agrees to service the other party's debt; that is, Company A would pay the US$ interest on Company B's loan and Company B the A$ interest on Company A's loan. At maturity the parties would reverse the initial exchange. In other words, Company A would pay US$65 million to Company B in return for Company B paying A$100 million to Company A, enabling both parties to repay their underlying loan obligations to the respective lenders.

**Exhibit 3.26** sets out in diagrammatic form the basic structure of this currency swap. **Exhibit 3.27** sets out the detailed cash flows and effective cost calculations of the transaction described. **Exhibit 3.28** sets out a typical transaction confirmation confirming entry by a company into a currency detailing the typical terms and conditions of such transactions.

The currency swap structure is similar to that of an interest rate swap. The major difference relates to the exchange of principal amounts at the commencement and conclusion of a transaction. This exchange is designed to provide the parties to the swap with access to the desired foreign currency amounts.

The forward exchange commitment leg of a currency swap transaction that entails the purchase and sale of foreign currency is very similar to that of a normal currency forward contract. However, currency swaps provide a greater degree of structural flexibility relative to a currency forward contract. For example, in a swap the normal par forward structure (the reversal of the currency exchange is

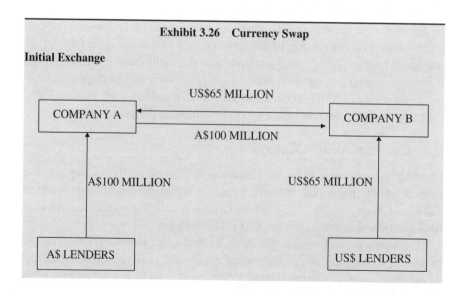

**Exhibit 3.26    Currency Swap**

**Initial Exchange**

US$65 MILLION

COMPANY A          COMPANY B

A$100 MILLION

A$100 MILLION          US$65 MILLION

A$ LENDERS          US$ LENDERS

**Periodic Payments**

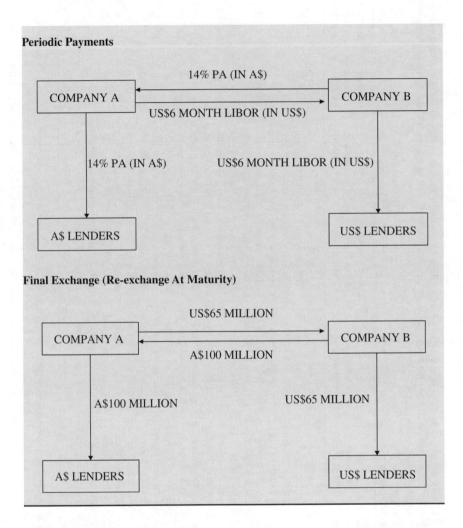

**Final Exchange (Re-exchange At Maturity)**

at the initial rate of exchange) means that the premium or discount built into the rate under a currency forward is settled through periodic payments (effectively the interest differential). The structure also has the advantage that for balance sheet purposes, the reported size of the borrowing before and after the swap is the same as the forward rate corresponding to the spot rate at inception of the transaction. Swaps are also easier to administer than a series of outright forwards. This is because the individual forwards are at different rates expressed as swap points deducted or added from the spot rate. Matching the cash flows in the foreign currency mean uneven cash flows in the base currency where currency forwards are used.

## Exhibit 3.27 Currency Swap – Cash Flows

The following cash flows are for a 3 year US$/A$ currency swap. Company A borrows A$100 million for 3 years at a rate of 14.00% pa and enters into a swap with Company B which borrows US$65 million for 3 years on a floating rate basis at a cost of US$ six month LIBOR. The swap is undertaken on the following terms: Company B pays A$ 14.00% pa in return for receiving $ 6 month LIBOR.

| Year | Company A Currency Swap | | | | Company B Currency Swap | | | |
|---|---|---|---|---|---|---|---|---|
| | Underlying Loan Cash Flows (A$ million) | Swap Receipts (A$ million) | Swap Payments (US$ million) | Net Cash Flows (US$ million) | Underlying Loan Cash Flows (US$ million) | Swap Receipts (US$ million) | Swap Payments (A$ million) | Net Cash Flows (A$ million) |
| 0 | +100.00 | −100.00 | +65.00 | +65.00 | +65.00 | −65.00 | +100.00 | +100.00 |
| 0.5 | −7.00 | +7.00 | −(US$ 6 month LIBOR × US$65 m × fraction of year) | −(US$ 6 month LIBOR × US$65 m × fraction of year) | −(US$ 6 month LIBOR × US$65 m × fraction of year) | +(US$ 6 month LIBOR × US$65 m × fraction of year) | −7.00 | −7.00 |
| 1.0 | −7.00 | +7.00 | −(US$ 6 month LIBOR × US$65 m × fraction of year) | −(US$ 6 month LIBOR × US$65 m × fraction of year) | −(US$ 6 month LIBOR × US$65 m × fraction of year) | +(US$ 6 month LIBOR × US$65 m × fraction of year) | −7.00 | −7.00 |
| 1.5 | −7.00 | +7.00 | −(US$ 6 month LIBOR × US$65 m × fraction of year) | −(US$ 6 month LIBOR × US$65 m × fraction of year) | −(US$ 6 month LIBOR × US$65 m × fraction of year) | +(US$ 6 month LIBOR × US$65 m × fraction of year) | −7.00 | −7.00 |
| 2.0 | −7.00 | +7.00 | −(US$ 6 month LIBOR × US$65 m × fraction of year) | −(US$ 6 month LIBOR × US$65 m × fraction of year) | −(US$ 6 month LIBOR × US$65 m × fraction of year) | +(US$ 6 month LIBOR × US$65 m × fraction of year) | −7.00 | −7.00 |
| 2.5 | −7.00 | +7.00 | −(US$ 6 month LIBOR × US$65 m × fraction of year) | −(US$ 6 month LIBOR × US$65 m × fraction of year) | −(US$ 6 month LIBOR × US$65 m × fraction of year) | +(US$ 6 month LIBOR × US$65 m × fraction of year) | −7.00 | −7.00 |
| 3.0 | −7.00 | +7.00 | −(US$ 6 month LIBOR × US$65 m × fraction of year) | −(US$ 6 month LIBOR × US$65 m × fraction of year) | −(US$ 6 month LIBOR × US$65 m × fraction of year) | +(US$ 6 month LIBOR × US$65 m × fraction of year) | −7.00 | −7.00 |
| 3.0 | −100.00 | +100.00 | −65.00 | −65.00 | −65.00 | +65.00 | −100.00 | −100.00 |

### Notes

1. (+) indicates a receipt while (−) indicates a payment. All cash flows are in US$ or A$ millions.
2. The accrual on the fixed rate payments assumes equal interest rate payments for simplicity.
3. LIBOR is equal to 6 month LIBOR set each semi-annually calculated on the relevant fraction of a year (actual days/360 in the case of $ LIBOR or based on the applicable day count). It is also assumed LIBOR on the loan and the swap are the same; that is, are set on the same day by the same rate setting mechanism.

---

**Exhibit 3.28    Currency Swap Confirmation**

To [Party A]

The purpose of this letter agreement is to confirm the terms and conditions of the Swap Transaction entered into between us on the Trade date specified below (the "Swap Trans-action"). This letter agreement constitutes a confirmation as referred to in the Interest Rate and Currency Exchange Agreement specified below.

The definitions and provisions contained in the 1991 ISDA Definitions (as published by the International Swap Dealers Association, Inc.) are incorporated into this Confirmation. In the event of any inconsistency between those definitions and provisions and this Confirmation, this Confirmation will govern.

This confirmation supplements, forms part of, and is subject to, the Interest Rate and Currency Exchange Agreement dated [ ], as amended and supplemented from time to time (the "Agreement") between you and us. All provisions contained in the Agreement govern this confirmation except as expressly modified below.

**General**

| | |
|---|---|
| Trade Date | 15 May 2001 |
| Effective Date | 17 May 2001 |
| Termination Date | 17 May 2004 subject to the [Following/Modified/Preceding Business] day Convention |

**Notional Principal Amounts**

| | |
|---|---|
| A$ Notional Amount | A$100 million |
| US$ Notional Amount | US$65 million (calculated as the US$ equivalent of A$ Notional Amount at the Agreed Exchange Rate) |
| Agreed Exchange Rate | A$1.00 = US$0.6500 |

**A$ Payments**

| | |
|---|---|
| A$ Payer | Company B |
| A$ Payment Dates | Every 17 November and 17 May commencing 17 November 2001 and terminating on 17 May 2004 subject to the [Following/Modified/Preceding Business] day Convention |
| A$ Rate | 6.25% pa payable semi-annually in accordance with the Fixed Rate Day Count Fraction on the A$ Notional Amount |
| Fixed Rate Day Count Fraction | Semi-annual bond equivalent basis calculated on an actual/365 day year |

**US$ Payments**

| | |
|---|---|
| US$ Payer | Company A |
| US$ Payment Dates | Every 17 November and 17 May commencing 17 November 2001 and terminating on 17 May 2004 subject to the [Following/Modified/Preceding Business] day Convention |

| US$ Rate | US$ LIBOR of the Designated Maturity reset semi-annually plus the Spread payable semi-annually in accordance with the Floating Rate Day Count Fraction on the US$ Notional Amount |
| --- | --- |
| Designated Maturity | 6 months |
| Spread | Nil |
| Floating Rate Day Count Fraction | Semi-annual money market basis calculated on an actual/ 360 day year |

**Principal Exchanges**

| Initial Exchange | For value on the Effective Date (subject to the [Following/ Modified/Preceding Business] day Convention), Company A shall pay to Company B the A$ Notional Amount and Company B shall pay to Company A the US$ Notional Amount |
| --- | --- |
| Exchange at Maturity | For value on the Termination Date (subject to the [Following/ Modified/Preceding Business] day Convention), Company B shall pay to Company A the A$ Notional Amount and Company A shall pay to Company B the US$ Notional Amount |

**Other Terms**

| Netting of Payments | Not applicable |
| --- | --- |
| Documentation | Standard ISDA |
| Calculation Agent | Party B |
| Governing Law | London |

**Account Details**
Payments to Party A
US$ Account for Payment
A$ Account for Payment
Payments to Party B
US$ Account for Payment
A$ Account for Payment

**Offices**
Party A
Party B

**Broker/Arranger (if applicable)**

Please confirm that the forgoing correctly sets forth the terms of our agreement by executing the copy of this Confirmation enclosed for that purpose and returning it to us or sending us a letter or telex substantially similar to this letter which letter or telex sets forth the material terms of the Swap Transaction to which this confirmation relates and indicates agreement to those terms.

Party B

## 9.3   Currency Swaps – Quotations

Currency swaps are quoted in a similar manner to interest rate swaps. Currency swaps of a given maturity are quoted as a fixed rate (expressed as either an absolute rate or as a spread over the relevant fixed rate government bond in the currency) against the receipt of US$3 or 6 month LIBOR flat (that is, plus or minus no margin). For example, Yen currency swaps might be quoted as 3.00% pa against US$6 month LIBOR. Alternatively, the same currency swap could be quoted as the relevant yen bond plus a margin of 60 bps pa against US$ 6 month LIBOR flat.

Currency swap quotations are commonly available for:
- Fixed foreign currency versus US$ LIBOR floating currency swaps.
- Floating to floating cross currency (basis) swaps.

All other structures are constructed from a combination of these structures and interest rate swaps in the relevant currencies[27].

## 9.4   Currency Swap – Structural Variations

A number of structural variations on the standard currency swaps are available including:
- The principal exchanges in a currency swap can be eliminated. Instead of an initial exchange, a spot foreign exchange transaction can be used to allow each party to generate its desired currency position. However, the elimination of the initial exchange does not obviate the need to set a reference spot rate between the relevant currencies. This rate is the rate at which the re-exchange at maturity is to be effected. Where an initial exchange is not undertaken, the spot rate must be set using a defined market rate as quoted by a specified dealer at a particular time. The most common reason for not undertaking an initial exchange is that the swap is being undertaken against an existing borrowing. In this situation, the currency swap is not combined with funding. This means that there are no new cash flows that can be used to support the initial currency swap exchange. The final re-exchange can also be eliminated. This is achieved by the parties undertaking appropriate spot foreign exchange transactions and by the difference in value (reflecting the appreciation or depreciation of the currencies) being paid by one party to the other. The spot foreign exchange transaction in conjunction with the settlement amount will give the same result as if the re-exchange had been effected at the original nominated rate. The elimination of the final re-exchange may be designed to lower the credit risk of the transaction. Where the exchanges

---

[27] See discussion below in relation to types of swap structures.

and final re-exchange in a currency swap are eliminated, the currency swap is often referred to as a cash settled currency swap.

- A wide variety of structured currency swaps is also feasible. One interesting example of a structured currency swap is the semi-fixed currency swap. These transactions were developed in Asia and other emerging markets. The major driver was the high interest rate differential between the local currency and US$. This cost discouraged entities located in the emerging countries from hedging their foreign currency (US$) liabilities into their domestic currency. The semi-fixed currency swap is designed to make it more attractive for a local entity to hedge. **Exhibit 3.29** sets out an example of this type of transaction.

---

**Exhibit 3.29    Structured Currency Swap**

Assume a borrower based in Thailand (Company A) seeks to hedge its US$ borrowing into Thai Bhat ("THB") to eliminate the currency risk on this debt. The current interest rate in THB is 12% pa and 6.00% pa in US$. Company A is reluctant to incur the additional 6.00% pa cost (the interest rate differential) to hedge its currency exposure.

Company A enters into the following structured currency swap. The currency swap is generally standard with Company A paying THB and receiving US$ cash flows. The only difference is the THB interest rate paid under the swap is as follows:
- If the US$/THB exchange rate stays below a pre-determined level (US$1 = THB 40.00) then Company A pays a below market rate (8.00% pa in THB).
- If the US$/THB exchange rate is above a pre-determined level (US$1 = THB 40.00) then Company A pays an above market rate (15.00% pa in THB).

The transaction structure is set out below:

**INITIAL EXCHANGE**

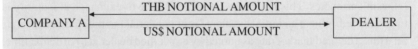

**PERIODIC PAYMENTS**

**FINAL EXCHANGE**

The overall position of Company A is as follows:
- The currency risk is hedged fully by the swap.
- Company A has uncertainty as to its cost of THB funding although the possible outcomes are known.

The structure basically combines a standard US$/THB currency swap with the sale by Company A of a digital option on the exchange rate (a digital option is a form of *exotic* currency option[28]). Company A has sold a digital put option on the exchange rate with a strike of US$1 = THB 40. The premium received reduces the THB cost of the swap. However, if the THB depreciates below the strike price, then Company A has to make a fixed payment under the digital option. This payment is made in the form of the higher rate paid in THB under the currency swaps.

The structure was used prior to the Asian currency crisis in 1997. Following the crisis, there has also been interest in this structure as it allows borrowers to hedge without paying the full (often very large) interest differential between the local currency and US$ in certain conditions. The structure is designed particularly for exporters, as a lower exchange rate naturally benefits these parties in the form of higher export revenues that act as a natural hedge against higher interest costs if the currency depreciates.

## 10  Types of Swaps

The various types of swap transactions theoretically feasible are set out in **Exhibit 3.30**. Two types of swaps require special comment:
- **Floating-to-floating currency swaps (cross currency basis swaps)** – theoretically cross-currency floating-to-floating swaps should not exist because a floating-to-floating swap is nothing more than a series of 3 or 6 month forward foreign exchange contracts rolled over until maturity. In practice, a floating-to-floating currency swap can be a far better alternative to a forward foreign exchange transaction. This is because it avoids the spread between bid and offer rates on every rollover date and the cash flow effect of the difference between the contracted forward rate and the spot rate at rollover. **Exhibit 3.31** sets out the structure of a floating-to-floating A$ and US$ currency swap.
- **"Cocktail" (Combination) Swaps** – these structures involve combinations of various types of swaps including both interest and currency swaps. They are used to construct various types of structures (for example fixed-to-fixed currency swap). Examples of such transactions are shown in **Exhibit 3.32**.

---

[28] See Das, Satyajit (2004) Structured Products Volume 1; John Wiley & Sons (Asia), Singapore at Chapter 10.

### Exhibit 3.30    Swap Transactions – Types

| Type | Interest Rate From | Interest Rate To | Currency | Example |
|---|---|---|---|---|
| Interest Rate Swap | Floating | Fixed | Same | Swapping from floating rate loan into fixed rate |
| Floating To Floating (Basis) Swap | Floating | Floating | Same | Swapping the interest rate basis of a loan from US$ 3 month LIBOR to US$ 1 month CP rates |
| Fixed To Fixed Interest Rate Swap | Fixed | Fixed | Same | Swapping the cash flow basis of a fixed rate loan from normal coupon payments to a zero coupon rate basis |
| Fixed To Floating Currency Swap | Floating | Fixed | Different | Swapping a US$ floating rate loan to fixed rate Yen |
| Fixed To Fixed Currency Swap | Fixed | Fixed | Different | Swapping a fixed rate US$ loan to fixed rate Yen |
| Floating To Floating Currency (Cross Currency Basis) Swap | Floating | Floating | Different | Swapping floating rate US$ LIBOR to floating rate Yen LIBOR |

### Exhibit 3.31    Cross Currency Basis Swap

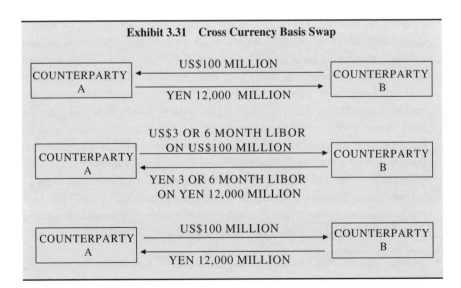

### Exhibit 3.32   "Cocktail" (Combination) Swap Transactions

**1.  Structuring A Fixed Yen to US$ Fixed Currency Swap**

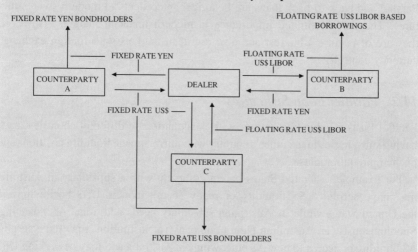

**2.  Structuring A Floating US$ LIBOR to US$ Commercial Paper ("CP") Basis Swap**

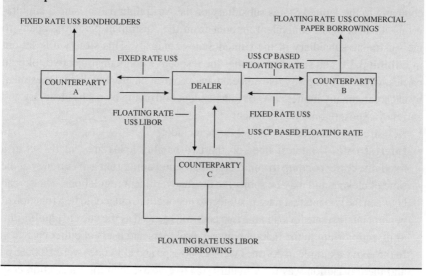

## 11    Parallel & Back-to-Back Loans

### 11.1    Background

Parallel and back-to-back loans are historical antecedents to modern swap structures. They are of limited importance in modern financial markets. However, they are of historical interest and also useful in markets with foreign exchange currency controls.

### 11.2    Parallel Loan Structures

Parallel loans involve two entities with headquarters in different countries; each having subsidiaries in the other's country with mirror-image liquidity positions and financing requirements.

For example, a United States parent company with a subsidiary in Australia may have surplus US$ liquidity or ready access to new US$ borrowings in the United States while its Australian subsidiary needs additional A$ financing. Simultaneously, an Australian parent company (or institution) may have surplus A$ liquidity or access to new A$ borrowings in Australia and may be seeking US$ financing for its United States subsidiary (or to support a portfolio investment). A parallel loan transaction consists of a US$ loan from the United States parent company to the United States subsidiary of the Australian parent, and a simultaneous A$ loan of an equivalent amount from the Australian parent company to the Australian subsidiary of the United States company. This structure is set out in **Exhibit 3.33**. The structure satisfies the respective financing objectives of both parties, while avoiding any relevant exchange control inherent in direct investment by each parent, any higher costs of independent borrowing by each subsidiary and currency exposure on the investment.

Key structural aspects of parallel loans include:

*   **Interest rates** – interest rates on the two parallel loans are usually set at a fixed rate corresponding to commercial rates prevailing for each currency at the time of closing and may be subject to local government regulations. The spread between the two interest rates is subject to negotiation, but would be a function of general interest rate levels in the two countries as well as the current equilibrium or disequilibrium in the market between providers and users of either currency. In the above example, if A$ rates were 15.00% pa and US$ rates were 10.00% pa and the transaction was for a maturity of five years, then the transaction cash flows would be as set out in **Exhibit 3.34**. The 5.00% pa differential would be paid by the United States multinational company. From an economic perspective, the Australian company receiving the 5.00% pa differential is essentially compensated for any opportunity loss that might otherwise be suffered as a

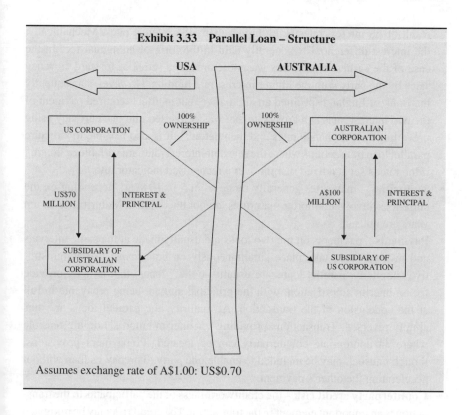

Exhibit 3.33    Parallel Loan – Structure

Assumes exchange rate of A$1.00: US$0.70

Exhibit 3.34    Parallel Loan – Cash Flows

| Year | Amount Received (Paid) By Subsidiary Of Australian Company (US$ million) | Amount Received (Paid) By Subsidiary Of US Multinational Company (A$ million) |
|---|---|---|
| 0 | +70 | +100 |
| 1 | −7 | −15 |
| 2 | −7 | −15 |
| 3 | −7 | −15 |
| 4 | −7 | −15 |
| 5 | −77 | −115 |

**Note:**
(+) indicates a receipt, while (−) indicates a payment.

result of A$ interest rates being higher than US$ interest rates. Mechanically, the interest differential is generally paid in the form of an annual fee. In the case of the earliest swaps, this was structured as a series of forward currency sales by the party with the higher interest rate funding. However, subsequently the Bank of England specified an alternative that in effect required payment of the two interest rates at a gross rate that was converted into one currency using prevailing spot exchange rates and then netted[29]. It is also feasible to structure parallel loan transactions where the relevant interest rates are variable or floating if the rate is set at a fixed margin over a recognised indicator rate.

- **Maturities** – maturities generally range from 5 to 10 years depending on the currencies involved. Shorter maturities are not uncommon. Maturities over ten years are unusual.
- **Payments** – payments on the two loans are usually made at the same intervals and in most cases take place simultaneously on both loans. For administrative simplicity, parallel loans are usually 'bullet" loans; that is, they provide for no interim amortisation, with the principal amount being repayable in full at the conclusion of the transaction. At maturity, the parallel loans are thus simply reversed. Transactions providing for interim amortisation are feasible where an appropriate counterparty can be located. Prepayment provisions, though unusual, may be included to enable one party to prepay its loan without accelerating the other's payment.
- **Counterparty credit risk** – the creditworthiness of the participants to the transaction is an important element in the transaction The credit risk may be mitigated by the inclusion of offset rights that allow each party the right to offset payments not received against payments due. Parallel loans (as distinct from back-to-back loans) do not include a right of offset. If either counterparty considers the other's subsidiary less than credit-worthy in its own right, then specific security or a parent guarantee is usually negotiated.
- **Credit enhancement** – a top-up provision is often included to keep the principal amounts outstanding in balance where exchange rates move significantly during the life of the loans. A top-up clause usually requires the lenders to make additional advances or repayments on one of the loans whenever the spot exchange rate moves past a trigger point. For example, in the A$ and US$ parallel loan example, additional A$ may have to be lent if the spot rate moves 10 cents lower, or paid back if the rate moves a corresponding amount higher.

---

[29]  See Price, John and Henderson, Schuyler K. (1984) Currency and Interest Rate Swaps; Butterworths, London at 13–14.

## 11.3 Back-to-Back Loans

Parallel loans differ from back-to-back loans. Parallel loans do not include a right of offset or cross-collateralisation between loans. In contrast, back-to-back loans include a right of offset. As exchange control regulations of many countries prohibit rights of offset, parallel loans are more common than back-to-back loans.

The back-to-back loan differs from a parallel loan in structure. Under the back-to-back loan, the United States multinational company in the United States would lend to the Australian company in Australia, whereas under a parallel loan structure the two parties would lend funds to their respective subsidiaries. This structure is set out in **Exhibit 3.35**.

The back-to-back loan entails the United States multinational company lending US$ to the Australian company in return for the Australian company lending the United States company A$. This is accompanied by an inter-company loan to their respective subsidiaries. Both loans are priced in line with market yields in the respective markets. Consequently, the transaction can be regarded as an initial exchange of currencies with an accompanying agreement to repay the respective loans. It is in a form that could be regarded as a forward sale of US$ for A$ on the one hand and a forward sale of US$ for A$ on the other. The structure resembles a modern currency swap transaction.

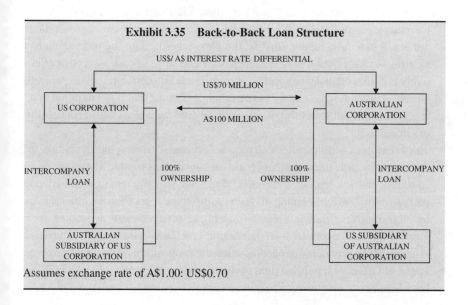

**Exhibit 3.35 Back-to-Back Loan Structure**

US$/ A$ INTEREST RATE DIFFERENTIAL

US$70 MILLION

US CORPORATION

A$100 MILLION

AUSTRALIAN CORPORATION

INTERCOMPANY LOAN

100% OWNERSHIP

100% OWNERSHIP

INTERCOMPANY LOAN

AUSTRALIAN SUBSIDIARY OF US CORPORATION

US SUBSIDIARY OF AUSTRALIAN CORPORATION

Assumes exchange rate of A$1.00: US$0.70

Significant structural differences between parallel and back-to-back loans include:
- A back-to-back loan entails cross-border funds flows that raise withholding tax issues.
- There is only one loan document in a back-to-back loan.

The general terms of a back-to-back loan are very similar to those for a parallel loan, although protection against withholding taxes may be included.

## 11.4 Parallel, Back-to-Back Loans and Currency Swaps – Comparison

A parallel loan, back-to-back loan and a currency swap (the structural successor to back-to-back loans) are similar techniques generally used to achieve similar objectives. In fact, currency swaps have for most purposes superseded parallel loans. However, a number of differences should be noted which might influence a company's choice between a parallel loan, back-to-back loan or a currency swap:

- **Accounting Treatment** – accountants differ on how parallel and back-to-back loans should be reported by the parent company on its balance sheet. Even if a right of offset exists, some accountants feel that both loans should appear in the balance sheet rather than being treated as off-balance sheet items. Such treatment inflates the company's balance sheet. It may produce adverse consequences under existing loan covenants and may therefore make a back-to-back loan or currency swap preferable. Where the back-to-back loan or currency swap does not entail new fund raising (that is, the party entering into the transaction has existing liquidity), the transaction entails the exchange of cash assets that effectively provides off-balance sheet financing. The future commitment to exchange currencies is analogous to a forward exchange contract that is not required to be reported on the balance sheet. It may require disclosure as a contingent liability or commitment.
- **Tax Treatment** – in a parallel loan transaction, each borrower has an unambiguous tax-deductible interest expense and each lender has taxable interest income. In a back-to-back loan or a currency swap, the annual payments paid by one party to the other (representing in effect the differential between the interest rates in the respective currencies) may or may not be tax-deductible depending upon local law. Either a parallel loan transaction or a back-to-back loan or currency swap might be preferable depending upon the tax position of each counterparty.
- **Right of Offset** – an implied right of offset often exists in the case of a back-to-back loan or currency swap whereas no such right exists between parallel loans.

If this right of offset is important as a credit matter then a currency swap or back-to-back loan might be preferable.

- **Regulatory Factors** – the constituting documents of the counterparty may permit entry into a parallel loan, but not into a back-to-back loan or currency swap, or vice versa.
- **Cash Flow Structure** – two major structural differences between parallel, back-to-back loans and currency swaps are significant:
  1. In a currency swap, no initial cash movements are necessary since the swap is normally based on prevailing spot rates, thereby allowing each party to obtain the relevant currency through the spot foreign exchange (FX) market.
  2. Swaps offer greater flexibility than parallel or back-to-back loans.

## 11.5  The Modern Role of Parallel or Back-to-Back Loan Structures

Parallel and back-to-back loan structures are best regarded as earlier technical forms of swap transactions. The evolution of parallel loans into back-to-back structures and the recognition that the transactions could be unbundled essentially into spot and forward currency contracts provided some of the important insights that underpin the modern swap market.

However, despite their structural obsolescence, parallel loans in particular continue to enjoy a secular role in the context of freeing blocked funds. Harking back to their original rationale of bypassing exchange controls, parallel loans continue to be used to circumvent exchange restrictions in countries that do not allow the free transfer of capital across their boundaries.

The modern parallel loan tends to be more custom-designed to the needs of the transaction although the basic structure remains very close to the original transaction mechanics. The market operates primarily against US$ although transactions not involving the US$ are not uncommon.

## 12  Summary

OTC derivative products are a key component of the global derivatives market. OTC products (primarily, forwards, options and swaps) are available on interest rates, currencies, equity indexes and a wide variety of commodities. The key feature of the OTC traded markets is the ability of transactions to be customised to counterparty requirements. This allows a high degree of matching to underlying instruments to be achieved, reducing the problem of basis risk. This capacity has enabled OTC derivative markets to be highly creative and develop a wide variety of products designed to assist counterparties in both the management and assumption of risk. The disadvantage of OTC markets is the lack of standardisation that creates problems of trading liquidity and lack of transparency of pricing. The absence of a central market with settlement and clearing mechanisms exposes each counterparty directly to the default risk of the other party to any OTC transaction.

# PRICING & VALUING DERIVATIVE INSTRUMENTS

# 4
# Derivatives Pricing Framework

## 1 Overview

The pricing of derivatives is central to the design, structuring, trading and application of derivative products. This is because the value or cost of derivatives drives all derivatives trading and applications. Derivatives are based on the underlying asset. The pricing and valuation of derivatives is *derived* from the cash prices of the underlying assets traded in capital markets.

Derivatives pricing consists of a number of inter-related techniques and approaches. In this Chapter, the overall framework of pricing and valuation is outlined. The structure of this Chapter is as follows:

- The general framework for pricing is outlined.
- The concept of arbitrage free or risk neutral valuation is explained.
- The application of this approach is discussed.
- The assumptions underlying this approach are considered.
- The literature and research into derivative pricing is analysed.

Within the overall framework, a number of precise techniques and models are required. Each of the specific technical processes defines a specific aspect of derivative pricing[1]. Each of these aspects and models is dealt with in this Part. Chapter 5 covers interest rates and yield curves that are used in derivative valuation. Chapter 6 covers the pricing of forward and futures contracts. Chapter 7 covers the pricing of options. Chapter 8 continues the discussion of option pricing, focusing on the

---

[1] For a discussion of the mathematical concepts underlying derivative pricing, see Kritzman, Mark (1995) The Portable Financial Analyst; Probus Publishing, Chicago, Illinois.

pricing of interest rate options including the use of interest rate term structure models. Chapter 9 deals with the estimation of volatility and correlation used in derivative pricing. Chapter 10 covers the pricing of interest rate and currency swaps. Chapter 11 covers the economics and determination of swap spreads. The Chapters in this Part deal with the pricing of individual derivative instruments on a stand-alone basis. Trading/hedging and portfolio management of derivative instruments is covered in Part 4 (Chapters 12 to 16 inclusive).

## 2   General Framework[2]

Pricing and valuation in capital markets is based on modern portfolio theory[3]. Modern portfolio theory examines the notion of risk in financial markets within a mean variance framework. The return of any security or transaction is compared to its risk. The risk of any security or transaction is taken to be given by the variance or the standard deviation (volatility) of the returns on that security. The investor or counterparty is assumed to maximise an utility function seeking the highest possible level of return for a given level of risk, or the lowest level of risk for a given target return level.

The principal mechanism of risk management within this framework is diversification. The investor or counterparty manages risk by adding securities or transactions where the returns on the securities or transactions are less than perfectly correlated with the returns on other securities or transactions within the portfolio. This type of action has the effect of reducing *portfolio* variance or risk. This classical framework of analysis does not specifically identify the concept of hedging or pricing *of individual transactions*.

The process of pricing and risk management of derivatives is not predicated on classical portfolio concepts. It is based on the concept of *specific* replication of transactions and the concept of *hedging*. Derivatives pricing is based substantially on the concept of entering into transactions to replicate the cash flow profile of the relevant transaction to create a hedge. The objective is to set up a hedge that

---

[2]   See Smith, Lance "Risk-Reward Relationships – Foundations of Derivatives" in Das, Satyajit (Editor) (1997) Risk Management and Financial Derivatives: A Guide to the Mathematics; LBC Information Services, Sydney; McGraw-Hill, Chicago; MacMillan Publishing, England at Chapter 1.

[3]   For a discussion of portfolio theory, see Markowitz, Harry (1959) Portfolio Selection: Efficient Diversification of Investments; John Wiley, New York; Sharpe, William (1985) Investments-Third Edition; Prentice-Hall, Englewood Cliffs, NJ at Chapters 6, 7 and 8; Cuthbertson, Keith (1996) Quantitative Financial Economics: Stocks, Bonds and Foreign Exchange; John Wiley, Chichester at Chapters 2, 3, 4 and 18.

effectively makes the derivatives transaction free of risk to the party entering into the transaction. The price of the derivative transaction is therefore the cost of the hedge. This is because the investor or counterparty is essentially indifferent as between the derivative and the replicating portfolio (that reproduces the cash flow profile of the derivative contract).

The general approach has a number of implications including:

- **Pricing** – derivatives are generally priced at values where the dealer is able to establish the required hedges. The cost of the derivative is effectively the cost of the hedge portfolio.
- **Hedging** – there is no substantive difference between pricing and hedging (trading) to construct the portfolio to replicate the derivative. The derivative trader will typically price *off the hedge*. This means that inefficiencies and institutional restrictions in capital markets will directly be reflected in derivative pricing.
- **Valuation** – the concept of valuation of an *existing* derivative position is identical to that of pricing. It is the price of the transaction over its remaining term to maturity (as determined off a replicating hedge portfolio). The current value is compared to the contractual price agreed to at the time of entry into the transaction. The value of the transaction is taken to be the difference between the original value of the transaction and the current value.
- **Arbitrage** – given that the pricing of the derivative portfolio is based on the cost of the replicating portfolio, any difference in value between the derivative and the replicating portfolio creates the opportunity for arbitrage. This will entail the trader selling the portfolio (derivative or replicating portfolio of assets) that is expensive, and purchasing the one that is cheaper to lock in a theoretically risk free profit. Capital market restrictions on arbitrage impede the efficiency of derivative pricing.
- **Pricing versus risk management** – pricing (synonymous with hedging) and risk management are different activities. Pricing is driven by the trader identifying the structure and risk of the derivative transaction and entering into a series of transactions to replicate its cash flow profile. The trader uses the replicating portfolio to price the derivative. The cost or price of the derivative is the cost of establishing and managing the replicating or hedge portfolio. In contrast, the process of risk management is concerned with establishing both the *hedged* risk (the risk mitigated or managed by the trader) and the *unhedged* risk (that is the risk where the hedge does not perform as expected or is unable to be maintained). The risk management process is concerned with ensuring that these risks are maintained within acceptable risk tolerance levels.

## 3  Arbitrage Free Pricing

This framework enables the pricing of derivatives within a risk neutral valuation framework. This is referred to as an arbitrage free price of the derivative.

Arbitrage free pricing (also referred to as risk neutral valuation) is taken to encompass three discrete principles:

- **Replication** – this is focused on creating portfolios to replicate the cash flow or return profile of the derivative contract. This will typically entail trading in the underlying asset (either purchasing or short selling the asset) and trading in interest rates (to finance the asset purchase or invest the proceeds of the short sale). This can be stated as:

    [Derivative Contract] = [Position in Asset + Borrowing or Lending Cash]

- **Value neutrality** – this directly follows from the principle of replication. It states that where a derivative is replicated by a position in the asset and cash, the value of the derivative must exactly equal the present value of the replicating portfolio. This is based on the fact that the two portfolios are identical in terms of cash flow and/or return characteristics. This can be stated as:

    Value of [Derivative Contract]

    = Value of [Position in Asset + Borrowing or Lending Cash]

- **Arbitrage** – this directly follows from the principles of replication and value neutrality. If the derivative can be replicated by positions in the asset and cash then if there is a difference in value, traders can theoretically sell the expensive portfolio (either the derivative or asset and cash) and purchase the cheaper replicating portfolio (asset plus cash or the derivative). This transaction would lock in risk free arbitrage returns that in turn should force the markets to an equilibrium state where value neutrality holds.

The overall process of pricing is summarised in **Exhibit 4.1**. The critical element underlying arbitrage free pricing is the process of replication. In practice, there are two separate types of replication[4]:

- **Static** – this assumes that the derivative position can be replicated and hedged by *holding* a position in the asset and cash through to maturity. This assumes that the position is established and maintained *without change* through to maturity of the

---

[4]   For a discussion of hedging see Hua, Philip and Wilmott, Peter "A Classification of Hedging Strategies" (31 May 1999) Derivatives Week 6–7.

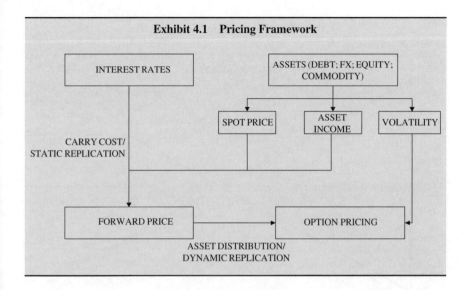

Exhibit 4.1    Pricing Framework

derivative contract. This is also called model independent hedging. This refers to the fact that the hedge is independent of the pricing model and assumptions incorporated in pricing the instruments. Replication of forwards is the best example of static hedging.

- **Dynamic** – this assumes that the derivative position can be replicated by establishing a position in the asset and cash. The hedge is then dynamically adjusted over time to maintain the hedge. This means that the hedge will typically only hold for small changes in the underlying asset price and for small periods of time. The hedge will need to be frequently re-balanced as market prices of the asset change over time. Dynamic hedging introduces significant risks in trading and pricing derivatives. This type of hedge is often referred to as a model dependent hedge. This reflects the fact that the hedge is based on the pricing model utilised to establish the value of the derivative instrument. This entails dependency upon the model or pricing inputs. Incorrect inputs may lead to inaccurate hedging. Replication of options is the best example of dynamic hedging.

Forwards are typically priced using a static hedge. The forward position is replicated by a long position in the asset that must be financed or a short position whose proceeds must be invested. The cost of the forward is the cost of borrowing (return or investment) adjusted for any income on the asset. The cost of borrowing the asset for the purpose of the short sale may also need to be incorporated.

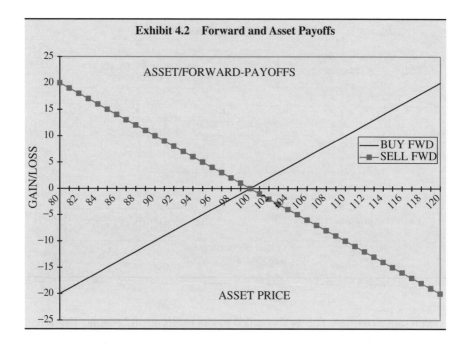

**Exhibit 4.2    Forward and Asset Payoffs**

The hedge is relatively simple. It is easy to establish and maintain. It is relatively low risk in nature. It makes a number of assumptions that in practice may be difficult to satisfy. In practice, the hedge is generally robust and efficient. The effectiveness of the static hedge derives from the fact that the payoff profiles for the forward contract is linear and identical to that of the asset (as at maturity of the forward contract). **Exhibit 4.2** sets out the payoffs of both a purchased and sold position in the asset or the forward. This characteristic enables static hedging of forwards.

Options require dynamic hedges. This reflects the fact that the payoff of the option is non-linear reflecting the asymmetric payoff of this instrument.

**Exhibit 4.3** sets out the payoff of the option both at maturity and prior to maturity. The familiar "hockey stick" shape of the option payoffs is only accurate at maturity. Prior to maturity, the option payoff is non-linear and convex in structure. This is the feature of options that requires dynamic hedging.

If the option is in-the-money at maturity, then the option approximates a bought (in the case of a call option) or sold (in the case of a put option) position in the underlying asset. If the option is out-of-the-money at maturity then the option approximates a zero position in the asset. This means if a trader has sold a call option, then at maturity it will need to hold 1 unit of the asset per option sold if the option expires in-the-money. The trader will not require any holding of the asset

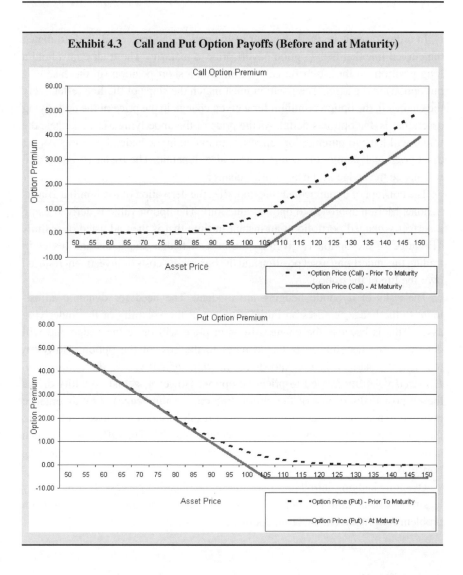

**Exhibit 4.3   Call and Put Option Payoffs (Before and at Maturity)**

if the option expires out-of-the-money. If a trader has sold a put option, then at maturity it will need to have a short position in 1 unit of the asset per option sold if the option expires in-the-money. The trader will not require any holding of the asset if the option expires out-of-the-money. The asset positions are used to hedge the trader's positions in the option. However, the trader does not know the final price of the asset prior to maturity. This means that the trader does not know the required position in the asset (that is, the constitution of the replicating portfolio).

In order to replicate the behaviour of the option, the trader will seek to match the curved line that is the option payoff prior to maturity. The trader must hold a long position (in the case of a call option) and a short position (in the case of a put option) in the asset. The position must match the slope of the line (effectively the change in the option premium for a given change in the price of the underlying asset; that is, the option's delta). As the price of the underlying asset changes, the trader will have to purchase or sell assets to maintain the hedged position. As the asset price is dynamic, the hedge is now also dynamic. The trader is required to re-balance the hedge as the asset price changes.

The concept of dynamic hedging underlies the derivation of the familiar Black-Scholes-Merton approach to option valuation[5]. The option value is derived using a perfectly hedged portfolio at an instant in time that is then adjusted over time. The price of the option is given as the cost of hedge (the gains and losses in trading the underlying asset position and the borrowing costs or investment returns) over the life of the option.

The risks of dynamic hedging are evident. The need for dynamic adjustment to the hedge requires an initial estimate of the volatility of the underlying asset. This is because the changes in asset price will drive the hedge and will determine the hedging costs that equates to the cost of the option. However, the *actual* volatility is not known *at the time of entry into the transaction*. *Expected* volatility is used to price the option. However, actual volatility drives the ex post realised cost of the option (the cost of the hedge). Any divergence between expected and actual volatility will result in gains and losses relative to the agreed price of the option using expected volatility. The difference between actual volatility and expected volatility will create hedging errors in the replicating portfolio.

Dynamic hedging introduces risks into the replication process. It is inherently less robust than static hedging. The risks of dynamic hedging create significant problem for pricing and hedging options[6].

# 4   Pricing Framework

All derivatives (forwards and options) are priced and hedged within the arbitrage pricing framework. This is the case irrespective of asset class or underlying instrument.

---

[5]   See Chapter 7.
[6]   For a discussion of the risks of dynamic hedging of options, see Chapter 16.

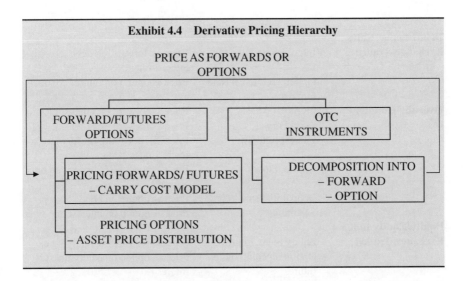

**Exhibit 4.4   Derivative Pricing Hierarchy**

The overall derivative pricing framework is set out in **Exhibit 4.4**. In practice, the process of pricing is as follows:

- Forward and futures contracts are priced using a static replication strategy (the carry cost model).
- Options are priced using a dynamic replication strategy (using volatility to generate expected changes in asset prices to derive the cost of the dynamic hedge).
- OTC instruments (such as swaps) are decomposed into the underlying derivative elements (forward etc) and then priced as the constituent elements.

**Exhibit 4.5** sets out the pricing approach to individual instruments.

**Exhibit 4.5   Pricing of Individual Instruments**

| Asset Class | Instrument | Pricing Approach |
|---|---|---|
| **Currency** | | |
| **Exchange-Traded** | Currency Futures | Price as forward on currency |
| | Option on Currency Futures | Price as option on futures contract |
| **Over-the-Counter** | Currency Forward | Price as forward on currency |
| | Currency Swap | Price as portfolio of forwards on currency |
| | Currency Option | Price as option on currency |

| **Debt/Interest Rates** | | |
|---|---|---|
| **Exchange-Traded** | Interest Rate Futures | Price as forward on debt securities/ interest rates |
| | Option on Interest Rate Futures | Price as option on futures contract |
| **Over-the-Counter** | FRAs | Price as forward on interest rates |
| | Bond Forwards | Price as forward on bond |
| | Interest Rate Swaps | Price as portfolio of forwards on interest rates |
| | Caps & Floors | Price as portfolio of options on interest rates |
| | Bond options | Price as option on bond |
| | Swaptions | Price as option on interest rate swap |
| **Equity/Equity Index** | | |
| **Exchange-Traded** | Equity index futures | Price as forward on equity index |
| | Option on equity index futures | Price as option on equity index futures |
| **Over-the-Counter** | Equity swaps | Price as portfolio of forwards on the equity index |
| | Equity options/warrants | Price as option on the underlying stock or equity index |
| **Commodity** | | |
| **Exchange-Traded** | Commodity futures | Price as forward on commodity |
| | Option on commodity futures | Price as option on commodity futures |
| **Over-the-Counter** | Commodity forwards | Price as forward on commodity |
| | Commodity swaps | Price as portfolio of forwards on commodity |
| | Commodity options | Price as option on commodity |

# 5   Derivative Pricing – Key Assumptions

All derivatives are priced using the hedging approach. The strength of this approach is that if an effective and efficient hedge can be devised then any derivative instrument can be priced. Once the hedge is determined, the problem can be reduced to an expected value calculation to which an established set of mathematical and statistical techniques can be applied.

A major advantage of this approach is that it enables the value of derivative contracts to be determined *without any assumption regarding the risk tolerance of traders or investors*. This is because the pricing approach inherently assumes the ability to create a riskless hedge. The weakness of this approach is that the conditions required to establish and maintain a riskless hedge are difficult to meet in practice. In this Section, the key assumptions underlying derivative pricing are considered. The primary focus is on identifying the assumptions and examining the consequence of failure of any of the assumptions.

The assumptions underlying derivative valuations include:

- **Asset trading** – the following assumptions are generally made about asset trading:

  1. *Transaction costs* – derivative pricing assumes that there are no transaction costs in trading. This includes the absence of bid-offer spreads, commissions and transaction costs (clearing charges etc). The presence of transaction costs has a number of implications. The costs may prevent trading or arbitrage as the transaction costs are greater than the risk free arbitrage profit opportunity. This means that the arbitrage free profit is not achieved. In addition, transaction costs dictate that the replicating portfolio cannot be adjusted as frequently as required, reducing the efficiency of the hedge and increasing the cost and risk of the hedge.

  2. *Credit risk* – derivative pricing also assumes that the underlying assets (with the exception of risky bonds such as corporate or non-sovereign securities) have no inherent credit risk. In addition, it is assumed that counterparties to derivative transactions are able to *always* perform their obligations; that is, they are not subject to credit risk. Mechanisms for reducing credit risk (bilateral collateral or margining on an exchange) may be employed to reduce risk but add to the cost and uncertainty of the hedge and the cash flows of the replicating portfolio.

  3. *Taxation* – derivative pricing assumes that all transactions are unaffected by tax or other fiscal charges. The presence of taxes means that positions that have identical economic outcomes have different *pre-tax* and *after-tax* results. This means that traders and investors will experience trading biases that will decrease asset trading efficiency and the creation of risk free portfolios and hedges.

  4. *Divisibility of assets* – derivative pricing requires assets to be infinitely divisible to enable perfect hedges to be established for the purposes of replication. This means that hedges will be inherently less than efficient and will leave residual risk that must be managed and priced.

- **Asset markets** – the following assumptions are generally made about the functioning of asset markets:

  1. *Complete markets* – derivative pricing is based on complete markets, that is, all possible instruments are available and are readily tradable. This includes

no restrictions on short selling of any security or assets. Inability to borrow assets for the purposes of short selling, the cost of borrowing the asset (including the uncertainty of borrowing cost over the required life of the hedge), the inability to earn interest on the total proceeds of the short sale and the presence of restrictions may prevent the construction of replicating portfolios and efficient hedges.

2. *Liquidity* – derivative pricing assumes that all assets and instruments can be traded with unlimited liquidity; that is, the trader can execute all trades irrespective of size without constraint in terms of trading liquidity. Restrictions on liquidity would prevent construction of hedges and leave residual risks that must be priced and managed. This creates difficulties in risk free arbitrage pricing.

3. *Borrowing and lending cash* – derivative pricing assumes that the trader is able to borrow and lend unlimited amounts as required to finance asset positions or invest the proceeds of short sales at known and fixed interest rates. It moreover assumes that this is done at *risk free rates*. It is unlikely that this can be achieved in practice. This is because while it is possible to lend at the risk free rate, it is unlikely that non-sovereigns can borrow at the risk free rate. In addition, it is unlikely that the traders can borrow *unlimited* amounts. This is likely to restrict the construction of efficient risk free hedges at known costs.

4. *Interest rates* – derivative pricing requires the availability of known, fixed and zero coupon rates (that entail no assumptions about re-investment or future borrowing rates). This is dictated by the fact that the cost of borrowing must be known accurately to facilitate derivative pricing. In practice, it may not be possible, depending on the market, to borrow or lend for the required maturity at known and fixed zero coupon interest rates. This exposes the hedger to interest rate risk (effectively uncertainty in the cost of the hedge portfolio). This has the effect of reducing the efficiency of the hedge and creates difficulties in pricing derivatives.

- **Asset prices** – the following assumptions are generally made about the behaviour of asset prices:

  1. *Continuous asset markets* – derivative pricing assumes continuous asset trading where the asset price changes in infinitely small increments in continuous time. This assumes a variety of behaviours including independence of price changes and the absence of jumps/discontinuous price changes. It also assumes a prescribed and known asset price process that generates known distributions with known volatility. In practice, the conditions of perfect continuous asset markets are difficult to satisfy. The failure to meet the required condition (particularly price discontinuity) is potentially a significant barrier

to the creation of efficient dynamic hedges. This is because it is difficult to rebalance the hedge as required to match movements in the underlying asset without significant hedging errors and additional trading costs. The costs must be incorporated in derivative pricing.

2. *Asset price distribution* – derivative pricing assumes that the distribution of the asset price is known and conforms to a known distribution with identifiable characteristics such as a log normal distribution. It is unlikely that asset price distributions consistently follow a known standard distribution generating pricing errors.

3. *Volatility* – derivative pricing assumes that the dispersion of the future asset prices defined by volatility or the standard deviation of the distribution is known and fixed. It is clear that volatility is itself variable and difficult to estimate with accuracy in practice. This makes replication of the option difficult as the hedging is model dependent. Errors in parameter estimates (such as volatility) create hedging errors. This creates differences between the theoretical price of the option and the actual realised replication cost.

• **Asset pricing** – the following assumptions are generally made about the nature of asset pricing:

1. *Arbitrage free pricing* – derivative pricing assumes that all assets and derivatives are efficiently priced and there are no risk free arbitrage possibilities. This is unlikely to be the case because of the failure of some of the assumptions already identified.

2. *Holding period risk* – derivative pricing assumes that all prices are arbitrage free and that the market price converges to the arbitrage free price. However, holding period risk (also referred to as horizon risk) refers to the fact that the market price may *not* converge to the theoretical price until maturity (which may be a long period of time). This may lead to absence of arbitrage activity as they are unable to maintain positions that are theoretically risk free for the required holding period as a result of margin calls.

In practice, it is unlikely that all of these assumptions are likely to be satisfied in practice. This means that in practice it is most unlikely that a derivative can be replicated with the degree of accuracy and efficiency dictated by the theory of arbitrage free pricing. This is particularly the case where the replication must be dynamic, as with options[7].

---

[7]  For a discussion of the impact of market imperfections on derivative pricing and trading see Musiela, Marek and Rutowski, Marek (1996) Martingale Methods in Financial Modelling; Springer, Berlin at Chapter 4.

This dictates that in practice, it is essential to understand the process of replication and hedging combined with an understanding of the risks of and potential breakdowns in the efficiency in hedges as a result of failures in the assumption underlying derivative pricing. Understanding model risk and the capacity to stress test these models is critical to derivative pricing and risk management.


# 6   Derivatives Pricing – Epistimology[8]

There is now a significant body of research literature covering derivative pricing. This body of research (much of it over the last 30 years) is concerned with both theoretical and applied research into derivative pricing. Much of this research work is focused on seeking to solve real world problems in derivative pricing. In this Section, a brief overview of the literature and knowledge base of derivative pricing is set out[9].

**Exhibit 4.6** sets out the overall structure of derivative literature. It may be divided into three major areas of concern:
- **Concept of risk neutrality** – this focuses on the use of risk neutrality to derive the value of derivatives. This includes work on the concept of no arbitrage and the use of martingale processes[10].
- **Interest rate and yield curves** – this focuses on the creation of complete yield curves for valuation purposes. This is taken to include the derivation of zero coupon yield curves, interpolation techniques to complete yield curves and the

---

[8]   For a review of derivatives research trends see Chance, Don M. "Research Trends in Derivatives and Risk Management Since Black-Scholes" (May 1999) Journal of Portfolio Management 35–46. For a review of the literature of option pricing, see Smith Jr., Clifford W. "Option Pricing: A Review" (1976) Journal of Financial Economics vol 3 15–24; Smithson, Charles "Wonderful Life" (October 1991) Risk 37–44; Smithson, Charles "Extended Family (1)" (October 1995) Risk 19–21; Smithson, Charles "Extended Family (2)" (November 1995) Risk 52–53; Smithson, Charles "Extended Family" (December 1997) Risk 158–163; Whaley, Robert "Building on Black-Scholes" (December 1997) Risk 149–156; Smithson, Charles "Extended Family" (September 1998) Risk-Black Scholes Merton Supplement 14–18.

[9]   Please note that the classification is somewhat arbitrary. There are a number of ways in which the literature is capable of being arranged.

[10]   See Harrison, J. Michael and Kreps, David M. "Martingales and Arbitrage in Multiperiod Securities Markets" (1979) Journal of Economic Theory vol 20 381–408; Harrison, J. Michael and Pilska, Stanley R. "Martingales and Stochastic Integrals in the Theory of Continuous Trading" (1981) Stochastic Processes and their Applications vol 11 261–271.

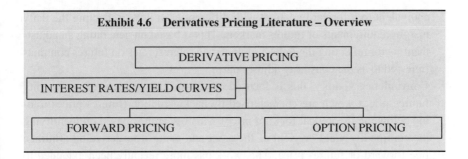

Exhibit 4.6 Derivatives Pricing Literature – Overview

term structure of interest rates. In practice, this area overlaps in part with interest rate modelling for the purpose of pricing interest rate options.

- **Forward Pricing** – this is focused on the pricing of forward contracts on different asset classes.
- **Option Pricing** – this is focused on deriving the price of options on different underlying assets.

**Exhibit 4.7** sets out the structure of the forward pricing research literature. The primary components include:

- **Carry cost model** – this is focused on using the concept of carry cost to derive the value of a forward contract (effectively the price of the asset adjusted for the cost of financing and storing the asset, less any income on the asset). This was derived originally for agricultural commodities. In a parallel development, the concept of interest rate parity was utilised to derive the price of foreign exchange forwards. This generalised model can be translated across all asset classes.
- **Futures pricing model (convexity adjustment)** – this is focused on derivation of the price of the futures contract using the insight that the futures contract is

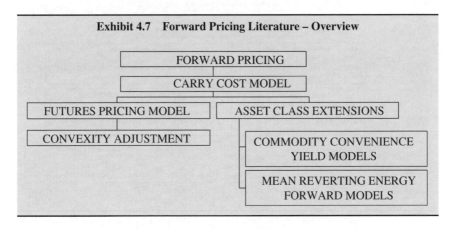

Exhibit 4.7 Forward Pricing Literature – Overview

equivalent to a forward contract with different cash flows reflecting the daily margin requirements of futures markets. This is based on generating an adjustment factor reflecting the impact of uncertain interest rates on futures contracts (referred to as the convexity adjustment).

• **Convenience yields** – this is focused on the special problem of commodity futures prices which are characterised by backwardation (futures prices trading below the theoretical forward price). This research is based on identifying the commodity yield or yield of the asset and using it to derive an arbitrage free forward or futures price. This work has more recently been extended to encompass mean reverting processes used to price forward contracts on energy contracts.

**Exhibit 4.8** sets out the structure of the literature on option pricing and contingent claims theory. This body of research is easily the most substantial area in derivative pricing. This body of research may be categorised into a number of different but closely inter-related areas of knowledge including:

• **Early option pricing models** – this body of research established the expected value concepts and the use of distribution of asset returns to derive the value of an option.

• **Black-Scholes-Merton ("BSM") option pricing models** – this consists of the seminal work of Fisher Black, Myron Scholes and Robert Merton in developing

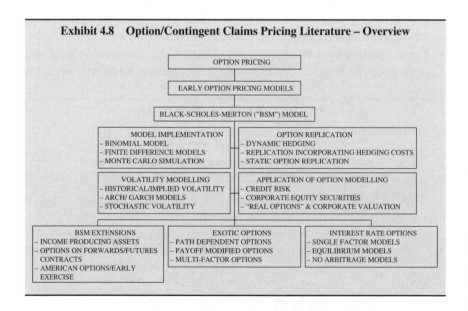

**Exhibit 4.8    Option/Contingent Claims Pricing Literature – Overview**

the notion that an option can be perfectly hedged using the underlying asset. This enabled the development of a risk free replicating portfolio that allowed the derivation of a closed form solution for the price of an option.

- **Model implementation** – this area of research is focused on implementing the BSM option pricing framework using different mathematical and numerical techniques. These include the use of binomial models, finite difference models, Monte Carlo simulation techniques and approximation techniques. It also includes work with jump diffusion models and different types of distributions to derive option valuations.
- **Option replication** – this area focuses on the actual hedging and trading of options by replicating the option position with a position in the asset that is dynamically managed over time. The work focuses on the process of dynamic hedging and use of dynamic hedging in portfolio insurance. More recent work focuses on replicating the portfolio where the transaction costs are incorporated. Other work focuses on the practice of static replication (effectively using a portfolio of *options* to replicate another option).
- **Volatility modelling** – the focus in this area is on estimating volatility that is a required input into option pricing models. It focuses on different approaches to volatility estimation such as historical volatility, implied volatility, the use of autoregressive models (ARCH/GARCH models) and the use of stochastic volatility (that is, volatility is itself a random variable). Other work focuses on the behaviour of volatility such as volatility smiles/skews and volatility term structure.
- **Applications of option modelling** – this focuses on the application of option concepts to contingent claims problems outside of pure derivatives. This focuses on the use of option pricing to model credit risk, the value of corporate securities and the valuation of "real" options (such as research and development projects, abandonment or scale up options, exploration rights, resource projects etc)[11].

---

[11] See Brennan, Michael J. and Schwartz, Eduardo S. "A New Approach to Evaluating Natural Resources" (Spring 1985) Midland Corporate Finance Journal vol 3 no 1 37–48; Ireland, Louise "Refining the Pricing Theory" (July 1990) Corporate Finance 11–13; Kulatilaka, Nalin and Marcus, Alan J. "Project Valuation Under Uncertainty: When Does DCF Fail?" (Fall 1992) Journal of Applied Corporate Finance vol 5 no 3 92–100; Hotchin, Simon and Dentskevich, Paul "The Risk-Based Way to Asset Valuation" (1996) Corporate Finance Risk Management & Derivatives Yearbook 15–17; Leslie, Keith J. and Michaels, Max P. "The Real Power of Real Options" (1997) The McKinsey Quarterly Number 3 4–22; Leslie, Keith J. and Michaels, Max P. "The Real Power of Real Options" (January 1998) Corporate Finance 13–20; Copeland, Thomas E. and Keenan,

- **BSM model extensions** – this research work concentrates upon generalising the BSM approach to cover different types of options. This covers work on pricing options on different asset classes/instruments (including forward/futures contracts), income producing assets and American options where there is the possibility of early exercise.
- **Exotic option pricing** – this research focuses upon using the general option pricing model to price "exotic" (that is, non-standard) options. This includes work on path dependent options (average, lookback, barrier, preference etc options), payoff modified options (binary or digital options) and multi-factor options (compound, quanto, basket, rainbow, exchange etc options)[12].
- **Interest rate options** – this work focused upon the pricing of interest rate options. This focuses upon problems of interest rate term structure and declining volatility and modelling of options on bonds and interest rates. The work is focused on different classes of models such as simple one-factor models, equilibrium models and arbitrage free/no arbitrage models.

**Exhibit 4.9** sets out the structure of derivative pricing and risk management literature. This area of research focuses on the following:
- **Hedging issues** – this body of literature focuses upon the use of derivatives to hedge financial risk. It is concerned with the benefits of hedging and the impact of hedging upon the value of the firm[13].
- **Value-at-risk ("VAR") and risk management** – this work is concerned with the use of VAR techniques (which are founded in derivative pricing and

---

Philip T. "Making Real Options Real" (1998) The McKinsey Quarterly Number 3 129–141; Kemna, Angelien G.Z. "Case Studies on Real Options" (1993) Financial Options vol 22 259–270; Trigeorgis, Leon "The Nature of Option Interactions and the Valuation of Investments with Multiple Real Options" (1993) Journal of Financial and Quantitative Analysis vol 28 1–20; Triantis, Alexander "The Hidden World of Real Options" (October 1999) Risk 52–54; Trigeorgis, Lenos (Editor) (1999) Real Options and Business Strategy: Applications to Decision Making; Risk Books, London; Amram, Martha and Kulatilaka, Nalin (1999) Real Options-Managing Strategic Investment in an Uncertain World; Risk Books, London; Rogers, Jamie (2002) Strategy, Value and Risk – The Real Options Approach; Palgrave, Basingstoke.

[12] For a discussion of exotic options, see Das, Satyajit (2004) Structured Products Volume 1; John Wiley & Sons (Asia), Singapore at Chapters 5 to 11 (inclusive).

[13] For a discussion of use of derivatives in hedging and risk management, see Das, Satyajit (2004) Structured Products Volume 1; John Wiley & Sons (Asia), Singapore at Chapters 1 to 3 (inclusive).

classical portfolio theory) to model risk of derivatives trading and market risk generally[14].

**Exhibit 4.9   Derivatives Pricing and Risk Management Literature – Overview**

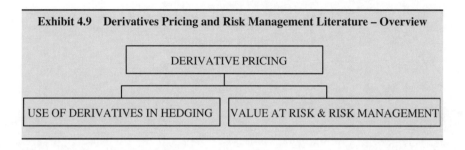

## 7  Summary

Derivatives pricing is based on the concept of arbitrage free pricing. It requires the construction of a replicating portfolio (consisting of the asset and cash) that reproduces the return characteristics of the derivative contract. This replicating portfolio is used to construct a hedge for the derivative to create a risk free portfolio. The cost of the hedging portfolio equates to the cost of the derivative. The replicating portfolio is either static (forward contract) or must be dynamically managed (option contracts). In practice, restriction in the functioning and structure of real markets and the breakdown in model assumptions may create divergences between the theoretical price of the derivative and the actual replication cost. This residual risk (which is generally difficult to eliminate in practice) requires the risk of the hedge and the pricing model to be understood and compensated for in the price of the derivative.

---

[14] For a discussion of risk management, see Das, Satyajit (2004) Structured Products Volume 1; John Wiley & Sons (Asia), Singapore at Chapters 1 to 12 (inclusive).

# 5
# Interest Rates & Yield Curves

## 1  Overview

Interest rates and the process of discounting future cash flows to price and value financial transactions is fundamental to capital markets. Accurate, consistent and reliable interest rates are essential to all financial transactions. This is true irrespective of the type and complexity of the instrument.

In practice, interest rates are required in derivatives pricing and valuation for two reasons:

- Interest rates drive the price of debt instruments and therefore are required to determine the underlying asset price for derivatives on debt instruments or interest rates.
- Interest rates are required to determine the cost of carry in pricing forwards on all asset classes.

In practice, interest rates are also required for the following applications:

- **Pricing and valuation of financial instruments or transactions** – this entails the valuation of instruments, such as bonds or derivatives on fixed income instruments, by allowing analysis of the returns from different sets of cash flows through comparison of their discounted present value. In addition, the use of interest rates to value and price derivatives in other asset classes, such as currency, equity, and commodities.
- **Relative value and arbitrage** – this covers the use of interest rates and discounting to assess the relative value of traded or untraded instruments and to identify arbitrage opportunities.
- **Assessing or forecasting economic expectations** – this involves the analysis of various types of information available from the yield curve, such as

forward rates, to assess market expectations of the path of future interest rates and the term structure of future interest rates. This allows the formation and testing of expectations about future economic activity and inflation rates.

The process of deriving interest rates or discount factors is not simple and unambiguous. Several techniques have been developed to assist in the determination of the interest rates to be utilised. In this Chapter the issues relating to the derivation of interest rates and yield curves for use in the pricing and valuation of transactions are examined.

The structure of this Chapter is as follows:
- The representation of interest rates and discount factors including quotation conventions are outlined.
- The use of interest rates in pricing is examined.
- Measures of interest rate sensitivity (duration, PVBP and convexity) are described.
- The interest rates to be utilised (par, forward and zero) are analysed.
- The calculation of forward and zero coupon rates from the available yield curve is described.
- The problem of deriving a suitable yield to enable the calculation of the various interest rates is outlined. This includes approaches to interpolation (linear and splines) and the issues in practical curve construction.
- Yield curve construction in practice is described.

# 2   Interest Rates[1]
## 2.1   Interest Rate Calculations[2]

Interest rates are the pure price of time. Interest rates are designed through the discounting process to equate cash flows occurring at different future dates to facilitate valuation and comparison of different transactions. It is an economic measure of forgone consumption. In effect, it is the price required by one entity willing to defer

---

[1]   For a discussion of interest rates, see Cohen, Roger "Interest Rates, Bond Pricing, Duration and Convexity" in Satyajit (Editor) (1997) Risk Management & Financial Derivatives: A Guide to the Mathematics; LBC Information Services, Sydney; McGraw-Hill, Chicago; MacMillan Publishing, England at Chapter 2.

[2]   For a discussion of the mathematics of interest, see Knox, David M., Zima, Petr and Brown, Robert l. (1984) Mathematics of Finance; McGraw-Hill, New York; Crapp, Harvey R. and Marshall, John (1986) Money Market Maths; Allen and Unwin, Sydney; Marshall, John (1991) Money Equals Maths; Allen and Unwin, Sydney; Cartledge, Peter (1991) A Handbook of Financial Mathematics; Euromoney Books, London; Sherris, Michael (1996) Money and Capital Markets: Pricing, Yields and

consumption from another seeking access to immediate consumption. An interest rate can be considered to equate to the rate of growth or decay of an asset over a time period. In effect, it is the effective measure of value of an asset today (present value) to its value at a future date (future value).

A complexity relating to interest rate calculations derives from the different manner in which interest rates may in practice be represented. There are numerous different interest calculation conventions. Market convention on certain key aspects of interest rate calculations varies significantly between various domestic and international capital markets. The primary differences are in the following areas:
- Payment of interest (simple versus compound; discount versus coupon basis).
- Compounding of interest payments (annual, semi-annual, quarterly, continuous etc).
- Day basis factor used in accruing and compounding of interest and accrued interest calculations.

## 2.2   Interest Rate Payments

### 2.2.1   Overview

Interest rates are calculated in several ways. The major forms include:
- Simple interest.
- Discount basis.
- Compound interest.

### 2.2.2   Simple Interest

Simple interest entails calculating interest without allowance for interest on interest. This is done by adding the amount of simple interest to the present value to calculate the future value of the cash flow. Simple interest calculations are rarely used in financial transactions. **Exhibit 5.1** sets out the formula for simple interest and an example of a simple interest calculation.

### 2.2.3   Discount Basis

An alternative manner of representing interest rates is simple discount basis. The discount basis is calculated by subtracting a discount amount from the principal

Analysis – Second Edition; Allen and Unwin, Sydney; Martin, John (1996) Derivatives Maths; IFR Publishing, London at Chapter 3; Van Deventer, Donald R. and Imai, Kenji (1997) Financial Risk Analytics; Irwin, Chicago at Chapter 1; (2001) Applied Math For Derivatives Maths; John Wiley & Sons, Singapore at Chapter 3.

---

**Exhibit 5.1    Simple Interest**

1. **Simple Interest Calculation**

   Simple Interest = Principal × Interest Rate (% pa) × Number of Days/365

   Future value = Principal + Simple Interest

2. **Example**
   Assume a $1,000,000 investment paying simple interest at 8.00% pa for a period of 6 months (184 days). The interest payable is:

$$\$1,000,000 \times .08 \times 184/365 = \$40,328.77$$

   The future value of this investment is:

$$\$1,000,000 + \$40,328.77 = \$1,040,328.77$$

---

payable at a future date. The present value is simply the principal amount adjusted by the amount of the discount. Discount rates are utilised in some markets to price and value short term discount securities. **Exhibit 5.2** sets out the formula for calculating the price of a short-term security on a discount basis and an example of a discount calculation.

Simple discount rates are used to determine present values from future values. This means that an equivalent yield to maturity for a given discount rate can be calculated. **Exhibit 5.3** sets out the formula for converting discount basis to a yield to maturity basis and an example of a conversion calculation.

The difference between the equivalent interest rate and discount rate increases with the absolute level of the discount rate and the term of the security.

### 2.2.4   Compound Interest

Compound interest calculations entail incorporating interest on interest earned. In effect, compound calculations assume that interest payments received are re-invested together with the invested principal. This is repeated at each interest payment date. The critical aspect of compound interest calculations is the re-investment rate that is assumed. In the traditional approach, the re-investment rate is assumed to be the same interest rate for each interest rate period. This re-investment rate is assumed equivalent to the interest rate or yield to maturity (also referred to as YTM).

---

**Exhibit 5.2    Discount Basis**

**1.  Discount Calculation**

Discount = Principal × Discount Rate (% pa) × Number of Days/365

Present Value = Principal − Discount

**2.  Example**

Assume an investment in a security with a face value of $1,000,000 at a discount of 8.00% with a maturity of 6 months (184 days). The discount amount is:

$1,000,000 × .08 × 184/365 = $40,328.77

The present value of this security is:

$1,000,000 − $40,328.77 = $959,671.23

---

**Exhibit 5.3    Conversion of Discount Rates to Yield to Maturity**

**1.  Conversion of Discount Rates to Yield to Maturity**

$$R = D/[1 - D \times N/365]$$

Where

R = Yield to Maturity
D = Discount Rate
N = Number of days

**2.  Example**

Assume a discount rate of 8% on a 6 month security (184 days). The equivalent yield is:

$$.08/[1 - .08 \times 184/365] = .0834 \text{ or } 8.34\% \text{ pa}$$

---

The yield to maturity is equivalent to the internal rate of return ("IRR") of cash flows. This is equivalent to the rate of return at which the future cash flows must be discounted to equate to the present value of the transaction. This is often expressed as the rate of return that results in the transaction having a net present value of zero.

The IRR calculation used to derive the yield to maturity has a number of weaknesses. These include:

- The calculation assumes that all cash flows are re-invested (in the case of cash inflows) or financed (in the case of outflows) at *the same rate*. The rate is the IRR rate itself.

- The IRR calculation does not allow a term structure of rate to be incorporated assuming a flat term structure equal to the IRR rate itself.

**Exhibit 5.4** sets out the formula for calculation of future values and present value utilising compound interest. **Exhibit 5.5** sets out the formulae for the determination of the yield to maturity given a series of known cash flows. **Exhibit 5.6** sets out a comparison of the future value calculated using simple interest and compound interest.

---

**Exhibit 5.4   Compound Interest Calculations**

**1.   Future Value**

$$FV = PV \times (1 + r)^t$$

Where

FV = Future value
PV = Present value
t   = Length of time to the cash flow
r   = Yield to maturity or discount rate

**2.   Present value**

$$PV = [FV/(1 + r)^t]$$

Where

FV = Future value
PV = Present value
t   = Length of time to the cash flow
r   = Yield to maturity or discount rate

---

**Exhibit 5.5   Yield to Maturity**

$$\sum_{t=1}^{n}[(C_t)/(1 + r)^t] = 0$$

Where
$C_t$ = Cash flow (e.g. interest and/or principal payments) at time t
t   = Length of time to the cash flow
n   = Length of time to final maturity
r   = Yield to maturity or discount rate

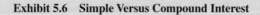

**Exhibit 5.6    Simple Versus Compound Interest**

In the graph below the future value of $100 compounded at a rate of 6.00% pa over different
time periods is displayed:

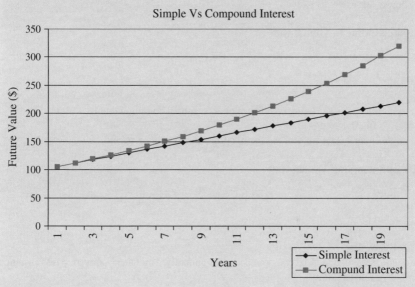

## 2.3   Interest Rate Compounding

Interest rates are frequently quoted on the basis of different compounding frequencies. The compounding frequency refers to how often interest is paid and therefore
can be reinvested (compounded) to increase earnings. In practice, the compounding
periods used commonly include annual, semi-annual, quarterly, weekly or daily
compounding. It is frequently necessary to convert interest rates from one particular interest rate basis to its equivalent utilising a different interest rate basis.
For example, it may be necessary to convert semi-annually compounded yields
to annually compounded yields. **Exhibit 5.7** sets out the formulae for converting
interest rates from a variety of bases into its equivalent utilising other interest rate
yield bases.

   An important form of compounding used in derivative pricing is continuous compounding. Continuously compounded rates refer to interest rates where
the compounding period is decreased (that is, the time increment between
interest payments is decreased) until it becomes infinitesimal. Continuously compounded rates are not used in the market and do not typically appear in *actual*

---

### Exhibit 5.7   Compounding Conversions

**1.   Compounding Conversions**

The generalised formula for converting interest rate to a different compounding basis is as follows:

**Compounding to Annual Rate**

$$r_a = (1 + r_n/n)^n - 1$$

Where:

$r_a$ = Interest Rate (in decimal form) on a pa annual compounding or effective basis.

$r_n$ = Interest Rate (in decimal form) compounded every n period.

**De-compounding Annual Rate**

$$r_n = [(1 + r_a)^{(1/n)} - 1] \times n$$

where all terms are the same as above.

**2.   Example**

Assume a rate of 6.00% pa compounded semi-annually. This can be converted into an annual effective rate as follows:

$$(1 + .06/2)^2 - 1 = .0609 \text{ or } 6.09\% \text{ pa compounded annually.}$$

The annual rate of 6.09% may be de-compounded into a quarterly rate as follows:

$$[(1 + .0609)^{(1/4)} - 1] \times 4 = .0596 \text{ or } 5.96\% \text{ pa compounded quarterly.}$$

---

financial transactions. However, they are frequently used in financial calculations for a number of reasons:

- Derivative pricing is often undertaken in a continuous time framework (to enable the use of stochastic processes) requiring the use of continuous interest rates.
- The mathematics (in particular the derivatives) of continuously compounded interest rates are simpler than that of discrete rates. This is the result of the ability to use exponential growth and decay terms where continuously compounded rates are used.

**Exhibit 5.8** sets out the mathematics of continuously compounded rates.

**Exhibit 5.9** sets out examples of calculating interest rate yield equivalents on different interest rate basis for a range of interest rates.

---

### Exhibit 5.8   Continuously Compounded Interest Rates

**1. Continuous Interest Rates**

Where the compounding period is decreased, at a rate r compounded continuously, then after 1 year the growth or future value can be expressed as:

$$\lim_{n \to \infty}(1 + r/n)^n = e^r$$

Where

r = Interest rate
n = Compounding Period
e = Exponential term (approximately 2.7128)

This means that using $r_c$ (a continuously compounded interest rate) will result in:

$$FV = PV \times e^{r_c t}$$

$$PV = FV \times e^{-r_c t}$$

Where

FV = Future value
PV = Present value
t   = Length of time to the cash flow
$r_c$   = rate compounded continuously

The relationship of discrete and continuously compounded rates is as follows:

$$r_c = \ln(1 + r_a)$$
$$r_a = e^{r_c} - 1$$

Where

$r_a$ = rate compounded annually
$r_c$ = rate compounded continuously
ln = natural logarithm

**2. Example**

Assume an annual effective interest rate of 6.00% pa. This is equivalent to a continuously compounded interest rate of:

$$\ln(1 + .06) = 0.0583 \text{ or } 5.83\% \text{ pa}$$

Assume a continuously compounded interest rate of 6.00% pa. This is equivalent to an annual compounded interest rate of:

$$e^{.06} - 1 = 0.0618 \text{ or } 6.18\% \text{ pa}$$

The future value $100 at the end of 3 years at a rate of 6.00% pa continuously compounded is:

$$PV \times e^{rt} = 100 \times e^{.0600 \times 3} = 119.72$$

The present value $100 at the end of 3 years at a rate of 6.00% pa continuously compounded is:

$$FV \times e^{-rt} = 100 \times e^{-0.0600 \times 3} = 83.53$$

---

### Exhibit 5.9    Compounding Conversions – Example

The following Tables set out the equivalent interest rates (in % pa) for different compounding assumptions:

| Interest Rate | **5.00** | | | |
|---|---|---|---|---|
| **Compounding Assumption** | | | | |
| Continuous | 4.99 | 4.97 | 4.94 | 4.88 |
| Monthly | 5.00 | 4.98 | 4.95 | 4.89 |
| Quarterly | 5.02 | 5.00 | 4.97 | 4.91 |
| Semi-annually | 5.05 | 5.03 | 5.00 | 4.94 |
| Annually | 5.12 | 5.09 | 5.06 | 5.00 |

| Interest Rate | **10.00** | | | |
|---|---|---|---|---|
| **Compounding Assumption** | | | | |
| Continuous | 9.96 | 9.88 | 9.76 | 9.53 |
| Monthly | 10.00 | 9.92 | 9.80 | 9.57 |
| Quarterly | 10.08 | 10.00 | 9.88 | 9.65 |
| Semi-annually | 10.21 | 10.13 | 10.00 | 9.76 |
| Annually | 10.47 | 10.38 | 10.25 | 10.00 |

| Interest Rate | **15.00** | | | |
|---|---|---|---|---|
| **Compounding Assumption** | | | | |
| Continuous | 14.91 | 14.73 | 14.46 | 13.98 |
| Monthly | 15.00 | 14.82 | 14.55 | 14.06 |
| Quarterly | 15.19 | 15.00 | 14.73 | 14.22 |
| Semi-annually | 15.48 | 15.28 | 15.00 | 14.48 |
| Annually | 16.08 | 15.87 | 15.56 | 15.00 |

## 2.4   Day Count Basis

Interest can been accrued on debt obligations using different assumed day count basis. **Exhibit 5.10** summarises the major features of the primary methods of interest rate calculations. **Exhibit 5.11** sets out the basis for conversion of a particular day count basis to another.

---

**Exhibit 5.10    Day Count Basis in Interest Rate Calculations**

**1.   Actual/365 or 365/365 Basis (Bond Equivalent Basis)**

This calculation assumes a year of 365 days and accrues on the basis of actual days elapsed.

Assume a security with a coupon of 8.00% pa. On a full year basis this security pays an interest amount (based on a principal amount of $100 million) of:

$8,000,0000 (calculated as $100 million × 8.00% pa × 365/365)

Accrued interest on this security would be calculated in the following manner. Assume the security has the following characteristics:

Maturity :            18 February 2010
Last Coupon Date:    18 February 2001
Settlement Date:     23 August 2001

The accrued interest on this security would equal:

$4,076,712 (calculated as $100 million × 8.00% × 186/365 − where the
number of days between 18 February 2001 and 23 August 2001 is 186)

The only significant difference between 365/365 day basis and actual/365 day basis occurs in leap years.

**2.   Annual Eurobond Basis (AIBD Basis)**

This calculation assumes a year of 360 days with 12 months each of 30 days.

Assume the above security with a coupon of 8.00% pa. On a full year basis, this security pays an interest amount (based on a principal amount of $100 million) of:

$8,000,0000 (calculated as $100 million × 8.00% pa × 360/360)

Accrued interest on this security on an annual bond basis for the facts outlined above would be calculated using the actual number of days in broken months and an even 30 days in whole months. The accrued interest on this security would equal:

$4,066,667 (calculated as $100 million × 8.00% × 183/360 − where the
number of days between 18 February 2001 and 23 August 2001 is 183
calculated as Number of Bond Days = 10 + 150 + 23 = 183)

**3.   Annual Money Market (LIBOR Basis)**

Interest is calculated on an Actual/360 day basis.

---

Assume the above security with a coupon of 8.00% pa. On a full year basis, this security pays an interest amount (based on a principal amount of $100 million) of:

$8,111,111 (calculated as $100 million × 8.00% pa × 365/360)

Accrued interest on this security on an annual money basis for the facts outlined above would be calculated using the actual number of days in the accrual period. The accrued interest on this security would equal:

$4,133,333 (calculated as $100 million × 8.00% × 186/360 − where the number of days between 18 February 2001 and 23 August 2001 is 186)

---

### Exhibit 5.11    Day Count Basis Conversions

**1.  Day Count Conversion**

The generalised formula for converting interest rates to a different day count basis is as follows:

**Money Market to Bond Equivalent Basis**

$$r_{bond} = r_{moneymarket} \times 365/360$$

Where:

$r_{bond}$ = Interest Rate on a bond equivalent (Actual/365 day) basis.
$r_{moneymarket}$ = Interest Rate on a money market (Actual/360 day) basis.

**Bond Equivalent to Money Market Basis**

$$r_{moneymarket} = r_{bond} \times 360/365$$

Where all terms are the same as above.

**2.  Example**

The following examples set out examples of conversion of day count basis:

| Original Day Count (Days) | 360 | 365 |
|---|---|---|
| Day Equivalent Basis | | |
| 360 Day | 5.0000 | 4.9315 |
| 365 Day | 5.0694 | 5.0000 |

| Original Day Count (Days) | 360 | 365 |
|---|---|---|
| Day Equivalent Basis | | |
| 360 Day | 10.0000 | 9.8630 |
| 365 Day | 10.1389 | 10.0000 |

| Original Day Count (Days) | 360 | 365 |
|---|---|---|
| Day Equivalent Basis | | |
| 360 Day | 15.0000 | 14.7945 |
| 365 Day | 15.2083 | 15.0000 |

## 3 Discount Factors

The concept of interest rates and discount factors or present value is interrelated. Central to the concept of interest rates and discount factors is the fact that value in financial transaction is given by cash flow that is defined in terms of two vectors: amount and the time at which the cash flow occurs[3].

The concept of discounting the cash flows that may occur at different points of time is designed to enable the value of these individual items to be calculated at a determined point of time (for example today) to allow comparability. This requires the cash flow to be moved in time to determine an *equivalent* cash flow at the relevant date. Using the fundamental homogeneity and uniformity of cash, the current value of cash can be given by its present value. This is an amount that if invested at the relevant interest rate will give a value equivalent to the stated cash flow at the date on which the cash flow occurs in the future.

This can be stated more precisely as:

$$C_{t0} = C_{t1} \times df_{t1}$$

Where

$C_{t0}$ = Cash flow at time t0
$C_{t1}$ = Cash flow at time t1
$df_{t1}$ = Discount Factor (or present value) for cash flows as at time t1

The discount factor ("df") generated or utilised to calculate a discount factor is essentially the present value of $1 at a specific future time. In theoretical terms, this is merely the price of the relevant zero coupon bond, discounted at the appropriate interest rate for the maturity.

**Exhibit 5.12** sets out the mathematical relationship of discount factors to the relevant interest rate for each future period. Discount factors where interest rates are

---

[3]  To be strictly accurate an additional vector that is required to define value is any contingency or conditionality relating to the cash flow, e.g. in the case of an option or risky (default risk) cash flow.

---

**Exhibit 5.12   Discount Factors and Interest Rates**

**1.  Simple Interest**

$$df = 1/(1 + r_{t1} * n/365)$$

Where

df = Discount factor for time t1 at rate $r_{t1}$
$r_{t1}$ = Interest rate as at time t1
n  = Number of days (or t1 − t0)

**2.  Compound Interest**

$$df = 1/(1 + r_{t1})^{(n/365)}$$

Where all terms are the same as above.

**3.  Continuously Compounded Interest**

$$df = e^{-r_{t1} \times n/365}$$

Where all terms are the same as above.

---

positive will be less than 1 and greater than 0. Discount factors are inversely related to yield with reference to maturity. **Exhibit 5.13** sets out the shape of the interest rate curve and the discount rate curve. Discount factors are equally applicable to forward rates.

The advantage of discount factors is that each discount factor is unique. It is not affected by market quotation conventions prevalent in relation to interest rates such as the periodicity of compounding (annual, semi-annual, quarterly or continuous) or the day count basis utilised (actual/365, actual/360 or bond basis).

In effect, the problem of yield curves can be expressed as the problem of either deriving term structure of interest rates or discount factors.

# 4   Interest Rates and Pricing

## 4.1   Valuing Cash Flows

Within the framework outlined, valuation of cash flows entails the following steps:
- Identify the amount and timing of individual cash flows (or series of cash flows).

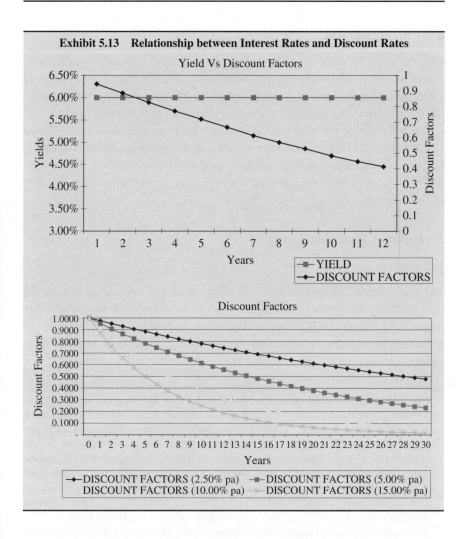

Exhibit 5.13    Relationship between Interest Rates and Discount Rates

- Identify the interest rate or discount factor appropriate for the relevant maturity.
- Discount the cash flows using the appropriate interest rate or discount factor to determine the present value of the cash flows.

The value of the stream of the cash flows is simply the sum of the present values of individual cash flows.

The approach outlined is generic and is applicable to all financial derivatives and financial transactions generally.

## 4.2   Pricing Bonds[4]

Valuations can be made for either individual cash flows or series of cash flows. The most common example of a combination of cash flows is a bond or security where the issuer receives the proceeds at the time of issue and then makes periodic interest payments (the coupons) and repays the principal at maturity.

The valuation of the bond (effectively the price to be paid *today* for the future cash flows) is based on discounting cash flows at an appropriate discount rate from the time at which the cash flows are to be paid to the valuation date. Conversely, given the value of the bond it is feasible to solve for the implied yield to maturity on the security[5].

# 5   Interest Rate Sensitivity

## 5.1   Overview

The key driver of value identified is interest rates. Any participant in financial markets that either owns or has issued financial instruments or has entered into transactions affected by interest rates is thus exposed to the changes in rates[6]. It is feasible to measure the sensitivity of individual cash flows or instruments to changes in interest rates. This measure equates to the risk of the instrument.

---

[4]   For a discussion of bond valuation, see Fabozzi, Frank J. "Bond Pricing and Return Measures" in Fabozzi, Frank J. and Fabozzi, T. Dessa (Editors) (1995) The Handbook of Fixed Income Securities – Fourth Edition; Irwin Professional Publishing at Chapter 4; Cohen, Roger "Interest Rates, Bond Pricing, Duration and Convexity" in Satyajit (Editor) (1997) Risk Management & Financial Derivatives: A Guide to the Mathematics; LBC Information Services, Sydney; McGraw-Hill, Chicago; MacMillan Publishing, England at Chapter 2. For information on the mathematics and valuation of bonds see Homer, Sidney and Leibowitz, Martin L. (1972) Inside the Yield Book; Prentice-Hall & New York Institute of Finance, New York; Fong, H. Gifford and Fabozzi, Frank J. (1985) Fixed Income Portfolio Management; DowJones-Irwin; Homewood, Illinois; Dattatreya, Ravi E. (Editor) (1991) Fixed Income Analytics; Probus Publishing; Chicago, Illinois; Fabozzi, Frank J., Pitts, Mark and Dattatreya, Ravi E. "Price Volatility Characteristics of Fixed Income Securities" in Fabozzi, Frank J. and Fabozzi, T. Dessa (Editors) (1995) The Handbook of Fixed Income Securities – Fourth Edition; Irwin Professional Publishing at Chapter 5; Van Deventer, Donald R. and Imai, Kenji (1997) Financial Risk Analytics; Irwin, Chicago at Chapter 1; Hagenstein, Frank and Bangemann, Tim (2002) Active Fixed Income and Credit Management; Palgrave, Chichester at Chapters 2, 3 and 5.

[5]   This is the IRR of the cash flows of the bond/security.

[6]   For an investor, issuer or counterparty that will hold the position to maturity this exposure is not obvious. However, on a *mark-to-market basis*, the value of the position – that is, what it is worth today – changes in response to changes in market interest rates.

A variety of risk measures designed to measure the risk to changes in interest rates have emerged. In this Section, the principal interest rate risk measures (duration, PVBP/ DVO1 and convexity) are outlined.

## 5.2 Duration[7]

### 5.2.1 Duration – Concept

Term to maturity is widely utilised as a measure of the length or maturity of securities. However, it only indicates when the final payment falls due. It ignores the time pattern of any payment received in the intermediate time span preceding the final payment. The deficiency of the concept of term to maturity can be overcome utilising duration as a measure of the term and the risk of a security or set of cash flows.

### 5.2.2 Duration – Measurement

There are two types of duration:
* Macaulay's duration.
* Modified duration.

*Macaulay's Duration*
Duration, as proposed in 1938 by Frederick R Macaulay, is the weighted average of the times in the future when cash flows (interest and principal payments) are to be received. Mathematically, duration can be measured as follows:

$$D = \sum_{t=1}^{n}[(C_t \times t)/(1+r)^t]/[(C_t)/(1+r)^t]$$

Where

$D$ = Duration

$C_t$ = Cash flow (e.g. interest and/or principal payments) at time t

---

[7] For a discussion of duration and other risk measures, see Kopprasch, Robert W. (September 1985) Understanding Duration and Volatility; Salomon Brothers Inc, New York; Bierwag, Gerald O. (1987) Duration Analysis; Ballinger Publishing, Cambridge, Massachusetts; Sturm, Frederick W. "Duration as a Risk Management Tool" (Autumn 1987) Journal of International Securities Markets 17–32; Fabozzi, Frank J., Pitts, Mark and Dattatreya, Ravi E. "Price Volatility Characteristics of Fixed Income Securities" in Fabozzi, Frank J. and Fabozzi, T. Dessa (Editors) (1995) The Handbook of Fixed Income Securities – Fourth Edition; Irwin Professional Publishing at Chapter 5; Green, Dr. A John "The Use of Duration with Interest Rate Derivatives" (April 1996) The Australian Corporate Treasurer 2–4; Van Deventer, Donald R. and Imai, Keni (1997) Financial Risk Analytics; Irwin, Chicago at Chapters 3 and 4.

t  = Length of time to the cash flow

n  = Length of time to final maturity

r  = Yield to maturity or discount rate

An example of the calculation of Macaulay's duration is set out in **Exhibit 5.14**. For bonds with a series of cash flows, duration is less than the final maturity. If there is a single payment (a zero coupon bond), then duration and maturity are equal.

Duration measures the weighted average of the times in the future when cash flows are to be received. Conceptually, it is the pivot or balancing point of the future cash flows. This is set out in diagrammatic form in **Exhibit 5.15**[8]. Macaulay's duration creates a single index type measure for any set of cash flows. This enables different sets of future cash flows to be compared. The essential risk measure is that longer duration is associated with greater risk reflecting the greater interest rate sensitivity of cash flows.

*Modified Duration*

Hicks independently developed modified duration in 1939 without any reference to Macaulay's duration. Modified duration provides a useful measure of the interest rate sensitivity or volatility of a given security. Mathematically, modified duration can be expressed as:

$$D_{mod} = D/(1 + r/f)$$

Where

D   = Macaulay duration

r    = Yield to maturity (in decimal form)

f    = Frequency of cash flow payments per year

r/f  = Periodic yield (in decimal form).

For semi-annual coupon bonds, this formula becomes: $D_{mod} = D/(1 + r/2)$

**Exhibit 5.16** calculates the modified duration for the example discussed above.

Mathematically, modified duration represents the first derivative of the price of the security with regard to yield to maturity. Modified duration can be used to

---

[8]    See Cohen, Roger "Interest Rates, Bond Pricing, Duration and Convexity" in Satyajit (Editor) (1997) Risk Management & Financial Derivatives: A Guide to the Mathematics; LBC Information Services, Sydney; McGraw-Hill, Chicago; MacMillan Publishing, England at Chapter 2 at 37.

For example, assume a five year bond with a 6.00% pa coupon rate payable semi-annually and yielding 6.50% pa to maturity. Assume that interest payments are received at the end of each of the ten semi-annual periods and that the principal payment is received at the end of the fifth year. The calculation of the duration of the bond is set out in the Table below:

### Exhibit 5.14 Macaulay's Duration – Calculation

| Period | 0 | 1 | 2 | 3 | 4 | 5 | 6 | 7 | 8 | 9 | 10 | Sum |
|---|---|---|---|---|---|---|---|---|---|---|---|---|
| Coupon | | 3.000 | 3.000 | 3.000 | 3.000 | 3.000 | 3.000 | 3.000 | 3.000 | 3.000 | 3.000 | |
| Principal | | | | | | | | | | | 100.000 | |
| Total Cash Flows | | 3.000 | 3.000 | 3.000 | 3.000 | 3.000 | 3.000 | 3.000 | 3.000 | 3.000 | 103.000 | |
| Discount Factor | 1.000 | 0.969 | 0.938 | 0.909 | 0.880 | 0.852 | 0.825 | 0.799 | 0.774 | 0.750 | 0.726 | |
| $(C_t \times t)/(1+r)^t$ | | 2.906 | 5.628 | 8.177 | 10.559 | 12.783 | 14.857 | 16.788 | 18.582 | 20.247 | 748.060 | 858.586 |
| $C_t/(1+r)^t$ | | 2.906 | 2.814 | 2.726 | 2.640 | 2.557 | 2.476 | 2.398 | 2.323 | 2.250 | 74.806 | 97.894 |

Duration in this case is calculated as: $[858.586/97.894] = 8.77$ semi-annual periods or 4.39 years.

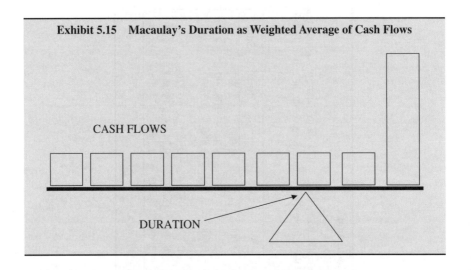

Exhibit 5.15   Macaulay's Duration as Weighted Average of Cash Flows

CASH FLOWS

DURATION

Exhibit 5.16   Modified Duration – Calculation

Assume the same facts as in **Exhibit 5.14**:
- Macaulay's duration is 4.39 years.
- Yield to maturity is 6.50% pa semi-annually.

Modified duration is given by: $[4.39/(1 + .065/2)] = 4.25$

estimate the percentage price volatility of a fixed income security. The relationship
is as follows:

$$\Delta P/P \times 100 = -D_{mod} \times \Delta R$$

This implies that the percentage price change is equal to the negative modified
duration multiplied by the yield change (in absolute percentage points). For example, in the example in **Exhibit 5.14** and **5.15**, the price volatility of the specified
bond is 4.25%. This means that for an increase in rates of 10 bps, the price of
the bond would be expected to decrease by 42.5 bps. This equates to the price
volatility of the bond or its interest rate sensitivity. In practice, modified duration
is a commonly used measure of interest rate risk.

### 5.2.3   Duration and the Zero Coupon Rate Yield Curve

It is feasible in theory to calculate duration utilising either normal conventional
par (coupon) yields or zero coupon interest rates for pure discount securities.

For example, the original Macaulay formulation for reasons of computational convenience uses yield to maturity as the discount rate throughout, rather than estimate interest rates for each future period. The rates are used to discount the security payments to present value. However, it is not reasonable to assume that yields to maturity for different terms are the same. In addition, rates at different points of the yield curve will not always change by the same amount. This reflects the fact that yields to maturity are complex averages of the underlying zero coupon yields. In general a given shift in the zero coupon rate curve will result in the yields at different maturity changing by different amounts.

To understand the interaction between duration and the zero coupon rate yield curve, it is necessary to define the following terms:

- **Zero coupon rate** – the rate of exchange between a cash flow now and a cash flow at a single date in the future, that is, the yield on a pure discount bond or zero coupon security.
- **Coupon or par yield to maturity** – the standard internal rate of return formula which discounts all payments on a coupon bond at the same rate.

The difference between the two interest rates lies in the fact that actual realised returns only equal the normal redemption par yield to maturity if reinvestment rates on intermediate cash flows, typically the coupon, are actually equal to the redemption yield. In practice, reinvestment rates on coupon cash flows will rarely equal the redemption yield. Forward rates are the true measure of the reinvestment rates. The forward rates implicit in the yield curve at any point in time do not guarantee that these reinvestment rates are actually achieved. In contrast, determining present values using zero coupon rates that are implicit in normal par redemption yields does not involve any assumptions as to the reinvestment rate, as no intermediate cash flows are involved [9].

### 5.2.4  Duration – Behaviour

The relationship between duration, maturity and coupon is complex[10]. The general relationships are as follows:
- There is an inverse relationship between coupon and duration. High coupon bonds effectively have shorter duration than lower (or zero) coupon bonds of the same maturity.

---

[9]   See discussion regarding the nature of par and zero rate later in this Chapter.

[10]  See Fisher, Lawrence and Weil, Roman L "Coping with the Risk of Interest Rate Fluctuations: Returns to Bondholders from Naive and Optional Strategies" (1971) 44 Journal of Business 418.

- As the term to maturity extends, the disparity between duration and maturity for a given coupon also increases.
- Duration falls when market yields rise because the present value of distant future payments falls relatively more than those closer to the present. As would be expected, when interest rates fall, duration rises for exactly the opposite reason.

**Exhibit 5.17** sets out an example explaining the relationship between duration, maturity and coupon.

### 5.2.5   Duration – Qualifications

There are a number of qualifications to duration as a risk measure including:
- Duration assumes a flat term structure of interest rates.
- Duration also assumes parallel shifts of the yield curve.
- Duration is a proxy for price risk only for relatively small changes in interest rates. Therefore, as market interest rates change, the duration of the relevant security also changes requiring adjustment of any offsetting hedge.

In using duration as a measure of interest rate risk or as basis for hedging (that is, immunisation by assuming an offsetting asset or liability with an equivalent duration to reduce portfolio duration to zero), these weaknesses of duration

---

**Exhibit 5.17   Duration – Behaviour**

Assume a bond with the following characteristics:

| | |
|---|---|
| Coupon | 6.00% pa payable semi-annually |
| Maturity | 10 years |
| Yield to maturity | 6.25% pa semi-annually |

The Table below calculates the price and duration of the bond:

| | |
|---|---|
| **Coupon** | 6.00% |
| **Maturity Date** | 15-Feb-11 |
| **Settlement Date** | 15-Feb-01 |
| **Yield** | 6.25% |
| **Price** | 98.162 |
| **Accrued Interest** | 0.000 |
| **Total Price** | 98.162 |
| **Macaulay Duration** | 7.64 |
| **Modified Duration** | 7.41 |

The Graphs below shows the relationships between duration and maturity, duration and coupon and duration and yield.

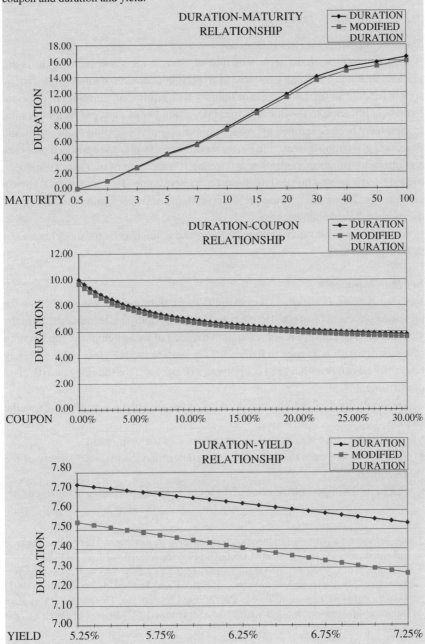

should be recognised. Some of the different types of duration are specifically designed to overcome the identified weaknesses.

## 5.2.6   Duration – Types

### Single Versus Multiple Factor Duration

If the assumptions of flat term structure of interest rates and parallel shifts are violated then it is not usually possible to effect immunisation of interest rate risk by simply holding an offsetting asset or liability with equivalent duration. In response to this qualification to the duration measure, a number of multiple factor duration models have been developed to provide a more complex mapping of the stochastic processes governing interest rate movements. For example, one approach proposes a multi-factor duration model where duration is a measure of two factors, namely, the long-term interest rate and the short-term interest rate. This approach implicitly seeks to model changes in the yield curve shape and the resultant effect on the duration of the relevant security[11].

The difference between a single factor model and a two-factor model is set out in **Exhibit 5.18**.

### Key Rate Duration[12]

Key rate duration is a special form of multi-factor duration introduced to allow the duration concept to be utilised to measure the risk of non-parallel movements in the yield curve. The concept revolves around the idea of measurement of the duration of a security with reference to *individual key portions of the yield curve*. The key rates utilised can be either zero coupon rates or par rates for the relevant risk class of instrument.

The application of the key rate duration approach entails a number of specific steps:

* Identify the interest rates that affect the price of the instrument.
* Specify the *key* rates that will be used to determine the price sensitivity of the instrument.
* Calculate the impact on the price of the security of a 1 bps change in each key rate.

---

[11]   See Schaefer, Stephen, "Immunisation and Duration: A Review of Theory, Performance and Applications" (1984) Midland Corporate Finance Journal vol 2 no 3 41–58.

[12]   The concept of key rate duration is attributed to Dattatreya, Ravi " A Practical Approach to Asset/Liability Management" in Fabbozzi, Frank J. and Konishi, Atsuo (Editors) (1991) Asset/Liability Management; Probus Publishing, Chicago; Ho, Thomas S.Y. "Key Rate Duration: Measures of Interest Rate Risk" (September 1992) Journal of Fixed Income 29–44.

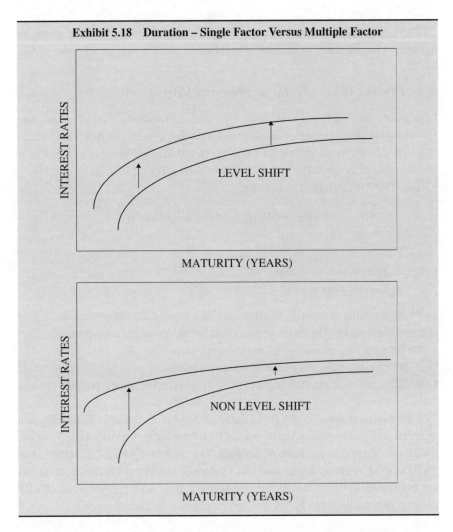

**Exhibit 5.18    Duration – Single Factor Versus Multiple Factor**

The key rate duration calculated measures the price change of the security for a change in the key rate. By repeating the calculation for each key rate in the specified yield curve, a series of price changes along the complete yield curve is determined. The process isolates the price sensitivity of the instrument for very small movements in the yield curve at each key segment as a result of the perturbation of the specified curve[13].

---

[13] The concept of key rate duration is similar to a cash flow approach to measurement of interest rate risk and hedging, see Luedecke, Bernd P "Measuring Displaying

The key rate duration of a note is, consistent with other forms of duration, dynamic with reference to changes in yield curve and the passage of time.

## 5.3   Present Value of a Basis Point ("PVBP")

In practice, the PVBP of a cash flow or security is frequently used as a substitute for or complement to modified duration in measuring interest rate risk. The concept of PVBP is the change in market value given a 0.01% pa increase in yield. It is also referred to as the dollar value of 1 basis point ("DVO1").

The PVBP is calculated as follows:

$$PVBP = MV(r) - MV(r \pm 0.01\% \text{ pa})$$

Where

MV = Market value function
r    = Current market yield

PVBP is similar to duration and provides a measure of the interest rate sensitivity of future cash flows. The characteristics and behaviour of PVBP includes:
• PVBP generally increases as time to expiry increases.
• PVBP tends to be greater for lower coupon bonds.
• PVBP is not constant. It changes with yield movements and the passage of time.

Like modified duration, PVBP is a standardised representation of the risk of a financial instrument (that is, the higher the PVBP the higher the risk). Like duration, PVBP can be used as the basis of hedging. This is done by PVBP matching. The PVBP of the position is determined and a sufficient number of say futures contracts are transacted to offset the PVBP (the hedge ratio). This creates a zero PVBP position or a position that is not sensitive to changes in interest rates.

## 5.4   Convexity[14]

Modified duration and PVBP are only accurate for small changes in the underlying rate or yield to maturity. This relates to the non-linearity of price movement

---

and Hedging the Market Risk on a Swap" in Das, Satyajit (Editor) (1991) Global Swap Markets; IFR Publishing, London. This approach is described in Chapter 14.

[14]  See Klotz, Richard G. (October 1985) Convexity of Fixed Income Securities; Salomon Brothers, New York; Frye, Jon "The Real Shape of Convexity" (October 1990) Risk 42–49.

for a given movement in yield. This is referred to as the convexity problem. **Exhibit 5.19** sets out the non-linear relationship between price and yield for fixed income securities.

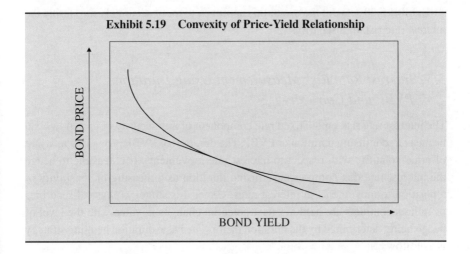

**Exhibit 5.19    Convexity of Price-Yield Relationship**

For a given movement in yield or interest rate, the quantum of the corresponding change in price (present value of the cash flow(s)) is different depending upon the absolute rate level from which the rate displacement occurs and also the magnitude of the rate displacement. This reflects the fact that measures of price or interest rate risk such as modified duration and PVBP are measures of the rate of changes in the price of the security *at the current yield or rate level*[15].

Convexity measures the curvature of the price yield relationship. It is a second order measure of price yield sensitivity. It is the second derivative of price with respect to yield. In effect, the presence of convexity means that for a small displacement in rates, modified duration/PVBP is a reasonable measure of price risk. However, for larger displacements, the curvature of the price function needs to be approximated. This is usually done by a second order Taylor series approximation of the curve.

The major significance of convexity is that it should be used in combination with modified duration to approximate percentage change in price given a percentage

---

[15]  Mathematically, as the first derivative modified duration or PVBP measures the rate of change at the current yield level. This equates to the slope of the tangent line to the price function at the current rate. As rates change, the slope of this line also changes.

change in yield. This relationship is set out below:

$$\Delta\text{Price}/\text{Price} = -D_{\text{mod}} \times \Delta\text{Yield} + [\text{Convexity}/2 \times (\Delta\text{ yield})^2]$$

**Exhibit 5.20** sets out the use of this approach to more accurately measuring the interest rate risk of a security.

## 5.5 Interest Rate Risk Measurement Using Duration, PVBP and Convexity

The interest rate risk on the fixed rate component of any security or cash flows can be measured utilising duration or PVBP. The duration or PVBP provides a measure of price volatility with respect to interest rate movements. It is feasible to hedge the interest rate risk component, utilising duration as a measure of sensitivity of a position to movements in interest rates. Under this strategy, physical securities or futures contracts are held to offset potential changes in value with the level of hedge being determined by the duration factor. The basic duration hedging strategy is as follows:

$$\text{Change in PV of Hedging Portfolio} = - \text{ Change in PV of Security or Cash Flow Portfolio}$$

The use of duration as a means of estimating interest rate risk varies between a single factor model and a multi factor model. This relationship is set out in **Exhibit 5.21**.

The concept of duration-based hedging assumes that cash flows generated by the securities or instruments form a portfolio of assets and liabilities that will vary with interest rates and with maturity. The use of duration-based hedging seeks to solve the problem of ensuring solvency, irrespective of interest rate movements, by matching the duration of the asset and liability cash flow streams. The underlying assumption is that irrespective of interest rate movements, and despite the fact that the cash flows are not perfectly matched, changes in values in the asset and liability portfolio would substantially offset each other.

The use of duration matching implicitly divides underlying market interest rate movements into two components:

• Systematic movements where rates for all maturities move in some statistically determined constant proportion to one or two index rates, such as the long and short interest rates depending on whether single or multi-factor duration measures are utilised.

## Exhibit 5.20 Duration/Convexity Adjusted Risk Measurement

Assume a bond with the following characteristics:

| | |
|---|---|
| Coupon | 6.00% pa payable semi-annually |
| Maturity | 10 years |
| Yield to maturity | 6.25% pa semi-annually |

The Table below calculates the price, duration, PVBP and convexity of the bond:

| | |
|---|---|
| **Coupon** | 6.00% |
| **Maturity Date** | 15-Feb-11 |
| **Settlement Date** | 15-Feb-01 |
| **Yield** | 6.25% |
| **Price** | 98.162 |
| **Accrued Interest** | 0.000 |
| **Total Price** | 98.162 |
| **Macaulay Duration** | 7.64 |
| **Modified Duration** | 7.41 |
| **PVBP** | 0.07 |
| **Convexity** | 68.31 |

The Table below compares the actual change in bond prices against forecast changes in bond prices using modified duration or modified duration adjusted for convexity:

| | | | |
|---|---|---|---|
| Expected Change in Yield | 0.01% | 0.10% | 1.00% |
| Modified Duration | 7.41 | 7.41 | 7.41 |
| Convexity | 68.31 | 68.31 | 68.31 |
| Actual Price Change (based on change in bond price using current yield adjusted for expected change in yield) | −0.073 | −0.724 | −6.945 |
| Δ Price/Price (based on modified duration) | −0.074 | −0.741 | −7.405 |
| Δ Price/Price (based on modified duration adjusted for convexity) | −0.074 | −0.737 | −7.064 |
| Difference (Actual Price Change Versus Modified Duration) | 0.00 | 0.02 | 0.46 |
| $ Difference (per $1m) | $14 | $170 | $4,604 |
| Difference (Actual Price Change Versus Modified Duration Adjusted for Convexity) | 0.00 | 0.01 | 0.12 |
| Difference (Per $1m) | $14 | $135 | $1,188 |

The modified duration measure adjusted for convexity is a more accurate measure of actual changes in bond prices for large changes in yield than modified duration itself.

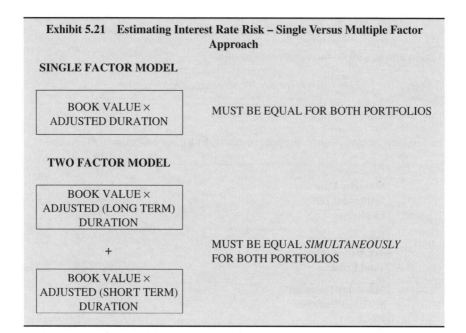

Exhibit 5.21   Estimating Interest Rate Risk – Single Versus Multiple Factor Approach

- Non-systematic movements that are the residual interest rate movements unexplained by movements in the indexes utilised. These are assumed to be randomly or normally distributed.

Duration matching only provides a formula to hedge away systematic market movements. Inefficiencies in hedge performance may result from the non-systematic risk component that cannot be effectively hedged under this approach.

Duration matching is utilised in preference to maturity matching because it is usually felt to reduce basis risk. It can also overcome imperfections in the hedge market such as the lack of availability of securities or instruments of the appropriate maturity. It may also reduce the actual cost of hedging as generally significantly lower levels of hedges will need to be maintained.

## 6   Types of Interest Rates

Interest rates have been considered as homogenous in the discussion to date. In practice, the type of interest rates utilised vary in terms of two dimensions:
- Types of interest rates.
- Credit risk.

In this Section, the types of interest rates are considered. The credit risk aspects of interest rates are considered later in this Chapter.

There are in practice three separate types of interest rates:

- **Par (or Coupon) rates** – defined as the interest rate on a coupon paying instrument out of today calculated as the internal rate of return of the cash flows. This rate is used to discount all payments on a coupon bond or instrument. The same interest rate is used for all cash flows of the instrument irrespective of maturity.
- **Forward rates** – defined as the interest rate on a coupon paying instrument out of a nominated date in the future.
- **Zero rates** (also known as zero coupon rates, spot rates or pure interest rates) – defined as the interest rate on an instrument which pays no coupon and entails the exchange of a cash flow today for another (larger) cash flow at a nominated future date.

The par rate is generally the only observable interest rate in markets. Forward rates and zero rates are usually not directly observable. However, in jurisdictions where there are traded markets in interest rate futures and/or zero coupon securities[16], it may be possible to directly observe certain forward and zero rates.

The three types of rates are interrelated. The rates are different aspects of the same set of interest rates. In practice, the par interest rates that are observable are utilised to calculate the implied forward and zero rates. The formal interrelationship between par, forward and zero rates can be stated as follows:

- Forward interest rates are the interest rates at which par yields are reinvested.
- Zero rates are the par interest rates with the reinvestment risk removed.
- Forward rates between two points in time are implied by the zero rates at those two points.

The difference between the rates (in particular par and zero rates) can be seen from a consideration of their role in valuation. Valuation of all financial transactions assumes the use of identified and specific interest rates or discount factors to discount or present value cash flows identified with individual transactions. The two alternative types of interest rates available are:

- Par rates to maturity.
- Zero rate to maturity.

---

[16] For example, the US Treasury STRIPS market which allows the unbundling of a bond into individual coupon and principal components and allows separate trading in these components (see Kalffsky, Thomas E and Plum, John D. (March 1985) STRIPS: The New Treasury Zeros; Salomon Brothers Inc., New York; Gregory, Beorah W. and Livingston, Miles "Development of the Market for U.S. Treasury STRIPS" (March-April 1992) Financial Analysts Journal 68–74). Equivalent markets exist in a number of currencies, e.g. Sterling (for example, see Philips, Patrick "Understanding Gild-edged STRIPS" (1997) Financial Products Issue 77 14–22), France, Canada. See Bruce, Rupert "Stripteasing European Government Bonds" (February 1995) Institutional Investor 25–27.

The par rate to maturity is usually directly observable being the market quoted rate for the required maturity. In the case of derivative transactions, the relevant par rate to maturity is typically the quoted swap rate for the relevant maturity, or if unavailable, the interpolated yield based on available swap yield curve information. In contrast, the zero rate is not directly observable and is usually estimated from the existing par rate curve for the relevant instrument.

Traditionally, financial instruments have been valued utilising par yield to maturity. However, use of par rates creates a number of problems including:

- Coupon effect.
- Assumptions on reinvestment rates.
- Absence of an unambiguous and unique interest rate for each maturity.

The coupon effect refers to the phenomenon observed in markets that the par interest rates of bonds or other financial instruments with the same maturity but different coupons may vary significantly. These differences may be caused by factors such as the interest rate risk or differential interest rate volatility of the securities, liquidity, tax or clientele effects.

Utilisation of the par rate implies that the actual realised return only equals the normal redemption par yield to maturity if reinvestment rates on all intermediate cash flows, typically the coupons, are actually equal to the redemption yield. The realised yield will only be equal to the par yield where the security is a zero coupon security; that is, a security which has no intermediate cash flows. This is because there is no potential reinvestment risk in the transaction. In practice, reinvestment rates on coupon cash flows will not equal the redemption yield. Theoretical forward rates are the only true measure of available reinvestment rates. However, the forward rates implicit in the yield curves at any point in time do not guarantee that these reinvestment rates are actually achieved.

In addition, the use of coupon of par rates creates an ambiguous relationship between yield and maturity. The use of par rate technology does not facilitate the identification of a *unique* interest rate and discount factor for a particular maturity.

For example, assume the following yield curve exists:

| Maturity (years) | Par yield % pa |
|---|---|
| 0.25 | 7.25 |
| 0.50 | 7.55 |
| 1.00 | 7.92 |
| 1.50 | 8.23 |
| 2.00 | 9.05 |

Under these circumstances, a 2-year security that pays intermediate coupons every six months will be valued by discounting all payments at 9.05% pa. However, for an identical security with a maturity of 1.5 years, all cash flows including coupons would be discounted at a different rate (8.23% pa). Consequently, the rates applicable for 0.50, 1.00 and 1.50 years can be 9.05% pa or 8.23% pa depending on the final maturity of the security being valued. The par rate to maturity valuation does not imply an unambiguous relationship between the interest rate and the relevant maturity.

The identified problems of par rate to maturity technology are substantially overcome by utilising zero rates. Zero rates are defined as the interest or discount rate that applies between a cash flow now and a cash flow at a single date in the future. This is equivalent to the yield on a pure discount bond or zero coupon security (hence the reference to zero rate). Utilising zero rates allows, for example, a two year yield to be directly related to a pure two year security being a pure zero coupon security with a single cash flow in two years time.

The zero rate eliminates the coupon effect. The use of zero rates to discount or present value cash flows does not involve any assumptions as to the reinvestment rate applicable to any intermediate cash flows. In addition, the zero coupon rate has the advantage that each maturity is identified with a single unambiguous interest rate, being the rate of a pure single payment instrument. These factors allow zero rates to be utilised to value and ultimately manage entire portfolios of financial instruments (bonds and derivatives) as a series of cash flows each of which is valued at a unique rate.

## 7 Forward Rates[17]

Forward interest rates can be calculated from the current yield curve. If suitably spaced yields and either synthetic or actual securities are available, then forward rates can be estimated.

The forward rates can be calculated based on the theoretical construct that securities of different maturity can be expected to be substitutes for one another. Investors at any time have three choices. They may invest in an obligation having a maturity corresponding exactly to their anticipated holding period. They may invest in short-term securities, reinvesting in further short-term securities at each maturity over the holding period. They may invest in a security having a maturity longer than the anticipated holding period. In the last case, they would sell the security at the end of

---

[17] For a discussion of the derivation and behaviour of forward interest rates see Chapter 6.

the given period, realising either a capital gain or a loss. According to a version of the pure expectations theory of interest rate term structure, the investor's expected return for any holding period would be the same regardless of the alternative or combination of alternatives selected. The return would be a weighted average of the current short-term interest rate plus future short rates expected to prevail over the holding period; this average is the same for each alternative.

Forward rates may be calculated from the currently prevailing cash market yield curve. Any deviation from the implied forward rates would create arbitrage opportunities which market participants would exploit. This arbitrage is undertaken by buying and selling securities at different maturities to synthetically create the intended forward transaction. By simultaneously borrowing and lending the same amount in the cash market, but for different maturities, it is possible to lock in an interest rate for a period in the future. If the maturity of the cash lending exceeds the maturity of the cash borrowing, the implied rate over the future period, the forward-forward rate, is a bid rate for a forward investment. If the maturity of the cash borrowing exceeds the maturity of the cash lending, then the resulting forward-forward rate is an offer rate for a forward borrowing.

**Exhibit 5.22** sets out the process of generating forward rates. **Exhibit 5.23** sets out the mathematical relationship between par interest rates and forward rates. **Exhibit 5.24** sets out an example of calculating forward rates.

Forward rates have the following characteristics:

- Forward rates are above (below) the par rates where the yield curve is positive (negative). This means that the forward rates cross from one side to the other of the par curve where the yield curve changes shape.
- Forward rates have greater momentum than par rates; that is, the rate of change of the forward rates is more attenuated than that of the par curve.
- Forward rates can be more volatile than par rates; that is, a small change in par rates can lead to a proportionately larger change in the forward rate.

It is important to note that forward rates, when regarded as forecasts of future short-term interest rates, require a number of theoretical and practical assumptions. From a theoretical perspective, this approach assumes the absence of transaction costs and assumes the validity of the pure expectations theory of the term structure of interest rates. In particular, the forward rate as calculated from the current cash market yield curve contains no compensation for risk and in particular includes no liquidity premium. In practice, the last condition is violated as forward rates are generated from the observed interest rate term structure that typically incorporates a liquidity premium.

**Exhibit 5.22 Relationship of Forward Rates to Par Rates**

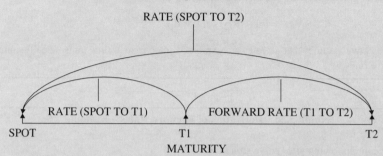

RATE (SPOT TO T2)

RATE (SPOT TO T1)     FORWARD RATE (T1 TO T2)

SPOT                        T1                        T2
                      MATURITY

Forward-forward Rate (borrowing rate for dealer/lending rate for client)

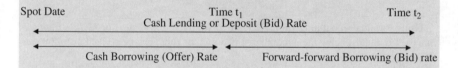

Spot Date                    Time $t_1$                    Time $t_2$
                  Cash Lending or Deposit (Bid) Rate

    Cash Borrowing (Offer) Rate         Forward-forward Borrowing (Bid) rate

Forward-forward Rate (lending rate for dealer/borrowing rate for client)

Spot Date                    Time $t_1$                    Time $t_2$

        Cash Borrowing (Bid) Rate    Forward-forward Lending (Offer) rate

                  Cash Borrowing (Offer) Rate

**Exhibit 5.23 Derivation of Forward Rates**

$$(1 + R_{t1})^{t1} * (1 + R_{t1 \times 2})^{t2-t1} = (1 + R_{t2})^{t2}$$

Where

$R_{t1}$ = the par interest rate to time t1
$R_{t2}$ = the par interest rate to time t2
$R_{t1 \times 2}$ = the forward interest rate between time t1 and t2
t1, t2 = the time to maturity in days from the present divided by 365

Rearranging to solve for the forward interest rate:

$$R_{t1 \times 2} = [(1 + R_{t2})^{t2}/(1 + R_{t1})^{t1}]^{1/(t2-t1)} - 1$$

The above assumes that all rates are expressed in consistent time units, usually annual effective rates.

---

**Exhibit 5.24    Derivation of Forward Rates – Example**

Assume the following yield curve structure:

| Maturity (days) | Interest Rate (% pa Compounded Annually) |
|-----------------|-------------------------------------------|
| 92              | 4.75                                      |
| 184             | 5.00                                      |

Using formula set out in **Exhibit 5.23**, the forward rate for 92 days *in 92 days from spot date* (3 × 6 months being the 3 month rate in 3 months time) can be derived as follows:

$$R_{92 \times 184} = [(1 + .05)^{(184/365)}/(1 + .0475)^{(92/365)}]^{1/(184/365 - 92/365)} - 1$$

$$= .052506 \text{ or } 5.2506\% \text{ pa}$$

---

# 8   Zero Rates – Calculation[18]

## 8.1   Basic Methodology

The actual computation of the zero rate yield curve is complex. In theory, for each future payment of a coupon security, there exists a zero rate that discounts that payment to its present value. These rates constitute the zero rate curve. The points along this curve represent the yield to maturity of a zero coupon bond for the appropriate maturity rate. This zero coupon yield curve is estimated from the

---

[18]   See Smith, David "By the Bootstraps" (June 1990) Risk vol 3 no 6 40–42 ; "Zero Coupon Yields" (1995) Capital Market Strategies 5 51–54; Martin, John (1996) Derivatives Maths; IFR Publishing, London at Chapter 9; Kawaller, Ira G. and Marshall, John F. "Deriving Zero-Coupon Rates: Alternatives to Orthodoxy" (May/June 1996) Financial Analysts Journal 51–55; Martin, John (2001) Applied Math for Derivatives; John Wiley & Sons, Singapore at Chapter 9; Flavell, Richard (2002) Swaps and Other Derivatives; John Wiley & Sons, Chichester at Chapter 3. For a discussion of the use of zero rates in swap valuation, see Cooper, Ronald "Swap House Switch to New Values" (January 1987) Euromoney 32–33.

existing par yield curve. This is completed by calculating equilibrium zero coupon rates that value each component of the cash flow of conventional coupon securities in an internally consistent fashion such that all par bonds would have the same value as the sum of their cash flow components.

The zero coupon rates are calculated using an iterative methodology whereby the zero coupon rate is determined from a known yield curve for the successive points in time (often referred to as bootstrapping). An alternative technique for deriving the zero rates is using the implied forward rates.

## 8.2 Calculating Zero Coupon Rates – Bootstrapping

The bootstrapping approach involves a series of distinct steps:
- Separate a coupon bond into a series of zero coupon bonds.
- Utilise available zero rates to price components.
- Solve for the unknown zero rate within the constraint that the market value of the bond must be equal to the value of the components using zero rates.

**Exhibit 5.25** shows the simple calculation of a zero coupon rate. In a similar way, breakeven zero rates for each subsequent maturity are derived through iteration. Known zero rates are used to derive the succeeding zero using the same logic to generate a complete yield curve of zero rates from the par rate curve. The process is repeated until a complete set of zero coupon rates is available.

---

**Exhibit 5.25    Derivation of Zero Rates – Bootstrapping**

Assume the following yield curve:

| Maturity (days) | Interest Rate (% pa semi-annually) |
|:---:|:---:|
| 181 | 7.00 |
| 365 | 8.00 |

Assume that the 6 month rate is a zero coupon rate. The 1 year rate relates to a security that has semi-annually cash flows. The cash flows of this security are set out below:

| Days | Principal | Cash Flows Coupon (at 8.00% pa) | Total |
|:---|:---|:---:|---:|
| 0.00 | −1,000,000 | | −1,000,000 |
| 181 | | 39,671 | 39,671 |
| 365 | 1,000,000 | 40,329 | 1,040,329 |

The 1 year bond can be separated into two separate zero coupon bonds:
- $39,671 face value 6 month zero coupon bond.
- $1,040,329 face value 1 year zero coupon bond.

The two zeros, if held together, precisely replicate the cash flow characteristics of the 1 year coupon bond.

The individual zeros must be valued using the *zero coupon rate* for the relevant maturity (to avoid the possibility of arbitrage). This means that as the six month security has a yield of 7.00% pa (which is a known zero coupon rate) (not 8.00% pa that is the par rate of the 1 year security) then the first coupon is discounted accordingly at 7.00% pa. The second zero must be discounted at the 1 year zero coupon rate. This rate is unknown. However, the value of the package of the two zeros (effectively the coupon paying 1 year security) is known (being the market value of the security – par or $1,000,000). This means that the present value of the 1 year zero can be calculated as the current price of the security less the value of the 6 month zero. Once the present value of the 1 year zero and the face value is known, the 1 year zero rate can be derived. This calculation is set out below.

| Period (Days) | Par Rate (% pa Semi-annual Compounding) | Par Rate (% pa Annual Compounding) | Bond Cash Flows ($) | Zero Rate (% pa Semi-annual Compounding) | Zero Rate (% pa Compounding) | Bond Cash Flows Discounted at Zero Rates |
|---|---|---|---|---|---|---|
| 0.00 | | | −1,000,000 | | | |
| 181 | 7.00 | 7.12% | 39,671 | 7.00 | 7.12 | 38,341 |
| 365 | 8.00 | 8.16% | 1,040,329 | 8.02 | 8.18 | 961,659 |
| | | | | | | 1,000,000 |

The 1 year zero coupon rate derived is 8.02% pa semi-annual compounding (8.18% pa annual). The 1 year payment must be discounted at a rate higher than the par rate to maintain the equilibrium price of $1 million.

The relevant zero coupon rate discount factor for the 1 year is the present value of the final cash flow in 1 year divided by the final cash flow ($961,659/1,040,329 = 0.9244$). This discount factor can be used directly or can be used to solve for the zero rate.

## 8.3  Calculating Zero Coupon Rates – Forward Rates

As an alternative, it is possible to determine the zero coupon rate curve by using the forward rates implicit in the current yield curve and assuming compounding of intermediate cash flows at the implicit forward rates. The basic concept is to use forward rates to reinvest intermediate cash flows to synthesise a zero coupon bond and derive the zero rate that equates the two cash flows. **Exhibit 5.26** sets out an example using the same data as in **Exhibit 5.25**. In theory, both approaches should yield identical results provided a consistent yield curve is utilised.

## 8.4   Zero Coupon Rates – Characteristics

**Exhibit 5.27** sets out examples of zero rates for hypothetical yield curves. The following characteristics of zero coupon rates and the corresponding zero coupon yield curve should be noted:

- Theoretical zero coupon rates are above (below) the relevant par or coupon yield curve for a normal or positively (inverse or negatively) sloped yield curve. This reflects the fact that a coupon bond is a collection of zero coupon bonds and the

---

**Exhibit 5.26   Derivation of Zero Rates – Forward Rates**

Assume the same rates as in **Exhibit 5.25**. The available 6 month and 1 year rate is used to derive a forward-forward rate (6 × 12 or the rate for 6 months in 6 months time). This forward rate is 9.23% pa annual (9.03% pa semi-annual). This forward rate is used to re-invest the coupon on the 1 year bond received after 6 months. The zero coupon rate is derived from the known current value of the security ($1,000,000) and the future value (represented by the maturing principal, two coupons and the re-investment income on the 6 month coupon calculated at the forward rate). This is set out below:

| Period (Year) | Bond Cash Flows ($) | Re-investment on Income Bond ($) | Adjusted Cash Flows ($) | Zero Rate (% pa Semi-annual Compounding) | Zero Rate (% pa Annual Compounding) |
|---|---|---|---|---|---|
| 0.00 | −1,000,000 | | −1,000,000 | | |
| 181 | 39,671 | | | 7.00 | 7.12 |
| 365 | 1,040,329 | 1,846 | 1,081,846 | 8.02 | 8.18 |

The 1 year zero rate discount factors can also be derived directly using forward discount factors (calculated using the derived forward rate). The relationship between spot and forward discount factors is as follows:

$$df_{t2} = df_{t1} \times df_{t1 \times t2}$$

Where

$df_{t2}$ = discount factor for period t2 out of spot
$df_{t1}$ = discount factor for period t1 out of spot
$df_{t1 \times t2}$ = forward discount factor for period t1 to t2

This allows the 1 year discount factor to be derived by using the 6 month discount factor and multiplying it by the discount factor calculated from the forward rate for 6 × 12 forward rate (in the above example). The product is effectively the zero rate discount factor for 1 year. This can be used to then derive the 1 year zero rate if required.

yield to maturity on a coupon bond is simply the average of the zero coupon rates on the constituent zero coupon securities. Consequently, if yields are increasing in a normally sloped yield curve, then each constituent zero element of the coupon bond will have a yield that is less than or equal to that on a zero with a maturity that is the same as the coupon bond. This dictates that the yield on the coupon bond must be less than a zero of the maturity. A reverse logic is applicable in the case of negatively sloped or inverse yield curves.

- The steeper the curve, the steeper the zero coupon rate curve.
- Zero coupon rates can be more volatile than par rates as each zero rate is dependent on each forward rate leading up to the maturity of the zero coupon rate. A movement in any of the rates results in a movement in the zero coupon rate.

---

### Exhibit 5.27   Zero Rate Curves – Examples

The accompanying graphs set out the derivation of zero coupon rates from a given yield curve utilising the iterative methodology specified. The tables are calculated using the following assumptions:
- Linear interpolation is used to determine the full yield curve.
- Coupons (payable semi-annually) are assumed to equal the par yield applicable to a specified maturity.

1.  **Example 1**

| Year | Par Rate (% pa) | Zero Rate (% pa) |
|------|-----------------|------------------|
| 0.50 | 5.750 | 5.750 |
| 1.00 | 6.000 | 6.004 |
| 1.50 | 6.050 | 6.054 |
| 2.00 | 6.100 | 6.105 |
| 2.50 | 6.175 | 6.184 |
| 3.00 | 6.250 | 6.264 |
| 3.50 | 6.325 | 6.345 |
| 4.00 | 6.400 | 6.426 |
| 4.50 | 6.575 | 6.624 |
| 5.00 | 6.750 | 6.825 |
| 5.50 | 6.813 | 6.894 |
| 6.00 | 6.875 | 6.964 |
| 6.50 | 6.938 | 7.035 |
| 7.00 | 7.000 | 7.109 |
| 7.50 | 7.017 | 7.123 |

| | | |
|---|---|---|
| 8.01 | 7.033 | 7.139 |
| 8.50 | 7.050 | 7.155 |
| 9.01 | 7.067 | 7.173 |
| 9.50 | 7.083 | 7.191 |
| 10.01 | 7.100 | 7.210 |

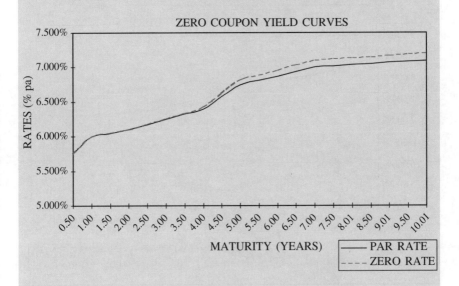

ZERO COUPON YIELD CURVES

MATURITY (YEARS) —— PAR RATE
---- ZERO RATE

## 2. Example 2

| Year | Par Rate (% pa) | Zero Rate (% pa) |
|---|---|---|
| 0.50 | 8.500 | 8.500 |
| 1.00 | 8.400 | 8.398 |
| 1.50 | 8.275 | 8.268 |
| 2.00 | 8.150 | 8.137 |
| 2.50 | 8.075 | 8.059 |
| 3.00 | 8.000 | 7.979 |
| 3.50 | 7.975 | 7.954 |
| 4.00 | 7.950 | 7.928 |
| 4.50 | 7.775 | 7.726 |
| 5.00 | 7.600 | 7.524 |
| 5.50 | 7.513 | 7.426 |
| 6.00 | 7.425 | 7.327 |
| 6.50 | 7.338 | 7.227 |
| 7.00 | 7.250 | 7.125 |

| 7.50 | 7.225 | 7.102 |
| 8.01 | 7.200 | 7.077 |
| 8.50 | 7.175 | 7.052 |
| 9.01 | 7.150 | 7.025 |
| 9.50 | 7.125 | 6.997 |
| 10.01 | 7.100 | 6.969 |

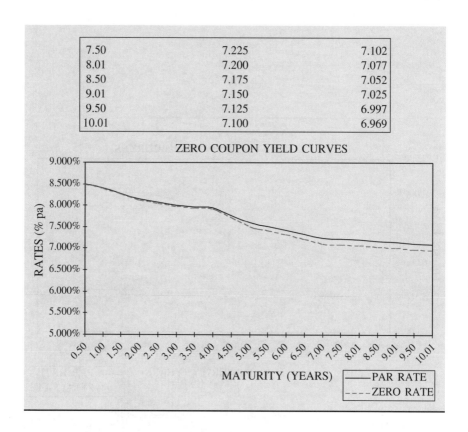

# 9   Yield Curve Modelling[19]

All par rates and zero rates assume and require the existence of a known and complete yield curve for all required maturities. The problems in derivation of interest rates and discount factors revolve around the issues in generating a complete yield curve of rates for generation of the suitable zero rates used for valuation.

**Exhibit 5.28** sets out a typical yield curve that illustrates the difficulties with defining the complete yield curve under most conditions. The curve highlights the

---

[19]   See Adams, Kenneth J. "Fitting Yield Curves to Market Data" (May 1994) The Pacific ALM Journal vol 1 no 2 27–34; Adams, Kenneth J. and Van Deventer, Donald R. "Fitting Yield Curves and Forward Rate Curves with Maximum Smoothness" (June 1994) The Journal of Fixed Income 52–62; (1995) Fitting Interest Rate Curves; Matlab Financial Computing Brief; Natick, Ma; Van Deventer, Donald R. and Imai, Keni (1997) Financial Risk Analytics; Irwin, Chicago at Chapters 2.

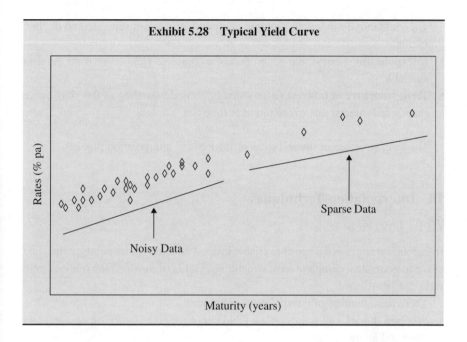

**Exhibit 5.28    Typical Yield Curve**

following problems:
- **Data noise** – the yield curve may be obscured by the presence of noisy data points where there may be a number of rates for similar or identical maturities that has the effect of increasing the difficulty of determining the *true* interest rate for any maturity.
- **Data sparseness** – the yield curve may be sparse; that is, there are significant gaps between observable interest rates. This makes it difficult to specify interest rates for maturities *between* the observed data points.

The yield curve described is fairly typical with the problem of noise at the shorter maturities and sparseness in longer maturities. The problems described may be caused by a number of factors including the institutional structure of the market, the regulatory framework, liquidity factors and tax factors that affect trading and valuation of financial instruments.

It should be noted that the analysis assumes homogeneity in terms of default risk or credit quality of the complete set of interest rates; that is, the rates are all risk free rates or of an identical credit quality. In practice, the interest rates may not be homogenous. This problem is considered below in the context of yield curve construction in practice.

The yield curve modelling problem is separable into two separate and distinct problems:

- **Interpolation** – that is, the generation of a complete yield curve from the data available.
- **Term structure of interest rates** – that is, an understanding of the yield curve shapes and interest rate evolution over time.

The term structure of interest rates influences the interpolation process.

# 10   Interpolation Techniques

## 10.1   Overview

Interpolation requires the use of available interest rates at various points in the yield curve to generate a complete term structure of yields from which the relevant zero rates can be stripped.

There are a number of interpolation techniques:

- **Stepped model** – all points on the yield curve are given by the nearest actually observed interest rates.
- **Linear interpolation** – all points on the yield curve are derived using a straight line drawn between each actually observed interest rate.
- **Non-linear interpolation** – all points on the yield curve are fitted to actually observed interest rates using either regression or spline techniques.

In practice, linear and non-linear techniques are the most important interpolation practices used. Each of these are discussed below.

The need and importance of creating an accurate and consistent yield curve using the choice of interpolation techniques available is best achieved when the yield curve generated satisfies the following criteria:

- **Fit** – that is, the yield curve generated is consistent with and closely tracks observed market interest rates.
- **Low in noise** – that is, the curve has the appropriate degree of fit in that it is not volatile in response to noisy data (usually where the curve is over fitted).
- **Consistent** – that is, the par, forward and zero rate derived from the curves are consistent with the observed and theoretical behaviour of these rates. In essence, they are arbitrage free.
- **Smoothness** – which is, the par, forward and zero rates derived are smooth in that they do not show sudden and unexpected changes and volatility.

In practice, all the criteria identified are unlikely to be satisfied *simultaneously*. In addition, the appropriate trade-off between the criteria is not readily definable. This necessarily introduces a substantial degree of subjectivity in the choice of method and the generation of the yield curve.

## 10.2 Linear Interpolation

Linear interpolation requires the use of straight lines between any two points of the observed yield curve to estimate the interest rate between these points. **Exhibit 5.29** sets out an example of linear interpolation.

It is important to note that linear interpolation *on interest rates* is equivalent to *exponential interpolation* on discount factors. Consequently, it is usually done with interest rates rather than discount factors.

The major advantage of linear interpolation is its simplicity and ease of calculation. The disadvantages include:

- The tendency to produce inaccurate rates where the yield curve is changing slope reflecting an inherent tendency for discontinuity (kinks) at each maturity point where the yield curve is not linear in slope.
- The difficulty of generating rates where there is sparse or noisy data.
- The prospect of generating yield curves that are inconsistent with term structure models of interest rates and the concept of yield curves which change shape continuously.

---

**Exhibit 5.29    Linear Interpolation**

Given the following 7 and 10 year interest rates, the benchmark interpolated rate for a 8 year maturity is calculated as follows:

| Maturity (years) | Rates (% pa) |
|:---:|:---:|
| 7 | 7.30 |
| 10 | 7.47 |

The interpolated yield for 8 years is calculated as follows:

| Maturity (years) | Maturity | Days (between) | Blending Factor |
|:---:|:---:|:---:|:---:|
| 7 | 15 April 2004 | | 555/(389+555) = 0.588 |
| | | 389 | |
| 8 | 9 May 2005 | | |
| | | 555 | |
| 10 | 15 November 2006 | | 389/(389+555) = 0.412 |

| Maturity (years) | Interest Rate (% pa) | Blending Factor | Blended Rate (% pa) |
|---|---|---|---|
| 7 | 7.30 | 0.588 | 4.292 |
| 10 | 7.47 | 0.412 | 3.078 |
| | | 8 year Interpolated Yield | 7.370 |

Please note that the 8 year rate is exactly 8 years from the spot date. The 7 and 10 year rates are not exactly 7 or 10 years out of the spot date but are the current *on-the-run* market rates for the relevant maturity. Please also note the over-weighting of the rate closest to the 8 year maturity (7 year rate in this example).

An alternative method calculates the interpolated rate as follows:

8-year rate = 7-year rate × [(difference between 7-year and 10-year rate)
            × ((days from 7-year to 8-year)/(days between 7-year and 10-year))]

In the above example, this equates to:

8-year rate = $7.30 + [(7.47 - 7.30 = 0.17) \times (389/944)] = 7.37\%$ pa.

## 10.3   Non-Linear Interpolation Models

### 10.3.1   Overview

The concept of non-linear interpolation is predicated on the use of mathematical techniques to generate a fitted yield curve through observed interest rate points. This is undertaken with the objective of fitting a yield curve that reflects the optimality criteria identified and is consistent with the term structure of interest rate assumptions usually made. There are two primary types of models generally utilised – regression based models or cubic spline based models.

### 10.3.2   Regression Based Models

A number of models have emerged which seek to use regression techniques, usually non-linear least square regression techniques, to create a fitted yield curve. The models are generally similar in approach differing in the following respect:

• The form of the equation.
• The number of terms.

Two available models are the Bradley-Crane model and the Elliott-Echols model (described in **Exhibit 5.30**). An example using an exponential regression based model is set out in **Exhibit 5.31**.

## Exhibit 5.30    Regression Based Yield Curve Interpolation Models

### 1. Bradley-Crane Model

The Bradley-Crane model has the following form:

$$\ln(1 + R_M) = a + b_1(M) + b_2 \ln(M) + e$$

Where

$R_M$ is observed interest rate for maturity M

M is the maturity of the interest rate

The model implies that the natural logarithm (ln) of one plus the observed yields for term to maturity of length M are regressed on two variables, the term to maturity and the natural log of the term of maturity. The last term (e) represents the unexplained yield variation. Once the estimated values of a, $b_1$ and $b_2$ are obtained, specific maturities of interest can be substituted to obtain estimated yields at these maturity points.

Source: Stephen P Bradley and Dwight B Crane, "Management of Commercial Bank Government Security Portfolios: An Optimisation Approach under Uncertainty" (Spring 1973) Journal of Bank Research 18.

### 2. Elliott-Echols Model

The Elliot-Echols model has the following form:

$$\ln(1 + R_i) = a + b_1(1/M_i) + b_2(M_i) + b_3(C_i) + e_i$$

Where

$R_i$ is the yield to maturity

$M_i$ is the term to maturity

$C_i$ is the coupon rate of the ith bond

The model implies that the natural logarithm (ln) of one plus the observed yields are regressed on three variables, the inverse of maturity, the term to maturity and the coupon. The last term (e) represents the unexplained yield variation. Once the estimated values of a, $b_1$, $b_2$ and $b_3$ are obtained, specific maturities and coupons can be substituted to obtain estimated yields at these maturity points.

The Elliot-Echols Model is useful where it is sought to fit yield curves directly to yield data for individual bonds rather than to homogenised yield series. This might be desirable as a means of avoiding possible distortions created in the process of arriving at the synthetic yield series.

Source: Michael E Echols and Jan Walter Elliott, "A Quantitative Yield Curve Model for Estimating the Term Structure of Interest Rates " (1976) Journal of Financial and Quantitative Analysis 87.

---

**Exhibit 5.31**[20]    **Regression Based Interpolation Model – Example**

## 1.  General Approach

Regression based models require the fitting of a functional form to the yield curve. The function is chosen so that it reflects the general shape of the term structure. Parameters that specify the exact form of the function are evaluated to minimise the difference between observed market data and the values given by the function.

The curve is fitted as follows:

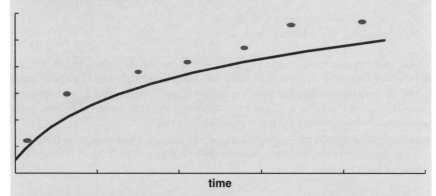

time

The yield curve is specified as a function of rates $r_1, r_2, r_3, \ldots, r_n$ and time t.

$$df(t) = F(t, r_1, r_2, r_3, \ldots, r_n)$$

Where df(t) is the discount factor at time t.

The form of the function is found by a least squares minimisation of the differences between the observed market rates and the values given by the function. This requires minimisation of:

$$\sum_{i=1}^{n} [F(t_i, r_1, r_2, \ldots, r_n) - \text{Market Price}(t_i)]^2$$

This now gives a function for which discount factors can be obtained for any term.

## 2.  Example – An Exponential Curve for Yield

Here we specify the curve of the form:

$$df(t) = a_1 e^{-r_1 t} + a_2 e^{-r_2 t} + \cdots + a_n e^{-r_n t}$$

To obtain the term structure function, values for the coefficients $a_1, a_2, \ldots, a_n$ must be found. This is done using the least squares minimisation shown above. Once these are obtained, we have a function for the yield at any time.

To illustrate this consider a term structure function containing seven terms

$$df(t) = a_1 e^{-r_1 t} + a_2 e^{-r_2 t} + \cdots + a_7 e^{-r_7 t}$$

---

[20]  The author would like to thank Roger Cohen for his permission to include this example.

The values of $r_1, r_2, r_3, r_4, r_5, r_6$ and $r_7$ are specified. Market rates for 1 through 10 years are used as observations. To define the yield curve, only the coefficients $a_1, a_2, a_3, a_4, a_5, a_6$ and $a_7$ need to be found. This is done using the minimisation above.

The market rates are as follows:

| Time (years) | Yield (% pa) |
|:---:|:---:|
| 1 | 7.52 |
| 2 | 7.57 |
| 3 | 7.7 |
| 4 | 7.8 |
| 5 | 7.88 |
| 6 | 7.95 |
| 7 | 7.995 |
| 8 | 8.03 |
| 9 | 8.05 |
| 10 | 8.06 |

The fitted curve is set out below:

| Time (y) | Yield | Fitted | Weights | W(fy)^2 | Error |
|:---:|:---:|:---:|:---:|:---:|:---:|
| 1 | 7.52 | 7.5211 | 1 | 1.26E-06 | -0.00112 |
| 2 | 7.57 | 7.5658 | 1 | 1.75E-05 | 0.004184 |
| 3 | 7.70 | 7.6998 | 1 | 3.01E-08 | 0.000174 |
| 4 | 7.80 | 7.8059 | 1 | 3.44E-05 | -0.00587 |
| 5 | 7.88 | 7.8853 | 1 | 2.78E-05 | -0.00527 |
| 6 | 7.95 | 7.9456 | 1 | 1.95E-05 | 0.00442 |
| 7 | 8.00 | 7.9914 | 1 | 1.28E-05 | 0.003575 |
| 8 | 8.03 | 8.0255 | 1 | 2.01E-05 | 0.004486 |
| 9 | 8.05 | 8.0496 | 1 | 1.39E-07 | 0.000372 |
| 10 | 8.06 | 8.0651 | 1 | 2.59E-05 | -0.00509 |
| | | | **Residual** | **0.000159** | |

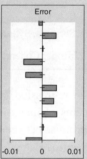

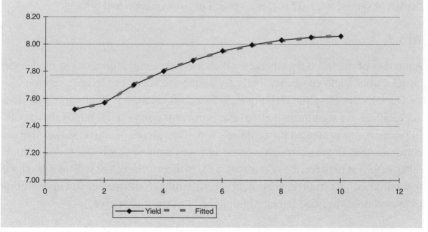

| Coefficient (I) | ai | Ri |
|---|---|---|
| 1 | 5.627834 | 0.00274 |
| 2 | 4.530894 | 0.019178 |
| 3 | −1.28394 | 0.082192 |
| 4 | −0.25905 | 0.246575 |
| 5 | −0.69042 | 1 |
| 6 | 2.108328 | 2 |
| 7 | 4.998892 | 10 |

This gives a smooth curve through the known data points. At each known rate, the difference between the market and that given by the curve is small (less than 0.006). The defined discount function is:

$$df(t) = 5.627834e^{-0.00274t} + 4.530894e^{-0.019178t} - 1.28394e^{-0.082192t}$$
$$- 0.25905e^{-0.246575t} - 0.69042e^{-t} + 2.108328e^{-2t} + 4.998892e^{-10t}$$

Using this function, discount factors – and hence yields – can be obtained for any time t.

Source: Cohen, Roger "Example of Regression Based Model" in Das, Satyajit (with Cohen, Roger) "Interest Rates and Yield Curve Modelling: An Introduction" in Satyajit (Editor) (1997) Risk Management & Financial Derivatives: A Guide to the Mathematics; LBC Information Services, Sydney; McGraw-Hill, Chicago; MacMillan Publishing, England at 70–72.

The regression based models are generally useful in avoiding some of the problems of linear interpolation techniques. In practice, the models represent a compromise between too few terms (which tends to create a smooth curve) and too many terms (which tends to overfit the curve creating a noisy curve). The major problem of the regression based model is that the fitted curve may not pass through market observed rates. This creates problems in valuation and pricing.

### 10.3.3 Cubic Splines

A number of models have emerged which use polynomial functions to model and create a fitted yield curve. The basic technique used is that of a cubic spline.

The concept of spline techniques is based on creating a yield curve that does not oscillate to a significant degree (that is, it is not noisy) and is relatively smooth. In practice, this is created using splines which are pieces of elastic shapes that are constrained as to pass through a given series of points but are allowed to assume other shapes in between the points specified. In theory, the spline will take the shape that minimises its strain energy that is consistent with the mathematical definition of smoothness specified in determining the fit of the yield curve.

Using splines there are two choices in fitting a yield curve:
- **Use a single high order polynomial** – this is generally not favoured because there is an inherent tendency for the curve to take untractable shapes between data points[21].
- **Use a number of lower order polynomials that are then linked to create a complete yield curve** – this is generally the favoured methodology because of its inherent flexibility and satisfaction of the condition that it pass through all observed interest rate data points.

The latter technique is referred to as a piecewise cubic spline technique. Using this technique, the complete yield curve is generated as follows:
- The observed yield curve in terms of observed data points is divided into a series (n − 1 where n is the number of observed data points) of pairs; in effect, a series of paired adjacent yield curve points and rates.
- The yield curve between any of these observed pairs is then specified as a polynomial that is unique.
- Each polynomial which specifies the yield curve shape between two unique points is related to the adjacent or neighbour polynomial so that the slope and/or the rate of change of slope is equal at the common data point between the two polynomials. In effect, the first and (optionally) the second derivative of the two polynomials are equated.

**Exhibit 5.32** sets out the mechanics of implementing a piecewise cubic spline interpolation methodology. The process generates a spline that passes through the data points which by definition is the smoothest interpolated function that fits the observed data.

The major advantages of piecewise cubic splines include:
- The fitted yield curve passes through observed data points and avoids the discontinuity or kinks where the yield curve changes slope.
- The curve is generally smooth.
- The curve provides a robust estimation technique in a variety of market conditions.

The disadvantages of piecewise cubic splines include:
- The need for sufficient data points to allow a good fitted curve to be generated.
- The computation is somewhat complex.

---

[21] This is similar to the regression based model described in **Exhibit 5.31**.

---

### Exhibit 5.32 Piecewise Cubic Spline Interpolation[22]

The piecewise cubic spline is calculated for the following three interest rates (R) as at time $t_1$, $t_2$ and $t_3$. The technique is also applicable to discount factors. The yield curve segment is set out in the following diagram:

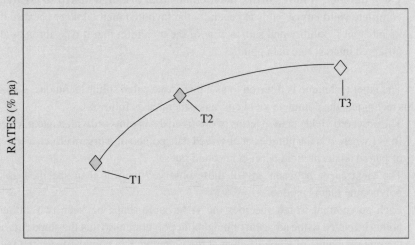

TERM TO MATURITY (YEARS)

The yield curve is divided into two separate pieces that are described by unique splines. The section between $t_1$ and $t_2$ is described by:

$$Rt_1 = a + bt_1 + ct_1^2 + dt_1^3$$

The section between $t_2$ and $t_3$ is described by:

$$Rt_3 = m + nt_3 + pt_3^2 + qt_3^3$$

There are eight constants within the two polynomials that must be calculated. It is now necessary to ensure that the two polynomials go through the common data point and that their slope and the rate of change of slope is equal. This is done as follows:

The section at $t_2$ is described by both the above polynomials:

$$Rt_2 = a + bt_2 + ct_2^2 + dt_2^3$$

$$Rt_2 = m + nt_2 + pt_2^2 + qt_2^3$$

The first and second derivatives at $t_2$ must be equal, therefore:

$$b + 2ct_2 + 3dt_2^2 = n + 2pt_2 + 3qt_2^2$$

$$2c + 6dt_2 = 2p + 6qt_2$$

---

[22] See Cox, David "Yield Curves and How to Build Them" (1995) Capital Market Strategies 4 29–33; Van Deventer, Donald R. and Imai, Keni (1997) Financial Risk Analytics; Irwin, Chicago at Chapter 2.

Two extra equations are necessary so the equation can be solved. This is done by setting second derivatives equal to zero as follows:

$$2c + 6dt_2 = 2p + 6qt_2 = 0$$

The final constraints imply that the yield curve is instantaneously straight at the left-hand side of the yield curve and at maturity.[23] There are six equations that can now be solved using multiple regression or matrix algebra techniques to generate the optimal piecewise cubic spline.

The solution of cubic polynomials with multiple regression techniques exhibit the problems of multi-collinearity (that is, the function introduces uncertainty due to the linkages between each segment of the yield curve) and when solved using multiple regression techniques the definition of accuracy of the result is not unambiguous.

### 10.3.4   Interpolation Techniques – Comparison

**Exhibit 5.33** sets a comparison of linear interpolation and non-linear interpolation (using cubic splines). There are significant differences in the derived rates.

**Exhibit 5.33   Interpolation Techniques – Comparison**

Assume the following yield curve:

| Maturity (Years) | Interest Rates (% pa) |
|---|---|
| 0.5 | 5.75 |
| 1.0 | 5.91 |
| 3.0 | 6.10 |
| 5.0 | 6.25 |
| 7.0 | 6.40 |
| 10.0 | 6.75 |
| 12.0 | 7.10 |

The available rates are used to derive the complete yield curve. Two methods of interpolation are used: linear and cubic splines. The interpolated yield curve is set out below:

| Maturity (Years) | Interest Rates (% pa) (Known) | Linear Interpolated Rates (% pa) | Cubic Spline Interpolated Rates (% pa) |
|---|---|---|---|
| 0.05 | 5.75 | 5.75 | 5.75 |
| 1.0 | 5.91 | 5.91 | 5.91 |

---

[23]   A further option is to set the first derivative of the polynomial defining the final segment of the curve to equal zero implying a flat yield curve at the longest maturity; see Van Deventer, Donald R. And Imai, Keni (1997) Financial Risk Analytics; Irwin, Chicago at Chapters 2 and 47.

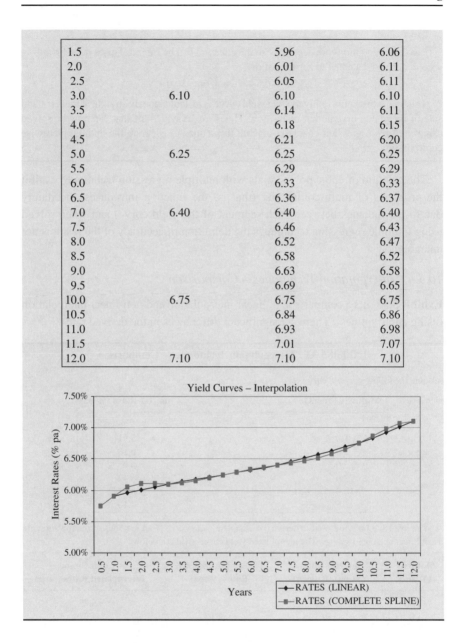

| | | | |
|---|---|---|---|
| 1.5 | | 5.96 | 6.06 |
| 2.0 | | 6.01 | 6.11 |
| 2.5 | | 6.05 | 6.11 |
| 3.0 | 6.10 | 6.10 | 6.10 |
| 3.5 | | 6.14 | 6.11 |
| 4.0 | | 6.18 | 6.15 |
| 4.5 | | 6.21 | 6.20 |
| 5.0 | 6.25 | 6.25 | 6.25 |
| 5.5 | | 6.29 | 6.29 |
| 6.0 | | 6.33 | 6.33 |
| 6.5 | | 6.36 | 6.37 |
| 7.0 | 6.40 | 6.40 | 6.40 |
| 7.5 | | 6.46 | 6.43 |
| 8.0 | | 6.52 | 6.47 |
| 8.5 | | 6.58 | 6.52 |
| 9.0 | | 6.63 | 6.58 |
| 9.5 | | 6.69 | 6.65 |
| 10.0 | 6.75 | 6.75 | 6.75 |
| 10.5 | | 6.84 | 6.86 |
| 11.0 | | 6.93 | 6.98 |
| 11.5 | | 7.01 | 7.07 |
| 12.0 | 7.10 | 7.10 | 7.10 |

Yield Curves – Interpolation

## 10.3.5   Yield Curve Interpolation – Other Techniques

A number other forms of interpolation models are sometimes used. This includes basis splines, Laguerre functions and interest rate models.

Basis splines are similar to the piecewise cubic spline technique described. The major benefit in using basis splines is that it avoids some of the problems with piecewise cubic splines described above. This is the result of the fact that basis splines go to zero at defined points, reducing the linkage issues identified above. Typically, third order basis splines are used as they satisfy the required criteria of smoothness.

Basis splines are generated in a systematic manner with second order splines being generated from first order splines and third order splines being generated from second order splines. **Exhibit 5.34** sets out the mechanics of using basis splines to create a yield curve. The process follows the following logic:

- Each spline function is specified with a defined range. Outside this range it has a zero value. The points at which the spline is zero are referred to as knot points.
- One spline will end where another spline commences across the yield curve.
- Where knot points have been specified, each spline is weighted using multiple regression techniques. This is predicated on the fact that market bond prices can be expressed in terms of the sum of the discounted bond cash flows and the discount factor at each point in the yield curve coinciding with a cash flow is capable of definition in spline functions and weights. This will allow the bond price today to be expressed as a function of unknown function weights and the product of the spline function values and the bond cash flows. This allows the regression to be performed nominating the bond price as the dependent variable and the function cash flows products as the independent variable. The regression process is then used to estimate the function weights.

The basis spline arguably has better properties for fitting yield curves than the simpler piecewise cubic spline techniques. However, the basis spline technique has a number of disadvantages including:

- It is complex and is computationally difficult.
- The shape of the fitted yield curve is sensitive to the location of the knot points. It appears necessary to ensure an even number of bonds are available between the knot points which in practice is difficult to satisfy.
- Basis splines demonstrate instability and volatility and provide inaccurate estimates where there are gaps in the yield curve and sparse data.

An alternative interpolation technique is to utilise Laguerre functions. **Exhibit 5.35** sets out a description of interpolation techniques using Laguerre functions.

**Exhibit 5.34    Basis Spline Interpolation**

The basis spline is calculated by specifying the following:
  Firstly, discount factors are specified as the sum of weighted spline functions:

$$DF(t) = \sum_{I=1}^{1} W_1 S_1(t)$$

Where

  $DF(t)$ = Discount factor for time t
  $W_1$    = Function weight
  $S_1 I$   = Spline function 1

  Secondly, the bond price is specified as the sum of the discounted bond cash flows:

$$P_i = \sum_{j=1}^{1} C_i \sum_{I=1}^{L} W_1 S_1(t)$$

Where

  $P_i$ =  Price of bond I
  $C_i$ =  Bond I cash flow at time j

  Finally, prices are expressed as the function weights and cashflow function product which allow determination of the unknown weights:

$$P_i = \sum_{j=1}^{1} W_i \sum_{I=1}^{L} C_i S_1(t)$$

Source: Cox, David "Yield Curves and How to Build Them" (1995) Capital Market Strategies 4 29–33.

---

**Exhibit 5.35    Polynomial Based Yield Curve Models – Laguerre Model**

Laguerre functions consist of a polynomial multiplied by a polynomial decay function in the following form:

$$I_t = (a_0 + a_1 t + a_2 t^2 + \cdots + a_n t^n) * e^{-bt}$$

Where

  $I_t$ is the interest rate for maturity t
  t is the time to maturity
  $a_n$, b are constants

Where Laguerre functions are utilised for term structure modelling the decay function eventually dominates the polynomial component. This means that the long term rates stabilise as predicted by a Laguerre function. This property provides Laguerre models with an advantage over other models where the estimates of long term rates continues to increase or decrease with time.

The advantages of Laguerre functions include:
- They provide a range of flexible shapes that are consistent with observable interest rate data.
- They are consistent with theoretical work on yield curve shape and there is some evidence for their applicability to interest rate data.

Source: B F Hunt, "Modelling the Term Structure" (Paper presented at Conference on Options on Interest Rates (organised by IIR Pty Ltd) at Sydney, March 1992).

A newer approach to modelling the yield curve entails the use of term structure models. The key feature of these models is the use of assumed stochastic processes to drive the term structure of interest rates. These models have the following characteristics:
- The models entail explicit recognition of the uncertain element in interest rate structure; that is, interest rates are probabilistic rather than deterministic.
- The models entail linking the term structure of interest rates to specified stochastic processes and nominated stochastic factors.
- The evolution of these factors over time in accordance with the assumed process determines interest rates.
- The model generated interest rates satisfy certain no arbitrage conditions.

There are a large number of competing models.[24] **Exhibit 5.36** sets out an example of these types of interest rate models. The model described is a relatively simple single factor model incorporating mean reversion. The major variations include two factor models (such as a short term and a long term interest rate), the inclusion or exclusion of mean reversion, and the imposition of arbitrage free conditions. Models commonly utilised include the Heath-Jarrow- Morton model[25] and the Hull-White model[26].

---

[24] For a detailed discussion on yield curve models see Chapter 8.

[25] See Heath, D, Jarrow, R and Morton, A, "Contingent Claim Valuation with a Random Evolution of Interest Rates" (1991) Review of Futures Markets 54–76; "Bond Pricing and the Term Structure of Interest Rates: A New Methodology" (1992) Econometrica 60, 1 77–105

[26] See Hull, John (2000) Option Futures and Other Derivatives – Fourth Edition; Prentice-Hall Inc., Upper Saddle River, NJ at Chapter 21.

---

**Exhibit 5.36    Interest Rate Models**

The Vasichek model specifies the following stochastic model for interest rates:

$$dr = \alpha(\gamma - r)dt + \sigma dz$$

Where

   dr = Change in the short term interest rate
   $\alpha$  = Parameter (greater than 0) which describes the speed at which r revert to a
        long run average value
   $\gamma$  = Long run value of r
   r  = Short term interest rate
   dt = short time interval
   $\sigma$  = Volatility of r
   dz = Random variable chosen from a normal distribution with mean 0 and variance dt

   The process specified identifies that the change in the short term rate r over the interval dt will have two components:
1. A deterministic component ($\alpha$ ($\gamma - r$)dt) whereby r will revert to a long run value at a speed parameter ($\alpha$).
2. A stochastic component ($\sigma dz$) which will change randomly.

   The structure of the first term implies that if r is close to (away from) its long run value, the deterministic term will be small (large). This term reflects mean reversion where interest rates tend towards some normal rate. The stochastic term will be larger as the time over which change occurs increases. The structure is designed to be consistent with the general pattern of evolution of interest rates in capital markets.
   The specified process for interest rate changes allows the derivation of valuation formula for a discount bond that in turn facilitates the solution for the value of interest rate derivative products.

Source: Vasichek, O. A. "An Equilibrium Characterisation of the Term Structure" (1977) Journal of Financial Economics 5 177–88.

---

   The major application of these models is in pricing interest rate derivatives, in particular interest rate options. The research into interest rate models is largely predicated on these demands. They are also related integrally to the non-linear interpolation techniques identified above. This relationship is predicated on the fact that an appropriate curve is fitted to observed market data. The fitted curve then allows the construction of an interest rate yield curve model that obtains estimates that are consistent with the market data. In this sense, the interest rate models reflect an extension of the interpolation techniques to allow the provision of solutions, both analytical and numerical, for the value of interest rate derivative products.

## 11 Term Structure of Interest Rates

Interest rates deal with the process of valuation of cash flows at different future times. Term structure deals with the pure price of time in the application of different interest rates at different future times. The process of interpolation assumes implicitly or explicitly a term structure model of interest rates. Understanding of the term structure of interest rates is essential in yield curve modelling[27].

The term structure of interest rates can be defined as the structure of interest rate applicable for cash flows of a homogenous credit quality for different maturities. **Exhibit 5.37** sets out the commonly observed shapes of yield curves. The types of term structure (or yield curve shapes) observed include:

- **Positive** – interest rates increase with maturity.
- **Negative** – interest rates decrease with maturity.
- **Flat** – interest rates are the same across all maturities.
- **Humped** – interest rates increase with maturity but peak and decrease from their maximum level with further increases in maturity.

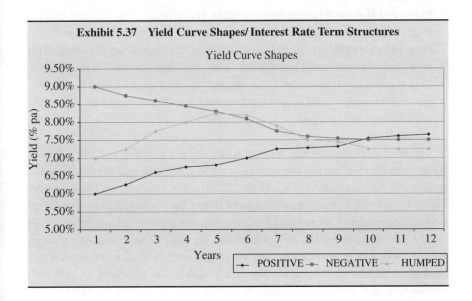

**Exhibit 5.37    Yield Curve Shapes/ Interest Rate Term Structures**

---

[27] For a summary of interest rate term structure theories see McEnally, Richard W. and Jordan, James V "The Term Structure of Interest Rates" in Fabozzi, Frank J. and Fabozzi, T. Dessa (Editors) (1995) The Handbook of Fixed Income Securities – Fourth Edition; Irwin Professional Publishing, Chicago at 779–830.

The following theories of the determinants of the term structure of interest rates are usually considered:

- **Expectations Hypothesis** – in it pure form, the expectations hypothesis states that expected interest return from securities of all maturities are equal. This implies that the return for a particular maturity represents the expected holding period return from investing in shorter term securities that are reinvested at maturity at the implied forward rates. This is based on the implicit assumption that the implied forward rate is the market consensus expected short term interest rate as of the future date. In effect, this theory is consistent with the assumption that longer term interest rates are an average of expected short term interest rates.
- **Liquidity Preference Hypothesis** – this states that investors prefer shorter maturities in preference to longer maturities and require a premium in the form of a higher interest rate or lower price (the liquidity premium). This is consistent with the assumption of increased price risk with increases in maturity reflecting the potential instability in their capital values upon liquidation prior to maturity if required. The liquidity premium is usually assumed to increase with maturity but at a decreasing rate.
- **Preferred Habitat/Market Segmentation Hypothesis** – this assumes that the market for shorter dated securities is segmented from that for longer dated securities reflecting the investment preferences of the underlying investors. This arises from investor asset liability matching requirements and risk preferences. This implies that differences in the market structure as embodied in differential demand/supply equilibrium for securities of different maturities dictate the interest rate term structure.

The theories of interest rate term structure are not mutually exclusive. Newer attempts to develop models to encompass the key determinants of term structure usually combine elements of each of the theories. For example, the biased expectations hypothesis states that interest rates reflect the combined impact of future interest rate expectations and also liquidity premia for increased maturities.

The interest rates models described above are not true term structure theories but represent new ways of modelling the yield curve. In reality, the interest rate models are consistent with the key theoretical approaches identified because each represents a special case of stochastic processes used to generate the yield curve.

**Exhibit 5.38** sets out a summary of the relationship between the observable interest rate term structures and the theoretical models identified. In practice, the yield curve interpolation model utilised must be consistent with the observed interest rate term structure prevalent in the relevant market to avoid inaccuracies and poor predictive performance.

**Exhibit 5.38 Summary of Interest Rate Term Structure**

| Type of Term Structure | Flat | Positive | Negative | Humped |
|---|---|---|---|---|
| Expectation Theory | Short term interest rates are expected to remain the same | Short term interest rates are expected to increase | Short term interest rates are expected to decrease | Short term interest rates are expected to increase and then decrease |
| Liquidity Premium | No liquidity premia | Positive liquidity premia | Negative liquidity premia | Positive liquidity premia followed by negative liquidity premia |
| Preferred Habitat/ Market Segmentation | Equilibrium in demand supply across all maturities | Excess of supply over demand in longer maturities | Excess of supply over demand in shorter maturities | Excess of supply over demand in intermediate maturities |
| Biased Expectations | Short term rates are expected to decrease but are offset by increasing liquidity premia | Short term rates are expected to remain the same or increase moderately and are accentuated by increasing liquidity premia | Short term rates are expected to decrease but the rate of decrease is offset by an increasing liquidity premia | Short term rates are expected to stay the same or increase and then decrease (the decrease being sharper than the increase) with the increase being accentuated by and the fall retarded by an increasing liquidity premia |

## 12  Yield Curve Construction in Practice[28]

The process of derivation of appropriate interest rates and discount factors can be reduced into two separate and distinct processes. The first process entails the use of yield curve modelling processes to derive a complete set of interest rates. The second process entails the generation of zero rates or discount factors from the yield curve that can be utilised for the valuation of financial instruments.

In practice, a number of additional considerations are relevant. A major factor underlying the uncertainties is the incomplete and imperfect nature of financial markets generally and the difficulties in nominating objective criteria to select optimal models for constructing accurate yield curves. These problems include the following:

* The difficulty in identifying yield curves that are homogenous in terms of credit or default risk. In practice, a series of interest rates derived from similar but not perfectly credit homogenous yield curves are combined.
* The problems of defining the characteristics of fit for an estimated yield curve because the criteria of fit, consistency and smoothness can be applied at different levels. For example, there are in reality multiple curves that can be fitted to satisfy the smoothness criteria including the par curve, the forward curve, the zero curve or the discount factors generated off any off these curves. Linear interpolation often creates irregular forward curves while splines can create regular smooth curve for one or more of these sets of interest rates or discount factors *but not for all curves.*

The problems identified are not necessarily capable of perfect solution. In practice, practitioners use compromises reflecting trade-offs between market structure, data integrity, estimation accuracy, computational efficiency and cost effectiveness. A major criteria is the issue of hedge-ability; that is, the capacity to hedge the components of the yield curve and the interest rate risks assumed in the course of pricing, valuing and trading financial instruments off the selected yield curve. In essence, practitioners will favour the construction of a yield curve that

---

[28]  See Flavell, Richard "Discount Function Construction" (27 July 1994) IFR Swaps Weekly Issue 27 4–5; Cox, David "Yield Curves and How to Build Them" (1995) Capital Market Strategies 4 29–33; Smit, Linda and van Niekerk, Frik "Curve Building" (April 1997) Risk – South Africa Supplement XIV–XVI; Zangari, Peter "An Investigation into Term Structure Estimation Methods for RiskMetrics" (Third Quarter 1997) RiskMetrics Monitor – J. P. Morgan/Reuters at 3–31; Flavell, Richard (2002) Swaps and Other Derivatives; John Wiley & Sons, Chichester at Chapter 3.

not only is nearest the theoretical paradigm but one which facilitates trading and hedging activities[29].

Driven by this set of constraints, most practitioners utilise two separate yield curves for valuation purposes:

- **Risk free curve** – this is usually constructed from the available series of interest rates on government securities of the relevant tenor. The risk free curve is used to value government securities and related derivatives.
- **Risk adjusted (the swap) curve** – this is usually constructed from a mixture of instruments including short term inter-bank rates, near term short term interest rate futures contracts or forward rate agreement ("FRA") prices/rates and interest rate swap rates. The swap curve is used to value credit risk affected (that is, non-government risk financial instruments) incorporating appropriate adjustment spreads where the underlying instrument is considered to have fundamentally different risk or other characteristics.

The derivation of the risk free curve follows the established procedures identified. Key considerations include depending on the market noisy data (reflecting a large number of government securities of identical or similar maturity with different coupons trading at different yields) and data sparseness (where there may be significant gaps in the yield curve). In practice, these are overcome by constructing a fitted curve (using one or other of the techniques identified) and generating the required zero rates from that curve.

The generation of the swap curve is more complex. The curve is constructed by combining a series of interest rates from different instruments. The following example is indicative of both the approach and the key considerations that are relevant. The problem of yield curve construction in other markets is more complex than in the US example, reflecting the relative maturity, liquidity and efficiency of the US market.

In practice, the swap curve in US$ is constructed using a number of distinct steps as follows:

- **Step 1** – a curve based on short term market cash deposit rates is constructed for the very short end. The cash rate (usually based on an inter-bank rate such as LIBOR) to the first Eurodollar delivery date (the near month contract) is taken.

---

[29] For a discussion of problems in yield curve estimation in different contexts see Dybvig, Philip H. and Marshall, William J. "Pricing Long Bonds: Pitfalls and Opportunities" (January February 1996) Financial Analyst's Journal 32–39; Dillon, Tom and McKee, Scott "A Question of Clarity" (June 1998) Risk – Latin Risk Special Report at 14–15; "Interest rate Swaps: Seeking a Curve" (June 1998) Risk 33.

Some interpolation is usually required as the period may not coincide with the traded maturity for cash that is usually overnight, one week, one, three, six etc months.

- **Step 2** – the cash rates are then combined with the Eurodollar futures rates. The cash rate (usually interpolated) is combined with the near month futures rate. The zero rates derived are then combined with successive futures rates. The number of successive Eurodollar futures contracts used varies but in practice will be between 12 and 20 quarterly contracts (3 to 5 years) [30]. For each contract, the traded futures price is deducted from 100 to determine the forward rate that is then incorporated into the yield curve. This process is repeated for each contract. The rates derived from the futures rate may need to be adjusted for convexity and year end (turn-of-year) effects.

- **Step 3** – beyond the futures contracts, available interest rate swap rates are utilised to complete the yield curve. In order to compute zero rates using the available swap rates, it is necessary to use bootstrapping to derive the implied zero rates. This is based on the zero rates for all maturities before the date of the relevant swap rates. These are obtained from the previously constructed zero rates from the combination of cash and futures rates. The swap rates used are a combination of available market rates and interpolated swap rates for other maturities.

The approach described is generic although the example used is US$. The major differences between US$ and yield curves derived in other currencies include:

- **Availability of instruments** – in currencies other than the major traded currencies (US$, yen, Euro etc), the range of instruments is more limited. For example, interest rate futures may not be available or may not trade with sufficient liquidity to be used except for shorter maturities. In many emerging markets, currency forward contracts are used to derive implied local currency zero rates for use in curve construction reflecting the scarcity of available instruments. In addition, the sparseness of yield curve points available dictates the need for interpolation between available points to create a complete cash and swap curve for the purpose of curve derivation.

- **Transition points** – the lack of availability of instruments or their trading characteristics will dictate significant differences between the transition points (between cash and futures and futures and swaps) in different currencies.

---

[30] It is likely in currencies other than US$, the number of futures contracts used would be lower, say 4 to 8 contracts (1 to 2 years) reflecting the fact that the futures markets in the relevant currency do not allow trading beyond this maturity and/or the liquidity of the market. Technically, in the US$ market, it is theoretically possible to trade Eurodollar futures out to 10 years (40 successive quarters) which would mean it would be possible to derive a 10 year yield curve from the futures rates.

The approach described requires careful consideration of the following factors:

- **Dominance rules** – dominance rules (that is the rate to be used when rates from two or more sources are available) need to be specified. Typically, dominance rules specifying the transition from cash rate to futures/FRA rates and the futures/FRA rates to swap rates need to specified. The dominance rules are usually driven by consideration such as trading liquidity, transaction/trading costs, balance sheet impact of trading in physical versus derivative instruments and regulatory capital considerations. The selection of the transition points is relatively arbitrary reflecting institutional and market considerations as well the margining and convexity issues.

- **Overlapping dates** – this can be illustrated by comparing and contrasting the use of FRAs versus futures. The FRAs out of spot will trade at regular runs ($3 \times 6$; $6 \times 9$ etc) which allows the calculation of the relevant forward interest rates and discount factors that can be incorporated in the yield curve. In contrast, the Eurodollar futures contracts are standardised. They are traded to pre-specified dates and are cash settled against 3 month LIBOR. As the dates may not be precisely three months apart, the prospect exists for gaps or overlaps between the end of the reference period and the maturity date of the next Eurodollar contract. The practical import of this is that the discount factors cannot be multiplied or forward rates compounded as the interest periods are not exactly linked. This requires adjustments to the futures rates.

- **Nature of instruments** – the instruments used in deriving the curve are different including differences in credit risk and instrument features. For example, the use of futures contracts introduces a number of factors including payment of deposits and margins, the differential credit risk of the clearing house and in the case of some futures contracts (such as the Eurodollar contract) the problems of the fixed tick point value (1 bps is always equal to US$25) or the negative convexity[31].

- **Convexity Adjustment** – the forward rates embodied in a futures price reflect some of the inherent biases in futures prices, including the impact of margin payments and (if present) the negative convexity. Where interest rates are expected to increase, the holder of a short (long) futures position will receive (be required to pay) margin payments which can be invested (must be funded) at higher interest rates. This uncertainty forces the futures rate to trade above the theoretical arbitrage free forward rate (futures price to trade below the theoretical futures price). In practice, the bias in futures prices and the negative convexity necessitate additional adjustments based on the expected volatility of interest rates.

---

[31] See discussion in Chapter 13 regarding the impact on hedging.

There are a variety of convexity adjustments available for use[32]. Where a convexity adjustment is utilised, the *adjusted forward rate* is used rather than the market futures rate.

- **Turn-of-year Effect** – this refers to the fact that in some markets there is a phenomenon where the rates are generally higher over the end of the calendar or financial year. This reflects year end adjustment to positions. In practice, it is possible to adjust the curve building process for the fact that the rates will be higher for a period of time at the end of the year. This usually entails specifying the period and the rate differential (based on expectation conditioned by historical experience) that is then used to adjust the rates used in deriving the curve and zero rates/discount factors[33].

The presence of these factors means that the generation of the relevant yield curve is unlikely to be objectively verifiable. The major practical problem to arise relates to the fact that more than one equally tractable yield curve can be created from the same set of market data, reflecting differences in interest rate selection and mode of adjustment for the problems identified. In practice, the problems are generally likely to be confined to the shorter end and the transition points from one set of interest rates to the next source. A major area is the transition from the futures/FRA rates to the swap rates.

Given that the zero rates are likely to be different, either a selection must be made between the yield curves or adjustment made to the set of rates to be used. One possible basis for selection between the curves is by application. Where an adjustment is to be made, it is necessary to either segment the curve to ensure the absence of overlap or create blended curves. There are problems with each approach:

- The use of different curves differentiated by application will create different values and prices for different transactions, opening up the possibility of value loss.
- The adjustments will either create discontinuity in the curve and irregularities in the rates or require complex and highly subjective adjustments.

In practice, there is little uniformity in approach to these issues. Each institution generally employs its own set of techniques to deal with the problem, reflecting the nature of the market and the purpose for which the generated zero rates are to be utilised.

---

[32] See discussion in Chapter 6.
[33] See discussion in Chapter 6.

In practice, the problems of deriving in yield curves are less significant than might be imagined. This is because the key issue is one of replication and the ability to hedge the zero rates derived. As long as it is possible to trade in the instruments used to derive the curve, then the curve can be hedged and replicated. This means that in practice, traders focus on the ability to trade the underlying instruments in order to enable them to efficiently hedge the transactions priced and trade off the zero rates derived.

**Exhibit 5.39** sets out an example of the process described using the example of constructing a zero coupon curve in A$.

---

**Exhibit 5.39   Constructing a Yield Curve in Practice[34]**

This is an example of how to construct a A$ zero coupon curve using bills[35], bill futures and swaps[36]. We use the bootstrap method. Interpolation is based on keeping the forward rates constant. Internal calculations will be in terms of continuously compounding rates and discount factors.

**1.   The Instruments**
For the curve, we use instruments whose prices are available in the marketplace. These are bills, bill futures and swaps. We will assume that the bill futures take precedence where there is any overlap[37].

To keep the procedure general, all times will be in days or years. This means that dates can be omitted. In a real application, dates would be converted to days. The spot date is assumed to be day zero. All days/years are relative to the spot date unless otherwise specified.

**Bills**
These are pure discount instruments whose maturity is a fixed number of days out from the spot date.

| Time to Maturity (Days) | Rate (% pa) |
|:---:|:---:|
| 1 | 6.00 |
| 30 | 6.00 |
| 60 | 5.98 |
| 150 | 6.00 |

---

[34]   The author would like to thank Roger Cohen for his permission to include this example.

[35]   A$ bills are bankers acceptances equivalent to A$ inter-bank rates (similar to US$ LIBOR). A$ bills are equivalent to bank certificates of deposit and are issued and traded on a discount basis.

[36]   This example uses the Australian dollar curve. However, the procedure is identical in other currencies. For example, in US$, the LIBOR cash rates, Eurodollar futures rates and US$ swap rates would be used.

[37]   This is a realistic assumption as they are the most liquid of the instruments used. Also, short dated swaps are usually hedged using bill futures.

The price of a bill is just its face value discounted over the appropriate number of days. Thus we can directly obtain discount factors for bills. If the bill has d days to maturity then the discount factor is:

$$df = \frac{1}{(1 + r\frac{d}{365})}$$

This gives a continuously compounded zero rate of

$$r(\text{zero}) = \frac{-365}{d} \ln(df)$$

| Time to Maturity (Days) | Rate (% pa) | Discount Factor | Zero Rate (% pa Continuous Compounding) |
|---|---|---|---|
| 1 | 6.00 | 0.999836 | 5.999507 |
| 30 | 6.00 | 0.995093 | 5.985254 |
| 60 | 5.98 | 0.990266 | 5.950799 |
| 150 | 6.00 | 0.975936 | 5.927221 |

### Bill Futures

Bill futures are just like bills, except that they start out of a forward date. In this example, we have a strip of bill futures. Where one bill future matures, the next begins. From the table below, the first bill future starts at day 40 and matures on day 132. The next starts on day 132 and expires on day 223 and so forth. The yield of a bill future is just 100 minus its price.

| Days to Start | Days to Expiry | Price | Yield (% pa) |
|---|---|---|---|
| 40 | 132 | 94.000 | 6.00 |
| 132 | 223 | 93.920 | 6.08 |
| 223 | 314 | 93.660 | 6.34 |
| 314 | 405 | 93.350 | 6.65 |
| 405 | 496 | 93.110 | 6.89 |
| 496 | 587 | 92.940 | 7.06 |
| 587 | 678 | 92.790 | 7.21 |
| 678 | 769 | 92.640 | 7.36 |
| 769 | 860 | 92.520 | 7.48 |
| 860 | 951 | 92.420 | 7.58 |
| 951 | 1042 | 92.330 | 7.67 |
| 1042 | 1133 | 92.220 | 7.78 |

It is a simple matter to get the forward discount factor and the forward rate continuously compounded for a bill future. These are given by the same formulae as for bills. If the bill future starts at $d_s$ and expires at $d_e$, then

$$df_s^e = \frac{1}{(1 + r\frac{(d_e - d_s)}{365})}$$

$$r_s^e(\text{zero}) = \frac{-365}{(d_e - d_s)} \ln(df_s^e)$$

These are forward discount factors and rates. They need to be linked to spot rates. This will be illustrated below when we combine all the components of the curve.

| Days to Start | Days to Expiry | Price | Yield[38] | Zero Rate (% pa Continuous Compounding) | Discount Factor |
|---|---|---|---|---|---|
| 40 | 132 | 94.000 | 6.00 | 5.955082 | 0.985102 |
| 132 | 223 | 93.920 | 6.08 | 6.034379 | 0.985068 |
| 223 | 314 | 93.660 | 6.34 | 6.290415 | 0.984439 |
| 314 | · 405 | 93.350 | 6.65 | 6.595475 | 0.983691 |
| 405 | 496 | 93.110 | 6.89 | 6.831492 | 0.983112 |
| 496 | 587 | 92.940 | 7.06 | 6.998586 | 0.982703 |
| 587 | 678 | 92.790 | 7.21 | 7.145964 | 0.982342 |
| 678 | 769 | 92.640 | 7.36 | 7.293288 | 0.981981 |
| 769 | 860 | 92.520 | 7.48 | 7.411109 | 0.981693 |
| 860 | 951 | 92.420 | 7.58 | 7.509266 | 0.981452 |
| 951 | 1042 | 92.330 | 7.67 | 7.597587 | 0.981236 |
| 1042 | 1133 | 92.220 | 7.78 | 7.705509 | 0.980972 |

## Swaps

Swaps are priced as fixed coupon instruments whose coupon is equal to the swap rate. In other words they are par bonds. Conventionally, swaps of three years and less pay quarterly coupons while swaps of longer maturity pay coupons semi-annually. It is convention to quote rates for swaps of maturity one to five years, then for seven and ten year swaps. For maturities of six, eight and nine years, we shall interpolate the rates linearly.[39]

| Maturity (Years) | Swap Rate (% pa) | Payment Frequency (payments/year) |
|---|---|---|
| 1 | 6.50 | 4 |
| 2 | 7.00 | 4 |
| 3 | 7.20 | 4 |
| 4 | 7.25 | 2 |
| 5 | 7.35 | 2 |
| 6 | 7.415 | 2 |
| 7 | 7.48 | 2 |
| 8 | 7.52 | 2 |
| 9 | 7.56 | 2 |
| 10 | 7.60 | 2 |

The swaps will be priced when the curve is assembled.

---

[38] Please note no adjustment has been made for convexity or turn-of-year effects.

[39] It may be more appropriate to use higher order interpolation. Alternatively, the curve can be built using only the quoted swap rates. The other rates obtained from the curve.

## 2. Putting it Together

We have chosen to construct the curve giving precedence to bill futures where there is overlap. Thus the bill of 150 days will be omitted. The 60 day bill will not be used explicitly, but will be used to obtain a bill rate to the beginning of the bill futures strip. Swaps of three years and less are not needed either.

Up to 30 days, the bills provide zero coupon instruments directly. Once a rate at 40 days is known, the bill futures can be used to compute the curve out to 1133 days. The swaps are then required for further dates.

As we know zero rates from the bills to 30 and 60 days, a 40 day bill rate can be implied by interpolation. In this example we assume that forward rates are constant. Using the 30 and 60 day bill rates, the discount factor and forward rate from 30 to 60 days is given by:

$$\text{df}_{30}^{60} = \frac{\text{df}_0^{60}}{\text{df}_0^{30}} = \frac{0.990266}{0.995093} = 0.995149$$

$$r_{30}^{60} = \frac{365}{(60 - 30)} \ln(\text{df}_{30}^{60}) = 5.916344\%$$

This forward rate is used from 30 to 40 days (as the interpolation keeps the forward rates flat). Thus the 40 day discount factor and zero rate can be obtained.

$$\text{df}_0^{40} = \text{df}_0^{30} e^{-0.05916344.10/365} = 0.993481$$

The process so far has used bill rates directly to obtain the zero curve to 30 days. The 60 day bill is used to obtain the curve to the beginning of the bill futures strip. The futures can be combined directly to generate the curve out to 1133 days.

|                 | Days (Start) | Days (Expiry) | Zero Rate (% pa) | Spot Discount Factor | Forward Discount Factor | Forward Rate (% pa) |
|-----------------|--------------|---------------|------------------|----------------------|-------------------------|---------------------|
| **Bill**        | 30           | 60            | 5.985254         | 0.995093             | 0.995149                |                     |
| **Bill**        | 60           |               | 5.950799         | 0.990266             |                         | **5.916344**        |
| **Futures Splice** | 40        | 60            | 5.968027         | **0.993481**         | 0.99838                 | **5.916344**        |
| **Futures**     | 40           | 132           | 5.968027         | **0.993481**         | 0.985102                | 5.955082            |
|                 | 132          | 223           | 5.959005         | 0.97868              | 0.985068                | 6.034379            |
|                 | 223          | 314           | 5.989763         | 0.964067             | 0.984439                | 6.290415            |
|                 | 314          | 405           | 6.076895         | 0.949065             | 0.983691                | 6.595475            |

The forward discount factors for the bill futures have already been obtained above. These can be combined with the discount factor to the beginning of the futures strip to build the curve. For the first future

$$\text{df}_0^{132} = \text{df}_0^{40} \text{df}_{40}^{132} = 0.993481 \times 0.985102 = 0.97868$$

and the continuous zero rate is

$$r_0^{132} = \frac{-365}{132} \ln(0.97868) = 5.959005\%$$

This can be continued for all the bill futures.

| Maturity (Days) | Discount Factor | Zero Rate (% pa Continuous Compounding) |
|---|---|---|
| 1 | 0.9998 | 5.9995 |
| 30 | 0.9950 | 5.9852 |
| 60 | 0.9903 | 5.9507 |
| 132 | 0.9787 | 5.9590 |
| 150 | 0.9759 | 5.9272 |
| 223 | 0.9641 | 5.9898 |
| 314 | 0.9491 | 6.0769 |
| 405 | 0.9336 | 6.1934 |
| 496 | 0.9178 | 6.3105 |
| 587 | 0.9019 | 6.4172 |
| 678 | 0.8860 | 6.5150 |
| 769 | 0.8701 | 6.6071 |
| 860 | 0.8541 | 6.6922 |
| 951 | 0.8383 | 6.7703 |
| 1042 | 0.8226 | 6.8426 |
| 1133 | 0.8069 | 6.9119 |

Exhibit 5.40. The Zero Curve to the End of the Bill Futures Strip

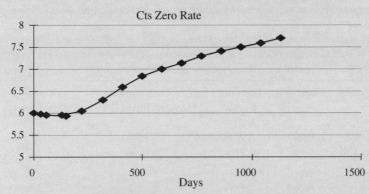

The swaps are now required. The first swap to be used is the four year swap. The swap rate of 7.25% implies the following cashflows

| Years | Cashflow |
|---|---|
| 0 | −100.000 |
| 0.5 | 3.625 |
| 1 | 3.625 |
| 1.5 | 3.625 |
| 2 | 3.625 |
| 2.5 | 3.625 |
| 3 | 3.625 |
| 3.5 | 3.625 |
| 4 | 103.625 |

As the curve has already been generated out to 1133 days (or 3.104 years), this can be used to value the cashflows to three years. The remaining two cashflows are required to generate the curve.

| Years | Days to Maturity | Cashflow | Discount Factor | Net Present Value |
|---|---|---|---|---|
| 0 | 0 | −100.000 | 1 | −100 |
| 0.5 | 182 | 3.625 | 0.970623 | 3.51851 |
| 1 | 366 | 3.625 | 0.940189 | 3.408186 |
| 1.5 | 547 | 3.625 | 0.908889 | 3.294723 |
| 2 | 731 | 3.625 | 0.876684 | 3.177981 |
| 2.5 | 912 | 3.625 | 0.845036 | 3.063255 |
| 3 | 1096 | 3.625 | 0.81323 | 2.947957 |
| 3.5 | 1278 | 3.625 | | |
| 4 | 1462 | 103.625 | | |

The NPV of the swap must equal exactly zero if the cash flow on the spot date is included. Of the cashflows where the curve is available, the NPV is −80.5894. The complete equation is

$$df_{1278} \times 3.625 + df_{1462} \times 103.625 = 80.5894$$

This cannot be solved directly as there are two unknown discount factors. If we use our interpolation rule keeping the forward rate constant, then an iterative solution can be generated.[40]

This gives a solution for the forward rate of $r_{1096}^{1462} = 8.022778$ and discount factors $df_{1278} = 0.781339328$ and $df_{1462} = 0.750369643$. This solves the equation for the swap price above. This procedure is then repeated for all the other swaps.

| Instrument | Years[41] | Discount Factor | Continuous Forward Rate (% pa) | Continuous Zero Rate (% pa) |
|---|---|---|---|---|
| Spot | | 1.0000 | | |
| 1 Day Bill | 0.003 | 0.9998 | 5.9995 | 5.9995 |
| 30 Day Bill | 0.082 | 0.9951 | 5.9848 | 5.9853 |
| | | | | |
| Futures | 0.110 | 0.9935 | 5.9163 | 5.9680 |
| | 0.362 | 0.9787 | 5.9551 | 5.9590 |
| | 0.611 | 0.9641 | 6.0344 | 5.9898 |
| | 0.860 | 0.9491 | 6.2904 | 6.0769 |
| | 1.110 | 0.9336 | 6.5955 | 6.1934 |
| | 1.359 | 0.9178 | 6.8315 | 6.3105 |
| | 1.608 | 0.9019 | 6.9986 | 6.4172 |
| | 1.858 | 0.8860 | 7.1460 | 6.5150 |
| | 2.107 | 0.8701 | 7.2933 | 6.6071 |

---

[40]  Any common numerical method such as Newton-Raphson can be used.

[41]  Note that the number of years is not exactly integral for the swaps. This is because when this example was generated, it was assumed that there were 365 days per year. Exact calendar dates were used.

|        |        |        |        |        |
|--------|--------|--------|--------|--------|
|        | 2.356  | 0.8541 | 7.4111 | 6.6922 |
|        | 2.605  | 0.8383 | 7.5093 | 6.7703 |
|        | 2.855  | 0.8226 | 7.5976 | 6.8426 |
|        | 3.104  | 0.8069 | 7.7055 | 6.9119 |
|        | 3.501  | 0.7813 | 8.1037 | 7.0471 |
| 4y Swap | 4.005 | 0.7504 | 8.0228 | 7.1699 |
|        | 4.501  | 0.7223 | 7.6876 | 7.2269 |
| 5y Swap | 5.005 | 0.6948 | 7.6876 | 7.2733 |
|        | 5.501  | 0.6689 | 7.6782 | 7.3098 |
| 6y Swap | 6.005 | 0.6435 | 7.6782 | 7.3407 |
|        | 6.501  | 0.6190 | 7.8404 | 7.3789 |
| 7y Swap | 7.005 | 0.5950 | 7.8404 | 7.4121 |
|        | 7.504  | 0.5725 | 7.7330 | 7.4334 |
| 8y Swap | 8.008 | 0.5506 | 7.7330 | 7.4523 |
|        | 8.504  | 0.5295 | 7.8649 | 7.4763 |
| 9y Swap | 9.008 | 0.5089 | 7.8649 | 7.4981 |
|        | 9.504  | 0.4892 | 7.9816 | 7.5233 |
| 10y Swap | 10.008 | 0.4699 | 7.9816 | 7.5464 |

**Exhibit 5.41. The Complete Zero Coupon Curve**

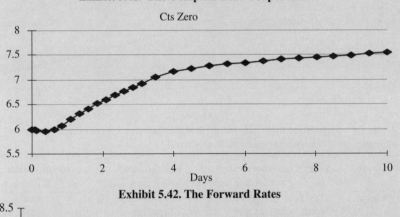

**Exhibit 5.42. The Forward Rates**

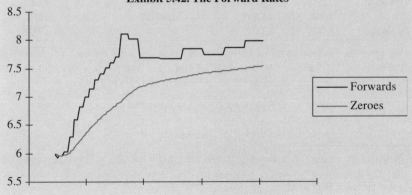

The graph showing the forward rates illustrates the interpolation method. The forward rates are stepped. They change discontinuously. Where there are frequent and liquid instruments (the bills and bill futures), the change is regular. Once the instruments become less liquid, there is some irregularity in these rates. The zero coupon rates are much smoother. It is rare that a long dated forward instrument will require pricing. If it does, the spread will have to be large to account for the irregularity in the forward rates. Alternatively an interpolation method where the forwards are kept smooth will need to be employed.

### 3. Obtaining Discount Factors

Once the curve has been generated, we have discount factors (and rates) at the points where cashflows from the underlying instruments occur. The curve will price these instruments. This in itself is not useful as the prices are already used in the curve construction. Indeed this is a circular situation. The value of the zero curve is in having a model which gives discount factors at any time in the future. To obtain these, we can either graphically retrieve them, or use the interpolation method implicit in the curve.

**Exhibit 5.43. The Discount Factors**

Discount Factors

Days

Using the interpolation method to obtain discount factors requires minor calculation. As an example, we will obtain the discount factor at 7.4 years.

| Instrument | Years[42] | Discount Factor | Continuous Forward Rate (% pa) | Continuous Zero Rate (% pa) |
|---|---|---|---|---|
| 7y Swap | 7.005 | 0.5950 | 7.8404 | 7.4121 |
| | 7.504 | 0.5725 | 7.7330 | 7.4334 |
| 8y Swap | 8.008 | 0.5506 | 7.7330 | 7.4523 |

We know the discount factor to 7.005 years. We also know that the forward rate for any period between 7.005 and 8.008 years is 7.7330% (as our interpolation method keeps the forward constant). We can obtain the discount factor from 7.005 to 7.4 years

$$\text{df}_{7.005}^{7.4} = e^{-0.07733t} = 0.969952$$

---

[42] Note that the number of years is not exactly integral for the swaps. This is because when this example was generated, it was assumed that there were 365 days per year. Exact calendar dates were used.

This then allows the discount factor and zero rate to be calculated.[43]

| Instrument | Years[44] | Discount Factor | Continuous Forward Rate (% pa) | Continuous Zero Rate (% pa) |
|---|---|---|---|---|
| 7y Swap | 7.005 | 0.5950 | 7.8404 | 7.4121 |
| **7.4y** | **7.4** | **0.577089** | **7.7330** | **7.429182** |
|  | 7.504 | 0.5725 | 7.7330 | 7.4334 |
| 8y Swap | 8.008 | 0.5506 | 7.7330 | 7.4523 |

Discount factors can be obtained to any dates by this process.

## 4. Pricing Cashflows

Arbitrary cashflows can now be valued by obtaining the discount factors to the dates where the cashflows occur. To price any instrument, decompose it into cashflows, then use this method. If there are liquidity or other conditions, the zero curve can be modified to account for these. Also the difference between market prices and the price on the curve can be calculated. This is useful to assess the premium or discount the market is building in to non-standard instruments. As an example, corporate bonds can be valued on a zero coupon curve built using Government bonds. The discount for credit liquidity and other factors can be quantified.

Source: Cohen, Roger "Constructing A Zero Coupon Curve" in Das, Satyajit (with Cohen, Roger) "Interest Rates and Yield Curve Modelling: An Introduction" in Satyajit (Editor) (1997) Risk Management & Financial Derivatives: A Guide to the Mathematics; LBC Information Services, Sydney; McGraw-Hill, Chicago; MacMillan Publishing, England at 84–93.

# 13   Summary

The pricing, valuation and trading of financial instruments, irrespective of whether it is a simple fixed income security or a derivative transaction, requires the availability of interest rate or discount factors extending across the maturity spectrum. In practice, the trader must choose between different interest rates to value these transactions. In practice, transaction cash flows are discounted using zero rates derived from the relevant yield curve. The zero rate itself requires the construction of the yield curve using mathematical techniques within a framework of economic

---

[43]   In this equation, t = 0.394520.

[44]   Note that the number of years is not exactly integral for the swaps. This is because when this example was generated, it was assumed that there were 365 days per year. Exact calendar dates were used.

theory that is consistent with observed interest rate behaviour. While the requirement for accurate zero rates is now recognised, deficiencies in market structure and data availability present significant challenges to the derivation of accurate, consistent and computationally efficient yield curves.

# 6
# Pricing Forward & Futures Contracts

## 1 Overview

The pricing of forwards follows the basic arbitrage free approach. The pricing of forwards is based on replicating the forward position through trading in the spot asset and a separate financing transaction. The process allows the forward price to be derived as the risk neutral price represented by the cost of the asset adjusted for the financing charges incurred. The process also enables the dealer to hedge a forward position assumed in trading. The process of hedging can be used to arbitrage price differences that may exist.

A forward contract can be replicated statically in theory; that is, the hedge does not need to be managed. However, in practice, estimation difficulties and market imperfections create complexities in forward pricing and hedging.

The pricing of forward contracts is required for the following purposes:
- Valuation and pricing of forward/futures contracts and instruments (such as swaps) constituted from forward contracts.
- Valuation of options as the option contract is generally on the underlying asset as at a future date (in effect, a forward price of the asset).

In this Chapter, the process of pricing forwards and futures contracts is examined. The structure of this Chapter is as follows:
- A generic forward pricing model is described.
- Specific forward pricing models covering different asset classes (currency, interest rates/debt instruments, equity and commodity) are outlined.
- The pricing of futures contracts, incorporating the effect of (uncertain) margin calls is considered.

# 2   Forward Pricing Approach – Carry Cost Model[1]

## 2.1   Carry Cost Model

The basic approach to pricing forwards is to replicate the forward position with a position in the underlying asset in the spot market, and finance the position. The forward price is the price of the asset adjusted for the financing charges. This model is known as the *cost of carry* model[2].

The basic carry cost model functions as follows[3]:

- Where a dealer enters into a forward sale of an asset, in order to hedge the risk of the position, the dealer must trade in the spot market. The dealer can replicate the forward sale by purchasing the asset in the spot market and holding it through to the forward date. On the forward date, the dealer delivers the asset to the forward buyer in return for payment of the agreed forward price. In establishing the hedge, the dealer incurs the cost of the asset and the cost of financing the asset[4]. Where the asset pays income, the dealer earns the income on the asset which offsets (in part or full) the financing cost of holding the asset. The arbitrage free forward price is therefore the cost of the asset adjusted for this financing (carry) cost.

- Where a dealer enters into a forward purchase of an asset, in order to hedge the risk of the position, the dealer must trade in the spot market. The dealer

---

[1]   For a discussion of the pricing of forward and futures contracts, see Martin, John (1996) Derivatives Maths; IFR Publishing, London at Chapters 4–7; Martin, John "Pricing Forwards and Futures Contracts" in Das, Satyajit (Editor) (1997) Risk Management & Financial Derivatives: A Guide to the Mathematics; LBC Information Services, Sydney; McGraw-Hill, Chicago; MacMillan Publishing, England at Chapter 4; Van Deventer, Donald R. and Imai, Kenji (1997) Financial Risk Analytics; Irwin, Chicago at Chapter 1; Hull, John (2000) Option Futures and Other Derivatives – Fourth Edition; Prentice-Hall Inc., Upper Saddle River, NJ at Chapter 3; Martin, John (2001) Applied Math for Derivatives; John Wiley & Sons, Singapore at Chapters 4 to 7. See also Kopprasch, Robert "Derivatives Valuation: Futures" (Fall 1994) Derivatives Quarterly 45–51.

[2]   This model is attributable to Working, Holbrook "The Theory of Price of Storage" (1949) American Economic Review 39 1254–1261; Working, Holbrook "A Theory of Anticipatory Prices" (1958) American Economic Review 48 188–199.

[3]   All examples are presented from the point of view of the dealer. This is for a number of reasons. In practice, counterparties transact through dealers who make markets in forward contracts. The dealer hedges exposures generated from transactions in the market as required. In addition, the process of pricing is symmetric and can be priced from the point of view of a counterparty using an identical logic.

[4]   Non-financial holding costs such as storage, important for commodities, are ignored. This is discussed later in the Chapter.

can replicate the forward purchase by selling the asset in the spot market. This entails a short sale where the dealer borrows the asset for the purpose of the short sale. The dealer holds the short position in the asset through to the forward date. On the forward date, the dealer purchases the asset from the forward seller and pays the agreed forward price. The asset received is then used to replace the asset to the original owner who lent the asset to the dealer for the purpose of the short sale. In establishing the hedge, the dealer receives the cash proceeds from the short sale that is then invested through to the forward date. Where the asset pays income, the dealer loses the income on the asset (the original owner of the asset must be compensated for the lost income on its asset). The lost income offsets (in part or full) the income received on the cash received from the short sale of the asset. The dealer may also incur borrowing charges on the borrowing of the asset for the purposes of the short sale. This would have the effect of reducing the income received by the dealer. The arbitrage free forward price is therefore the cost of the asset adjusted for this financing (carry) cost.

**Exhibit 6.1** and **Exhibit 6.2** set out the process undertaken by the dealer to hedge a forward position assumed. **Exhibit 6.3** sets out a numerical example of

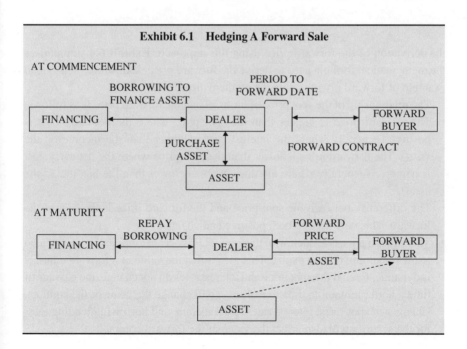

**Exhibit 6.1 Hedging A Forward Sale**

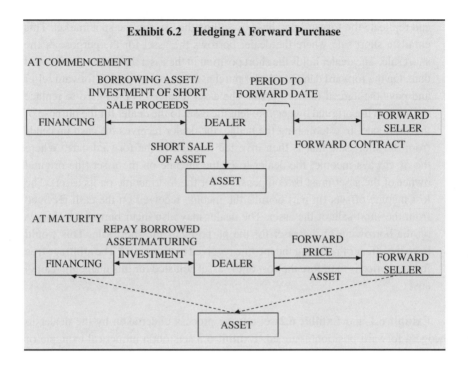

**Exhibit 6.2   Hedging A Forward Purchase**

the derivation of the forward price using this approach. **Exhibit 6.4** summarises the mathematical formula used to derive the forward price. **Exhibit 6.5** sets out an example of forward pricing using the mathematical formula.

The relationship of the spot price of the asset and the forward price is as follows:

- The forward price is greater than the spot price where the net carry cost is positive (generally where the interest cost is higher than the income on the asset). The forward price is lower than the spot price where the net carry cost is negative (generally where the interest cost is lower than the income on the asset).
- The difference between the spot price and the forward price is the cost of the forward. This cost may be both positive and negative.
- The forward price is a function of the time. This is because the carry cost is related to the remaining time to expiry. This means that the value of a forward contract is dynamic. Even if the spot price and interest rates do not change, the passage of time (shorter remaining time to maturity) will change the value of the contract. Changes in spot rates, interest rates, asset income and borrowing/lending rates for the security will also affect the value of the forward contract.

---

### Exhibit 6.3    Forward Pricing – Example 1

**1.  Assumptions**

Assume the following data:

| | |
|---|---|
| Asset: | Generic asset |
| Spot Price ($): | 100.00 |
| Term to Forward Date: | 1 year |
| Interest Rate (% pa): | 10.00 |

It is initially assumed that the asset pays no income. This assumption is amended later.

The above assumptions are utilised to derive the value of a forward contract – a forward sale and forward purchase.

**2.  Pricing A Forward Sale – No Income**

Assume the dealer enters into a forward sale. The dealer will hedge by purchasing the asset and financing the holding through to the forward date. The resulting cash flows ($) are summarised in the Table below:

| Transaction | Time ($t_0$ or spot) | Time ($t_1$ or forward date) |
|---|---|---|
| **Asset Transactions** | | |
| Purchase/sale of asset | −100 | +110 |
| **Financing Transactions** | | |
| Borrow/Repay Cash | +100 | −110 |
| **Net Cash Flows** | 0 | 0 |

The table illustrates that the arbitrage free forward price based on these assumptions would be $110 (effectively the spot cash price of the asset ($100) plus the financing cost ($10 calculated as $100 at 10.00% pa)).

**3.  Pricing A Forward Purchase – No Income**

Assume the dealer enters into a forward purchase. The dealer will hedge by short selling the asset and investing the proceeds through to the forward date. The resulting cash flows ($) are summarised in the Table below:

| Transaction | Time ($t_0$ or spot) | Time ($t_1$ or forward date) |
|---|---|---|
| **Asset Transactions** | | |
| Purchase/sale of asset | +100 | −110 |
| **Financing Transactions** | | |
| Investment of Cash | −100 | +110 |
| **Net Cash Flows** | 0 | 0 |

The table illustrates that the arbitrage free forward price based on these assumptions would be $110 (effectively the spot cash price of the asset ($100) plus the investment return ($10 calculated as $100 at 10.00% pa)).

Note that under the assumptions made both the forward sale and purchase have the same valuation. However, in practice, the asset will pay income and trading in the asset and borrowing/lending cash will result in transaction costs. In the following examples, asset income and transaction costs are incorporated in the analysis.

## 4.   Forward Pricing – Income Paying Asset

Assume the asset pays income of 5.00% pa. This can be incorporated into the analysis of the forward sale and forward purchase as follows:

- In the case of the forward purchase, the asset income ($5 calculated as $100 at 5.00% pa) is a cash inflow that has the effect of reducing the carry cost of holding the asset:

| Transaction | Time ($t_0$ or spot) | Time ($t_1$ or forward date) |
|---|---|---|
| **Asset Transactions** | | |
| Purchase/sale of asset | −100 | +105 |
| Asset Income | | +5 |
| **Financing Transactions** | | |
| Borrow/Repay Cash | +100 | −110 |
| **Net Cash Flows** | 0 | 0 |

- In the case of the forward sale, the asset income ($5 calculated as $100 at 5.00% pa) is a cash outflow (the lender of the asset for the short sale suffers a loss of income that must be compensated by the dealer) that has the effect of reducing the investment income from the investment of the proceeds of the short sale of the asset:

| Transaction | Time ($t_0$ or spot) | Time ($t_1$ or forward date) |
|---|---|---|
| **Asset Transactions** | | |
| Purchase/sale of asset | +100 | −105 |
| Asset Income | | −5 |
| **Financing Transactions** | | |
| Investment of Cash | −100 | +110 |
| **Net Cash Flows** | 0 | 0 |

## 5.   Pricing Incorporating Transaction Costs

In practice, trading in the asset, borrowing/lending cash and borrowing the security for the purposes of short selling will incur transaction costs. These costs must be incorporated in the pricing of the forward.

Assume the following data that now incorporates bid offer spreads:

| | |
|---|---|
| Spot Price ($): | 100.00/100.50 |
| Term to Forward Date: | 1 year |
| Interest Rate (% pa): | 10.00/10.125 |
| Asset income (% pa): | 5.00 |
| Commission/Transaction Tax (%): | 0.30 |
| Asset lending/borrowing cost (% pa): | 0.50/1.00 |

The forward prices generated are as follows:

| Forward | Purchase | Sale |
|---|---|---|
| **Price of Asset ($)** | 99.70 | 100.80 |
| **Carry Cost Adjustments ($)** | | |
| Funding Cost/Income | 9.97 | 10.21 |
| Asset Income/Payment | 5.00 | 5.00 |
| Asset Borrowing Cost/Lending Income | 1.00 | 0.50 |
| Net Carry Cost | 3.97 | 4.71 |
| **Forward Asset Price ($)** | 103.97 | 105.21 |
| **Cost of Forward ($)** | 3.97 | 4.71 |

Notes:
1. Price of the asset is calculated using the market bid or offer price at which the dealer is assumed to transact (buy at offer/sell at bid).
2. All asset transactions are assumed to incur commission expenses at the assumed commission rates.
3. All borrowing and lending is done at market rates.
4. Asset lending and asset borrowing is assumed to be done at market rates and based on the bid side of the market price.
5. Asset income is regarded as fixed at 5.00% pa of bid asset price.

---

**Exhibit 6.4    Forward Pricing – Formula[5]**

**1.   Discrete Time Models**
**1.1  Asset Paying No Income**

$$F = S \times (1 + r)^{t_1}$$

Where

$F$ = Forward price
$S$ = Spot asset price
$r$ = Interest rate for maturity $t_1$
$t_1$ = Maturity of forward contract

---

[5]   Please note that the pricing formula ignores non-interest holding costs. These are discussed in the context of commodity forwards later in the Chapter. Also care should be taken in using the formula because the mathematical formulation assumes all elements of the carry cost (interest cost, income, (if applicable) borrowing/lending fees, commissions etc) are proportionate to the spot asset price. This may or may not be the case (see **Exhibit 6.3**). If this does not hold true, then the rate of income, fees etc must be adjusted or the specific cash flows used to derive the forward price to avoid errors.

### 1.2 Asset Paying Known Income

$$F = S \times (1 + (r - y))^{t_1}$$

Where

F = Forward price
S = Spot asset price
r = Interest rate for maturity $t_1$
$t_1$ = Maturity of forward contract
y = income on asset over period to maturity of forward contract

Alternatively, the forward price can be calculated by adjusting the spot price of the asset by deducting the present value of the income as follows[6]:

$$F = S_{\text{ex-income}} \times (1 + r)^{t_1}$$

Where

F                = Forward price
S                = Spot asset price
$S_{\text{ex-income}}$ = $S - y/(1 + r)^{t_1}$
r                = Interest rate for maturity $t_1$
$t_1$            = Maturity of forward contract
y                = income on asset over period to maturity of forward contract

### 1.3 Value of Existing Forward (Asset Pays Known Income)

$$\text{Value of forward contract} = \Phi[S - F_{\text{contract}}/(1 + (r - y))^{t_1}]$$

Where

$F_{\text{contract}}$ = the contracted Forward price
$\Phi$                = binary variable set equal to 1 for a forward sale and $-1$ for forward purchase

All other parameters are as above.

### 2.   Continuous Time Model
### 2.1 Asset Paying Known Income

$$F = S \times e^{(r-y)t_1}$$

Where

F = Forward price
S = Spot asset price
R = Interest rate for maturity $t_1$ expressed as continuously compounded rates
$t_1$ = Maturity of forward contract
y = income on asset over period to maturity of forward contract
e = exponential term

---

[6]   See **Exhibit 6.26** for an example of this approach.

## 2.2 Value of Existing Forward

$$\text{Value of forward contract} = \Phi\left[S \times e^{-y \cdot t_1} - F_{contract} \times e^{-r \cdot t_1}\right]$$

Where

$F_{contract}$ = the contracted forward price

$\Phi$ = binary variable set equal to 1 for a forward sale and −1 for forward purchase

All other parameters are as above.

---

### Exhibit 6.5   Forward Pricing – Example 2[7]

#### 1.  Assumptions
Assume the following data:

| | |
|---|---|
| Spot Price ($): | 100.00 |
| Term to Forward Date: | 0.5 years |
| Interest Rate (% pa continuously compounded): | 5.00 |
| Asset income (% pa continuously compounded): | 0.00 |

The following prices/valuations utilise the continuously compounded model.

#### 2.  Forward Price
The forward price is:

$$F = 100 \times e^{.05 \times .5} = \$102.53$$

#### 3.  Valuation of Forward Contract
Assume the forward contract (entered into at $102.53) must be revalued at the following rates:

| | |
|---|---|
| Spot Price ($): | 101.00 |
| Term to Forward Date: | 0.1 year |
| Interest Rate (% pa continuously compounded): | 4.80 |
| Asset income (% pa continuously compounded): | 0.00 |

The value of the forward is given by:

$$\text{Value of forward position} = 101 - 102.53 \times e^{-.048 \times .1} = 101 - 102.04 = \$1.04$$

This represents a gain to a forward seller and a loss to the forward buyer of $1.04.

---

The basis for pricing the forward contract assumes that the dealer entering into the trade incurs no market risk. This is because the position in the forward is exactly matched by the position assumed in the spot market for the asset. This means that changes in the asset price results in gains and losses on the spot and forward position that exactly offset. This allows the forward price to be derived

---

[7]  For convenience, asset income and transaction costs have been ignored.

as the cost of the hedge (the spot price adjusted for the carry cost). The pricing assumes that there is no credit or default risk on the forward transaction. If credit risk is to be incorporated, then this is undertaken as a separate adjustment. The pricing approach makes a number of assumptions that in practice may be violated:

- **Ability to trade** – the model assumes the ability to freely trade in the underlying assets.
- **Short sales** – the model assumes (in the case of a forward purchase) the ability to short sell the asset. It also assumes the ability to borrow the asset for the purpose of short selling. It is assumed that the borrowing of the asset covers the full term of the forward contract and is at a known and fixed cost.
- **Financing** – the model assumes that the dealer can finance its holding of any asset at a known fixed cost (where the future value of the borrowing and lending is known with certainty – in effect, zero coupon rates).
- **Known income** – the model assumes that the income on the asset is known, fixed, accrues on a continuous basis and does not have any tax uncertainty.

## 2.2 Financing/Securities Borrowing

Financing asset positions is central to forward pricing. This reflects the fact that a key driver of forward prices is the financing cost/investment return (where the asset is bought or where the asset is sold short as a hedge) and the return/cost of lending out or borrowing assets required as a hedge. In practice, this means that the process of forward pricing is closely related to the repurchase and securities borrowing markets (known collectively as the repo markets). Appendix A to this Chapter sets out a discussion of the structure and functioning of the repo markets.

This has two implications for forward pricing:

- The financing cost to be utilised.
- The ability to borrow the assets required to short sell for hedging purposes.

In practice, the cost of financing is related to the *individual borrower* and its credit quality. This means that theoretically each borrower would derive forward prices that are different, based on the specific borrowing cost of each entity. However, in practice, a homogenous rate is utilised to create a *market* forward rate. This rate is either of the following rates:

- **Implied repo rate**[8] – that is, the rate at which the underlying asset can be sold and re-purchased to create a secured or collateralised borrowing[9].

---

[8] See Hull, John (2000) Option Futures and Other Derivatives – Fourth Edition; Prentice-Hall Inc., Upper Saddle River, NJ at 664.

[9] As the asset secures the borrowing, the rate applicable should be the same, irrespective of the credit quality of the borrowing entity.

- **Zero rate** – in the absence of a repo rate (for example, where a repo market in the asset is not available or lacking in liquidity), the derived zero rate for the maturity[10].

The issues with borrowing an asset for the purposes of short selling are more complex. In practice, there are a number of barriers to short selling, including:

- **Regulatory factors** – it may be illegal to short sell assets under the law or regulations applicable in the relevant jurisdiction.
- **Credit risk** – the lender of the asset would, in the absence of any form of credit enhancement, incur a credit exposure equal to the face value of the asset to the borrower of the asset. However, in practice, the lender will seek collateral in the form of the cash received by the borrower from the sale of the asset. This cash is held as security against the future obligation to replace the asset lent at the end of the borrowing term[11]. However, the price of the asset is liable to fluctuations and the lender is exposed to the *forward* price of the asset. The lender will seek a collateral amount *exceeding* the value of the asset at the time of entry into this transaction. This amount (referred to as the *haircut*) is set at a percentage of the asset value. This means that the full proceeds of the short sale may not be available to the short seller.
- **Length of borrowing assets** – the lender of the asset will typically only lend the asset for relatively short periods of time (overnight to a few weeks)[12]. The cost of borrowing assets also rises sharply with the term of the borrowing. This reflects the lender's loss of flexibility in dealing with the asset where it has been lent out to a third party. This creates difficulties for dealers seeking to borrow the asset for a term matching the maturity of the forward contract (where this is longer than the term of the typical asset borrowing). Inability to borrow the asset for the requisite term makes it difficult to maintain the short position (that is, the ability to re-borrow the asset at the maturity of any borrowing arrangement) or uncertainty about the cost of the borrowing.

---

[10]  This equates to about an A/AA rated credit inter-bank transaction; see Chapters 5 and 11. In theory, the risk free rate should be used. However, in practice, for the dealer the risk free rate is not relevant. This reflects the fact that the dealer generally will not be able to borrow at the risk free rate. This means in practice, the repo or swap (effectively the inter-bank rate) is utilised.

[11]  This is the structure used in the repo market for borrowing an asset for short selling.

[12]  It is important to note that the borrowing may be for a short term although it may be renewed or rolled at maturity. However, the short term creates uncertainty about the ability to maintain the short and the cost of borrowing the asset.

- **Cost of borrowing assets** – the charge for borrowing the asset can vary depending upon the supply and demand for the asset. Where the demand for borrowing the asset exceeds supply, the price of borrowing can increase sharply[13]. This creates problems for dealers seeking to quantify the cost of a hedge, as the combination of short maturity of the borrowing and the uncertainty of cost makes the cost of maintaining a short over a longer time frame difficult to estimate.

- **Accounting and taxation factors** – the accounting and tax treatment of repo agreements varies between jurisdictions. The repo transaction may be treated as a sale and re-purchase of an asset. This may have the effect of triggering accounting and/or tax gains or losses. This may not be acceptable to the party lending the asset. Similarly, where the asset pays income that has tax implications (tax credit or withholding tax), the tax incidents of the income may dictate the ability or willingness of a party to lend the asset or the cost of lending the asset[14]. These factors have the ability to significantly affect the supply and demand for assets in the repo markets. This creates additional uncertainty and risks in the ability to borrow and short sell assets.

The barriers to short selling may create difficulties in establishing and maintaining hedges required by entry into forward purchases. The difficulties must be incorporated into the cost of the hedge and the forward price. This, in turn, affects the pricing of forward contracts and the ability to arbitrage to force price equilibrium.

## 2.3   Cash-Forward Arbitrage[15]

Price equilibrium in forward markets is established by arbitrage. There are two forms of arbitrage:

- **Cash and carry** – this entails the arbitrageur taking advantage of a forward price above the theoretical or equilibrium forward price. This is done by buying the

---

[13]   In the US Treasury bond market, dealers often short existing on-the-run bonds against purchase orders in the new issued bonds during the auction period to roll their inventory into the new on-the-run bonds. During this period, on occasion, the demand for borrowing a security may far exceed the availability of stock available for lending. This means that the cost of borrowing can increase sharply (the bond is said to be "on special"). The cost of borrowing can substantially erode the earnings on the cash proceeds of the short itself.

[14]   This is particularly important in equity markets.

[15]   For a discussion of cash futures arbitrage, see Jones, Frank J. "The Integration of Cash and Futures Markets for Treasury Securities" (1981) The Journal of Futures Markets vol 1 no 1 33–57.

asset and financing the asset through to the forward date (effectively, a synthetic forward purchase) against a simultaneous sale of the asset at the high forward price to lock in an arbitrage profit.

- **Reverse cash and carry** – this entails the arbitrageur taking advantage of a forward price below the theoretical or equilibrium forward price. This is done by short selling the asset and investing the proceeds through to the forward date (effectively, a synthetic forward sale) against a simultaneous purchase of the asset at the low forward price to lock in an arbitrage profit.

In each case, the action of the arbitrageur should force the price of the spot asset and the forward contract into equilibrium.

**Exhibit 6.6** sets out the process of arbitrage. **Exhibit 6.7** sets out the process of arbitrage in a diagrammatic form.

Several aspects of cash-forward arbitrage require comment:

- **"Fair" price** – the process of arbitrage results generally in the forward price adjusting to a level that eliminates arbitrage possibilities. However, it does not necessarily return to its prior equilibrium price level. This is because the concept of forward price has no significance outside the arbitrage model. In effect, the *fair* value of the forward is only the outcome of a set of market variables at a given point in time. The equilibrium forward price is the price outcome that offers no risk free arbitrage opportunities.
- **Arbitrage in the presence of transaction costs** – where there are transaction costs (in practice this will generally be the case) then the spread between the bid and offer forward price defines the arbitrage possibilities. In effect, as long as the forward price stays within a range, then there is no available arbitrage reflecting the fact that the transaction costs prevent arbitrage. This is referred to as the arbitrage "gate".

---

| Exhibit 6.6    Cash Forward Arbitrage – Example |
|---|

**1. Cash and Carry Arbitrage**[16]

Assume the following data:

| | |
|---|---|
| Asset: | Generic asset |
| Spot Price ($): | 100.00 |
| Term to Forward Date: | 1 year |
| Interest Rate (% pa): | 10.00 |
| Asset Income (% pa): | 5.00 |

---

[16] For convenience, the calculations ignore transaction costs, costs or returns of lending or borrowing assets and commissions.

This would equate to a *theoretical* forward price of $105.00. However, assume that the forward market is not in equilibrium and the forward is trading at $107.00. This enables the construction of a cash and carry arbitrage as follows:
- The dealer enters into the following transactions simultaneously:
  1. Purchase the asset
  2. Borrow to finance the asset through to the forward date.
  3. Sell the forward contract.
- At maturity, the dealer delivers the asset purchased into the sold forward contract to close out the forward position.

The cash flows from the series of transactions are set out in the table below:

| Transaction | Time ($t_0$ or spot) | Time ($t_1$ or forward date) |
|---|---|---|
| **Asset Transactions** | | |
| Purchase/sale of asset | −100 | +107 |
| Asset Income | | +5 |
| **Financing Transactions** | | |
| Borrow/Repay Cash | +100 | −110 |
| **Net Cash Flows** | 0 | +2 |

The $2 represents a risk free (ignoring any counterparty credit risk on the transactions) profit for the arbitrageur. This is likely to attract a large number of arbitrageurs and capital to this arbitrage opportunity. This will result in the market moving to equilibrium as follows:
- The spot price may rise as increased buying takes place.
- The cost of finance may increase as there is increased demand for funds.
- The forward price may fall as increased selling takes place.

Generally, a combination of the above will move the market towards an equilibrium price. Assume the following movements in market parameters:

Spot Price ($):          101.00
Term to Forward Date:   1 year
Interest Rate (% pa):     10.50
Asset income (% pa):     5.00

The *new* equilibrium forward price generated is as follows:

| | Forward Price |
|---|---|
| **Price of Asset ($)** | 101.00 |
| **Carry Cost Adjustments ($)** | |
| Funding Cost | −10.61 |
| Asset Income | +5.00 |
| Net Carry Cost | 5.61 |
| **Forward Asset Price ($)** | 106.61 |

Assume that the forward price adjusts to $106.61 to eliminate arbitrage opportunities.

## 2. Reverse Cash and Carry Arbitrage

Assume the following data:

| | |
|---|---|
| Asset: | Generic asset |
| Spot Price ($): | 100.00 |
| Term to Forward Date: | 1 year |
| Interest Rate (% pa): | 10.00 |
| Asset Income (% pa): | 5.00 |

This would equate to a *theoretical* forward price of $105.00. However, assume that the forward market is not in equilibrium and the forward is trading at $103.00. This enables the construction of a reverse cash and carry arbitrage as follows:
- The dealer enters into the following transactions simultaneously:
  1. Short sell the asset
  2. Invest the proceeds of the asset through to the forward date.
  3. Buy the forward contract.
- At maturity, the dealer purchases the asset under the forward contract to close out the asset borrowing position.

The cash flows from the series of transactions are set out in the table below:

| Transaction | Time ($t_0$ or spot) | Time ($t_1$ or forward date) |
|---|---|---|
| **Asset Transactions** | | |
| Purchase/sale of asset | +100 | −103 |
| Asset Income | | −5 |
| **Financing Transactions** | | |
| Investment of Cash | −100 | +110 |
| **Net Cash Flows** | 0 | +2 |

The $2 represents a risk free (ignoring any counterparty credit risk on the transactions) profit for the arbitrageur. This is likely to attract a large number of arbitrageurs and capital to this arbitrage opportunity. This will result in the market moving to equilibrium as follows:
- The spot price may fall as increased selling takes place.
- The investment return available may decrease as there is increased demand for investments.
- The forward price may increase as increased buying takes place.

Generally, a combination of the above will move the market towards an equilibrium price. Assume the following movements in market parameters:

| | |
|---|---|
| Spot Price ($): | 99.00 |
| Term to Forward Date: | 1 year |
| Interest Rate (% pa): | 9.50 |
| Asset income (% pa): | 5.00 |

The *new* equilibrium forward price generated is as follows:

|                                | Forward Price |
|--------------------------------|:-------------:|
| **Price of Asset ($)**         |     99.00     |
| **Carry Cost Adjustments ($)** |               |
| Investment Return              |     +9.41     |
| Asset Income                   |     −5.00     |
| Net Carry Cost                 |      4.41     |
| **Forward Asset Price ($)**    |    103.41     |

Assume that the forward price adjusts to $103.41 to eliminate arbitrage opportunities.

**Exhibit 6.7    Cash-Forward Arbitrage**

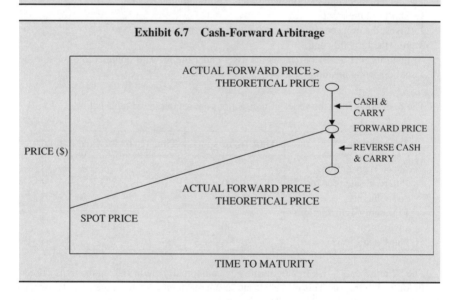

The process of arbitrage described is critical to the achievement of an equilibrium forward price. In practice, the (potential) restriction on shorting assets means that it is easier to undertake a cash and carry arbitrage transaction than a reverse cash and carry transaction (that requires short selling). This means that in practice the forward price may trade with a bias relative to the theoretical forward price.

## 2.4   Forward Prices – Behaviour

### 2.4.1   Cash-Forward Convergence

A central feature of the behaviour of forward prices is the process of convergence. This describes the phenomenon where the forward price converges to the price

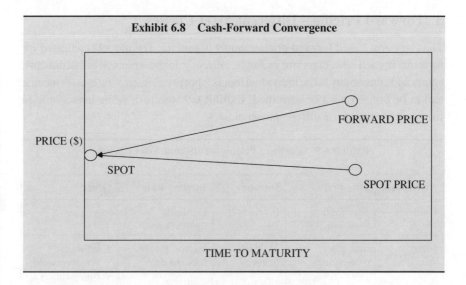

Exhibit 6.8    Cash-Forward Convergence

PRICE ($)

FORWARD PRICE

SPOT

SPOT PRICE

TIME TO MATURITY

of the spot asset at maturity of the forward. This reflects the fact that at maturity, the forward contract is equivalent to a spot position in the asset. Lack of convergence would create arbitrage opportunities. **Exhibit 6.8** describes the process of convergence.

### 2.4.2   Forward Prices and the Expected Spot Price

The relationship of the forward price to the *expected* and *actual* spot price at maturity is complex. The forward price is the arbitrage free price that can be established and hedged through the process of replication. It does not have any other relationship to the expected forward price or the actual spot price at maturity. It is common to assume that the forward price is an unbiased estimator of the expected forward price[17]. However, a number of structured products are focused on seeking to benefit from the expected differences between *implied* (arbitrage free) forward rates and *expected actual* forward rates[18].

---

[17]  For a discussion of the evidence, see Hull, John (2000) Option Futures and Other Derivatives – Fourth Edition; Prentice-Hall Inc., Upper Saddle River, NJ at 74–76 (and the references cited therein); see also Howard, Charles T. "Are T-Bill Futures Good Forecasters of Interest Rates?" (1982) Journal of Futures Markets vol 1 no 4 305–315; Peijan, Achim and Gemperle, Albert "The German Yield Curve as a Forecasting Instrument" (1994) Swiss Bank Corporation/Prospects 3 5–7.

[18]  For example, see Das, Satyajit (2004) Structured Products Volume 1; John Wiley & Sons (Asia), Singapore at Chapters 14, 15, 16, 17, 18 and 19.

## 3   Forward Pricing – Different Asset Classes

The carry cost based forward pricing model is generic. The model is adjusted for forwards in each asset class (for example, currency, interest rates/debt instruments, equity and commodity). The individual inputs (spot price, interest rate, asset income etc) to be utilised must be identified. **Exhibit 6.9** summarises the inputs utilised for pricing forwards on different asset classes.

<table>
<tr><td colspan="5">Exhibit 6.9   Forward Pricing – Different Asset Classes</td></tr>
<tr><th>Asset Class</th><th>Spot Price</th><th>Income</th><th>Interest Rate[19]</th><th>Other</th></tr>
<tr><td>Currency</td><td>Spot foreign exchange rate</td><td>Foreign interest rate</td><td>Domestic interest rate</td><td></td></tr>
<tr><td>Interest rates/debt</td><td>Spot price of securities</td><td>Yield to maturity</td><td>Interest rate to forward date</td><td>• Either use prices or yields<br>• Borrowing cost for securities (for short sales)</td></tr>
<tr><td>Equity</td><td>Spot stock price</td><td>Dividend</td><td>Interest rate in currency of stock</td><td>• Borrowing cost for securities (for short sales)</td></tr>
<tr><td>Commodity</td><td>Spot commodity price</td><td>Convenience yield (asset lease rate)</td><td>Interest rate (US$ or commodity currency)</td><td>• Holding costs</td></tr>
</table>

## 4   Forward Pricing – Foreign Exchange/Currency Contracts

### 4.1   Currency Forward Pricing[20]

The pricing of currency forward contracts is concerned with pricing short and long dated currency forward contracts. In addition, currency swaps can be decomposed into a portfolio of forward currency contracts and priced off the forward

---

[19]  Please note all interest rates used are assumed to be zero coupon rates for the relevant maturity.

[20]  See Riehl, Heinz and Rodriguez, Rita M. (1977) Foreign Exchange and Money Markets; McGraw-Hill, New York at Chapters 2, 3 and 5; Brown, Brendan (1983) The Forward Market in Foreign Exchange; Croon Helm, London; (August 1983) Foreign Exchange and Money Market Operations; Swiss Bank Corporation at 60–79; Antl, Boris "Pricing the Hedge to Cut the Cost" (May 1983) Euromoney 230–233; Anthony, Steve (1989) Foreign Exchange in Practice; The Law Book Company, Sydney at Chapter 7 and 9;

currency contracts. The other major form of currency forwards is futures contracts on currencies.

Pricing of currency forwards is based on the carry cost model. The spot foreign exchange rate is adjusted for the carry cost – defined as the difference between the interest cost (the interest rate in the domestic currency) and the income on the asset (the interest rate in the foreign currency). The carry cost equates to the interest rate differential between the two currencies. This approach is often referred to as the interest parity theorem or covered interest arbitrage.

The pricing logic follows the underlying process by which the forward currency position can be replicated using currency transactions and money market transactions. This can be illustrated with an example. Assume a forward purchase of yen against a sale of US$ for value in 1 year. This forward can be replicated as follows:

• For value spot date, enter into the following transactions:
    1. Borrow US$ for 1 year term at US$1 year interest rates.
    2. Enter into a spot transaction to convert the US$ into yen at the spot FX rate.
    3. Place the yen on deposit for 1 year at yen interest rates.

• As at forward date, the spot transactions have the following cash flow consequences:
    1. The US$ borrowing must be repaid (both principal borrowed and interest to be paid).
    2. The yen deposit matures releasing cash (both the principal invested and interest accrued).

The cash flow at the forward date is equivalent to the cash flow under a normal forward. This means that under standard no-arbitrage conditions, the equilibrium forward price must be equal to the future values of the yen deposit and the US$ borrowing. The relationship of the future values is driven by the interest rate differential between the currencies. **Exhibit 6.10** sets out the relationship underlying the currency forward pricing model.

The process described can be presented in a different but equivalent manner using the argument of synthetic assets or liabilities combining spot and forward currency transactions and borrowing/lending transactions in the underlying currencies. For example, in the above example, a yen 1 year deposit is exactly the same

Modest, David "Currency Forwards and Futures" in Antl., Boris (Editor) (1989) Management of Currency Risk: Volume 1; Euromoney Publications, London at Chapter 24; DeRosa, David F. "Forwards and Futures Contracts on Foreign Exchange" (Fall 1994) Derivatives Quarterly 24–30; Martin, John (2001) Applied Math for Derivatives; John Wiley & Sons, Singapore at Chapter 6.

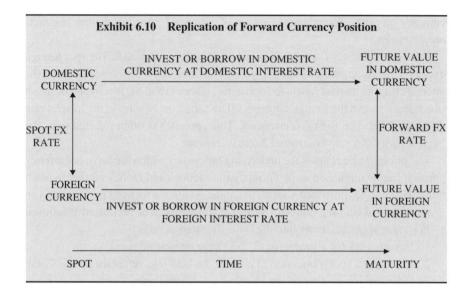

**Exhibit 6.10    Replication of Forward Currency Position**

as a 1 year US$ investment of an equivalent yen amount (calculated at the spot rate between US$ and yen) at the US$ interest rate where the US$ is hedged. This is the case where the future value (principal plus accrued interest) on the US$ deposit is fully hedged back through a yen/US$ forward (sell US$/buy yen) entered into at the time the US$ was placed on deposit at the commencement of the transaction. This reflects the fact the US$ investment cash flows are fully hedged back into yen, and there is only exposure to yen, not to US$. As the two transactions are equivalent (both are yen deposits) the yield on both transactions should be identical. This means the currency forward rate must adjust for the interest rate differential between the currencies.

In pricing currency forwards, it is traditional to differentiate between short dated (less than 1 year) forwards and longer dated transactions (referred to as LTFX (long term foreign exchange) (greater than 1 year in maturity)). The underlying valuation approach is similar in the two instruments. However, there are some differences in pricing approach, hedging and the risk of the two types of transactions.

## 4.2   Pricing Short Dated FX/Currency Forwards

The basis of utilising interest rate differentials to price forward currency contracts is based upon the concept of arbitrage between various foreign exchange and money markets. This approach predicts that the returns obtainable in any particular currency sold in the forward markets against a base currency would normally be equal to those obtainable in the base currency. If discrepancies occur, then opportunities for risk free profit exist and are quickly exploited by market participants. The process of arbitrage forces the forward rates on currencies to reflect the interest rate differential between the respective currencies[21]. **Exhibit 6.11** sets out an example of forward currency pricing based on arbitrage between foreign exchange and money markets. **Exhibit 6.12** sets out the formula used to derive the value of a currency forward.

In pricing currency forwards, it is necessary to specify the domestic currency and foreign currency carefully. This reflects the fact that currency rates may be quoted in the following formats:

- **Direct quotation** – foreign currency units per unit of US$ e.g. US$1 = Yen 105.00. Most currencies are quoted in this manner.
- **Indirect quotation** – US$ per unit of foreign currency e.g. Euro 1 = US$1.10. US$/Euro, US$/Sterling, US$/A$ and US$/NZ$ are quoted in this manner.

The importance of this specification is in identifying the correct domestic and foreign currencies to derive the forward rates.

---

**Exhibit 6.11    Pricing Short Dated Currency Forwards – Example**

**1.  Assumptions**
Assume the following rates and prices:

| | |
|---|---|
| Spot Rate: | US$1 = Yen 105.00 |
| Forward Maturity: | 1 year |
| 1 year US$ Interest Rate: | 6.50% pa |
| 1 year Yen Interest Rate: | 3.00% pa |

The above information is used by the trader to calculate a 1 year forward price for US$ against yen.

All rates are assumed to be annual effective rates calculated on an actual/365 day basis. For convenience, bid-offer spreads are ignored for the purposes of the calculation. The bid-offer spreads can be incorporated in the calculation by using the appropriate rates for buying or selling the currency and borrowing/lending funds as appropriate in the relevant currencies.

**2.   Pricing Using Arbitrage Between Foreign Exchange and Money Markets**
Traders are faced with two choices:
- An investment of US$1 million yielding 6.50% pa.
- An investment in Yen 105 million (US$1 million converted at the spot rate of US$1 = Yen 105) investment yielding 3.00% pa.

---

[21] In some cases, a currency forward may be transacted at off-market rates to *roll over* exchange rate gains and losses into the price of the contract. These structures (known as *historic rate rollovers*) are discussed in Das, Satyajit (2004) Structured Products Volume 1; John Wiley & Sons (Asia), Singapore at Chapter 13.

The different amount of initial investment reflects the current spot exchange rate between A$ and US$ at which the relevant currencies could be exchanged for each other to provide the initial investment capital.

The two investments respectively provide a final termination value reflecting the return of principal plus interest earned of US$1,065,000 and Yen 108,150,000 respectively. The forward US$/Yen rate is the rate that equates the two future values. This implies a forward exchange rate of US$1 = Yen 101.55 or a Yen premium on spot of Yen 3.45.

In practice, currencies with lower interest rates relative to the other currencies in the relevant currency paid will trade at a premium to the spot rate (designed to equate the effective interest return). Conversely, currencies with higher interest rates relative to the other currencies in the relevant currency pair will trade at a discount to the spot rate.

This discount or premium equates the effective interest rate differential between the two markets. If the forward exchange rate does not reflect the existing interest rate differential, then the opportunity exists for borrowing in one currency with a simultaneous investment in another to yield an arbitrage profit.

The cash flows are summarised in the Table below:

| Spot Date | Time Period = 1 year | Forward Date |
|---|---|---|
| US$1,000,000 Converted at Spot Rate of US$ 1 = Yen 105 ↓ Yen 105,000,000 | Invested at 6.50% pa → Invested at 3.00% pa → | US$1,065,0000 Yen 108,150,000 |
| Spot Rate (US$1) | | 1 year Forward Rate (US$1) |
| Yen 105 | | Yen 101.5493 ↑ (Calculated as Yen 108,150,000/US$1,065,000) |

### 3. Currency/Money Market Arbitrage

If the forward exchange rate prevailing in the market for 1 year was US$1 = Yen 101.00, then it would be profitable to borrow US$1 million, sell the currency spot for Yen 105 million and lodge the Yen in an investment yielding 3.00% pa. The proceeds of the investment, both principal and interest (Yen 108,150,000), would be sold forward for value in 1 year at the market forward rate of US$1 = Yen 101. This series of transactions would provide the investor with an effective US$ termination value of US$1,070,792, (calculated as Yen 108,150,000 converted at the locked in forward rate of US$1 = Yen 101). This represents an increase of US$5,792 (US$1,070,792 versus US$1,065,000) on a direct US$ investment or an effective yield of 7.08% pa that is significantly higher than the current market yield for US$ investment of 6.50% pa.

The potential arbitrage profit would encourage traders to undertake the transaction described. This would drive the market towards an equilibrium forward exchange rate. The increased supply of Yen for 1 year investment, increased demand for 1 year US$ borrowings and increased forward selling of Yen against US$ would force the US$ and Yen interest rates and forward exchange rate to adjust until the arbitrage opportunity was eliminated.

## 4. Implied Interest Rates

The process of deriving forward rates can be used to derive the *implied* interest rate in a particular currency[22]. The process can be illustrated with an example. Assume that in the above example, the Yen interest rate for 1 year is not known. The following data is available:

Spot Rate:                          US$1 = Yen 105.00
1 year forward rate:                US$1 = Yen 99.25
1 year US$ Interest Rate:           6.50% pa

The forward rate would be derived using the cash flows summarised in the Table below:

| Spot Date | Time Period = 1 year | Forward Date |
|---|---|---|
| US$1,000,000 Converted at Spot Rate of US$1 = Yen 105 ↓ Yen 105,000,000 | Invested at 6.50% pa → | US$1,065,0000 |
| | Invested at x% pa → | Yen 105,701,250 ↑ (Calculated as US$1,065,000 converted at Yen 99.25) |
| **Spot Rate (US$1)** Yen 105 | | **1 year Forward Rate (US$1)** Yen 99.25 |

This known investment of Yen 105 million and a given future value of Yen 105,701,250 in 1 year enables the derivation of the implied interest rate in yen for 1 year of 0.67% pa.

---

### Exhibit 6.12    Currency Forward Pricing Formula

### 1. Currency Forward Pricing Formula

For directly quoted currencies (i.e. US$1 =) the forward rate is calculated as follows[23]:

$$F_{t_1} = S_{t_0} \times [((1 + r_f)^{t_1})/((1 + r_{US\$})^{t_1})]$$

---

[22] This process is significant in certain emerging markets lacking well developed money markets. Implied interest rates derived from available market foreign exchange rates are used as a money market benchmark rate. This rate is used in settling derivative transactions such as FRAs, swaps and caps/floors in those currencies (see Chapter 3). This rate may also be used to construct yield curves for valuation (see Chapter 5).

[23] Note that the pricing is based on compounded interest rates. For short dated transactions (less than 6 months), simple interest calculations are frequently used to derive the forward

Where

$F_{t_1}$ = Forward currency rate at time $t_1$
$S_{t_0}$ = Spot currency rate at time $t_0$
$r_f$ = zero coupon interest rate in foreign currency for maturity $t_1$
$r_{US\$}$ = zero coupon interest rate in US\$ for maturity $t_1$
$t_0$ = spot date
$t_1$ = time to maturity of forward contract expressed as number of days $(t_1 - t_0)/365$
or 360 days

For indirectly quoted currencies (i.e. 1 Foreign currency unit = US\$), the forward rate is calculated as follows:

$$F_{t_1} = S_{t_0} \times [((1 + r_{US\$})^{t_1})/((1 + r_f)^{t_1})]$$

Where all parameters are as defined above.

### 2. Example
Two examples using the above formula are set out below:

| Base Currency | | US\$ | | A\$ |
|---|---|---|---|---|
| Foreign Currency | | Yen | | US\$ |
| Quotation Convention | | Direct | | Indirect |
| Spot Price | Yen | 105.00 | US\$ | 0.7200 |
| Value Date | | 31-Dec-02 | | 31-Dec-02 |
| Maturity Date | | 30-Jun-03 | | 30-Jun-03 |
| Term (days) | | 181 | | 181 |
| Interest Rate – (% pa) | US\$ | 6.000% | US\$ | 6.000% |
| Interest Rate – (% pa) | Yen | 1.675% | A\$ | 7.500% |
| Day Count Basis (either 360 or 365) | | 360 | | 365 |
| Forward Rate | Yen | 102.82 | A\$ | 0.7150 |
| Cost of Forward (Premium/Discount) | | −2.18 | | −0.0050 |

---

rate as follows:

(For direct quotation currencies) $F_{t_1} = S_{t_0} \times [(1 + r_f \times t_1)/(1 + r_{US\$} \times t_1)]$

For short maturities (because of the minimal impact of compounding), there will be minimal difference between the two approaches. However, for longer maturities, there will be significant differences between the two techniques. It is preferable to use the compounding techniques for all forwards.

## 4.3  Pricing LTFX Contracts[24]

### 4.3.1  Pricing Approaches

The model that traders exploit arbitrage opportunities for risk-free profit holds for short-term forward exchange contracts (contracts up to 1 year in most markets). This is particularly the case in freely convertible currencies where there are well-developed money markets. This is especially the case when international markets in the relevant currencies also exist. International markets are unregulated and outside the control of national authorities. This means that the markets are efficient. Under these conditions, arbitrage forces forward rates to reflect the interest rate differentials between currencies. However, for LTFX contracts, arbitrage is more difficult. LTFX rates do not necessarily reflect the activity of arbitrageurs between the various capital and foreign exchange markets.

The failure of arbitrage at longer maturities reflects a variety of factors:

- **Higher transaction costs** – this makes it difficult for market participants to undertake long-term arbitrage because of the higher costs involved. The costs include balance sheet holding costs for assets incurred in the process of arbitrage, as well as the commitment of credit lines for extended periods of time.
- **Ability to borrow/lend on a zero coupon basis for the term** – a factor impeding arbitrage is the difficulty in locating securities or investments that are required for the arbitrage process. The securities or investments required must have particular cash flow characteristics, that is, they must have a *known terminal value* of the investment or borrowing cost (that is zero coupon rates). In the case of short-term forward exchange contracts, the availability of zero coupon instruments means that the terminal value of the investment or the cost of the borrowing is known in advance. However, where this simple one payment, one period situation is replaced by either a single payment, multi-period situation, or alternatively a multi-period, multi-payment situation, the process of determining the terminal value of the investment becomes more complex.

In practice, the problem of guaranteed future value instruments is overcome by the use of zero coupon swap rates. This transforms the problem into a problem

---

[24] See Hilley, John L., Beidleman, Carl R., and Greenleaf, James A. "Why There Is No Long Forward Market in Foreign Exchange" (January 1981) Euromoney 94–103; Beidleman, Carl R., Hilley, John L., and Greenleaf, James A. "Alternatives in Hedging Long Date Contractual Foreign Exchange Exposure" (Summer 1983) Sloan Management Review 45–54.

of the derivation and hedging of the zero coupon rate curve. The problem of transaction costs is not as readily overcome. This dictates that LTFX markets are less efficient. LTFX prices approximate interest differentials but may exhibit larger bid offer spreads (that is higher transaction costs), reflecting the difficulty of arbitrage.

The difficulties and higher cost of hedging LTFX contracts mean that traders are less willing to trade in the absence of a similar matching or offsetting counterparty. This means that LTFX forward prices reflect the supply and demand for the currency at the forward dates. Short dated forwards reflect the fully arbitraged prices governed by prevailing interest rate differentials between the relevant currencies.

In practice, LTFX contracts are priced using an identical approach to short dated forward contracts. The rates used are the zero coupon swap rates in the relevant currencies for the appropriate maturity.

There are a number of other ways in which the LTFX contract may be priced and hedged. The most important approaches include:
- Zero coupon currency swap method.
- Fully arbitraged cash flow method.

### 4.3.2 Long Dated FX/Currency Forwards – Priced As Currency Swaps

LTFX transactions can be equated to fixed-to-fixed zero coupon currency swaps and priced accordingly. **Exhibit 6.13** sets out an example of structuring and pricing a LTFX transaction as a fixed-to-fixed zero coupon currency swap.

---

**Exhibit 6.13    Pricing LTFX as Zero Coupon Swaps**

**1.   Assumptions**
Assume the swap entails payments based on the following rates:

| | |
|---|---|
| Spot Rate (A$1 = US$) | 0.7000 |
| US$ Swap Rate | 6.00% |
| A$ Swap Rate | 10.00% |

Assuming an A$ notional principal of A$100, under a normal fixed to fixed currency swap, this would entail the following case flows:
- Initial and final exchange of principal of A$100 and US$70.
- Payment of US$4.20 annually in exchange for payments of A$7.

## 2. Cash Flows – Conventional Currency Swap

The cash flows are set out in the Table below:

| Year | A$ Cash Flows | US$ Cash Flows |
|------|---------------|----------------|
| 0 | 100.00 | −70.00 |
| 1 | −10.00 | 4.20 |
| 2 | −10.00 | 4.20 |
| 3 | −10.00 | 4.20 |
| 4 | −10.00 | 4.20 |
| 5 | −110.00 | 74.20 |

## 3. Cash Flows – Zero Coupon Currency Swaps

In the case of the zero coupon swap structure, intermediate cash flows are replaced with a single cash flow on maturity. The intermediate A$ payments of A$10 are assumed to be compounded at the swap rate of 10.00% pa to give a maturity value of A$161.05, reflecting compounded interest together with the repayment of the original principal received under the swap. Similarly, the intermediate US$ cash flows are compounded at the swap rate of 6.00% pa, giving a maturity value of US$93.68, reflecting principal plus compounded interest.

The cash flows are set out in the Table below:

| Year | A$ Cash Flows | Balance at Start of Period (A$) | Interest Compounded on Balance (A$) | A$ Zero Coupon Swap Cash Flows |
|------|---------------|---------------------------------|-------------------------------------|--------------------------------|
| 0 | 100 | 100.00 | | 100.00 |
| 1 | −10 | 110.00 | 10.00 | |
| 2 | −10 | 121.00 | 11.00 | |
| 3 | −10 | 133.10 | 12.10 | |
| 4 | −10 | 146.41 | 13.31 | |
| 5 | −110 | 161.05 | 14.64 | −161.05 |

| Year | US$ Cash Flows | Balance at Start of Period (US$) | Interest Compounded on Balance (US$) | A$ Zero Coupon Swap Cash Flows |
|------|----------------|----------------------------------|--------------------------------------|--------------------------------|
| 0 | −70.00 | 70.00 | | −70.00 |
| 1 | 4.20 | 74.20 | 4.20 | |
| 2 | 4.20 | 78.65 | 4.45 | |
| 3 | 4.20 | 83.37 | 4.72 | |
| 4 | 4.20 | 88.37 | 5.00 | |
| 5 | 74.20 | 93.68 | 5.30 | 93.68 |

This would imply a five year outright currency forward rate of A$1.00 = US$0.5817 (calculated as US$93.68/A$161.05) or a discount on the spot rate of 0.1183 or 1183 points.

**4.  Structural Issues**

A number of aspects of this transaction should be noted:

- If the initial cash flows are ignored (they are exactly equivalent to a spot currency transaction), then the cash flow pattern is identical to a five year LTFX contract entailing the purchase or sale of A$ for US$.

- The swap structure assumes compounding at the swap rate. In practice, the zero coupon swap rate would have been used (reflecting re-investment at implied forward rates in the relevant currency).

- The zero coupon currency swap is structured on the basis of exchanges of fixed rate cash flows in both currencies. This type of pricing cannot be applied to a currency swap between a fixed rate and floating rate. This is because the floating rate cash flows are uncertain and the maturity value unknown at the time the transaction is entered into. In practice, as most currency swaps are quoted against US$ LIBOR, the US$ interest rate swap market can be utilised to imply fixed US$ rates that can form the basis of this pricing methodology.

- This technique reflects full arbitrage between the two capital markets through the currency swap market[25].

In this case, the price of the forward exchange contract for five years has been calculated. A similar methodology, utilising applicable zero coupon swap rates for the different maturities, could be utilised to engineer forward prices for all maturities.

---

### 4.3.3   Long Dated FX/Currency Forwards – Fully Arbitraged Cash Flow Pricing Methodology

The fully arbitraged cash flow method of pricing LTFX contracts uses a structure that avoids any reinvestment risk on intermediate cash flows[26]. The fully arbitraged cash flow method creates a set of fully arbitraged forward rates utilising the current yield curve. This is achieved by structuring a series of borrowings or investments spread out over the entire exposure period, with the amount borrowed or invested for each maturity taking into account any intermediate cash flows, interest payments due under borrowings, or investments related to exposures in other periods. In essence, the total liabilities in each period, that is the principal plus all interest payments received, are structured to equal all assets in that same period. This creates a series of self-liquidating cash transactions whereby all currency risk and investment risk is avoided. **Exhibit 6.14** sets out an example of the fully arbitraged cash flow method for pricing LTFX contracts.

---

[25]  See discussion in Chapter 11.

[26]  The fully arbitraged cash flow method was first described in Antl, Boris "Pricing the Hedge to Cut the Cost" (May 1983) Euromoney 230–233.

## Exhibit 6.14 Fully Arbitraged Cash Flow Methodology

### 1. Assumptions
In this example, fully arbitraged forward rates are created to cover future receipts of A$1 million every year for five years.
The rates applicable are as follows:

**Exchange rates:**

Spot Rate (A$1 = US$)     0.7000

**Interest rates:**

| Year | 1.00 | 2.00 | 3.00 | 4.00 | 5.00 |
|---|---|---|---|---|---|
| US$ Swap Rate (% pa) | 6.25 | 6.40 | 6.60 | 6.80 | 7.10 |
| A$ Swap Rate (% pa) | 16.00 | 14.75 | 14.50 | 14.35 | 14.25 |

### 2. Fully Arbitraged Cash Flow Methodology
The self-liquidating cover must be structured by first computing the principal amount to be borrowed for the longest period. In this example, this is equal to A$875,274 that reflects the exposure amount of A$1,000,000 discounted at the rate of 14.25% pa. This implies a cash flow in five years from commencement of the transaction equal to A$1,000,000 being the sum of the principal plus the interest payment. This process is then repeated for each of the shorter periods. The amount borrowed for four years reflects the fact that the sum of the interest payment from the five year loan, plus the final payment for the four year borrowing, must equate to A$1,000,000. Based on a four year interest rate of 14.35% pa, this is equal to A$765,434. This provides a maturity value (principal plus interest) of A$875,274, which in conjunction with the interest payment of A$124,726 on the five year borrowing, provides the required A$ cash flow of A$1,000,000. This process is repeated for each maturity. The total A$ borrowing can then be determined. In this example, this equates to A$3,393,997.
The A$ cash flows are summarised in the Table below:

| Year<br>Interest<br>Rates | 1<br>16.00% pa | 2<br>14.75% pa | 3<br>14.50% pa | 4<br>14.35% pa | 5<br>14.25% pa | |
|---|---|---|---|---|---|---|
| **Years** | | | | | | **Total** |
| 0 | 502,217 | 582,572 | 668,501 | 765,434 | 875,274 | 3,393,997 |
| 1 | (582,572) | (85,929) | (96,933) | (109,840) | (124,726) | (1,000,000) |
| 2 | | (668,501) | (96,933) | (109,840) | (124,726) | (1,000,000) |
| 3 | | | (765,434) | (109,840) | (124,726) | (1,000,000) |
| 4 | | | | (875,274) | (124,726) | (1,000,000) |
| 5 | | | | | (1,000,000) | (1,000,000) |

The other side of the hedge, the investment, operates as follows. The A$ borrowing proceeds are converted into US$, at the spot rate, and invested *in the same proportion as the borrowings undertaken*. In the example, the US$ proceeds (US$2,375,798 calculated as the A$ present value of A$3,393,997 converted at the spot rate of A$1 = US$0.70) are invested in the amounts set out. For example, the amount invested for one year US$351,552 equates to 14.80% of the total amount available for investment (the same proportion as the A$ borrowing for one year (A$502,217) as a percentage of the total A$ borrowing (A$3,393,997)). The proceeds of the investment are equal to the sum of investments maturing in each period plus any coupons received.

The US$ cash flows are summarised in the Table below:

| Year | 1 | 2 | 3 | 4 | 5 | |
|------|---|---|---|---|---|---|
| Interest Rates | 6.25% pa | 6.40% pa | 6.60% pa | 6.80% pa | 7.10% pa | |
| Ratios (%) | 14.80 | 17.16 | 19.70 | 22.55 | 25.79 | |
| **Years** | | | | | | **Total** |
| 0 | (351,552) | (407,800) | (467,951) | (535,804) | (612,691) | (2,375,798) |
| 1 | 373,524 | 26,099 | 30,885 | 36,435 | 43,501 | 510,444 |
| 2 | | 433,899 | 30,885 | 36,435 | 43,501 | 544,720 |
| 3 | | | 498,836 | 36,435 | 43,501 | 578,771 |
| 4 | | | | 572,238 | 43,501 | 615,739 |
| 5 | | | | | 656,193 | 656,193 |

The forward exchange rates are then calculated as a function of the cash flows in the two currencies, that is, the A$ receipts divided by the US$ amounts maturing each year:

| Year | A$ | US$ | Exchange Rates | Forward Points |
|------|-----|------|----------------|----------------|
| 0 | 3,393,997 | (2,375,798) | 0.7000 | |
| 1 | (1,000,000) | 510,444 | 0.5104 | −0.1896 |
| 2 | (1,000,000) | 544,720 | 0.5447 | −0.1553 |
| 3 | (1,000,000) | 578,771 | 0.5788 | −0.1212 |
| 4 | (1,000,000) | 615,739 | 0.6157 | −0.0843 |
| 5 | (1,000,000) | 656,193 | 0.6562 | −0.0438 |

### 3. Fully Arbitraged Cash Flow Methodology – Constant Ratio Forward Rates

In the above example, the US$ investments are invested *in the same proportion as the A$ borrowings undertaken*. However, in practice there is no need for the pattern of investment to be identical to the pattern of borrowing. By altering the proportion of the investment, an entirely new set of forward rates, which are capable of being totally hedged at market interest rates, can be created. These rates are often referred to as *slanted* LTFX rates. The specific ratios nominated can be manipulated to create a desired set of foreign exchange rate matching specific asset – liability management requirements. The example below uses a constant 20% to create a specific set of forward rates.

The A$ cash flows are as above. The altered US$ cash flows are summarised in the Table below:

| Year | 1 | 2 | 3 | 4 | 5 | |
|---|---|---|---|---|---|---|
| **Interest Rates** | 6.25% pa | 6.40% pa | 6.60% pa | 6.80% pa | 7.10% pa | |
| **Ratios (%)** | 20.00 | 20.00 | 20.00 | 20.00 | 20.00 | |
| **Years** | | | | | | **Total** |
| 0 | 475,160 | 475,160 | 475,160 | 475,160 | 475,160 | 2,375,798 |
| 1 | 504,857 | 30,410 | 31,361 | 32,311 | 33,736 | 632,675 |
| 2 | | 505,570 | 31,361 | 32,311 | 33,736 | 602,978 |
| 3 | | | 506,520 | 32,311 | 33,736 | 572,567 |
| 4 | | | | 507,470 | 33,736 | 541,207 |
| 5 | | | | | 508,896 | 508,896 |

The forward exchange rates are then calculated as a function of the cash flows in the two currencies, that is, the A$ receipts divided by the US$ amounts maturing each year:

| Year | A$ | US$ | Exchange Rates | Forward Points |
|---|---|---|---|---|
| 0 | 3,393,997 | (2,375,798) | 0.7000 | |
| 1 | (1,000,000) | 632,675 | 0.6327 | −0.0673 |
| 2 | (1,000,000) | 602,978 | 0.6030 | −0.0970 |
| 3 | (1,000,000) | 572,567 | 0.5726 | −0.1274 |
| 4 | (1,000,000) | 541,207 | 0.5412 | −0.1588 |
| 5 | (1,000,000) | 508,896 | 0.5089 | −0.1911 |

The fully arbitraged cash flow method effectively creates forward foreign exchange rates utilising the zero coupon rates in the relevant currencies. A specific feature of the fully arbitraged cash flow method is the technique for pricing implicitly identifies the hedging transactions required; it allows a party entering into these transactions to specifically construct hedges required to insulate it from any exposure to reinvestment rates in either currency.

## 4.4 Pricing FX/Currency Forwards in Regulated Markets

The methodology described requires free access to the currency markets (spot and forward) and the money market in both currencies. However, in regulated markets, access to one or more of these elements may be subject to controls. This creates significant difficulties in using the interest rate parity or covered arbitrage approach to derive the arbitrage free forward price. This arises because of the difficulties in undertaking the arbitrage transactions designed to force equilibrium pricing.

These problems are most often encountered in emerging markets. Typical restrictions include:
- Restrictions on spot and forward transactions other than where there is an approved underlying trade or investment transaction.
- Limitations on borrowing or lending in the domestic currencies.

These restrictions impact upon pricing of forward currency contracts in a number of ways:
- **Multi-tier markets** – differential access to different market components drives differential pricing between market segments. A common differentiation is based on offshore and onshore forward price segments. The major driver of the differential pricing is based on the different prevailing interest rates between the onshore and offshore money markets.
- **Market driven pricing** – this reflects markets in instruments such as non-deliverable forwards ("NDFs")[27] where the regulation structure prevents traditional replication and hedging. NDF markets are driven by the availability of surrogate (usually correlation based) hedges and the matching of underlying supply and demand for the currency as of the relevant forward date. **Exhibit 6.15** sets out some of the dynamics of these markets.

---

**Exhibit 6.15    Pricing Non-deliverable Currency Forwards**

There are significant markets in NDFs in emerging market currencies (in Asia, Eastern Europe and Latin America). The markets are driven primarily by the regulatory structure that typically prevents free funds transfer and access to the spot and forward currency market. Generally access is limited to approved transactions (trade transactions and certain specified capital transactions). The restrictions force market participants to use NDFs to hedge or speculate on future currency movements. Generally, the markets are outside the relevant jurisdictions with all cash flows taking place in US$ or other freely convertible currencies.

In NDF markets, the dealers cannot hedge positions assumed in dealing with clients, as they do not have access to the spot and forward currency markets or the local currency money market. This means that the dealers must operate as follows:
- **Run matched books** – that is, the dealer merely matches buy and sell transactions in the relevant currency and the specific maturity to avoid any price risk (the matching approach).

---

[27]  See Chapter 3.

- **Correlation hedges** – the dealer models the price movements of the currency and develops/manages hedges using another currency or currency basket that closely replicates the price movements in the subject currency (the correlation hedging).

The matching approach is restrictive as the dealer may not be able to accommodate client demands. In practice, this often reflects the fact that the future rate expectation in many emerging market currencies is one-sided. This means the demand or supply of a currency is skewed to the buy or sell side. This creates illiquidity and difficulties for participants and dealers.

Correlation hedges are risky as a change in a fundamental relationship or a policy shift may destroy the basis of the hedge. For example, a number of Asian currencies (the Thai Baht and Indonesian Rupiah) were pegged to a basket of US$, Yen and European currencies through much of the 1990s. However, in July 1997, the currencies were de-coupled from the basket and allowed to find their own level after the central banks were unable to defend the target currency levels. Hedges based on the previous correlation relationships failed in this environment.

In practice, a mixture of approaches are utilised by dealers to price NDFs. In practice, the identified difficulties limit the maturity and size of transactions feasible in these markets. Pricing in the NDF markets reflect a number of factors:

- **Interest rate differentials** – the prevailing interest rate differentials are used to estimate a starting point for forward prices.
- **Expected price movements** – the forward rates will reflect the theoretical forward price adjusted for expected appreciation or depreciation as follows:

NDF Forward Price = Arbitrage Free Price + Expected Appreciation (Depreciation)

The expected appreciation and depreciation is obviously market driven and subjective. However, the market NDF prices allow the *backing out* of the *expected* appreciation or depreciation in the currency[28]. The departure from theoretical prices can be very significant (both discounts and premiums).

- **Market structure** – the structure of buyers and sellers drives the size of discount or premium to the theoretical market. Typically, for most structurally weak emerging market currencies, the forwards trade at a discount to the theoretical forward price. The size of this discount reflects the implied interest rate (the high forward discount means that the money market rate implied is higher than the domestic money market rate) required to attract investors in the currency. The investments are typically in the form of synthetic foreign currency deposits. The major depositors are often speculators (including hedge funds), local exporters that have flexibility in leading or lagging foreign currency payables/receivables and non-resident persons from the relevant jurisdictions who have natural currency demand. A secondary source of demand may be traders with profitable speculative positions wishing to lock in profits.

The pricing of NDFs is difficult to model theoretically. In practice, NDF prices are volatile. This creates difficulties in verification of prices and valuation of open positions.

---

[28] This is frequently expressed as an implied interest rate for the currency based on the NDF rates. The implied rates will differ from prevailing *actual* money market rates.

# 5   Forward Pricing – Interest Rate/Debt Contracts

## 5.1   Interest Rate/Debt Forwards – Pricing Approach[29]

Interest rate forwards generally consist of forwards on bonds and FRAs. Interest rate swaps can be decomposed into a series of interest rate forwards/FRAs. Other interest rate forward products include non-generic and structured products such as CMT forwards or yield curve swaps[30]. The other major form of interest rate forwards is futures contracts on short term interest rates and bonds.

Interest rate forwards are priced off forward-forward interest rates. This forward-forward interest rate is implied by the cash market yield curve. The forward interest rate is replicated through cash market transactions. The pricing of interest rate forwards reflects the dealer's ability, at least theoretically, to hedge the transaction through the relevant cash market transactions. In practice, interest rate forwards can be priced either using the price of the securities or interest rates (reflecting the inverse relationship between the price and yield).

## 5.2   Interest Rate/Debt Forward Pricing Models – Price Based Models

The price based model for pricing interest rate forwards is used primarily with bond forwards. The approach uses the spot price of the bond and adjusts it for the cost of carry (the interest cost of funding the bond and the interest income received from the bond). The interest rate used for the cost of funding the bond is usually the repo rate (at least for maturities where the repo market operates). **Exhibit 6.16** sets out an example of deriving the price of a bond forward using the price based model.

---

**Exhibit 6.16    Pricing Interest Rate Forwards – Price Model**

**1.  Assumptions**
Assume the following bond:

| | |
|---|---|
| Maturity: | 15 November 2010 |
| Coupon: | 7.50% pa (payable semi-annually) |

---

[29]   See Martin, John (2001) Applied Math for Derivatives; John Wiley & Sons, Singapore at Chapter 5.

[30]   See Das, Satyajit (2004) Structured Products Volume 1; John Wiley & Sons (Asia), Singapore at Chapter 17.

Assume that the bond is to be priced for forward delivery (3 months). The settlement and rate information are as follows:

| | |
|---|---|
| Settlement Date: | 27 June 2001 |
| Forward Date: | 27 September 2001 (92 days) |
| Bond Yield: | 7.65% pa (semi-annual compounding) |
| 3 month Interest Rate: | 6.10% pa (payable quarterly) |

All prices are calculated based on $100 face value of the bond.

## 2. Forward Bond Price
The current price of the bond is as follows:

| | |
|---|---|
| Bond Price: | 98.9961 |
| Accrued Interest: | 0.8764 |
| Total Price: | 99.8724 |

The forward price is given by:

Forward Bond Price = Spot Price of Bond + (Funding Cost − Interest Income)

Funding cost on this position is given by: $99.8724 \times 6.10\% \times 92/365 = 1.5356$.

Interest income is the difference between the accrued interest on the settlement date (27 June 2001) and the forward date (27 September 2001): $2.7514 − 0.8764 = 1.8750$

The forward price can then be derived as follows:

Forward Bond Price = $98.9961 + (1.5356 − 1.8750) = 98.6567$

This equates to a forward yield of 7.7054% pa.

Please note that simple interest is used to determine the funding cost. For longer maturities, it will be necessary to utilise compound interest.

## 5.3 Interest Rate/Debt Forward Pricing Models – Interest Rate Based Models

### 5.3.1 General Approach

Interest rate forwards (such as FRAs) are priced off forward-forward interest rates. Forward interest rates can be calculated from the current yield curve where suitably spaced yields and money market securities are available.

The forward rates are calculated on the theoretical basis that securities of different maturity can be expected to be substitutes for one another. Investors at any time have three choices. They may invest in an obligation having a maturity corresponding exactly to their anticipated holding period. They may invest in short-term securities, reinvesting in further short-term securities at each maturity over the holding period. They may invest in a security having a maturity longer than the anticipated holding period. In the last case, they would sell the security at the end of the given period, realising either a capital gain or a loss. According to a version of the pure expectations theory, an investor's expected return for any holding period would be the same regardless of the alternative or combination of alternatives selected. The return would be a weighted average of the current short-term interest rate plus future short rates expected to prevail over the holding period; this average is the same for each alternative.

Forward rates may be calculated from the currently prevailing cash market yield curve, as any deviation from the implied forward rates would create arbitrage opportunities that traders would exploit. This arbitrage is undertaken by buying and selling securities at different maturities to synthetically create the intended forward transaction. By simultaneously borrowing and lending the same amount in the cash market, but for different maturities, it is possible to lock in an interest rate for a period in the future. If the maturity of the cash lending exceeds the maturity of the cash borrowing, then the implied rate over the future period, the forward-forward rate, is a bid rate for a forward investment. If the maturity of the cash borrowing exceeds the maturity of the cash lending, then the resulting forward-forward rate is an offer rate for a forward borrowing.

**Exhibit 6.17** sets out the process of generating forward rates from trading in money market instruments. **Exhibit 6.18** sets out an example of pricing an interest rate forward off the hedge utilising borrowing and lending transactions. **Exhibit 6.19** sets out the formula for derivation of forward interest rates.

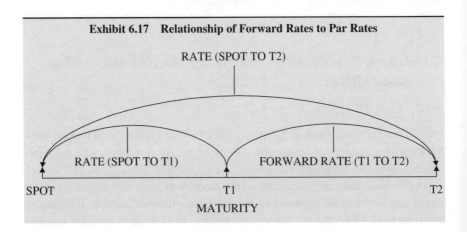

**Exhibit 6.17     Relationship of Forward Rates to Par Rates**

RATE (SPOT TO T2)

RATE (SPOT TO T1)          FORWARD RATE (T1 TO T2)

SPOT                              T1                              T2

MATURITY

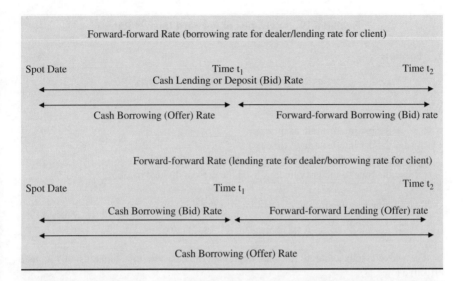

**Exhibit 6.18   Pricing Interest Rate Forwards Using Cash Market Transaction**

Assume that Bank B is approached by a client to quote for and provide an interest rate forward/FRA to hedge a loan drawdown for three months commencing in three months time for an amount of $10 million. B is long the interest rate forward or selling a 3 × 6 FRA.

Current interest rates (all rates are % pa compounded annually) are:

3 months:    11.00/11.20% pa
6 months:    11.80/12.00% pa

B would price and hedge its FRA as follows:
- B borrows $10 million for six months at 12.00% pa and lends it for three months at 11.00% pa (note that it lends (borrows) at the market bid (offer) rates).
- B then buys the interest rate forward (sells the $10 million 3 × 6 FRA) to essentially provide it with a replacement for the investment which matures in three months time.
- B seeks to earn a spread of 0.25% pa on the interest rate forward or FRA, that is, it must earn 12.25% pa over the six months. Therefore, B quotes a rate of 13.51% pa.

After the transaction is executed, at the end of three months, B would need to re-lend the maturing $10 million for three months. The interest rate forward/FRA would be settled and the cash payment by or to the client would have the effect of locking in the rate of 13.51% pa. The interest rate forward/FRA could also be structured as a physical transaction whereby B actually provided funding for its client at the forward rate.

If B had been asked to hedge an investment, by selling the forward interest rate/buying an FRA, B would have lent $10 million for six months at 11.80% pa and funded the loan for three months at 11.20% pa with the interest rate forward FRA locking in its refinancing cost. Using the same profit margin as above, the FRA rate quoted would be 11.90% pa.

**Exhibit 6.19   Derivation of Forward Interest Rates**

**1.   Formula**

$$(1 + R_{t_1})^{t_1} * (1 + R_{t_1 x_2})^{t_2 - t_1} = (1 + R_{t_2})^{t_2}$$

Where

$R_{t_1}$   = the par interest rate to time $t_1$
$R_{t_2}$   = the par interest rate to time $t_2$
$R_{t_1 x_2}$ = the forward interest rate between time $t_1$ and $t_2$
$t_1, t_2$   = the time to maturity in days from the present divided by 365

Rearranging to solve for the forward interest rate:

$$R_{t_1 x_2} = [(1 + R_{t_2})^{t_2} / (1 + R_{t_1})^{t_1}]^{1/(t_2 - t_1)} - 1$$

The above assumes that all rates are expressed in consistent time units, usually annual effective rates.

**2.   Example**
Assume the following yield curve structure:

| Maturity (days) | Interest Rate (% pa Compounded Annually) |
|---|---|
| 92 | 4.75 |
| 184 | 5.00 |

Using formula set out above, the forward rate for 92 days *in 92 days from spot date* ($3 \times 6$ months being the 3 month rate in 3 months time) can be derived as follows:

$$R_{92 \times 184} = \left[(1 + .05)^{(184/365)} / (1 + .0475)^{(92/365)}\right]^{1/(184/365 - 92/365)} - 1$$
$$= .052506 \text{ or } 5.2506\% \text{ pa}$$

Interest rate forwards can also be priced off a type of forward-forward arbitrage. This type of arbitrage is predicated on the fact that forward foreign exchange prices are determined by interest differentials between the relevant currencies, reflecting the yield curves in the respective currencies. This therefore provides another mechanism to hedge by entering into an interest rate forward/FRA to hedge the interest rate exposure under a covered interest rate arbitrage transaction, that is, to lock in the interest rate leg for the arbitrage. **Exhibit 6.20** sets out an example of this type of transaction.

---

**Exhibit 6.20    Synthetic Forward-Forward Interest Rate Transactions**

A borrower wishes to lock in a two month borrowing cost in NZ$ for NZ$10 million. Normally, the borrower would achieve this objective by selling an interest rate forward/ buying a NZ$ $1 \times 3$ month FRA (2 month NZ$ interest rates in one month forward). However, we assume that NZ$ interest rate forwards/FRAs are not directly available, although A$ FRAs for the required term as well as A$ and NZ$ currency forwards are available.

The current market rates are[31]:

| | |
|---|---|
| A$/NZ$ Spot | A$1.00 = NZ$1.1660 |
| 1 month forward | A$1.00 = NZ$1.1710 |
| 3 months forward | A$1.00 = NZ$1.1840 |
| A$ interest rate forwards/FRAs ($1 \times 3$) | 13.24% pa |

In these circumstances the borrower could synthesise a NZ$ interest rate forward/FRA as follows:
- Buy NZ$10,000,000 against a sale of A$8,539,710 for value in one month at the quoted rate of NZ$ 1.1710.
- Sell NZ$10,334,133 against a purchase of A$8,728,153 for value in three months at the quoted rate of NZ$1.1840.
- Enter into a two month A$ interest rate forward/FRA commencing in one month at a rate of 13.24% pa.

The series of transactions would provide the borrower with a known fully hedged cost of NZ$ funds. Under the transaction, the borrower would draw down A$ funding for two months in one month at a rate of 13.24% pa guaranteed under the interest rate forward/FRA. The A$ would be converted into NZ$ through the A$ and NZ$ forward foreign exchange contract. The A$ amount drawn down is determined by the need to generate NZ$10 million of funding. At maturity, the borrower would repay NZ$10,334,133 which would be converted into A$8,728,153 through the forward contract. The A$ amount at maturity corresponds to the amount required to meet the principal and interest commitment on the A$ liability. The overall transaction results in a guaranteed borrowing cost for NZ$10 million for two months in one month's time of 20.05% pa.

---

## 5.3.2    Forward Interest Rates – Types and Behaviour[32]

Given any two interest rates at particular maturities, it is feasible to generate a forward interest rate. This means that given a complete yield curve, multiple forward

---

[31]  Bid-offer spreads are omitted for ease of exposition.

[32]  For a discussion of the volatility of futures contracts, see "The Analysis of Value and Volatility in Financial Futures" in Fabozzi, Frank J. (Editor) (1992)

rates can be generated. **Exhibit 6.21** sets out the complete combination of rates that can be derived from a complete yield curve.

Forward rates also have specific characteristics. The following major characteristics of forward rates should be noted:

- Forward rates lie above (below) the par rates where the yield curve is positive (negative). This means that the forward rates cross from one side to the other of the par curve where the yield curve changes shape. **Exhibit 6.22** sets out the shape of forward curves.
- Forward rates have greater momentum than par rates; that is the rate of change of the forward rates is more attenuated than that of the par curve. For an upward sloping yield curve, the steeper the yield curve the greater the slope/steepness of the forward curve. This is most marked for short dated forwards i.e. forwards on 3 or 6 month rates. Where the underlying security is longer dated (i.e. a forward on a 10 year bond), the relative steepness of the forward curve is significantly less pronounced.
- Forward rates can be more volatile than par rates; that is, a small change in par rates can lead to a proportionately larger change in the forward rate. **Exhibit 6.23** analyses the volatility of forward rates.

## 5.4    Pricing Interest Rate Futures

Interest rate futures contracts are priced similarly to interest rate forwards. The interest rate futures price is based on replication of the futures position with cash borrowing and investments. The equilibrium futures price is achieved through cash-futures arbitrage.

In a competitive market, a risk-free arbitrage should earn a return equal to the risk-free rate. Using this principle, a risk-free position combining cash and futures can be established. The futures price is determined so that the return on the combined position earns the risk-free rate over the holding period. If the trade consists of a short position in the Eurodollar futures maturing in three months, and a long position in the physical six months Eurodollar deposit market, the physical Eurodollar position is financed for three months (prior to its delivery into the contract) at the three month rate. In this trade, the cost of financing and the rate of return of the six month position are known. Arbitrage will determine the futures price. In equilibrium, it will be bid to a level such that the rate of return represented

---

Investing: The Collected Works of Martin L. Leibowitz; Probus Publishing, Chicago at 1065–1093; Anderson, Ronald W. "Some Determinants of the Volatility of Futures Prices" (1985) The Journal of Futures Markets vol 5 no 3 331–348.

Exhibit 6.21   Forward Rates – Example

| Year | Interest Rate (% pa) | Start Date (years) | 10.0 | 9.5 | 9.0 | 8.5 | 8.0 | 7.5 | 7.0 | 6.5 | 6.0 | 5.5 |
|------|------|------|------|------|------|------|------|------|------|------|------|------|
| 0.50 | 6.00 | 0.5 | 7.959 | 7.911 | 7.896 | 7.850 | 7.804 | 7.726 | 7.670 | 7.518 | 7.507 | 7.365 |
| 1.00 | 6.25 | 1.0 | 8.040 | 7.995 | 7.984 | 7.940 | 7.897 | 7.820 | 7.768 | 7.610 | 7.607 | 7.461 |
| 1.50 | 6.40 | 1.5 | 8.119 | 8.076 | 8.070 | 8.029 | 7.990 | 7.914 | 7.866 | 7.702 | 7.708 | 7.557 |
| 2.00 | 6.50 | 2.0 | 8.202 | 8.161 | 8.160 | 8.123 | 8.089 | 8.015 | 7.972 | 7.801 | 7.822 | 7.664 |
| 2.50 | 6.75 | 2.5 | 8.232 | 8.190 | 8.192 | 8.154 | 8.119 | 8.042 | 7.996 | 7.808 | 7.832 | 7.650 |
| 3.00 | 6.90 | 3.0 | 8.273 | 8.231 | 8.236 | 8.200 | 8.166 | 8.085 | 8.039 | 7.829 | 7.861 | 7.648 |
| 3.50 | 6.95 | 3.5 | 8.352 | 8.313 | 8.327 | 8.295 | 8.268 | 8.190 | 8.152 | 7.926 | 7.984 | 7.748 |
| 4.00 | 7.00 | 4.0 | 8.435 | 8.401 | 8.424 | 8.400 | 8.382 | 8.309 | 8.285 | 8.041 | 8.142 | 7.880 |
| 4.50 | 7.10 | 4.5 | 8.484 | 8.451 | 8.482 | 8.463 | 8.451 | 8.377 | 8.363 | 8.076 | 8.222 | 7.870 |
| 5.01 | 7.21 | 5.0 | 8.512 | 8.479 | 8.518 | 8.500 | 8.493 | 8.413 | 8.403 | 8.035 | 8.233 | 7.540 |
| 5.51 | 7.24 | 5.5 | 8.621 | 8.597 | 8.658 | 8.661 | 8.685 | 8.632 | 8.693 | 8.283 | 8.932 | |
| 6.01 | 7.38 | 6.0 | 8.582 | 8.549 | 8.612 | 8.607 | 8.624 | 8.533 | 8.574 | 7.640 | | |
| 6.51 | 7.40 | 6.5 | 8.718 | 8.701 | 8.808 | 8.850 | 8.954 | 8.982 | 9.517 | | | |
| 7.01 | 7.55 | 7.0 | 8.585 | 8.539 | 8.632 | 8.629 | 8.673 | 8.450 | | | | |
| 7.51 | 7.61 | 7.5 | 8.612 | 8.561 | 8.692 | 8.718 | 8.898 | | | | | |
| 8.01 | 7.69 | 8.0 | 8.541 | 8.450 | 8.590 | 8.540 | | | | | | |
| 8.51 | 7.74 | 8.5 | 8.541 | 8.405 | 8.640 | | | | | | | |
| 9.01 | 7.79 | 9.0 | 8.492 | 8.170 | | | | | | | | |
| 9.51 | 7.81 | 9.5 | 8.816 | | | | | | | | | |
| 10.01 | 7.86 | | | | | | | | | | | |

| Year | Interest Rate (% pa) | Final Maturity (years) Start Date (years) | 5.0 | 4.5 | 4.0 | 3.5 | 3.0 | 2.5 | 2.0 | 1.5 | 1.0 |
|------|------|------|------|------|------|------|------|------|------|------|------|
| 0.50 | 6.00 | 0.5 | 7.346 | 7.239 | 7.144 | 7.110 | 7.081 | 6.939 | 6.668 | 6.601 | 6.502 |
| 1.00 | 6.25 | 1.0 | 7.451 | 7.344 | 7.251 | 7.231 | 7.227 | 7.085 | 6.751 | 6.700 | |
| 1.50 | 6.40 | 1.5 | 7.559 | 7.452 | 7.362 | 7.365 | 7.403 | 7.278 | 6.802 | | |
| 2.00 | 6.50 | 2.0 | 7.685 | 7.582 | 7.502 | 7.552 | 7.703 | 7.752 | | | |
| 2.50 | 6.75 | 2.5 | 7.672 | 7.539 | 7.418 | 7.452 | 7.655 | | | | |
| 3.00 | 6.90 | 3.0 | 7.676 | 7.501 | 7.301 | 7.250 | | | | | |
| 3.50 | 6.95 | 3.5 | 7.818 | 7.626 | 7.352 | | | | | | |
| 4.00 | 7.00 | 4.0 | 8.050 | 7.900 | | | | | | | |
| 4.50 | 7.10 | 4.5 | 8.201 | | | | | | | | |
| 5.01 | 7.21 | 5.0 | | | | | | | | | |
| 5.51 | 7.24 | 5.5 | | | | | | | | | |
| 6.01 | 7.38 | 6.0 | | | | | | | | | |
| 6.51 | 7.40 | 6.5 | | | | | | | | | |
| 7.01 | 7.55 | 7.0 | | | | | | | | | |
| 7.51 | 7.61 | 7.5 | | | | | | | | | |
| 8.01 | 7.69 | 8.0 | | | | | | | | | |
| 8.51 | 7.74 | 8.5 | | | | | | | | | |
| 9.01 | 7.79 | 9.0 | | | | | | | | | |
| 9.51 | 7.81 | 9.5 | | | | | | | | | |
| 10.01 | 7.86 | | | | | | | | | | |

### Exhibit 6.22    Forward Rate – Slope of Yield Curve

**1.  Positive Yield Curve**

| Time to Maturity (Years) | Time to Maturity (Days) | Interest Rates (% pa) | Forward Rates (% pa) |
|---|---|---|---|
| 0.50 | 182 | 5.2500 | 5.7479 |
| 1.00 | 366 | 5.5000 | 6.5613 |
| 1.50 | 547 | 5.8500 | 6.8467 |
| 2.00 | 731 | 6.1000 | 6.8580 |
| 2.50 | 912 | 6.2500 | 8.3519 |
| 3.00 | 1096 | 6.6000 | 7.6628 |
| 3.50 | 1277 | 6.7500 | 7.1477 |
| 4.00 | 1461 | 6.8000 | |

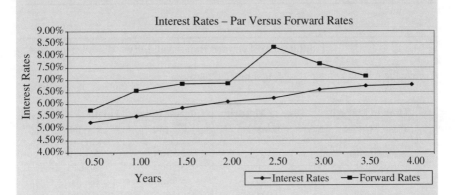

**2.  Negative (Inverse) Yield Curve**

| Time to Maturity (Years) | Time to Maturity (Days) | Interest Rates (% pa) | Forward Rates (% pa) |
|---|---|---|---|
| 0.50 | 182 | 7.7500 | 7.0549 |
| 1.00 | 366 | 7.4000 | 6.9473 |
| 1.50 | 547 | 7.2500 | 6.8533 |
| 2.00 | 731 | 7.1500 | 6.2962 |
| 2.50 | 912 | 6.9800 | 5.4406 |
| 3.00 | 1096 | 6.7200 | 6.5085 |
| 3.50 | 1277 | 6.6900 | 5.5834 |
| 4.00 | 1461 | 6.5500 | |

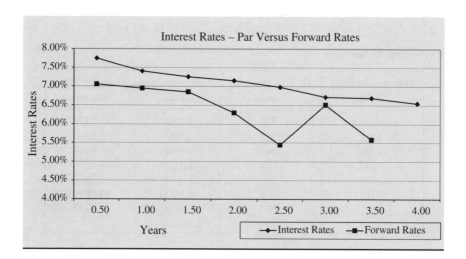

**Exhibit 6.23    Forward Rate – Volatility**

Assume the following interest rates and forward rates:

| Time to Maturity (Years) | Time to Maturity (Days) | Interest Rates (% pa) | Forward Rates (% pa) |
|---|---|---|---|
| 0.50 | 182 | 5.2500 | 5.7479 |
| 1.00 | 366 | 5.5000 | 6.5613 |
| 1.50 | 547 | 5.8500 | 6.8467 |
| 2.00 | 731 | 6.1000 | 6.8580 |
| 2.50 | 912 | 6.2500 | 8.3519 |
| 3.00 | 1096 | 6.6000 | 7.6628 |
| 3.50 | 1277 | 6.7500 | 7.1477 |
| 4.00 | 1461 | 6.8000 | |

Assume now that the 3.50 year rate changes by 10 bps (from 6.75% to 6.85% pa). This affects the forward rates for 6 months out of 3 and 3.50 years. The recomputed rates are summarised below:

| Time to Maturity (Years) | Time to Maturity (Days) | Interest Rates (% pa) | Forward Rates (% pa) |
|---|---|---|---|
| 3.00 | 1096 | 6.6000 | 8.3764 |
| 3.50 | 1277 | 6.8500 | 6.4536 |
| 4.00 | 1461 | 6.8000 | |

In each case, the 10 bps change in the interest rate results in a larger (around 70 bps) change in the forward rate. This reflects the fact that the 10 bps change over the term (3.5 years) is compressed into a short period (6 months), causing the large movement in that interest rate.

Where the forward is on a longer term underlying security (say a 3.5 year forward into a 10 year security), the fact that the change in rate can be effectively amortised over the life of the security means that the volatility of that forward rate change is significantly lower. This is illustrated below:

| Time to Maturity (Years) | Time to Maturity (Days) | Interest Rates (% pa) | Forward Rates (% pa) |
|---|---|---|---|
| 3.50 | 1277 | 6.7500 | 6.8175 |
| 10.50 | 4930 | 6.8000 | |

| Time to Maturity (Years) | Time to Maturity (Days) | Interest Rates (% pa) | Forward Rates (% pa) |
|---|---|---|---|
| 3.50 | 1277 | 6.8500 | 6.7825 |
| 10.50 | 4930 | 6.8000 | |

by the difference between the futures price and the deposit will be equal to the cost of financing the deposit over the three month period. This calculated rate is sometimes called the break-even borrowing cost.

If the futures price is greater than the equilibrium level, then arbitrageurs will earn a positive return with no risk by purchasing the cash deposit, selling the futures and carrying the position at the three-month rate. This will drive down the futures price relative to the cash price until the holding period return equals the cost of financing the trade. If the futures price is below the equilibrium price, then arbitrageurs will buy the futures, sell the cash and invest the proceeds at a net positive spread. This will tend to drive the futures price up relative to the cash market, resulting in an equilibrium price such that the rate of return on the trade equals the three-month borrowing rate. In both cases, the synthetic asset consists of cash deposits or equivalent securities that are either lengthened or shortened by going long or short in the futures market. A long position in a futures contract or a strip of futures lengthens the cash position by purchasing deposits today for future delivery. A short futures position essentially sells off the back end of a cash deposit, thereby shortening it.

**Exhibit 6.24** sets out an example of cash futures arbitrage. The example highlights the process of arbitrage through which interest rate futures are forced to
equilibrium levels. The approach outlined is applicable irrespective of the term of
the underlying security (short term or longer term bonds).

---

**Exhibit 6.24    Interest Rate Futures – Cash Futures Arbitrage**

Assume the following trading condition exists on 1 September 2002:

Eurodollar Rate for 104 days (to 14 December 2002)      6.34% pa
Eurodollar Rate for 195 days (to 15 March 2003)        7.00% pa

The implied equilibrium futures rate for the December 2002 Eurodollar contract that
expires on 14 December 2002 is 92.17 or 7.83% pa. This futures price reflects the fact that the
purchase of a 91 day investment (commencing 14 December 2002) and the purchase of a 195
day deposit and the sale of the December Eurodollars contract are equivalent transactions.

Assume the December Eurodollar is trading at 92.59 (7.41% pa). Under these circumstances, it is feasible to structure a cash and carry cash-futures arbitrage transaction as
follows:

• Purchase a Eurodollar Deposit for 195 days at 7.00% pa.
• Borrow Eurodollar for 104 days (to futures expiry) at 6.34% pa.
• Sell the December Eurodollar contract at 92.59.

The results of these transactions (based on an assumed face value of US$1,000,000) are
as follows:

| Interest Earnings | US$ |
|---|---|
| US$1,000,000 @ 7.00% × 195/360 | 37,916.67 |
| **Interest Expense** | |
| US$1,000,000 @ 6.34% × 104/360 | 18,315.56 |
| US$1,000,000 @ 7.41% × 91/360 | 18,730.83 |
| | 37,046.39 |
| **Net Gain** | 870.28 |

The above calculation ignores the interest cost of funding the interest payment of
US$18,315.56. Assuming a funding cost of 7.41% pa for 91 days, this equates to US$343.07
(US$18,315.56 @ 7.41% 91/360). This reduces the net gain to $527.21.

The party entering into the transaction can utilise the higher than equilibrium futures
price to create a 195 day synthetic borrowing at a lower cost than the equivalent investment
rate.

Alternatively, it would be possible to construct a synthetic 104 day investment at above
market rates as follows:

• Purchase one deposit at 7.00% pa for US$1,000,000.00 (future value at 15 March 2003
  of US$1,037,916.67).
• Sale of Eurodollar Deposit at 7.41% pa (as at 14 December 2002) for US$1,018,833.07
  (locked in rate through sale of December 2002 Eurodollar Contract).

The transaction produces a gain of US$18,833.07. This gain equates to a yield over 104 days of 6.52% pa, an arbitrage gain of 0.18% pa.

If the December Eurodollar Futures Contract is trading below equilibrium levels at 92.01, then a reverse cash and carry transaction could be engineered by purchasing a 104 day Eurodollar deposit, purchasing the December Eurodollar Contract and borrowing Eurodollars for 195 days.

The results of the transaction are as follows:

| Interest Earnings | US$ |
|---|---|
| US$1,000,000 @ 6.34% × 104/360 | 18,315.56 |
| US$1,000,000 @ 7.99% × 91/360 | 20,196.94 |
| **Total Earnings** | 38,512.50 |
| **Interest Expense** | |
| US$1,000,000 @ 7.00% × 195/360 | 37,916.67 |
| **Net Gain** | 595.83 |

The disequilibrium in the futures price effectively allows the creation of a 195 day security yielding 7.11% pa, an arbitrage gain of 0.11% pa. This calculation again ignores interest on the interim interest payment (in this case a receipt). This additional interest equates to US$369.92 (US$18,315.56 @ 7.99% pa × 91/360), increasing the net gain to US$965.75.

In practice, the pricing of interest rate futures is affected by a number of additional factors. Some of these factors affect all futures contract. However, a number of the factors are unique to interest rate futures.

Generic factors that affect the pricing of interest rate futures include:

- **Mark-to-market of futures contract** – a risk associated with futures positions is the need to immediately make good losses in the value of a futures contract (the mark-to-market). This creates cash flows (funding cost or investment return uncertainty) that must be incorporated into the pricing of the futures contract. This is known as the convexity adjustment[33].

- **Delivery** – the futures contract may not be capable of delivery. The non-availability of delivery as a mechanism for settlement of the contract may affect the ability to arbitrage the contract and therefore the achievement of an arbitrage free price outcome. Where delivery is feasible, uncertainty with respect to the exact instrument that will be delivered and the prices at the point of each settlement can also play a role in price determination for futures.

---

[33] The convexity adjustment is described later in this Chapter.

Specific factor affecting interest rate futures contracts include:

- **Convexity issues** – there are several convexity aspects of interest rate futures contracts:
  1. **Margins** – this refers to the adjustment where the theoretical forward interest rate is adjusted for the impact on funding or re-investing the cash flows resulting from the contract being marked to market periodically.
  2. **Fixed tick point value** – short dated interest rate futures contracts often have fixed tick point values (for example, the Eurodollar futures contract has a fixed value of 1 bps = US$25). This means the futures contract has negative convexity. This means that where the futures contract used to hedge a convex financial instrument (such as deposit or bond) there is a mismatch in the price changes between the underlying transaction and the futures contract. This must be adjusted for in hedging. This is also known as the convexity adjustment[34].
  3. **Unnatural time lag** – this refers to a problem of discrepancies between the term of the forward and the payment pattern on the instrument. Where the derivative (the forward) is structured so that the payoffs correspond to the payment pattern on the underlying instrument (bond or swap), then it is appropriate to set the expected rate used to calculate the implied spread to the derived forward rate. Where the payoffs do not follow the same payment pattern, then a convexity adjustment to the forward rate is required. This is relevant for a number of products such as arrears reset and constant maturity transactions[35].
- **Delivery and conversion factors** – this refers to deliverable bond futures contracts where a system of conversion factors is used to derive the cheapest to deliver ("CTD") bond[36]. The futures contract trades as a forward on the CTD bond. However, the CTD calculation is somewhat arbitrary and creates problems and uncertainties on delivery that affect the pricing of the bond futures contracts.

## 5.5   Interest Rate/Debt Forward Pricing – Key Issues

Pricing of interest rate forwards is straightforward. This reflects the fact that given a set of interest rates, the forward prices or rates can be derived relatively simply.

The major issues with the derivation of forward interest rates include:

- **Yield curve to be utilised** – in practice the treasury yield curve is used for forwards on government securities or rates. The swap curve is used for most

---

[34]  This issue is discussed in detail in Chapter 13.
[35]  This issue is discussed in detail in Das, Satyajit (2004) Structured Products Volume 1; John Wiley & Sons (Asia), Singapore at Chapters 14 and 17.
[36]  See discussion in Chapter 2.

other forward transactions. The key issue here is that for many transactions, the appropriate rate should be derived off the *yield curve for the relevant credit quality* – that, in practice, is difficult[37].

- **Availability of yield curve and rates** – in many markets the actual underlying rates may not be available or might be difficult to define, creating significant difficulties in determining the forward rates. This is the case with many less liquid markets such as emerging markets.

# 6  Forward Pricing – Equity & Equity Indexes

## *6.1  Equity & Equity Index Forwards – Pricing Approach*[38]

Equity forwards generally consist of forwards on individual shares or more commonly equity indexes (baskets of shares). Equity swaps can be decomposed into a series of equity forwards. The other major form of equity forwards is futures contracts on equity indexes or less commonly individual equity stocks.

Equity forwards are priced using the carry cost model. The spot price (individual equity price or equity index value) is adjusted for the interest cost through to the forward date and the income on the asset (the dividends). The basic models used focus on either using a continuous income model or using discrete dividends to derive the forward price. The major issues in deriving the forward price relate to the interest rate used and also the dividend assumed.

The interest rate assumed is the swap rate in the currency in which the shares are denominated. This generally does not cause problems. However, there are a number of situations in which the interest rate used is ambiguous. These include:

- **Dual listed stocks** – these are equity stocks that are listed in two jurisdictions and traded in the currencies of the relevant jurisdiction[39]. The applicable interest rate is not clear. It would appear logical to treat the two stocks as *separate stocks* and utilise the interest rate in the currency in which the specific stock is being quoted.
- **American Depository Receipts ("ADRs") or Global Depository Receipts ("GDRs")**[40] – these are effectively certificates of deposits issued by a custodian against shares held by the trustee. The receipts are separate from the underlying shares themselves and can be traded independently but derive their value from the underlying shares. The primary motivation for ADRs and GDRs is

---

[37] See discussion in Chapter 5.
[38] See Martin, John (2001) Applied Math for Derivatives; John Wiley & Sons, Singapore at Chapter 7.
[39] Examples include Royal Dutch/Shell, Rio Tinto and BHP Billiton.
[40] The term ADR is used in the US and GDR generally based in London.

the capacity for investors to trade the underlying stock in their chosen currency (ADRs/GDRs are usually traded in a currency that is different from the denomination of the underlying shares) and in their preferred form (parcel size, listing, time zone). The issue in pricing forwards on ADRs is the fact that the ADRs/GDRs are traded in a currency different from that on the underlying shares. However, the ADR/GDR value is derived from the value of the underlying shares (effectively the local currency value of the underlying shares translated into the equivalent foreign currency value at the current applicable currency rate for settlement date). The applicable interest rate in this case should be the interest rate in the currency of the underlying shares. However, the ADR/GDR may not trade at theoretical price levels. This means that the forward price may vary between the local currency market and the ADR/GDR market[41].

The dividend rate creates significant estimation issues. These are detailed in a separate Section below.

## 6.2   Equity/Equity Index Pricing Models

There are two feasible approaches to deriving the equity forward price. The first entails treating the dividend income as a continuous income stream. The alternative methodology entails treating the dividend as a discrete cash flow. **Exhibit 6.25** sets out an example using the continuous dividend income model. **Exhibit 6.26** sets out an example using the discrete income models. Both examples are based on individual stocks. The approach in pricing an equity index forward is similar. Specific issues arising from the underlying asset being an equity index is discussed in the next Section.

---

**Exhibit 6.25    Pricing an Equity Forward – Continuous Income Model**

**1.   Assumptions**
Assume the following:

| | |
|---|---|
| Share Price | $100.00 |
| Spot Date | 1 April 2002 |
| Forward Date | 1 October 2002 |
| Time to Maturity | 183 days |
| Interest Rates | 6.00% pa |
| Dividend | $2 per share (payable in one instalment) |

---

[41]  This represents an arbitrage opportunity that is exploited by a number of dealers.

**2. Calculation of Forward Price**

The first step in the determination of the forward price is to determine the dividend rate. The dividend yield in this instance is calculated as:

Dividend yield (% pa) $= [1 + (\text{Dividend } (\$2)/\text{Share Price } (\$100)]^{365/183} - 1 = 4.03\%$ pa

It is important to note the importance of annualising the dividend. This is to ensure the dividend is on the same basis as the interest rate. The dividend used is the *dividend that the owner of the share would be entitled to over the life of the forward contract.*

This allows the derivation of the forward price as follows:

| | |
|---|---:|
| Spot Price of Asset | $100.00 |
| Value Date | 01-Apr-02 |
| Maturity Date | 01-Oct-02 |
| Term (days) | 183 |
| Interest Rate (% pa) | 6.00 |
| Asset Return (% pa) | 4.03 |
| Day Count Basis (either 360 or 365) | 365 |
| Forward Asset Price | $100.98 |
| Cost of Forward | $0.98 |

**Exhibit 6.26   Pricing an Equity Forward – Discrete Income Model**

**1. Assumptions**

Assume the same data as in **Exhibit 6.25**. Also assume that the dividend is payable on 27 August 2002

**2. Calculation of Forward Price**

The first step in the determination of the forward price is to discount or present value the dividend to the spot date. The discounted dividend is then used to adjust the spot price of the asset.

| | |
|---|---:|
| Spot Date | 1-Apr-02 |
| Income date | 27-Aug-02 |
| Number of days | 148 |
| Spot Price | $100.00 |
| Income Amount – $ | $2.00 |
| Interest rate (% pa) | 6.00 |
| Discount Factor | 0.9767 |
| Time (years) | 0.41 |
| Income Present Value | $1.95 |
| Adjusted Spot Price | $98.05 |

This allows the derivation of the forward price (using the adjusted spot price) as follows:

| Spot Price of Asset | $98.05 |
|---|---|
| Value Date | 01-Apr-02 |
| Maturity Date | 01-Oct-02 |
| Term (days) | 183 |
| Interest Rate (% pa) | 6.00 |
| Asset Return (% pa) | 0.00 |
| Day Count Basis (either 360 or 365) | 365 |
| Forward Asset Price | $100.96 |
| Cost of Forward | $0.96 |

In practice, the discrete income model is preferred for the following reasons:

- **Dividend Timing** – it is easier to accommodate specific dividend timing as actual cash flows and payment dates are used. This is particularly important as dividend amounts do not accrue in the manner of interest rates. The discrete income approach also enables a term structure on interest rates to be incorporated.
- **Dividend Growth** – changes in dividend can be readily incorporated into the pricing model.
- **Flexibility** – the discrete income approach is much more flexible and allows a greater degree of control over the inputs. It also has the merit of allowing all assumptions underlying the calculation to be transparent.

## 6.3   Pricing Equity Index Forwards[42]

The approach to pricing equity index forwards or futures contracts is similar. The underlying asset for an equity index is the basket of stocks constituting the index. This means that a position in the equity index forward must be hedged with a long or short position *in all the index stocks*. The income on the asset is the combined dividends on all index stocks.

The key differences relative to pricing individual equity forwards are as follows:

- **Replication issues** – replication of the index may be difficult and a smaller replication portfolio (constituting a tracking basket) may be used. In addition, the composition of the index may change, creating difficulties in replication. This incurs tracking error risk (effectively correlation risk) and affects forward prices. There are issues in respect of short selling equities that affect all equity forwards that are discussed below.

---

[42] The issues discussed here are relevant to the process of equity index cash future arbitrage that is common in many markets, see Das, Satyajit (2004) Structured Products Volume 2; John Wiley & Sons (Asia), Singapore at Chapter 1.

- **Difference in transaction costs** – trading in stock index futures and the underlying stock have different transaction costs. The differences between the trading costs influences forward pricing. For example, it might be more attractive to trade one instrument (usual the equity index futures contract) as a surrogate for trading in the stocks. This may result in pricing slippage as the higher costs and/or differences in liquidity may result in the trader factoring these into the forward price.
- **Dividends** – it is preferable to use the actual cash dividends on each individual stock where possible in pricing the index futures contract. However, it is often more convenient to use a dividend yield (in particular where the number of index stocks is very large). Where a dividend is utilised, it is desirable to adjust for any seasonable pattern in the payment of dividends in pricing the equity index forward.

## 6.4  Equity/Equity Index Pricing Models – Key Issues

Equity and equity index pricing models generally make similar assumptions to forward pricing models. Difficulties in short selling and the presence of transaction costs affect the pricing of equity/equity index forwards.

In relation to short selling, it is common in equity markets to have a number of regulations that place limitations on short selling including:
- **Concept of eligible security** – some stock exchanges only allow short selling of some securities that meet minimum market capitalisation and turnover requirements.
- **Limits on short sales** – there might be cumulative limits on the level of short sales on any particular stock (% of outstanding shares).
- **Uptick or down tick rules** – some exchanges require short sales to be identified and it may not be done at a price lower than the last sale price. This has the effect of restricting short selling, in particular, in a falling market.

As with other assets, the availability of stock for borrowing for the purpose of short selling is often restricted. This is exacerbated in equity markets by tax factors. The factors include tax credits on dividends and realisation of gains/losses in stock lending transactions.

An additional problem unique to equity forwards is the problem of estimation of dividends[43]. This is because unlike interest rates (that are the income term in both currency and interest rate forwards), they are not known with certainty. This creates

---

[43] For a discussion of these and other related risks, see Das, Satyajit "Pricing & Risk Management of Equity Derivatives Transactions: Part 1" (1998) Financial Products Issue

significant problems including:

- **Amount** – the dividend amount is completely discretionary and is subject to the company having distributable earnings or reserves. The problem increases with the maturity of the forward.
- **Timing uncertainty** – the entitlement and/or payment dates are determined by the company and are not known in advance.
- **Accrual issues** – dividends do not accrue to the holder of the shares in a smooth and continuous manner over the life of the holding. Entitlement arises from ownership of the share on a specific date. Typically, the share price falls by the amount of the dividend on the date the shares go ex-dividend. This means timing of dividends is critical to the forward contract value, as a small change in timing may result in receipt or loss of the dividend.
- **Tax treatment** – derivative pricing is generally done pre-tax. Dividends attract a variety of treatments. Dividends can be free of tax, partially free of tax, or taxable. The specific treatment will depend upon the jurisdiction, the company paying the dividend and the receiver of the dividend. This means that the pre-tax dividend amount needed for the forward price calculation is difficult to establish with certainty. An additional issue in this context is that the tax treatment may change at any time[44].

The difficulty in estimation of dividends is a central issue in the pricing of equity forwards. In practice, traders are forced to rely on historical dividend rates and projection based on equity analyst forecasts. However, the risk of changes in dividends is significant in the pricing of equity and equity index forwards.

# 7 Forward Pricing – Commodity Contracts

## 7.1 Commodity Forwards – Pricing Approach

Commodity forwards generally consist of forwards on individual commodities or commodity indexes (baskets of commodities). Commodity swaps can be decomposed into a series of commodity forwards. The other major form of commodity forwards is futures contracts on individual commodities or commodity indexes.

---

87 18–23 and "Pricing & Risk Management of Equity Derivatives Transactions: Part 2" (1998) Financial Products Issue 89 18–26.

[44] An example of the problem caused by changes in tax treatment of dividends is discussed in Chapter 7 in the context of pricing equity options.

Commodity forwards are priced using the carry cost model. However, there are differences in pricing commodity forwards relative to the pricing of forwards on financial assets. The differences are driven by the fundamental differences in the underlying asset[45]. The key differences between real asset (commodities) and financial assets (currencies, debt/interest rates, and equities) include:

- **Real (physical) assets** – unlike financial assets, holding of commodities because of their physical nature incur additional costs (such as storage, insurance and transport). Commodities are also affected by changes in the asset (deterioration, loss or change in quality).

- **Consumption and production issues** – real commodities are required to be produced and consumed. Production and consumption are driven by complex factors and subject to (often large) time lags. In addition, individual commodities are often related in a complex manner to other commodities through complementary and substitute behaviour.

- **Price behaviour** – commodity prices display certain systematic price behaviour[46]. The most important aspects of this behaviour includes:
  1. **Mean reversion** – If high, commodity prices tend to decline, and if low, tend to rise towards some long run mean or equilibrium levels. This reflects a combination of supply and demand shifts driven by price changes as well as timing lags in equilibrating supply and demand.
  2. **Seasonal price movements** – some commodity prices appear to demonstrate a strong seasonal price cycle. This is driven by seasonal consumption and production cycles (for example, heating oil demand rises in winter).

---

[45] For a discussion of the special issues in pricing commodity derivatives, see Pilipovic, Dragana (1998) Energy Risk: Valuing and Managing Energy Derivatives; McGraw-Hill, New York.

[46] See Pilipovic, Dragana (1998) Energy Risk: Valuing and Managing Energy Derivatives; McGraw-Hill, New York at Chapters 1, 4 and 5, See also Gabillion, Jacques "Analysing the Forward Curve" in (1995) Managing Energy Price Risk; Risk Publications, London at Chapter 1; Duffie, Darrell and Gray, Stephen "Volatility in Energy Prices" in (1995) Managing Energy Price Risk; Risk Publications, London at Chapter 2; Frankel, Oliver "Special Issues in Valuing Metal Derivatives" in (1997) Managing Metals Price Risk; Risk Publications, London at Chapter 9; Harris, Chris "Long Term Metal Price Development" in (1997) Managing Metals Price Risk; Risk Publications, London at Chapter 10; Nagarajan, Shankar "Power Forward Price Curves: A Managerial Perspective" in (1999) Managing Energy Price Risk – Second Edition; Risk Publications, London at Chapter 12; Duffie, Darrell, Gray, Stephen and Hoang, Philip "Volatility in Energy Prices" in (1999) Managing Energy Price Risk – Second Edition; Risk Publications, London at Chapter 14.

Price cycles are evident in other assets. The cycles appear to be more marked in commodity markets.

- **Market structure** – commodity markets are often regulated and certain facilities (such as borrowing for the purpose of short selling) are not as readily available as in other financial assets.

The presence of these factors must be incorporated in pricing models for commodity forwards.

In this Section, forward pricing models for commodities are outlined. A forward pricing model incorporating storage costs is first outlined. The problem of backwardation in commodity forwards is then identified. The use of convenience yields is then developed as a basis of pricing commodity forwards. In the final section, a forward pricing model incorporating mean reversion is outlined.

## 7.2 Commodity Forward Pricing Model – Basic Model (Incorporating Storage Costs)

The basic forward price of a commodity is usually determined in accordance with an arbitrage-based forward pricing model. This is similar to the carry cost model of pricing forward prices. The forward price of a commodity is a price set today to be paid in the future for the purchase or sale of the identified commodity. For example, a forward purchaser of a commodity could arrange to purchase the required quantity of the commodity today at the current market price, fund and store it until the delivery date, and deliver the commodity to the forward purchaser on the agreed forward date. A forward seller could replicate a forward sale by selling the commodity on the spot market and investing the proceeds until the forward purchase date, when the maturing investment could be utilised to fund the purchase of the agreed amount of the commodity. The cost associated with the immediate purchase, funding and storage until delivery forms a basis of the pricing of the forward contract.

The major factors determining the forward price are:

- Spot price of the commodity.
- Current interest rates as embodied in the yield curve.
- Storage costs.

The information that is available in the market can be used to calculate the forward price, utilising the essential condition that a forward contract can be replicated by entering into a series of transactions that would have the same economic effects as the forward contract.

The first two parameters are consistent with the pricing models used with other assets. The two major differences are the omission of an asset income term (the commodity is not assumed to pay any income[47]) and the inclusion of storage costs. Storage costs are taken to include:

- **Storage or holding costs** – this includes the cost of physical storage of the commodity.
- **Insurance costs** – this covers the cost of taking out and maintaining insurance cost against physical loss of the commodity.
- **Location or transportation costs** – this covers the cost of transporting the physical commodity from buyer to seller. Location costs describe the fact that the completion of a physical purchase or sale may require the commodity to be transported to a specific location. This may be in the form of actual physical transportation of the relevant commodity, or a *location swap* where specific amounts of a commodity *in different locations* are exchanged between two counterparties. The location swaps may incur costs that must be factored into the forward price.
- **Wastage or loss** – this covers the deterioration or loss during the period of holding. This may arise from evaporation (oil products), transport loss (electricity or natural gas transported through a pipeline), oxidisation (metals) or perishability (agricultural products)[48].

**Exhibit 6.27** sets out an example where the forward price of a commodity is calculated using the forward price model incorporating storage costs.

---

**Exhibit 6.27    Pricing a Commodity Forward**

**Discrete Time Models**

$$F = S \times (1 + (r + h))^{t_1}$$

Where

F = Forward price
S = Spot asset price
R = Interest rate for maturity $t_1$
$t_1$ = Maturity of forward contract
h = Storage and other holding costs

---

[47] This assumption is adjusted with the introduction of the convenience yield later in this Chapter.

[48] Certain *non-storable* commodities have an infinite rate of wastage (i.e. the commodity is only capable of utilisation at the time of production). These include: electricity and telecommunication capacity (minutes or packets of data).

**Forward Pricing Example**[49]
Assume the following data:

| | |
|---|---|
| Spot Price ($): | 100.00 |
| Term to Forward Date (years): | 0.50 |
| Interest Rate (% pa): | 6.00 |
| Holding Cost (% pa): | 2.00 |

The forward price is:

$$F = 100 \times (1 + (.06 + .02))^{0.5} = \$103.92$$

## 7.3   Commodity Forward Pricing Model – Backwardation

Commodity forward price is affected by a variety of other factors (other than the spot price, interest cost and storage costs). The additional factors are usually examined through an analysis of the commodity forward price curve.

The relationship between spot and forward commodity prices at a given point in time (referred to as the commodity price curve) can take three basic shapes:
- **Contango** – forward price higher than the spot price.
- **Backwardation** – forward price lower than the spot price.
- **Flat** – the spot price is the same as the forward price.

**Exhibit 6.28** sets out possible shapes of the commodity price curve.

Under the basic model (see **Exhibit 6.27**), the forward price of a commodity should always be above the spot price (that is, in contango). This reflects the fact that the process of replication of the forward position will normally incur costs. The major component of the holding cost is the interest expense of funding the holding of the spot commodity. In addition, the holding of a position in the physical commodity will result in expenditure on storage costs. However, actual forward market prices for commodities are often lower than the spot price; that is, in backwardation[50]. For example, a number of commodities such as crude oil and certain agricultural commodities exhibit consistent backwardation of the forward curve. The problem of backwardation is incorporated in commodity forward pricing using convenience yields predicated on the theoretical relationship between the spot and forward rates.

---

[49]  For convenience, transaction costs have been ignored.
[50]  See Walton, David (28 May 1991) Backwardation in Commodity Markets; Goldmans Sachs & Co, London.

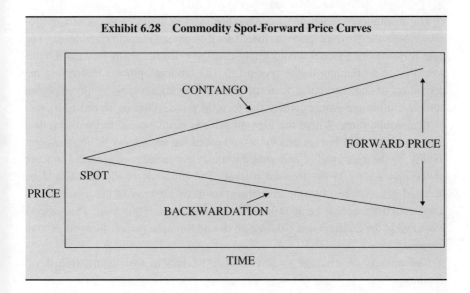

Exhibit 6.28   Commodity Spot-Forward Price Curves

## 7.4   Relationship Between Spot and Forward Commodity Prices – Model[51]

The normal contango shape of the commodity price curve is usually based on the following:

* The pure carry cost model described above.
* The fact that the market is net long hedgers and speculators have to be enticed to take short positions.

This implies that the forward price exceeds current spot price. In practice, the factors determining the relationship between spot and forward commodity prices are more complex. A number of factors dictate that the actual forward price deviates significantly from that derived utilising the pure forward price model. The factors include the difficulty of undertaking arbitrage transactions of the type described.

---

[51] See Walton, David (28 May 1991) Backwardation in Commodity Markets; Goldmans Sachs & Co, London; Das, Satyajit "Forward March" (February 1993) Risk 41–49; Litzenberg, R. and Rabinowitz, N. "Backwardation in Oil Futures Markets: Theory and Empirical Evidence" (January 1995) Journal of Finance vol 50 no 5 1,517–1,545; Schwartz, E. "The Stochastic Behaviour of Commodity Prices: Implications for Valuation and Hedging" (July 1997) Journal of Finance vol 52 no 3 923–972.

The institutional structure of commodity markets impedes the arbitrage process where the forward price is forced to its contango equilibrium level. The pure forward price model would imply that the price for oil in forward months would be at a premium to the spot price. The arbitrage process underlying the derivation of the theoretical forward price of the commodity would imply an attractive arbitrage process where the forward price would be forced to its theoretical equilibrium. Where the forward price is at a discount to the theoretical forward price, the arbitrage process would entail the arbitrageur selling the commodity in the spot market and simultaneously repurchase an identical amount of the commodity in the forward market. The proceeds of the sale would be invested in an interest bearing investment until the maturity of the forward contract, with the proceeds being utilised to fund the forward purchase. This process would yield the arbitrageur a risk free profit and force the market forward price to increase.

The process of arbitrage to force forward prices to their equilibrium level assumes:

• Free purchase and sale of securities including short sales of the commodity.
• Availability of storage and holding facilities for the commodity.
• Absence of market frictions such as trading costs and taxes.

Many of these conditions are not satisfied in the traded market for commodities. A major violation is the inability of arbitrageurs (with the possible exception of large commodity producers and a few large trading companies) to enter into short sales of commodities. Where short sales are possible, the cost of financing or borrowing a commodity to be sold short is high. In essence, it is only possible to be long or flat commodities. This effectively eliminates certain types of arbitrage activities. The only economic means of creating a short position in a commodity is in the futures market for the commodity, if one exists. The inadequacies in the institutional structure of commodity markets dictate that the arbitrage process does not function in accordance with theory.

Other factors that affect the behaviour of the commodity forward prices include:

• Impact of futures supply/demand expectations.
• Price/volume elasticity of the commodity.
• Price expectations.

The factors that in practice drive the commodity forward price are set out in **Exhibit 6.29**.

The theoretical attempts to explain the phenomenon of backwardation in the commodity market are complex and varied. There are a number of possible

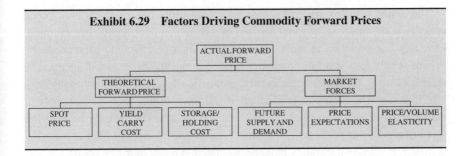

Exhibit 6.29    Factors Driving Commodity Forward Prices

approaches to modelling this relationship:
- **Expectations hypothesis** – under the expectations hypothesis, the current price of a forward contract should be equal to the market consensus expectation of the spot price on the delivery date. This is based on the condition that implies that speculators can neither expect to win or lose from a position in the forward market.
- **Net hedging theory** – the net hedging theory suggests that the relationship between the spot and forward market will depend on the variable net hedging demand in the market. Both the expectations hypothesis and net hedging theory imply that the forward prices will sometimes be higher and sometimes lower than the current spot price of the commodity. Neither theory is satisfactory.
- **Keynesian normal backwardation** – the theory of normal backwardation put forward by John Maynard Keynes (termed normal backwardation) is probably the most interesting basis for determining the relationship between spot and forward prices in commodity markets. The theory of normal backwardation implies the use of convenience yields to value commodity forwards.

## 7.5   Commodity Convenience Yields

The theory of normal backwardation and convenience yields combines the market factors outlined above to derive an interesting basis of pricing commodity forwards.

A common explanation for the occurrence of backwardation is a shortage of supply of a commodity for immediate delivery. An adverse supply shock or a positive demand shock that raises the price of commodity also encourages consumers to substitute future consumption away from that commodity, and producers to increase planned output. The anticipated supply and demand responses in reaction to a price shock may cause the current spot to increase by more than anticipated future spot prices, leading to backwardation.

The actual forward price of a commodity therefore often reflects anticipated changes in the future supply and demand of a particular commodity. For example, increases in production in most commodities cannot be affected instantaneously. Where supply falls short of demand, the price in the spot market will increase to market clearing levels. Simultaneously, production levels of the commodity may also increase. The increases in production and the resulting increase in supply in the spot market may be subject to considerable time lags. The backwardation in the forward market may reflect this lag where the increased supply of the commodity is *expected* to more accurately balance demand and result in lower prices.

A major factor influencing the level of forward prices will be the price/volume elasticity of the commodity. For example, the absolute level of prices for a particular commodity will affect demand for the product. For example, following the oil shocks, consumers of energy products made considerable advances in structuring their energy consumption in a manner that allows them to switch between different energy products. A price rise in oil products may result in switching behaviour where major consumers of oil increase their purchase of coal or natural gas products in preference to oil based energy sources. Similarly, a fall in oil prices may induce a reverse switching behaviour. The forward price must impound expectations as to these types of changes in the supply and demand for commodities.

Backwardation in commodity markets may reflect the price expectations of investors anticipating a fall in commodity prices. Where investors anticipate prices of the commodity will fall because of an improvement in the supply/demand balance for a particular commodity, they will tend to defer their consumption of the commodity, waiting for the price fall.

In addition, a number of commodities are subject to seasonal pricing cycles that may also impact upon the actual levels of forward prices and the premium or discount to the spot price.

Keynes advanced a further reason for backwardation in commodity markets (termed normal backwardation). Under this theory, it is argued that the long run average futures price for a commodity will in general be below the long run average spot price. This reflects the fact that commodity producers are prepared to pay a positive insurance premium (the difference between expected or current spot price and current forward price) to guard against the risk of unforeseen adverse price movements.

The theory of normal backwardation does not depend on any deficiency in the commodity market. It suggests that backwardation exists because the commodity forward market provides a mechanism for risk transfer. Under this market structure, a group of risk averse participants subject to price uncertainty (namely producers who are committed to supplying the commodity) seek insurance from another group of risk averse traders (investors). The positive risk premium (the difference between the anticipated futures spot price and the forward price) is an insurance premium paid by producers to investors to entice investors to undertake forward purchases.

The theory of normal backwardation implies that the degree of backwardation will be a function of:

- Volatility of commodity prices.
- Degree of risk aversion of producers and investors.
- Cost of trading and inventories.

Typically, backwardation tends to be greatest in markets where commodity prices are very volatile, where producers are very sensitive to commodity price fluctuations, and where it is costly to have large holdings of inventories. This is the characteristic of markets in oil, hogs and cattle. If any of these conditions fail to hold, then the excess return will diminish. Backwardation is usually greatest in markets in which commodities are consumed as they are produced and holdings of stocks are small, because they are expensive to store or unsuitable for storage. That makes particular commodities more prone to supply disruptions and, as a result, physical possession often commands a premium embedded in the spot price.

A feature of backwardation in commodity markets is that investors with no interest in holding physical quantities of commodities are able to make investments in commodity markets yielding returns theoretically above the riskless rate. Assuming reasonable stability in the price curve over time, an investor can buy a distant forward contract for a commodity and then transfer this contract into a more distant month as the original contract approaches maturity. This generates a running yield on the commodity holding. The size of the interest-like earning accruing to the investor would depend on the degree of backwardation.

This return embedded within the commodity forward price curve is commonly referred to as *convenience yields*. **Exhibit 6.30** sets out the spot-forward commodity price relationship incorporating convenience yields.

The concept of convenience yield is equivalent to a net earning or yield accruing to the owner of a physical commodity. In a simple sense, this can be equated to the return that can be earned by a commodity owner by lending out the commodity asset[52]. For example, in a backwardated market, the discount evident in forward prices relative to the spot price represents a positive (negative) yield for consumers (producers). In a contango market, the premium of forward prices over spot prices represents a negative (positive) yield to consumers (producers).

---

[52] For example, lending of gold is quite common; see Das, Satyajit (2004) Structured Products Volume 2; John Wiley & Sons (Asia), Singapore at Chapter 9.

The role of convenience yields in the factors that, in practice, drive the commodity forward price are set out in **Exhibit 6.31**.

The use of convenience yields conceptually simplifies the derivation of the forward commodity price. The availability of estimates of convenience yields allows forward prices to be derived by applying the adjusted carry cost model incorporating the convenience yield parameters to generate a series of forward prices for a particular commodity as required. It requires estimates of the convenience yield.

Convenience yield estimates can be obtained by several approaches:
- Analysis of historical data.
- Fitting convenience yield process to current observed sets of forward prices.

---

**Exhibit 6.30    Pricing a Commodity Forward – Incorporating Convenience Yields**

$$F = S \times (1 + (r + h - c))^{t_1}$$

Where

F = Forward price
S = Spot asset price
R = Interest rate for maturity $t_1$
$t_1$ = Maturity of forward contract
h = Storage and other holding costs
c = convenience yield

In practice this can be simplified further by eliminating storage costs (h). These costs are assumed to be incorporated into the convenience yield. This allows re-statement of the forward price as:

$$F = S \times (1 + (r - c))^{t_1}$$

---

**Exhibit 6.31    Factors Driving Commodity Forward Prices (Incorporating Convenience Yields)**

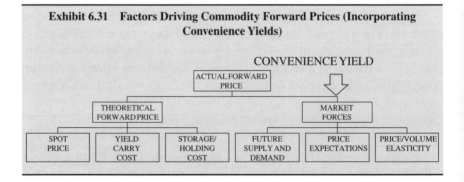

**Exhibit 6.32** sets out the basic procedure used to derive the convenience yield from available spot and forward commodity prices. The major difficulty in estimation of convenience yields relates to the fact that it is necessary to have both the spot *and the forward price* in order to derive the convenience yield. In practice, the convenience yield is required *to calculate the forward price* in the first instance. This means that in practice, an estimate of the *expected* convenience yield (based on historical data or other estimation procedure) is used. This is not dissimilar to the problem of volatility estimation in option pricing.

Research indicates that convenience yields have certain observable behaviours[53]. Convenience yields appear to be inversely related to the level of inventories. In addition, there is evidence of mean reversion in convenience yields.

There is evidence of significant differences in the levels of convenience yield between commodities. Oil and base metals (such as copper) are industrial commodities that are consumed shortly after production. Precious metals are held as repositories of value in anticipation of future price appreciation. This means that certain commodities are not consumed and the bulk of production continues to exist. In commodities that are rapidly consumed, the market is backwardated in general reflecting:

- Relatively low levels of stocks of the commodity.
- Lack of infrastructure to store the commodity.
- High possession value of the commodity, particularly during periods of market dislocation.

In the oil market, most independent refiners are inherently capital constrained and are forced to rely on near-term surety of supply rather than longer-term hedging strategies. This results in a persistent pattern of purchasing crude at a time close to the consumption requirement. This necessitates that the independent refiners sacrifice the added yield from capturing the natural backwardation of the market.

In a variety of industries that are regulated, the impact of the regulatory framework affects the level of convenience yields. In industries where consumers are assured supply or a regulatory mechanism exists, allowing higher prices of the commodity to be passed on to the ultimate consumer, buying activities are concentrated in the near months forcing a backwardated curve with the resultant convenience yield structures. In markets that are structured as cartels or supply

---

[53] Research mentioned in Dr Desmond Fitzgerald "Pricing Energy Derivatives"; paper presented at conference "Pricing and Structuring Energy Swaps", IIR Pty Ltd, in London, England on 2 March 1992.

is regulated, short-term demand shocks or supply shocks may lead to sharp back-wardation. This is driven by the expectation of increased future production and/or consumer conservation, as the regulatory body is expected to move to equalise demand and supply in the market.

### Exhibit 6.32     Calculating Convenience Yield

Assume the following spot and forward prices exist for a commodity:

| Term (Days) | Commodity Price ($) |
|---|---|
| Spot | 21.05 |
| 55 | 20.82 |
| 88 | 20.74 |
| 117 | 20.70 |
| 150 | 20.62 |
| 179 | 20.42 |
| 212 | 20.30 |
| 238 | 20.09 |
| 272 | 20.02 |
| 303 | 19.90 |
| 331 | 19.85 |
| 360 | 19.81 |
| 392 | 19.80 |

Assume that the following interest rates are applicable:

| Term (Days) | Interest Rates (% pa) |
|---|---|
| Spot | |
| 55 | 5.50 |
| 88 | 5.60 |
| 117 | 5.65 |
| 150 | 5.70 |
| 179 | 5.75 |
| 212 | 5.85 |
| 238 | 5.88 |
| 272 | 6.00 |
| 303 | 6.02 |
| 331 | 6.10 |
| 360 | 6.10 |
| 392 | 6.15 |

The spot price, the term to maturity and the interest rate can be used to derive the *theoretical* forward commodity price as follows:

| Term (Days) | Commodity Price ($) | Interest Rate (% pa) | Arbitrage Free Forward Price ($) |
|---|---|---|---|
| Spot | 21.05 | | |
| 55 | | 5.50 | 21.22 |
| 88 | | 5.60 | 21.33 |
| 117 | | 5.65 | 21.43 |
| 150 | | 5.70 | 21.54 |
| 179 | | 5.75 | 21.64 |
| 212 | | 5.85 | 21.77 |
| 238 | | 5.88 | 21.86 |
| 272 | | 6.00 | 22.00 |
| 303 | | 6.02 | 22.11 |
| 331 | | 6.10 | 22.23 |
| 360 | | 6.10 | 22.33 |
| 392 | | 6.15 | 22.46 |

The arbitrage free forward prices differ from the *actual* market forward price as set out below. This difference is caused by the convenience yield. That can be calculated as the convenience yield that, given the spot price, the term and the interest rate, would generate the actual market forward price. This is set out in the Table below:

| Term (Days) | Commodity Price ($) | Arbitrage Free Forward Price ($) | Difference Attributable to Convenience Yield ($) | Convenience Yield (% pa) |
|---|---|---|---|---|
| Spot | 21.05 | | | |
| 55 | 20.82 | 21.22 | (0.40) | 12.439 |
| 88 | 20.74 | 21.33 | (0.59) | 11.489 |
| 117 | 20.70 | 21.43 | (0.73) | 10.678 |
| 150 | 20.62 | 21.54 | (0.92) | 10.533 |
| 179 | 20.42 | 21.64 | (1.22) | 11.678 |
| 212 | 20.30 | 21.77 | (1.47) | 11.825 |
| 238 | 20.09 | 21.86 | (1.77) | 12.692 |
| 272 | 20.02 | 22.00 | (1.98) | 12.424 |
| 303 | 19.90 | 22.11 | (2.21) | 12.477 |
| 331 | 19.85 | 22.23 | (2.38) | 12.284 |
| 360 | 19.81 | 22.33 | (2.52) | 11.991 |
| 392 | 19.80 | 22.46 | (2.66) | 11.617 |

## 7.6 Commodity Forward Prices – Mean Reverting Forward Prices

Commodity prices exhibit mean reversion and seasonal price trends. A number of models for pricing commodity forward contracts, incorporating the impact of these factors, have been developed[54].

**Exhibit 6.33** sets out the model suggested by Pilipovic. The Pilipovic mean reversion model defines the forward price in terms of extent of backwardation or contango. This is in terms of both the short and longer term commodity forward price curve. Where the spot price is higher, then the long term equilibrium price, the convenience yield, is positive. This results in the short end of the forward curve being backwardated. The reverse is true where the opposite conditions hold and the short end of the forward curve would be in contango. Where the market price of risk on the equilibrium price is greater than the equilibrium price drift, then the longer term forward curve would generally be backwardated. The reverse would again be true if the opposite conditions hold and the long end of the commodity forward price curve would be in contango[55].

The models are valuable in capturing the behaviour of the underlying commodity and it price evolution. The major difficulty with the models is the need to estimate a number of parameters (the long-term equilibrium price, mean reversion rate, cost of risk, volatility of equilibrium price and rate of return or drift rate) that are not directly available from the market. The need to estimate these factors (typically from historical price information) is problematic. The historical estimates may not hold for the period in question. The problems in this context are not dissimilar to the problems associated with interest rate term structure models, where similar variables must be estimated from market data.

---

[54] See Pilipovic, Dragana (1998) Energy Risk: Valuing and Managing Energy Derivatives; McGraw-Hill, New York at Chapter 5. See also Gabillion, Jacques "Analysing the Forward Curve" in (1995) Managing Energy Price Risk; Risk Publications, London at Chapter 1; Amin, Kausik, Ng, Victor, and Pirrong, S. Craig "Valuing Energy Derivatives" in (1995) Managing Energy Price Risk; Risk Publications, London at Chapter 3; Hillard, J. and Reis, J. "Valuation of Commodity Futures and Options Under Stochastic Convenience Yield, Interest Rates and Jump Diffusions in the Spot" (1998) Journal of Financial and Quantitative Analysis vol 33 no 1 61–86; Amin, Kausik, Ng, Victor, and Pirrong, S. Craig "Arbitrage Free Valuation of Energy Derivatives" in (1999) Managing Energy Price Risk – Second Edition; Risk Publications, London at Chapter 13.

[55] See Pilipovic, Dragana (1998) Energy Risk: Valuing and Managing Energy Derivatives; McGraw-Hill, New York at 97.

---

**Exhibit 6.33   Pricing a Commodity Forward – Incorporating Mean Reversion**

$$F_{t,T} = (S_t - L_t)e^{-(\alpha+\lambda\varepsilon)\tau} + L_t e^{(\mu-\lambda\varepsilon)\tau}$$

Where

F = Forward price
t = Time of observation
T = Time of contract estimation
S = Spot asset price
L = Equilibrium price
$\alpha$ = Mean reversion rate
$\lambda$ = Cost of risk
$\varepsilon$ = Volatility of long term equilibrium price
$\tau$ = Time to expiration T − t
$\mu$ = Rate of return or drift rate

Source: Pilipovic, Dragana (1998) Energy Risk: Valuing and Managing Energy Derivatives;
McGraw-Hill, New York at 87–97.

---

# 8   Pricing Futures Contracts

## 8.1   Pricing Approach

Pricing of futures contracts is similar to but not identical to the pricing of forward contracts. Futures contracts and default free forward contracts are similar
but distinct instruments as a result of the different cash flow patterns. The cash
flow patterns derive from the fact that the forward contract has no cash flows until
the forward or settlement date. Futures contracts have cash flows deriving from
the requirement of marking the contracts to market, resulting in daily positive or
negative cash flows[56]. In effect, a futures contract is a forward contract that is
simultaneously cash settled and rolled to the original contract maturity on every
day (or whenever the contract is marked-to-market).

In practice, the approach to pricing futures contracts is to price the contract as
a *forward contract* (that is assuming all cash flows are deferred to maturity of the
contract). The price is then adjusted for the impact of early cash flows.

---

[56] This was identified by Cox, John C., Ingersoll, Jonothan E., and Ross, Stephen A.
"The Relation Between Forward Prices and Futures Prices" (1981) Journal of Financial
Economics 9 321–346; Jarrow, Robert and Oldfield, George "Forward Contracts and
Futures" (1981) Journal of Financial Economics 9 373–382.

It is possible to demonstrate via arbitrage arguments that where the risk free interest rate is constant and the same for all the maturities (or through an extension to the basic argument where interest rates are a known function of time), the forward price and the futures price for a contract with the same delivery dates is the same[57]. Where interest rates vary unpredictably, forward and futures prices diverge. The difference between the forward and futures price is driven by the correlation or relationship between the spot price and interest rates and the volatility of interest rates.

The relationship between forward and futures prices can be illustrated conceptually. **Exhibit 6.34** sets out the relationship between forward and futures prices. **Exhibit 6.35** shows the quantitative impact of the argument by examining the impact of mark-to-market cash flows on a futures contract and an identical replicated position using a FRA (a forward interest rate contract).

---

**Exhibit 6.34    Relationship Between Forward and Futures Prices**

**1.    Perfect Positive (+1) Correlation Between Asset Price and Interest Rates**
Assume a trader has a bought position in a futures contract enabling the purchase of the asset. The futures position behaves as follows:
- If the asset price increases, then the trader makes a mark-to-market gain on the position. The gain is invested at higher interest rates (based on the perfect positive correlation between the asset price and interest rates).
- If the asset price decreases, then the trader makes a mark-to-market loss on the position. The loss is financed at lower interest rates (based on the perfect positive correlation between the asset price and interest rates).

In contrast, interest rate movements do not affect the trader holding an identical bought position using a forward contract.

Using an arbitrage free argument, it is possible to demonstrate that the bought futures contract is more attractive than the comparable forward position and will accordingly be more expensive (futures price greater than the forward price).

Generalising this conclusion, where the spot asset price is positively correlated with interest rates, futures prices will be higher than forward prices.

**2.    Perfect Negative (−1) Correlation Between Asset Price and Interest Rates**
Assume a trader has a bought position in a futures contract enabling the purchase of the asset. The futures position behaves as follows:
- If the asset price increases, then the trader makes a mark-to-market gain on the position. The gain is invested at lower interest rates (based on the perfect negative correlation between the asset price and interest rates).

---

[57]  For a detailed proof see Hull, John (2000) Option Futures and Other Derivatives – Fourth Edition; Prentice-Hall Inc., Upper Saddle River, NJ at 85–86.

- If the asset price decreases, then the trader makes a mark-to-market loss on the position. The loss is financed at higher interest rates (based on the perfect negative correlation between the asset price and interest rates).

In contrast, interest rate movements do not affect the trader holding an identical bought position using a forward contract.

Using an arbitrage free argument, it is possible to demonstrate that the bought forward contract is more attractive than the comparable futures position and will accordingly be more expensive (futures price lower than the forward price).

Generalising this conclusion, where the spot asset price is negatively correlated with interest rates, futures prices will be lower than forward prices.

The difficulty with this approach to deriving the pricing difference between forward and futures contracts is the necessity of establishing the correlation between the asset price and interest rates. In practice, this is difficult. The only asset for which this is readily feasible is interest rates (such as Eurodollar forward contracts). In this case, there is perfect negative correlation between the futures price and the underlying asset (a 1 bps change in interest rate results in a .01 price change in the contract value).

Other factors that might impact upon the pricing of futures contracts relative to the pricing of forward contracts include:

- Differences in transaction costs.
- Settlement basis (that is, the ability to settle by delivery) which may affect convergence.
- Differences in liquidity between the markets.
- Delivery option (such as those in deliverable bond futures contracts).
- Impact of taxes (including treatment of margin payments).

In practice, the factors are difficult to quantify and may not be explicitly captured in futures pricing models.

The differences between forward and futures prices are relatively minor for contracts where the maturity is short. This allows the differences to be ignored or quantified relatively simply (using crude and often arbitrary adjustments). Where the maturity of the contract is longer, the difference between the forward and futures price is more significant. In these situations, it is necessary to adjust the forward price using a convexity adjustment to calculate the futures prices. Alternatively, where the futures prices are available, the future price must be adjusted by the convexity adjustment to derive the forward price. This is relevant where the futures price is used for example in building a zero coupon curve. The methodology for calculating the convexity adjustment is set out in the following Section.

**Exhibit 6.35    Relationship Between Interest Rate Forward and Interest Futures Prices[58]**

Assume the following market data:

Spot Date:        1 December 2001
Forward Date:   1 December 2002

A trader sell an interest rate futures contract and also enters into a series of borrowing and lending contracts to replicate the futures position.

The futures contract covers a period from 1 December 2002 to 1 March 2003 (90 days out of the forward date). The borrowing and lending transactions are to 1 December 2002 (365 days out of spot) and 1 March 2003 (455 days out of spot).

The interest rates prevailing are as follows:

| Term (days) | Interest Rates (% pa) |
|:-----------:|:---------------------:|
| 365         | 6.00                  |
| 455         | 6.50                  |

Based on these rates, the forward rate is 8.55% pa. Assume the futures contract is trading at 91.45 (100.00 − 8.55).

The forward (a sold forward or bought FRA position) can be replicated by borrowing funds for 455 days and lending funds for 365 days. The cash flow position (assuming $1,000,000 principal amount) is set out below:

| Term | Cash Flows ($) | | Net Cash Flows ($) |
|:---:|:---:|:---:|:---:|
| | **Borrowing** | **Investment** | |
| 1 December 2001 | 943,396 | (943,396) | |
| 1 December 2002 | | 1,000,000 | 1,000,000 |
| 1 March 2003 | (1,020,440) | | (1,020,440) |

The transaction depicted provides the trader with a guaranteed funding cost of 8.55% pa. All cash flows are deferred till maturity of the contracts, thereby ensuring that the price will not change.

Alternatively, the trader may sell interest futures contracts at 91.45 (8.55% pa). However, in this case the trader must post an initial margin or deposit (assumed to be $500). In addition, as interest rates change and the futures price changes, the contract is marked to market and variation margins are received or paid. To simulate the behaviour of the futures contracts

---

[58]   This example draws on the approach taken by Martin, John "Pricing Forwards and Futures Contracts" in Satyajit (Editor) (1997) Risk Management & Financial Derivatives: A Guide to the Mathematics; LBC Information Services, Sydney; McGraw-Hill, Chicago; MacMillan Publishing, England at 140–141.

cash flows, the following analysis assumes that rates decline over the life of the contract to 6.00% pa. The resulting cash flows are summarised in the Table below:

| Term (years) | Interest Rates (% pa) | Futures Price | Current Forward Rate (% pa) | Mark-to-Market ($) | Funding Requirement ($) | Interest Received on Initial Margin ($) | Interest Paid on Total Funding Requirement ($) | Net Interest ($) |
|---|---|---|---|---|---|---|---|---|
| 0 | 6.00 | 91.45 | 8.55 | | (500) | | | |
| 0.25 | 6.00 | 92.09 | 7.91 | (1,600) | (2,100) | 6 | (32) | (25) |
| 0.5 | 6.00 | 92.73 | 7.27 | (1,600) | (3,700) | 6 | (56) | (49) |
| 0.75 | 6.00 | 93.37 | 6.63 | (1,600) | (5,300) | 6 | (80) | (73) |
| 1 | 6.00 | 94.00 | 6.00 | (1,575) | (6,875) | 6 | (103) | (97) |
| | | | | | Total | 25 | (270) | (245) |

Notes:
1. All futures price are assumed to take place instantaneously at quarter end.
2. It is assumed that interest rates are the same for overnight rates and 3 months.
3. The mark to market is based on $25 per .01 price movements (.01% pa).
4. Interest received is calculated as the current interest rates minus 1% pa.

The effective futures cost incorporating the additional cost of funding the margin payments is summarised below:

| Date | Cash ($) | Futures Cost ($) | Adjusted Cash Flows ($) |
|---|---|---|---|
| 1-Dec-02 | 1,000,000 | (245) | 999,755 |
| 1-Mar-03 | (1,020,440) | | (1,020,440) |

This equates to an effective interest rate cost of 8.66% pa.
The comparison between the forward rate and the futures contract is summarised below:

| | |
|---|---|
| Forward Rate | 8.55% pa |
| Futures Rate | 8.66% pa |
| Difference | 0.11% pa |

The convexity adjustment is used in practice primarily in connection with short-term interest rate futures contracts (such as Eurodollar futures) that trade out to longer maturities. The fact that other futures contracts do not trade out to longer maturities means that the difference is ignored or estimated simply.

## 8.2 Pricing Interest Rate Futures – Convexity Adjustment

In practice, the term convexity adjustment is used to cover three specific adjustments made to forward or futures rates. These are:
- Margins.
- Fixed tick point value.
- Unnatural time lag.

The convexity adjustment discussed in this Section refers to the adjustment where the theoretical forward interest rate is adjusted for the impact on funding or re-investing the cash flows resulting from the contract being marked to market periodically[59]. **Exhibit 6.36** sets out the convexity adjustment generally used in practice[60].

---

**Exhibit 6.36    Pricing Futures Contracts – Convexity Adjustment**

**1.   Convexity Adjustment Formula**[61]
The convexity adjustment is given by the following:

$$(B(t_1, t_2)/(t_2 - t_1)) \times [B(t_1, t_2) \times (1 - e^{-2at_1}) + 2aB(0, t_1)^2] \times (\sigma^2/4a)$$

Where

$t_1$    = Time (years) to forward date from spot date
$t_2$    = Time (years) to forward maturity from spot date
$a$    = Mean reversion rate
$\sigma$    = Volatility of the rate
$B(t_1, t_2) = (1 - e^{-a(t_2 - t_1)})/a$
$B(0, t_1) = (1 - e^{-a(t_1 - 0)})/a$

Where $a = 0$ the convexity adjustment is given by:

$$\sigma^2 t_1 t_2/2$$

---

[59] The convexity adjustment required for the fixed tick point (which affects using futures contracts as a hedge) is discussed in Chapter 13. The unnatural time lag (the pattern of payments under a contract) is discussed in Das, Satyajit (2004) Structured Products Volume 1; John Wiley & Sons (Asia), Singapore at Chapters 14 and 17.

[60] See Hull, John (1997) Futures, Options and Other Derivatives – Third Edition; Prentice Hall, Upper Saddle River, NJ at 450–452.

[61] The formula is that suggested by John Hull, See Hull, John (1997) Futures, Options and Other Derivatives – Third Edition; Prentice Hall, Upper Saddle River, NJ at 450–452, 419, 420; see also See Hull, John (2000) Option Futures and Other Derivatives – Fourth Edition; Prentice-Hall Inc., Upper Saddle River, NJ at 547–551, 563, 595.

## 2. Example

The assumed inputs are as follows:

| | |
|---|---|
| Settlement Date | 1-Dec-01 |
| Time to Settlement Date | 1-Dec-11 |
| Time to Forward Maturity | 1-Mar-12 |
| Time to Settlement Date ($t_1$) | 10.01 |
| Time to Forward Maturity ($t_2$) | 10.25 |
| Future Price | 94.00 |
| Futures Rate (Quarterly) | 6.00% |
| Futures Rate (Annual) | 6.14% |
| Futures Rate (Continuously compounded) | 5.96% |
| Zero Rate to Settlement Date | 6.00% |
| Mean Reversion Rate (a)[62] | 0.05 |
| Interest Rate Volatility ($\sigma$)[63] | 0.30% |
| $B(t_1, t_2)$ | 0.2478 |
| $B(0, t_1)$ | 7.8727 |

The convexity adjustments derived are set out below:

Convexity Adjustment (Using Mean Reversion)   0.000284
Convexity Adjustment (No Mean Reversion)    0.000462

The convexity adjustment (using the mean reversion) is used to adjust the futures rate to derive the forward rate as follows:

Adjusted Forward Rate (Continuous)    5.93% pa
Adjusted Forward Rate (Annual)      6.11% pa
Adjusted Forward Rate (Quarterly)    5.97% pa
Difference                    0.03% pa

### Sensitivity of Convexity Adjustment

In the Tables below the convexity adjustment is calculated for different maturities and at different volatility:

$\sigma = 0.30\%$ pa

| | | | | | | | |
|---|---|---|---|---|---|---|---|
| Time to Settlement Date (years) | 0.50 | 1.00 | 2.00 | 3.00 | 5.01 | 7.01 | 10.02 |
| Time to Forward Maturity (years) | 0.75 | 1.25 | 2.25 | 3.25 | 5.25 | 7.26 | 10.27 |
| Future Price | 94.00 | 94.00 | 94.00 | 94.00 | 94.00 | 94.00 | 94.00 |
| Futures Rate (Quarterly) | 6.00 | 6.00 | 6.00 | 6.00 | 6.00 | 6.00 | 6.00 |
| Futures Rate (Annual) | 6.14 | 6.14 | 6.14 | 6.14 | 6.14 | 6.14 | 6.14 |
| Futures Rate (Continuous) | 5.96 | 5.96 | 5.96 | 5.96 | 5.96 | 5.96 | 5.96 |

---

[62] For a discussion of the mean reversion rate, see Chapter 8.
[63] For a discussion of volatility, see Chapter 9.

**σ = 0.30% pa**

| Zero Rate to Settlement Date (% pa) | 6.00 | 6.00 | 6.00 | 6.00 | 6.00 | 6.00 | 6.00 |
|---|---|---|---|---|---|---|---|
| Mean Reversion Rate | 0.05 | 0.05 | 0.05 | 0.05 | 0.05 | 0.05 | 0.05 |
| Convexity Adjustment (% pa) | 0.000 | 0.001 | 0.002 | 0.004 | 0.009 | 0.016 | 0.028 |

**σ = 0.60% pa**

All other parameters are as above.

| Time to Settlement Date (years) | 0.50 | 1.00 | 2.00 | 3.00 | 5.01 | 7.01 | 10.02 |
|---|---|---|---|---|---|---|---|
| Time to Forward Maturity (years) | 0.75 | 1.25 | 2.25 | 3.25 | 5.25 | 7.26 | 10.27 |
| Convexity Adjustment (% pa) | 0.001 | 0.002 | 0.007 | 0.015 | 0.037 | 0.065 | 0.114 |

**σ = 1.00% pa**

All other parameters are as above.

| Time to Settlement Date (years) | 0.50 | 1.00 | 2.00 | 3.00 | 5.01 | 7.01 | 10.02 |
|---|---|---|---|---|---|---|---|
| Time to Forward Maturity (years) | 0.75 | 1.25 | 2.25 | 3.25 | 5.25 | 7.26 | 10.27 |
| Convexity Adjustment (% pa) | 0.002 | 0.006 | 0.020 | 0.042 | 0.102 | 0.180 | 0.316 |

**σ = 1.50% pa**

All other parameters are as above.

| Time to Settlement Date (years) | 0.50 | 1.00 | 2.00 | 3.00 | 5.01 | 7.01 | 10.02 |
|---|---|---|---|---|---|---|---|
| Time to Forward Maturity (years) | 0.75 | 1.25 | 2.25 | 3.25 | 5.25 | 7.26 | 10.27 |
| Convexity Adjustment (% pa) | 0.004 | 0.013 | 0.046 | 0.094 | 0.230 | 0.405 | 0.712 |

## 8.3 Pricing Interest Rate Futures – Turn-of-Year Adjustment

The pricing on interest rate futures contracts sometimes requires an adjustment for the year-end turn affect[64].

The turn effect refers to the fact that rates generally are higher for a brief period at the end of each (financial) year. The turn period is generally taken to be a period of between 2 and 4 days between the last business day of the current calendar year and the first business day of the new year (depending on which day 31 December falls)[65]. There can be year end financing pressures as financial

---

[64] For a discussion of the year end turn effect, see Burghardt, Galen and Kirshner, Susan "One Good Turn" (November 1994) Risk 44–54.

[65] The turn effect is most often noted in relation to US$. However, it is equally evident in other currencies.

institutions adjust their year end balance sheets (so-called window dressing). This causes volatility in short term rates. Contracts that span the year end (such as the 1 month LIBOR and 3 month Eurodollar contracts in US$) are affected by these factors. The effects can be substantial e.g. a 100 bps increase in the spread between the non-turn and turn forward deposit rates can have a 2–4 bps effect on the value of the 3 month Eurodollar contract trading out of December[66]. It may also have significant effects on various market spreads (such as Treasury-Eurodollar spread as well as the inter-month contract spreads in interest rate futures contracts).

The market futures rates presumably build in the market expectations of the turn. If a participant has a different view on the turn rates, then it would be necessary to adjust the relevant contract rates. This would typically be done by specifying the turn rate expected and adjusting the forward/futures prices or rates to reflect the assumptions.

## 9 Summary

Forward contracts are priced using a carry cost model that calculates the forward price as the spot price adjusted for the cost of holding the asset (the interest and other costs of acquiring and holding the asset adjusted for any income on the asset). This price is predicated on the ability of traders to replicate the transactions by trading in the underlying asset and borrowing or lending cash. The hedge should be static and enable a good hedge of the underlying forward position. The ability to arbitrage the relationship between the spot and forward prices should force, in theory, equilibrium arbitrage free prices.

In practice, the application of the model to individual types of assets is affected by inefficiencies in trading in the spot market (such as restrictions on short selling). The inefficiencies prevent arbitrage and allow mis-pricing between the spot and forward prices. Additional problems derive from the fact that for some assets (equities), the income term is not readily available and must be estimated. In the case of commodity forwards, the nature of the underlying asset markets and the price behaviour further complicates pricing. Futures contracts are treated as forward contracts and adjusted for the impact of funding any mark-to-market gains and losses using a convexity adjustment.

---

[66]  See Burghardt, Galen and Kirshner, Susan "One Good Turn" (November 1994) Risk at 49.

## Appendix A: Repo (Security Repurchase/Borrowing and Lending) Markets[67]

### A.1.  Overview

The repurchase agreement or repo market is in effect a collateralised money market in which individual institutions borrow cash and lend a liquid marketable security as collateral against the loan. The repo market's economic function is based on its role in financing dealers' inventory of securities (for example bonds) and covering short positions by facilitating the lending and borrowing of securities.

The relationship between repo markets and forward pricing derives from the fact that the trader must purchase or short the underlying asset in order to replicate a forward contract. Where the asset is purchased, it must be funded. Where it is sold short, the trader must borrow the asset in order to undertake the short sale. The repo market provides the basic mechanism for financing asset holdings and borrowing assets for the purpose of short sales.

The relationship exists in both the exchange-traded and OTC derivatives markets. For example, in the OTC swap market, given that in maintaining hedges against swap positions, financial institutions need to fund securities or alternatively borrow bonds to cover short positions held against swap risk positions, the repo market play a significant role in swap portfolio management[68].

In this Appendix the basic mechanism of repo transactions is outlined.

### A.2.  Repo Transactions

A repo agreement is an immediate sale and a simultaneous commitment to repurchase securities at an agreed date in the future. There are basically two types of repo agreements:

- **Repos** – where the institution lends the collateral and borrows cash; that is, the institution is said to "repo" the collateral.
- **Reverse repo** – where the institution borrows the collateral security and lends the cash; that is, they reverse the repo.

---

[67] For an overview of the repo markets, see Corrigan, Daniel, Georgiou, Christopher and Gollow, Jonothan (1999) Repo: The Ultimate Guide; Pearls of Wisdom Publishing Ltd, London; see also Shanahan, Terry "The Repo Market" (Summer 1991) Journal of International Securities Market 169–180; Corrigan, Daniel "Repos: Some Fundamental Issues (September 1994) Capital Market Strategies Issue No. 2 33–42.

[68] See Chapter 11 and 13.

In each case, a rate of interest is paid for the use of funds by the borrower (the repo rate).

The structure of a generic repo transaction is set out in **Exhibit 6.A.1**. An example of a repo transaction is set out in **Exhibit 6.A.2**.

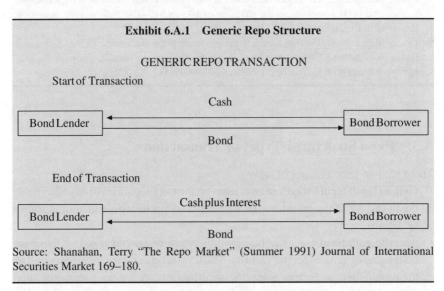

**Exhibit 6.A.1    Generic Repo Structure**

GENERIC REPO TRANSACTION

Start of Transaction

Cash

| Bond Lender | ← Bond → | Bond Borrower |

End of Transaction

| Bond Lender | ← Cash plus Interest → Bond ← | Bond Borrower |

Source: Shanahan, Terry "The Repo Market" (Summer 1991) Journal of International Securities Market 169–180.

**Exhibit 6.A.2    Repo Transaction – Example**

Assume a repo transaction using the following bond:

Security:              Government Bond
Nominal Amount:   $10,000,000
Coupon:              6% pa payable semi-annually
Maturity:             15/11/2012
Yield to Maturity:   6.75% pa

Assume the following details of the repo:

Trade Date:          22 March 2002
Value Date:          24 March 2002
Termination Date:   25 March 2002
Repo Term:          Overnight (1 day)
Repo Rate:           5.85% pa

The bond value on value date is as follows:

Clean Price:          94.36
Accrued Interest:    2.14

Total Price:     96.50
Cash Price:     $9,649,817

The repo transaction would operate as follows:
- On 24 March 2002, the bond lender transfers $10 million face value government bonds to the bond borrower in return for payment of $9,649,817. The cash amount equates to the value of the collateral[69].
- On 25 March 2002, the bond lender repays the original amount of $9,649,817 and in return receives the $10 million of bonds back. In addition, the bond lender pays the bond borrower interest of $1,568.10 (calculated as $9,649,817 × 5.85% pa × 1/360).

## A.3.   Repo Structures-Types of Transaction

There are two general types of repos:
- **General collateral** – these are cash loans against any securities of any acceptable credit quality to the investor. The transaction is primarily a collateralised loan or deposit.
- **Specific collateral** (security borrowing/lending or special repos) – these are cash loans against a specific security. The transaction is primarily motivated by the requirement to borrow a specific security (usually for the purpose of short selling).

The term repo is used generically to cover all types of repurchase agreements. In practice, there are three general transaction structures utilised:
- **Repurchase agreements** – a repurchase agreement entails the bond lender selling the bond and pre-arranging to repurchase it *at the same price* it was sold together with an interest payment reflecting interest cost of borrowing funds for the relevant period. A repurchase agreement is structured so that the original bond owner receives any coupons paid on the bond. **Exhibit 6.A.3** sets out this structure in diagrammatic form.
- **Sale and buy-back** – a sale and buy-back transaction requires the bond lender to agree to sell the bonds today and repurchase them at a later date. The sale price of the bonds will include the accrued coupon interest to the sell date. The buy-back price will also be adjusted to include accrued coupon interest to the buy-back

---

[69] Please note that for convenience no adjustment for a *haircut* (in effect over collateralisation) has been made. If a haircut was applied, the amount advanced in exchange for the bond would be reduced by the amount of the haircut. Interest on the repo would be based on this lower amount advanced.

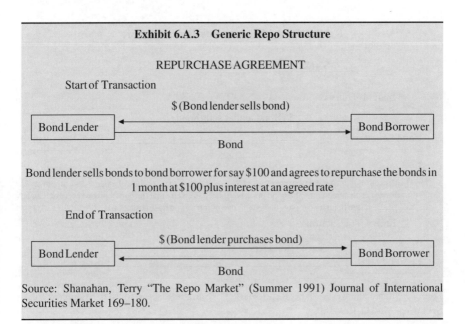

**Exhibit 6.A.3   Generic Repo Structure**

REPURCHASE AGREEMENT

Start of Transaction

$ (Bond lender sells bond)

| Bond Lender | ← | Bond Borrower |

Bond

Bond lender sells bonds to bond borrower for say $100 and agrees to repurchase the bonds in 1 month at $100 plus interest at an agreed rate

End of Transaction

$ (Bond lender purchases bond)

| Bond Lender | ← | Bond Borrower |

Bond

Source: Shanahan, Terry "The Repo Market" (Summer 1991) Journal of International Securities Market 169–180.

date. In order to ensure that the borrower of the funds pays the appropriate rate of interest (the repo interest rate), the clean price of the buy-back (the price of the bond including no accrual) is set at a level that on an internal rate of return basis provides the relevant interest rate in the transaction. **Exhibit 6.A.4** sets out this structure in diagrammatic form.

- **Securities lending** – in a bond lending transaction, the cash borrower agrees to borrow the cash for a fixed period of time at a fixed rate of interest, with the bonds being lodged as collateral to lower the overall risk of the transaction. At maturity of the transaction, the cash borrower pays back the loan with interest and receives the bond back. The original bond owner receives all coupons paid on the bond over the loan period. Bond lending transactions can be structured where the bonds are lodged for several days or weeks, the rate of interest on the cash loan being reset daily. **Exhibit 6.A.5** sets out this structure in diagrammatic form.

The structures are similar. The different structures are used to take advantage of different tax treatments of the cash flows and differing legal treatment of security rights and bond ownership. In substantive terms, the economic effect of the different structures is similar.

In financing securities held as hedges against derivative transactions/portfolios or borrowing bonds to create short positions, financial institutions will typically

**Exhibit 6.A.4    Sale and Buy-Back Structure**

SALE AND BUY-BACK AGREEMENT

Start of Transaction

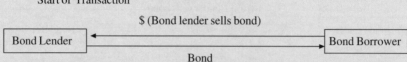

$ (Bond lender sells bond)

Bond

Bond lender sells bonds to bond borrower for say $100 and agrees to repurchase the bonds in 1 month at $100 plus interest at an agreed rate (the bond price is adjusted to ensure that the bond borrower receives and the bond lender pays the agreed rate of interest on the transaction).

End of Transaction

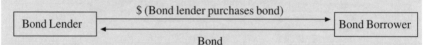

$ (Bond lender purchases bond)

Bond

Source: Shanahan, Terry "The Repo Market" (Summer 1991) Journal of International Securities Market 169–180.

**Exhibit 6.A.5    Securities Lending Structure**

BOND LENDING TRANSACTION

Start of Transaction

Cash

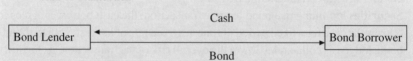

Bond

Bond borrower agrees to borrow bond against a cash borrowing of say $100 for a fixed period by the bond lender at an agreed rate of interest

End of Transaction

Cash plus Interest

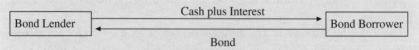

Bond

Source: Shanahan, Terry "The Repo Market" (Summer 1991) Journal of International Securities Market 169–180.

use repurchase agreements or sale and buy back structure to finance a long position. In contrast, financial institutions will borrow securities, usually as an open trade, that is, for an uncertain period, to cover short positions held as a hedge.

## A.4. Market Dynamics

Several aspects of the operation of the repo markets should be noted including:
- Types of securities.
- Settlement mechanics.
- Documentation.
- Pricing and rate structure.
- Credit risk aspects.

Repo facilities are generally available for bonds (primarily, government securities and to a more limited extent for other bonds[70]) and to a more limited extent equity securities[71].

The most substantial repo markets are in government bonds. The typical bonds utilised in relation to the repurchase agreements as they impact upon derivative trading are government securities. In practice, repo markets exist across government bond markets in a number of currencies. In most markets, it is customary where it is necessary to create a short bond position to short the current "on-the-run" government security. This reflects the fact that the derivative market typically prices "off" the most liquid government stock of the relevant maturity. However, a danger that needs to be carefully managed in regard to such short positions is that cost of borrowing such bonds to cover the short position can often escalate to very high levels. This reflects the fact that bond borrowers in the repo market tend to be dealers and use the securities to short the bond market, either hedging portfolio positions or positioning against increases in interest rates. Where large short positions exist in a particular security, bonds may be difficult to borrow, resulting in high cost of borrowing that can adversely effect the efficiency of the hedge. Repo market makers also try to avoid repo bonds that have an intervening coupon payment during the term of the repo transaction.

---

[70] Other bonds encompass corporate bonds (infrequently), agency debt (in the US) and asset or mortgage backed securities (primarily Pfandbriefe in Europe).

[71] See Hopton, David "Securities Lending and Borrowing" in Bishop, Elizabeth (Editor) (1991) Equity Trading; Euromoney Books, London at Chapter 10; see also Kim. T.J. "Trying to Interest Companies in Equity Repos" (May 1996) Global Finance 25; Brooks, Alison "Equity Repo Comes of Age" (October 1996) Risk 27–30.

Settlement of repo transaction is undertaken through the book entry system of the relevant depository, clearing or settlement system in one of two ways:

- **Bilateral** – where the counterparties to the repo trade deliver securities/cash directly to each other through the clearing or settlement system.
- **Tri-party** – where counterparties trade directly as principals with each other and then confirm, deliver/settle and manage the collateral through a third party (such as a custodian or settlement/clearing agent).

The major advantage of the tri-party structure is the ability to use multiple securities simultaneously. A related advantage is the ability to outsource the collateral management functions (settlement, mark-to-market collateral calculations, margining and collateral substitution).

The majority of repo trading is governed under the PSA/ISMA Global Master Agreement (under English law) or domestic equivalents in use in certain jurisdictions. The agreements allow counterparts to mark-to-market the collateral, make margin calls and terminate the transaction in case of default and set off exposures[72].

The fundamental reason for utilising the repo market is that it provides cheaper financing and diversifies funding sources. Depending on maturity, bond repos can be utilised to reduce the cost of financing inventory by anywhere between 0.125% pa and 0.75% pa, depending on the currency and term of financing. Similarly, the cost of borrowing bonds is considerably cheaper through the repo market than alternative sources such as Cedel and Euroclear that usually charge higher fees to lend bonds, depending on currency.

Even for highly rated financial institutions (AA/AAA), use of financing and repurchase agreements allows them to raise funds opportunistically at rates significantly better than the money market. For example, where institutions carry inventory of a particular security that is sought after to cover bond shorts, it may be possible to raise funds at levels often 100 bps pa below inter-bank rates. Other advantages of raising funds through repo transactions include the capacity to arrange funding from overnight to one year, although the market is deepest for shorter-rated repos. The repo market also facilitates borrowing odd sums of cash that may be difficult to arrange by means of more formal money market transactions.

Equity repo rates are generally higher than the applicable rates for bond repos.

---

[72] For a discussion of documentation issues, see Corrigan, Daniel, Georgiou, Christopher and Gollow, Jonothan (1999) Repo: The Ultimate Guide; Pearls of Wisdom Publishing Ltd, London at Chapter 7.

The formulas utilised for calculating the implied repo rate are summarised in **Exhibit 6.A.6**. The linkages between the repo market and the futures market allow market professionals to utilise what are known as "basis trades" to create cash and carry or reverse cash and carry positions. This is typically utilised to arbitrage cash futures relationships.

The credit risk on a repo transaction is akin to that applicable to any collateralised loans. In general terms, the risk on a repo agreement is relatively low. A significant concern in this regard is the value of the collateral. The collateral price

---

**Exhibit 6.A.6  Pricing Formula for Repo Transactions**

Formula for implied repo rate with zero or one interim coupon:

$$(P + A_1)(1 + rD_1/360) = C \times (1 + rD_2/360) + DP + A_2$$

[Cost to purchase and finance bond] = [Interim coupon and reinvested earnings and amount received from contract delivery]

Rearranging the terms:

$$r = DP + A_2 - (P + A_1 + C)/(P + A_1)(D_1/360) - C(D_2/360)$$

Where:

$P$ = bond purchase price (flat price)
$A_1$ = accrued interest at time of purchase
$r$ = implied repo rate (as a decimal $r = 0.05 = 5\%$)
$D_1$ = days from purchase settlement to futures deliveries
$C$ = actual interim coupon received (equals 0 if no coupon received)
$D_2$ = days from interim coupon receipt to futures delivery
$DP$ = delivery price = (factor × futures quote for factor contracts) (price using futures yield for yield contracts)
$A_2$ = accrued interest on the bond on futures delivery day

Formula for the net basis:

$$NB = (P + A) \times (R - r) \times D/360$$

Where:

$NB$ = Net basis
$P$ = bond purchase price (clean price)
$A$ = accrued interest at time of purchase
$R$ = repo rate
$r$ = implied repo rate
$D$ = days from bond purchase to futures delivery

Source: Shanahan, Terry "The Repo Market" (Summer 1991) Journal of International Securities Market 169–180.

will be affected by interest rate movements in financial markets, causing potentially significant deviations of the value of the repo cash loans resulting in a risk exposure to either party to the transaction.

The credit risk in repo transactions is managed through the extent of collateralisation. Repo markets are utilised on a "full accrual" pricing for valuing collateral. This means a bond user would be valued at market price plus accrued interest minus a reasonable margin (known as a "haircut") to allow for adverse bond market movements. This haircut is related to the volatility of the collateral and is designed to protect the lenders from becoming exposed to the borrower as a result of any decline in value of the collateral. Repo agreements can be structured to provide for margin calls to maintain collateral coverage[73].

If a coupon is payable prior to the repo maturity, then the ultimate owner of the security gets the benefit of the coupon payment in an offsetting adjustment made in the value of the repo loan.

## A.5.  Repo Markets[74]

Markets for repo transactions have traditionally been a prominent part of US$ capital markets. However, increasingly active repo markets are developing in most currencies, particularly in government bonds[75]. The market in most major currencies is now reasonably liquid with a number of dealers and brokers active in matching borrowers and lenders.

The investors in repo transactions include banks, corporations, fund managers and central banks and supranational institutions. The primary motivation of investors includes:

- **Yield enhancement** – return on repo transactions provide returns that are comparable and sometimes better than equivalent money market transactions. The capital efficiency of repos means that the risk-adjusted returns are enhanced.

---

[73] For a discussion of repo risks, see Singer, Richard "Lending Insecurity" (October 1996) Risk 32–34; Muehring, Kevin "The Fed's Repo Man" (April 1997) Institutional Investors 159–161; Celarier, Michelle "Both a Lender and a Borrower Be" (January 1998) Euromoney 62–64; Crabbe, Matthew "G-10, IOSCO Highlight Securities Lending Risks" (July 1999) Risk 11.

[74] See Lewis, Julian "Repos: The $50 billion Secret" (June 1991) Euromoney 38–43; D'Amario, Peter "New Opportunities in the Repo Markets" (June 1996) Corporate Finance 12–15.

[75] See Powell, Scott "All Abroad the Merry-Go-Round" (June 1992) Euromoney 53–60; Heron, Dan "Gilt Not Proven" (October 1996) Risk 21–24; Elliot, Margaret "Repo's Gone Global and Hip" (February 1997) Derivatives Strategy 14–19.

- **Credit risk management** – the repo markets allow diversification of credit risk and the collateralised nature of the transactions reduces credit risk significantly. In addition, for banks, repo transactions attract favourable treatment under capital regulations making them efficient in terms of capital usage.

Lenders also use repos to obtain securities for the purpose of short sales.

Borrowers in repo markets include banks and other financial institutions who use repos as an alternative to the inter-bank money markets as a funding mechanism for positions. Fund managers (including hedge funds) that lack access to the inter-bank and deposit markets use repos to generate cost effective funding, using their security holdings as collateral.

# 7
# Option Pricing[1]

## 1  Overview

Option contracts provide the purchaser with the right to either buy from (a call option) or sell to (a put option) the writer of the option at an agreed price (the strike price) a fixed amount of an underlying asset on (European style exercise) or any time before (American style exercise) a pre-nominated date (the expiry date). The purchaser pays the writer a fee (the premium) in return for effectively guaranteeing a maximum purchase price (call option) or minimum sales price (put option).

---

[1] There is a large amount of literature on option pricing. The books listed here are the ones that the author finds most useful in practice. The list is not comprehensive. The major reference works include: Briys, Eric Bellalah, Mondher, Mai, Huu Minh and De Varenne, Francois (1998) Options, Futures and Exotic Derivatives: Theory, Application and Practice; John Wiley & Sons, Chichester; Hull, John (2000) Option Futures and Other Derivatives – Fourth Edition; Prentice-Hall Inc., Upper Saddle River, NJ; Wilmott, Paul (1998) Derivatives: The Theory and Practice of Financial Engineering; John Wiley & Sons, Chichester; Wilmott, Paul, Dewynne, Jeff and Howison, Sam (1993) Option Pricing: Mathematical Models and Computations; Oxford Financial Press, Oxford. Other useful books include: Cox, J. and Rubinstein, M. (1985) Options Markets; Prentice-Hall, Inc; Jarrow, Robert A. and Rudd, Andrew (1983) Option Pricing; Richard D. Irwin: Homewood, Illinois; Ritchen, Peter (1987) Options-Theory, Strategy and Applications; Scott, Foresman and Company: Glenview, Illinois; Tompkins, Robert (1994) Options Explained[2]; MacMillan Press: England; Chriss, Neil A. (1997) Black-Scholes and Beyond: Option Pricing Models; Irwin Professional Publishing, Chicago; Das, Satyajit (Editor) (1997) Risk Management & Financial Derivatives: A Guide to the Mathematics; LBC Information Services, Sydney; McGraw-Hill, Chicago; MacMillan Publishing, England; Martin, John (1996) Derivatives Maths; IFR Publishing, London; Rubinstein, Mark (1999) Rubinstein On Derivatives; Risk Books, London; Martin, John (2001) Applied Math for Derivatives; John Wiley & Sons, Singapore at Chapters 12 to 15. For a simple intuitive introduction to option pricing, see Swiss Bank Corporation (1994) Understanding Derivatives; Prospects Special: Basel, Switzerland.

Option valuation is concerned with the determination of the fair value of the premium. The distinguishing feature of option valuation is the asymmetric nature of the payoff of the instrument. The structure of the payoff dictates that the purchaser has unlimited potential profit, with the loss limited to the premium paid. The writer in contrast has a limited gain (the premium received), but an unlimited loss. The structure of the payoffs means the actual value of the option is contingent on the future asset price either at maturity (for an European option) or the *path* or sequence of asset prices between the entry into the option and the option expiry (for an American option because of the risk of early exercise).

The nature of the payoffs complicates the process of risk neutral valuation for option instruments. In the case of a forward, the forward instrument payoffs can be replicated by a spot position in the asset that is then financed or invested. For example, a forward purchase is hedged by a spot purchase of the asset which is the financed through till the forward maturity. This replication is allowed by the *symmetric* nature of the payoffs to the parties entering into the forward. In the case of an option, the asymmetric nature of the payoff dictates both a more complex method of replication of the option position (the option must be replicated dynamically) and the determination of the fair value of the instrument.

In this Chapter, the process of option valuation is examined. The process of pricing interest rate options (which present special problems in valuation) is discussed in Chapter 8. The estimation of volatility is considered in Chapter 9. The sensitivities of the value of the option to each of the parameters used to value the option are examined in Chapter 15. The process of option replication through trading in the spot asset is considered in Chapter 16.

The structure of this Chapter is as follows:

- The basic concepts of option valuation including the key determinants of option value are considered.
- The concept of risk neutral option value is developed using a simple probability and expected value based framework.
- The approach of risk neutral mathematical option valuation is introduced.
- Two approaches to option valuation (the Black-Scholes model and the binomial model) are examined.
- The assumptions underlying the model and their violation in financial markets are analysed.
- The adaptation of the basic model for different problems of valuation (early exercise, dividend paying stock as well as the different asset classes) is described.

# 2  Option Valuation Concepts

## 2.1  Option Pricing Nomenclature

The value of an option is known at maturity because one of the key determinants of option value, the asset price at maturity, is known. At maturity, the price of an option is usually given as:

**Call Option**     $P_C = \text{Maximum } [0; S_m - K]$
**Put Option**      $P_P = \text{Maximum } [0; K - S_m]$

Where

$P_C$ = Premium/value of call option
$P_P$ = Premium/value of put option
$S_m$ = Spot price of asset at maturity
$K$  = Strike price of option

The maximum function is necessitated by the choice of option exercise that rests with the purchaser who will not exercise the option unless it is economically advantageous to do so.

In determining the value of an option, it is usual to distinguish between:
• *Intrinsic* value.
• *Time* value.

An option's intrinsic value is based on the difference between its exercise price and the current price of the underlying debt instrument. If the option is currently profitable to exercise, then it is said to have intrinsic value. A call (put) option has intrinsic value if the current price of the instrument is above (below) the option's exercise price. The intrinsic value is given by:

For a call option: $S_t - K$
For a put option: $K - S_t$

Where

$S_t$ = Spot price at time t

The concept of intrinsic value requires additional clarification in the context of the applicable exercise rules. In the case of a European option, as exercise is only permitted at maturity, intrinsic value prior to that date requires the strike price to be discounted to the relevant date. This is usually given as $Ke^{-rf.t}$ (that is, the strike price discounted back to the date of valuation at the continuously compounded risk free rate). The discounted strike price is then compared to the spot price of the asset. To a degree, the concept of an intrinsic value of a European option prior to maturity is redundant, as the option is incapable of being exercised prior to maturity. The computation of the *theoretical* intrinsic value of the European option prior to maturity is only relevant as a means for identifying the *sources* of value for the option. In the case of an American option where the possibility of early exercise is present and permissible, the exercise price does not need to be discounted as it will be paid in full at the date of exercise.

Whether or not the option has intrinsic value, it may have time value. Time value is defined as:

$$\text{Option Premium } = \text{ Intrinsic Value } + \text{ Time Value}$$

Therefore

$$\text{Time Value } = \text{ Option Premium } - \text{ Intrinsic Value}$$

The time value of the option reflects the amount buyers are willing to pay for the possibility that at some time prior to expiration, the option may become profitable to exercise.

The values identified are subject to a number of value constraints:

Option Premium $\geq 0$
Intrinsic Value $\quad \geq 0$
Time Value $\quad \geq 0$

Three other option valuation terms are relevant:
• In-the-money.
• At-the-money.
• Out-of-the-money.

It is customary for market participants to refer to particular options as belonging to one of the three groups. An option with an exercise price at or close to the current *forward* price of the underlying security is said to be at-the-money. An option with intrinsic value is referred to as being in-the-money, while an out-of-the-money option is one with no intrinsic value but presumably with some time value.

## 2.2 Factors Affecting Option Values

The fundamental direct determinants of option value include:
* The current price of the underlying asset (S).
* The exercise price of the option (K).
* The time to expiry (T).
* The volatility of prices on the underlying asset ($\sigma$).
* Interest rates (Rf)[2].

Other factors affecting option valuation include the type of option (that is, whether the option is American or European) as well as payouts (income) from holding the underlying instrument.

S and K affect the intrinsic value of the option. The time to expiry affects both time value (increased probability of the options having value) and intrinsic value (a decrease in the effective strike price in present value terms). Volatility affects time value of the option. Interest rates affect the intrinsic value through its impact on the present value of the strike price.

The general effect of each of the five major relevant variables on the value of an option (where all other variables are held constant) is summarised in **Exhibit 7.1**[3].

**Exhibit 7.1   Factors Affecting Option Valuation**

| Factor | Effect of Increase in Factor on Value of | |
|---|---|---|
| | Call | Put |
| Spot Price | Increase | Decrease |
| Strike Price | Decrease | Increase |
| Volatility | Increase | Increase |
| Time to Expiry | Increase | Increase (for small increase only); Decrease (for large increases) |
| Interest Rate | Increase | Decrease |

The effect of changes in the spot price of the instrument, option strike prices and time to expiry on the pricing of options are relatively easily understood.

---

[2] It is customary to specify the interest rate as the *risk free rate* (effectively, a government bond rate for the relevant maturity). However, in practice the swap rate for the relevant maturity is likely to be used. This reflects the fact that this rate will more typically reflect the actual borrowing cost or investment return for the trader.

[3] A quantitative example of the impact of factor changes on the value of an option is set out in **Exhibit 7.10**.

In the case of a call option, the higher the price of the underlying instrument, the higher the intrinsic value of the option if it is in-the-money and hence the higher the premium. If the call is out-of-the-money, then the higher the underlying instrument's price the greater the probability that it will be possible to exercise the call at a profit, and hence the higher the time value or premium of the option. In the case of put options, the reverse will apply.

The impact of changes in strike or exercise price is somewhat similar. For an in-the-money call option the lower the exercise price, the higher the intrinsic value, while for an out-of-the-money call, the lower the exercise price, the greater the probability of profitable exercise, and hence the higher the time value. A similar but opposite logic applies in the case of put options.

The impact of time to expiration and option valuation is predicated on the fact that the longer an option has to run, the greater the probability that it will be possible to exercise the option profitably, hence the greater the time value of the option. As the time to expiry increases, the decrease in the strike price (in present value terms)[4] means that the intrinsic value of the call option increases. However, the put option becomes further out of the money and becomes progressively less likely to be exercised and decreases in value.

The impact of volatility derives from the fact that the greater the expected movement in the price of the underlying instrument, the greater the probability that the option can be exercised at a profit and hence the more valuable the option or its time value. In essence, the higher the volatility, the greater the likelihood that the asset will either do very well or very poorly which is reflected in the price of the option.

The impact of interest rates is less clear intuitively. The role of interest rates in the determination of option premiums is complex and varies from one type of option to another. In general, however, the higher the interest rate, the lower the *present value* of the exercise price the call buyer has contracted to pay in the event of exercise[5]. In essence, a call option can be thought of as the right to buy the underlying asset at the discounted value of the exercise price. Consequently, the greater the degree of discount, the more valuable is the right, hence, as interest rates increase and the degree of discount increases commensurately, the corresponding option value increases. In fact, a higher interest rate has a similar influence to that of a lower exercise price. A similar but opposite logic applies in the case of a put option. The higher interest rate decreases the value of the put option as it reduces

---

[4]   This is equivalent to a higher forward price.
[5]   This is equivalent to a higher forward price.

the current (present valued or discounted) value of the exercise price that the buyer has contracted to receive.

An alternative way of looking at the impact of changes in interest rates is to view the option as a means for replicating the exposure to the asset. For example, a call option provides exposure to the asset in a manner analogous to a purchase of the asset. If interest rates increase, then the call option increases in attractiveness as a means of replicating the asset exposure. This is because the lower cash outlay entailed by the premium means that the cost (in forgone interest) is lower if the option is utilised. This means that the price of the call option is bid up. In the case of a put option, such a transaction can be viewed as an alternative to selling the asset. In this case an increase in interest rates reduces the premium of a put option, as the proceeds of the sale are not received until the option is exercised and entails higher opportunity costs where interest rates increase. Decreases in interest rates have a similar impact, but in reverse.

## 3   Risk Neutral Option Valuation

The development of a formal model for the valuation of options requires an understanding of the concept of risk neutral valuation techniques. The application of risk neutral valuation arguments is identical to that used in the context of the valuation of forward contracts.

The risk neutral approach is predicated on two central premises:
- The value of any option must be equal to the expected payoffs under the instrument.
- The value of the option can be determined by replicating the payoff or economic profile of an option using a position in the underlying asset and cash. This means that a short (long) position in the option can be hedged by the offsetting position in the asset and cash to create a riskless portfolio that should return the risk-free rate of interest.

The risk neutral valuation approach allows determination of the value of an option by arbitrage arguments. This implies that the value of the option can be determined independent of risk preferences of the parties to the transaction, as well as any expectations about the *direction* of underlying asset prices. As in the case of pricing of forward contracts, the creation of this risk neutral portfolio to replicate the payoff profile of the derivative allows the value of the derivative instrument to be determined, because both the asset and the derivative contract have the same value driver – the changes in the price of the underlying asset. The use of risk neutrality is central to both the valuation and trading or synthetic creation of options[6].

# 4   A Simple Option Pricing Model

Within the framework of risk neutrality outlined, a very simple intuitive option pricing model can be derived. This model exhibits all the characteristics and dimensions of option valuation generally.

The central unknown in valuing an option is the *forward* asset price as of the expiry date (this assumes a European style exercise). As with any other unknown variable in financial valuation, determination of value of the underlying contract is feasible by estimating the range of possible values and the probabilities attached to individual possible outcomes.

**Exhibit 7.2** sets out a basic option pricing model utilising this fundamental approach.

The basic model requires, consistent with all option valuation models, the following input parameters:

- The possible values or prices that can be assumed by the underlying asset at option expiry.
- The probabilities attached to the possible values that can be assumed by the asset at option expiry.
- The risk free interest rate to allow discounting of the expected values of the option.

In the basic option pricing model described, the asset price at the forward date is restricted to 5 possible values. For a real world transaction the range of possible value is large and theoretically infinite, although in reality, many of the value states

---

[6]  The concept of risk neutrality in option price was introduced by Black, Scholes and Merton in their pioneering work on option pricing; see Black, Fischer and Scholes, Myron. "The Pricing of Options and Corporate Liabilities" (1973) Journal of Political Economy 81 399–417. Option pricing generally uses risk neutrality to create a replicating portfolio to simulate the derivative payoffs within a framework where prices of underlying assets are available in the market and arbitrage opportunities do not exist. It has been shown that this no arbitrage condition is equivalent to a Martingale process; see Harrison, J. Michael and Kreps, David M. "Martingales and Arbitrage in Multi-period Securities Markets" (1979) Journal of Economic Theory 20 381–408; Harrison, J. Michael and Pliska, Stanley R. "Martingales and Stochastic Integrals in the Theory of Continuous Trading" (1981) Stochastic Processes and Their Applications 11 261–271.

**Exhibit 7.2    Simple Option Pricing Model**

Assume the following scenario:

Current Spot Price of Asset (S)     = $100
1 year Risk Free Interest Rate (Rf) = 10.00% pa

This implies an arbitrage free forward of $110 assuming that the asset does not pay any income. The *actual* spot price of the asset in 1 year time is not known but is expected to be in the range set out below, and the probability of the asset price being at any particular level is also specified:

| Expected Asset Price in 1 Year ($) | Probability (%) |
|:---:|:---:|
| 90 | 10 |
| 100 | 20 |
| 110 | 40 |
| 120 | 20 |
| 130 | 10 |

The above table assigns a designated probability to all possible forward asset price states (effectively the assumed distribution of forward asset prices).

This data can now be utilised to price the following call option:

K  = $110
T  = 1 year
Rf = 10.00% pa

The fair value of the option today should, consistent with the risk neutral argument, be the expected payoff of the option contract, which is as follows:

| Expected Asset Price in 1 Year ($) | Probability (%) | Value of Call Option ($) | Probability Adjusted Expected Value of Call Option ($) |
|:---:|:---:|:---:|:---:|
| 90 | 10 | 0 | 0 |
| 100 | 20 | 0 | 0 |
| 110 | 40 | 0 | 0 |
| 120 | 20 | 10 | 2 |
| 130 | 10 | 20 | 2 |
| | | Total | 4 |

The expected value of the call option in this case is $4 at maturity of the option which must be discounted back at 10.00% pa for 1 year to provide the present value of the option. The current value of the option is $3.64.

are unlikely or have very low probabilities. However, the requirement dictated by this model for both identification of each of the possible asset price states and the probability attached to each possible asset price state, is tedious.

In practice, the process of generating the possible forward asset prices and their probabilities is simplified by the introduction of an assumed asset price distribution.

# 5   Asset Price Distributions

The concept of a distribution of forward prices is central to option pricing theory. The seminal work of Black, Scholes and Merton in their path breaking option pricing model is as much about their work in simplifying the generation of the forward asset price as it is about the valuation of options.

Black, Scholes and Merton introduce a simple assumption in generating the forward asset price distribution. In effect, they assume that if the spot price of the asset and the *distribution of asset price changes (the asset returns)* are known, then it would be possible to determine the complete distribution of forward asset prices. To generate the distribution of asset price changes it is assumed that the stock prices follow a process that is termed a continuous *random walk*. The introduction of this assumption means that the changes in the price of or continuously compounded returns on the underlying asset are normally distributed and that the forward asset price is lognormally distributed.

The introduction of these assumptions has a number of very significant implications. The forward asset prices and the probabilities of a particular asset price can now be calculated utilising the characteristics of a normal distribution. The major feature of a normal distribution is that the *complete* distribution of asset prices and probabilities can be expressed in terms of two variables:

- The mean expected return ($\mu$).
- The standard deviation of the expected return ($\sigma$).

In the Black-Scholes-Merton approach, the mean expected return is taken to be the risk free rate of interest. In effect, the price of the underlying asset is expected to drift towards the forward price. The standard deviation of the expected return, which equates to the volatility of asset prices (identified above as a key determinant of option values), is defined to be the standard deviation of the logarithmic returns on the underlying asset to the maturity of the option[7].

---

[7]   The estimation of volatility is a particularly vexed issue and is dealt with in detail separately in Chapter 9. In the remainder of this Chapter, volatility is assumed to be a known term.

The advantage of utilising a normal distribution is evident in that the two variables identified can also be used to infer the probability of the asset price taking on particular values. For example, once the mean and standard deviation are known, the following probabilities are also known:

- 67% probability that the forward asset price will be between the mean (the forward price) $\pm 1\sigma$.
- 95% probability that the forward asset price will be between the mean (the forward price) $\pm 2\sigma$.
- 99% probability that the forward asset price will be between the mean (the forward price) $\pm 3\sigma$.

The introduction of the concept of log normality should also be explained. **Exhibit 7.3** sets out the comparative shape of a normal against log normal distribution.

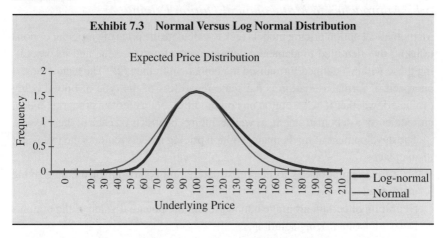

**Exhibit 7.3    Normal Versus Log Normal Distribution**

The log normal distribution differs from the symmetrical normal distribution in that it exhibits a skew with its mean, median and mode all differing from that in a normal distribution. The major advantage of using a log normal distribution is that a log normally distributed variable can only take positive values (between zero and infinity) in contrast to a normal distribution that allows variables to take on both positive and negative values.

The introduction of the assumptions allows the generation of a *complete distribution* of forward asset prices and their probabilities. This in turn allows *all* possible positive intrinsic values of the option at maturity to be generated. The intrinsic values are then weighted by their respective probabilities to determine the expected value of the option that is then discounted to the present to calculate the option's fair value.

The introduction of the concept of the distribution of forward asset prices transforms the problem of option valuation in several respects:

- It makes the valuation of the option independent of the *direction* of asset price movements.
- It converts the problem of option valuation into a problem of estimation of the *volatility* of the returns on the asset (more particularly, the annualised standard deviation of the log of the price changes).

The introduction of the asset price distribution assumption allows the development of mathematical option pricing models.

# 6 Option Pricing Theory

## 6.1 Approaches to Mathematical Option Pricing

Mathematical option pricing models seek to calculate the price of particular options utilising the identified fundamental determinants of option value and incorporating these within a defined formalised mathematical framework. The technological approach of formal valuation is the same regardless of the type of option being evaluated, whether it be an option on commodities, equity stocks or market index, currencies, or a debt instrument, as well as futures contracts on each of these assets.

The development of mathematical option pricing models requires the following distinct steps:

- Specific assumptions as to market structure and behaviour of the underlying instrument.
- Definition of certain arbitrage boundaries on the potential value of the option.
- Derivation of a pricing solution.

## 6.2 Market Assumptions

Mathematical option pricing models can be developed to synthesise the many factors that affect the option premium within identified arbitrage boundaries. In order to develop such mathematical option pricing models, it is necessary to make a number of restrictive assumptions including[8]:

- Asset trading is continuous with all asset prices following continuous and stationary stochastic processes.
- The asset has no intermediate cash flows (for example, dividends, interest etc).

---

[8]   See discussion in Chapter 4.

- The asset price moves in a continuously random manner.
- The distribution of the asset's return is log normal.
- The variance of the return distribution is constant over the asset's life.
- The risk free rate of interest is constant over the option's life.
- The option is European.
- No restrictions or costs of short selling.
- No taxes or transaction costs.

Most of these assumptions are self-explanatory and are consistent with efficient capital market theory. Stochastic process refers to the evolution of asset prices through time modelled as random, and characterised by continuous series of price changes governed by the laws of probability as prescribed. By continuous processes, it is usually implied that the price of the underlying asset can vary over time but does not have discontinuities or jumps[9]. The stationary stochastic process, as assumed, is one that is determined the same way for all time periods of equal length. Specifically, the traditional approach to option valuation assumes that the price of the underlying asset has a particular type of probability distribution, assumed to be a log normal distribution. It is also assumed that the standard deviation of this distribution is constant over time.

## 6.3   Boundary Conditions

Mathematical option pricing requires identification of certain boundaries that can be placed on the values of options based on arbitrage considerations. The concept of arbitrage in this context relies upon dominance, where a portfolio asset is said to dominate another portfolio if for the same cost it offers a return that will at least be the same. The underlying assumption in this context is that if these boundary conditions are breached, arbitrage activity would force the prices of the underlying assets and options within the arbitrage boundaries, as arbitrageurs would enter into transactions designed to take advantage of riskless profit opportunities.

**Exhibit 7.4** sets out the major boundary conditions on the price of an option. In the interest of clarity, in this Section, the boundary conditions to option value are stated with reference to generalised assets. There are nine major arbitrage boundaries discussed in **Exhibit 7.4**. Put-call parity for options is a special arbitrage condition that is discussed below.

---

[9]   This means that the price movement over time of the asset could be graphed without lifting the pen from the paper.

## Exhibit 7.4    Boundary Restrictions on the Value of an Option[10]

### 1. Notation
The following notation is used in outlining the boundary conditions:

| | |
|---|---|
| S | = asset price |
| Sm | = asset price at maturity |
| K | = strike price |
| T | = time to maturity |
| Rf | = risk free interest rate |
| $\sigma$ | = volatility of returns from asset |
| $P_{ca}$ | = price of American call |
| $P_{ce}$ | = price of European call |
| $P_{pa}$ | = price of American put |
| $P_{pe}$ | = price of European put |
| PV(K) | = present value of amount K (that is, $Ke^{-Rf \cdot T}$) |
| C | = Intermediate cash flow on asset |

### 2. Arbitrage Boundaries
**Boundary Condition**

$$P_{ce} \text{ or } P_{ca} \geq 0$$
$$P_{pe} \text{ or } P_{pa} \geq 0$$

This states that the value of an option is greater than or equal to 0. Option exercise is voluntary; consequently, purchasers will never exercise an option if the value of the option entails a loss and therefore option prices cannot take on negative values.

**Boundary Condition**
At maturity of the option:

$$P_{ce} \text{ or } P_{ca} = 0 \text{ or } Sm - K$$
$$P_{pe} \text{ or } P_{pa} = 0 \text{ or } K - Sm$$

The value of a call or put option will be either 0 or its intrinsic value at maturity. If this condition is not satisfied, arbitrage opportunities exist. For example, if a call at maturity sells for less than Sm − K, arbitrageurs could lock in a profit by borrowing enough to purchase the call and exercising it immediately, making a riskless profit after paying back the loan.

**Boundary Condition**
Prior to maturity of the option:

$$P_{ca} \geq 0 \text{ or } S - K$$
$$P_{pa} \geq 0 \text{ or } K - S$$

---

[10]  The description of option boundary conditions draws on Rowley, Ian "Pricing Options Using the Black-Scholes Model" (May 1987) Euromoney Corporate Finance 108–112.

If at any time prior to maturity an American option contract sells for less than its intrinsic value then an arbitrage opportunity exists to purchase the option and exercise immediately while buying or selling the physical asset to lock in a riskless profit.

**Boundary Condition**

$$P_{ca} \geq P_{ce}$$
$$P_{pa} \geq P_{pe}$$

An American option cannot sell for a premium value less than an identical European option. The American style of option confers all the benefits of the European contract plus the capacity of early exercise.

**Boundary Condition**

For an asset that has no intermediate cash flow, it can be economically demonstrated that it is superior to sell the option prior to maturity rather than being exercised early.

The validity for this arbitrage condition can be established by constructing the following two portfolios:
1. Buy an European call for $P_{ce}$ and invest PV of strike price PV(K)
2. Buy S

The payoff from these two portfolios is set out below as at maturity of the options is:

| Portfolio Value | Out-of-the-money (Sm < K) | In-the-money (Sm ≥ K) |
|---|---|---|
| $P_{ce}$ + PV(K) | 0 + K | (Sm − K) + K |
| S | Sm | Sm |

At maturity, the portfolio consisting of the European call and the present value of the strike price is never worth less than the asset, so the current cost of the first portfolio can never be less than that of the second. This implies that an American call option will usually never be exercised prior to maturity as the investor would only receive the intrinsic value of the option (S − K) which is less than $S - Ke^{-RfT}$ for any positive interest rate. Consequently, a rational investor will always sell a call option rather than exercise the option.

**Boundary Condition**

For an asset that has intermediate cash flows, it can be economically demonstrated that early exercise is possible.

The proof of this strategy can be established by constructing portfolios that are similar to above. The two portfolios are as follows:
1. Buy an European call for $P_{ce}$ and invest PV of strike price PV(K + C) where C is the intermediate cash flow from holding the asset.
2. Buy S

The payoff from these two portfolios at maturity of the options is set out below:

| Portfolio Value | Out-of-the-money (Sm < K) | In-the-money (Sm ≥ K) |
|---|---|---|
| $P_{ce}$ + PV(K + C) | 0 + K + C | (Sm − K) + K + C |
| S | Sm + C | Sm + C |

The payoff table indicates that at maturity, the portfolio of the call and cash never pays less than the second portfolio consisting of the stock. The first portfolio gives a higher return when the option expires out-of-the-money. Consequently, the first portfolio cannot sell for less than the second portfolio. This means that whenever a European call is in-the-money prior to maturity, the lowest value it can trade for will be equal to the stock price minus the investment required to receive an amount equal to the strike price, plus any intermediate cash flow at maturity; that is, $S - PV(K + C)$. The lower limit on the value of the European call must be the lower limit on an American option's value.

This implies an optimal exercise policy for an American option on an asset with intermediate cash flows. If the lower limit on the call value $[S - PV(K + C)]$ is greater than the amount received by exercising $(S - K)$ then it is better to sell than exercise. However, if $[S - PV(K + C)]$ is less than $(S - K)$, then the American call should be exercised rather than sold prior to maturity.

An American call should therefore only be exercised early where the discounted value of the strike price and intermediate cash flows are greater than the strike price. In essence, it is $PV(C)$ that determines whether the option is sold or exercised. This implies that an American option, where the underlying asset has high intermediate cash flows, is more likely to be exercised early.

**Boundary Condition**

$$P_{ce} \text{ or } P_{ca} \leq S$$
$$P_{pe} \text{ or } P_{pa} \leq S$$

This can be illustrated with an example. A call option cannot be worth more than the underlying asset because if the option were worth more than the asset, then a riskless arbitrage profit could be made by writing a call and using the proceeds to buy the asset. If the call is exercised, the asset can be delivered and the strike price received in return, while if the call is unexercised at maturity, the asset which has a positive value will be held, thereby allowing the arbitrageur to make a positive profit without incurring any risk.

**Boundary Condition**

$P_{ce}$ or $P_{ca}$ must be worth less than an identical option with a lower exercise price; and, $P_{pe}$ or $P_{pa}$ must be worth less than an identical option with a higher exercise price.

In this case, the call with the low exercise price offers a greater chance of being in-the-money. Consequently, it cannot sell for a price which is lower than an option which has less chance of being in-the-money. The reverse is true for put options.

**Boundary Condition**

$P_{ce}$ or $P_{ca}$ or $P_{pe}$ or $P_{pa}$ cannot be worth less than an identical option with a shorter time to maturity.

Intuitively, the longer the maturity on the option, the greater the opportunity for there to be a sufficiently large change in the asset price to push the option into the money. Consequently, an option with a longer maturity cannot sell for less than an equivalent option with a shorter maturity. If this condition is violated, then an arbitrage can be set up whereby the arbitrageur writes the shorter-dated option while purchasing the option with the longer maturity to lock in a riskless arbitrage profit.

## 6.4 Put-Call Parity

Put-call parity that defines the relationship between the price of a European call option and a European put option with the same exercise price and time to expiration is an additional arbitrage boundary on option values[11]. Utilising the same notation as that used previously, put-call parity can be stated as follows:

$$P_{ce} + PV(K) = P_{pe} + S$$

This implies that buying a call and investing PV of $K(Ke^{-Rf \cdot T})$ is identical to buying a put and buying the asset. **Exhibit 7.5** sets out the proof of put-call parity. **Exhibit 7.6** sets out the use of put-call parity to create synthetic asset and option positions. For European options, arbitrage possibilities will exist if the put-call parity conditions are not fulfilled. An example of put-call parity arbitrage is set out in **Exhibit 7.7**.

---

### Exhibit 7.5   Put-Call Parity – Proof

The proof of this relationship can be established by setting up two portfolios:
1. Buy an European call for premium $P_{ce}$ and invest PV(K)
2. Buy an European put for premium $P_{pe}$ and buy the asset for S

The payoffs on the two portfolios at maturity are as follows:

| Portfolio Value | Out-of-the-money (Sm < K) | In-the-money (Sm > K) |
|---|---|---|
| $P_{ce}$ + PV(K) | 0 + K | (Sm − K) + K |
| $P_{pe}$ + S | (K − Sm) + Sm | 0 + Sm |

At maturity, the two portfolios are equal irrespective of whether the option expires in or out-of-the-money.

---

Where the underlying asset pays out a cash flow of C, put-call parity can be restated as:

$$P_{ce} + PV(K + C) = P_{pe} + S$$

It is important to note that the put-call parity theorem is only valid for European options. Synthetic positions for American options are not always pure. For example, if S decreases and an American put is exercised, then it is possible to lose the

---

[11] For a discussion of put-call parity, see Margrabe, William "Ask Dr. Risk: Put-Call Basics" (August 1999) Derivatives Strategy 54–55.

---

### Exhibit 7.6    Put-Call Parity – Synthetic Positions

The put-call parity condition can be restated as follows:

**Synthetic call (reversal)**

$$P_{ce} = P_{pe} + S - PV(K)$$

**Synthetic put (conversion)**

$$P_{pe} = P_{ce} - S + PV(K)$$

**Long asset/forward**

$$S = P_{ce} - P_{pe} + PV(K)$$

**Short asset/forward**

$$-S = P_{pe} - P_{ce} - PV(K)$$

---

### Exhibit 7.7    Put-Call Parity Arbitrage

Assume that the forward on an asset for 1 month forward is trading at 86.14/86.15. Call options on the contract with strike price 86.00 on the contract are trading at 0.28/0.33. Put options with an identical strike price are trading at 0.02/0.07. Both options are on the forward contract. In these circumstances, it is possible to create a synthetic 86.00 call at less than 0.28 as follows:

* Buy 86.00 put at 0.07.
* Buy forward at 86.15.
* Sell 86.00 call at 0.28.

   This transaction effectively creates a call at less than the 0.28 received. This can be proved as follows: the sold call and the bought put are equivalent to a synthetic short forward position at a price of 86.00. The position creates a net cash flow to the grantor of 0.21. Of the 0.21, 0.15 is lost through the bought forward position at 86.15 that is above the synthetic short price of 86.000. However, the forward loss of 0.15 is more than offset by the 0.21 gain on the option.

---

difference between K and S immediately, not at the forward date. This means that put-call parity for American options can be stated as follows[12]:

$$P_{ca} - S + PV(K) < P_{pa} < P_{ca} - S + K$$

---

[12]   For a mathematical proof see Hull, John (2000) Option Futures and Other Derivatives – Fourth Edition; Prentice-Hall Inc., Upper Saddle River, NJ at 178–179.

## 6.5   The Concept of a Riskless Hedge

The derivation of the mathematical option pricing model also requires understanding of the concept of a riskless hedge. By definition, a riskless portfolio consists of an asset and a corresponding option held in proportion to the prescribed hedge ratio continuously adjusted where the portfolio is perfectly hedged against movements in asset prices, as changes in the call price and the asset price are mutually offsetting.

Certain riskless portfolio positions are set out below:

| Position | Hedge |
|----------|-------|
| Long position in calls | Short $\Delta$ assets for each call held |
| Short position in calls | Long $\Delta$ assets for each call sold |
| Long position in puts | Long $\Delta$ assets for each put held |
| Short position in puts | Short $\Delta$ assets for each put sold |

Delta $(\Delta)$[13] refers to the sensitivity of the option premium to changes in the asset price.

Utilising the constructs of portfolio theory or the capital asset pricing model, it can be predicted that a riskless portfolio should earn no more than a risk free rate of return. It is important to note that outside the context of this riskless hedge construct, the values derived by mathematical option pricing models are not meaningful. Mathematical option pricing models, such as Black-Scholes, utilise the concept of the riskless hedge to set up portfolios of the asset and cash that are managed dynamically over time to replicate the payoff of an option. It is then possible to utilise the techniques of stochastic calculus to derive a mathematical solution to the valuation problem[14].

# 7   The Black-Scholes Option Pricing Model[15]

Black and Scholes (1973) were the first to provide a close form solution for the valuation of European call options. The mathematical derivation of the Black and

---

[13]  See discussion in Chapter 15.

[14]  For a discussion regarding the implications if it is not possible to replicate the option dynamically, see Kamal, Michael and Derman, Emanual "Correcting Black-Scholes" (January 1999) Risk 82–85.

[15]  See Black, Fischer and Scholes, Myron "The Pricing of Options and Corporate Liabilities" (1973) Journal of Political Economy 81 399–417. For a detailed discussion of the Black-Scholes model, see Chriss, Neil A. (1997) Black-Scholes and Beyond: Option

Scholes option pricing model is beyond the mathematical capabilities assumed for this text[16]. **Exhibit 7.8** sets out the Black Scholes formula[17]. **Exhibit 7.9** sets out an example of utilising the Black and Scholes Option Pricing Model to calculate the price of an option. **Exhibit 7.10** sets out an example outlining the changes in the option premium for changes in the underlying inputs.

---

**Exhibit 7.8    Black-Scholes Option Pricing Model**

The Black and Scholes option pricing model is usually specified as follows:

$$P_{ce} = S.N(d1) - Ke^{-Rf.T}.N(d2)$$

Where

$$d1 = [\ln(S/K) + (Rf + \sigma^2/2)T]/\sigma\sqrt{T}$$
$$d2 = [\ln(S/K) + (Rf - \sigma^2/2)T]/\sigma\sqrt{T} = d1 - \sigma\sqrt{T}$$

A number of aspects of the formula require explanation:
- $N(d1)$ and $N(d2)$ are cumulative normal distribution functions for $d1$ and $d2$.
- ln is the logarithm of the relevant number.
- $Ke^{-Rf.T}$ is the amount of cash needed to be invested over period or time T at a continuously compounded interest rate of Rf in order to receive K at maturity.

The price of a European put option can be derived by utilising put-call parity:

$$P_{pe} = Ke^{-Rf.T} \cdot N(-d2) - S \cdot N(-d1)$$

---

Pricing Models; Irwin Professional Publishing, Chicago. For discussion about the development of the model and specific aspects in practice, see Black, Fischer "The Holes in Black-Scholes" (March 1988) Risk 30–33; Black, Fischer "How We Came up with the Option Formula" (Winter 1989) Journal of Portfolio Management 4–8; Black, Fischer "How to Use the Holes in Black-Scholes" (1989) Continental Bank Journal of Applied Corporate Finance vol 1 no 4 67–73; Black, Fischer "The Holes in Black-Scholes" (March 1998) Risk 30–33; Black, Fischer "Living up to the Model" (1990) (March) 11–13. See also Mason, R.C. "Building on Black Scholes" (November 1988) Risk 13–17.

[16]  For a derivation of Black-Scholes option pricing model, see Hull, John (2000) Option Futures and Other Derivatives – Fourth Edition; Prentice-Hall Inc., Upper Saddle River, NJ at 485–486; 268–270; Gillespie, Tom "Mathematical Techniques" in Das, Satyajit (Editor) (1997) Risk Management & Financial Derivatives: A Guide to the Mathematics; LBC Information Services, Sydney; McGraw-Hill, Chicago at Chapter 19.

[17]  The Black Scholes formula is often referred to as the Black-Scholes-Merton option pricing model in recognition of Robert Merton's work in developing the model, see Merton, Robert "The Theory of Rational Option Pricing" (1973) Bell Journal of Economics and Management Science 28 141–183.

Two aspects of the Black and Scholes Option Pricing Model require comment:
- The calculation of the cumulative normal distribution function [N(d)] is undertaken either utilising a N(d) table or directly utilising numerical procedures. Appendix A to this chapter sets out the methodology for the calculating cumulative normal distribution function.

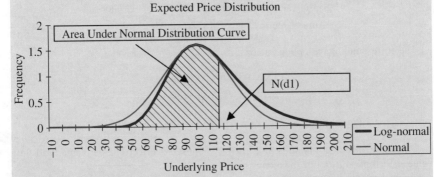

Expected Price Distribution

- The Model requires specification of the volatility of prices on the underlying instrument (parameter $\sigma$ in the above equation)[18].

---

**Exhibit 7.9    Using Black-Scholes Option Pricing Model**

Calculate the price for a call and put option on an asset based on the following information:

S   = 105.00
K   = 100.00
T   = six months (0.5 years)
Rf  = 10% pa (0.10)
$\sigma$   = 20% pa (0.20)

Using the above inputs, we can compute the call option price as follows:
$$d1 = [\ln(105/100) + (0.1 + 0.20^2/2)0.5]/.20\sqrt{.5} = 0.769$$
$$d2 = 0.769 - 0.141 = 0.628$$

Using the Normal Cumulative Distribution Table
$$N(0.769) = 0.7791$$
$$N(0.628) = 0.7349$$

---

[18] Techniques for the estimation of volatility, including discussion of the various issues thereto, is detailed in Chapter 9.

Therefore, the call option value is:

$$P_{ce} = 105 \times 0.7791 - 100 \times e^{-0.10 \times 0.50} \times 0.7349 = 11.90$$

The value of the call option is $11.90 or 11.33% of Asset Price.
The value of the call can be dissected as follows:

$$\text{Intrinsic value} = 105 - 100 \times e^{-0.10 \times 0.50} = 9.88$$
$$\text{Time value} = 11.90 - 9.877 = 2.02$$

The corresponding put option value is:

$$N(-0.769) = 0.2209$$

$$N(-0.628) = 0.2651$$

$$P_{pe} = 100 \times e^{-0.10 \times 0.50} \times 0.2651 - 105 \times 0.2209 = 2.02$$

The value of the put option is $2.02 or 1.93% of Asset Price. The put value is all time value as the option is out-of-the money.

---

**Exhibit 7.10     Using Black-Scholes Option Pricing Model – Sensitivity to Changes in Factors**

**1. Assumptions**

In this example, individual inputs (asset price, strike price, time to maturity, volatility and interest rate) are changed and the impact on the value of the option considered[19].

**2. Option Value**

Assume the option in **Exhibit 7.9**. Key details are summarised below:

| Pricing Inputs | | |
|---|---|---|
| Underlying Asset Price ($) | 105.00 | |
| Strike Price ($) | 100.00 | |
| Option Maturity (years) | 0.50 | |
| Volatility (% pa) | 20.00 | |
| Risk Free Rate (% pa) | 10.00 | |
| Call (0)/Put (1) | 0 | 1 |
| European (0)/American (1) Exercise | 0 | |
| Income on Asset (% pa) | 0.00 | |
| | **Call** | **Put** |
| Option Premium ($) | 11.90 | 2.02 |

---

[19] Please note that only increases are considered. This is because there would be a symmetric change in the case of a decrease.

### 3. Change in Asset Price

Assume the asset price increases to $106 (from $105). The option premiums are as follows:

|  | Call | Put |
|---|---|---|
| Option Premium ($) | 12.69 | 1.81 |

The call option premium increases by $0.79 ($11.90 to $12.69). This is the result of an increase in the intrinsic value of the option by $1.00 (as intrinsic value is given by $S - Ke^{-rf \cdot t}$ therefore an increase in S of $1 will translate into an equivalent increase in intrinsic value) and a decrease in time value of $0.21.

The decrease in time value results from the fact that the forward price of the asset has changed. The original forward price of $110.38 ($Se^{rf \cdot t}$ or $105e^{.10 \times 0.5}$) increases to $111.43 ($106e^{.10 \times 0.5}$). This shifts the distribution of forward prices to the right. Given that the strike price remains constant, the call option goes further into the money. As the call option goes further into the money, the behaviour of the option begins to approximate that of the asset. For example, in an extreme case, if the asset price increases to $150 then the option premium becomes $54.88 (entirely intrinsic value). The price of the option directly reflects changes in the asset price (for example, if the asset price moves to $149 then the option premium falls to $53.88). In effect, as the option moves deeper into the money, its behaviour is identical to that of the asset. Time value is not a characteristic of assets and therefore as the option moves into the money, the time value of the option decreases.

The time value of an option is maximised where the option has a strike exactly equal to the forward rate (at-the-money forward). At this level, the option has pure time value and no intrinsic value. For European options, the premiums of the call and put option are identical under these circumstances. In this example, this would be where the option had a strike price of $110.38 (the forward price as calculated above). The call and the put option would have a value of $5.92 (pure time value).

The put option premium decreases by $0.21 ($2.02 to $1.81). This is the result of the shift in the distribution to the right. This means that the asset price has to move by a larger amount in order to trigger the put option. The required move is less likely resulting in a lower time value.

### 4. Change in Strike Price

Assume the strike price increases to $101 (from $100). The option premiums are as follows:

|  | Call | Put |
|---|---|---|
| Option Premium ($) | 11.21 | 2.28 |

The call option premium decreases by $0.69 ($11.90 to $11.21). The put option premium increases by $0.26 (from $2.02 to $2.28).

The decrease in the call option is driven by a decrease in the intrinsic value of $0.95 (as intrinsic value is given by $S - Ke^{-rf \cdot t}$ therefore an increase in K of $1 will translate into a decrease in intrinsic value of $1 \times e^{-.10 \times 0.5}$). This decrease is offset by an increase in the time value. This reflects the fact that while the distribution does not change, the strike price intercept moves to the right bringing the call option closer to being at-the-money.

This is the opposite of what happened when the asset price increased. This has the effect of increasing the time value of the option.

The put option increase is purely an increase in time value. The increase in the strike price means that the smaller move (that is more likely) is required to trigger the put option, resulting in a higher time value of the put option.

### 5. Change in Time to Maturity

Assume the time to expiry increases by fixed time increments. The option premiums are as follows:

| Option Maturity (years) | Call | Put |
|:---:|:---:|:---:|
| 0.50 | 11.90 | 2.02 |
| 1.00 | 17.09 | 2.58 |
| 2.00 | 25.84 | 2.72 |
| 3.00 | 33.43 | 2.49 |
| 5.00 | 46.22 | 1.86 |
| 10.00 | 69.00 | 0.77 |

The increase in time to expiry has the effect of increasing both the call and put option premium at least for small increases in maturity. Where the increase in the time to expiry is large, the call option continues to increase in value, while the put option decreases in value.

The increase in time has two effects:

- The increase in time has the effect of making large price changes and extreme outcomes (that will provide large payoffs under the options) more likely. This is because there is higher likelihood of a draw from the distribution (at a given volatility level) of an extreme price change. This results in the time value of both the call and the put (initially) increasing.
- The increase in the time to expiry also increases the forward price of the asset. This has the effect of shifting the distribution of forward prices to the right. This in turn increases the intrinsic value of the call and pushes it further into the money, with the effect of decreasing time value (for the reasons previously outlined). The increase in the forward price also has the effect of pushing the put option further out of the money, resulting in a loss of time value (that ultimately dominates the price behaviour of the put option).

### 6. Change in Volatility

Assume the volatility increases to 21% pa (from 20% pa). The option premiums are as follows:

| | Call | Put |
|:---|:---:|:---:|
| Option Premium ($) | 12.12 | 2.24 |

The call and put option premiums increase by $0.22 ($11.90 to $12.12 and $2.02 to $2.24). The change in premium is driven by the increased probability of large price changes that increase the time value of both options.

The impact of volatility changes can be illustrated below. The first graph shows the distribution using an initial volatility level. The second graph shows the distribution at a higher volatility level[20]. As is evident, the distribution at higher volatility level is *fatter*. This equates to higher probabilities for large price changes and larger expected values for both the call and put options, which increases the time value of each.

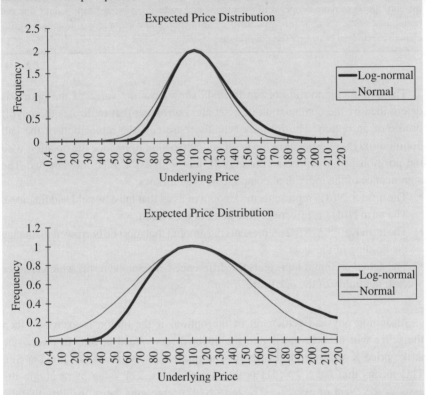

### 7. Change in Interest Rate

Assume the interest rate increases to 11% pa (from 10% pa). The option premiums are as follows:

|  | Call | Put |
|---|---|---|
| Option Premium ($) | 12.25 | 1.90 |

The call option premium increases by $0.35 ($11.90 to $12.25). The put option premium decreases by $0.12 (from $2.02 to $1.90).

---

[20] In order to highlight the impact in a perceptible manner, the volatility has been doubled.

The increase in the call option is driven by a change in intrinsic value as well as time value. The present value of the strike price falls from \$95.12 ($Ke^{-rf.t}$ or $100 \times e^{-.10 \times 0.5}$) to \$94.65 ($Ke^{-rf.t}$ or $100 \times e^{-.11 \times 0.5}$) as a result of the higher interest rate, creating an increase in intrinsic value of \$0.47. This is partially offset by the loss in time value (\$0.12) as a result of the higher forward asset price and the shift of the distribution to the right, with the call option moving deeper into the money and suffering a loss of time value. The put option loses time value as it is now further out of the money and a larger, less likely price change is required to trigger the put option.

The actual components of the formula show how the value of the option is determined by the combination of asset and borrowing that replicates the payoff profile of an option. The formula actually represents the replication of the call option through investment in the asset and borrowing to finance the position with the position being adjusted over time in line with asset price movements. The significance of the individual components is as follows:

- The term $S. N(d1)$ represents the amount of asset that must be held and financed. The term $N(d1)$ is effectively the delta of the option.
- The term $Ke^{-Rf.T}.N(d2)$ represents the amount that must be borrowed to finance the holding of the asset.
- The actual premium represents the difference between the terms which ensures cash neutrality of the portfolio.

Assuming physical settlement of the option, if the option is exercised then the seller will have to transfer to the buyer assets valued at Sm. In effect, the strike price K will need to be satisfied through delivery of assets valued at Sm. This means that the $S \cdot N(d1)$ is intuitively the present value of receiving the asset in the event of exercise. The term $N(d2)$ represents the probability that the option will be exercised. The second term $(-Ke^{-Rf.T} \cdot N(d2))$ would under this approach represent the present value cost of the strike price to be paid in the event of exercise. In a risk neutral world, if the option is likely to be exercised, then the difference between the two terms would represent the expected payout of the option that in turn would equate to the premium to render the transaction a zero return transaction.

This is evident by the fact that if the option is deep in-the-money then both $N(d1)$ and $N(d2)$ approach 1. This means that the call value approaches $S - Ke^{-Rf.T}$. Similarly, as the option approaches expiry, that is T approaches 0, both $N(d1)$ and $N(d2)$ approach 1 and $e^{-Rf.T}$ also approaches 1. This means that the call value approaches $S - K$.

# 8 Binomial Option Pricing Model[21]

## 8.1 Concept

The binomial option pricing model utilises an identical logical approach to Black-Scholes. However, in contrast to Black-Scholes, the binomial approach assumes that the security price obeys a binomial generating process. The binomial approach also assumes that the option cannot or will not be exercised prior to expiration (that is, the option is European).

The valuation process begins by considering the possibility that the price can move up or down over a given period by a given amount. This enables calculation of the value of the call option at expiration of the relevant period (which is always the greater of zero or the price of the instrument minus the exercise price – effectively the intrinsic value of the option). The riskless hedge technique starts at expiration and works backwards in time to the current period for a portfolio consisting of the physical security sold short, or one sold futures contract on the relevant asset and one bought call option on the relevant asset.

Since the portfolio is riskless, it must return the risk free rate of return over the relevant period. The derivation of the value of the call option using this approach is predicated on the fact that the call option must be priced so that the risk free hedge earns exactly the risk free rate of return.

**Exhibit 7.11** sets out a simple example of pricing an option using a 1 step binomial model.

---

**Exhibit 7.11    One Step Binomial Option Pricing Model**

In order to illustrate the logic of a binomial option pricing model, consider the following example:

$$S = \$100$$

The asset price is expected to increase or decrease by 10% to $110 or $90 respectively over the next 1 year. Assume a call option utilising the following parameters:

K  = $105
T  = 1 year
Rf = 10% pa

---

[21] The binomial model was suggested by: Cox, John C., Ross, Stephen, Stephen A. and Rubinstein, Mark "Option Pricing: A Simplified Approach" (1979) Journal of Financial Economics 7 229–263; see also Rendleman, Richard J. and Bartter, Brit, J. "Two State Option Pricing" (1979) Journal of Finance 34 1093–1110.

The value of the call option can be ascertained based on the expected increase or decrease in the asset price as follows:

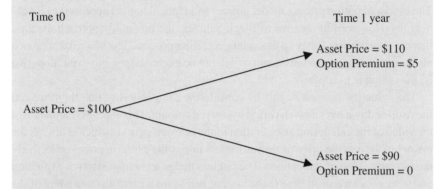

Time t0                                                                    Time 1 year

Asset Price = $110
Option Premium = $5

Asset Price = $100

Asset Price = $90
Option Premium = 0

To determine the fair value of the option it is necessary to create a riskless hedge, entailing investment in the asset to offset the position in the call such that the portfolio value is known with certainty, *irrespective of whether the asset price increases or decreases.*

The construction of the riskless portfolio requires the following steps:
- Assume the position consists of 1 sold call that is offset by holding $\Delta$ units of the asset.
- The value of $\Delta$ is determined on the basis that it will equate to a value that makes the portfolio riskless. This entails that the value of portfolio will be the same for both an increase and a decrease in the asset price. Therefore:

$$\$110\Delta - \$5 = \$90\Delta$$

$$\Delta = 0.25$$

This means that to hedge or replicate 1 sold call it would be necessary to hold .25 units of the asset. Irrespective of whether the asset price moves up or down, the portfolio has a value of $22.5 at the expiry of the option.

Based on the intuition that a riskless portfolio should earn the risk free rate of interest, it is now possible to derive the fair value of the option based on the following steps:
- The value of the riskless portfolio constructed must in present value terms be:

$$e^{-Rf \cdot T} 22.5 = e^{-.10 \times 1} 22.5 = \$20.36$$

- The fair value of the option can now be calculated using the known value of the portfolio of assets at commencement of the transaction (.25 $\times$ $100 = $25) as follows:

Value of Asset Portfolio – Option premium = Value of Riskless Portfolio

$25 – Option Premium = $20.36

Option premium = 4.64

The fair value of the call option is $4.64. If the option was trading at a value higher (lower) than the fair value, then the riskless portfolio would cost less (more) than the option premium to create allow the creation of a portfolio which yields more than the risk free rate of return (a mechanism for borrowing at less than the risk free rate). In either case, the value difference would attract arbitrage to realign the value of the option to eliminate the possibilities for arbitrage.

## 8.2   Generalised Binomial Option

In the binomial model, the time period to option expiry is divided into a series of discrete intervals. This contrasts with the continuous time model of Black Scholes. As the number of intervals to maturity increases, the resulting increase in final stock prices begins to approximate the continuous log normal distribution. This allows a more generalised version of the model to be created. **Exhibit 7.12** sets out the generalised version of the binomial model for pricing options. **Exhibit 7.13** sets out a multi step binomial option model using the generalised model created for a call option. **Exhibit 7.14** sets out a multi step binomial model for a put option.

---

**Exhibit 7.12   Generalised Binomial Option Pricing Model**

In order to generalise the Binomial Option Pricing Model, it is necessary to define the factor amount the asset price can go up or down at each step of the binomial tree, and the probability of an up or a down move.
It can be shown that[22]:

$$u = e^{\sigma\sqrt{t/n}}$$
$$d = e^{-\sigma\sqrt{t/n}} = 1/u$$
$$p = (e^{rf.t/n} - d)/(u - d)$$

Where
u  = the factor amount the stock price can go up
d  = the factor amount the stock price can go down
e  = the exponential term
$\sigma$  = the volatility of logs of the returns of the asset price
t  = time to expiry of the option
n  = number of steps
p  = the probability of an upward move in the asset price
rf = the risk free rate of interest

---

[22]  See Hull, John (2000) Option Futures and Other Derivatives – Fourth Edition; Prentice-Hall Inc., Upper Saddle River, NJ at Chapter 9 for a full proof and derivation of these relationships.

The value of an option in a 1 step tree can therefore be stated as:

$$P = e^{-rf.t/n}[p.P_u + (1 - p)P_d]$$

Where

$P_u$ = the option value on an increase in the asset price
$P_d$ = the option value on a decrease in the asset price

The model can be extended using a similar logic for multiple steps.

---

**Exhibit 7.13   Multi-Step Binomial Model for European Call Option**

Assume the following parameters for a European call option:

S  = $100
K  = $100
T  = 1 year
Rf = 10% pa
$\sigma$  = 20% pa

Assume also the number of steps (n) to be used is 2.
In order to use the binomial model, it is necessary to calculate u, d, and p.

$$u = e^{.20\sqrt{1/2}} = 1.151910$$
$$d = 1/u = 0.868123$$
$$p = (e^{.10.1/2} - 0.868123)/(1.151910 - 0.868123) = .645371$$

This allows the construction of the binomial tree as follows:

Time = 0                    Time = 0.5 years                    Time = 1 year

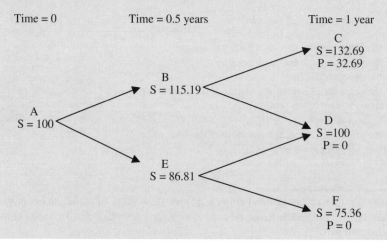

C
S = 132.69
P = 32.69

B
S = 115.19

A
S = 100

D
S = 100
P = 0

E
S = 86.81

F
S = 75.36
P = 0

In order to now derive the value of the option, it is necessary to work back through the tree, solving for the price of the option at each node of the tree. In the above case the major node which is relevant is Node B where the value of the option can be given as:

$$P = e^{-.10.1/2}[.645371(32.69) + (1 - .645371)0] = \$20.07$$

This allows restatement of the tree as follows:

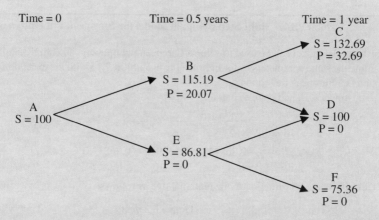

The value of the option at commencement (Node A) can now be calculated as follows:

$$P = e^{-.10.1/2}[.645371(20.07) + (1 - .645371)0] = \$12.32$$

The complete tree therefore is as follows:

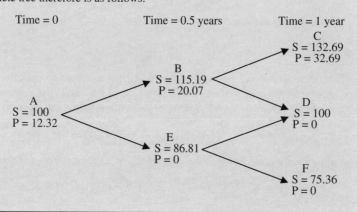

## 8.3   Numerical Solution Issues

The simple binomial models with small numbers of steps are relatively easy to solve. However, it is necessary to increase the number of steps significantly to increase the accuracy of the estimate of the value of the option. In general a large number of steps must be utilised in valuing options using the binomial approach. The large number of paths places substantial demands on numerical techniques

---

**Exhibit 7.14   Multi-Step Binomial Model for European Put Option**

The binomial model can be used to value a European put option in an entirely similar way. Assume the same parameters as for the example in **Exhibit 7.13** with the exception that the option is a European put option.

The inputs u, d, and p are as before:

$$u = e^{.20\sqrt{1/2}} = 1.151910$$
$$d = 1/u = 0.868123$$
$$p = (e^{.10.1/2} - 0.868123)/(1.151910 - 0.868123) = .645371$$

This allows the construction of the binomial tree as follows:

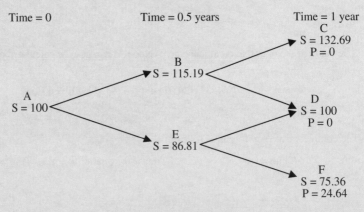

In order to now derive the value of the option, it is necessary to work back through the tree, solving for the price of the option at each node of the tree. In the above case the major node which is relevant is Node E, where the value of the option can be given as:

$$P = e^{-.10.1/2}[.645371(0) + (1 - .645371)24.64] = \$8.31$$

This in turn allows calculation of the value of the put at commencement (Node A) as:

$$P = e^{-.10.1/2}[.645371(0) + (1 - .645371)8.31] = \$2.80$$

The complete tree therefore is as follows:

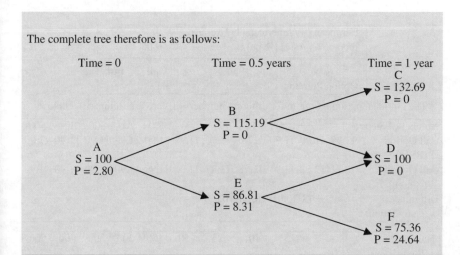

Time = 0          Time = 0.5 years         Time = 1 year

C
S = 132.69
P = 0

B
S = 115.19
P = 0

A
S = 100
P = 2.80

D
S = 100
P = 0

E
S = 86.81
P = 8.31

F
S = 75.36
P = 24.64

to solve through the tree to estimate the price of the option. For example, for a binomial tree with 50 steps there are:

- $n + 1$ terminal stock prices ($n$ = the number of steps) or 51 (50 + 1) terminal stock prices
- $2^n$ possible paths or $2^{50}$ ($1.13 \times 10^{15}$) possible price paths.

The large number of paths is necessary to ensure that the *correct numerical solution* is achieved. **Exhibit 7.15** sets out the process of convergence using a numerical solution for a binomial option pricing model.

---

**Exhibit 7.15    Numerical Solution of a Binomial Option Pricing Model**

Assume the same option in **Exhibit 7.9**. As the option is a European option, the Black-Scholes option pricing model gives the correct price. A binomial model (with varying numbers of steps) can be used to see the number of steps required to converge to the correct solution.

Key details of the option are summarised below:

| Pricing Inputs | | |
|---|---|---|
| Underlying Asset Price ($) | 105.00 | |
| Strike Price ($) | 100.00 | |
| Option Maturity (years) | 0.50 | |
| Volatility (% pa) | 20.00 | |
| Risk Free Rate (% pa) | 10.00 | |
| Call (0)/Put (1) | 0 | 1 |

| European (0)/American (1) Exercise | 0 | |
|---|---|---|
| Income on Asset (% pa) | 0.00 | |
| | **Call** | **Put** |
| Option Premium ($) | 11.90 | 2.02 |

The binomial option premium for different numbers of steps are summarised below:

| Number of Steps | 1 | 2 | 5 | 10 | 25 | 50 | 100 | 200 | 300 | 400 | 500 |
|---|---|---|---|---|---|---|---|---|---|---|---|
| Call Option (BSM) | 11.90 | 11.90 | 11.90 | 11.90 | 11.90 | 11.90 | 11.90 | 11.90 | 11.90 | 11.90 | 11.90 |
| Call Option (Binomial) | 12.31 | 12.38 | 11.91 | 11.78 | 11.87 | 11.90 | 11.90 | 11.90 | 11.90 | 11.90 | 11.90 |
| Difference (Call Option) | 0.41 | 0.48 | 0.01 | (0.12) | (0.03) | – | – | – | – | – | – |

| Number of Steps | 1 | 2 | 5 | 10 | 25 | 50 | 100 | 200 | 300 | 400 | 500 |
|---|---|---|---|---|---|---|---|---|---|---|---|
| Put Option (BSM) | 2.02 | 2.02 | 2.02 | 2.02 | 2.02 | 2.02 | 2.02 | 2.02 | 2.02 | 2.02 | 2.02 |
| Put Option (Binomial) | 2.44 | 2.50 | 2.03 | 1.91 | 1.99 | 2.03 | 2.02 | 2.03 | 2.02 | 2.02 | 2.02 |
| Difference (Put Option) | 0.42 | 0.48 | 0.01 | (0.11) | (0.03) | 0.01 | – | 0.01 | – | – | – |

The process of convergence is set out in graphical format below:

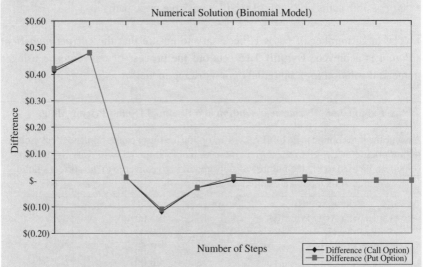

Numerical Solution (Binomial Model)

The analysis highlights the importance of using a sufficient number of steps to ensure that the numerical solution converges to the true underlying values.

## 8.4 Binomial Models – Features

The binomial option pricing model contains the Black and Scholes formula as a limiting case. If in the binomial option pricing model the number of sub-periods is allowed to tend to infinity, then the binomial option pricing model tends to the option pricing formula derived by Black and Scholes. In effect, the two models are identical, with the binomial model being a numerical implementation of the Black-Scholes model.

The major advantage of the binomial model is that as the time to maturity is segmented into a series of discrete time steps, the model can take into account specific option values *prior to maturity*. This allows the binomial approach to be used to provide a solution not only for the closed form European option pricing problem, but also for the more difficult American option pricing problems when numerical simulation approaches must be employed. In essence, the binomial pricing approach is useful as it can accommodate more complex option pricing problems, such as non-constant interest rates and volatility, debt options and exotic options such as path dependent structures.

# 9 Option Pricing Models – Alternative Approaches

The binomial approach is an example of numerical approaches to option pricing. There are a number of other numerical and approximation approaches that are used in practice[23]. These include:

* **Multinomial tree structures** – binomial approaches are one example of using a tree (also called a lattice) to price options. The option can extended in a

---

[23] For a discussion of different option pricing models and their historical development, see Chance, Don M. "Research Trends in Derivatives and Risk Management Since Black-Scholes" (May 1999) Journal of Portfolio Management 35–46; Smith Jr., Clifford W. "Option Pricing: A Review" (1976) Journal of Financial Economics Vol 3 15–24; Smithson, Charles "Wonderful Life" (October 1991) Risk 37–44; Smithson, Charles "Extended Family (1)" (October 1995) Risk 19–21; Smithson, Charles "Extended Family (2)" (November 1995) Risk 52–53; Smithson, Charles "Extended Family" (December 1997) Risk 158–163; Whaley, Robert "Building on Black-Scholes" (December 1997) Risk 149–156; Smithson, Charles "Extended Family" (September 1998) Risk Black Scholes Merton Supplement 14–18. For a discussion of developments in numerical techniques, see Broadie, M. and Detemple, Jerome "Recent Advances in Numerical Methods for Pricing Derivative Securities" in Rogers, L.C.G. and Talay, D. (Editors) (1997) Numerical Methods in Finance; Cambridge University Press, Cambridge, at 43–66.

number of ways:

1. *Alternative tree structures* – this would include trees where the probabilities are held constant (at say 0.5) regardless of volatility or the number of time steps[24].
2. *Trinomial tree structures* – this allows the price to take three possible steps (up, unchanged, down)[25]. This structure is set out in **Exhibit 7.16**.

- **Finite difference methodologies** – finite difference schemes, when applied to option pricing, allow the option value to be calculated by solving for the differential equation that the option must satisfy[26]. The approach is not dissimilar to the binomial/multinomial schemes described. Finite difference models create a rectangular grid of prices with an identical number of prices at each price step[27]. The differential equation that the option must satisfy is then specified. This is then converted into a set of difference equations. The difference equations are then solved using iteration methodologies[28].
- **Monte Carlo simulation** – Monte Carlo simulation techniques involve the generation of a large number of possible price paths. The paths are intended to represent possible prices of the underlying asset with the same likelihood as in reality. The price paths generated are used to determine the value of the option at

---

[24]  See Hull, John (1997) Futures, Options and Other Derivatives – Third Edition; Prentice Hall, Upper Saddle River, NJ at 350, 351.

[25]  See Hull, John (2000) Option Futures and Other Derivatives – Fourth Edition; Prentice-Hall Inc., Upper Saddle River, NJ at 405–406.

[26]  Finite difference methodologies were suggested by Schwartz, Eduardo S. "The Valuation of Warrants: Implementing a New Approach" (1977) Journal of Financial Economics 4 79–93; see also Brennan, Michael J. and Schwartz, Eduardo S. "Finite Difference Methods and Jump Processes Arising in the Pricing of Contingent Claims: A Synthesis" (1978) Journal of Financial and Quantitative Analysis 13 462–474; Courtadon, Georges A. "A More Accurate Finite Difference Approximation for the Valuation of Options" (1982) Journal of Financial and Quantitative Analysis 17 697–703.

[27]  This means that at each point three price outcomes are possible (trinomial tree); see Hull, John and White, Alan "Valuing Derivative Securities Using the Explicit Finite Difference Models" (1990) Journal of Financial and Quantitative Analysis 25 79–83.

[28]  For a more detailed discussion on implementing finite difference models, see Hull, John (2000) Option Futures and Other Derivatives – Fourth Edition; Prentice-Hall Inc., Upper Saddle River, NJ at 415–425; Wilmott, Peter (1998) Derivatives: The Theory and Practice of Financial Engineering; John Wiley & Sons, Chichester at Chapters 46–48; Wilmott, Paul, Dewynne, Jeff and Howison, Sam (1993) Option Pricing: Mathematical Models and Computations; Oxford Financial Press, Oxford at 17–19.

maturity, or more frequently in the case of a path dependent option. The average payoff is then discounted back to the start[29]. A variety of techniques are used to improve the accuracy of the price paths and the speed of the calculation. These include[30]:

1. *Variance reduction methodologies* – these include the use of antithetic variates [the value of the option is calculated twice for each simulation run (once normally; the second as a mirror image; that is, with changed signs) and the average of the two value used], control variates [where a simpler option with a known analytic solution is used as a control case for a more complex option with Monte Carlo simulation being run for both with the value of the complex option being adjusted for the relationship between the known and Monte Carlo simulation values for the simpler option] and moment matching [the samples created can be re-sampled (for example using quadratic techniques) to ensure the samples have the same mean and standard deviation as the underlying distribution][31].

2. *Quasi-Monte Carlo methodologies* – this involves using low discrepancy sequences[32] being used to generate sample prices that are more evenly distributed than under a truly random simulation where a small number of samples do not generally fill the sampling space evenly, as samples are drawn without regard to previous sample points[33]. The approaches are used to increase the speed and efficiency of Monte Carlo simulations.

---

[29] This approach was suggested by Boyle, Phelim P. "Options: A Monte Carlo Approach" (1977) Journal of Financial Economics 4 323–338; for a discussion of implementing Monte Carlo models, see Hull, John (2000) Option Futures and Other Derivatives – Fourth Edition; Prentice-Hall Inc., Upper Saddle River, NJ at 406–415; Wilmott, Peter (1998) Derivatives: The Theory and Practice of Financial Engineering; John Wiley & Sons, Chichester at Chapter 49.

[30] For a discussion of Monte Carlo simulation in practice, see Brotherton-Ratcliffe, R. "Monte Carlo Motoring" (December 1994) Risk 53–58; Newton, Nigel J. "Continuous Time Monte Carlo Methods and Variance Reduction" in Rogers, L.C.G. and Talay, D. (Editors) (1997) Numerical Methods in Finance; Cambridge University Press, Cambridge, at 22–42; Lehoczky, John P. "Simulation Methods for Option Pricing" in Dempster, Michael A.H. and Pliska, Stanley R. (1997) (Editors) Mathematics of Financial Derivatives; Cambridge University Press, Cambridge, at 528–544; Paskov, Spassimir H. "New Methodologies for Valuing Derivatives" in Dempster, Michael A.H. and Pliska, Stanley R. (1997) (Editors) Mathematics of Financial Derivatives; Cambridge University Press, Cambridge, at 545–582.

[31] Other techniques used include importance and stratified sampling.

[32] For example, Faure, Sobol or Halton sequences.

[33] This approach is also known as quasi-random or the pseudo random number approach.

- **Approximation techniques**[34] – approximation techniques are based on using an option with a known solution to infer the solution to a more complex option pricing problem. A variety of approaches are feasible and include approximating the underlying function with a polynomial or approximating the differential equation that the option must satisfy and solving the approximation. For example, in the case of American options, since the European and American options must both satisfy the same differential equation, the difference between the two premium must also satisfy the same differential equation. This allows the value of the American option to be estimated by using a quadratic approximation technique[35].

- **Other mathematical techniques** – these involve a variety of advanced mathematical techniques to price options using complex integration or standard numeric integration techniques.

---

### Exhibit 7.16    Trinomial Trees

The structure of a trinomial tree is set out below. At each node the price is allowed to increase (Su), decrease (Sd) or stay at the same level (Sm).

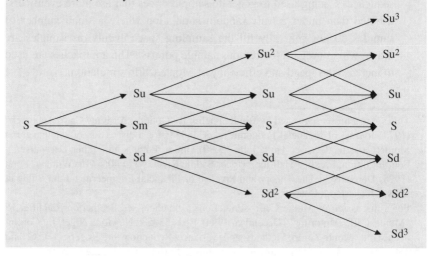

---

[34] Approximation techniques have fallen into disuse and are less common as the availability of increased computing power has allowed more accurate and robust numerical methods to be utilised. Approximation is still used for some exotic option structures.

[35] See Geske, Robert and Johnson, H.E. "The American Put Option Valued Analytically" (1984) Journal of Finance 39 1511–1524; MacMillan, L.W. "Analytic Approximation for the American Put Option" (1986) Advances in Futures and Options Research 1 119–139; Barone-Adesi, Giovanni and Whaley, Robert E. "Efficient Analytic Approximation of American Option Values" (1987) Journal of Finance 42 301–320.

For a non-income paying asset, parameter values for setting up the trinomial tree are as follows[36]:

$$u = e^{\sigma \sqrt{3.\Delta t}}$$

$$d = 1/u$$

$$p_d = -\sqrt{\Delta t/12\sigma^2}(r - \sigma^2/2) + 1/6$$

$$p_m = 2/3$$

$$p_u = \sqrt{\Delta t/12\sigma^2}(r - \sigma^2/2) + 1/6$$

Where

u  = the factor amount the stock price can go up
d  = the factor amount the stock price can go down
e  = the exponential term
$\sigma$  = the volatility of logs of the returns of the asset price
t  = time to expiry of the option
n  = number of steps
$\Delta t$ = the length of each time step
$p_u$ = the probability of an upward move in the asset price
$p_m$ = the probability of no change in the asset price
$p_d$ = the probability of a downward move in the asset price
r  = the risk free rate of interest

For an asset paying income, the term r is replaced by $r - y$ (where $y$ = income on the asset).

# 10    Option Pricing Models – Issues in Application

The major attraction of option pricing models based on the Black-Scholes approach (including its binomial and various numerical implementations) include:

- The fact that all input variables other than volatility are directly observable.
- The models do not make any reference to the investor's attitudes to risk.

While the model plays a central role in option valuation trading, the underlying assumptions do not necessarily hold true in practice. In particular, violations of the model's assumptions exist in the following areas:

- Asset price behaviour.
- Constant and measurable volatility.
- Constancy of interest rates.
- No intermediate cash flows.
- The issue of early exercise.

---

[36]   See Hull, John (2000) Option Futures and Other Derivatives – Fourth Edition; Prentice-Hall Inc., Upper Saddle River, NJ at 405.

Some of these violations are significant (like assumptions about asset price behaviour and volatility) while others are relatively minor (constancy of interest rate (except in the case of debt options where it is problematic), intermediate cash flows and early exercise) in terms of their impact on the validity of the models.

The key assumption violated in practice is that price changes are continuous through time (that is, the assumption that there are no jumps or discontinuities between successive asset prices), independent and log normally distributed over time with constant variance. The assumption of independence of asset price changes as required by efficient market theory is not wholly convincing. The empirical evidence and support for the log normal distribution of asset prices and its constancy over time are also not completely convincing[37]. It is clear that option prices are sensitive to the stochastic processes assumed and changes in the assumptions produce significant, large percentage changes in option prices[38].

Empirical research[39] highlights that *true* distributions differ from theoretical normal distribution in two respects:

- The distributions of actual asset price changes are characterised by *fat tails*; that is, the distributions display larger extreme price changes (both positive and negative) than implied by a theoretical normal distribution. This means that the theoretical models would *under price* out-of-the-money and in-the-money option. This reflects the fact that the theoretical distribution allocates a lower probability to very high intrinsic values than is the case in reality.
- Asset price behaviour appears to be characterised by discontinuities in the asset price changes or jumps. This contributes to the fat tails of the distribution.

The violation of the asset price behaviour assumptions underlying Black and Scholes has prompted the development of variations on the basic model. They include alternative stochastic processes including absolute diffusion, displaced diffusion, jump processes and diffusion-jump processes[40]. **Exhibit 7.17** sets out an example of a model using jump diffusion processes.

---

[37] For a discussion of the log normality of asset price changes, see Das, Satyajit (2004) Risk Management; John Wiley & Sons (Asia), Singapore at Chapter 2 where the evidence is considered in the context of value at risk calculations that also rely on the assumption of log normality.

[38] See Smith, Andrew "The Taming of the Skew" (February 2001) FOW – Risk & Reward 28–30.

[39] See Rowe, David "What to Do When Price Changes are Not Normal" (November 1999) Risk 60.

[40] For example, see Merton, Robert C. "Option Pricing When Underlying Stock Returns Are Discontinuous" (1976) Journal of Financial Economics 3 125–144; Cox, John C. and Ross, Stephen A. "The Valuation of Options for Alternative Stochastic Processes"

Empirical tests show that the alternative models are not able to provide better predictions of actual prices than the Black and Scholes type of model on a consistent basis. The price differences resulting from differing assumptions as to the underlying asset price movements in fact are *no* greater than the price differences that result from different assumptions of volatility.

The asset price volatility factor required as an input to option pricing models must be forward looking; that is, a forecast of the probable size (although not necessarily the direction) of asset price changes between the present and the maturity of the option. The problem in volatility estimation (the determination of the true constant volatility of the asset price) is sought to be overcome in practice by utilising two types of volatility – historical and implied.

Historical volatility is based on past prices of the underlying asset, computed as the standard deviation of log relatives of daily price returns (usually annualised) over a period of time. Using historical volatility requires the selection of the period over which price data is to be sampled. It is possible to use price information over long periods (up to five years or longer) to derive the volatility estimate. This assumes that volatility is constant over long periods. It is also possible to use a much shorter period (less than 30 days) to get a good estimate of the current level of volatility. It is necessary to adjust the volatility input into the option pricing formula on a regular basis where short-term volatility is used, on the basis that the volatility actually varies significantly.

Implied volatility is determined by solving an option pricing model (such as Black-Scholes) in reverse; that is, calculating the volatility which would be needed in the formula to make the market price equal to fair value as calculated by the model. Where this method is used, the implied volatility equates the model premium to the actual premium observed in the option market. An interesting problem with implied volatility measures is that options with different strike prices but with the same maturity often have different implied volatility[41]. In addition, volatility appears to be characterised by a defined term structure.

Historical volatility is a measure of past, already experienced price behaviour. To the extent the option pricing model is validated, implied volatility reflects market expectations of future price behaviour during the life of the option. Both measures are important and comparisons of the two measures can reveal interesting

(1976) Journal of Financial Economic 3 145–166; Jarrow, Robert and Rudd, Andrew "Approximate Option Valuation for Arbitrary Stochastic Processes" (1982) Journal of Financial Economic 10 347–369. See also Leib, Barclay "The Return of Jump Modelling" (May 2000) Derivatives Strategy 28–32.

[41] This is the phenomenon of the volatility smile that is dealt with in Chapter 9.

insights into the market in the underlying asset. However, no normative rule for derivation of the volatility estimate is available. In addition, the models usually assume constant volatility. This assumption is clearly breached in practice as volatility changes over time often very significantly. Some attempted solutions to the volatility measurement model have sought to explicitly take into account the stochastic nature *of volatility* itself by using multi-factor numerical techniques which utilise two stochastic variables, namely, the asset and the volatility[42].

The assumption that interest rates are constant is particularly problematic in the case of options on debt instruments. This is because interest rate changes drive asset price changes where the asset itself is an interest bearing security. In addition, the volatility of asset prices in the case of debt instruments is a function of remaining maturity and, in turn, interest rates that reflect the shape of the yield curve. As maturity diminishes, the volatility of the asset also diminishes and constant variance cannot be assumed.

The impact of intermediate cash flows depends on the pattern of payments and the certainty with which the cash flows can be predicted. The Black-Scholes model does not appear to be very sensitive to assumptions about intermediate payouts that are certain. Where the intermediate cash flows are uncertain, however, the closed form Black-Scholes approach appears to break down.

The Black and Scholes model is not applicable to American options. It sets a lower limit for the price of the American call, but the model does not encompass the additional problem of determining the optimal time to exercise the option where the possibility of early exercise is not excluded.

The problems of both intermediate cash flows and early exercise can be solved with some adjustments to the standard models. The adjustments are examined below in detail.

Empirical tests[43] of the Black and Scholes model indicate that the model is relatively robust and provides accurate pricing for at-the-money options with medium to long maturity. The model appears to systematically misprice out-of-the-money and in-the-money options, and options where volatility increases or time to maturity is very short. In general, however, the model appears to successfully capture the essential determinants of option prices and United States studies show that traders

---

[42]  A discussion of issues pertaining to estimation of volatility is set out in Chapter 9.

[43]  See Rowley, Ian "Option Pricing Models: How Good is Black-Scholes?" (June 1987) Euromoney Corporate Finance 30–34; Hull, John (2000) Option Futures and Other Derivatives – Fourth Edition; Prentice-Hall Inc., Upper Saddle River, NJ at 448–449 (and the references cited therein).

cannot make consistent above normal returns on an after tax, post commission basis by setting up hedged portfolios.

Different models that seek to overcome some deficiencies of Black and Scholes introduce new assumptions and do not necessarily produce improvements in pricing predictions.

The increased effort in improving and developing variations on available theoretical option pricing models creates the added problem of model selection[44]. Clearly, there is no simple basis for selecting between the various techniques as the actual benefit from a particular model will depend on the user's objective. The selection of a model in practice depends on the user's assumptions concerning the underlying asset price process. As there is no universal or true underlying process of asset prices, there can be no universal option pricing model and therefore no definitive fair value price for options.

In practice, models such as Black-Scholes (including its numerical equivalents such as the binomial etc models) have been successful because of the logical simplicity, computational efficiency and robustness. Market participants have sought to deal with the failure of model assumptions in real markets by a series of adjustments to the models in practice including:

- Adjusting the volatility utilised for options with different maturity or different strikes to adjust for the under valuation of in or out-of-the-money options.
- Increasing volatility for shorter dates options to adjust for the potential impact of large jumps and consequent changes in the price of the underlying asset.

The strength of the option pricing models identified may ultimately lie in their capacity to compress the four observable variables into one other variable (implied volatility) that can then be interpreted. However, the problem of model pricing performance has led to option traders using a range of pricing techniques and risk management techniques to manage the risk of trading in options[45].

| Exhibit 7.17   Jump Diffusion Option Pricing Models |

**1. Approach**
Jump diffusion models typically use both a diffusion process (the price moves continuously over time as assumed under the Black-Scholes Approach) and occasional large jumps in the asset price. Generally, the models assume that after each jump, the asset price follows a

---

[44] For a framework for assessing error in option pricing models, see Jacquier, Eric and Jarrow, Robert "Vital Statistics" (April 1995) Risk 62–64.

[45] For a market practitioner oriented review of model trends, see Cookson, Richard "Moving in the Right Direction" (October 1993) 22–26. For a view on model risk issues, see Derman, Emanuel "Model Risk" (May 1996) Risk 34–37.

diffusion process. A variety of processes (such as Poisson processes) are used to model the asset price movement.

## 2.  Example[46]

Assume the following option:

| Pricing Inputs | | |
|---|---|---|
| Underlying Asset Price ($) | 100.00 | |
| Strike Price ($) | 125.00 | |
| Option Maturity (years) | 0.50 | |
| Volatility (% pa) | 20.00 | |
| Risk Free Rate (% pa) | 10.00 | |
| Call (0)/Put (1) | 0 | 1 |
| European (0)/American (1) Exercise | 0 | |
| Income on Asset (% pa) | 0.00 | |
| | **Call** | **Put** |
| Option Premium ($) | 0.82 | 19.73 |

The option is now re-priced using the jump diffusion process. The resulting option premiums are summarised below:

| Expected Number of Jumps Per year ($\lambda$) | 2 | 5 | 10 | 25 | 50 |
|---|---|---|---|---|---|
| Fraction (%) of Volatility Accounted for by Jumps | 10 | 10 | 10 | 10 | 10 |
| Call Option | 0.82 | 0.82 | 0.82 | 0.82 | 0.82 |
| Put Option | 19.73 | 19.73 | 19.73 | 19.73 | 19.73 |

| Expected Number of Jumps Per year ($\lambda$) | 2 | 5 | 10 | 25 | 50 |
|---|---|---|---|---|---|
| Fraction (%) of Volatility Accounted for by Jumps | 25 | 25 | 25 | 25 | 25 |
| Call Option | 0.83 | 0.83 | 0.82 | 0.82 | 0.82 |
| Put Option | 19.73 | 19.73 | 19.73 | 19.73 | 19.73 |

| Expected Number of Jumps Per year ($\lambda$) | 2 | 5 | 10 | 25 | 50 |
|---|---|---|---|---|---|
| Fraction (%) of Volatility Accounted for by Jumps | 50 | 50 | 50 | 50 | 50 |
| Call Option | 0.86 | 0.84 | 0.83 | 0.83 | 0.82 |
| Put Option | 19.77 | 19.74 | 19.73 | 19.73 | 19.73 |

The jump process has the greatest impact where the option is out of the money and there are few jumps, but the jumps contribute a large fraction of the overall volatility.

---

[46]  The example uses a jump diffusion model where the model is specified by the following stochastic differential equation for asset price evolution:

$$dS/S = hcos t \cdot dt + (1 - jumpfrac)^{1/2}V \cdot dZ(t) + jumpfrac^{1/2}V/\lambda \cdot W(t) \cdot dP_\lambda(t)$$

Where S = asset price; hcos t = riskfree rate − asset income; t = time to option expiry; jumpfrac = fraction of volatility accounted for by jumps; V = annualised volatility of the price of the underlying asset; dZ = a Wiener process; $\lambda$ = expected number of jumps in a year; $dP_\lambda$ = independent Poisson process with parameter $\lambda$; W(t) = independent standard random variables.

# 11 Options Pricing Models – Extensions to the Standard Models[47]

In this Section, the amended versions of the basic option pricing model are considered. The basic models are designed to deal with European options on non-income producing assets. **Exhibit 7.18** sets out a hierarchy of option pricing models covering different instruments and asset classes. The extensions described extend the basic model in a number of specific areas:

* Adjustment for intermediate cash flows using either continuous income or discrete income.

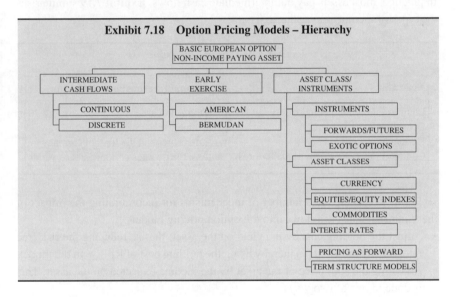

**Exhibit 7.18    Option Pricing Models – Hierarchy**

---

[47] For a discussion of different option pricing models, see Chance, Don M. "Research Trends in Derivatives and Risk Management Since Black-Scholes" (May 1999) Journal of Portfolio Management 35–46; Smith Jr., Clifford W. "Option Pricing: A Review" (1976) Journal of Financial Economics vol 3 15–24; Smithson, Charles "Wonderful Life" (October 1991) Risk 37–44; Smithson, Charles "Extended Family (1)" (October 1995) Risk 19–21; Smithson, Charles "Extended Family (2)" (November 1995) Risk 52–53; Smithson, Charles "Extended Family" (December 1997) Risk 158–163; Whaley, Robert "Building on Black-Scholes" (December 1997) Risk 149–156; Smithson, Charles "Extended Family" (September 1998) Risk Black Scholes Merton Supplement 14–18. See also Meisner, James F. and Labuszewski, John W. "Modifying the Black-Scholes Option Pricing Model for Alternative Underlying Instruments" (November-December 1984) Financial Analysts Journal 23–30.

- Early exercise.
- A change in the underlying asset or instruments. This covers *a forward or futures contract* on the asset or forms of exotic optionality[48].
- Coverage of specific asset classes such as equity, currency, debt or commodities. This is divided into two separate groups of assets – currency, equity/equity indexes and commodities and debt/interest rates. This classification is dictated by the special problem created by debt options[49].

## 12  Intermediate Cash Flows

In practice, most assets pay out intermediate cash flows. **Exhibit 7.19** summarises the types of income on various assets.

| Exhibit 7.19   Income on Assets | |
| --- | --- |
| **Asset Class** | **Income/Intermediate Cash Flow** |
| Equities/equity market indexes | Dividends |
| Debt/Interest rates | Coupons |
| Currencies | Interest rate on the foreign currency |
| Commodities/Commodity Price Indexes | Asset lease rates or convenience yields |

In practice, there are a number of mechanisms for incorporating the impact of these intermediate cash flows into the option pricing models:

- Adjust the holding cost by the yield on the asset; that is, reducing the risk free rate (Rf) by the yield (y) thereby using the holding cost of $Rf - Y$ in the model.
- Adjusting the spot price of the asset by the income expected on the asset. This is done in one of two ways:
  1. Where the income is assumed to be continuous by adjusting the asset by replacing S by the term $Se^{-Y.T}$ where Y = the continuously compounded expected rate of return on the asset. **Exhibit 7.20** sets out a valuation model adapting the standard Black-Scholes model (suggested by Robert Merton) for an asset that pays continuous income. **Exhibit 7.21** sets out an example of using the model. An example of applying this type of model is set out below using a currency option where the risk free interest rate in the foreign currency ($Rf_f$) is used instead of Y in the formula in **Exhibit 7.27**.

---

[48] Pricing of exotic options is covered in Das, Satyajit (2004) Structured Products Volume 1; John Wiley & Sons (Asia), Singapore at Chapters 5 and 7 to 11 (inclusive).
[49] Pricing of debt options is covered in Chapter 8.

2. Where the income is discrete and known the spot price of the asset may be adjusted. This is done by discounting the known income to the commencement of the transaction and subtracting the discounted income from the spot price to derive an ex-income asset price that is then used as S in the model. **Exhibit 7.25** sets out an example of this type of adjustment with regard to an equity option.

---

**Exhibit 7.20    Valuation Model for European Option Asset Paying Continuous Income**

For a call option:

$$P_{ce} = Se^{-Y \cdot T} \cdot N(d1) - Ke^{-Rf \cdot T} \cdot N(d2)$$

Where

$$d1 = [\ln(S/K) + (Rf - Y + \sigma^2/2)T]/\sigma\sqrt{T}$$
$$d2 = [\ln(S/K) + (Rf - Y - \sigma^2/2)T]/\sigma\sqrt{T} = d1 - \sigma\sqrt{T}$$

Where all terms are as defined previously and Y = the continuously compounded expected rate of return on the asset.

For a put option:

$$P_{pe} = Ke^{-Rf \cdot T} \cdot N(-d2) - Se^{-Y \cdot T} \cdot N(-d1)$$

---

**Exhibit 7.21    Valuation Model for European Option Asset Paying Continuous Income – Example**

Assume the same option in **Exhibit 7.9**. Key details of the option are summarised below:

| Pricing Inputs | | |
|---|---|---|
| Underlying Asset Price ($) | 105.00 | |
| Strike Price ($) | 100.00 | |
| Option Maturity (years) | 0.50 | |
| Volatility (% pa) | 20.00 | |
| Risk Free Rate (% pa) | 10.00 | |
| Call (0)/Put (1) | 0 | 1 |
| European (0)/American (1) Exercise | 0 | |
| Income on Asset (% pa) | 0.00 | |
| | **Call** | **Put** |
| Option Premium ($) | 11.90 | 2.02 |

Assume the asset pays income of 4.00% pa. This income is re-stated the continuously compounded expected rate of return on the asset as follows:

$$Y = \ln(1 + 0.04) = .0392 \text{ or } 3.92\% \text{ pa continuously compounded}$$

The option premium incorporating the income is:

| Pricing Inputs | | |
|---|---|---|
| Underlying Asset Price ($) | 105.00 | |
| Strike Price ($) | 100.00 | |
| Option Maturity (years) | 0.50 | |
| Volatility (% pa) | 20.00 | |
| Risk Free Rate (% pa) | 10.00 | |
| Call (0)/Put (1) | 0 | 1 |
| European (0)/American (1) Exercise | 0 | |
| Income on Asset (% pa) | 3.92 | |
| | **Call** | **Put** |
| Option Premium ($) | 10.35 | 2.52 |

The fall in the call option premium reflects the lower intrinsic value (lower ex income asset price) partially offset by a higher time value as the option moves closer to at the money. The put option increases in value because of higher time value. The higher time value reflects the fact the forward asset price distribution has shifted to the left (a lower forward price) and the put is closer to at-the-money and therefore has a higher chance of exercise.

Where a binomial option pricing model is used to value the option, the value of the asset must be adjusted at the node at which the income is paid (in practice the date at which the entitlement to the income is lost such as an ex-dividend or ex-coupon date). The value of the asset is reduced by the amount of the income flow.

This creates a number of problems. The tree of asset prices becomes non-recombining; that is, an up move followed by a down move is no longer the same as a down move followed by an up move in the asset price. The tree also becomes larger as a result of the non-recombining nature of the tree. This is exacerbated where there are several cash flows. A common approach to improve the numerical efficiency of the solution of the binomial tree under these circumstances is to treat the asset as the asset price (ex-dividend) that is modelled through the tree. The present value of the future income (for example dividends) is added to the modelled asset price at each node[50].

# 13   Early Exercise/American Options

The market for options includes both European and American options. An American option will generally not be exercised early as the economic rationale favours the sale of the option. Under certain circumstances, early exercise is possible.

---

[50]   See Hull, John (2000) Option Futures and Other Derivatives – Fourth Edition; Prentice-Hall Inc., Upper Saddle River, NJ at 273–277.

In practice, the risk of early exercise is particularly evident in the following cases:

- For in-the-money call options where the asset pays a high yield or income payment. This is because the benefit of receiving the high yield or the capture of the cash flow of the income payment on the asset may yield a superior return to the uncertain value of the asset and call at maturity. This is particularly relevant for equity options with a large dividend payable prior to option expiry, where payment of the dividend would substantially reduce the value of the asset reducing the value of the call option. A similar logic applies to currency call options on a currency that has high interest rates where the option is likely to be exercised early.
- In the case of put options, a deep in-the-money put can economically be exercised early, with the proceeds received invested at the risk free rate to yield a superior return to the uncertain intrinsic value of the put at maturity.

The valuation of American options is usually undertaken in two ways:

- Using a modified version of the Black-Scholes option pricing model.
- Using the binomial approach to option pricing.

The Modified Black-Scholes European Option Pricing Formula relies on the intuition that the standard Black-Scholes model provided a lower estimate of the value of the American option. It is identical to Black Scholes except that the formula checks to see if the value it is returning is below the intrinsic value of the option. Where the Black-Scholes European Option value is below the intrinsic price of the option, then the Modified Black-Scholes American Formula returns the intrinsic value of the option as follows :

Black-Scholes American Option Value = Maximum (Black-Scholes
European Value; Intrinsic Values)

The binomial option pricing model is well suited to estimating the fair value of an American exercise option. This reflects the fact that the approach incorporates all possible paths taken by the asset price, as well as the distribution of asset prices at the expiry of the option. This allows American options to be priced through a process where it is possible to calculate option values at each node of the tree, and to test for the feasibility of early exercise. If the option at any node has a higher intrinsic value (that is, the value on early exercise) than the theoretical value of the option, then the higher intrinsic value is used in the solution back through the tree, effectively incorporating the risk of early exercise.

**Exhibit 7.22** sets out an example of using a binomial option pricing model to value an American put option. **Exhibit 7.23** sets out the value of the option previously priced as a European option in **Exhibit 7.9** where it is an American option.

An alternative approach is to use quadratic approximation methods to value American options. Under this approach, it is assumed that an American option is equal to a European option plus a separate early exercise option. The quadratic approximation method determines the early exercise option value and then adds it to the value calculated by the Modified Black-Scholes European Formula. The early exercise option value is determined by an iterative process[51].

A variation on the American option is the Bermudan option that is only capable of exercise on a nominated number of discrete dates prior to expiry. In effect, it is some way between an American and a European option. Bermudan options are priced using a binomial option pricing model that tests for the risk of early exercise at the relevant nodes of the tree.

---

**Exhibit 7.22   Multi-Step Binomial Model for American Put Option**

The use of a multi-step binomial option pricing model for an American Put Option can be illustrated with the example given in **Exhibit 7.14**. Assume all the factors stated in that example, with the exception that the option is now an American put.

The complete tree therefore is as follows:

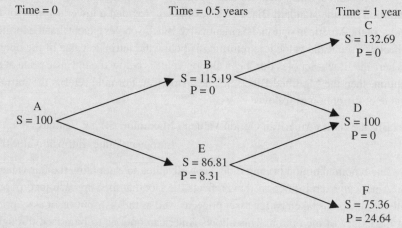

In solving back through the tree it is feasible to compare the value of a European put option with *the intrinsic value of the option* if the option is exercised at that node.

In this example, as at Node E the value of the European option is 8.31. However, if the option is exercised, it will have an intrinsic value of 13.19 (100 − 86.81). This means that the holder of the option would at this point rationally exercise the put option early.

---

[51]   See Barone-Adesi, G. and Whaley, R.E. "Efficient Analytic Approximation of American Option Values" (June 1987) Journal of Finance vol 42 301–320.

In order to value the American put, the intrinsic value of the option at node E is substituted for the theoretical European value. This in turn allows calculation of the value of the put at commencement (Node A) as:

$$P = e^{-.10.1/2}[.645371(0) + (1 - .645371)13.19] = 4.45$$

The complete tree therefore is as follows:

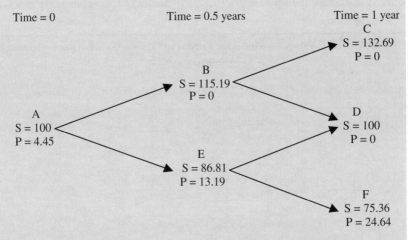

| Time = 0 | Time = 0.5 years | Time = 1 year |

C
S = 132.69
P = 0

B
S = 115.19
P = 0

A
S = 100
P = 4.45

D
S = 100
P = 0

E
S = 86.81
P = 13.19

F
S = 75.36
P = 24.64

The difference between the value of the American put (4.45) and the value of the European put (2.80) of 1.65 can be attributed to the value of the right of early exercise.

## 14   Options on Forward/Futures Contracts

Where the option is on a forward or futures contract the basic Black-Scholes model can be altered to adjust for the changed nature of the underlying asset. **Exhibit 7.24** sets out Black's version of the original basic Black and Scholes' model for a premium paid European option on a futures contract[52]. **Exhibit 7.25** sets out an example of utilising the Black option pricing model to derive the price of an option on a forward contract.

The intuition behind the Black reformulation of the Black and Scholes option pricing model in the context of futures is that the investment in a futures contract

---

[52]   See Black, Fischer "The Pricing of Commodity Contracts" (March 1976) 3 Journal of Financial Economics 167–179.

requires no commitment of funds (deposits, margins etc are ignored). In contrast, an option on an asset entails investment in the physical asset, for example a share in the case of an equity option imposes a cost. This means that nothing is paid or received (up-front) in setting up the hedge that entails buying or selling the futures contract. The value of a call option on a futures contract should be lower than the value of a call option on the physical asset as the futures price should already impound the carrying costs associated with the physical commodity. The futures price is in essence the forward price that will naturally reflect any carry costs over

---

**Exhibit 7.23   Valuation Model for European Option Asset Paying Continuous Income – Example**

Assume the same option in **Exhibit 7.9**. Key details of the option are summarised below:

| Pricing Inputs | | |
|---|---|---|
| Underlying Asset Price ($) | 105.00 | |
| Strike Price ($) | 100.00 | |
| Option Maturity (years) | 0.50 | |
| Volatility (% pa) | 20.00 | |
| Risk Free Rate (% pa) | 10.00 | |
| Call (0)/Put (1) | 0 | 1 |
| European (0)/American (1) Exercise | 0 | |
| Income on Asset (% pa) | 0.00 | |
| | **Call** | **Put** |
| Option Premium ($) | 11.90 | 2.02 |

Assume the option is American. The revised option premium (solved using a binomial tree with 500 steps) is as follows:

| Pricing Inputs | | |
|---|---|---|
| Underlying Asset Price ($) | 105.00 | |
| Strike Price ($) | 100.00 | |
| Option Maturity (years) | 0.50 | |
| Volatility (% pa) | 20.00 | |
| Risk Free Rate (% pa) | 10.00 | |
| Call (0)/Put (1) | 0 | 1 |
| European (0)/American (1) Exercise | 1 | |
| Income on Asset (% pa) | 0.00 | |
| | **Call** | **Put** |
| Option Premium ($) | 11.90 | 2.27 |

---

**Exhibit 7.24    Black Option Pricing Model for Forward/Futures
Contracts**

For a call option:

$$P_{ce} = e^{-Rf \cdot T}[F \cdot N(d1) - K \cdot N(d2)]$$

Where

$$d1 = [\ln(F/K) + (\sigma^2/2)T]/\sigma\sqrt{T}$$

$$d2 = [\ln(F/K) - (\sigma^2/2)T]/\sigma\sqrt{T} = d1 - \sigma\sqrt{T}$$

Where all terms are as defined previously and F = forward or future prices of the underlying asset.

For a put option:

$$P_{pe} = e^{-Rf \cdot T}[K \cdot N(-d2) - SN(-d1)]$$

---

**Exhibit 7.25    Black Option Pricing Model for Forward/Futures
Contracts – Example**

Assume the following information:

Forward Price      = F  = 100
Strike Price       = K  = 100
Time to Maturity = T  = 12 months (1.00 years)
Risk Free Rate    = Rf = 10% pa (0.10)
Volatility          = $\sigma$  = 20% pa (0.20)

Using the above inputs, we can compute the call option price as follows:

$$d1 = 0.10$$

$$d2 = -0.10$$

Using the N(x) table:

$$N(d1) = N(0.10) = 0.5398$$

$$N(d2) = N(-0.10) = 0.4602$$

$$N(-d1) = N(-0.10) = 0.4602$$

$$N(-d2) = N(0.10) = 0.5398$$

Therefore, the call and put prices are as follows:

$$P_{ce} = e^{-0.10 \times 1.00}[100 \times 0.5398 - 100 \times 0.4602]$$
$$= 7.20 \text{ or } 7.20\% \text{ of Future Asset Value}$$

$$P_{pe} = e^{-0.10 \times 1.00}[100 \times 0.5398 - 100 \times 0.4602]$$
$$= 7.20 \text{ or } 7.20\% \text{ of Future Asset Value}$$

the relevant period. The usual qualifications concerning early exercise of American options apply[53].

The Black option pricing model involves the assumption that $\sigma$ (in this case the volatility of the forward/futures contract) is constant. This assumption is unlikely to hold in practice because of the mean reverting process. This dictates that when the period to option expiration is large, the price of the forward or futures contract is not greatly sensitive to current interest rates. However, as the time to option expiry decreases, the current level of interest rates becomes progressively more important in determining the forward or futures price, with the result that the volatility of the forward or futures price may increase with time. This is most relevant in the case of options on forward interest rates[54].

The computational method where the Black model is used to price options *on futures contracts* will need to be adjusted depending on the type of margining system applicable. When the margining system dictates that proceeds are not paid

---

[53] The adjustments required for the possibility of early exercise, discussed above, apply where the option is American style allowing the possibility of exercise prior to maturity. These must be solved using a binomial version of the Black Forward/Futures pricing model.

[54] In practice, the Black option pricing model can be applied if some adjustments designed to minimise the impact of this phenomenon are adopted. Utilising this approach, applied volatility for forward interest rates are calculated usually from traded futures options or from traded caps, floors etc. The debt option being valued is then priced utilising the implied volatility generated. This multiple use of the Black model, firstly, to calculate implied volatility and, secondly, to price the option, allows errors that may be caused by the use of the inexact model to be reduced. More importantly, they ensure that the calculated option prices are reasonably consistent with traded option prices. In general, the mean reverting property of interest rates causes the implied volatility to decrease with option maturity. The relationship between volatility and maturity of caps, floors and collars etc is difficult to observe since most of these over-the-counter instruments have maturities beyond the longest maturity of traded Eurodollar futures. However, in practice, this relationship can be extrapolated. This issue is discussed in Chapter 8.

up-front to option writers, prices have to be higher to compensate the seller for the fact that the premium is not received at the beginning, and consequently is not available for investment. If it is assumed initially that the premium is paid over to the seller of the option only at maturity, then the premium would have to be increased by the additional interest that could have been earned over the life of the option if the premium were available for investment. The value of the call option will become:

$$P_{ce} = F \cdot N(d1) - K \cdot N(d2)$$

In addition, the put-call parity relationship where proceeds are not paid up-front for open futures contracts is different:

$$P_{pe} = P_{ce} - F + K$$

In practice, the adjustment process is not simple because if nothing changes, part of the premium will be paid over to the writer of the option as the time value decays to zero over the life of the option.

# 15   Options on Currency/Foreign Exchange[55]

In theory, the Black model for pricing options on forward contracts is capable of being used to value currency options. In practice, the way several interest rates are involved, in ways differing from the assumption of the Black-Scholes model, dictate the use of different models. The principal model used is the Garman-Kohlhagen model[56]. The model argues that it is the interest rate *differential between domestic*

---

[55]   To date, the focus on option valuation has been general, rather than focused on specific types of assets. In this and the following Sections, adjustments to the option pricing model dictated by the *type* of underlying asset are examined. The amendments are specifically designed to encompass the particular characteristics of each asset class. The adjustments required for the possibility of early exercise, discussed above, apply to these cases where the option is American style, allowing the possibility of exercise prior to maturity. These must be solved using a binomial version of the pricing model. Similarly, the use of an amended model where the underlying asset is a futures contract on the asset, as described above, is also applicable to each of the asset classes described.

[56]   See Garman, Mark B. and Kohlhagen, Steven W. "Foreign Currency Option Values" (1983) 2 Journal of International Money and Finance 231–237. For an alternative model see Grabbe, J Orlin, "The Pricing of Call and Put Options on Foreign Exchange" (1983) 2 Journal of International Money and Finance 239–253. As noted above, the Garman-Kohlhagen formulation represents a special case of the Merton continuous yield income option pricing model.

*and foreign risk free rates* that reflects the expected price drift of the underlying asset, rather than a single interest rate that is appropriate in a single asset option[57]. The Garman-Kohlhagen model is set out in **Exhibit 7.26**. An example of pricing a currency option using the model is set out in **Exhibit 7.27**.

---

**Exhibit 7.26    Garman-Kohlhangen Model for Valuation of Currency Option**

For a call option:

$$P_{ce} = Se^{-Rf_f T} \cdot N(d1) - Ke^{-Rf_d T} \cdot N(d2)$$

Where

$$d1 = [\ln(S/K) + (Rf_d - Rf_f + \sigma^2/2)T]/\sigma\sqrt{T}$$
$$d2 = d1 - \sigma\sqrt{T}$$

Where all terms are as defined previously except as set out below:

$Rf_d$ = the risk free interest rate in the domestic currency
$Rf_f$ = the risk free interest rate in the foreign currency

For a put option:

$$P_{pe} = Ke^{Rf_d T} \cdot N(-d2) - Se^{Rf_f T} \cdot N(-d1)$$

---

The difference between the Black model and the Garman-Kohlhagen model[58] gains importance where the difference between the two rates is very small, or when one or other rate is large. The latter is particularly relevant in the case of American

---

[57] The Black-Scholes model employs interest rates in two different contexts: firstly, to discount future values; and secondly, as an arbitrage based surrogate for the drift of the deliverable instrument. The first use takes place outside the $N(\cdot)$ while the second takes place inside, reflecting the distribution of maturation values. Garman and Kohlhagen show that it is only interest rate differential controls the distribution features while the interest rates control the discounting of future values.

[58] Garman and Kohlhagen also show that by substituting the forward currency price at the option expiry (relying on the interest parity condition that the fully arbitraged forward rate should equal the spot rate adjusted by the interest differential between the currencies) into the model, it is possible to derive the Black option pricing model on forward/futures contracts, thereby showing that currency options can be treated on the same basis as options on forwards generally.

---

**Exhibit 7.27    Garman-Kohlhangen Model for Valuation of Currency Option – Example**

Assume the following facts relating to US$/Yen.

S    = Yen 115.00
K    = Yen 110.00
T    = 6 months (0.5 years)
$Rf_f$  = 3% pa (0.03) (the yen interest rate)
$Rf_{fd}$ = 6% pa (0.06) (the US$ interest rate)
$\sigma$    = 12.00% pa (0.12)

The calculations are as follows:

$$d1 = 0.743$$
$$d2 = 0.658$$

Therefore:

$$N(0.743) = 0.771$$
$$N(0.658) = 0.745$$
$$N(-0.743) = 0.229$$
$$N(-0.658) = 0.255$$

The value of the US$ call/ Yen put option is:

$$P_{ce} = Se_f^{-Rf \cdot T} \cdot N(d1) - Ke_d^{-Rf \cdot T} \cdot N(d2) = 115.e^{-0.03 \times 0.5} \times 0.771$$
$$- 110.e^{-0.06 \times 0.5} \times 0.745 = 7.92$$

The fair value of the call in Yen is 7.92.
   The value of the US$ put/Yen call option is:

$$P_{ce} = Ke_d^{-Rf \cdot T} \cdot N(-d2) - Se_f^{-Rf \cdot T} \cdot N(-d1) = 110 \cdot e^{-0.06 \times 0.5} \times 0.255$$
$$- 115.e^{-0.03 \times 0.5} \times 0.229 = 1.28$$

The fair value of the put in Yen is 1.28.

---

options because the high interest rate may influence the early exercise of the option.

In practice, the difference between the two models is more subtle and potentially more significant. The Garman-Kohlhagen approach assumes that the forward currency rate is fully arbitraged and trades at interest rate parity (that is, the forward rate reflects interest rate differentials between currencies). In practice, this condition may not be satisfied for long maturity currency forwards (in developed markets) and currency forwards generally (in emerging and regulated markets)[59]. Under these conditions, it is preferable to use the Black forward pricing model approach where the *actual market currency forward rate* (irrespective of whether it reflects interest rate differentials) is directly used as the underlying forward price. This has the additional merit of relating the option pricing directly to the hedging source (the currency forward itself).

# 16   Options on Equity/Equity Market Indexes

## 16.1   Approach

Options where the underlying asset is an individual equity stock or equity market index requires the model to be adjusted for a number of factors:
- Dividends paid on the underlying asset.
- Potential dilutionary impact of conversion.

## 16.2   Dividend Adjustment

In order to incorporate the potential impact of the income stream the two approaches described above are used:
- Where the dividend income is assumed to be continuous, by adjusting the asset by replacing S by the term $Se^{-Y \cdot T}$ where $Y = $ the continuously compounded expected dividend rate on the asset. **Exhibit 7.20** sets out a valuation model adapting the standard Black-Scholes model for an asset that pays continuous income.
- Where the dividend income is discrete and known, the spot price of the asset may be adjusted by discounting the known dividend to the commencement of the transaction, and subtracting the discounted income from the spot price to derive an ex-income asset price which is then used as S in the model. **Exhibit 7.28** sets out an example of this type of adjustment with regard to an equity option.

In practice, the ssecond approach is preferred. This reflects the ability to specifically incorporate dividend payment timing, dividend payment pattern (seasonal dividends) and changes in dividend rates over time.

---

[59] See discussion in Chapter 6.

---

**Exhibit 7.28   Valuation of Equity Option – Example**

**1.   Assumptions**
Assume the following call option on a stock:

Spot price of stock $\quad$ = S $\quad$ = \$5.00
Strike price of option = K $\quad$ = \$5.50
Time to expiry $\qquad$ = T $\quad$ = 6 months (0.5 years)
Risk free rate $\qquad$ = Rf = 6.00% pa (0.06)
Stock volatility $\qquad$ = $\sigma$ $\quad$ = 20.00% pa (0.20)

The last dividend paid on the stock was \$0.20 per share. Assume that the stock is expected to pay a dividend of \$0.20 per share just prior to option maturity.

**2.   Option Valuation**
In order to value the option, it is necessary to adjust the spot price of the asset for the expected dividend. The present value of this dividend discounted at the risk-free rate of return is:

$$\text{Present value of dividend} = \$0.20e^{-0.06 \times 164/365} = \$0.1947$$

Where the number of days to the dividend payment date is 164 days.
Therefore, the ex-dividend share price on \$4.8053 (calculated \$5.00 − \$0.1947).
Key details of the option are summarised below:

| Pricing Inputs | | |
|---|---|---|
| Underlying Asset Price (\$) | 4.8053 | |
| Strike Price (\$) | 5.50 | |
| Option Maturity (years) | 0.50 | |
| Volatility (% pa) | 26.00 | |
| Risk Free Rate (% pa) | 6.00 | |
| Call(0)/Put (1) | 0 | 1 |
| European (0)/American (1) Exercise | 0 | |
| Income on Asset (% pa) | 0.00 | |
| | **Call** | **Put** |
| Option Premium (\$) | 0.15 | 0.68 |

The Black-Scholes option-pricing model values the stock call option at \$0.15.

---

## 16.3   Dividend Estimation – Issues

The major issue with the income stream attaching to the asset is the uncertainty relating to future dividends in terms of:

- **Dividend amount** – the dividend payments that are the income stream on the asset are discretionary and are subject to change. This is in contrast to other assets (fixed income and currency) where the income stream is known. The problem of dividend amount estimation is not capable of being addressed as they are outside the control of the option buyer and seller. In practice, traders use historical dividends and analyst projections to generate *forward dividend estimates*.

- **Timing of dividend payments** – the dividend payments are discrete, lumpy and the timing is uncertain and determined by the company. The problem of dividend timing estimation is not capable of being addressed as they are outside the control of the option buyer and seller. In practice, past dividend payment patterns are used to generate future *expected* dividend timing.
- **Non-accrual of dividends** – unlike interest rates that accrue continuously to the holder of an investment, dividends are only payable to the holder of a stock over a specific period (the dividend record date and the day when the stock become ex-dividend or the holder's entitlement to the dividend ceases). This means that stock value generally decreases by the same amount when the stock becomes ex-dividend. The impact of this on equity option pricing is that the dividend timing is extremely critical to the income term incorporated into the option calculation. As the dividend does not accrue continuously, an error in dividend timing can have a significant impact upon the price of the option. This is corrected by identifying the relevant dividend payable over the time to expiry of the option and the specific timing of each cash flow.
- **Taxation treatment of dividend income** – the taxation of dividend streams is complex. Where the jurisdiction has an integrated corporate/investor tax framework, the dividend may be tax-free in the hands of the recipient at least where the company declaring the dividend has already paid tax on the underlying income. The tax position will also be a function of the status of the recipient – including distinctions between individual and corporate shareholders as well as domestic and foreign shareholders. This means that there are additional sources of risk – the tax position of the company, the tax regulations and the ability of the recipient to benefit from the tax credit.

The impact of uncertain dividends is evident in two specific areas:
- **Pricing of options** – the income term has a material impact on the spot forward price relationship. The impact on the pricing of the option is generated by the price of the forward. That has the impact of changing the relativity of the option strike and the implied forward asset price.
- **Early exercise of options** – the impact of dividends on the risk of early exercise is well understood. Unanticipated changes in dividends will also affect the risk of early exercise and hence the price of an American option.

**Exhibit 7.29** sets out an example of the impact of dividend rate uncertainty on the pricing of equity options. **Exhibit 7.30** sets out an example of the impact of dividends on early exercise of equity options. **Exhibit 7.31** sets out a case study involving UK equity warrant transactions highlighting the dividend tax risk in equity option pricing.

---

**Exhibit 7.29    Equity Option Pricing – Impact of Dividend Uncertainty**

**1.   Equity Forward Pricing**
Assume a stock is trading at on the following terms:

| | |
|---|---|
| Spot price | $20.00/share |
| Dividends (cents/share) | 30 |
| Dividend (yield) | 1.50% pa |
| Spot Date | 15 March 2001 |

The forward price of the share assuming continuously paid dividends and an interest rate of 6.00% pa is as follows:

| Time to maturity (years) | Dates | Forward Price ($) |
|---|---|---|
| 1 | 15 March 2002 | 20.90 |
| 2 | 15 March 2003 | 21.84 |
| 3 | 15 March 2004 | 22.83 |
| 4 | 15 March 2005 | 23.85 |
| 5 | 15 March 2006 | 24.93 |

Note that this assumes a flat term structure of rates and ignores the exact timing of the dividends.

Assume that the dividend payment dates are 31 May and 30 November each year and each dividend is 15 cents per share. By present valuing each dividend and adjusting the spot price of the asset, we can generate a series of new forward prices to reflect the exact timing of cash flows:

| Time to maturity (years) | Dates | Present Value of Dividends ($) | Adjusted Spot Price ($) | Forward Price ($) |
|---|---|---|---|---|
| 1 | 15 March 2002 | 0.29 | 19.71 | 20.89 |
| 2 | 15 March 2003 | 0.57 | 19.43 | 21.84 |
| 3 | 15 March 2004 | 0.83 | 19.07 | 22.84 |
| 4 | 15 March 2005 | 1.07 | 18.93 | 23.90 |
| 5 | 15 March 2006 | 1.30 | 18.70 | 25.03 |

The differences increase as maturity becomes longer. At 5 years, the difference is around 0.40%. Where the dividends are not paid evenly over the year and the full term structure of interest rates is incorporated, the differences may be more marked.

The analysis assumes that the dividends are *known as to amount and timing*. The impact of changes in dividends can be illustrated by varying the dividend yield. Assuming a spot price of $20.00 and interest rates of 6.00% pa (continuous dividends are used for convenience), the implied forward prices are as follows:

**Dividend Yields**

| Maturity (years) | 0.00% | 0.50% | 1.00% | 1.50% | 2.00% | 2.50% | 3.00% |
|---|---|---|---|---|---|---|---|
| 1 | $21.20 | $21.10 | $21.00 | $20.90 | $20.80 | $20.70 | $20.60 |
| 2 | $22.47 | $22.26 | $22.05 | $21.84 | $21.63 | $21.42 | $21.22 |
| 3 | $23.82 | $23.48 | $23.15 | $22.82 | $22.50 | $22.17 | $21.85 |
| 4 | $25.25 | $24.78 | $24.31 | $23.85 | $23.40 | $22.95 | $22.51 |
| 5 | $26.76 | $26.14 | $25.53 | $24.92 | $24.33 | $23.75 | $23.19 |

The impact in terms of forward price is significant, particularly at longer maturities.

## 2. Changes in the Taxation of Dividends

The tax impact on dividends can be best understood in terms of its impact on the *effective pre-tax dividend yield*. Traditional derivative pricing assumes no taxes, or in practice, more generally operates on a pre-tax basis. The problem is that in the case of derivatives this assumption is inherently flawed. Consequently, in pricing equity derivatives, the tax impact must be incorporated. In effect, using the above example, a dividend of $0.30/share, assuming it is fully tax free as a result of having a tax credit attached which is available to the institution, is equivalent to:

Dividend Amount/(1 − Tax Rate)

Assuming a tax rate of 35%:

$0.30/(1 − .35) = $0.46 or an implied dividend yield of 2.31%

The forward would typically be calculated using *the implied pre-tax dividend yield or rate*. The problem is if the tax credit is unavailable, for whatever reason (change in tax rules; change in tax status; change in company's tax paying status etc), then the impact is the same as the dividend yield falling in terms of the pricing of the forward. This can be illustrated by recalculating the implied forwards at different tax rates (assuming that the holder of the stock will get a tax credit equivalent to the assumed tax rate):

| Dividend Yield | | | | | | Tax Rate | 35.00% |
|---|---|---|---|---|---|---|---|
| **Unadjusted** | 0.00% | 0.50% | 1.00% | 1.50% | 2.00% | 2.50% | 3.00% |
| **Including Tax Effect** | 0.00% | 0.77% | 1.54% | 2.31% | 3.08% | 3.85% | 4.62% |
| **Maturity (years)** | | | | | | | |
| 1 | $21.20 | $21.05 | $20.89 | $20.74 | $20.58 | $20.43 | $20.28 |
| 2 | $22.47 | $22.15 | $21.82 | $21.50 | $21.19 | $20.87 | $20.56 |
| 3 | $23.82 | $23.31 | $22.80 | $22.30 | $21.81 | $21.32 | $20.84 |
| 4 | $25.25 | $24.52 | $23.82 | $23.12 | $22.44 | $21.78 | $21.13 |
| 5 | $26.76 | $25.81 | $24.88 | $23.98 | $23.10 | $22.25 | $21.42 |

| Dividend Yield | | | | | | Tax Rate | 20.00% |
|---|---|---|---|---|---|---|---|
| Unadjusted | 0.00% | 0.50% | 1.00% | 1.50% | 2.00% | 2.50% | 3.00% |
| Including Tax Effect | 0.00% | 0.63% | 1.25% | 1.88% | 2.50% | 3.13% | 3.75% |
| Maturity (years) | | | | | | | |
| 1 | $21.20 | $21.08 | $20.95 | $20.83 | $20.70 | $20.58 | $20.45 |
| 2 | $22.47 | $22.21 | $21.95 | $21.68 | $21.42 | $21.17 | $20.91 |
| 3 | $23.82 | $23.40 | $22.99 | $22.58 | $22.17 | $21.78 | $21.38 |
| 4 | $25.25 | $24.66 | $24.08 | $23.51 | $22.95 | $22.40 | $21.86 |
| 5 | $26.76 | $25.98 | $25.22 | $24.48 | $23.75 | $23.05 | $22.35 |

The zero tax case is the same as the forward calculated with no tax adjustment above.

As is evident, changes in both the dividend rate and the tax treatment have a major impact on the pricing of the forwards.

## 3. Option Pricing

The impact of uncertain dividends on option prices as noted above is evident through the altered forward price (irrespective of whether the change is created by changes in dividends paid or changes in the tax regime). The impact on options can be illustrated with an example. Assume the following parameters:

| | |
|---|---|
| Spot Price | $20.00 |
| Dividends | $0.30/share per annum or 1.50% pa |
| Strike Price | $20.00 |
| Volatility | 20.00% |
| Interest Rate | 6.00% pa |

The option premium for European and American exercise call and put options and the sensitivity to dividend rate changes are set out in the following Table:

### European Call Option Premium (Numbers in Brackets are for American Call Option Premium)

| Maturity (years) | 0.5 | 1 | 3 | 5 |
|---|---|---|---|---|
| Dividend Rate (0.50%) | 1.41 (1.41) | 2.13 (2.13) | 4.28 (4.28) | 5.93 (5.93) |
| Dividend Rate (1.50%) | 1.35 (1.35) | 2.01 (2.01) | 3.86 (3.86) | 5.18 (5.18) |
| Dividend Rate (2.50%) | 1.29 (1.29) | 1.89 (1.89) | 3.46 (3.46) | 4.50 (4.51) |

### European Put Option Premium (Numbers in Brackets are for American Put Option Premium)

| Maturity (years) | 0.5 | 1 | 3 | 5 |
|---|---|---|---|---|
| Dividend Rate (0.50%) | 0.86 (0.92) | 1.07 (1.13) | 1.28 (1.66) | 1.23 (1.87) |
| Dividend Rate (1.50%) | 0.90 (0.95) | 1.14 (1.24) | 1.44 (1.78) | 1.44 (2.02) |
| Dividend Rate (2.50%) | 0.94 (0.98) | 1.22 (1.30) | 1.61 (1.90) | 1.67 (2.19) |

**Exhibit 7.30    Early Exercise of Equity Options – Impact of Dividend Uncertainty**

In practice, the risk of early exercise is particularly evident in the following types of options:
- For in-the-money call options where the asset pays a high yield or income payment. This is because the benefit of receiving the high yield or the capture of the cash flow of the income payment on the asset may yield a superior return to the uncertain value of the asset and call at maturity. This is particularly relevant for an equity option with a large dividend payable prior to option expiry, where payment of the dividend would substantially reduce the value of the asset, reducing the value of the call option.
- In the case of put options, a deep in-the-money put can economically be exercised early, with the proceeds received invested at the risk free rate to yield a superior return to the uncertain intrinsic value of the put at maturity.

This pattern of early exercise is exacerbated by the risk of changes in dividend policy. For example, the payment of a large special dividend, as a mechanism for returning capital to shareholders, may have the impact of significantly increasing the risk of early exercise. The rise of early exercise manifests itself in both the value of the option and hedging risk.

Assume an option with the following parameters:

| | |
|---|---|
| Spot Price | $20.00 |
| Dividends | $0.25 due some 6 weeks after settlement date |
| Strike | $20.00 |
| Maturity | 6 months |
| Risk Free Rate | 6.00% pa |
| Volatility | 20.00% |

The value of a put option on this security would be priced as follows:

| | European | American |
|---|---|---|
| Option Premium | 0.93 | 1.01 |
| Delta | −0.42 | −0.47 |

Assume the company announces a special dividend of $1.00 payable in addition to the dividend some 6 weeks after the settlement date of the option. The shift in value of the put option is as follows:

| | European | American |
|---|---|---|
| Option Premium | 1.43 | 1.55 |
| Delta | −0.57 | −0.63 |

The loss to the trader holding a short position in the option results from the mark-to-market loss on the position, plus the need to now short an additional amount of the underlying (the rise in the delta). This re-hedging is now done at a lower market price, locking in higher hedging losses than would have been the case had the special dividend not been paid. This impact of changes in dividends is both significant in terms of it impact on pricing as well as its impact on early exercise.

| |
|---|
| **Exhibit 7.31    Equity Option Pricing – Impact of Dividend Tax Treatment**[60] |

## 1.  Background

In the 1990s, the tax treatment of dividends for foreign investors created opportunities for equity warrant (equity call option) transactions. The transactions involved exposure for the warrant sellers (primarily, investment banks with operations in London) to changes in the tax treatment of the dividend.

The major motivation for these warrant transactions was the following problems encountered by foreign investors with investments in UK shares:

*   **Dividend withholding taxes** – dividends paid to foreign investors were subject to withholding tax (at rates of typically 10–15% and in some instances higher). Theoretically, this withholding tax was recoverable against tax liabilities of the investor in its domestic jurisdiction. However, recovery was subject to time delays, complex foreign tax rules (that in some cases would result in loss of the withholding tax altogether) or the tax status of the investor (a non-tax paying investor would not be able to recover the withholding tax). This meant that foreign investors rarely received the full value of the dividend.
*   **Dividend tax treatment** – UK dividends were tax free in the hands of domestic investors where the dividend was paid from taxed income (referred to as the Advanced Corporation Tax system). This was designed to avoid double taxation of corporate income. This tax credit was only available to *UK taxpayers*. This meant that foreign investors receiving this credit did not benefit from the tax exemption.

The transactions described below were designed to assist foreign investors to overcome these problems of UK share ownership.

## 2.  Equity Warrant Transaction

The basic transaction structure[61] is based around the foreign investor re-structuring its exposure to the UK stocks that it wishes to hold as follows:

*   The foreign investor sells it direct shareholding.
*   The foreign investor buys an equity warrant giving it the right to purchase the UK stock. The call option is structured to be deep-in-the-money. This is designed to give the investor an exposure to the stock equivalent to ownership of the stock itself.
*   The equity warrant is written by a *UK resident* investment bank. The bank hedges its position in the warrant by purchasing the underlying stocks and trading these in the market.

The effect of this transaction is as follows:

*   The foreign shareholder no longer receives dividends from the UK shares. The only earning is from the warrant exercise itself (effectively the appreciation of the stock above its strike price). This income will usually be in the form of a cash settlement (this should not attract withholding tax or the dividend tax credit problems identified).

---

[60] For a discussion of the particular transactions, see "Is This Marriage a Mistake?" (31 January 1998) The Economist 90; "Blind Faith" (31 January 1998) The Economist 90; "What Really Happened at UBS?" (October 1998) Derivatives Strategy 18–32.

[61] Please note that a variety of similar transactions (such as equity swaps and stock lending transactions) were also used to achieve similar objectives.

- The bank hedging the warrants with the position in the UK stocks receives the dividends. However, as it is *UK resident*, it is not subject to withholding tax and gets the full benefit of the tax free status of the dividend.

The structure of the transaction is set out below.

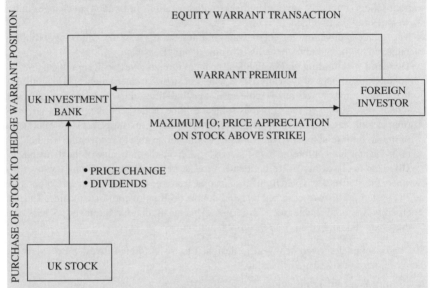

EQUITY WARRANT TRANSACTION

### 3. Valuation of Equity Warrants – Initial

The key to the transaction economic lies in the valuation of the warrants. In this Section, the initial valuation of the warrants is outlined.

In valuing the warrants, the following hypothetical warrants are valued[62]:

Spot price of stock   = S   = $100.00
Strike price of option = K   = $25.00
Time to expiry   = T   = 5 years
Risk free rate   = Rf = 8.00% pa (0.08)
Stock volatility   = $\sigma$   = 20.00% pa (0.20)
Dividend rate   = y   = 3.50% pa (0.035) equivalent to 3.44% pa continuously compounded

The structure of the warrant with its low strike price is designed to replicate ownership of the underlying stock. The long time to expiry of the warrant is designed to allow to replicate long term share ownership.

---

[62] Please note that the pricing is based on purely hypothetical options using assumed parameters to illustrate the issues.

The key issue in valuation is the dividend yield to be used. The UK tax credit system dictates that the UK bank will receive the dividend free of tax (where the company itself has paid tax on the underlying income). This means that the dividend yield used as a model input should be equal to the *equivalent pre-tax dividend yield*; that is, the dividend yield should be grossed up to a pre-tax number equal to dividend yield /(1 − tax rate). This is required to ensure that both the risk free rate and the dividend yield are on comparable terms (pre-tax).

Given that the UK bank is assisting the foreign investor to improve its after tax investment return, there would usually be a sharing of the benefits of the transaction. This would be built into the transaction by adjusting the extent of the tax benefit transferred to the foreign investor. This is typical of tax arbitrage transactions of this type.

Assume in this case, the applicable UK tax rate is 35%. This would equate to a grossed up dividend yield of 5.29% pa (calculated as 3.44%/(1 − .35)). Assume that the gross up tax rate applied is 30% rather than the real tax rate of 35% (equivalent to a grossed up pre tax dividend rate of 4.91% (calculated as 3.44%/(1 − .30)). The difference represents the profit to the investment of structuring and facilitating the transaction.

The valuation of the option is summarised below:

| Pricing Inputs | |
| --- | --- |
| Underlying Asset Price ($) | 100.00 |
| Strike Price ($) | 25.00 |
| Option Maturity (years) | 5.0 |
| Volatility (% pa) | 20.00 |
| Risk Free Rate (% pa) | 8.00 |
| Call (0)/Put (1) | 0 |
| European (0)/American (1) Exercise | 0 |
| Income on Asset (% pa) | 4.91 |
| | **Call** |
| Option Premium ($) | 61.45 |

The foreign investor pays $61.45 to purchase the warrant. The warrant price is significantly lower than the actual current stock price. The difference reflects the transfer of 5 years of dividends from the foreign investor to the UK owner of the shares. In present value terms, the dividends are approximately $13.97 per share (excluding the benefit of the tax credits) and around $19.96 (including the tax benefit, assuming a 30% tax gross up rate). This, together with the discounted strike price, equates to the difference between the current stock price and the price of the warrant.

The important point to note is that the seller of the warrant (the UK investment bank) is giving the foreign shareholder the benefit of the cash dividends received from the shares *and the tax credits* (up to the gross up rate) *over the full life of warrant*. This is built into the warrant price.

In the books of the UK bank, the position would be revalued using the full tax gross up rate (35%) and pre-tax equivalent dividend yield of 5.29%. This would equate to a value of the warrant of $59.99. The difference of $1.46 would be treated as the mark-to-market value of the position (effectively the profit on the transaction).

### 4. Valuation of Equity Warrant – After Tax Change

In mid 1997, the UK tax authorities announced (unexpectedly) a change in taxation regime for dividends[63]. Under the new regime, financial institutions would not receive the benefit of the tax credit on dividends. The changed tax treatment means that the dividend receipts are now taxed in the hands of the UK bank. This is applicable to all future dividends received. This means that the dividend rate required to be used in the model to revalue the warrant is 3.44% pa (this is now the *pre-tax dividend amount*).

The value of the option is now given as:

| Pricing Inputs | |
|---|---|
| Underlying Asset Price ($) | 100.00 |
| Strike Price ($) | 25.00 |
| Option Maturity (years) | 5.0 |
| Volatility (% pa) | 20.00 |
| Risk Free Rate (% pa) | 8.00 |
| Call (0)/Put (1) | 0 |
| European (0)/American (1) Exercise | 0 |
| Income on Asset (% pa) | 3.44 |
| | **Call** |
| Option Premium ($) | 67.44 |

The immediate result is a mark-to-market loss for the investment bank. This loss is equal to $5.99 (relative to the premium received of $61.45) and $7.45 (relative to the previous valuation of $59.99). In each case, the loss is significant (9.75% of the initial warrant premium received).

The result of this tax change was to create large losses in the portfolios of UK banks that had structured these particular types of transactions.

An important aspect of dividend tax risk is that it is generally not a risk that can be hedged. Traders are generally unable to immunise themselves effectively from this risk, particularly in long dated equity derivative transactions.

---

The significant sensitivity to dividend rate changes is evident. In considering the impact of dividend uncertainty (amount, timing and tax treatment), it is important to note that the construction of the position may affect the overall exposure. For example, where the derivative is hedged with an offsetting position in the under-lying stock(s), then the effect of the change of dividends may be hedged at least partially by the value shift in the spot price. However, there may well be a mis-match. The critical thing about the dividend risk is that it is generally not a risk that can be hedged. Traders are generally not able to immunise themselves effectively

---

[63]  See Dunbar, Nicholas "Ex-Dividend" (August 1997) Futures & Options World 19.

from the risk, in particular in long dated equity derivative transactions. The risk poses problems for pricing, valuation and risk management.

## 16.4  Adjusting Equity Values for Corporate Actions/Transactions

### 16.4.1  Overview

A second consideration in relation to equity options is the potential dilutionary impact of conversion. Companies have the capacity to undertake a wide variety of transactions that can have an impact on the equity securities issued by the entity. These transactions, that are all within the power of the corporation to implement, have the capacity to alter its share price, often very significantly, without having a corresponding impact on the *economic value of the shareholders' investment*.

However, in changing the share price of the company, these transactions can in turn affect the value of derivative instruments traded on the underlying securities. The effects on derivative pricing can be, *in relative terms*, more significant than for the underlying equity securities themselves because of the inherent leverage of derivative instruments. This requires the values of the equity derivative to be adjusted to incorporate the expected impact of the company's action. In this Section, the calculation of the impact of these changes on the pricing and valuation of equity derivatives is examined, and appropriate methods of adjusting the valuation process are considered.

This exists as a problem in the case of equity options or warrants issued by the company, the equity securities of which underlie the options. It is not a problem in exchange-traded or over-the-counter options *on existing equity securities*. This is because it is only in the first case that the exercise of the option results in the issue of *additional equity*. As the standard option pricing model assumes that the exercise of the option does not impact the value of the underlying asset, it is necessary to adjust the model.

The underlying logic of valuation adjustment is that the counterparty to the derivative transaction, such as a forward or option, receives at maturity or upon exercise the pre-agreed value of equity securities, *irrespective of the actions taken by the company*. In most derivative transactions, the value of the contract incorporates adjustments for the expected dividend payments. The additional adjustment is designed to specifically adjust for the impact of other corporate actions, predicated on the counterparty to the derivative transaction receiving value equivalent to the number of underlying equity securities that the counterparty would have been entitled to at the commencement of the transaction and prior to the actions of the issuer.

The types of corporate transactions that have the potential to affect the company's share prices include:

- **New issues of equity securities** – that is, the company may issue new equity securities or instruments convertible or exchangeable into equity securities to raise capital. These may be issued through public issues, private placements or through rights/entitlement issues.
- **Stock splits** – that is, where the equity securities on issue are replaced with a larger number of equity securities with lower value.
- **Stock dividends** – that is, the payment of a dividend in the form of equity securities rather than in cash.

## 16.4.2   Equity Issues

The issue of new equity securities, or instruments convertible into equity securities, has the effect of altering the price of the underlying shares. This is irrespective of whether the new equity securities are issued by way of public issue or private placement. Where the equity securities are issued by way of a rights or entitlement issue, there are additional complexities and considerations that are discussed separately below.

The issue of new equity securities will affect the value of the underlying *existing* equity securities as follows[64]:

- The number of shares will increase (by the issued shares or shares into which the issued instrument can be exchanged).
- The value of the company is increased by the consideration (for example, cash) received as a result of the issue.

The adjustment of the underlying shares can be undertaken as follows:

$$S_{post} = [(N \times S_{pre}) + (N_i \times S_{issue})]/[N + N_i]$$

Where

$S_{post}$ = Share price post the issue
$S_{pre}$ = Share price pre issue
$S_{issue}$ = Consideration received per share under the new issue
$N$ = Number of shares outstanding prior to the new issue
$N_i$ = Number of shares issued in the new issue

---

[64] See Damodaran, Aswanth (1995) Damodaran on Valuation: John Wiley, New York at 336–339.

**Exhibit 7.32** sets out an example of the calculation adjusting for the impact of a new equity issue. Where options are traded on the underlying equity securities, the spot price of the shares should be adjusted to reflect the impact of the new issue.

| Exhibit 7.32 Calculation of Impact on Share Price of New Issue | |
|---|---|
| Number of Shares on Issue | 102,000,000 |
| New Shares Issued | 20,000,000 |
| Share Price Before Issue ($) | 5.45 |
| Share Price of Issue ($) | 5.00 |
| Market Capitalisation (Prior to Issue) ($) | 555,900,000 |
| Capital Raised ($) | 100,000,000 |
| Expected Share Price Post Issue ($) | 5.38 |

## 16.4.3 Rights Issues

A rights or entitlements issue is an offer of shares to the *existing shareholders* in proportion to their existing shareholding. **Exhibit 7.33** sets out the key terms associated with rights issues.

The rights issue structure raises two separate issues:
- The value of the rights themselves.

| Exhibit 7.33 Rights/Entitlement Issues – Key Terms | |
|---|---|
| **Term** | **Concept** |
| Rights Issue | Entitlement to purchase shares pro rata to existing shares as of Books Closing Date on issue terms. |
| Issue Terms | The ratio of new shares to be issued as a proportion to existing shares. |
| Renounceable Issue | Shareholders are entitled to sell the rights if they do not want to take them up. |
| Application Price/ Rights Price | The price at which shares are to be issued under the rights issue. |
| Books Closing Date | Final date for determination of shareholders on the share register entitled to participate in the rights issue. |
| Cum Rights Price | The share price incorporating the entitlement to subscribe under the terms of the rights offering. |
| Ex Rights Date | The date on which the rights are separated from the existing shares allowing the rights trading to commence. |

| Ex Rights Price | The share price after the ex rights date. |
|---|---|
| Applications Closing Date | The date as of which the eligible shareholders must pay the Application Price where the shareholder is accepting the rights. Rights trading ceases as of the Application Closing Date. |
| Renunciation Closing Date | A date after Application Closing Date as of which the purchasers of the Rights have to pay the Application Price, if accepting. |

- The impact of the rights issues on holders of derivative securities such as options over the underlying equity securities.

The rights themselves are technically call options, conveying the right to the holder to purchase the underlying shares at a fixed price (the Application Price) within the given time period for the exercise of the right (the Application Closing Date). This option can be priced using conventional approaches to option pricing. In essence, the valuation of the right is based on the derivation of the underlying option price in terms of calculating the intrinsic value and time value of the option. The latter is generally ignored, reflecting the relatively short time to expiry. Rights issues may contain a "bonus element" where the rights issue is structured so that the shareholders have the opportunity to take up shares at a price set well below the prevailing market price of the issue.

The derivation of the intrinsic value can be calculated based on the concept of wealth indifference. This assumes that the investor will seek to maintain the original value of its investment *pre* and *post* rights issue. For example, assume the cum rights share price of a company is trading at $2.10. The rights are on a one-for-one basis with the shares to be issued for $1.50. This means that the investor can obtain 2 shares in the company for an outlay of $3.60 (the cum rights price plus the price payable for the share entitlement). This implies an ex rights share price of $1.80/share (the outlay divided by the number of shares). The right to purchase the shares is therefore $0.30 (the difference between the cum rights price and the ex rights price), reflecting the fact that shareholders would be disadvantaged economically by the same amount unless they took up their entitlement to the rights issue. However, by selling the rights for this sum, the investor maintains an indifference to the potential dilution.

**Exhibit 7.34** sets out more formally the derivation of the value of the rights. **Exhibit 7.35** sets out an example of the calculation of the value of rights issues.

---

**Exhibit 7.34    Calculation of Value of a Right**[65]

Assume the following terminology:

$R$    = the value of one right
$S_{ex}$ = the ex rights share price
$S_{cum}$ = the cum rights share price
$S_r$   = the application price to subscribe to shares under the rights offering
$N$    = the ratio of existing shares to new shares

The value of a right is:

$$R = S_{ex} - S_r$$

Where

$$S_{ex} = [N \cdot S_{cum} + S_r]/[N + 1]$$

By a process of combining the two above equations, the value of a right can be re-stated as follows:

$$R = N[S_{cum} - S_{ex}]$$

The dilution factor (D) of a rights issue is measured as:

$$D = S_{ex}/S_{cum}$$

---

The level of dilution is dependent on the issue price and the terms of the issue:

- The closer the ex rights share price is to the cum rights share price, the lower the dilution level.
- The lower the ratio of existing shares to new shares, the higher the dilution level.

In terms of derivatives on the underlying equity, the rights issue may have significant impact on the value of a forward or an option. The change in the underlying share price as a result of the rights issue may significantly affect the value of the derivative contract. A fair value adjustment to the price of the option is usually based on the counterparty to the derivative transaction receiving value equivalent

---

[65] See Peter Sullivan "Rights Issues: Issues in Getting Them Right" (December 1985) The Chartered Accountant in Australia 46–47.

**Exhibit 7.35    Calculation of Value of a Right – Examples**

**Example 1**

**Pre Issue Position**

| | |
|---|---|
| Shareholding | 100 |
| Share Price (Cum Rights) | $5.50 |
| Total Value | $550.00 |

**Terms of Rights Issue**

| | |
|---|---|
| Proportion (1: ?) | 5 |
| Number of New Shares | 20.00 |
| Share Price Under Rights Issue | $4.00 |
| Amount Raised | $80.00 |

**Case 1 – Exercise Rights**

| | |
|---|---|
| Total Number of Shares (Post Issue) | 120 |
| Share Price (Ex Rights) | $5.25 |
| Total Value (Post Issue) | $630.00 |

**Case 2 – Sell Rights**

| | |
|---|---|
| Share Price (Ex Rights) | $5.25 |
| Total Number of Shares | 100 |
| Total Value (Post Issue) | $525.00 |
| Sale of Rights | $25.00 |
| Total Value (Post Issue) | $550.00 |

| | |
|---|---|
| Rights Price (Per Right) | $1.25 |

**Example 2**

**Pre Issue Position**

| | |
|---|---|
| Shareholding | 100 |
| Share Price (Cum Rights) | $5.50 |
| Total Value | $550.00 |

**Terms of Rights Issue**

| | |
|---|---|
| Proportion (1: ?) | 6.5 |
| Number of New Shares | 15.38 |
| Share Price Under Rights Issue | $5.20 |
| Amount Raised | $80.00 |

**Case 1 – Exercise Rights**

| | |
|---|---|
| Total Number of Shares (Post Issue) | 115.38462 |
| Share Price (Ex Rights) | $5.46 |
| Total Value (Post Issue) | $630.00 |

| Case 2 – Sell Rights | |
|---|---|
| Share Price (Ex Rights) | $5.46 |
| Total Number of Shares | 100 |
| Total Value (Post Issue) | $546.00 |
| Sale of Rights | $4.00 |
| Total Value (Post Issue) | $550.00 |

| | |
|---|---|
| Rights Price (Per Right) | $0.26 |

to the number of underlying equity securities that the counterparty would have been entitled to at the commencement of the transaction, and prior to the actions of the issuer. In practical terms, this requires the execution of a number of potential strategies to maintain the investor's shareholding in the company. **Exhibit 7.36** sets out a worked example of both strategies. **Exhibit 7.37** sets out the formal formula for deriving the required adjustment to the option terms to maintain the economic position of the option holder.

---

**Exhibit 7.36    Adjusting an Equity Option for a Rights Issue**

Assume the shares of Company A are trading at $5.00. An investor owns a European call option covering 1,000 shares with a strike price of $5.25 with a remaining time to expiry of 6 months. The Company announces a 1:4 rights issue where it plans to issue 1 share for every 4 shares outstanding. The shares to be issued are priced at $4.00.

The cum rights price for the shares immediately prior to going ex-right is $4.80. This means that the investor can obtain 5 shares in the company for an outlay of $23.20 (the cum rights price for 4 shares plus the price payable for the share entitlement). This implies an ex rights share price of $4.64 per share (the outlay divided by the number of shares). The right to purchase the shares is therefore A$0.16 (the difference between the cum rights price and the ex rights price), reflecting the fact that shareholders would be disadvantaged economically by the same amount unless they took up their entitlement to the rights issue. However, by selling the rights for this sum, the investor maintains an indifference to the potential dilution.

The holder of the equity option has an entitlement to the net gains (losses) it would have accrued on a shareholding of 1,000 shares underlying this option. The adjustment required to preserve the value of the option can be determined in either of two ways:

1. **Alternative 1** – The investor can sell the rights on 1,000 shares. This would generate $160. This cash could be used to buy approximately 34 additional shares ($160/$4.64 (the ex rights price)). This would mean that the investor had a holding totalling 1,034 shares.

2. **Alternative 2** – The investor could sell 173 shares at the cum rights price ($4.80). This would generate cash of $829. The 827 shares continuing to be held by the investor would allow exercise of rights to purchase 207 shares (827/4). This would require an outlay of $829 that is equal to and could be financed by the previously identified sale of 173 shares. The final shareholding position of the investor would equal 1,034 shares in the company.

The adjustment for the option would be made based on the fact that the investor should be entitled to 1,034 shares, where previously the option entitled the investor to 1,000 shares. In effect, the strike price of the option is reduced to $5.08 (calculated as the total strike outlay ($5.25 × 1,000 = $5,250)/number of shares (1,034)).

---

**Exhibit 7.37    Formula for Adjusting an Equity Option for a Rights Issue**

**1.  Alternative 1**
The new number of shares covered by the option is given by[66]:

$$O = N_{pre}[(S_{cum} \times (N_r + N_e))/((N_e \times S_{cum}) + (N_r \times S_r))]$$

Where

$O$     = the new number of shares underlying the option
$N_{pre}$ = the number of existing shares pre the rights issue
$S_{cum}$ = the cum rights price immediately prior to going ex rights
$S_r$    = the application price to subscribe to shares under the rights offering
$N_r$    = the ratio of new shares issued for $N_e$ existing shares

This approach has the following features:
• The valuation of the rights is not required.
• The adjustment is capable of determination during the cum rights period.

**2.  Alternative 2**
The new number of shares covered by the option is given by:

$$O = N_{pre} \times [1 + R/S_{ex}]$$

Where

$O$     = the new number of shares underlying the option
$N_{pre}$ = the number of existing shares pre the rights issue
$R$     = the price of the rights per share
$S_{ex}$ = the price of the ex rights price

---

[66]  See Raoul Davie "Equity Moves" (October 1997) Asia Risk 38–39.

This approach has the following features:
* The rights need to be valued and the adjustment is based on the *market value* of the rights as established in trading.
* The two approaches will be equal only where the rights trade at their theoretical value.

### 16.4.4  Stock Splits/Stock Dividends

The company may choose to adjust the capitalisation of the entity by increasing the number of shares through a stock split whereby the existing number of shares is increased by a nominated ratio. The principal objective here is to lower the *nominal* value of the shares, as the existing market capitalisation is now represented by a larger number of outstanding and issued shares.

The company may also pay stock dividends to its shareholders where a declared dividend is met by an issue of shares in the company. The stock dividend may be used to conserve cash, and is economically equivalent to a cash dividend payment that is undertaken simultaneously with an equity issue to raise the amount of the dividend.

The adjustment of the underlying shares can be undertaken as follows:

$$S_{post} = [(N \times S_{pre})/[N_i]$$

Where

$S_{post}$ = Share price post the issue
$S_{pre}$ = Share price pre issue
$N$    = Number of shares outstanding prior to the new issue
$N_i$   = Number of shares outstanding after the split or stock dividend equivalent to N plus the new shares created.

Where options are traded on the underlying equity securities, the spot price of the shares should be adjusted to reflect the impact of the stock split of stock dividend.

## 17  Options on Commodities

Options on commodities create issues in pricing primarily through difficulties in the estimation of the convenience yield/asset payout rate. This reflects the substantial

difficulties in the estimation of this parameter. In practice, options on commodities may be priced in one of the following ways:
- Options on physical commodities using the continuous income version of the Black-Scholes model (see **Exhibit 7.20**) with the asset convenience yield being used as the income term Y.
- Options on forward commodities using the Black model for options on forward contracts (see **Exhibit 7.24**).

The latter approach has the advantage of already impounding the convenience yield or asset payout rate in the forward commodity price used in the model.

A number of commodity option pricing approaches incorporating the behaviour of commodity prices have emerged. These models incorporate features such the mean reverting nature of commodity prices, the volatility of convenience yields, and the discontinuous nature of commodity price movements[67].

# 18 Summary

Option contracts, because of their asymmetric payoff profiles, present a particular challenge in pricing. However, using the standard assumption of risk neutral valuation, it is possible to estimate the fair value of the option contract by determining the expected value of a portfolio consisting of the underlying asset and cash which is adjusted dynamically through time to replicate the payoff of the option. The basic model thus derived can then be adjusted in a number of ways to estimate the fair value of different types of options, as well as options on different asset classes.

---

[67] See Cortazar, G. and Schwartz, E. "The Valuation of Commodity Contingent Claims" (Summer 1994) Journal of Derivatives 27–29; Beaglehole, David and Chebanier, Alain "A Two Factor Mean Reverting Model" (July 2002) Risk 65–69.

# Appendix A
# Cumulative Normal Distribution Function[68]

Tables for the cumulative normal distribution function (N) are attached.
Alternatively, a polynomial approximation can be used:

Where $x \geq 0$

$$N(x) = 1 - N'(x)(a_1 k^1 + a_2 k^2 + a_3 k^3)$$

Where $x < 0$

$$N(-x) = 1 - N(x)$$

Where

$$k = 1/(1 + \alpha x)$$

$$\alpha = 0.33267$$

$$a_1 = 0.4361836$$

$$a_2 = -0.1201676$$

$$a_3 = 0.9372980$$

and

$$N'(x) = (1/\sqrt{2\Pi}) \cdot e^{-x2/2}$$

This provides values for $N(x)$ that are usually accurate to about four decimal places and are always accurate to within 0.0002.

---

[68]  See Abramowitz, M. and Stegun, I. (1972) Handbook of Mathematical Functions – Ninth Edition; Dover Publications, New York.

## Table for N(x)

This table shows values of N(x) for $x \geq 0$. When $x < 0$, the relationship $N(-x) = 1 - N(x)$ can be used. For example,

$$N(-0.12) = 1 - 0.5478 = 0.4522.$$

The table should be used with interpolation. For example:

$$N(0.7691) = N(0.76) + 0.91[N(0.77) - N(0.76)] = 0.7764 + 0.91 \times 0.0030 = 0.7791$$

$$N(0.6278) = N(0.62) + 0.78[N(0.63) - N(0.62)] = 0.7324 + 0.78 \times 0.0033 = 0.7350$$

| x | .00 | .01 | .02 | .03 | .04 | .05 | .06 | .07 | .08 | .09 |
|---|---|---|---|---|---|---|---|---|---|---|
| 0.0 | 0.5000 | 0.5040 | 0.5080 | 0.5120 | 0.5160 | 0.5199 | 0.5239 | 0.5279 | 0.5319 | 0.5359 |
| 0.1 | 0.5398 | 0.5438 | 0.5478 | 0.5517 | 0.5557 | 0.5596 | 0.5636 | 0.5675 | 0.5714 | 0.5753 |
| 0.2 | 0.5793 | 0.5832 | 0.5871 | 0.5910 | 0.5948 | 0.5987 | 0.6026 | 0.6064 | 0.6103 | 0.6141 |
| 0.3 | 0.6179 | 0.6217 | 0.6255 | 0.6293 | 0.6331 | 0.6368 | 0.6406 | 0.6443 | 0.6480 | 0.6517 |
| 0.4 | 0.6554 | 0.6591 | 0.6628 | 0.6664 | 0.6700 | 0.6736 | 0.6772 | 0.6808 | 0.6844 | 0.6879 |
| 0.5 | 0.6915 | 0.6950 | 0.6985 | 0.7019 | 0.7054 | 0.7088 | 0.7123 | 0.7157 | 0.7190 | 0.7224 |
| 0.6 | 0.7257 | 0.7291 | 0.7324 | 0.7357 | 0.7389 | 0.7422 | 0.7454 | 0.7486 | 0.7517 | 0.7549 |
| 0.7 | 0.7580 | 0.7611 | 0.7642 | 0.7673 | 0.7704 | 0.7734 | 0.7764 | 0.7794 | 0.7823 | 0.7852 |
| 0.8 | 0.7881 | 0.7910 | 0.7939 | 0.7967 | 0.7995 | 0.8023 | 0.8051 | 0.8078 | 0.8106 | 0.8133 |
| 0.9 | 0.8159 | 0.8186 | 0.8212 | 0.8238 | 0.8264 | 0.8289 | 0.8315 | 0.8340 | 0.8365 | 0.8389 |
| 1.0 | 0.8413 | 0.8438 | 0.8461 | 0.8485 | 0.8508 | 0.8531 | 0.8554 | 0.8577 | 0.8599 | 0.8621 |
| 1.1 | 0.8643 | 0.8665 | 0.8686 | 0.8708 | 0.8729 | 0.8749 | 0.8770 | 0.8790 | 0.8810 | 0.8830 |
| 1.2 | 0.8849 | 0.8869 | 0.8888 | 0.8907 | 0.8925 | 0.8944 | 0.8962 | 0.8980 | 0.8997 | 0.9015 |
| 1.3 | 0.9032 | 0.9049 | 0.9066 | 0.9082 | 0.9099 | 0.9115 | 0.9131 | 0.9147 | 0.9162 | 0.9177 |
| 1.4 | 0.9192 | 0.9207 | 0.9222 | 0.9236 | 0.9251 | 0.9265 | 0.9279 | 0.9292 | 0.9306 | 0.9319 |
| 1.5 | 0.9332 | 0.9345 | 0.9357 | 0.9370 | 0.9382 | 0.9394 | 0.9406 | 0.9418 | 0.9429 | 0.9441 |

| x | .00 | .01 | .02 | .03 | .04 | .05 | .06 | .07 | .08 | .09 |
|---|---|---|---|---|---|---|---|---|---|---|
| 1.6 | 0.9452 | 0.9463 | 0.9474 | 0.9484 | 0.9495 | 0.9505 | 0.9515 | 0.9525 | 0.9535 | 0.9545 |
| 1.7 | 0.9554 | 0.9564 | 0.9573 | 0.9582 | 0.9591 | 0.9599 | 0.9608 | 0.9616 | 0.9625 | 0.9633 |
| 1.8 | 0.9641 | 0.9649 | 0.9656 | 0.9664 | 0.9671 | 0.9678 | 0.9686 | 0.9693 | 0.9699 | 0.9706 |
| 1.9 | 0.9713 | 0.9719 | 0.9726 | 0.9732 | 0.9738 | 0.9744 | 0.9750 | 0.9756 | 0.9761 | 0.9767 |
| 2.0 | 0.9772 | 0.9778 | 0.9783 | 0.9788 | 0.9793 | 0.9798 | 0.9803 | 0.9808 | 0.9812 | 0.9817 |
| 2.1 | 0.9821 | 0.9826 | 0.9830 | 0.9834 | 0.9838 | 0.9842 | 0.9846 | 0.9850 | 0.9854 | 0.9857 |
| 2.2 | 0.9861 | 0.9864 | 0.9868 | 0.9871 | 0.9875 | 0.9878 | 0.9881 | 0.9884 | 0.9887 | 0.9890 |
| 2.3 | 0.9893 | 0.9896 | 0.9898 | 0.9901 | 0.9904 | 0.9906 | 0.9909 | 0.9911 | 0.9913 | 0.9916 |
| 2.4 | 0.9918 | 0.9920 | 0.9922 | 0.9925 | 0.9927 | 0.9929 | 0.9931 | 0.9932 | 0.9934 | 0.9936 |
| 2.5 | 0.9938 | 0.9940 | 0.9941 | 0.9943 | 0.9945 | 0.9946 | 0.9948 | 0.9949 | 0.9951 | 0.9952 |
| 2.6 | 0.9953 | 0.9955 | 0.9956 | 0.9957 | 0.9959 | 0.9960 | 0.9961 | 0.9962 | 0.9963 | 0.9964 |
| 2.7 | 0.9965 | 0.9966 | 0.9967 | 0.9968 | 0.9969 | 0.9970 | 0.9971 | 0.9972 | 0.9973 | 0.9974 |
| 2.8 | 0.9974 | 0.9975 | 0.9976 | 0.9977 | 0.9977 | 0.9978 | 0.9979 | 0.9979 | 0.9980 | 0.9981 |
| 2.9 | 0.9981 | 0.9982 | 0.9982 | 0.9983 | 0.9984 | 0.9984 | 0.9985 | 0.9985 | 0.9986 | 0.9986 |
| 3.0 | 0.9986 | 0.9987 | 0.9987 | 0.9988 | 0.9988 | 0.9989 | 0.9989 | 0.9989 | 0.9990 | 0.9990 |
| 3.1 | 0.9990 | 0.9991 | 0.9991 | 0.9991 | 0.9992 | 0.9992 | 0.9992 | 0.9992 | 0.9993 | 0.9993 |
| 3.2 | 0.9993 | 0.9993 | 0.9994 | 0.9994 | 0.9994 | 0.9994 | 0.9994 | 0.9995 | 0.9995 | 0.9995 |
| 3.3 | 0.9995 | 0.9995 | 0.9995 | 0.9996 | 0.9996 | 0.9996 | 0.9996 | 0.9996 | 0.9996 | 0.9997 |
| 3.4 | 0.9997 | 0.9997 | 0.9997 | 0.9997 | 0.9997 | 0.9997 | 0.9997 | 0.9997 | 0.9997 | 0.9998 |
| 3.5 | 0.9998 | 0.9998 | 0.9998 | 0.9998 | 0.9998 | 0.9998 | 0.9998 | 0.9998 | 0.9998 | 0.9998 |
| 3.6 | 0.9998 | 0.9998 | 0.9999 | 0.9999 | 0.9999 | 0.9999 | 0.9999 | 0.9999 | 0.9999 | 0.9999 |
| 3.7 | 0.9999 | 0.9999 | 0.9999 | 0.9999 | 0.9999 | 0.9999 | 0.9999 | 0.9999 | 0.9999 | 0.9999 |
| 3.8 | 0.9999 | 0.9999 | 0.9999 | 0.9999 | 0.9999 | 0.9999 | 0.9999 | 0.9999 | 0.9999 | 0.9999 |
| 3.9 | 1.0000 | 1.0000 | 1.0000 | 1.0000 | 1.0000 | 1.0000 | 1.0000 | 1.0000 | 1.0000 | 1.0000 |
| 4.0 | 1.0000 | 1.0000 | 1.0000 | 1.0000 | 1.0000 | 1.0000 | 1.0000 | 1.0000 | 1.0000 | 1.0000 |

# 8

# Interest Rate Options Pricing[1]

## 1 Overview

The Black-Scholes-Merton ("BSM") framework for option pricing is capable of adaptation to most asset classes (foreign exchange, equity and commodities). However, the application of this option pricing approach to interest rates/debt instruments presents special challenges. In this Chapter, a number of approaches to pricing of interest rate options are examined.

The structure of this Chapter is as follows:

- The distinctive features of options on interest rates/debt instruments are considered.
- Alternative approaches to pricing interest rate options are examined.
- Standard BSM models adapted to interest rates are outlined.
- Term structure models of interest rates are considered.
- The applicability of different models to pricing interest rate options is examined.

## 2 Debt Options – Distinctive Features

The basic mathematical option pricing models such as BSM were originally developed in the context of equity options. The basic model requires significant amendments where it is used to value options on other instruments such as futures contracts, currencies and debt instruments[2].

---

[1] There is a significant body of literature on interest rate option pricing. Useful reference works include: see Hull, John (2000) Option Futures and Other Derivatives – Fourth Edition; Prentice-Hall Inc., Upper Saddle River, NJ at Chapters 20, 21 and 22; Rebanato, Riccardo (1998) Interest Rate Option Models – Second Edition; John Wiley, New York; Wilmott, Paul (1998) Derivatives: The Theory and Practice of Financial Engineering; John Wiley & Sons, Chichester, at Chapters 31–40.

[2] In this context there is no distinction drawn between the actual Black-Scholes model itself and discrete time implementation of the approach such as the binomial type of models.

The pricing of options on interest rates and debt instruments are complex[3]. Several distinctive features of debt instruments must be incorporated into the pricing of debt options. Key features that require incorporation in the pricing mechanism include:

- The underlying security, in the case of debt instruments, usually involves payouts in the form of interest during the life of the option.
- The rate of interest cannot be assumed to be constant. Interest rate changes drive price changes in the underlying asset. Most interest rate security values do not depend on a single random variable but on a number of random interest rates (depending on the remaining time to maturity of the underlying security that may be variable).
- Debt instruments typically have a defined maturity. The limited and declining life represents special problems in option pricing. This is in contrast to other assets such as equities, currencies and commodities that do not have fixed lives (they are perpetual in nature).
- Volatility of the underlying debt instrument cannot be assumed to be constant.

Of the four features, all but the first feature creates considerable complexity in the pricing of options on debt instruments. These features of interest rate options are examined in detail in the following Sections.

The impact of intermediate cash flows on the underlying debt instrument will depend on whether the underlying asset for the debt option is a cash market debt security or a futures contract on the relevant instrument. Where the option is on a futures contract on the relevant debt instrument, the underlying debt instrument is typically a hypothetical security with known characteristics. There are no coupon interest payments over the life of the option.

Where the option is on a physical security, there may be coupon payments over the life of the option. The assumption made by models such as Black-Scholes is that there are no intermediate cash payouts. This can be relaxed using a modification of the formula that allows for payments that are proportional to the price of the underlying security (effectively a continuously compounded rate of return on the asset)[4].

The normal type of adjustment utilised may not be appropriate in the case of debt options. Where the option is on an underlying security that bears a coupon, the accrued interest is continuously added to the full price of the bond, representing

---

[3] The term options on interest rates and options on debt instruments are used interchangeably throughout the Chapter.

[4] See Merton, Robert C. "Theory of Rational Option Pricing" (Spring 1973) Bell Journal of Economics and Management Science 4 141–183. See also Chapter 7.

a continuous payout to the holder of the debt security. As the coupons are fixed in dollar amount not proportional to the price of the underlying debt security, the type of modification proposed would be inappropriate. An alternative approach to adjustment would be to deduct the present value of coupons on the underlying bond over the life of the option from the capital value of the security. The underlying asset price is then set at the *ex-coupon price of the bond* with the asset assumed to pay *no* income. The second approach is preferred in practice.

## 3   Interest Rate Options – Pricing Approaches

### 3.1   Interest Rate/Debt Options – Types

The problems created by the distinctive features of options on debt instruments are analysed in the context of fixed deliverable versus variable deliverable options.

In practice, options on debt instruments take one of two forms[5]:

- **Fixed deliverable option** – where the underlying debt instrument is a debt security *with specified maturity characteristics*. For example, a six month call option on a 90 day Eurodollar futures contract is a fixed deliverable option. The maturity of the underlying debt instrument is always a fixed 90 days commencing from the expiry date of the option.
- **Variable deliverable option** – where the underlying debt instrument is a *specified existing debt issue* with time dependent maturity characteristics. For example, a three year call option, say, on the 5.50% 15 August 2012 US Treasury bond is a variable deliverable option. This option requires delivery of that specific security or the option payoff is a function of the price of this specific security. The maturity of the underlying security obviously varies depending on the date of exercise of the option. For example, at expiry of the option, the remaining maturity of the underlying security will have reduced by 3 years.

Variable deliverable options create complex pricing issues. This reflects the fact that actual physical debt securities are affected by the passage of time. This is unlike other cash market assets that have infinite lives or futures contracts that are

---

[5]   It is important to distinguish between two classes of options on debt instruments: options on the cash market debt instrument (that is, the actual physical debt security) and futures on the relevant debt instrument. In practice, both types of options coexist and are available. This is despite the fact that in any market, a cash market, a futures market and one options market (either on the cash market instrument or the futures contract) would usually be sufficient to fulfil all risk transfer possibilities. The option on the cash market and the option on the futures market will generally serve similar functions.

not based on a particular wasting debt security (futures contracts have particular characteristics that are specified and constant). This has several implications:

- The underlying debt instrument itself has a shorter tenor or period to maturity as the option itself approaches expiration.
- At maturity, the value of the interest rate security converges to a known constant value (par or face value) and the volatility of the security approaches zero.

The distinctive features of debt options derive from the two characteristics of options on physical debt securities.

The basic option pricing model assumes that only one interest rate (the risk-free rate) is relevant. However, at any given point in time, a variety of interest rates for different maturities are observable. Each of these interest rates and consequently the shape of the yield curve as a whole is subject to change over time.

A major difficulty in relation to the pricing of debt options relates to the fact that the price of the underlying asset (the debt security) itself is a function of interest rates. It is also unlikely, depending on the type of option, that it is a function of the risk-free interest rate used to present value the exercise price of the option. An additional complication arises from the fact that where the option is a variable deliverable option, the exact interest rate required to value the underlying debt instrument itself is subject to change with the passage of time. The difficulties mean that the value of options on debt instruments or interest rates do not depend on a single random interest rate variable, but may depend on a *number* of different random interest rates.

The effect of changes in interest rates and the time to expiration are particularly complex. For options on assets, such as shares, as the risk-free rate increases, the value of the call option increases as the present value of the exercise price, in the event of exercise, declines. In effect, if the call option and the security itself are regarded as different ways for an investor to capture any gain on the security price, as rates rise the increased cost of carry on the underlying security will make the call more attractive, leading to an increase in its value.

However, in the case of debt options, it is unreasonable to assume (as is usually done in the case of equity options) that the price of the underlying debt security is independent of the level of interest rates. Significant movements in the price of the asset will occur as a result of changes in interest rates and in general, any cost of carry consideration would be minor relative to the change in the value of the underlying security. For example, it would be reasonable to assume that rate increases will usually have a negative impact on the price of call options on debt instruments, as a rise in interest rates will most likely cause a fall in the price of the underlying instrument or futures contract.

**Exhibit 8.1   Volatility Evolution – Bonds Versus Stock/Other Financial Assets**

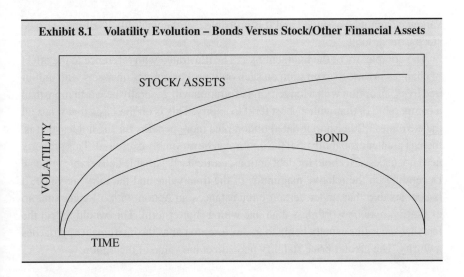

The assumption of constant variance or volatility of the price underlying debt instrument is also flawed[6]. This results from two factors:

- Volatility of debt securities (in the case of a variable delivery option) is likely to tend to zero. This reflects the fact that at maturity the value of a debt instrument itself must converge to a known value (the par value of the security). An additional factor in this regard is that the price volatility of a security is itself a complicated function of the actual volatility of interest rates of varying maturity and the time to maturity the security itself. **Exhibit 8.1** sets out the pattern of evolution of volatility for a debt instrument and other financial assets (with no fixed maturity).

- The stochastic process followed by interest rates appears to have a mean reversion quality – that is, there is an inbuilt drift that pulls them back to some long run average level.

Consequently, the volatility of debt instruments will generally be a function of the assumed stochastic process of interest rate movements, assumptions about the shape/future movement of interest rates across the whole yield curve, and the remaining life of the security at a given point in time. This dictates that constant

---

[6]  This derives in part from the assumption of a process for the underlying asset (interest rates/bond prices) that is modelled as a geometric Brownian motion process where the total standard deviation is related to $\sqrt{}$ time. This implies that the underlying interest rate or prices can take very large values. This is unlikely to hold true in the case of interest rates.

variance cannot be assumed and it is probable that the volatility itself may also be stochastic variable.

The complexity of the interactions can be illustrated with reference to the effect of changes in time to expiration on such options. For options on assets with unlimited lives, an option with a longer time expiration will generally be worth more than a comparable option with a short term to expiry. This is on the basis that it has all the attributes of the shorter dated option plus more benefits for the holder; that is, there is greater probability that the option can be profitably exercised. This property need not necessarily hold for debt options, particularly variable deliverable options. Depending on the relative magnitude of the time value and the intrinsic value, it is conceivable that under certain circumstances an option with a longer time to expiration may be worth less than one with a shorter term. This would reflect the fact that securities usually begin to trade closer to par as the instrument approaches maturity. The greater price stability may affect the value of the option.

## 3.2   Pricing Debt and Interest Rate Options – Approaches

In practice, the pricing of debt and interest rate options falls into two categories:

- **Options on instruments where the underlying asset is a standardised debt instrument** (with a fixed maturity, for example, options on futures and forwards on standard debt instruments) – the options can be valued with Black-Scholes type models, in particular, the Black option pricing model[7]. This is because some of the problems identified can be minimised although not eliminated[8].
- **Options on instruments where the underlying asset is non-standard** (with variable maturity, for example, options on physical bonds) – these are more problematic and usually entail the use of term structure or yield curve models.

# 4   Pricing Interest Rate Options Using Black's Model[9]

## 4.1   Black's Model

Where the underlying asset has a fixed maturity, BSM model approaches may be applied. This allows the valuation to be done using Black's option on a forward

---

[7]   See Black, Fischer, "The Pricing of Commodity Contracts" (1976) (March) 3 Journal of Financial Economics 167–179. See also Chapter 7.

[8]   Please note options on standardised debt instruments can also be priced using term structure models.

[9]   See Hull, John (2000) Option Futures and Other Derivatives – Fourth Edition; Prentice-Hall Inc., Upper Saddle River, NJ at Chapter 20.

pricing model. This type of approach is commonly used with pricing futures on debt instruments, short dated options on bonds, caps, floors and options on swaps/swaptions[10]. In the case of swaptions, Bermudan style swaptions pose problems of pricing similar to those affecting options on physical debt instruments. This is because the swap may be exercised on a number of dates but the final maturity of the underlying swap is fixed at the time of entry. This causes the actual maturity of the underlying swap to alter with time in a manner analogous to that for an option on a physical bond. These structures must be priced using interest rate term structure models.

In this Section, the use of the Black model to value bond options and caps/floors is considered.

Using this approach to valuation allows the use of an adapted version of Black. The basic adaptation required includes:

*   Income on the asset is incorporated by the option being treated as on the *forward price* of the underlying bond or forward interest rate.
*   The use of this model requires the volatility used to be the volatility of the *forward price* of the underlying bond or forward interest rates.

**Exhibit 8.2** sets out Black's model for a premium paid European option on a futures contract[11].

---

**Exhibit 8.2    Black Option Pricing Model for Forward Contracts**

For a call option:

$$P_{ce} = e^{-Rf.T}[F.N(d1) - K.N(d2)]$$

Where

$$d1 = [\ln(F/K) + (\sigma^2/2)T]/\sigma\sqrt{T}$$
$$d2 = [\ln(F/K) - (\sigma^2/2)T]/\sigma\sqrt{T} = d1 - \sigma\sqrt{T}$$

For a put option:

$$P_{pe} = e^{-Rf.T}[K.N(-d2) - SN(-d1)]$$

---

[10]   The use of the Black model to value options on swaps is considered in Das, Satyajit (2004) Structured Products Volume 1; John Wiley & Sons (Asia), Singapore at Chapter 15.

[11]   See Black, Fischer "The Pricing of Commodity Contracts" (March 1976) 3 Journal of Financial Economics 167–179. See also Chapter 7.

Where

F  = forward or future prices of the underlying asset.
K  = strike price
T  = time to maturity
Rf = risk free interest rate
σ  = volatility of returns from asset
$P_{ce}$ = price of European call
$P_{pe}$ = price of European put

## 4.2   Pricing Bond Options

In certain circumstances, the Black model approach is used to price options on physical bonds. This is predicated on ignoring some of the distinctive characteristics of options on physical debt instruments or seeking to adjust the basic framework.

The original model for pricing debt options within a Black-Scholes framework is based on continuous time bond price dynamics[12]. The model examined the problem of pricing an option on equities where the interest rate is stochastic rather than deterministic as in the standard BSM framework. The model does not explicitly indicate how specific properties of bonds (fixed maturity and known maturity value) are guaranteed. Subsequent models seek to overcome these deficiencies by seeking to model the bond price dynamics in a more complex way[13].

In practice, this approach to pricing is applied only where the term of the option is short relative to the term of the underlying bond into which the option is capable of exercise. This reflects the fact that the problems (the change in volatility and the need for a complete term structure of rates) are less important. **Exhibit 8.3** sets out an example of using the Black Model to price a short dated option on a bond.

[12] See Merton, Robert C. "Theory of Rational Option Pricing" (Spring 1973) Bell Journal of Economics and Management Science 4 141–183.
[13] For example, see Ball, Clifford A. and Torous, Walter N. "Bond Price Dynamics and Options" (December 1983) Journal of Financial and Quantitative Analysis 18 517–531; Brennan, M.J. and Schwartz, E.S. "An Equilibrium Model of Bond Pricing and a Test of Market Efficiency" (September 1982) Journal of Financial and Quantitative Analysis vol 17 no 3 301–29; Schaefer, S.M. and Schwartz, E.S. "Time Dependent Variance and the Pricing of Options" (December 1987) Journal of Finance 42 1113–28. For example, the Schaefer-Schwartz model utilises a process where the bond price volatility is related to a bond's duration as the basic model for the bond price dynamics.

---

**Exhibit 8.3    Pricing Bond Options – Option on Forward Price Model**

Assume the following bond:

Face value;    $100
Maturity:      15 November 2012
Coupon:        6.00% pa payable semi annually (each 15 May and 15 November)

The bond is trading currently (settlement date of 27 August 2002) as follows:

| | |
|---|---|
| Yield (% pa) | 6.36 |
| Price | $97.304 |
| Accrued Interest | $1.696 |
| Total Price | $99.000 |

Assume a European call and put option this bond with the following terms:

| | |
|---|---|
| Trade Date | 27 August 2002 |
| Expiry Date | 27 February 2003 |
| Time to expiry (days) | 184 |
| Strike Price | $99.000 |
| Yield (% pa) | 6.14 |

The information must now be re-arranged to allow the option price to be derived. The following should be noted:

- The assumed volatility is 8.00% pa (in price terms)[14]. This is the volatility of the forward bond price.
- The 6 month interest rate (risk free) is 6.00% pa (continuously compounded). The yield curve is also assumed to be flat to the option expiry date.
- The bond forward price must be determined. The bond pays a semi-annual coupon of $3.00 on 15 November 2002 (80 days from trade date) prior to the option expiry. The present value of the coupon is:

$$\$3.00 \times e^{-.06 \times (80/365)} = \$2.96.$$

This implies a forward bond price of:

$$(99.00 - 2.96) \times e^{0.06 \times (184/365)} = \$98.99.$$

- The precise terms of the bond option must be carefully defined. Please note that the strike price in this case is the "clean" bond price. The strike price for the purpose of valuing the option must be adjusted to include the accrued interest at the expiry date[15]. This produces a value for the strike price of $99 + $1.724 (accrued interest as at 27 February 2003) = $100.724.

---

[14] For a discussion of price versus yield volatility of bonds and methodologies for converting one to the other, see Chapter 9.

[15] If the strike price is the dirty price, then this would be the strike price directly.

The inputs into the model are as follows:

F = $98.99
K = $100.724
T = 0.50 years
Rf = 0.06 (6.00% pa)
$\sigma$ = 0.08 (8.00% pa)

The option premium for a call option derived using the Black model (see **Exhibit 8.2**) is $1.46 (1.47% of the forward bond price). The option premium for a put option derived using the Black model is $3.14 (3.17% of the forward bond price).

If the option were American, then a binomial model would be used to derive the option value.

## 4.3   Pricing Interest Rate Caps and Floors

### 4.3.1   Approach

Pricing caps, floors and collars using the Black model for options on forward/futures rates entails the following steps:

*   The cap, floor or collar agreement is analytically separated into a series of option contracts. An interest rate cap may be split up into a series of put option contracts on the prices of short term debt securities pricing off the relevant interest rate index (call options on the forward interest rate). An interest rate floor may be split up into a series of call option contracts on the prices of short term debt securities pricing off the relevant interest rate index (put options on the forward interest rate).
*   Each separate option is then valued using the identified model. In determining the price of each option, it is important to note that the input for the current spot price of the index is not the physical market price at the time the agreement is entered, but the then current futures or forward price on the relevant index. The volatility required is the volatility of the forward interest rates.
*   The option premium for each contract is calculated and then summed to give the actual price for the overall contract.

**Exhibit 8.4** sets out an example of using this approach to price a single period cap and floor using both the yield and price method. **Exhibit 8.5** sets out an example of pricing a multi-period cap and floor transaction.

---

**Exhibit 8.4   Pricing Single Period Cap/Floor Transactions – Option on Forward Rate Model**

**1.   Yield Approach**

Assume the dealer is required to calculate the premium for a $1 million 15% pa cap on 3 month LIBOR for one period of 3 months commencing in 3 months' time (3 × 6 months). Assume the forward rate for 3 month LIBOR in 3 months' time is 15.016% pa and the 3 month risk free rate is 15.00% pa. The assumed yield volatility is 17% pa. This information can be reformulated for input into the model as follows:

F  = 0.15016
K  = 0.1500
T  = 0.25
Rf = 0.15
$\sigma$  = 0.17

The price of the cap (call option on yield) can be calculated as follows:

d1 = 0.055
d2 = −0.030

Therefore:

N(0.055) = 0.5219
N(−0.03) = 0.4880

The price of the call is calculated as follows:

$$P_{ce} = e^{-0.15 \times .25}[0.15016 \times 0.5219 - .15 \times 0.4880] = 0.004978$$

The premium is stated in yield as the asset and strike price were specified in yield terms. It is necessary to restate the option premium as follows:

$$P_{ce} = [t.FV/(1 + F.t)] \times P_{ce}$$

where

t    = the interest rate period (.25 years)
FV = face value of the option (1,000,000)

Therefore, the value of the cap is as follows:

$P_{ce} = [.25 \times 1,000,000/(1 + .15016 \times .25)] \times .004978 = \$1,200$ or 0.12% of face value.

The price of the equivalent floor (put on interest rates) is as follows:

N(−0.055) = 0.4781
N(−0.03) = 0.5120

$$P_{pe} = 240{,}954.57 \times e^{-0.15 \times 0.25}[0.15 \times 0.5120 - 0.15016 \times 0.4781]$$
$$= \$1{,}162 \text{ or } 0.116\% \text{ of face value.}$$

## 2. Price Approach

Assume the dealer is required to calculate the premium for an 8% pa cap on 3 month LIBOR for one period of 3 months in one year's time (12 × 15 months). Assume the forward rate for 3 month LIBOR in one year is 7% pa. Assume the risk free rate for 1 year is 6.50% pa and the price volatility is 0.344% pa. This information can be reformulated for input into the model as follows:

F  = \$982,801 (\$1,000,000 face value 3 month security discounted at 7.00% pa)
K  = \$980,392 (\$1,000,000 face value 3 month security discounted at 8.00% pa)[16]
T  = 1.0
Rf = 0.065
$\sigma$  = 0.00344

The price of the cap is calculated as follows:

d1 = 0.715
d2 = 0.712

Therefore:

N(0.715) = 0.7627
N(0.712) = 0.7616
N(−0.715) = 0.2373
N(−0.712) = 0.2384

Therefore, the cap premium (put option on price) is:

$$P_{pe} = e^{-0.065 \times 1}[980{,}392(0.2384) - 982{,}801(0.2373)]$$
$$= \$475 \text{ or } 0.0475\% \text{ of face value.}$$

---

[16]  This assumes that the underlying trades as discount instruments. Where the market trades as par (i.e. principal plus the agreed interest), then the strike price is set at the face value of the transaction (in this example, \$1,000,000) and the forward price is calculated by taking the principal and the interest at the strike rate and discounting it back at the forward rate (in this example, \$1,020,000 (the principal plus accrued interest at 8.00% pa for 3 months – the exact number of days and day count convention would normally be used) discounted back for 3 months at 7.00% pa).

**Exhibit 8.5    Pricing Multi Period Cap/Floor Transactions – Option on Forward
Rate Model**

Assume a 3 year cap on the following terms:

| | |
|---|---|
| Face Value | $1,000,000 |
| Term | 3 years |
| Strike Rate – Cap | 6.00% pa |
| Strike Rate – Floor | 4.00% pa |
| Interest Rate | 3 month US$ LIBOR |

The contract is broken down into a series of *cap-lets* or *floor-lets* to facilitate pricing. The
3 year cap or floor would be broken down into 11 cap or floor lets. This corresponds to the
12 quarterly periods of the 3 year contract on 3 month rates minus the first period. The first
period is ignored, as the spot 3 month LIBOR is already known and there is no time to expiry
for the option[17].

The first step in pricing is to derive the forward rates from the yield curve. The complete
yield curve at the time of entry into the transaction is set out below (in both numerical and
graphical form):

| Maturity (years) | Swap Rates (% pa) | 3 Month Forward LIBOR Rates (% pa)[18] |
|---|---|---|
| 0.25 | 3.25 | 4.25 |
| 0.50 | 3.75 | 4.14 |
| 0.75 | 3.88 | 4.40 |
| 1.00 | 4.01 | 4.93 |
| 1.25 | 4.20 | 5.31 |
| 1.51 | 4.38 | 5.69 |
| 1.76 | 4.57 | 6.08 |
| 2.00 | 4.75 | 5.54 |
| 2.25 | 4.84 | 5.71 |
| 2.51 | 4.93 | 5.90 |
| 2.76 | 5.01 | 6.08 |
| 3.00 | 5.10 | 5.34 |
| 3.25 | 5.12 | 5.38 |
| 3.51 | 5.14 | 5.42 |
| 3.76 | 5.16 | 5.46 |
| 4.00 | 5.17 | 5.49 |
| 4.25 | 5.19 | 5.53 |
| 4.51 | 5.21 | 5.57 |

---

[17]  Please note that for forward starting cap and floor transactions the first period is also an
     option and must accordingly be priced.
[18]  3 month forward LIBOR rate out of the maturity date.

| Maturity (years) | Swap Rates (% pa) | 3 Month Forward LIBOR Rates (% pa) |
|---|---|---|
| 4.76 | 5.23 | 5.61 |
| 5.01 | 5.25 | 6.19 |
| 5.26 | 5.30 | 6.28 |
| 5.51 | 5.34 | 6.38 |
| 5.76 | 5.39 | 6.49 |
| 6.01 | 5.43 | 6.55 |
| 6.26 | 5.48 | 6.64 |
| 6.51 | 5.52 | 6.75 |
| 6.76 | 5.57 | 6.85 |
| 7.01 | 5.61 | 6.43 |
| 7.26 | 5.64 | 6.48 |
| 7.51 | 5.67 | 6.55 |
| 7.76 | 5.69 | 6.62 |
| 8.01 | 5.72 | 6.65 |
| 8.26 | 5.75 | 6.71 |
| 8.51 | 5.78 | 6.78 |
| 8.76 | 5.81 | 6.84 |
| 9.01 | 5.84 | 6.88 |
| 9.26 | 5.86 | 6.94 |
| 9.51 | 5.89 | 7.01 |
| 9.76 | 5.92 | 7.09 |
| 10.01 | 5.95 | 6.26 |

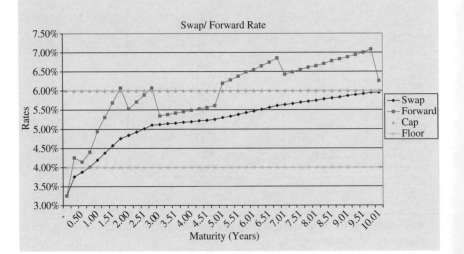

The information must then be re-arranged for use within the Black forward option pricing model to price each individual cap and floor-let. In this example, the volatility assumed is 20.00% pa (for all cap and floor-lets – see discussion in next Section). The individual cap and floor-let prices are summarised below:

| Maturity (years)[19] | Forward Rate (% pa) | Volatility (% pa) | Risk Free Rate (%pa)[20] | Cap Premium (% pa) | Floor Premium (% pa) |
|---|---|---|---|---|---|
| 0.25 | 4.25 | 20.00 | 3.25 | 0.00 | 0.01 |
| 0.50 | 4.14 | 20.00 | 3.75 | 0.00 | 0.03 |
| 0.75 | 4.40 | 20.00 | 3.88 | 0.00 | 0.02 |
| 1.00 | 4.93 | 20.00 | 4.01 | 0.03 | 0.01 |
| 1.25 | 5.31 | 20.00 | 4.20 | 0.08 | 0.01 |
| 1.51 | 5.69 | 20.00 | 4.38 | 0.14 | 0.01 |
| 1.76 | 6.08 | 20.00 | 4.57 | 0.22 | 0.00 |
| 2.00 | 5.54 | 20.00 | 4.75 | 0.16 | 0.01 |
| 2.25 | 5.71 | 20.00 | 4.84 | 0.21 | 0.01 |
| 2.51 | 5.90 | 20.00 | 4.93 | 0.26 | 0.01 |
| 2.76 | 6.08 | 20.00 | 5.01 | 0.30 | 0.01 |

The cap and floor contract value is given by the sum of the individual cap or floor-lets.

The first period of the cap or floor must also be considered. It is necessary to determine whether the cap strike is below (floor strike above) the current 3 month LIBOR rate. If this is the case, then the intrinsic value of payout/settlement amount must be calculated.

In this case, the cap strike (6.00% pa) is above the current 3 month LIBOR rate (3.25% pa). However, the floor strike (4.00% pa) is above the current 3 month LIBOR rate. This is equivalent to around 0.19% pa. This amount must be added to the value of the floor calculated as the sum of the floor-lets.

The final price of the 3 year cap and the floor is as follows:

Cap:    1.42% ($14,200 per $1,000,000 face value)
Floor:  0.32% ($3,200 per $1,000,000 face value)

These amounts would be paid by the purchaser of the cap or floor to the seller.

The price of a collar is a combination of the value of the cap and floor as follows:

Collar (bought cap/sold floor):          1.10% pa
Reverse Collar (sold cap/bought floor):  −1.10% pa (buyer receives this amount).

---

[19] Note that the expiry date of the individual cap or floor-lets is the start of the relevant interest rate period when the comparison between the market rate and the cap and floor rates is undertaken.

[20] Assumed to be the swap rate for the relevant maturity.

## 4.3.2   Caps/Floors – Volatility Inputs

The relevant volatility to be used in pricing interest rate caps/floors is the volatility of *forward interest rates*. There are two possible approaches to the volatility input utilised in cap/floor pricing models:
- A different volatility is used for each individual cap or floor-let (often referred to as spot volatility).
- A single volatility is used for all individual cap-lets or floor-lets (often referred to as flat volatility) [21].

In practice, it is desirable to utilise spot volatility structures[22]. This reflects the fact that the term structure of volatility is rarely flat, and individual cap and floor-lets may be deep in or out-of-the-money and affected by the shape of the volatility smile or skew[23]. **Exhibit 8.6** depicts a typical volatility curve for cap/floors that sets out the *humped* shape often exhibited.

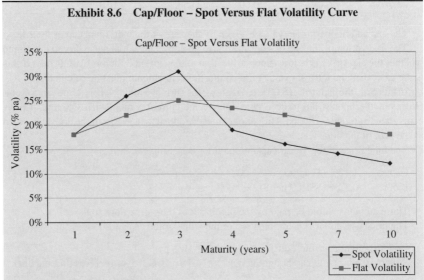

**Exhibit 8.6    Cap/Floor – Spot Versus Flat Volatility Curve**

Note: Maturity refers to final maturity in the case of flat volatility and maturity of the individual cap/floor-let in the case of spot volatility.

---

[21]   Flat volatility may be thought of as the cumulative average of the spot volatility.
[22]   Cap/floor volatility quotations in the market are typically flat volatility.
[23]   See discussion of behaviour of volatility in Chapter 9.

# 5  Interest Rate Term Structure Models[24]

## 5.1  Overview

The major identified problems with pricing options on interest rates or debt instruments are most evident in pricing options on physical debt instruments, particularly medium to long-term bonds. There are some problems in the pricing approaches in relation to short dated bond options, interest rate caps/floors and swaptions. This includes the assumption of a constant discount rate and constant volatility (which implies very large or small interest rates). In addition, there is an inherent problem of consistency of valuation approaches where some interest rate/debt instruments are priced using one approach, while other instruments are priced using a fundamentally different approach.

The problems have led to the development of interest rate term structure models to price options on interest rates/debt instruments. While strictly only necessary to price options on physical debt instruments (variable deliverable structures), in practice, these models are used increasingly to price *all* interest rate options within a consistent framework.

A variety of interest rate term structure models and approaches have emerged. An overview of some of the pricing approaches is summarised below[25].

## 5.2  Concept

Interest rate term structure models are based on modelling interest rate term structure movements. The pricing approaches seek to overcome clear deficiencies in the simple Black model where there is no model of the term structure of interest rates

---

[24]  The description of interest rate term structure models draws on Rowlands, Tim "Interest Rate Option Pricing Models" in Das, Satyajit (Editor) (1997) Risk Management & Financial Derivatives: A Guide to the Mathematics; LBC Information Services, Sydney; McGraw-Hill, Chicago; MacMillan Publishing, England at Chapter 6.

[25]  A detailed treatment of the pricing approaches requires an understanding of mathematical techniques that are beyond the scope of this book. For readers interested in examining the details of the various approaches, see Hull, John (2000) Option Futures and Other Derivatives – Fourth Edition; Prentice-Hall Inc., Upper Saddle River, NJ at Chapters 21 and 22; Rebanato, Riccardo (1998) Interest Rate Option Models – Second Edition; John Wiley, New York; Wilmott, Peter (1998) Derivatives: The Theory and Practice of Financial Engineering; John Wiley & Sons, Chichester, at Chapters 33, 34, 37, 38, 39 and 40. For an overview of this area, see Rowlands, Tim "Interest Rate Option Pricing Models" in Das, Satyajit (Editor) (1997) Risk Management & Financial Derivatives: A Guide to the Mathematics; LBC Information Services, Sydney; McGraw-Hill, Chicago; MacMillan Publishing, England at Chapter 6.

or the change in volatility with a reduction in the maturity of the underlying bond in the option pricing model. A further rationale of the models is to allow *all derivatives* on debt instruments to be priced within a consistent uniform framework[26].

The models themselves entail three distinct components:

- **Choice of yield curve process** – the models require the specification of a dynamic process to generate the term structure of interest rates and the instantaneous volatility to allow the derivation of the option price.
- **Model calibration** – the model inputs must generally be calibrated to actual market interest rates, prices and volatility.
- **Numerical implementation** – most of these models do not yield closed form solutions for the option value. Accordingly, numerical procedures must be employed to solve for the price of the option.

The main difficulty with the approaches is the requirement to estimate certain model inputs from the market. The estimation of the parameters required to solve these pricing formulae is difficult. This problem is complicated by the fact that option prices appear to be sensitive to changes in these parameters.

## 5.3 Types of Models

### 5.3.1 Overview

There are a number of distinctive types of interest rate term structure models. The major differences are driven by the following features:

- Equilibrium versus arbitrage free models.
- Single factor versus multi-factor models.

The classification is not mutually exclusive.
In practice, the trend is to arbitrage free multi factor models.

### 5.3.2 Equilibrium Versus Arbitrage Free Models

Equilibrium models assume certain economic variables and model the process for the short term risk free rate. The model uses the process specified to generate the relevant interest rates and create a complete term structure of interest rates and volatility over time, enabling the value of the option to be derived.

---

[26] For a review of the different models see Chance, Don M. "Research Trends in Derivatives and Risk Management Since Black-Scholes" (May 1999) Journal of Portfolio Management 35–46; Smith Jr., Clifford W. "Option Pricing: A Review" (1976) Journal of Financial Economics vol 3 15–24; Smithson, Charles "Wonderful Life" (October 1991)

Equilibrium models are useful for understanding potential relationships. However, equilibrium models suffer from a significant disadvantage. The model does not automatically fit the current term structure. This is because the initial term structure is a model *output* rather than input. This results in unsatisfactory pricing results as the projected yield curve may diverge significantly from the actual current yield curve[27].

The concept underlying arbitrage free models is that the initial current term structure is assumed and specified. The model defines how term structure evolves. This avoids the problem of equilibrium models.

Arbitrage free models typically require the selection of an interest rate process. The approach then models the evolution of interest rates over time. The evolution over time must satisfy a specified no arbitrage condition. This condition is that there should be no self financing strategy that generates a risk free gain (analogous to the risk neutral valuation methodology that underlies option valuation generally). The probability description of interest rates is usually specified to conform to the arbitrage free condition (no internal arbitrage) and also the current term structure of rates (no external arbitrage). The major advantage of arbitrage free models is that the model fits the initial yield curve. It also allows freedom to choose volatility in any way desired.

The arbitrage free models can be separated into two separate types of models – not preference free and preference free[28]. This derives from the fact that the

---

Risk 37–44; Smithson, Charles "Extended Family (1)" (October 1995) Risk 19–21; Smithson, Charles "Extended Family (2)" (November 1995) Risk 52–53; Smithson, Charles "Extended Family" (December 1997) Risk 158–163; Whaley, Robert "Building on Black-Scholes" (December 1997) Risk 149–156; Smithson, Charles "Extended Family" (September 1998) Risk Black Scholes Merton Supplement 14–18.

[27] Examples of equilibrium models include Cox, J.C., Ingersoll, J.E. and Ross, S.A. "A Theory of the Term Structure of Interest Rates" (1985) Econometrica 53 385–407; Longstaff, F.A. and Schwartz, E.S. "Interest Rate Volatility and the Term Structure of Factor General Equilibrium Model" (1992) Journal of Finance XLVII 1259–1282; Longstaff, F.A. and Schwartz, E.S. "A Two Factor Interest Rate Model and Contingent Securities Valuation" (1992) Journal of Fixed Income 16–23.

[28] Examples of arbitrage free but not preference free models include Brennan, M.J. and Schwartz, E.S. "An Equilibrium Model of Bond Pricing and a Test of Market Efficiency" (1982) Journal of Financial and Quantitative Analysis 17 301–329; Rendleman, R. and Bartter, B. "The Pricing of Options on Debt Securities" (1980) Journal of Financial and Quantitative Analysis 15 11–24; Vasicek, O.A. "An Equilibrium Characterisation of the Term Structure" (1977) Journal of Financial Economics 5 177–188. Examples of arbitrage free and preference free models include: Black, Fisher, Derman, E., and Toy, W., "A One Factor Model of Interest Rates and Its Application to Treasury Bond Options"

construction of an arbitrage free model using an interest rate process will require an estimate to be made of the market price of risk. This derives from the fact that the term structure derived from the model will be unlikely to fit the observed term structure. The market observed short rate is also not likely to fit the "risk free" rate (at least, in the same sense of the return on the replicating portfolio as used in BSM models) because in arbitrage free models it is a return on a money market account. In order to fit the observed rate, a premium over the "risk free" rate must be calculated (that is, the market price of risk). This must be estimated as it is not directly observable. The preference free models do not require a market price of risk to be estimated. The preference free arbitrage models take the current term structure of interest rates and interest rate volatility and fit the model to these market parameters. Preference free models specifically fit the observed term structure in a manner that is arbitrage free using numerical techniques[29].

### 5.3.3  Single Versus Multi Factor Models

The distinction between single and multi factor models derives from the number of factors used to derive the yield curve.

Single factor models use one factor (typically, the short term interest rate) to derive the complete yield curve. Multi factor models use additional factors together with the short term rate to generate the yield curve. This may include a number of random variables to generate the yield curve.

---

(1990) 46 (No 1) Financial Analysts Journal 33–39; Black, Fischer and Karasinski, Piotr "Bond and Option Pricing When Short Rates are Lognormal" (July-August 1991) Financial Analysts Journal 47 52–59; Brace, A., Gatarek, D., and Musiela, M. "The Market Model of Interest Rate Dynamics" (1997) Mathematical Finance vol 7 no 2 127–155; Heath, D., Jarrow, R., and Morton, A., "Contingent Claim Valuation with a Random Evolution of Interest Rates" (1991) Review of Futures Markets 54–76; Heath, D., Jarrow, R., and Morton, A. "Bond Pricing and the Term Structure of Interest Rates: A New Methodology For Contingent Claims Valuation" (1992) 60 (No 1) Econometrica 77–105; Ho, T.S.Y., and Lee, S.B. "Term Structure Movements and Pricing Interest Rate Contingent Claims" (1986) 41 (No 5) Journal of Finance 1011–29; Hull, J., and White, A. "Pricing Interest Rate Derivatives" (1990) Review of Financial Studies vol 3 no 4 573–592; Jamshidian, F. "LIBOR and Swap Market Models and Measures" (1997) Finance and Stochastics 1 293–330.

[29]  General equilibrium models can be adapted to fit the current term structure. For example, a significant contribution of John Hull and Alan White has been to show how these models can be fitted to the current term structure and used to price interest rate derivatives: see Hull, John and White, Alan "Pricing Interest Rate Derivatives" (1990) Review of Financial Studies 3 573–592.

Some models specify the whole term structure of interest rates as a random variable[30]. In the single factor case, the interest rate at different maturities (specified as a vector of interest rates) is the underlying variable. Instruments are valued directly at any forward date by discounting the cash flows back using the forward rates generated by the model.

## 5.4 Yield Curve Process

Central to the process underlying an interest rate term structure model is the specification of a yield curve process. This process generally involves specification of two elements:

- **Short-term interest rate** – the short-term rate (r) is modelled and used in conjunction with individual risk preferences to specify current term structure and the projected term structure.
- **Mean reversion** – the model will generally incorporate mean reversion effects. This means that the model of the drift of r is specified to have average drift with volatility superimposed upon the drift. The drift tendency is to pull interest rates to some long term average level. Mean reversion is responsible for decline in forward rate volatility as maturity of underlying instrument decreases. **Exhibit 8.7** sets out a model of the mean reversion effect.

There are complex choices between interest rate processes and a wide variety of models have emerged.

The interest rate process specifies the manner in which the interest rate evolves over time. Typically, geometric Brownian motion or a Wiener process is assumed to ensure that the resulting distribution is normal. **Exhibit 8.8** sets out a typical yield curve process used in interest rate term structure models. The process enables dr to be normally distributed as dz is normally distributed. The distribution of dr is a function of $\sigma$ (volatility estimated from historical data or some other source). Where $\mu$ is constant, the expected changes in r follow a linear pattern.

The problems with this type of process include rates may become very large or negative. As this is not consistent with market behaviour of rates, the interest rate process must be amended. This can be done in a number of ways. For example, a

---

[30] See Heath, D., Jarrow, R., and Morton, A. "Contingent Claim Valuation with a Random Evolution of Interest Rates" (1991) Review of Futures Markets 54–76; Heath, D., Jarrow, R., and Morton, A. "Bond Pricing and the Term Structure of Interest Rates: A New Methodology for Contingent Claims Valuation" (1992) 60 (No 1) Econometrica 77–105.

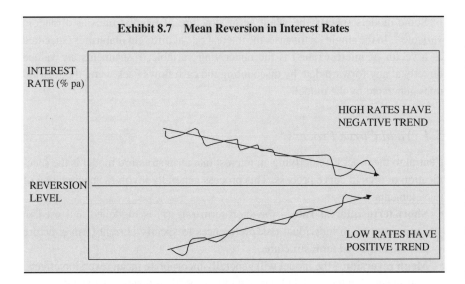

**Exhibit 8.7    Mean Reversion in Interest Rates**

INTEREST
RATE (% pa)

HIGH RATES HAVE
NEGATIVE TREND

REVERSION
LEVEL

LOW RATES HAVE
POSITIVE TREND

---

**Exhibit 8.8    Yield Curve Process – Simple**

A standard Black-Scholes type relative diffusion process would be as follows:

$$dr = \mu.dt + \sigma.dz$$

Where

- r  = spot interest rate
- dr = a change in r over dt
- $\mu$  = deterministic drift function per unit of time
- dt = unit of time (t)
- $\sigma$  = volatility of r per unit of time
- dz = a small change in a normal random variable with mean zero and standard deviation equal to $\sqrt{t}$

---

log normal distribution of interest rates may be used to avoid negative interest rate outcomes. However, this does not prevent interest rates becoming very high. In practice, a mean reverting process is utilised to overcome the problem of high or negative rates. **Exhibit 8.9** sets out a typical mean reverting interest rate process used in interest rate term structure models. In a mean reverting process, the model incorporates mean reversion with the r being pulled to level b at rate a. A normally distributed stochastic term ($\sigma \cdot dz$) is superimposed upon this overall drift creating volatility in rates and prices around this trend.

---

**Exhibit 8.9   Yield Curve Process – Mean Reverting**

A typical mean reverting process would be as follows[35]:

$$dr = a(b - r)dt + \sigma \cdot dz$$

Where

a = the parameter (greater than 0) which describes the speed at which r revert to the
long run average value

b = the long run value of r

All other terms are as in **Exhibit 8.8**.

---

The difficulty with this approach is that the change in r is path dependent (that is, change is dependent upon where rates currently are). This makes the process non-Markov[31]. This makes it difficult to derive analytical solutions and numerical solutions are required.

The interest rate processes described utilise single factor models. Multi factor models may use a variety of structures (two rates, time dependency or specification of the complete yield curve as a variable). **Exhibit 8.10** sets out some multi-factor interest rate processes.

In practice, the approaches used vary between practitioners[32]. The major models used are Hull-White ("HW") (time dependent single or two factor types of models) and Heath Jarrow Morton ("HJM")[33]/Brace Gatarek Musiela ("BGM")[34] multi factor models.

## 5.5   Model Calibration

The arbitrage free approach requires a process of model calibration. A basic requirement of both equilibrium and no arbitrage models is the need to estimate the required variables from market data. In the case of arbitrage free models the model parameters are constrained to fit:

- **Initial term structure** – that is, the current interest rates.

---

[31] A Markov process is one where only the present value of the variable is relevant to predicting the future and the past history of the variable is irrelevant.

[32] For a comparison see Ho, Thomas S.Y. "Evolution of Interest Rate Models: A Comparison" (Summer 1995) Journal of Derivatives 9–20.

[33] It can be shown that many of the other available models are special cases of the HJM framework/approach.

[34] Also known as the LIBOR market model.

[35] The model specified is the Vasicek model; see Vasicek, O.A. "An Equilibrium Characterisation of the Term Structure" (1977) Journal of Financial Economics 5 177–188.

- **Market option prices** – that is, the implied volatility of traded market instruments.

**Exhibit 8.11** sets out the overall process of calibration used in interest rate term structure models.

The process of calibration requires:

- **Selection of the calibrating instruments** – the process of calibration is structured so that the calibrating instruments chosen are similar to the instrument being valued.
- **Nomination of best-fit criteria** – the best-fit criteria is usually specified to minimise the difference between the market price and the model price. Weighting schemes may be employed to give greater emphasis on particular instruments.

---

**Exhibit 8.10    Yield Curve Process – Multi-Factor Models**

**1.    Multiple Rates**

The interest rate process can be specified as a function of a short term and a long term rate[36]:

$$dr = a(l - r)dt + \sigma_1 r dw$$

$$dr = \sigma_2 l dz$$

Where

$$dwdz = \rho dt$$

Where

$l$  = the long term rate
$\sigma_1$ = volatility of r
$\sigma_2$ = volatility of l
$\rho$  = correlation of r and l

The short rate (r) is a mean reverting log normally distributed rate where the mean reversion is to the log normally distributed long term rate (l).

**2.    Time Dependent**

The model can be made time dependent as follows[37]:

$$dr = (a(t) - ar)dt + dz$$

---

[36]  See Brennan, M.J. and Schwartz, E.S. "An Equilibrium Model of Bond Pricing and a Test of Market Efficiency" (1982) Journal of Financial and Quantitative Analysis 17 301–329. John Hull and Alan White have suggested a time dependent arbitrage free version of this approach, see Hull, John and White, A "Numerical Procedures for Implementing Term Structure Models II: Two Factor Models" (Winter 1994) Journal of Derivatives vol 2 no 2 37–48.

[37]  See Hull, J. and White, A. "Pricing Interest Rate Derivatives" (1990) Review of Financial Studies vol 3 no 4 573–592.

The coefficients are time dependent. The value selected ensures that the evolving interest rates fit the observed market term structure of rates such that the expected rates at forward dates are consistent with the observed forward rates.

## 1. Yield Curve As Variable

The whole term structure of interest rates can be specified as a random variable as follows[38]:

$$df(t, T) = a(t, T)dt + \sigma_f(t, T)dw(t)$$

Where

$df$    = a change in the forward rate (f)
$\sigma_f$    = volatility of f
$(t, T)$    = forward period t to T

The rate is defined as a function of the forward rate[39] that is modelled within an arbitrage free framework and calibrated to fit the existing term structures of rates and volatility.

**Exhibit 8.11    Interest Rate Term Structure Models – Model Calibration**

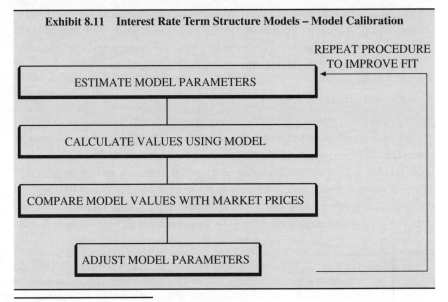

---

[38]    See Brace, A., Gatarek, D., and Musiela, M. "The Market Model of Interest Rate Dynamics" (1997) Mathematical Finance vol 7 no 2 127–155; Heath, D., Jarrow, R., and Morton, A. "Contingent Claim Valuation with a Random Evolution of Interest Rates" (1991) Review of Futures Markets 54–76; Heath, D., Jarrow, R., and Morton, A. "Bond Pricing and the Term Structure of Interest Rates: A New Methodology for Contingent Claims Valuation" (1992) 60 (no 1) Econometrica 77–105.

[39]    The Heath Jarrow Morton model was the first to suggest that the evolution of the term structure be modelled entirely in terms of the forward rate. The authors argued that the structure of forward rate volatility is more consistent and easier to estimate as the spot

The ability to calibrate the model to market prices is far from easy. There are also differences between models. For example, where the forward price is modelled (as in HJM), it is difficult to calibrate the model, as the continuously compounded forward rates modelled are not directly observable in the market and the model is not easy to calibrate to traded caps/floors. In contrast, BGM/LIBOR market model approaches are easier to calibrate as the model is expressed in terms of forward rates that are constructed so as to be consistent with traded cap prices.

The Black-Scholes model/Black model is central to the process of calibration. This is because any arbitrage free yield curve model must recover Black-Scholes/ Black price for plain vanilla instruments (such as cap/floors and swaptions).

## 5.6 Numerical Solution Issues

The model of the interest rates generates forward term structures of interest rates (short rate or forward rates) and volatility. The rates and volatility are then used to generate the distribution of prices of the underlying debt instrument to enable the option value to be derived. Most of the pricing models require numerical solution[40].

The process of numerical implementation entails several steps including:

* Tree construction
* Numerical solution.


The basic intuition underlying tree construction is the construction of a discrete time representation of stochastic process and the sequence of bond prices. It is conceptually similar to the binomial or trinomial approach to option pricing[41]. The difference between an asset tree and interest rate tree is that discounting in the interest rate tree is done using different rates at each node, and the volatility does not necessarily remain constant. The tree construction process may include

---

rate volatility reflects the behaviour of bond prices as maturity approaches. Basing the model on the forward rates avoids this problem. This creates an additional problem in that instantaneous forward rates are generally not directly observable in the market.

[40] See Hull, John (2000) Option Futures and Other Derivatives – Fourth Edition; Prentice-Hall Inc., Upper Saddle River, NJ at Chapters 21; Wilmott, Paul, Dewynne, Jeff and Howison, Sam (1993) Option Pricing: Mathematical Models and Computation; Oxford Financial Press: Oxford, England.

[41] The key development in this context was the publication of Ho, T.S.Y. and Lee, S.B. "Term Structure Movements and Pricing Interest Rate Contingent Claims" (1986) 41 (no 5) Journal of Finance 1011–29. Ho and Lee's approach started with the current term structure that was then allowed to shift to one of two possible steps – a binomial process. The model is then forced to be arbitrage free. This model was the first to allow the entire term structure to evolve within a binomial model structure.

a variety of techniques including trinomial trees. The tree may also include non-standard branching (to accommodate mean reversion) and changing the length of the tree step (to accommodate instruments such as Bermudan options to ensure that nodes coincide with key exercise dates).

The process of numerical solution will typically focus on backward induction techniques, solving partial differential equations using finite difference schemes/analytic solutions or Monte Carlo processes.

For example, in the case of discrete time models, the option is evaluated by starting at expiration and working backwards through the lattice or price tree of bond prices or interest rates utilising a procedure referred to as dynamic programming. Alternatively, numerical solutions of the partial differential equations developed using the various pricing approaches must be computed. This is sometimes undertaken using finite difference methods that value the option by solving numerically the differential equation that the option must satisfy by converting the differential equation into a set of different equations which are then solved using an iterative process. A final approach to pricing debt options should be noted – namely, the use of Monte Carlo simulation techniques. Using this technique, a model of interest rates can be developed and the movement of the term structure of interest rates during the life of the option would then be repeatedly simulated assuming a distribution of interest rates conforming to the risk adjusted parameter levels. The simulation run would generate payoffs for the option that would then be discounted to the present time using the average short term rates. The value of the option would be average of these discounted payoffs.

A major problem with implementation of interest rate term structure models in practice is the non-Markov nature of the models. This means that the numerical solutions required are complex. The trees used are usually non-recombinant and dense (bushy). This means that solutions are slow and expensive.

# 6 Interest Rate Term Structure Model – An Example

In this Section, an example of building and implementing an interest rate term structure model is discussed[42]. The model used is based on a simple interest rate process where equal probabilities (0.5) of an increase and decrease are assumed. A tree/lattice of interest rates is constructed including a variable drift component that is then solved using iteration methods to fit the current term structure of interest rates (zero coupon rates). A discount tree/lattice is also generated as part of the curve fitting process to allow individual cash flows to be discounted back. The tree

---

[42] The author would like to thank Tim Rowlands for his permission to include this example.

of rates is used to generate the option payoffs (initially in % terms that is converted to $ terms) that are then discounted to determine the option value. **Exhibit 8.12** sets out the example of implementing an interest rate term structure model[43].

---

**Exhibit 8.12    Interest Rate Term Structure Model – Example**

**1.  Assumptions**
In this example, a binomial tree or lattice model is used to price a cap-let based on a 3 month rate with an expiry of two years and a strike price of 7.00% pa. The caplet is priced using 8 steps within the binomial tree with each step representing a period of 3 months.

**2.  Interest Rate Process**
The interest rate process assumed is a simple lognormal process with the drift term being time dependent to allow the fitting of the current structure in an arbitrage free manner and with the volatility term being constant.

The interest rate term structure is:

$$dr = \mu(t)rdt + \sigma rdz$$

Where

r  = spot interest rate
dr = a change in r over dt
$\mu$  = deterministic drift function per unit of time
dt = unit of time (t)
$\sigma$  = volatility of r per unit of time
dz = a small change in a normal random variable with mean zero and standard deviation
     equal to $\sqrt{t}$

This is equivalent to[44]:

$$d\ln(r) = (\mu(t) - \tfrac{1}{2}\sigma^2)dt + \sigma dz$$

where

$\ln(r)$ = natural (base e) logarithm of r

---

[43]  This example shows a simple case to illustrate how an interest rate term structure model would be constructed and calibrated. In practice, the implementation of the model would be more complex. For example, the number of steps used would be greater.

[44]  This can be shown using Ito's Lemma. In this case, the spread of the distribution is determined by the value of $\sigma$ based on the standard deviation of the logarithms of the rate changes. The equivalent absolute change in the logarithm of the rate from one day to the next day is the logarithm of one rate minus the logarithm of the previous rate and the difference between two logarithms is equal to the logarithm of the rate changes. This process ensures that the rates cannot take negative values. This is because that if $\ln(r)$ trends down to be a negative number (i.e. $\mu$ is negative), this means the rate will still be positive as the exponential of a negative number is positive and lies between zero and one.

Integrating both sides (ignoring the time dependence of $\mu$) gives:

$$\ln(r_T) - \ln(r_0) = (\mu(T) - \tfrac{1}{2}\sigma^2)T + \sigma\sqrt{T}U(0, 1)$$

or

$$r_T = r_0 e^{(\mu(T) - \frac{1}{2}\sigma^2)T} + e^{\sigma\sqrt{T}U(0, 1)}$$

Where

$U(0, 1)$ is a standard normal variable (mean zero and standard deviation 1)

This expression has 3 components:
- The initial interest ($r_0$)
- The drift term ($e^{(\mu(T) - \frac{1}{2}\sigma^2)}$)
- The volatility term ($e^{\sigma\sqrt{T}U(0,1)}$)

## 3. Fitting to Current Term Structure

The drift term must be adjusted so that the rate tree/lattice matches the current term structure. This is rewritten as follows:

$$r_T = r_0 a_T e^{\sigma\sqrt{T}U(0, 1)}$$

Where $a_T$ is determined to fit the current term structure.

This fitting process is the reason for not being rigorous with the integration of the time dependent $\mu$ term. The standard normal variable $U(0, 1)$ is replaced with a binomial variable $B(0, 1)$ consistent with building a binomial tree/lattice.

A binomial variable ($b_{ni}$) is represented on a lattice at node 1 at time step n. It has value:

$$b_{ni} = (2i - n)/\sqrt{n}$$

It has probability:

$$P_{ni} = {}^nC_i 2^{-n}$$

Where the binomial co-efficient is:

$$^nC_i = n!/[i!(n - i)!]$$

and assuming a probability of one half for up and down movements. Consequently, this variable has mean zero and standard deviation one. (A further comment on the choice of probabilities is made below.) If the time to maturity T is split into n steps then each step has length:

$$\Delta t = T/n$$

Substituting into our expression for $r_T$,

$$r_T(n, i) = r_0 a_T e^{\sigma\sqrt{n\Delta T}(2i-n)/\sqrt{n}}$$

Which can be simplified as follows:

$$r_T(n, i) = r_0 a_T e^{\sigma\sqrt{\Delta T}(2i-n)}$$

## 4. Implementing the Model

Assume the following zero coupon rate curve (continuously compounded rates):

| Years | 0 | 0.25 | 0.50 | 0.75 | 1.00 | 1.25 | 1.50 | 1.75 | 2.00 | 2.25 |
|---|---|---|---|---|---|---|---|---|---|---|
| Rates (% pa) | 6.00 | 6.15 | 6.28 | 6.40 | 6.50 | 6.58 | 6.64 | 6.69 | 6.72 | 6.75 |

Based on a volatility of 12% pa, a set of rates (% pa) for each node can be generated using the formula previously derived:

| Node | 0 | 1 | 2 | 3 | 4 | 5 | 6 | 7 | 8 |
|---|---|---|---|---|---|---|---|---|---|
| 0 | 6.1500 | 6.7941 | 7.4597 | 8.0902 | 8.6896 | 9.2487 | 9.8558 | 10.335 | 11.0276 |
| 1 | | 6.0259 | 6.6162 | 7.1753 | 7.7070 | 8.2029 | 8.7413 | 9.1668 | 9.7806 |
| 2 | | | 5.8680 | 6.3639 | 6.8355 | 7.2753 | 7.7529 | 8.1302 | 8.6746 |
| 3 | | | | 5.6443 | 6.0625 | 6.4526 | 6.8762 | 7.2108 | 7.6937 |
| 4 | | | | | 5.3770 | 5.7229 | 6.0986 | 6.3954 | 6.8237 |
| 5 | | | | | | 5.0758 | 5.4090 | 5.6723 | 6.0521 |
| 6 | | | | | | | 4.7973 | 5.0308 | 5.3877 |
| 7 | | | | | | | | 4.4620 | 4.7607 |
| 8 | | | | | | | | | 4.2224 |
| $a_T$ | 1 | 1.040403 | 1.075797 | 1.098776 | 1.111456 | 1.114082 | 1.118078 | 1.104214 | 1.109543 |

The above Table represents a set of interest rates for periods of 3 months. The current spot rate (6.15% pa) (corresponding to $r_0(0,0)$) is modelled to increase to 6.7941% pa or down to 6.0259% pa.

The probability of an up or down movement is taken to 0.5 (50%). This reveals the reasons for using $a_T$. The formula value (based on a rigorous integration) could be used and the up and down probabilities adjusted to fit the term structure. Alternatively, the probabilities can be chosen and the rates for each node adjusted to fit the term structure (the option selected in this example). The second approach means that the probability at a node is the simple one set out above rather than depending on a combination of adjusted volatilities. The use of 0.5 as the probability makes the implementation much simpler.

The values for $a_T$ are derived using an iterative technique. This can be shown as follows:
- At the first step there are two rates ($r_1(1, 0)$ and $r_1(1, 1)$), each occurring with a probability of 0.5.
- The two quarter zero rate using these rates is given by:

$$e^{R_2 2\Delta t} = 0.5 \times e^{r_0(1,0)\Delta t} \times e^{r_1(1,0)\Delta t} + 0.5 \times e^{r_0(0,0)\Delta t} \times e^{r_1(1,1)\Delta t}$$

- Since $R_2$ should equal the two quarter spot rate from the current zero coupon curve (6.28% pa), the $a_1$ factor can be adjusted to ensure the $r_1$ rates until the above condition is met[45].

---

[45] This can be done with a numerical zero finding algorithm or a solver-type function in a spreadsheet.

The two individual terms in the expression correspond to the node specific discount rates. These rates can be used to discount cashflows occurring on the nodes back to zero.

This technique for building a tree/lattice follows an approach that is known as forward induction.

In this example, the discount rate (% pa) lattice has the following values:

| Discount Rates | 0 | 1 | 2 | 3 | 4 | 5 | 6 | 7 | 8 |
|---|---|---|---|---|---|---|---|---|---|
| 0 | 6.1500 | 6.4721 | 6.8013 | 7.1235 | 7.4367 | 7.7387 | 8.0421 | 8.3279 | 8.6279 |
| 1 | | 6.0879 | 6.3921 | 6.7413 | 7.0873 | 7.4188 | 7.7448 | 8.0522 | 8.3668 |
| 2 | | | 6.0146 | 6.2435 | 6.5610 | 6.8994 | 7.2439 | 7.5739 | 7.9088 |
| 3 | | | | 5.9220 | 6.0787 | 6.3420 | 6.6572 | 6.9831 | 7.3246 |
| 4 | | | | | 5.8130 | 5.9087 | 6.1215 | 6.3901 | 6.7018 |
| 5 | | | | | | 5.6902 | 5.7437 | 5.9001 | 6.1347 |
| 6 | | | | | | | 5.5626 | 5.5753 | 5.6966 |
| 7 | | | | | | | | 5.4250 | 5.4180 |
| 8 | | | | | | | | | 5.2914 |
| Expected Value | 6.15 | 6.28 | 6.40 | 6.50 | 6.58 | 6.64 | 6.69 | 6.72 | 6.75 |

The cap-let is now priced as follows:
- The first set of rates is used to determine the value of the cap-let.
- The second set of discount rates is used to determine the net present value.

The cap-let strike (7.00% pa) is compared to each of the final node rates to determine the option payoff. The payoff is then weighted by the probability of occurrence and then discounted back to the start of the transaction. The sum of these contributions is the caplet price.

The detailed calculations are summarised below:

| Node | Rate (% pa) | Maximum (r − K, 0) (% pa) | Value ($) Per $1 million[46] | Discount Rate (% pa)[47] | Probability | Contribution ($) |
|---|---|---|---|---|---|---|
| 0 | 11.0276 | 4.0276 | 10,608.96 | 8.6279 | 0.00391 | 33.10 |
| 1 | 9.7806 | 2.7806 | 6,951.48 | 8.3668 | 0.03125 | 183.76 |

---

[46] The value per $1 million is calculated as the % payoff applied to $1,000,000 for one quarter.

[47] In this case, each caplet contribution is discounted by the discount rate that applies to its node – in effect assuming stochastic discount rates. Under BSM models, a single discount factor is used for the period (i.e. interest rates are not stochastic). If the 2 year

| Node | Rate (% pa) | Maximum (r − K, 0) (% pa) | Value ($) Per $1 million | Discount Rate (% pa) | Probability | Contribution ($) |
|------|------|------|------|------|------|------|
| 2 | 8.6746 | 1.6746 | 4,186.51 | 7.9088 | 0.10938 | 390.91 |
| 3 | 7.6973 | 0.6973 | 1,734.21 | 7.3246 | 0.21875 | 327.66 |
| 4 | 6.8237 | 0 | 0 | 6.7018 | 0.27344 | 0 |
| 5 | 6.0521 | 0 | 0 | 6.1347 | 0.21875 | 0 |
| 6 | 5.3677 | 0 | 0 | 5.6966 | 0.10938 | 0 |
| 7 | 4.7607 | 0 | 0 | 5.4180 | 0.03125 | 0 |
| 8 | 4.2224 | 0 | 0 | 5.2914 | 0.00391 | 0 |
| | | | | | Price ($) | 935.43 |

The cap-let price is therefore $935.43 per $1 million face value.

The process would be repeated for the other cap-lets to derive the value of the cap. In this case a single constant volatility was used for the valuation. Use of different volatilities and thus different trees/lattices for the different caplets in a cap would allow the calibration of the cap price to the volatility term structure as well as the interest rate term structure.

Source: Rowlands, Tim "Interest Rate Option Pricing Models" in Das, Satyajit (1997) Risk Management & Financial Derivatives: A Guide to the Mathematics; LBC Information Services, Sydney; McGraw-Hill, Chicago; MacMillan Publishing, England 282–287.

# 7 Model Selection[48]

The wide range of models available currently, and the unsettled nature of the debate on pricing interest rate options, forces the practitioner to confront the awkward question of which model to utilise.

---

spot rate (6.72% pa) is used as the discount rate for each contribution, then the price of the cap-let is $955.69 per $1 million face value. The difference between the prices ($955.69 and $935.43) shows the relative size of the error made under a BSM model approach of constant discount rates.

[48] For a discussion of model selection issues, see Leong, Kenneth "In the Eye of the Beholder" (July-August 1990) Risk 38–40; Leong, Kenneth "The Emperor's New Clothes" (September 1990) 11–15; Leong, Kenneth "Exorcising the Demon" (October 1990) Risk 29–35; Leong, Kenneth "Price Versus Value" (November 1991) Risk 22–26; Leong, Kenneth "Model Choice" (1992) Risk 60–66; Leong, Kenneth "Model Choice" (September 1998) Black-Scholes-Merton Supplement 19–22.

The key criteria against which interest rate option pricing models must be benchmarked include:

- **Arbitrage free pricing** – the model used must generate prices that are consistent with market prices for standard instruments. This will ensure that arbitrage opportunities are minimised and also ensure that dealers are able to hedge position in the market easily without an unexplained value shift.
- **Hedge-ability** – the ability of the model to generate hedges that can be implemented in the market is central to the utility and value of the model.
- **Model transparency, consistency and flexibility** – the model methodology should be transparent and easily validated/verified. In addition, the model should ideally be able to price the full range of products consistently. This avoids problems of risk management where different models are used to price and trade different instruments. It should also be flexible in terms of specification of parameters, capable of accommodating new instruments, and able to operate under different market conditions.
- **Computational efficiency** – the model should be sufficiently fast to meet trading requirements (price discovery, transaction pricing, hedging and portfolio management, position revaluation) and risk management requirements (profit/loss calculations, sensitivities (greeks), stress testing). The essential issue is that the choice of model should not ideally constrain business activities.
- **Cost-benefit** – the cost of the system (both establishment and operation) must be related to the *true* benefits from the operation of the system.

The identified criteria are difficult to satisfy simultaneously in reality. In practice, the following trends are evident:

- Options on futures, particularly where the underlying debt instrument is a short term interest rate or security or the time to expiration is relatively short (particularly in relation to the life of the underlying debt instrument), are priced using the Black model.
- The pricing of caps and floors is generally undertaken using the Black model.
- Options on swaps or swaptions are priced using the Black model, particularly where the time to exercise is relatively short (particularly in relation to the life of the swap). However, interest rate term structure approaches are increasingly being used for certain types of structures, particularly Bermudan options.
- Options on bonds are priced using Black's model where the time to expiry is short relative to the life of the underlying bond. For longer dated bond options, interest rate term structure models are utilised.

- Other debt options, particularly long maturity options, such as those embedded in callable and puttable bonds, asset/mortgage-backed securities etc, are priced using interest rate term structure models.

Major dealers are increasingly implementing interest rate term structure models to price/value *all* interest rate products within a consistent framework.

The statement of practice should not be regarded as comprehensive but rather indicative of market practitioners' approaches. The approach to pricing in practice reflects a variety of factors including:

- None of the option pricing models described is perfect *for all situations*.
- Users will typically utilise models which are easy to implement and that are not expensive to build or cumbersome to use. For example, interest rate term structure models require estimation of parameters that may in practice be difficult to verify. In addition, term structure models will generally require numerical solution. This requires significant amounts of computer resources and can take time to produce results (albeit the increasing availability of very fast computers at ever decreasing costs is increasingly a factor).

The models form the basis of pricing and risk management systems within financial institutions, which are active in trading and hedging these instruments. This dictates that the need to actively manage the risk exposure of positions in a rapidly changing market means the risk managers are willing to sacrifice some theoretical niceties in favour of speed and direct relevance of the information generated by the model.

In fundamental terms, the pricing of these instruments using often complex mathematics must be taken in the context of market realities. In particular, the underlying market for debt instruments does not fully reflect the assumptions of perfect liquidity, no transaction costs and perfect information made in the pricing models themselves. Given the failures of the real market to conform to the theoretical constructions underlying option pricing models, no model can be used risklessly to arbitrage mispricing. In addition, there are difficulties in evaluating the performance of individual models using rigorous empirical approaches. The difficulty in model selection necessarily makes the mathematical techniques merely indications of relative value of options on particular instruments[49].

---

[49]   There is some recent anecdotal evidence of problems in using interest rate term structure models to price options on swaps, see Dunbar, Nicholas "Sterling Swaptions: Volatility by the Pound" (September 1999) Risk 23–28.

A major advantage of Black and Scholes (and Black's variation thereto)[50] is the capacity to compress four observable variables into one other variable, volatility, which can then be interpreted in the pricing, trading and hedging of these instruments. The enduring quality of the Black-Scholes model continues to be its ease of use despite its theoretical shortcomings under certain conditions.

## 8  Summary

Options on interest rates/debt instruments present significant challenges. Traditional BSM approaches are inadequate in relation to certain types of instruments where a complete term structure of rates and non-constant volatility are required to derive valuations.

Debt options are priced using two competing approaches. The first uses Black's model for pricing options on forward rates to price a wide range of options (short dated options on bonds, interest rate caps/floors, swaptions). This requires a number of simplifying assumptions. The second approach uses a term structure model to generate a complete model of the complete yield curve and its evolution through time to price options on interest rates/debt instruments.

The second approach is capable of accommodating certain types of options (long dated bond options, callable/puttable bonds and mortgage/asset backed securities) that are not easily dealt with under the first approach. The approach also has the benefit of enabling the consistent valuation of all interest rate/debt instruments within a single framework. However, the term structure models are complex and difficult to implement (due to their numerical nature) and must be calibrated to available interest rates and volatility. In practice, the two approaches co-exist in the market.

---

[50] This refers to both the closed form and the binomial implementation of these models.

# 9
# Estimating Volatility and Correlation[1]

## 1 Overview

The concept of volatility of asset prices and returns and correlation between asset prices and returns is central to financial markets. Volatility provides essential data about the probability of achieving certain outcomes in terms of price levels. This information is used in key decisions in financial markets such as asset allocation and construction of efficient asset or liability portfolios (in the context of a risk-return trade-off). In option pricing, an estimate of volatility is essential to the valuation of the instrument. Correlation is used for asset allocation decisions, hedging and pricing certain types of exotic options. Volatility and correlation estimates are also required for risk management in particular value-at-risk ("VAR") models[2].

---

[1] For a discussion of issues in volatility and correlation estimation, see Alexander, Carol "Volatility and Correlation: Measurement, Models and Application" in Alexander, Carol (Editor) Risk Management and Analysis – Volume 1: Measuring and Modelling Financial Risk; John Wiley & Sons, Chichester at 125–171; Hull, John (2000) Option Futures and Other Derivatives – Fourth Edition; Prentice-Hall Inc., Upper Saddle River, NJ at Chapters 15 and 17; Rebanato, Riccardo (1999) Estimating Volatility and Correlation; John Wiley, New York; Tompkins, Robert (1994) Options Explained[2]; MacMillan Press: England at Chapter 4–5; Wilmott, Peter (1998) Derivatives: The Theory and Practice of Financial Engineering; John Wiley & Sons, Chichester, at Chapters 22, 23 and 25. See also Cox, J. and Rubinstein, M. (1985) Options Markets; Prentice-Hall, Inc.; Englewood Cliffs, NJ at 6; Brown, Stephen J. "Estimating Volatility" in Figlewski, Stephen, Silber, William L. and Subrahmanyan, Marti G. (Editors) (1990) "Financial Options: From Theory to Practice"; Business One Irwin, Homewood Illinois at 516–537.

[2] See Das, Satyajit (2004) Risk Management; John Wiley & Sons (Asia), Singapore at Chapter 2.

This chapter focuses on the problem of estimation of volatility and correlation in the context of option pricing. The structure of the Chapter is as follows:

- A framework for volatility covering causes of volatility in asset markets and the relationship between volatility and option pricing is examined.
- Approaches to volatility estimation including historical volatility, implied volatility, and alternative approaches to volatility modelling are described.
- The behaviour of volatility, particularly the concept of the volatility smile and the term structure of volatility, are analysed.
- Emerging models of stochastic volatility and its use in option pricing are outlined.
- The estimation of correlation is analysed.
- Volatility and correlation estimation in practice is discussed.

## 2 Volatility Estimation – Framework

### 2.1 Overview

Volatility estimation in the context of option pricing must be considered within the broader context of asset price and return volatility. The framework for volatility estimation must recognise the causes of volatility in asset prices and the inter-relationship between volatility and option pricing models.

### 2.2 Causes of Volatility in Asset Prices

Price volatility in asset markets is caused by a variety of factors. The most important is release of new price sensitive information. A second cause of volatility is the process of trading in financial instruments.

Information releases generally fall into two categories – anticipated and unanticipated information. Anticipated information includes economic statistics as well as political or social information. This type of information release is anticipated. Market participants develop expectations regarding the content of the informational release. The impact of the information is often driven by whether or not the release corresponds to market expectations, reflecting the fact that asset prices will generally incorporate the content of expected information releases. The impact of information releases can be analysed, particularly with reference to past releases. It may be possible to develop probabilistic expectations of anticipated asset price volatility from the historical reaction of the market to prior actual data releases, in combination with probabilities in relation to a variety of range outcomes for the relevant information release. Unanticipated information releases typically relate to international events (wars, natural disasters etc) and other unanticipated or impossible to anticipate events. This type of information can have substantial and unpredictable impact on asset price volatility. The difficulty in predicting this type of informational release (by definition) makes it extremely complex to incorporate these types of factors in forecasting future asset price volatility[3].

A newer area of financial economics research (the study of market microstructure) seeks to isolate the impact of trading on volatility[4]. The research identifies the informational content of trading. It examines the interaction of information from trading with the institutional structure of markets and its impact on volatility in asset markets[5].

In seeking to isolate factors generating asset price volatility, the linkages between volatility in various market segments or across markets should be noted. Analysis indicates that there may be implied and historical volatility relationships between different markets. For example, bond market volatility across various currencies shows significant correlation. Similarly, equity market volatility across market may also display significant correlation. In certain currencies, volatility in the foreign exchange market is often a useful indicator of volatility in interest rate markets in the relevant currencies.

## 2.3   Relationship between Asset Volatility and Option Pricing

Mathematical option pricing models require estimation of volatility. The future volatility of the underlying asset price is a parameter that must be input into the model.

The volatility estimate used in option valuation is the annualised standard deviation of the logarithms of the asset returns (or the continuously compounded asset returns). The volatility estimate is a measure of the uncertainty about the returns on

---

[3]  For a recent analysis of the impact of release of information of volatility, see Ederington, Louis and Lee, Ja Hae "The Impact of Macroeconomic News on Financial Markets" (Spring 1996) Journal of Applied Corporate Finance vol 9 no 1 41–50.

[4]  For example, a number of studies found that volatility between close of trading on Friday and opening of trading the next Monday morning (when there is an interval of around 3 non-trading days) is only around 20% higher than that between close of trading on one day and open of trading the next day (when there are no intervening non-trading days) rather than the predicted three times higher, suggesting that volatility is higher when trading on exchanges is open than when it is closed; see Fama, E.E. "The Behaviour of Stock Market Prices" (January 1965) Journal of Business vol 38 34–105; French, K.R. "Stock Returns and the Weekend Effect" (1979) Journal of Financial Economics 55–69.

[5]  See Cohen, Kalman J., Maier, Steven F., Schwartz, Robert A., and Whitcomb, David K. (1986) The Microstructure of Securities Markets; Prentice-Hall, Englewood Cliffs, New Jersey; Schwartz, Robert A. (1988) Equity Markets; Harper & Row, New York.

the asset. It is used to generate the distribution of asset prices at the option expiry to calculate the fair value of the option.

There are several aspects of the volatility estimate that should be noted:

* The volatility parameter required to derive option values is forward looking; that is, the relevant volatility is the asset return volatility in the period to option expiry.
* Volatility is assumed to be constant between the pricing date and option expiry.
* Volatility is assumed to be time homogenous; that is, it is the same over the life of the option.
* Uncertainty about the asset price at option maturity is assumed to be directly proportional to the asset price at commencement.

The estimation of the volatility of the underlying asset price is particularly problematic because it is the only parameter of most mathematical pricing models that is not observable directly. The sensitivity of the option value to this parameter places additional demands on the estimation of volatility.

## 3 Volatility Estimation – Approaches

Estimation of the *true* volatility of the underlying asset price is difficult. In practice, a number of alternative approaches are used. The major approaches include:

* Historical/empirical approach.
* Implied volatility approach.

In recent times, a number of other approaches to option volatility have emerged. These include autoregressive conditional hetroskedasticity models ("ARCH")[6]/generalised ARCH ("GARCH")[7] or stochastic volatility models.

## 4 Historical/Empirical Volatility

### 4.1 Calculation of Historical Volatility

Under the historical or empirical approach, volatility estimates are calculated as the standard deviation of logarithms of the price changes of a sample time series of historical data for the asset price.

---

[6] See Engle, R.F. "Autoregressive Conditional Hetroskedasticity with Estimates of Variance of UK Inflation" (1982) Econometrica 50 987–1008.

[7] See Bollersev, T. "Generalised Autoregressive Conditional Hetroskedasticity" (1986) Journal of Econometrics 31 307–327.

The calculation procedure entails the following steps:
- The time series of historical data is specified. This will usually be the series of daily, weekly or monthly price observations for the relevant asset. For debt securities, either price or yield can be used.
- The price changes are calculated to measure the periodic (daily etc) return on the asset. In practice, the price relatives are utilised; that is, one plus the return or the observation at time t1 divided by the observation at the previous point in the time series t0. While the standard deviation can be calculated for either the returns or the price relatives, the first leads to inaccuracies reflecting the nature of the log normal distribution based on the effect of compounding. This means that the calculation using the price relatives is preferred. The difference is not significant for calculations involving relatively short data series, but becomes increasingly significant as the data series increases in size.
- The standard deviation of the price relatives is then calculated.

The interpretation of the standard deviation is as follows:
- The standard deviation computed equates to the volatility over the relevant time interval (for example, daily).
- The periodic observation is then scaled to give the annualised volatility of the asset price returns. This is done using the following relationship:

$$\sigma_{annual} = \sigma_{daily} \times \sqrt{\text{number of days}}$$

where the number of days would be set at either 250 or 260 days[8].

**Exhibit 9.1** sets out an example of the calculation of historical volatility.

## 4.2 Calculating Historical Volatility – Adjustments

In calculating the historical volatility of certain assets, the asset price sequence must be adjusted to reflect the non-homogenous nature of the data series. A major cause of this non-homogeneity is the entitlement to income on the underlying assets; for example, coupons in the case of debt instruments and dividends in the case of equity stocks.

The presence of income flows has the impact of reducing the comparability of succeeding price observations because the transition from cum-interest to ex-interest

---

[8]    Note that the daily volatility is scaled using the square root of the time interval. This reflects the fact that the assumed uncertainty about the asset price does not increase linearly.

**Exhibit 9.1    Volatility Estimation – Historical/
Empirical Approach**

Assume the following sequence of asset prices over a 20 day period:

| Period (Days) | Asset Price ($) |
|---|---|
| 0 | 8.2500 |
| 1 | 8.1800 |
| 2 | 8.2000 |
| 3 | 8.2000 |
| 4 | 8.2100 |
| 5 | 8.1200 |
| 6 | 8.1500 |
| 7 | 8.0700 |
| 8 | 8.1300 |
| 9 | 8.1700 |
| 10 | 8.2000 |
| 11 | 8.1600 |
| 12 | 8.1900 |
| 13 | 8.1200 |
| 14 | 8.0400 |
| 15 | 8.1900 |
| 16 | 8.0900 |
| 17 | 8.1200 |
| 18 | 8.1800 |
| 19 | 8.2700 |
| 20 | 8.1500 |

The price sequence in graphical form is as follows:

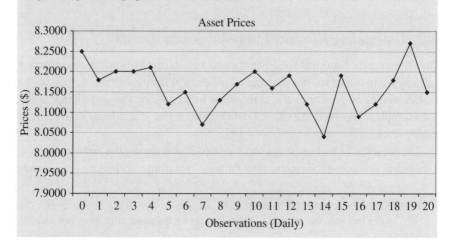

The price changes and the logarithms of the price changes are set out below:

| Period (Days) | Asset Price ($) | Price Relative $(S_t/(S_t-1))$ | Daily Return $[\ln(S_t/(S_t-1))]$ |
|---|---|---|---|
| 0 | 8.2500 | | |
| 1 | 8.1800 | 0.99152 | (0.00852) |
| 2 | 8.2000 | 1.00244 | 0.00244 |
| 3 | 8.2000 | 1.00000 | 0.00000 |
| 4 | 8.2100 | 1.00122 | 0.00122 |
| 5 | 8.1200 | 0.98904 | (0.01102) |
| 6 | 8.1500 | 1.00369 | 0.00369 |
| 7 | 8.0700 | 0.99018 | (0.00986) |
| 8 | 8.1300 | 1.00743 | 0.00741 |
| 9 | 8.1700 | 1.00492 | 0.00491 |
| 10 | 8.2000 | 1.00367 | 0.00367 |
| 11 | 8.1600 | 0.99512 | (0.00489) |
| 12 | 8.1900 | 1.00368 | 0.00367 |
| 13 | 8.1200 | 0.99145 | (0.00858) |
| 14 | 8.0400 | 0.99015 | (0.00990) |
| 15 | 8.1900 | 1.01866 | 0.01848 |
| 16 | 8.0900 | 0.98779 | (0.01229) |
| 17 | 8.1200 | 1.00371 | 0.00370 |
| 18 | 8.1800 | 1.00739 | 0.00736 |
| 19 | 8.2700 | 1.01100 | 0.01094 |
| 20 | 8.1500 | 0.98549 | (0.01462) |

The volatility is calculated as the standard deviation of the logarithms of the price changes. The data gives an estimate for the daily volatility of 0.00889 or 0.889%. Assuming that time is measured in trading days and that there are 250 trading days per year, the estimated annual volatility is 0.14051 or 14.051% pa (calculated as $0.00889 \times \sqrt{250}$).

or cum-dividend to ex-dividend will affect the price of the asset. In theory, the asset price should fall by the amount of the income entitlement (coupon or dividend ("D")). This necessitates intervention to adjust the price sequence when an asset goes ex entitlement as follows:

The price relative is restated as $\ln(S_t + D)/S_{t-1}$.

Some practitioners eliminate data around the ex entitlement data, particularly for equities, from the data series, reflecting the impact of a variety of factors, such as tax, on asset prices during these transitions and the resultant potential distortion in the volatility estimate.

## 4.3    Calculating Historical Volatility – Asset Class Extensions

The analysis focuses on the volatility of asset prices in general. This would encompass equity stocks, equity market indexes, commodity prices, commodity price indexes and currency values. In the case of debt instruments it is feasible to calculate the volatility of asset prices (being volatility of the price of the underlying debt security) and yield volatility (being the volatility of the interest rate index itself)[9].

**Exhibit 9.2** sets out calculation of both the price and yield volatility for a debt instrument (in this case a three month or 90 day discount instrument). In practice,

---

**Exhibit 9.2    Volatility Estimation – Historical/Empirical Approach
for Debt Instruments**

**1.  Assumptions**
Assume the following sequence of interest rates on a 3 month instrument and the equivalent price of a 90 day security:

| Period | Interest Rate | Asset Price |
|--------|---------------|-------------|
| 0      | 6.000%        | 98.5421     |
| 1      | 6.125%        | 98.5122     |
| 2      | 6.350%        | 98.4584     |
| 3      | 6.200%        | 98.4943     |
| 4      | 6.250%        | 98.4823     |
| 5      | 6.400%        | 98.4464     |
| 6      | 6.500%        | 98.4225     |
| 7      | 6.650%        | 98.3867     |
| 8      | 6.750%        | 98.3629     |
| 9      | 6.650%        | 98.3867     |
| 10     | 6.580%        | 98.4034     |
| 11     | 6.600%        | 98.3987     |
| 12     | 6.710%        | 98.3724     |
| 13     | 6.650%        | 98.3867     |
| 14     | 6.700%        | 98.3748     |
| 15     | 6.720%        | 98.3700     |
| 16     | 6.740%        | 98.3653     |
| 17     | 6.780%        | 98.3557     |
| 18     | 6.740%        | 98.3653     |
| 19     | 6.670%        | 98.3820     |
| 20     | 6.700%        | 98.3748     |

---

[9]   For a discussion of interest rate volatility, see Hargreaves, Guy D. "Volatility in Interest Rate Options" (paper presented to a conference "Options on Interest Rates", IIR Conferences, 9–10 March 1992, Sydney, Australia).

## 2. Price Volatility
The price changes and the logarithms of the price changes are set out below:

| Period (Days) | Asset Price ($) | Price Relative $(S_t/(S_t - 1))$ | Daily Return $[\ln(S_t/(S_t - 1))]$ |
|---|---|---|---|
| 0 | 98.54 | | |
| 1 | 98.51 | 0.99970 | (0.00030) |
| 2 | 98.46 | 0.99945 | (0.00055) |
| 3 | 98.49 | 1.00036 | 0.00036 |
| 4 | 98.48 | 0.99988 | (0.00012) |
| 5 | 98.45 | 0.99964 | (0.00036) |
| 6 | 98.42 | 0.99976 | (0.00024) |
| 7 | 98.39 | 0.99964 | (0.00036) |
| 8 | 98.36 | 0.99976 | (0.00024) |
| 9 | 98.39 | 1.00024 | 0.00024 |
| 10 | 98.40 | 1.00017 | 0.00017 |
| 11 | 98.40 | 0.99995 | (0.00005) |
| 12 | 98.37 | 0.99973 | (0.00027) |
| 13 | 98.39 | 1.00015 | 0.00015 |
| 14 | 98.37 | 0.99988 | (0.00012) |
| 15 | 98.37 | 0.99995 | (0.00005) |
| 16 | 98.37 | 0.99995 | (0.00005) |
| 17 | 98.36 | 0.99990 | (0.00010) |
| 18 | 98.37 | 1.00010 | 0.00010 |
| 19 | 98.38 | 1.00017 | 0.00017 |
| 20 | 98.37 | 0.99993 | (0.00007) |

The data gives an estimate for the daily volatility of 0.00023 or 0.023%. Assuming that time is measured in trading days and that there are 250 trading days per year, the estimated annual *price* volatility is 0.368% pa (calculated as $0.00023 \times \sqrt{250}$).

## 3. Yield Volatility
The yield changes and the logarithms of the yield changes are set out below:

| Period (Days) | Asset Price ($) | Price Relative $(S_t/(S_t - 1))$ | Daily Return $[\ln(S_t/(S_t - 1))]$ |
|---|---|---|---|
| 0 | 6.00 | | |
| 1 | 6.13 | 1.02083 | 0.02062 |
| 2 | 6.35 | 1.03673 | 0.03608 |
| 3 | 6.20 | 0.97638 | (0.02391) |
| 4 | 6.25 | 1.00806 | 0.00803 |
| 5 | 6.40 | 1.02400 | 0.02372 |
| 6 | 6.50 | 1.01563 | 0.01550 |

| Period (Days) | Asset Price ($) | Price Relative $(S_t/(S_t - 1))$ | Daily Return $[\ln(S_t/(S_t - 1))]$ |
|---|---|---|---|
| 7 | 6.65 | 1.02308 | 0.02281 |
| 8 | 6.75 | 1.01504 | 0.01493 |
| 9 | 6.65 | 0.98519 | (0.01493) |
| 10 | 6.58 | 0.98947 | (0.01058) |
| 11 | 6.60 | 1.00304 | 0.00303 |
| 12 | 6.71 | 1.01667 | 0.01653 |
| 13 | 6.65 | 0.99106 | (0.00898) |
| 14 | 6.70 | 1.00752 | 0.00749 |
| 15 | 6.72 | 1.00299 | 0.00298 |
| 16 | 6.74 | 1.00298 | 0.00297 |
| 17 | 6.78 | 1.00593 | 0.00592 |
| 18 | 6.74 | 0.99410 | (0.00592) |
| 19 | 6.67 | 0.98961 | (0.01044) |
| 20 | 6.70 | 1.00450 | 0.00449 |

The volatility is calculated as the standard deviation of the logarithms of the price changes. The data give an estimate for the daily volatility of 0.01499 or 1.499%. Assuming that time is measured in trading days and that there are 250 trading days per year, the estimated annual volatility is 0.23705 or 23.705% pa (calculated as $0.01499 \times \sqrt{250}$).

---

**Exhibit 9.3    Relationship Between Price and Yield Volatility**

The following formula can be used to convert yield volatility into its price volatility equivalent:

$$\text{Price Volatility} = (\Delta\text{Price}/\Delta\text{Yield}) \times \text{Yield} \times \text{Yield Volatility}$$

For example, the formula can be used to convert yield volatility of 20% for 91 day securities to its equivalent price volatility as follows:

$(\Delta\text{Price}/\Delta\text{Yield}) = 24.08$ for 0.0001% pa or 1 bps change in yield
(per $1,000,000 face value of the security at a yield of 7.00% pa)

Therefore:

$$\text{Price Volatility} = 24.08 \times 7.00\% \times 20.00\% = 0.337\% \text{ pa}$$

---

the two are related, with the interest rate changes driving the changes in the price of the debt instrument. **Exhibit 9.3** sets out the normal method for converting yield volatility to price volatility. Both yield based and price based measures of volatility are used for debt instruments. In theoretical terms, price volatility is proportional to absolute yield volatility and modified duration.

An observable feature of the relationship between yield and price volatility is that yield volatility increases in a market with decreasing yields whereas price volatility decreases (for similar movements in outright yield).

In practice, both types of yields are utilised with the preferred volatility estimate parameter being driven largely by market convention. In utilising yield volatility estimates, the following points should be noted:

- Yield volatility is usually assumed to be constant for fixed interest instruments of the same yield, implying a flat yield curve that does not change shape and trades at constant yield volatility across all maturities.
- The use of yield volatility has the potential to create confusion where the yield curve shape is itself volatile.
- Yield volatility is not affected by the changing duration associated with fixed coupon bonds.

Utilising price volatility estimates for debt instruments, the following points should be noted:

- The price volatility constantly changes with changing duration of the underlying fixed interest instrument.
- It is necessary to clarify where the price volatility being calculated are the basis of a "clean" (ex interest) or "dirty" (cum accrued interest) price.

In practice, price volatility is used in markets where the underlying security is traded in price (for example, the US Treasury bond market). In addition, yield volatility is used in preference to price volatility in a variety of markets for options on short term interest rates, because price volatility of these instruments is very low.

## 4.4 Considerations in Using Historical/Empirical Volatility[10]

The historical/empirical techniques for volatility estimation seek to quantify past market volatility and use this as a basis for forecasting future market volatility for asset prices.

The major difficulties with this approach include:

- Assumption that the volatility parameters estimated from past data are correct for future periods.
- Specifying the number of observations utilised.
- The availability of a variety of price observations.

---

[10] See Leong, Kenneth "Estimates, Guesstimates and Rules of Thumb" (February 1991) Risk 15–19; Leong, Kenneth "Mean Streets" (May 1991) Risk 45–48.

- Specifying the number of days utilised.
- Allocating relative importance to different components of the time series.

A major difficulty relates to the assumption implied by this technique that past volatility is a useful mechanism for deriving future asset price volatility. The assumed stationary nature of the volatility estimate is neither logical nor supported by empirical evidence. Volatility for a variety of assets demonstrates significant changes over time.

The period over which data is used to generate historical volatility is constantly debated. Proponents of using data over a long period (say, three to five years) implicitly assume that volatility is constant over long periods of time or alternatively tends towards a quantifiable average level of volatility. This is consistent with a hypothesis regarding the mean reverting nature of volatility.

Proponents of using data over a shorter period (between one and three months) base their position on the implied view that volatility itself is not constant but varies significantly, and prefer to use a shorter period to obtain a good estimate of the current level of volatility. Adherents to this theory would, as a consequence, regularly adjust the volatility parameter input into option pricing formulas.

It is clear that the larger the number of observations used to estimate volatility, the higher the probability that changes in, for example, general economic conditions or other exogenous factors, will impact upon the calculated volatility. This causes a violation of the assumption that the standard deviation of the asset's return is constant over the life of the option. The trade-off between increasing the period over which data is utilised in order to achieve more efficient estimates, and the probability that the volatility has altered, is difficult to resolve.

A further complication arises from the fact that the price data used can take a variety of forms including:

- Close-to-close prices.
- Open-to-close prices.
- Close-to-open prices.
- High or low prices.

The use of close-to-close prices is the most common measure used. This measure allows the full daily movement of the asset price to be captured and the impact of all information released over the relevant 24 hour period to be captured. The impact of non-trading days (such as holidays and weekends) tends to distort the data series as information may be released and impact upon prices, but is not captured until a later date. The process of annualisation does not adjust for this phenomenon.

Open-to-close prices provide a measure of intra day volatility that shows reaction to all information released during the trading day. Use of open-to-close prices creates problems of annualisation as it is necessary to be accurate to adjust for the concentration of information released within an average 24 hour period.

Use of close-to-open prices allows a measure of overnight volatility. It shows reaction to information release outside trading hours, and in certain cases, measures the interrelationship between the domestic market and international market in other time zones. The close-to-open price series suffers from the same difficulties as the open to close price series because of difficulties of annualisation.

High or low prices again facilitate capturing of the range of full day price movements in the volatility estimate. It is useful to traders who have intra day positions or are hedging positions intra day.

The major value of the variety of price series and the different estimates of volatility that can be derived lies in the capacity to compare the relative price volatility of the various series.

As noted above, the daily volatility is scaled by the square root of the time to maturity to derive the annualised volatility. There are at least three relevant choices as to the maturity estimate[11]:

- **Calendar days** – the number of actual calendar days between the time of valuation and option maturity.
- **Trading days** – the number of days over the option life on which trading in the relevant asset is open.
- **Economic days** – the number of days over the option life on which information *likely to impact the asset price* is released.

The last concept requires the information release to be *anticipated*. The asset price reacts to both anticipated and unanticipated information. In addition, the use of economic days would necessarily require an understanding of and specific identification of information *likely* to affect asset prices[12].

The distinction between calendar and trading days is more interesting. The volatility estimate used for short dated options is particularly problematic. For example, in the case of an option with a time to expiry of 7 days where there are intervening non-trading days (a weekend and perhaps a holiday), the proportion of non-trading days as a proportion of the life of the option is significant. Similarly,

---

[11] See Leong, Kenneth "Exorcising the Demon" (October 1990) Risk vol 3 no 9 29–35.
[12] For discussion of research on economic days, see Burghardt, Galen and Hanweck, Jr., Gerald A. "Calendar-Adjusted Volatilities" (Winter 1993) The Journal of Derivatives 23–32.

---

**Exhibit 9.4    Adjusting Volatility**

Assume an option with 7 days to expiry. Of these 7 days, 4 days are non-trading days. The market volatility on an annualised basis is 15.00% pa. The volatility of this option is rebased as follows to adjust for the short maturity:
- Rebase the annual volatility to a daily basis: $0.15/\sqrt{250} = 0.009487$
- Re-annualise the daily volatility to an annualised basis adjusted for the lower number of trading days (3 out of 7 or 42.86%). The adjustment is based on the fact that normally the annualisation uses 250 days in a year (or 68.49% of the calendar year). Therefore, the daily volatility is scaled by 156.43 days (42.86% of 365 days): $.009487\sqrt{156.43} = .118655$

The adjusted volatility used would be 11.8655% pa.

If the option had 5 days to expiry, all of which were trading days, then the adjustment would be to rebase it using 365 days (100% trading days) as follows: $.009487\sqrt{365} = .1812$ or 18.12% pa.

---

for a short dated option, there may be no non-trading days. In these cases, the use of the same volatility scaled over the calendar time to maturity appears inappropriate. In practice, some traders adjust the volatility estimate to reflect this factor. **Exhibit 9.4** sets out a common technique used to adjust the volatility estimate.

An additional problem relates to the impact of high value price changes in the calculation of historical volatility estimates. This problem may also be stated as the problem of allocating relative importance to the sequence of data. Consider an un-weighted set of data that contains a single large price change. If that data point is removed, for example where a trailing average for a fixed number of days of price observations is used to calculate the volatility estimate, then the removal of the particular data point will have the impact of substantially altering the volatility either up or down. **Exhibit 9.5** sets out an example of this phenomenon[13].

This problem, together with the desire to give greater weight to more recent data, has led to a number of weighting schemes being proposed. One example of this is the exponential weighting scheme proposed by JP Morgan in its RiskMetrics[TM] models[14]. **Exhibit 9.6** sets out the types of model for volatility estimation. **Exhibit 9.7** sets out an example of the implementation of weighting schemes.

---

[13]   This is often referred to as the *ghost features* of the time series.

[14]   For a discussion of the exponential scheme see JP Morgan (1996) RiskMetric[TM] – Technical Document – Fourth Edition; JP Morgan: New York at 77–101; see also Hull, John (2000) Option Futures and Other Derivatives – Fourth Edition; Prentice-Hall Inc., Upper Saddle River, NJ at 370–372.

**Exhibit 9.5    Impact of Changes in Data Series on Volatility Estimate**

Assume the following sequence of asset prices over a 20 day period:

| Period (Days) | Asset Price ($) |
| --- | --- |
| 0 | 10.68 |
| 1 | 8.25 |
| 2 | 8.18 |
| 3 | 8.20 |
| 4 | 8.20 |
| 5 | 8.21 |
| 6 | 8.12 |
| 7 | 8.15 |
| 8 | 8.07 |
| 9 | 8.13 |
| 10 | 8.17 |
| 11 | 8.20 |
| 12 | 8.16 |
| 13 | 8.19 |
| 14 | 8.12 |
| 15 | 8.04 |
| 16 | 8.19 |
| 17 | 8.09 |
| 18 | 8.12 |
| 19 | 8.18 |
| 20 | 8.27 |

The price sequence in graphical form is as follows:

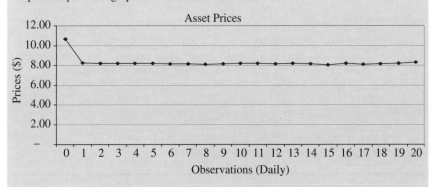

The sequence of asset price is identical to that set out in **Exhibit 9.1** except for the first and final price. In effect it is the same sequence *one day previously*.

The data give an estimate for the daily volatility of 5.83%. Assuming that time is measured in trading days and that there are 250 trading days per year, the estimated annual volatility is 92.25% pa.

This volatility should be contrasted with the significantly lower volatility of 14.05% pa *one day later* when the large price fluctuation at the start of the price series is eliminated. This occurs as the moving average of 20 days eliminates the first price observation in this series the next day.

---

**Exhibit 9.6    Volatility Estimation – Weighting Schemes**

The forecast from the exponential estimator for the variance of returns over the next day is given as:

$$\sigma_t^2 = \lambda \sigma_{t-1}^2 + (1 - \lambda)(x_t - x_{t-1})^2$$

Where

| | |
|---|---|
| $\sigma_t^2$ | = the volatility for day t |
| $\lambda$ | = decay factor (between 0 and 1) |
| $\sigma_{t-1}^2$ | = the volatility estimate made 1 day ago for day t − 1 |
| $(x_t - x_{t-1})$ | = The most recent observation on changes in the market price |

The decay factor is chosen to minimise the error between actual observed volatility and its forecast over the sample period utilised[15].

---

**Exhibit 9.7    Volatility Estimation – Example Weighting Schemes**

Assume the following:

| | |
|---|---|
| $\lambda$ | = decay factor = 0.94 |
| $\sigma_{t-1}$ | = the volatility estimate made 1 day ago for day t − 1 = 1.25% (0.0125) |
| $(x_t - x_{t-1})$ | = The most recent observation on changes in the in the market price = 1.75% (0.0175) |

Therefore:

$$\sigma_t^2 = 0.94 \times 0.0125^2 + (1 - 0.94) \times 0.0175^2 = 0.0165$$
$$\sigma_t = \sqrt{0.0165} = 0.012855 \text{ or } 1.2855\% \text{ per day}$$

---

[15] J.P. Morgan suggest a decay factor ($\lambda$) of 0.94 which across a range of different market variables generated volatility forecasts that are closest to the actual observed volatility; see JP Morgan (1996) RiskMetric$^{\text{TM}}$ – Technical Document – Fourth Edition; JP Morgan: New York at 77–101.

# 5 Implied Volatility

## 5.1 Calculation

The implied volatility approach calculates volatility implied by the current market value of options. This is undertaken by specifying the option price and calculating the volatility that would be needed in a mathematical option pricing formula such as Black-Scholes to derive the specified market price as a fair value of the option. **Exhibit 9.8** sets out an example of the calculation of implied volatility.

The calculation of implied volatility is usually done using an iterative procedure. **Exhibit 9.9** sets out two examples of iterative procedures commonly used[16].

---

**Exhibit 9.8   Volatility Estimation – Implied Volatility**

Assume the same option priced in **Exhibit 7.9**. Key details are summarised below:

| Pricing Inputs | | |
|---|---|---|
| Underlying Asset Price ($) | 105.00 | |
| Strike Price ($) | 100.00 | |
| Option Maturity (years) | 0.50 | |
| Volatility (% pa) | 20.00 | |
| Risk Free Rate (% pa) | 10.00 | |
| Call (0)/Put (1) | 0 | 1 |
| European (0)/American (1) Exercise | 0 | |
| Income on Asset (% pa) | 0.00 | |
| | **Call** | **Put** |
| Option Premium ($) | 11.90 | 2.02 |

Assume the call option is trading in the market at a price of $12.85 and the put option is trading at $2.55. Based on these prices, assuming the underlying asset price, strike price, maturity and risk free rate are known, the implied volatility can be calculated as follows:

| Pricing Inputs | | |
|---|---|---|
| Underlying Asset Price ($) | 105.00 | |
| Strike Price ($) | 100.00 | |
| Option Maturity (years) | 0.50 | |
| Risk Free Rate (% pa) | 10.00 | |
| Call (0)/Put (1) | 0 | 1 |
| European (0)/American (1) Exercise | 0 | 0 |

---

[16] For a discussion of other approaches, see Carrado, Charles and Miller, Thomas "Volatility Without Tears" (July 1996) Risk 49–52; Chance, Don "Leap into the Unknown" (May 1993) Risk 60–66; Weinberger, Ed "The Letter Box" (June 1993) Risk 54–55.

|                                        | Call   | Put    |
| -------------------------------------- | ------ | ------ |
| Option Premium ($)                     | 12.85  | 2.55   |
| Option Premium (% of Asset Price)      | 12.24% | 2.43%  |
| Implied Option Volatility (% pa)       | 24.14% | 22.34% |

### Exhibit 9.9    Iterative Procedures for Calculation of Implied Volatility

The following are two common methods used to calculate implied volatility:

**1. Bisection Method**

The process utilised is as follows:

- A low estimate for volatility is used to determine an option value.
- A high estimate for volatility is used to calculate a second option value.
- The next estimate is determined by an interpolation procedure:

$$\sigma_{low} + (P - P_{low}) \times [(\sigma_{high} - \sigma_{low})/(P_{high} - P_{low})]$$

Where

$\sigma_{high}$; $\sigma_{low}$ is equal to the high or low volatility estimate

$P$; $P_{high}$; $P_{low}$ is equal to the actual observed option premium, option premium for the high and low volatility estimate

- If the interpolated option value is below (above) the actual option premium then the procedure is repeated with the low (high) volatility estimate with the interpolated estimate.
- The procedure entailing the above steps is repeated until the volatility estimate corresponds to the actual price of the option.

**2. Newton Raphson Method**

This procedure is as follows:

- A reasonable estimate for the implied volatility is used to calculate the option premium.
- If the option premium does not correspond to the actual observed option price, then the first estimate is adjusted as follows:

$$(P - P_{first\ estimate})/(\delta C/\delta \sigma)$$

Where

$P - P_{first\ estimate}$ is the actual observed premium and the premium calculated using the first volatility estimate

$\delta C/\delta \sigma$ is the derivative of the option formula with respect to volatility evaluated at the first estimate of volatility:

$$S \times \sqrt{T}(1/\sqrt{2\pi})e^{-d^2/2}$$

Where

$S$  = price of underlying asset

$K$  = strike price

$T$  = time remaining to maturity

$R_f$ = risk free interest rate

$\sigma$  = volatility

$d$  = $[\ln(S/K) + (R_f + \sigma^2/2)T]/\sigma\sqrt{T}$

- The volatility estimate generated is then used to recalculate the option premium.
- The process is repeated until the implied volatility corresponding to the observed market premium is derived.

Source: Kritzman, Mark (1995) The Portable Financial Analyst; Probus Publishing; Chicago, Illinois at 113–122.

## 5.2  Considerations in Using Implied Volatility

The use of implied volatility is based on a circular process. The volatility implied in options currently trading, which measures the volatility level required to clear the market at a given point in time, is treated as being the true constant asset price volatility parameter.

There are additional technical difficulties:

- A major difficulty with implied volatility is that options with different strikes with the same maturity often demonstrate different implied volatility (the so-called smile effect).
- Where options of the relevant type or maturity are not traded this technique is unavailable.

The major value of implied volatility techniques as a method of volatility estimation is that it provides an observable measure of the relevant option market expectations as to volatility.

# 6  Volatility Modelling

## 6.1  ARCH Models[17]

Historical and implied volatility assume that volatility is stable, in that changes in volatility are unpredictable in that volatility *changes* are uncorrelated with previous changes in volatility.

---

[17]  For a discussion of ARCH/GARCH models, see Alexander, Carol "Estimating and Forecasting Volatility and Correlation Using ARCH and GARCH Models" in Das, Satyajit (1997) Risk Management & Financial Derivatives: A Guide to the Mathematics; LBC Information Services, Sydney; McGraw-Hill, Chicago; MacMillan Publishing, England at Chapter 9. See also Engle, Robert F. "Statistical Models for Financial Volatility" (January-February 1993) Financial-Analysts Journal 72–78 at 75; Hull, John (2000) Option Futures and Other Derivatives – Fourth Edition; Prentice-Hall Inc., Upper Saddle River, NJ at 372–381.

This condition would be satisfied if a regression of the squared value of the differences of the asset price changes or returns and the mean of the time series (the error squared) as at time t(n) and the error squared as at time t(n − 1) (the previous observation) showed no significant relationship. This lack of relationship would be evident in:

- The $\beta$ or slope of the regression line should not be significantly different from 0.
- The intercept of the regression line should approximate the average value of the errors squared.
- The residuals around the fitted values equal the differences between the actual values for the errors squared and the predicted values from the regression are randomly distributed around a zero expected value.

If the conditions were satisfied the residuals would be described as homoskedastic (that is, they are serially independent).

In practice, the residuals do not in fact satisfy the above conditions; that is, they are heteroskedastic. This is evident in the following:

- The regression coefficients may or may not be significant.
- The errors squared are related to prior values. For example, there are clusters of positive as well as negative residuals (where the regression underestimates (overestimates) the actual errors squared).
- The errors squared are related in a usually non-linear relationship.

The underlying logic of this approach is that of *volatility clustering* (the high value of the errors squared occur in clusters). Volatility clustering observable in financial markets suggests that volatility may follow a predictable pattern. Large asset price changes seem to be succeeded by a sequence of *further large changes*. This pattern causes volatility to be high after large asset price movements. Increasingly, a variety of statistical/econometric techniques are being applied to volatility estimation. One such technique is the ARCH/GARCH models.

The basic insight underlying ARCH type models is the concept that volatility follows clear patterns. Central to this approach is that the volatility of an asset today depends on the volatility of the asset yesterday, and the "shock" in the price of the asset yesterday. A central element in this approach is that the inter-temporal link in volatility changes over time is relatively constant or stationary. This implies that volatility changes are predictable on the basis of historical volatility. This approach is usually allied to an assumption that volatility regresses towards long-term long run means (that is, it shows a basic mean reversion tendency). ARCH models imply that the best estimate of volatility is not the volatility of the asset *today*. These models show how a change in volatility persists and decays gradually. For example, an increase in asset price leads to an underlying increase in asset volatility with a gradual decrease towards a mean level.

The ARCH models are predicated on correcting for the detected non-linearity through regressing the residuals at time t(n) on the errors squared as at time t2. The coefficients of this second regression are then used to adjust (by adding) to the coefficients of the original regression. This assumes that the variance (the average value of errors squared) is *conditional on the hetroskedasticity*. **Exhibit 9.10** sets out the basic procedure for deriving ARCH estimates.

---

### Exhibit 9.10 Arch Procedures

The ARCH methodology requires the following procedure:
1. The observed means are subtracted from their mean.
2. The difference calculated in the previous step (Step 1) is squared to calculate the errors squared.
3. The errors squared as at time t(n) are regressed against the errors squared as at time t(n − 1) (Regression 1).
4. The fitted errors squared as at time t(n) are subtracted from the observed errors squared as at time t(n − 1).
5. The residuals in the previous step as at time t(n) are regressed on the errors squared as at time t(n − 1) (Regression 2). Under the generalised least square approach, both sides of the regression equation should be divided by the fitted values from Regression 1.
6. The regression coefficients (intercept ($\alpha$) and slope ($\beta$) from the Regression 2 are added to the coefficients from Regression 1 (Regression 3).

The adjusted regression equation (Regression 3) provides a more efficient predictor of variance than the original regression equation. The increased efficiency is only to the degree that the residuals from the original model are heteroskedastic.

Source: Kritzman, Mark (1995) The Portable Financial Analyst; Probus Publishing: Chicago, Illinois at 123–129.

---

An important element of ARCH models is that it more readily explains "fat tailed"/leptokurtic distributions of asset price changes. The major applications of ARCH models have to date been modelling correlation between assets and forecasting volatility.

## 6.2 ARCH Models – Types

A number of variations on basic ARCH/GARCH techniques representing extensions of the basic model are also increasingly being used. These include[18]:
• AARCH – Augmented ARCH or Asymmetric ARCH.

---

[18] See Engle, Robert F. "Statistical Models for Financial Volatility" (January-February 1993) Financial-Analysts Journal 72–78 at 75.

- MARCH – Modified ARCH or Multiplicative ARCH.
- NARCH – Non-linear ARCH.
- PNP ARCH – Partially non-parametric ARCH.
- QTARCH – Qualitative Threshold ARCH.
- SP ARCH – Semi-parametric ARCH.
- TARCH – Threshold ARCH.

The models may have advantages over the basic ARCH models in fitting individual time series. In practice, the GARCH model is the general model used for modelling financial data. There remain questions as to the real benefits of the individual models in modelling and forecasting volatility[19].

# 7   Risk Reversal Volatility

Classical volatility estimates are to a degree non-directional. There is increasing interest in using observed market volatility as a mechanism for inferring information about the future direction of volatility and also of the spot asset price. One such technique is that of risk reversal volatility that is used for these purposes.

Risk reversal volatility uses implied volatility as a mechanism for deriving the market's view of the future path and volatility of asset prices. It is not a mechanism for deriving volatility estimates but is used in parallel with other techniques to provide additional information to calibrate volatility estimates. In particular, it provides valuable information regarding the pattern of volatility, in particular, the volatility smile[20].

Risk reversals may be defined as the following transactions:
1. The purchase of an out of the money call with the simultaneous sale of an out of the money put.
2. The purchase of an out of the money put with the simultaneous sale of an out of the money call.

Typically both transactions are done with the two options both usually having the same expiration date and being of equal size or more typically the same deltas (.25).

---

[19] For an interesting adaptation of ARCH/GARCH approaches to emerging markets where the markets may be controlled, see Jain, Jinendra "Finding the Right Price" (December 1998) Asia Risk 37–39.

[20] See McCauley, Robert and Melick, Will "Risk Reversal Risk" (November 1996) Risk 54–57; McCauley, Robert and Melick, Will "Propensity and Destiny" (November 1996) Risk 54–57.

Transaction 1 above yields a view of the market that is biased to increases in the asset price while transaction 2 evidences a view of the market that is biased to decreases in the asset price. This reflects the economic biases evident in the transactions. **Exhibit 9.11** sets out a diagrammatic view of the transactions using the payoff profiles. **Exhibit 9.12** sets out an example of risk reversal volatility estimation.

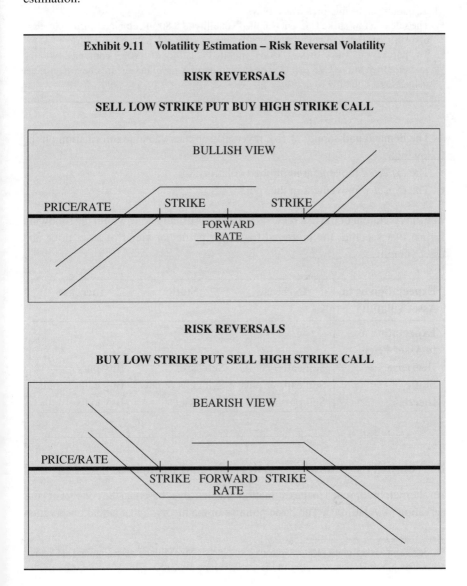

**Exhibit 9.11    Volatility Estimation – Risk Reversal Volatility**

**RISK REVERSALS**

**SELL LOW STRIKE PUT BUY HIGH STRIKE CALL**

BULLISH VIEW

PRICE/RATE      STRIKE            STRIKE

FORWARD
RATE

**RISK REVERSALS**

**BUY LOW STRIKE PUT SELL HIGH STRIKE CALL**

BEARISH VIEW

PRICE/RATE

STRIKE   FORWARD   STRIKE
RATE

---

**Exhibit 9.12   Volatility Estimation – Risk Reversal Volatility Example**

Assume the market is trading 3 month US$/JPY risk reversals as follows:
- 3 month US$/JPY volatility are quoted as 8.50/8.80%.
- 3 month US$/JPY 25 delta risk reversals (premium for JPY calls/US$ puts) are quoted as 0.00/0.20%.

These quotes can be interpreted as follows:
- The sale of a low strike US$ put (implied volatility of 8.80%) combined with a purchase of a US$ call (implied volatility of 8.80%) means a net risk reversal volatility of 0.00%.
- The purchase of a low strike US$ put (implied volatility of 8.70%) combined with the sale of a high strike US$ call (implied volatility of 8.50%) means the client pays a net risk reversal volatility of 0.20%.

---

The demand and supply of risk reversals supplies valuable information on the following:
- The *expected* movement in implied volatility.
- The *expected* movement in the spot.

The interpretation of the risk reversal volatility is usually done within the following format that specifies the preferred trades for particular views of asset price and asset volatility:

| Expectation as to Asset Volatility | Decrease | Static | Increase |
|---|---|---|---|
| **Expectation as to Asset Price** | | | |
| **Decrease** | Sell calls | Sell asset | Buy puts |
| **Static** | Sell calls & puts | Sell calls & puts | Buy calls & puts |
| **Increase** | Sell puts | Buy asset | Buy calls |

# 8   Volatility Estimation – Alternative Approaches

An alternative approach to the estimation of volatility is based on the concept of conservation of volatility[21]. The basic premise of the theory is that actual observation

---

[21]   See Tompkins, Robert (1994) Options Explained[2]; MacMillan Press: England at Chapter 5; Tompkins, Robert "Answer in the Cards" (June 1995) 55–57.

reveals that there are days with high volatility and there are days with low volatility. Any estimate or forecast of volatility is essentially an average of these two elements based on historical data. Utilising this approach, volatility is defined as follows:

$$\sigma = w_1\sigma_n + w_2\sigma_h$$

Where

$\sigma$ = volatility overall
$w_1$ = fraction of days of normal volatility
$\sigma_n$ = normal volatility
$w_2$ = fraction of days of high volatility
$\sigma_h$ = high volatility

This concept is similar to the concept of economic days. This is relevant insofar as it would be expected that days when economic information is released would generally be volatile days.

This approach is used to estimate volatility as follows:

- Existing historical price changes are segmented into two groups – high and normal volatility. This is done using a filter such as changes above a certain threshold level.
- The volatility for each series is calculated normally.
- The estimate for volatility is calculated using the traders' estimate of the number of days of normal versus high volatility in the period to the expiry of the option. The weights are calculated using this scheme and applied to the historical volatility estimates derived for the respective series.

# 9 Behaviour of Volatility

## 9.1 Concept

There are significant weaknesses in current approaches to estimation of volatility. However, increasingly research is identifying several aspects of the *behaviour of volatility*. The behaviour of volatility can be classified into two categories

- **Behaviour of implied volatility** – this consists of two characteristics of implied volatility:
  1. *Volatility smile* – the behaviour of volatility relative to the strike price or yield of the option.
  2. *Term structure of volatility* – the behaviour of volatility relative to time to expiry.

The volatility smile and term structure is typically combined into the volatility surface.

• **Historical volatility** – this relates to the pattern of historical volatility known as the volatility cone.

## 9.2 Volatility Smile[22]

In practice, at-the-money options generally are observed to trade with lower implied volatility relative to out-of-the-money options and to a lesser extent in-the-money options. This phenomenon is described as the volatility smile. It is also referred to as the volatility skew. **Exhibit 9.13** sets out examples of typical implied volatility smiles/skews.

The volatility smile or skew varies significantly between asset classes. For example, the volatility smile for currency options will typically take shapes 1 and 2. In contrast, the volatility smile for equity options may take shape 3. For example, out-of-the-money puts will have significantly higher implied volatility than out-of-the-money calls.

The volatility smile reflects a variety of factors including:

• Adjustments for the distributional assumptions underlying standard option pricing models.
• Directional assumptions regarding the movement in the underlying asset prices which is incorporated into the option volatility and price.
• Clientele effects and the demand for out-of-the-money options.
• The management of option hedging risks by traders.
• Liquidity effects.

The volatility smile is affected by the deviation of observed asset price movements from the assumed log normal distribution. In practice, asset price movements seem to be characterised by the following:

• The market distribution of asset prices changes appears to demonstrate fat tails (statistically described as the kurtosis of the distribution)[23]. This type of

---

[22] See Hull, John (2000) Option Futures and Other Derivatives – Fourth Edition; Prentice-Hall Inc., Upper Saddle River, NJ at Chapter 17. See also Murphy, Gareth "When Options Price Theory Meets the Volatility Smile" (March 1994) Euromoney 66–74.

[23] In practice, distribution of price changes in financial assets are characterised by fat tails and a greater height and concentration in the distribution. In effect, the real distribution is characterised by a greater number of both small and large price changes than consistent with a log normal distribution.

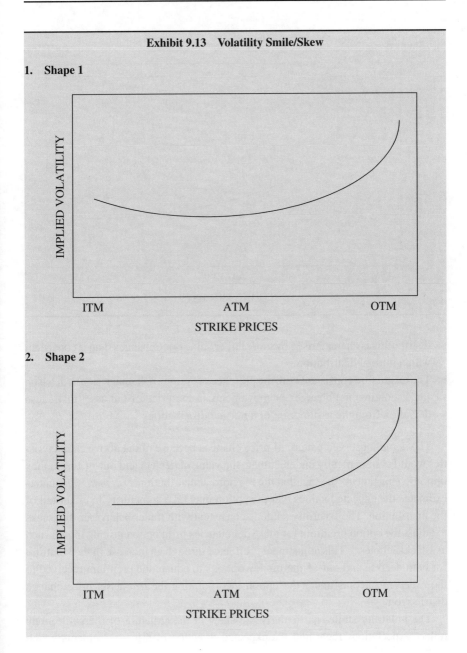

**Exhibit 9.13    Volatility Smile/Skew**

1.  **Shape 1**

2.  **Shape 2**

3.  Shape 3

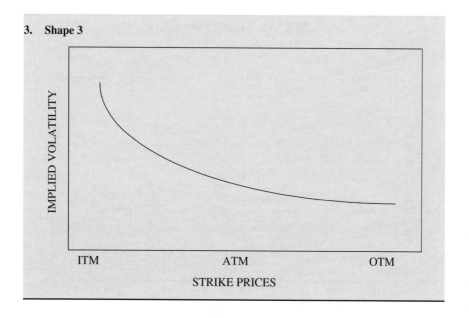

distribution is characterised by more larger value price changes than is consistent
with a normal distribution.
*   The fat tails are consistent with the presence of "jump" risk, that is non-stochastic
    (or discontinuous) changes or movements in the price of the asset that cause
    deviation from the assumption of a normal distribution.

The *actual* observed pattern of price changes because of the above characteristics would systematically underestimate the value of deep in and out-of-the-money
options. This reflects the fact that the log normal distribution *systematically* underestimates the expected values that the option may take at maturity in either tail of
the distribution. The volatility smile is consistent with trader behaviour that seeks
to adjust the option premium for these deficiencies in an option pricing model such
as Black-Scholes[24]. This adjustment is effected through an increase in the volatility
for both deep in and out-of-the-money options to equate the premium received to
the *expected* payouts under the option incorporating the *true* asset price change
distribution.

The volatility smile, particularly the skew in the structure of the smile, may
reflect expectations regarding the expected direction of price movements which

---

[24]   This approach is suggested by Fischer Black in "How to use the Holes in Black-Scholes"
       (1989) 1 (No 4) Continental Bank Journal of Applied Corporate Finance 59.

are incorporated in the option price and by implication, the implied volatility. For example, if the US$/JPY is expected to decline from its current level of US 1 = Yen 110 then US$ puts/JPY calls may be more valuable and US$ calls/JPY puts with a strike price at or above the spot rate may be correspondingly less valuable. The directional view may be reflected in the option price that will be higher than in the absence of this expectation, and reflected in the implied volatility.

The higher price and implied volatility can be considered to be the higher expected economic cost of hedging or dynamically replicating the option. The smile and the skew are also consistent with the inherent nature of log normal distributions that have a natural skew to the right hand tail, implying a higher probability of a rise than a fall in the asset price. Implied volatility, if it is sought to adjust for the skew, should be higher for options with strike prices below the implied forward rate (assumed to be the mean of the distribution) than for options with strike prices above the implied forward prices to correct for the natural bias in prices.

The market for options with different strike prices appears to exhibit significant biases in demand and supply (a clientele effect). Out-of-the-money options are attractive vehicles for speculative investment demand reflecting the following factors:

- The gearing or leverage of the out-of-the-money options (expressed as the asset price divided by the option premium) is higher.
- The low absolute cash investment entailed in the purchase of the option.

For equity put options, concern about the risk of large and unexpected price falls (crashes) may be reflected in implied volatility[25].

These factors dictate significant demand for out-of-the-money options. The supply of these types of options is constrained by the fact that option traders are reluctant to sell/write these out-of-the-money options. This reflects the difficulty of hedging or replicating these options in the event of a jump in the asset price (high gamma risk)[26].

In contrast, the position for in-the-money options is influenced by different factors. The dominating characteristic of these types of options is that they have a high delta and move closely with movements with the underlying asset prices. This allows in-the-money-options to be used as a direct substitute for the asset itself.

---

[25] This is termed "crashophobia" by Mark Rubinstein, see Hull, John (2000) Option Futures and Other Derivatives – Fourth Edition; Prentice-Hall Inc., Upper Saddle River, NJ at 440.
[26] See Chapter 16.

The primary demand for these options is from traders who need to trade in the underlying asset. The high delta of the options may enable the option to be substituted for the asset in the replication process. This has the effect of lowering the financing costs in replicating the option synthetically. Other traders or participants seeking to synthesise positions in the asset at lower cost may find these in-the-money options attractive. The supply of these options is limited. This reflects the reluctance to write a deep in-the-money option because, in the absence of a large or extreme price movement, the option will be exercised, requiring the seller to buy or sell the asset at a price that is disadvantageous to them. In addition, such options do not have significant time or volatility value, further reducing their attractiveness to the seller.

The interaction of supply and demand for these deep in-the-money-options results in the option price and implied volatility being bid up above comparable volatility for at-the-money options of the same maturity.

The volatility smile also incorporates the impact of traders seeking to manage the risk of option transactions. Traders seek to replicate options through a process of trading in the underlying asset. This approach to option portfolio management is consistent with standard option pricing models, such as Black-Scholes. The models derive the fair value of the option as the cost of dynamically hedging a short position in the option through a position in the asset that is adjusted continuously, including the funding cost of the position[27].

The process of option replication is, in practice, not free from risk. The primary risks are the possibility of a sudden gap or jump in asset prices (a large value price change) that requires a substantial adjustment to the position in the asset to be effected. This reflects the fact that the option delta has changed significantly. The option writer is also exposed to changes in volatility that will cause changes in both the value of the options and its delta, requiring re-hedging through trading in the asset. The risks usually referred to, the gamma and vega risk, cannot be hedged through trading in the asset. This is because the asset itself has low or no gamma (that is, the convexity of the asset price is significantly lower than the convexity of the option) and no vega risk. Gamma and vega risk can only be offset by trading in an option on the underlying asset.

In practice, the problems in hedging require traders to trade in options to manage the risks in their option portfolios. Traders typically trade in short dated at-the-money options to manage gamma and to a lesser extent vega risks. This creates

---

[27] This process referred to as delta hedging or dynamic option replication is discussed in detail in Chapter 16.

significant demand for these options, as traders rebalance hedges frequently in response to market movements in the asset price and volatility. The supply for these options is also strong, reflecting the high volatility or time value of these at-the-money options that makes them attractive for sellers.

The combination of the above factors results in differential liquidity of options with different strike prices for a given maturity. The volatility of at-the-money options is lower, reflecting the higher liquidity of these options from the greater balance between supply and demand for these options. In and out-of-the-money are less frequently traded, and the imbalance of demand relative to supply is reflected in the higher implied volatility relative to the at-the-money options. The resultant volatility smile is often skewed with out-of-the-money options demonstrating higher volatility than both at and in-the-money option. The volatility smile also appears to diminish with maturity, reflecting the reduced impact of the factors identified.

## 9.3   Term Structure of Volatility[28]

The term structure of volatility encompasses the relationship between volatility and the time to expiry of the option. In general terms, volatility for shorter time to expiry options is higher than the volatility for options with longer times to expiry. **Exhibit 9.14** sets out the general observed term structure of volatility.

The pattern of decreasing volatility relative to option maturity essentially reflects:
- The expectations of larger price movements in the very near future that drive the implied volatility levels to higher levels for short dated options.
- The proportionately larger impact on option values of large asset price changes in the asset price on short dated options, and the relatively higher risk to the seller of these options that must be compensated for through higher premiums and higher implied volatility.
- The mean reversion nature of volatility that seems to fall (rise) from high (low) absolute level towards a long run mean level.

## 9.4   Volatility Surfaces

The patterns of implied volatility (the smile and term structure) are combined into a volatility surface. **Exhibit 9.15** sets out an example of a typical volatility surface.

---

[28]   See Hull, John (2000) Option Futures and Other Derivatives – Fourth Edition; Prentice-Hall Inc., Upper Saddle River, NJ at Chapter 17.

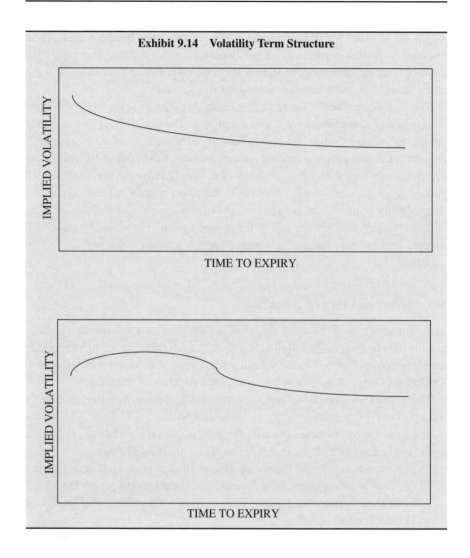

Exhibit 9.14    Volatility Term Structure

The surface is generated for the purpose of valuation of portfolios of options that may contain a range of options with substantially different strike prices and time to expiry. The surface is derived from observed implied volatility or specified volatility obtained from other sources. Interpolation procedures are used to complete points on the surface that are either unavailable or not traded. The volatility estimates generated from the surface are then used to determine the value of the options in the portfolio.

**Exhibit 9.15 Volatility Surface**

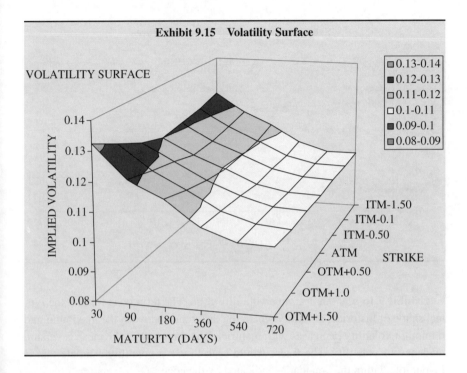

## 9.5 Volatility Cones[29]

The concept of the volatility cone is based on the fact that in projecting volatility over the life of the option, the trader may seek to project the average, highest and lowest volatility based on history. This is designed to ensure that the estimated volatility is unlikely to be exceeded (assuming the option is sold). This entails the projection of maximum, minimum and historical volatility for at the money options for different maturities[30].

The steps used to generate the volatility cone are as follows:
- The actual historical volatility for each relevant maturity (1 month, 3 months etc) is estimated from historical data.
- The average, maximum and minimum historical volatility for each maturity is then calculated.

[29] This approach is attributed to Galen Burghardt, see Tompkins, Robert (1994) Options Explained[2]; MacMillan Press: England at 179.

[30] For a discussion of volatility cones, see Tompkins, Robert (1994) Options Explained[2]; MacMillan Press: England at 179–186.

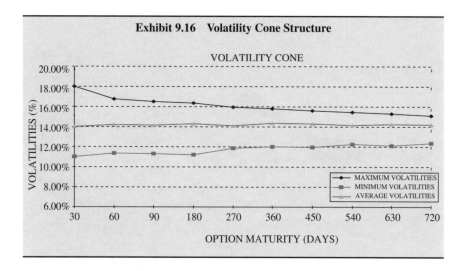

Exhibit 9.16    Volatility Cone Structure

**Exhibit 9.16** sets out a sample volatility cone. The term cone reflects the typical shape of historical volatility where the difference between the maximum and minimum volatility decreases with maturity. This may reflect the mean reversion tendency of volatility. The trader would seek to use a volatility estimate that is favourable within the boundaries indicated by the cone.

## 9.6    Forward Volatility

The concept of forward volatility is analogous to the concept of forward asset prices such as forward interest rates. It focuses on the implied forward volatility calculated as the forward variance. **Exhibit 9.17** sets out an example of the calculation of forward volatility.

# 10    Stochastic Volatility

## 10.1    Concept

Traditional option pricing models do not incorporate the observed structure of volatility (such as the volatility smile/skew or term structure). This is problematic for a number of reasons. The major problems arise from the potential mis-pricing or mis-valuation of option positions. It also creates difficulties in hedging option positions with traded options in the market (where the market prices incorporate the observed volatility behaviours). The hedging problem is present in all options but is

---

**Exhibit 9.17    Forward Volatility**

Assume volatility is trading as follows:

0.5 year (184 days):          16.40% pa (.1640)
1 year (365 days):            15.25% pa (.1525)

The forward volatility is given by the following relationship[31]:

$$\sigma_{forward} = \sqrt{[t_m \cdot \sigma_{tm}^2 - t_n \sigma_{tn}^2]/(t_m - t_n)}$$

Where
$\sigma_{forward}$ = forward volatility
$\sigma_{tm}, \sigma_{tn}$ = volatility for maturity n or m
$t_n$    = shorter maturity n
$t_m$    = longer maturity m

Applying the formula to the assumptions the derived forward volatility is given as follows:

Forward volatility (181 day forward in 184 days time)
$$= \sqrt{[365. \, 0.1525^2 - 184. \, 0.1640^2]/(365 - 184)} = 0.1398 \text{ or } 13.98\% \text{ pa}$$

---

exacerbated in the case of exotic options[32]. This is because the payoff on an exotic option is generally sensitive to the shape of the volatility smile or term structure. This reflects the fact that the payoff on these options is driven by different aspects of the future distribution of the asset price as compared to traditional options.

The attempts to incorporate the observed behaviour of volatility in option pricing models ranges from models incorporating alternative diffusion processes (such as jumps)[33] to models incorporating stochastic volatility[34]. The models effectively introduce a stochastic volatility term into the option pricing process. This replaces the traditional constant volatility term.

---

[31]  See Tompkins, Robert (1994) Options Explained[2]; MacMillan Press: England at 191.

[32]  See Das, Satyajit (2004) Structured Products Volume 1; John Wiley & Sons (Asia), Singapore at Chapters 5 and 7 to 11 (inclusive).

[33]  See Chapter 7; see also Cox, J.C. and Ross, S.A. "The Valuation of Options for Alternative Stochastic Processes" (March 1976) Journal of Financial Economics 145–166; Rubinstein, Mark "Displaced Diffusion Option Pricing" (March 1983) Journal of Finance 213–217.

[34]  For early examples of stochastic models, see Hull, J.C. and White, Alan "An Analysis of the Bias in Option Pricing Caused by a Stochastic Volatility" (1988) Advances in Futures and Options Research 3 27–61; Heston, S.L. "A Closed Form Solution for Options with Stochastic Volatility with Applications to Bonds and Currency Options" (1993) Review of Financial Studies Vol 6 No 2 327–343.

The major development has been the emergence of volatility models that incorporate the impact of the volatility smile and term structure. The stochastic volatility term is usually a function of the strike price and the term of the option. The volatility function is derived from available market prices for options. This entails calculating the implied option volatility using an option pricing model. This allows the construction of an option pricing model that uses and is consistent with market volatility structures. In this Section, these models of volatility incorporating the observed behaviour of volatility are considered.

## 10.2   Types of Volatility Models

There are in practice several different types of volatility models that allow incorporation of the observed market volatility[35]:
- **Volatility-by-spot** (also referred to as local volatility or implied tree/diffusion models).
- **Volatility-by strike** (also referred to as sticky volatility).
- **Volatility-by-delta** (also referred to as volatility-by-moneyness or sticky delta models).

In practice, the volatility-by-spot models are most commonly used[36].

## 10.3   Local Volatility/Implied Tree or Diffusion Models[37]

The local volatility/implied tree or diffusion models were first proposed in the early 1990s[38]. The concept requires the constant volatility term in option pricing models

---

[35]   See Derman, Emanuel, Kamal, Michael, Kani, Iraj, McClure, John and Zou, Joseph "Investing in Volatility" (June 1998) FOW – Black-Scholes-Merton Supplement 7–11; Derman, Emanuel "Regimes of Volatility" (April 1999) Risk 55–59. For an interesting discussion of the type of models, see also an interview with Eric Reiner in "Eric Reiner" (January 2000) Derivatives Strategy 36–40. The categorisation used is that suggested by Eric Reiner.

[36]   Other models (such as analytic jump-diffusion models) have also been proposed, see Andersen, Leif and Andreasen, Jesper "Jumping Smiles" (November 1999) Risk 65–68.

[37]   See Hull, John (2000) Option Futures and Other Derivatives – Fourth Edition; Prentice-Hall Inc., Upper Saddle River, NJ at 485–486; Rebanato, Riccardo (1999) Estimating Volatility and Correlation; John Wiley, New York at 4–8; Wilmott, Peter (1998) Derivatives: The Theory and Practice of Financial Engineering; John Wiley & Sons, Chichester, at Chapter 22. See also Blacher, Guillaume "Pricing with a Volatility Smile" (22–28 February 2000) Financial Products 8–9.

[38]   See Dupire, Bruno "Pricing with a Smile" (January 1994) Risk 18–20; Derman, Emanuel and Kani, Iraj "Riding on a Smile" (February 1994) Risk 32–39; Rubinstein, Mark "Implied Binomial Trees" (July 1994) Journal of Finance 771–818.

to be replaced by a volatility term that is a function of both the spot price and the time to expiry of the option. This is done by replacing the standard diffusion term with a local volatility diffusion term. **Exhibit 9.18** sets out the different diffusion terms used. The approach requires the volatility used to fit the current observed market volatility (that is consistent with the volatility smile and the volatility term structure).

The implementation of the model is driven by the manner in which the model volatility is fitted to the market volatility. This can be calculated analytically[39] or using an implied binomial tree[40].

The tree approach entails constructing a tree that is consistent with the market prices of options and implicitly, the implied volatility smile and term structure. The implied tree is effectively a binomial tree where the position of the nodes is determined to fit the observed volatility structure. This is done using numerical procedures (such as forward induction). The process entails using the observed volatility surface to determine the *local volatility surface*. The local volatility surface is in effect the forward volatility (in effect, the current market implied future volatility when the asset price is at a specific level and the time to expiry is specified). The local volatility is then used to re-shape the binomial tree that is then used to price all options.

## 10.4  Volatility-by-Strike and Volatility-by-Delta Models

The volatility-by-strike models assume that as asset prices change over time, the implied volatility for an individual option will stay approximately the same. This implies that, for example, as the asset price goes up, an option with a fixed strike price (that is at-the-money but now out-of-the-money) will continue to trade at the same volatility. Other options at different fixed strike prices will also continue to trade at their pre-existing different volatility. Restated in relative terms, for example, the implied volatility of at-the-money options will decrease by the difference between the implied volatility of the two options. This is contrary to what the volatility-by-strike model would predict.

The volatility-by-delta models assumes that volatility of options with the same "money-ness" (effectively, the option delta) trade at the same volatility. This implies

---

[39]  See Dupire, Bruno "Pricing with a Smile" (January 1994) Risk 18–20; Andersen, L.B.G. and Brotherton-Ratcliffe, R. "The Equity Option Volatility Smile: An Implicit Finite Difference Approach" (Winter 1997/98) Journal of Computational Finance 5–37.

[40]  See Derman, Emanuel and Kani, Iraj "Riding on a Smile" (February 1994) Risk 32–39; Rubinstein, Mark "Implied Binomial Trees" (July 1994) Journal of Finance 771–818.

---

**Exhibit 9.18   Local Volatility/Implied Tree Diffusion Process**

**1.   Standard Diffusion Process**

$$dS = (r - y)S\, dt + \sigma S\, dz$$

Where
- S   = the spot price of the asset
- dS = the change in the spot price over time dt
- r   = the continuously compounded or instantaneous interest rate
- y   = the continuously compounded or instantaneous return or income on the asset
- dt  = a small interval in time
- $\sigma$   = volatility of the asset price
- dz = a Wiener process with mean 0 and a variance equal to dt

**2.   Local Volatility Diffusion Process**

$$dS = (r(t) - y(t))S\, dt + \sigma(S, t)S\, dz$$

Where
- r(t)     = the continuously compounded or instantaneous forward interest rate at time t
- y(t)     = the continuously compounded or instantaneous return or income on the asset at time t
- $\sigma(S, t)$ = volatility of the asset price as a function of both spot price and time to expiry

All other parameters are the same as above.

---

that as the asset price changes over time, the applicable volatility is driven by changes in the option delta[41].

## 10.5   Stochastic Volatility Models – Assessment

The various volatility models that have emerged provide interesting insights into the nature of volatility. In practice, the implied tree or diffusion approach is the most commonly used[42].

---

[41]   This is a version of a rule often used in currency options where the implied volatility for a given strike is calculated as the at-the-money volatility plus a constant times the delta of the relevant strike minus the delta of the at-the-money option.

[42]   In part, this reflects implementation issues in respect of the other models. Models that create an implied distribution where volatility is a function of the spot price and time to

The major advantages of the models include:

- The ability to price conventional and exotic options within a consistent framework.
- The ability to hedge options, particularly exotic options, with conventional options[43].
- All Greeks and risk management measures are consistent and directly comparable.

The models are difficult to implement. This relates partly to data problems. The implied diffusion process assumes availability of implied volatility for all options (different strike and maturity). In practice, this condition is rarely satisfied. This requires the use of interpolation techniques (either linear or non-linear) to estimate implied volatility for the purpose of creating the implied tree. The models seem, in practice, to be sensitive to the estimate of unobserved volatility creating model problems. In addition, the models seem to perform differently in different asset classes[44].

At a more fundamental level, the volatility models are no more than the market consensus of future volatility including the volatility smile and term structure. There is no evidence that the implied volatility is a good and consistent predictor of future actual market volatility. In effect, as the market volatility changes day to day, the implied local volatility structure also varies.

In practice, the major benefit is the ability to use conventional options to hedge exotic options. However, where the options are dynamically hedged, the use of volatility models may in fact introduce significant additional model risks in hedging.

# 11  Volatility Estimation – In Practice[45]

Volatility estimation in practice is a complex activity, it requires an understanding of the following:

- The various volatility estimates available and their significance.
- Behaviour of volatility parameters.

---

maturity are available. In contrast, models that build the equivalent implied distribution for, say, a volatility-by-strike model are currently not commonly available.

[43]  In effect, this reduces model risk in hedging; see Chapter 16.

[44]  There is some evidence that volatility-by-delta is a good estimator for currency and long dated equity options.

[45]  See Spinner, Karen "Estimating Volatility" (March 1997) Derivatives Strategy 30–32.

484 until it was

In practice, market participants take into consideration the following types of volatility:

- Implied versus historical volatility.
- Implied versus predicted volatility.
- Implied or historical volatility versus actual volatility.

The difference between implied and historical volatility is useful in predicting potential changes in volatility, while differences between implied versus predicted volatility determines a variety of trading strategies used by market participants. The relationship of the implied historical volatility versus actual realised volatility provides the basis for adjusting expectations of future asset price volatility.

In practice, the attitude to volatility estimation and the relative importance assigned to each of these methodologies will depend to some extent on the activities of the market participant and the risks sought to be managed. For example, an intra-day trader will take a different view to a participant seeking to hedge longer term positions. Similarly, volatility estimation for hedging short versus long dated options may be different. Generation of volatility for the purposes of risk management, as distinct from option valuation, may also be different.

The volatility estimates available are in practice influenced by the underlying liquidity in assets. The lack of liquidity, signified by wider bid-offer spreads for particular securities, will generally be reflected in the pricing of options (that is, the implied volatility).

The emergence of volatility models has in practice changed the process of volatility estimation in option pricing. The emphasis is on understanding the market volatility (derived from market option prices) and ensuring that options (both conventional and exotic) are priced consistent with the observed volatility structure. This in part reflects the difficulties with volatility estimation generally. The volatility models assume both the availability of a sufficient number of option prices, and the fact that option positions are in effect hedged statically (that is, with other options).

# 12   Estimation of Correlation[46]

## 12.1   Concept

Correlation is a statistical measure of the degree to which two variables are related.

---

[46] See Bhansali, Vineer (1998) Pricing and Managing Exotic and Hybrid Options"; McGraw-Hill, New York at Chapter 4; Hull, John (2000) Option Futures and Other Derivatives – Fourth Edition; Prentice-Hall Inc., Upper Saddle River, NJ at 382–383;

Correlation is used in the pricing of certain forms of exotic options (primarily multi-factor options such as basket options, quanto options, exchange options, best-of and worst-of options, spread options and yield curve options)[47]. In these options, the price relationship between the assets determines the payoff requiring the correlation between the assets to be estimated. There are in practice two types of price relationship that are estimated using correlation:

- **Primary price relationship** – this is where the correlation between the assets has a direct impact on the option price; for example basket options, exchange options, best-of and worst-of options, spread options and yield curve options.
- **Secondary price relationship** – this is where the correlation affects the relationship between the asset price and movement in a second variable (typically, exchange rates) and therefore has a secondary effect on the option price; for example quanto options.

Correlation is used to design hedges. Correlation is also used in investment management for asset allocation decisions and risk management using VAR models.

## 12.2  Estimation Approaches

Correlation may be estimated from historical data. **Exhibit 9.19** sets out an example of estimating correlation from historical data using simple linear (ordinary least squares) regression methodology[48]. Alternative methodologies for estimation of correlation include exponential weighted moving average models[49] or GARCH Models[50].

---

Rebanato, Riccardo (1999) Estimating Volatility and Correlation; John Wiley, New York at 3.

[47] See Das, Satyajit (2004) Structured Products Volume 1; John Wiley & Sons (Asia), Singapore at Chapters 5 and 7 to 11 (inclusive).

[48] For a discussion of correlation estimation, see Gillespie, Tom "Mathematical Techniques" in Das, Satyajit (Editor) (1997) Risk Management & Financial Derivatives: A Guide to the Mathematics; LBC Information Services, Sydney; McGraw-Hill, Chicago at Chapter 19; Kritzman, Mark (1995) The Portable Financial Analyst; Probus Publishing: Chicago, Illinois at Chapter 10 or see any standard textbook on statistics.

[49] See Hull, John (2000) Option Futures and Other Derivatives – Fourth Edition; Prentice-Hall Inc., Upper Saddle River, NJ at 382–383.

[50] See Hull, John (2000) Option Futures and Other Derivatives – Fourth Edition; Prentice-Hall Inc., Upper Saddle River, NJ at 382–383; Engle, R. and Mezrich J. "GARCH for Groups" (August 1996) Risk 36–40.

## 12.3    Correlation Estimation – In Practice

In practice, the process of correlation estimation is problematic. Correlation estimates based on historical data tend to be unstable and are often a poor predictor of actual correlation over the relevant period. There are additional problems of asynchronous data. This arises from the fact that data used to compute correlation may not be obtained at the same point in time, as the relevant markets are not simultaneously open for trading. A further major problem with the estimation of volatility is that unlike volatility it is very difficult to determine *implied* correlation. This is because there are very few traded instruments from which a market correlation parameter can be derived.

---

**Exhibit 9.19    Estimation Correlation – Linear Regression Methodology**

**1. Assumptions**
Assume the following price for an individual stock and the relevant stock index over 20 days. The price changes in the stocks and index are also set out.

| Observation (Daily) | Stock Price ($) | Stock Price Changes (%) | Index Price | Index Price Changes (%) |
|---|---|---|---|---|
| 0 | 10.25 | | 1500.4 | |
| 1 | 10.26 | 0.098 | 1512.1 | 0.780 |
| 2 | 10.18 | −0.780 | 1511.8 | −0.020 |
| 3 | 10.12 | −0.589 | 1505.6 | −0.410 |
| 4 | 9.85 | −2.668 | 1477.6 | −1.860 |
| 5 | 9.87 | 0.203 | 1470.4 | −0.487 |
| 6 | 9.87 | 0.000 | 1475.2 | 0.326 |
| 7 | 9.92 | 0.507 | 1484.9 | 0.658 |
| 8 | 9.88 | −0.403 | 1481.7 | −0.216 |
| 9 | 9.91 | 0.304 | 1481.8 | 0.007 |
| 10 | 9.9 | −0.101 | 1480.2 | −0.108 |
| 11 | 9.95 | 0.505 | 1482.6 | 0.162 |
| 12 | 10.04 | 0.905 | 1484.1 | 0.101 |
| 13 | 9.98 | −0.598 | 1485.2 | 0.074 |
| 14 | 10.01 | 0.301 | 1489.2 | 0.269 |
| 15 | 10.01 | 0.000 | 1487.2 | −0.134 |
| 16 | 10.04 | 0.300 | 1490.6 | 0.229 |
| 17 | 9.98 | −0.598 | 1490.8 | 0.013 |
| 18 | 9.96 | −0.200 | 1485.2 | −0.376 |
| 19 | 9.94 | −0.201 | 1486.1 | 0.061 |
| 20 | 9.99 | 0.503 | 1490.4 | 0.289 |

The following graphs set out the stock and index values and the price changes:

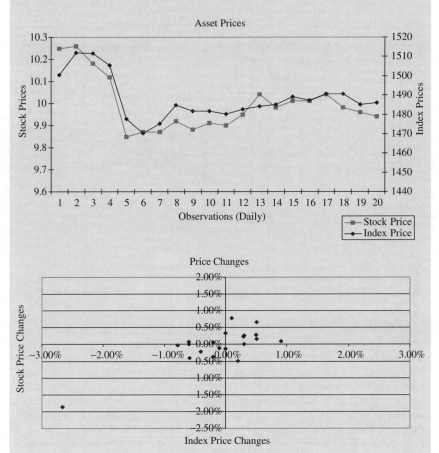

## 2. Linear Regression

The linear regression entails fitting a straight line (the regression line) to the price changes. The line is fitted so that the sum of the differences of the observed stock price changes from the values implied by the regression line is minimised.

The regression equation is specified as follows:

$$Y = \alpha + \beta X$$

Where

    Y = the predicted change in the stock price

    $\alpha$ = the intercept of the regression line with the vertical axis

    $\beta$ = the slope of the regression line

    X = the change in the index

The estimated regression line (using a least squares minimisation technique) is as follows:

$$Y = -0.09\% + 0.791X$$

The estimated correlation is taken to be the slope of the regression line ($\beta$) or 0.791. The fitted line is shown below:

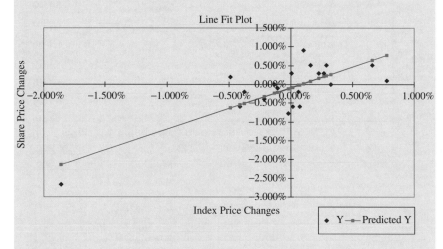

**3. Analysis**
In order to establish whether the regression equation provides a good fit to the data, it is usual to examine the variance. This is generally referred to as the $R^2$ or coefficient of determination. This measures the degree to which the regression equation is a good predictor of the dependent variable. $R^2$ has a value between 0 and 1. In this example, it is 0.626. A high (low) value for $R^2$ indicates a strong (weak) relationship between the dependent and independent variable. Other measures used include the standard error (in this example: 0.005) which measure the dispersion of the residuals around the regression line.

In order to overcome these problems, some practitioners have developed a number of approaches to estimation of correlation. These are similar in approach to different ways of estimating volatility. These include[51]:

* **Moving correlation window** – under this approach, a series of correlation estimates are calculated for successive overlapping time series data to create *distributions* of correlation. This may be combined with a term structure of correlation. The approach is similar to the concept of the volatility cone.

---

[51] For a discussion of these approaches, see Bhansali, Vineer (1998) Pricing and Managing Exotic and Hybrid Options"; McGraw-Hill, New York at Chapter 4.

- **Exponential smoothing** – this uses smoothed data to estimate correlation[52].
- **ARCH/GARCH models** – this uses ARCH/GARCH techniques to estimate time varying correlation estimates.
- **Co-integration techniques** – this uses statistical methods to extract the long run dynamic relationship between two time series.

# 13 Summary

Volatility and to a lesser extent, correlation estimates, are essential to the valuation of options. The relevant parameters are required to be estimates of the actual volatility and correlation to be experienced over the time to expiry of the option. The *future* volatility and correlation are not directly observable and must be estimated.

A common approach is to calculate historical volatility and correlation. In the case of volatility, implied volatility from traded option prices is also available. However, in practice, either historical or implied volatility or correlation provides an accurate estimate of the volatility and correlation to be experienced in the future. In relation to option volatility, a considerable body of knowledge exists about the behaviour of volatility (the smile and term structure effects). Increasingly, volatility models that seek to ensure that option prices are calculated consistent with observable market volatility are used. This ensures consistency of pricing and also accuracy/effectiveness of hedging. However, the fundamental problem of volatility estimation remains largely unresolved and problematic.

---

[52] See Hull, John (2000) Option Futures and Other Derivatives – Fourth Edition; Prentice-Hall Inc., Upper Saddle River, NJ at 382–383.

# 10
# Pricing Interest Rate & Currency Swaps

## 1 Overview

Swap transactions are in effect portfolios of forward contracts. Consistent with the general approach to the pricing of over-the-counter ("OTC") instruments, swaps are priced through a process where the transaction is decomposed into a series of individual forward contracts that are then priced separately. The price of the swap is given by the value of the portfolio of forwards. In the case of interest rate and currency swaps, an alternative methodology is to utilise the zero coupon rates to price the swaps. This approach is used with all types of swaps. In this Chapter, the pricing of interest rate and currency swaps is examined[1].

The structure of this Chapter is as follows:

- The overall approach to swap pricing is outlined.
- The pricing of interest rate swaps as a portfolio of forward contracts (including the use of futures contracts) and the use of zero coupon rates to value interest rate swaps is described.
- The pricing of cross currency swaps is outlined.
- The design of non-generic swap structures and the trading of interest rate and currency swaps are discussed.

## 2 Swap Pricing – Approach

The cost of a typical interest rate swap of a given maturity is quoted as a fixed rate (for example, 6.00% pa) against a floating rate index quoted flat (that is,

---

[1] For a discussion of the pricing of other types of swaps (equity swaps and commodity swaps) see Das, Satyajit (2004) Structured Products Volume 2; John Wiley & Sons (Asia), Singapore at Chapters 1 and 7.

with no margin over or under the index). In a number of markets, the price on a generic interest rate swap is quoted as a spread over a fixed rate index (spread to an underlying government bond rate) against the floating rate index flat. The price of a typical currency swap is quoted in a manner very similar to that utilised in the case of interest rate swaps. Typically, the price of a currency swap of a given maturity is quoted as a fixed rate (expressed as either an absolute rate or as a spread over the relevant government fixed rate index in the currency) against the receipt of US$3 or 6 month LIBOR. For example, A$ currency swaps might be quoted as 7.50% pa against US$3 month LIBOR. Alternatively, the same currency swap could be quoted as the relevant A$ bond plus a margin of 60bps versus US$6 month LIBOR flat[2].

Swap pricing is predicated on the following approaches:

- **Pricing the swap as a portfolio of forward contracts** – under this approach the swap contract is re-constituted as a portfolio of forward contracts. The forward contracts are then priced as individual forward contracts. The value of the swap is given by the portfolio of forward contracts[3].
- **Pricing the swap using zero coupon rates** – under this approach swap cash flows are restated as cash flows under equivalent bonds or similar securities (either floating rate or fixed rate bonds/notes). The swap cash flows are then valued as bonds or similar transactions using standard compound interest and present value concepts at the prevailing zero coupon rates[4]. The swap rate is determined as the rate that, at the prevailing zero coupon rates, results in the transaction (usually a simultaneous purchase and sale of bonds) having equivalent value at the commencement of the transaction[5].

---

[2]  For quotation conventions, see Chapter 3.

[3]  This equivalence has structuring implications for tax driven derivative transactions, see Das, Satyajit (2004) Structured Products Volume 2; John Wiley & Sons (Asia), Singapore at Chapter 19.

[4]  For a discussion of the derivation of the zero coupon curve, see Chapter 5.

[5]  The basic financial mathematics required to value swap transactions utilises standard time value of money or net present value/discounted cash flow concepts. The discussion in this section/chapter and the book assumes an understanding of net present value (NPV) and internal rate of return (IRR) concepts. For readers seeking to revise their understanding of these concepts, see Knox, David M., Zima, Petr and Brown, Robert L. (1984) Mathematics of Finance; McGraw-Hill, New York; Crapp, Harvey R. and Marshall, John (1986) Money Market Maths; Allen and Unwin, Sydney; Marshall, John (1991) Money Equals Maths; Allen and Unwin, Sydney; Cartledge, Peter (1991) A Handbook of Financial Mathematics; Euromoney Books, London; Sherris, Michael (1996) Money and Capital Markets: Pricing, Yields and Analysis – Second Edition; Allen and Unwin, Sydney; Martin, John (1996) Derivatives Maths; IFR Publishing, London at Chapter 3;

The two techniques are equivalent. This is because the zero coupon rate can be replicated by compounding a series of interest rate forward contracts. In practice, short dated swaps (particularly interest rate swaps) may be directly priced off the interest rate forwards available in the market. This is primarily via the use of interest rate futures contracts (such as the Eurodollar or Euro-ibor futures contract). These contracts are used to hedge the transactions. In practice, the futures rates are used to derive the zero coupon rate. This means that pricing swaps using the zero coupon rates in effect relates the swap price to the portfolio of forward contracts. In practice, therefore, *all* swaps are generally priced off zero coupon rates, although shorter dated swaps may be hedged by replicating the transaction in the futures or FRA markets.

In valuing swaps, the basic technique is used to price generic swaps (in effect, standard swap transactions). In practice, swaps must often be adjusted for a number of non-standard features (non-generic or non-standard swaps). The valuation methodology in respect of non-generic swaps entails two specific and distinct phases:

- The derivation of the price of a generic swap.
- The adjustment of the generic swap price by factoring in the price/cost impact of variations from the generic structure to generate a price for the non-generic swap.

In this Chapter, the methodology for pricing generic swaps is developed and then adapted for the pricing of non-generic swaps.

# 3 Interest Rate Swap Pricing – Forward Pricing

## 3.1 Interest Rate Swap Pricing – Pricing as Portfolio of Forward Contracts[6]

Interest rate swap transactions can be priced as a portfolio of forward contracts. This involves the following steps:

- The swap contract is decomposed into a series of forward contracts. For a swap starting on the normal commencement date (a spot start interest rate swap), this will generally entail decomposing the swap into a physical borrowing or

---

Van Deventer, Donald R. and Imai, Kenji (1997) Financial Risk Analytics; Irwin, Chicago at Chapter 1.

[6] See Hull, John (2000) Option Futures and Other Derivatives – Fourth Edition; Prentice-Hall Inc., Upper Saddle River, NJ at 133–135.

investment transaction for the first interest rate period and then a series of forwards.
- The individual interest rate forwards are then priced using conventional methodologies to derive forward-forward interest rates[7].
- The swap price is derived as the value of the portfolio of interest rate forwards.

In practice, the approach takes two forms:
- Pricing off interest rate forwards stripped from the current yield curve or FRA price available in the market.
- Pricing off interest rate futures contract prices/rates derived from the market.

The second approach is used because in practice the interest rate futures markets (on short term interest rates such as the Eurodollar or Euro-ibor futures contract) provide readily available information on market forward interest rates, and also because it is the most logical hedging avenue for traders. The use of interest rate futures contracts creates complexity in pricing the interest rate swap. The process of using interest rate futures contract prices/rates to determine the interest rate swap price is considered in the next Section.

**Exhibit 10.1** sets out an example of decomposing an interest rate swap. **Exhibit 10.2** sets out an example of deriving the interest rate swap price using the forward interest rates.

## 3.2 Interest Rate Swap Pricing – Pricing off Futures Contracts

### 3.2.1 Concept

Interest rate swaps are effectively portfolios of forward contracts. The functional capacity to replicate interest rate swaps by entering into a series of short-term interest rate futures contracts on the relevant interest rate index is a direct result of this relationship. Functional equivalence between strips of short-term interest rate futures contracts and interest rate swaps allows the two separate types of transactions to be used as substitutes or as the equivalent of the other. The functional equivalence of futures strips and interest rate swaps facilitates their use in two ways:
- The interest rate swap is priced off the strip of future contracts.
- The strip of futures contracts can be used to hedge interest rate swap transactions entered into.

---

[7] For a discussion of the derivation of forward interest rates, see Chapter 6.

Interest rate swaps with maturity up to approximately 3 to 5 years are typically priced off the implied yield curve derived from futures contracts. This reflects

---

**Exhibit 10.1    Interest Rate Swap – Decomposition into Forward Contracts**

Assume a borrower has a floating rate loan that is hedged into fixed rate for a period of 1 year. This is achieved using a 1 year interest rate swap where the borrower pays the fixed rate and receives US$3 month LIBOR to match its interest payments under its loan[8]. The position is set out below:

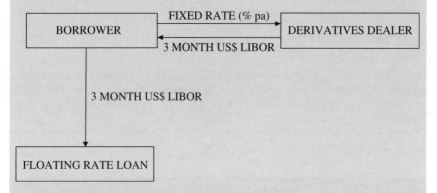

The position in cash flow terms can be summarised as follows:

| Period | Spot to 3 months | 3 to 6 months | 6 to 9 months | 9 to 12 months |
|---|---|---|---|---|
| Loan | – LIBOR | – LIBOR | – LIBOR | – LIBOR |
|  | $(0 \times 3)$ | $(3 \times 6)$ | $(6 \times 9)$ | $(9 \times 12)$ |
| Swap |  |  |  |  |
| Fixed rate | – Fixed Rate | – Fixed Rate | – Fixed Rate | – Fixed Rate |
| Floating Rate | + LIBOR | + LIBOR | + LIBOR | + LIBOR |
|  | $(0 \times 3)$ | $(3 \times 6)$ | $(6 \times 9)$ | $(9 \times 12)$ |
| Net Cash Flows | – Fixed Rate | – Fixed Rate | – Fixed Rate | – Fixed Rate |

The identical position can be achieved by the borrower entering into a series of FRAs/forwards as follows:
- The first interest rate (LIBOR 0 × 3) is already known.
- 3 forwards are entered into as follows: bought FRAs/forward sales on 3 month LIBOR $(3 \times 6; 6 \times 9; 9 \times 12)$. The net settlement on these contracts would offset any movement in the actual 3 month LIBOR under the loan.

---

[8]   The margin (if any) is ignored and will be an additional cost to the borrower.

The position is set out below:

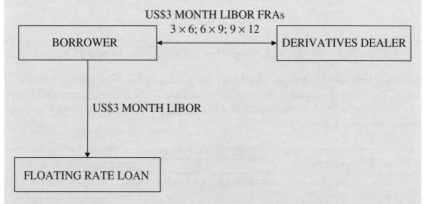

In effect, the two positions (the interest rate swap and the forwards) are identical and must be equivalent in value or price to avoid the possibility of arbitrage. This means that the fixed rate of the interest rate swap must be equal to the value of the portfolio of forwards.

---

**Exhibit 10.2    Interest Rate Swap – Pricing as Forward Contracts**

**1. Assumptions**

Assume a 3 year interest rate swap (fixed rate versus 3 month US$ LIBOR). The interest rates are as follows:

| Years (from Start) | Days (from Start) | Days in Interest Rate Period | Forward Interest Rates (% pa) |
|---|---|---|---|
| 0.25 | 92 | 92 | 7.25 |
| 0.50 | 183 | 91 | 7.33 |
| 0.75 | 275 | 92 | 7.29 |
| 1.01 | 368 | 93 | 7.34 |
| 1.26 | 459 | 91 | 7.44 |
| 1.51 | 550 | 91 | 7.61 |
| 1.76 | 641 | 91 | 7.77 |
| 2.01 | 732 | 91 | 7.93 |
| 2.25 | 823 | 91 | 8.09 |
| 2.50 | 914 | 91 | 8.16 |
| 2.75 | 1005 | 91 | 8.26 |
| 3.00 | 1096 | 91 | 8.39 |

Please note that the rate for the first 3 month period (7.25% pa) is the current interest rate for 3 months. All other rates are forward interest rates.

## 2. Interest Rate Swap Pricing

The interest rate swap price is derived from the interest rate for the first period and the 11 forward interest rates as follows:

| Days (from Start) | Days in Interest Rate Period | Forward Interest Rates (% pa) | Future Value at End of Interest Rate Period | Cumulative Future Value at End of Interest Rate Period |
|---|---|---|---|---|
| 92   | 92 | 7.25 | 1.0185 | 1.0185 |
| 183  | 91 | 7.33 | 1.0185 | 1.0374 |
| 275  | 92 | 7.29 | 1.0186 | 1.0567 |
| 368  | 93 | 7.34 | 1.0190 | 1.0768 |
| 459  | 91 | 7.44 | 1.0188 | 1.0970 |
| 550  | 91 | 7.61 | 1.0192 | 1.1181 |
| 641  | 91 | 7.77 | 1.0196 | 1.1401 |
| 732  | 91 | 7.93 | 1.0200 | 1.1629 |
| 823  | 91 | 8.09 | 1.0204 | 1.1867 |
| 914  | 91 | 8.16 | 1.0206 | 1.2112 |
| 1005 | 91 | 8.26 | 1.0209 | 1.2365 |
| 1096 | 91 | 8.39 | 1.0212 | 1.2627 |

Notes:
1. The future value at the end of each interest rate period is calculated as the future value of $1 at the applicable forward interest rate (except for the first period where the cash interest rate is used) for the number of days in the interest rate period. In effect, the calculation indicates the expected balance or future value of $1 at the end of the relevant interest period if borrowed or invested at the applicable interest rate. For example, for the first period the calculation is: $1 + .0725 \times 92/360 = 1.0185$.
2. The cumulative future value at the end of each interest rate period is the future value at the end of the previous period compounded at the applicable interest rate for the current period. In effect, this is calculated as the cumulative future value at the end of the previous period multiplied by the future value at the end of the current period. For the first period, the cumulative future value is the same as the future value for the period. In effect, the calculation assumes the compounded balance at the end of the previous period (principal plus interest) is re-borrowed/re-invested or rolled over for the current period. For example, for 183 days the calculation is: $1.0185 \times 1.0185 = 1.0374$.

The swap rate is calculated from the future value at the end of 3 years (1.2627). The swap rate is equivalent to the interest rate that equates a cash flow at commencement of $1 to a future value of $1.2627 at the maturity of 3 years. This rate is 7.96% pa compounded annually. This would equate to the rate on the interest rate swap of 7.74% pa compounded quarterly.

Please note that the swap rate is effectively the weighted average of the spot rate and the successive forward rates. As a result, the interest rate swap rate is higher than the early forward rates, but below the forward rates in the last part of the transaction. This reflects the positive slope in the yield curve. The position would be reversed in the case of a negatively sloped yield curve.

the perspective that the interest rate futures contracts provide accurate and market based information about current market forward interest rates. The market forward interest rates can be used to both price and hedge interest rate swaps (either directly or by hedging the zero coupon curve that the swap is priced off).

The practice is dependent upon the structure and liquidity of the short interest rate futures contracts. The key issues are the maturity of short term interest rate futures contracts and the liquidity in the trading of these contracts.

For example, the Eurodollar futures contract is traded out to a full ten years[9]. As a result of the liquidity provided in the futures market, US$ swap pricing has become highly influenced by the yields implied by the Eurodollar strip. The correlation between swap and strip prices is very high for short dated swaps (3 to 5 years). The correlation is reduced further out along the maturity spectrum. Increased futures execution risk, interest rate volatility and liquidity concerns are all factors that result in the reduced pricing relationship.

Several dealers use strips to price swaps beyond the traded Eurodollar contract maturities. It is theoretically feasible to price contracts out beyond these maturities by extending the linear relationship in the back contracts. The theoretical contracts would be hedged by stacking the contracts in the furthest traded Eurodollar contract. Although this pricing methodology and hedging strategy is only used by a small group of dealers, it is an emerging factor influencing the pricing of longer-term deals. To a large extent this practice relates to the period when Eurodollar futures were traded out to five years. With the extension in late 1993 for Eurodollar trading to initially seven years and subsequently for ten years, the actual ability to trade the underlying futures for more distant maturities eliminates, in part, the need for the theoretical pricing process.

A similar technique can be used to price interest rate swaps in other currencies where there is an active short term interest rate futures market. In practice, in other currencies such as the Euro, Yen, Sterling, A$ etc, the ability to use the futures strip is more restricted due to the more limited liquidity in those currencies. This means that the interest rate futures contracts are used for pricing and hedging *shorter dated* swaps (say out to 2 to 3 years).

---

[9]   Between 1990 and 1992, the Eurodollar futures contract covered 4 years. In 1992, the contract was extended to 5 years and in 1993 the contract was extended out to 10 years. For an interesting history of the Eurodollar contract, see McDonald, Dick "Eurodollar Futures at the Chicago Mercantile Exchange" (November 1995) Financial Derivatives & Risk Management Issue 3 35–40.

### 3.2.2 Pricing Interest Rate Swaps Using Interest Rate Futures – Mechanics

Where interest rate futures contracts are used to price the interest rate swap, the swap rate is the implied yield from a transaction being a borrowing or lending transaction undertaken in cash LIBOR up to the first futures contract and then at each successive rate of futures contracts thereafter. This is identical to the procedure set out in **Exhibit 10.2**. The major difference is that instead of forward or FRA rates, the rates implied by interest rate futures is used. The yield of a futures strip needs also to be adjusted for cash flows arising from initial and variation margin requirements/funding costs and commission charges. **Exhibit 10.3** sets out an example of the determination of the interest rate swap rate (a three year swap) from the yield on the futures strip adjusting for these various costs. The cost of using the futures strip is typically relatively low (in the order of a few bps pa).

---

**Exhibit 10.3    Pricing Interest Rate Swap off Eurodollar Futures Strip**

Assume the futures strip yield is 8.00% pa. The swap rate can be derived as follows:

| | |
|---|---|
| Futures Strip Yield | 8.00% pa |
| Cost of Funding Deposit | 0.03% pa |
| Cost of Funding Margins Calls | 0.01% pa |
| Brokerage Commissions | 0.01% pa |
| Effective Cost of Futures Strip | 8.05% pa |

**Notes:**
1. The futures strip yield is the effective rate at which the 3 year strip was entered into.
2. The cost of funding the initial margin/deposit is based on a deposit is $500 per contract where the cost is assumed to be 1% pa (being the difference between borrowing the funds and investing in Treasury Bills, that is, a negative carry investment).
3. Cost of funding margin calls is based on cash flow of $25 per basis point move in the Eurodollar futures contract yield, an assumed cost of borrowing of 8% pa and yields falling 10 bps each quarter for the life of the contract (12 quarters). This means that after 3 years the contract yields are 6.80% pa. This represents a substantial adverse movement in the position and highlights the relatively minor impact of margin funding costs on the transaction.
4. Commission cost is based on $15 per contract or a total cost of $18,000 over the life of the contract (3 years).

---

The use of interest rate futures creates a number of issues:
- The futures contract expiry dates may not correspond to the interest rate settlement dates on the interest rate swap itself.

- The liquidity of the futures market may not allow trading in *all* required interest rate futures contracts.

The structuring responses to these issues are considered in this Section. A number of pricing/valuation issues are considered in the following Section.

Where the date structure of the interest rate swap coincides perfectly with the specification of the futures contract and the dates (including the commencement date of the interest rate swap and futures contract), the strip of futures contract can be used as a perfect substitute for the interest rate swap. This would allow a highly efficient hedge to be created. In practice, the terms of the interest rate swap will depart significantly from the specifications of the futures contract used to hedge the interest rate swap. This requires considerable structuring of the hedging process.

The objective of using futures to replicate an interest rate swap position is to construct positions in the futures market that offset the dealer's position in the interest rate swap. The hedge is structured such that the dollar price change for a given movement in interest rates will be identical but opposite in direction on the hedge. This is the key element that facilitates use of the futures contracts to price and hedge. The efficiency of the hedge will be affected by the changing relationship between the value of the swap being hedged and the price at which the corresponding futures contracts trade, and how this relationship evolves over time. The difference between the cash and futures price is referred to as the "basis". Using futures to price and hedge interest rate swaps essentially entails substituting basis risk for absolute market risk on changes in interest rates.

Using futures to hedge interest rate swap positions requires considerable structuring of the hedge itself including:
- Adjusting and anticipating basis fluctuations.
- Determining appropriate hedge ratios.
- Selecting appropriate contract and delivery months.

Appropriate hedge management requires determination of possible gains and losses due to basis fluctuation. The effect of basis changes on the efficiency of the hedge can be viewed as the basis either increasing in value (strengthening) or decreasing in value (weakening). This necessarily means that a short hedger who buys the basis will have a net gain as the basis strengthens (that is, the basis becomes increasingly more positive or less negative). In contrast, a long hedger will have a net gain as the basis weakens (that is, where the basis has become increasingly more negative or less positive). Where the basis changes occur, the net profit or loss on the futures positions will not exactly offset the gain or loss in the cash position. This will effectively create a cash flow mismatch, with resulting economic gains or losses between the settlement on the interest rate swap contract and the settlement on the futures contract. Consequently, when dealers are using futures to price or hedge interest rate swaps, they must seek to adjust the hedge for the anticipated changes in basis by slightly over or under-hedging.

The hedge ratio is the number of futures contracts required to hedge the interest rate swap position to ensure that the hedge performs as expected. The hedge ratio must be determined to equate the price changes of the interest rate swap and the futures contract. The relative price changes will not be of the same magnitude because of differences in the contract specifications between the interest rate swap and the futures contract. The hedge ratio represents the principal face value of the futures contract held relative to the principal face value of the interest rate swap position.

There are a number of techniques for calculating the hedge ratio[10]. These include:

- **Duration model** – where the number of futures contracts used over the life of the hedge are designed to ensure that changes in the value of the futures position will offset the changes in the value of the cash position by equating the duration of the interest rate swap and the futures contract[11].
- **Volatility/PVBP or DVO1 matching** – where the hedge is structured to match the change in the dollar value of the interest rate swap to be hedged with the change in the dollar value of the futures contract[12].
- **Regression model** – where a regression relationship between the interest rate swap price movements and the futures contract price movements is established on the basis of historical data, with the hedge being structured as the value of the futures position that reduces the variability of price changes of the hedged position to the lowest possible level.

The models for calculating the hedge ratio each require assumptions to be made and will be appropriate in different situations. In the case of interest rate swaps, volatility or PVBP matching is commonly used to make the necessary hedge adjustments.

A critical decision for the intermediary using futures to hedge interest rate swaps is to:

- Select the contract to be used to effect the hedge.
- Select the delivery month in which the hedge will be placed.

---

[10] See further discussions in Das, Satyajit (2004) Structured Products Volume1; John Wiley & Sons (Asia), Singapore at Chapter 2.
[11] For a discussion of these terms and their use, see Chapter 5.
[12] For a discussion of these terms and their use, see Chapter 5.

Selection of the contract is usually based on the correlation between movements in the prices of the relevant futures contract and the price of the interest rate swap. For example, Eurodollar futures will be used to hedge LIBOR based interest rate swaps.

The selection of contract month is more problematic. Interest rate swaps traded to meet client requirements will rarely exactly match the traded futures delivery dates. The selection of the delivery month to be used generally depends on the following factors:

- Liquidity of the particular delivery month both at the time the position is established and at the time the position must be closed.
- Time horizon over which the hedge is designed to be maintained and relative pricing of contracts across delivery months or the basis relationship between contract dates.

A variety of hedging strategies is available in regard to delivery month selection. These range from placing the hedge in the nearest liquid contract months to the relevant interest rate swap, to using a basket of delivery months and contracts appropriately weighted to effect the hedge. Two hedging techniques (strip hedging versus stack hedging/structured arbitrage) require special mention.

Ideally, the dealer will price and hedge the interest rate swap with a series of interest rate futures exactly matching the interest rate setting dates under the swap. The interest rate futures transactions are economically identical to the interest rate swap, enabling efficient pricing and hedging. This is known as strip hedging where each roll of the interest rate swap is hedged with a futures contract where the settlement dates closely follow the relevant interest rate settlement dates of the interest rate swap.

The strip hedge operates in two phases:

- Initially, a series of futures contracts are bought or sold to hedge the interest rate settlements on the interest rate swaps. In essence, the strip is bought or sold.
- After the hedge is established, the hedge must be rolled periodically, usually at each interest rate settlement date. This involves lifting the futures leg by buying or selling the appropriate futures contract month and settling the corresponding leg of the interest rate swap.

An example of a strip hedging operation is set out in **Exhibit 10.4**.

Stack hedging refers to front loaded hedges where most of the futures positions are concentrated in certain contract months in an attempt to improve overall hedge performance. Front loading seeks to take advantage of the higher available liquidity in the nearby futures contract months. Utilising a stack hedge, an interest rate swap

---

**Exhibit 10.4  Pricing/Hedging Interest Rate Swaps Using Interest Rate Futures – Strip Hedge Example**

An investor wants to enter into an interest rate swap with a dealer to lock in investment rates for just under a year through to September 2002, commencing early October in 2001. B does not need to hedge the first leg in the futures as the investment is today and the rate is known. The first leg is priced at where either the investor or the dealer can make a Eurodollar deposit in the spot market. The subsequent legs of the interest rate swap are hedged in the futures market. At each settlement date under the interest rate swap, fresh deposits would be made by the investor, and the interest rate swap settlement made. The dealer would simultaneously close out its futures position with the gain or loss on the futures offsetting the interest rate swap settlement amount.

Assume the following rates prevail:

| | |
|---|---|
| 70 day Eurodollar deposit (maturing early December) | 10.45% pa |
| Buy December futures | 10.90% pa (futures price 89.10) |
| Buy March futures | 12.28% pa (futures price 87.72) |
| Buy June futures | 13.12% pa (future price 86.88) |

The price of the strip is provided by utilising the rate compounding method. The interest rates are first converted to an annual effective basis and converted to an actual/365 day count basis:

10.45% pa quarterly LIBOR basis = 11.02% pa annual actual/365 basis
10.90% pa quarterly LIBOR basis = 11.51% pa annual actual/365 basis
12.28% pa quarterly LIBOR basis = 13.04% pa annual actual/365 basis
13.12% pa quarterly LIBOR basis = 13.97% pa annual actual/365 basis

The strip rate is determined as follows:

$$[(1 + 0.1102 \times 70/365)(1 + 0.1151 \times 91/365) \times (1 + 0.1304 \times 91/365) \\ \times (1 + 0.1397 \times 91/365)] - 1 = 12.24\% \text{ pa compounded annually.}$$

The equivalent rate on the swap would be 11.55% pa compounded quarterly on LIBOR (actual/360 day) basis.

---

contract is hedged by entering into futures contracts that will expire prior to the some of the later settlement dates under the interest rate swap. The futures position will be rolled at each settlement date until the commencement of the relevant periods under the interest rate swap. **Exhibit 10.5** sets out an example of a stack hedge.

The risk of a stack hedge is that the basis between the months could alter; that is, the yield curve could change shape. This may mean that deferred contract months will either become more expensive or cheaper relative to nearby contracts,

---

**Exhibit 10.5    Pricing/Hedging Interest Rate Swaps Using Interest Rate Futures – Stack Hedge Example**

A borrower enters into a 2 year Euro 250 million interest rate swap with a dealer where it pays fixed rates and receives 3 month Euro-ibor. The dealer decides to use a stack hedge to hedge the 2 year swap. This decision is based on the fact that the liquidity in the 3 month Euro-ibor futures is low, other than in the near contract months.

On 6 June 2001 (the commencement date of the swap), the dealer establishes a futures hedge that is fully stacked in the front month contract. The number of contracts is based on an assumed hedge ratio of 0.9760 and a Euro-ibor futures contract with face value of Euro 1 million. The initial and subsequent transactions necessary to keep the stack hedge in place are shown below:

| Date | Hedge |
|---|---|
| 16 June 2001 | Sell 1708 September 2001 Euro-ibor contracts (1708 = seven 3 month interest periods to be hedged as to 244 contracts per period (calculated as Euro 250 million/Euro 1 million × 0.9760). |
| 16 September 2001 | Close out the September 2001 position and sell 1464 (6 × 244) December 2001 contracts. |
| 16 December 2001 | Close out the December 2002 position and sell 1220 (5 × 244) March 2002 contracts. |
| 16 March 2002 | Close out the March 2002 position and sell 976 (4 × 244) June 2002 contracts. |
| 16 June 2002 | Close out the June 2002 position and sell 732 (3 × 244) September 2002 contracts. |
| 16 September 2002 | Close out the September 2002 position and sell 488 (2 × 244) December 2002 contracts. |
| 16 December 2002 | Close out the December 2002 position and sell 244 (1 × 244) March 2003 contracts. |
| 16 March 2003 | Close out the March 2003 position. |

The hedge could be stacked in other futures contract months. For example, the dealer could have strip hedged the first three contract months and stacked the remainder of the hedge in the fourth contract month.

---

exposing the stack hedger to altered inter-contract month price spreads when rolling the stack hedge. This can result in a marked decline in hedge efficiency. Stack hedges can also expose dealers to trading liquidity risk because of the size of the hedge position[13].

---

[13]  See Das, Satyajit (2004) Risk Management; John Wiley & Sons (Asia), Singapore at Chapter 8. This risk is very significant as illustrated by the case of MG Corporation (see **Exhibit 8.5**).

The price of the interest rate swap would still be determined as for the strip hedge. An additional allowance may be made for the risks of rolling the hedge. This would include additional costs such as higher transaction costs, execution risks (exacerbated by the size of the position in any contract month), higher degree of yield curve risk and the risk of not being able to roll the contract at fair value.

Stack hedges can be viewed as a substitute to strip hedging techniques. For example, instead of purchasing or selling a strip of futures, a stack hedge can be executed; the stack hedge is gradually rolled out as futures contracts expire, and the amount of contracts maintained is adjusted at each settlement date. The use of stack hedging reflects liquidity in the back months of short term interest rate futures contracts. Near month liquidity is significant with the liquidity in the back months declining sharply. This necessitates the use of hedge stacking techniques. The position varies significantly as between currency markets.

Strip hedging has a number of advantages over stack hedging including:
- Fewer transactions and therefore lower commission costs.
- More certainty about the final performance of the hedge.
- Lower hedge management requirements.

A front loaded stack hedge has a number of advantages over a strip hedge including:
- The fact that a stack hedge involves trading in the more liquid contracts may minimise transaction costs as reflected by the lower bid-offer spreads in the more liquid months.
- By maintaining the hedge in the liquid nearby contract months, the hedger has increased flexibility in adjusting the hedge position in response to changing market conditions and corporate objectives.

A structured arbitrage option is an alternative to stack hedging where there is little or no trading in a particular futures month, particularly in the more distant months. In this situation, the structured arbitrage trade entails a dealer taking both sides of the futures transactions and incorporating the side that would usually have been taken by a counterparty into its futures portfolio. The rationale in such structured arbitrage is that it is always possible to enter into a futures trade at a price. Usually, the counterparty will trade, particularly in the more distant lightly traded months, at a price designed to give the other trader an arbitrage or a particularly attractive price. The structured arbitrage is predicated on taking that arbitrage internally and rolling out of that arbitrage by either creating a synthetic security, or alternatively maintaining the position until such time as it can be liquidated.

### 3.2.3 Pricing Interest Rate Swaps Using Interest Rate Futures – Pricing Issues[14]

Given the equivalence of futures strips and interest rate swaps, economic theory would dictate that the effective yields generated by both transactions should be closely correlated. In order to analyse the performance of a futures strip versus an interest rate swap, the likely cash flows and net gains (losses) on interest rate swaps and the corresponding three year futures strip can be simulated. The results of the analysis indicate that the yield on the futures strip is on average lower than the yield on the comparative interest rate swap.

The value of an interest rate swap priced off futures contracts is calculated in a manner not significantly different from that used where forward contracts are used. The major differences identified arise from transaction costs, potential basis risk arising from mismatches in the interest rate settlement dates, and liquidity/trading considerations that necessitate specific hedging structures.

In practice, the price of the interest rate swap must be also be adjusted for a number of other factors:

- The margining feature of futures contracts.
- The convexity problem in using futures contracts arising from the fixed basis point value (US$25 for the Eurodollar contract) of most short term interest rate futures contracts.

In the next Sections, the identified issues are considered. They are examined with specific reference to US$ interest rate swaps priced off/hedged in Eurodollar futures contracts. The analysis presented is applicable in all other currencies where a similar approach is used.

### 3.2.4 Pricing Interest Rate Swaps Using Interest Rate Futures – Cash Requirements

A feature of Eurodollar futures strips is the requirement that the contracts be marked-to-market on a daily basis and immediately cash margined if the position is out-of-the-money. The margin requirement means that the hedging corporation may be required to make substantial margin payments.

An important point to note is that cash requirements between a futures strip and an interest rate swap should not vary substantially in terms of amount, only timing.

---

[14] See Das, Satyajit "Futures Strips Gaining in Interest" (July 1991) Corporate Finance 12–16; Kawaller. Ira G. "Comparing Eurodollar Strips to Interest Rate Swaps" (Fall 1994) Journal of Derivatives 67–79.

This reflects the fact that with the futures contract, as the position goes out-of-the-money, variation margin calls would have to be posted and immediately cash settled. In contrast, with an interest rate swap, the cash flow (representing the difference between the fixed and floating interest rate) would not be realised until the relevant payment date (typically quarterly or semi-annually).

An additional difference is that with an interest rate swap, the settlement payment at any payment date relates *only to the immediate interest period* (three or six months). In contrast, in the case of a futures strip, the margin settlement would relate to *all* futures contracts that are open; that is, all potential cash settlements *over the full term of the transaction*.

This cash margin requirement impacts on several levels including:
- Potential requirement to fund large margin payments from available liquidity sources.
- Funding costs in respect of such margin payments.
- The interest rate risk of the funding of margin payments.

The cash requirement and cost of funding such margin variations can be analysed using simulation methodology. **Exhibit 10.6** sets out an analysis of the cash requirements of an interest rate futures strip. **Exhibit 10.7** analyses the cash requirements on futures strips for larger moves in future yields.

Two specific aspects of the cash flow impact using futures to hedge interest rate swap positions should be noted:
- Adjustment for the funding cost of holding the strip.
- The concept of "tailing" of the hedge.

In using futures strip rates to price interest rate swaps, the impact of the cash requirements/funding cost of margin calls must be adjusted for. Futures contracts do not trade at the same prices/rates as equivalent forward contracts[15]. This reflects the impact of the financing or convexity. For example, if a portfolio is short interest rate futures and interest rates rise in all maturities, the portfolio will receive variation margins that can be invested at comparatively high short-term rates. As interest rates fall, the trader has to pay variation margins but this can be funded at comparatively lower short-term interest rates. This benefit may be cumulative as rates rise and fall over the life of a particular futures contract, and even where the contract itself settles at the original price at which the contract was traded, the portfolio may have benefited from price oscillation. This difference reflects the

---

[15] See Chapter 6.

**Exhibit 10.6    US$ Interest Rate Futures Strip – Variation Margin Cash Requirement – Example 1**

Assume a US$100 million face value hedge for a term of 3 years requiring an initial purchase of 1,200 contracts. At the end of each quarter, as futures contracts mature, 100 contracts expire and are closed out. The Table below summarises cash flow requirements of this position on a particular day in each quarter if Eurodollar futures yields move by 1, 5 or 10 bps. Note how the effect of a movement yield is felt most dramatically in the early period of the hedge when the number of contracts open is larger.

| Contract Month | Number of Contracts | Cash Flow ($) if Futures Yields Fall (bps) | | |
|---|---|---|---|---|
| | | 1 | 5 | 10 |
| Jun-01 | 1200 | −30,000 | −150,000 | −300,000 |
| Sep-01 | 1100 | −27,500 | −137,500 | −275,000 |
| Dec-01 | 1000 | −25,000 | −125,000 | −250,000 |
| Mar-02 | 900 | −22,500 | −112,500 | −225,000 |
| Jun-02 | 800 | −20,000 | −100,000 | −200,000 |
| Sep-02 | 700 | −17,500 | −87,500 | −175,000 |
| Dec-02 | 600 | −15,000 | −75,000 | −150,000 |
| Mar-03 | 500 | −12,500 | −62,500 | −125,000 |
| Jun-03 | 400 | −10,000 | −50,000 | −100,000 |
| Sep-03 | 300 | −7,500 | −37,500 | −75,000 |
| Dec-03 | 200 | −5,000 | −25,000 | −50,000 |
| Mar-04 | 100 | −2,500 | −12,500 | −25,000 |

**Exhibit 10.7    US$ Interest Rate Futures Strip – Variation Margin Cash Requirement – Example 2**

**1. Assumptions**
Assume that a dealer enters into the sold future strip to hedge an interest rate swap. Following entry, interest rates fall immediately and stay at this level throughout the life of this transaction.

In order to simulate the potential cash requirement of margin calls resulting from large interest rate movements, the following transaction is examined:

| | |
|---|---|
| Face Value Amount | 1,200 Eurodollar futures contracts |
| Face Value Amount | US$100 million |
| Term | 3 years |
| No of Contracts | 1,200 Eurodollar futures contracts |
| Initial Yield | 8.00% pa. |

The futures position requires lodgement of a deposit of US$600,000 (based on the assumed deposit provision of US$500 per contract).

Assume that changes in Eurodollar strip yield rate changes had the following characteristics:

| | |
|---|---|
| Average Change | 0.58% pa |
| Range of Changes | −1.59% to 2.04% pa |
| Standard Deviation | 0.43% pa. |

Assuming a normal distribution curve, based on the above information there is a 95% probability that US$ Eurodollar strip yields would not move up or down by more than approximately 166.25 bps over a period of three months. In the transaction being analysed, this means that there is a 95% probability that the maximum change in Eurodollar strip yields over a three month period will be 166.25 bps. Assuming that the futures strip yield achieved initially was 8.00% pa, this means rates should not be outside the range 6.34% pa to 9.66% pa. As a fall in interest rates will generate a negative margin payment requirement, the simulation focuses on a fall in interest rates to 6.34% pa.

## 2. Projected Cash Requirements

If Eurodollar rates fall to 6.34% pa then the following cash requirements will need to be met:

| | US$ |
|---|---|
| Margin Call | 4,987,563 |
| Margin Funding Cost (3 months at 8.00% pa) | 99,751 |
| Initial Deposit | 600,000 |
| Deposit Funding Cost (3 months at 1.00% pa) | 1,500 |
| Commission (US$15/contract) | 1,500 |
| Total | 5,090,314 |

**Notes:**
1. Initial deposit cash flow is committed irrespective of interest rate movements.
2. Deposit funding cost represents the difference between the funding cost and the rate earned on the deposit by lodging in the form of government securities.

The maximum cash flow requirement is based on holding 1,200 contracts in the first three month period of a three year US$100 million hedging transaction. If interest rates fall to 6.34% pa and remain at this level, then the need to maintain and fund substantial margin requirements adds to the cost of the position. In this example, assuming a funding cost of 8.00% pa, the additional cost would be approximately 20 bps pa. This would make the futures strip approximately 13 bps pa more expensive than the equivalent interest rate swap (this assumes cost of funding such a margin payment over the full three year life of the transaction).

The analysis indicates that in the case of a large movement in interest rates, a hedger may be required to meet substantial cash margin requirements. In the transaction analysed, the maximum cash requirement identified was approximately US$5 million on a 3 year

US$100 million transaction. However, the actual cash requirement of establishing and maintaining such a futures position is likely to be substantially lower. This reflects the fact that the movement in rates assumed is very large and occurs in the first 3 months of the futures strip.

convexity adjustment[16]. This means that the market futures prices must be adjusted by the convexity adjustment to equate to the corresponding forward price. It is this adjusted forward rate that should be used in determining the futures strip rate for an interest rate swap.

The concept of tailing is used to describe a technique used commonly in futures markets to protect the funding cost of any adverse movement in margins required on the futures position.

This is driven by the fact that in using short-term interest rate futures to hedge interest rate swap positions, substantial positions in the futures markets may be required to be maintained, resulting in significant funding costs on margins required to be posted by the clearing house. The notion of a "tail" is that an opposing position is taken in the futures contract to protect against adverse movements in the average principal hedge required within the portfolio and the resultant increase in margins as a result of a subsequent increase in funding costs. The futures position taken is designed to protect the tail position. Important variables in determining the efficiency of the tailing include the overnight cost of funds, the length of time the funding is required and the size of the interest rate futures position held.

For example, if interest rates rise in the principal bought futures position requiring a substantial margin payment to be made, then the cost of funding the margin will be offset by positive cash flow on the short interest rate futures tail position. Tailing is an extremely important concept in interest rate swap portfolios where interest rate futures are used as a major hedging technique. It is conceivable that the tail becomes substantial enough to require *its own tail*. As opposing positions are booked in and out of the portfolio, the size of the tail typically stabilises, although substantial tails can develop where the portfolio acquires a significantly positive or negative bias in the nature of the underlying futures positions held.

The use of tailing to hedge an interest rate exposure is very similar to constructing a modified duration matched hedge. A tailed futures hedge offsets changes in value

---

[16] For a discussion of the calculation of the futures to forward convexity adjustment, see Chapter 6.

of future assets or liabilities in a similar manner to the way in which a duration matched hedge offsets changes in asset and liabilities as a result of interest rate movements.

### 3.2.5   Pricing Interest Rate Swaps Using Interest Rate Futures – Convexity Adjustments[17]

*Convexity Bias*

The use of futures contracts to hedge interest rate swaps displays a systematic pattern. This pattern favours a position where the dealer under the interest rate swap receives fixed rate and pays the floating rate (3 month LIBOR) and hedges by selling a strip of Eurodollar interest rate futures contracts. This position will result in profits accruing to the dealer irrespective of the movement in interest rates. If rates increase, then the gain on the short futures position will be greater than the loss on the swap. If rates decrease, then the loss on the short futures position will be less than the gain on the swap. This position is the result of the convexity difference between the interest rate swap and the interest rate futures strip. The interest rate swap is characterised by positive convexity (that is, the PVBP of the swap will increase as rates fall and decrease as rates increase). In contrast, the interest rate futures contract has no convexity (contract PVBP is fixed at US$25). This difference between the swap and the futures contracts is referred to as the convexity bias.

Interest rate swaps are priced off/hedged by offsetting futures contracts positions. The positions are determined based on a hedge ratio that equates the PVBP of both transactions. The gain or loss on the swap is only realised at each interest rate settlement period. This means that the value change of the swap depends upon the difference between the swap rate and the forward rate, and on the discount rate to present value the cash difference. In contrast, the value and the value change of the Eurodollar futures contract is always in present value terms and is fixed in

---

[17]   For a discussion of the convexity bias, see Rombach, Ed "Not So Perfect" (October 1990) Risk 11–13; Burghardt, Galen and Hoskins, Bill "A Question of Bias" (March 1995) Risk 63–70; Burghardt, Galen and Hoskins, Bill "The Convexity Bias in Eurodollar Futures: Part 2" (Summer 1995) Derivatives Quarterly 59–72; Rombach, Ed "Zen and the Art of Trading the Convexity Bias" (December 1995) Financial Derivatives & Risk Management Issue 4 17–22; Rombach, Ed "Arbitraging the Convexity Bias" (29 May 1996) IFR Financial Products Issue 43 16–17; Kirkos, George and Novak, David "Convexity Conundrums" (March 1997) Risk 60–61; Baker, James "Futures Convexity Adjustments" (24 September 1998) Financial Products 13–15.

value terms. This means that it is only dependent upon the changes in the forward rate. This creates the convexity bias.

**Exhibit 10.8** sets out the differences in convexity between a Eurodollar futures contract and an equivalent forward interest rate contract or FRA. **Exhibit 10.9** sets out an example of the impact of the convexity bias on pricing and hedging an interest rate swap using the futures strip.

---

**Exhibit 10.8    Convexity Difference between Eurodollar Futures and FRAs/Swaps**

**1.   Eurodollar Futures Versus FRA**

The following Table compares the PVBP of 1 Eurodollar futures contract with the PVBP of a FRA on 3 month LIBOR. All calculations are on US$1 million.

| Interest Rate (% pa) | PVBP of Futures Contract ($) | PVBP of FRA Contract ($) | Difference ($) |
|---|---|---|---|
| 3.00 | 25.00 | 24.90 | 0.10 |
| 3.50 | 25.00 | 24.84 | 0.16 |
| 4.00 | 25.00 | 24.77 | 0.23 |
| 4.50 | 25.00 | 24.71 | 0.29 |
| 5.00 | 25.00 | 24.65 | 0.35 |
| 5.50 | 25.00 | 24.59 | 0.41 |
| 6.00 | 25.00 | 24.53 | 0.47 |
| 6.50 | 25.00 | 24.47 | 0.53 |
| 7.00 | 25.00 | 24.41 | 0.59 |
| 7.50 | 25.00 | 24.35 | 0.65 |
| 8.00 | 25.00 | 24.29 | 0.71 |
| 8.50 | 25.00 | 24.22 | 0.78 |
| 9.00 | 25.00 | 24.17 | 0.83 |

**2.   Eurodollar Futures Versus Interest Rate Swap**

The following Table compares the PVBP of Eurodollar futures contract with the PVBP of a 5 year interest rate swap against 3 month LIBOR. All calculations are on US$1 million. In the case of the futures, a total of 20 futures contracts are used.

| Interest Rate (% pa) | PVBP of Futures Contracts ($) | PVBP of 5 Year Interest Rate Swap ($) | Difference ($) |
|---|---|---|---|
| 3.00 | 500.00 | 457.84 | 42.16 |
| 3.50 | 500.00 | 451.38 | 48.62 |
| 4.00 | 500.00 | 445.06 | 54.94 |
| 4.50 | 500.00 | 438.88 | 61.12 |

| 5.00 | 500.00 | 432.83 | 67.17 |
| 5.50 | 500.00 | 426.91 | 73.09 |
| 6.00 | 500.00 | 421.12 | 78.88 |
| 6.50 | 500.00 | 415.46 | 84.54 |
| 7.00 | 500.00 | 409.91 | 90.09 |
| 7.50 | 500.00 | 404.48 | 95.52 |
| 8.00 | 500.00 | 399.17 | 100.83 |
| 8.50 | 500.00 | 393.96 | 106.04 |
| 9.00 | 500.00 | 388.86 | 111.14 |

**Exhibit 10.9    Pricing/Hedging an Interest Rate Swap Using the Futures Strip – Convexity Bias Impact**

Assume a dealer pays fixed on a US$100 million 2 year swap at 8% pa semi-annual bond basis and hedges with a strip of Eurodollar futures at 8.03% pa. The true gain to the dealer is unlikely to be 3 basis points because the dealer has taken on negative convexity by entering into this trade.

With a yield of 8% pa, the dealer would need to buy a total of 726 contracts in order to match the duration of the swap[18]. If swap yields dropped the next day to 7% pa, then the gain on the futures position would total US$1,815,000. At these lower yields, the PVBP of the swap increases to US$18,581 from $18,140. Consequently, the 100 bps move in yield results in a loss on the interest rate swap of US$1,836,500. The net loss due to a rate movement is US$21,500 that equates to slightly over 1bps per annum over the life of the swap.

Source: See Leibovitch, Richard "The US Dollar Swap Market" in Das, Satyajit (Editor) (1991) The Global Swaps Market; IFR Publishing, London at Chapter 3.

*Convexity Bias – Valuation*[19]

In practice, the convexity bias is observable. It is taken to be the rate on an interest rate swap for the relevant maturity compared to the futures strip for the same maturity. Consistent with the convexity bias, the interest rate swap rates trade

---

[18]   The modified duration of a two year swap yielding 8% pa is 1.814 resulting in the PVBP of $18,142 on a $100 million notional value. Since Eurodollars have a PVBP of $25, it would take 726 contracts to match the PVBP of the swap.

[19]   See Burghardt, Galen and Hoskins, Bill "A Question of Bias" (March 1995) Risk 63–70 at 65–68; Burghardt, Galen and Hoskins, Bill "The Convexity Bias in Eurodollar Futures: Part 2" (Summer 1995) Derivatives Quarterly 59–72 at 61–64; Rombach, Ed "Zen and the Art of Trading the Convexity Bias" (December 1995) Financial Derivatives & Risk Management Issue 4 17–22 at 18–20.

at a rate that is below the equivalent futures strip. This difference ranges from very low levels to significant levels at longer maturities (from 1 bps at the short end to 10–15 bps at the long end). The differences are also quite volatile. The determination of the *correct* value of the bias is important in enabling dealers to make the appropriate adjustment to the futures strip rate to arrive at the swap rate to be quoted.

The bias is driven by the following factors:

• Volatility in interest rates (the forward rates and term zero coupon rates).
• The correlation between the change in the forward rates and the zero rates (this will tend to be positive with changes in the forward rate being strongly correlated to changes in zero rates).

There are a number of possible approaches to determining the theoretical value of the convexity bias. One feasible approach is an empirical approach. This would look at the level and distribution of the convexity bias in past periods. This approach does not provide any basis for adjusting the convexity bias estimate for different market conditions (different volatility and correlation). An alternative approach may use risk simulations to estimate the likely value under different market conditions using actual simulated hedge results. In practice, some simpler approaches are available.

A simple but intuitively appealing approach uses the value of the drift in the spread between the futures and forward rates to estimate. This is based on the intuition that at maturity of the futures contract, the forward and the futures contract value must converge. The drift therefore is the amount that the spread must decrease over each contract period to compensate for the convexity bias[20]. **Exhibit 10.10** sets out this approach to estimation of the convexity bias[21].

The estimation of the convexity bias requires the following volatility and correlation estimates:

• **Volatility Estimates** – in practice, the volatility used will be the implied volatility in cap/floor agreements or swaptions for the relevant maturity. Historical volatility for swaps or forward rates may also be considered.
• **Correlation Estimates** – the correlation estimates generally display stability.

The convexity bias estimates are sensitive to the volatility and correlation parameters used. The convexity bias estimates are also likely to be sensitive to changes

---

[20] This is conceptually similar to measuring the expected error where modified duration is used to hedge interest rate risk and no adjustment for convexity is incorporated.

[21] This approach is suggested by Burghardt, Galen and Hoskins, Bill "A Question of Bias" (March 1995) Risk 63–70 at 67–68; Burghardt, Galen and Hoskins, Bill "The Convexity Bias in Eurodollar Futures: Part 2" (Summer 1995) Derivatives Quarterly 59–72 at 61–64.

in the shape of the yield curve. In practice, the convexity bias is likely to be significant[22]. This is particularly true for longer maturity transactions.

---

**Exhibit 10.10   Estimation of the Convexity Bias**

**1.  Approach[23]**

The convexity bias may be estimated in two steps:
- Determine the drifts (amount that the spread must decrease over each contract period to compensate for the convexity bias) as follows:

$$\text{Drift} = \sigma_f \times \sigma_z \times \rho_{fz}$$

Where

$\sigma_f$ = volatility of forward rate changes

$\sigma_z$ = volatility of zero coupon rates changes

$\rho_{fz}$ = correlation between forward rate changes and zero coupon rate changes

- Using the drift factors cumulatively to generate the convexity bias assuming that the forward and futures rate must converge at the futures expiry date.

**2.  Example**

Assume the following volatility and correlation estimates[24]:

| Forward Dates | 3 months forward | 6 months forward |
|---|---|---|
| $\sigma_f$ (% pa) | 0.75 | 0.90 |
| $\sigma_z$ (% pa) | 0.25 | 0.60 |
| $\rho_{fz}$ | 0.99 | 0.97 |

The drift factors are set out below:

| Forward Dates | 3 months forward | 6 months forward |
|---|---|---|
| Drift Factor (annual) (% pa) | 0.19 | 0.52 |
| Drift Factor (per quarter) (% pa) | 0.05 | 0.13 |

The drift factors are used to derive the convexity bias. Assuming where the futures/forward contracts have 3 months to expiry that the drift factor is 0.05, the futures rate must be 5 bps higher than the forward rate with 3 months to expiry (this is axiomatic as the forward

---

[22] For example, see Burghardt, Galen and Hoskins, Bill "A Question of Bias" (March 1995) Risk 63–70; Burghardt, Galen and Hoskins, Bill "The Convexity Bias in Eurodollar Futures: Part 2" (Summer 1995) Derivatives Quarterly 59–72; Rombach, Ed "Zen and the Art of Trading the Convexity Bias" (December 1995) Financial Derivatives & Risk Management Issue 4 17–22.

[23] See Burghardt, Galen and Hoskins, Bill "A Question of Bias" (March 1995) Risk 63–70 at 67–68; Burghardt, Galen and Hoskins, Bill "The Convexity Bias in Eurodollar Futures: Part 2" (Summer 1995) Derivatives Quarterly 59–72 at 61–64.

[24] Please note that these numbers are hypothetical and are not designed to provide any indication of actual volatility or correlation levels.

rate and the futures rate are assumed to be the same at maturity). This process is then extended to get the convexity bias at 6 months. Assuming that the rate of drift between 3 and 6 months is 13 bps, the futures rate must be 18 bps higher than the forward rate with 6 months to expiry (5 bps + 13 bps).

This process is repeated to construct the complete set of required convexity bias estimates.

*Convexity Bias – Monetisation*[25]

The identified difficulty in estimating the theoretical or fair value of the convexity bias leads to trading to take advantage of perceived mis-pricing. This trading is particularly focused in longer maturities at the long end of the Eurodollar futures strip. This trading consists of two types of activities:

• Trading perceived mis-valuation of the convexity bias.
• Monetisation strategies involving the use of options to adjust for the convexity bias.

The first type of application consists of either receiving fixed rate in swaps and selling the futures strip where the convexity bias is perceived to be too low, or paying fixed in swaps and buying the futures strip where the convexity bias is considered too high. Variations in this strategy use forward starting swaps. Other variations include calendar spreads. This assumes that changes in the bias will affect the spread between the contracts. However, the spreads are also subject to changes in yield curve shape.

The monetisation strategies are more complex. They are predicated on the assumption that the convexity bias position is analogous to an option straddle. For example, the position of a bank receiving fixed on a 5 year swap at say 5 bps below the 5 year futures strip is equivalent to a long straddle on interest rates. This reflects the fact that as rates fall, the gains on the swap will exceed the losses on the futures contracts, and as rates increase, the losses on the swap will be lower than the gains on the hedge because of the convexity bias.

This position results in several types of trading. Where the convexity bias is perceived to be large, traders pay fixed under a swap and hedge by buying a futures strip. The position is similar to selling an expensive straddle. Where the convexity is perceived to be small, traders receive fixed under the swap and hedge by selling the futures strip. This is designed to lock in a purchase of volatility, effectively the purchase of a relatively cheap straddle.

---

[25] For a discussion of trading strategies, see Rombach, Ed "Zen and the Art of Trading the Convexity Bias" (December 1995) Financial Derivatives & Risk Management Issue 4 17–22; Rombach, Ed "Arbitraging the Convexity Bias" (29 May 1996) IFR Financial Products Issue 43 16–17.

In each case, the option positions would realise value over the life of the hedge or swap. This is because entering into the swap against the futures strip effectively locks in a gain or a loss over the life of the transactions. The simplest way to conceptualise this is to assume that interest rate volatility is zero. In this case, traders paying fixed under the swap and hedging by buying a futures strip will generate a gain in cash terms equal to the convexity bias. Assuming a 5 year swap rate of 6.50% versus a strip rate of 6.55% pa (convexity bias of 5 bps) in present value terms, the realised gain would equal approximately $207,500 per US$100 million face value. Conversely, traders receiving fixed under the swap and hedging by selling the futures strip would generate an equivalent cash loss.

The monetisation strategies seek to capture value by neutralising the expected profit and loss on the transactions. Where traders receive fixed under the swap and hedge by selling the futures strip, the transaction would generate an equivalent cash loss. The value of the straddle offsets the inherent time decay on the swap through the time decay on the sold options. If the bias is large, then this is achieved through the sale of the options. If the bias is small, then the value of the straddle is likely to be realised through the dynamic management of the futures hedges to maintain PVBP matches between the swap and the futures hedge. As rates decrease, additional futures must be sold to maintain the hedged position. As rates increase, the futures position must be bought back to maintain the hedged position. This will trigger trading gains that should be greater than the convexity bias present value loss on the matched swap and futures position.

In a refinement of this basic strategy, option strangles (incremental ratios of out-of-the-money puts and calls) can be sold at specific strike prices. The options are designed to automatically adjust the hedge. For example, if rates increase, then the short put positions would be exercised against the trader, reducing the futures hedge position as required. If rates fall, then the short call positions would be exercised against the trader, increasing the futures hedge position as required. The premium on the option strangles should approximate the projected time value decay of the convexity bias in the swap-futures hedge portfolio.

In effect, the monetisation strategies are designed to add convexity to the futures hedge[26]. This translates into improving the efficiency of the hedge and captures the value of the convexity bias.

*Convexity Bias – Applications*
Historically, traders have priced interest rate swaps against futures strips without adjustment for the convexity bias. This was not problematic where the strip is used to price short dated swaps. As the Eurodollar futures market has extended maturity

---

[26] This is effectively the gamma of the hedge, see Chapter 15.

(currently 10 year and potentially longer dated swaps are capable of being priced off the Eurodollar prices/rates), the need to incorporate the impact of the convexity bias is evident.

The convexity bias has a number of implications:

*   **Pricing** – where futures strip yields are used to price interest rate swaps, an adjustment for the convexity bias must be incorporated. The convexity cost of a swap versus strip position may be estimated using the expected interest rate volatility and correlation. The convexity bias will increase at longer maturities. This has implications for how portfolios of swaps are valued and marked-to-market.
*   **Hedging** – Eurodollar strips will provide a less effective hedge the further out the maturity is extended. When a swap is initially offset with a Eurodollar strip, the amount of contracts in the futures hedge will only be appropriate for the swap rate at the time the trade is done. As absolute yields change, the number of contracts in the hedge will need to change to reflect the change in duration of the underlying swap. In effect, adjusting for the convexity bias.
*   **Trading** – the convexity bias is driven by interest rate volatility and correlation. Fluctuations in the convexity bias may not correspond to expectations of interest rate volatility (for example, as implied from cap/floors and swaptions creating trading/arbitrage opportunities).

# 4   Interest Rate Swap Pricing – Zero Coupon Pricing

## 4.1   Approach[27]

An alternative methodology for pricing interest rate swaps is using zero coupon rates. The basic valuation procedure for an interest rate swap is predicated on the transaction being characterised or restated in equivalent security terms. The transaction can be deconstructed into equivalent hypothetical securities for the purposes of determining the market value of the transaction. In effect, the swap is treated as an exchange of two securities – a fixed rate and a floating rate security.

---

[27] For a discussion of the valuation of interest rate swaps see Kopprasch, Robert W., Macfarlane, John, Ross, Daniel R. and Showers, Janet (1985) The Interest Rate Swap Market: Yield Mathematics, Terminology and Conventions; Salomon Brothers Inc., New York; Martin, John (1996) Derivatives Maths; IFR Publishing, London at Chapter 9; Miron, Paul and Swannell, Philip (1991) Pricing & Hedging Swaps; Euromoney Books, London at Chapter 5, 6 and 7; Schachter, Barry "Swap Pricing and Swap Mispricing" (Summer 1996) Derivatives Quarterly 59–61; Martin, John (2001) Applied Math for Derivatives; John Wiley & Sons, Singapore at Chapters 9 and 10; Flavell, Richard (2002) Swaps and Other Derivatives; John Wiley & Sons, Chichester at Chapters 2 to 6.

The swap can therefore be conceptualised as follows:

*   A fixed rate payer is selling a fixed rate security and buying a floating rate security.
*   A fixed rate receiver is buying a fixed rate security and selling a floating rate security.

The process of decomposition is set out in **Exhibit 10.11**.

---

**Exhibit 10.11    Interest Rate Swap – Decomposition into Security Positions**

**1.  Receiving Fixed/ Paying Floating**

Assume an interest rate swap where the derivative dealer enters into a swap where the dealer receives fixed rate at 6.00% pa on US$100 million for 5 years. The swap is decomposed as follows:

1.  The component of the interest rate swap where the derivative dealer receives fixed rate US$ can be restated as a long position or bought US$ bond with a face value of US$100,000,000 with a fixed coupon of 6.00% pa semi-annually in US$ with a maturity of 5 years.

2.  The component of the swap where the derivative dealer pays floating rate is restated as a short position or sold US$ bond with a face value of US$100,000,000 paying a floating rate coupon semi-annually of US$6 month LIBOR with a maturity of 5 years.

**INTEREST RATE SWAP**

US$6 MONTH LIBOR ON US$100 MILLION

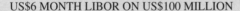

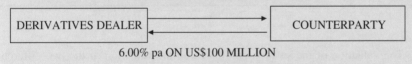

6.00% pa ON US$100 MILLION

**IS EQUIVALENT TO SYNTHETIC SECURITY POSITIONS**

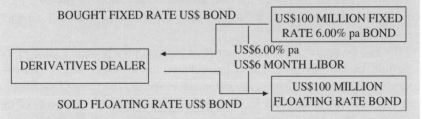

**2.  Paying Fixed/ Receiving Floating**

Assume an interest rate swap where the derivative dealer enters into a swap where the dealer pays fixed rate at 6.00% pa on US$100 million for 5 years. The swap is decomposed as follows:

1. The component of the interest rate swap where the derivative dealer pays fixed rate US$ can be restated as a short position or sold US$ bond with a face value of US$100,000,000 with a fixed coupon of 6.00% pa semi-annually in US$ with a maturity of 5 years.

2. The component of the swap where the derivative dealer receives floating rate is restated as a long position or bought US$ bond with a face value of US$100,000,000 paying a floating rate coupon semi-annually of US$ 6 month LIBOR with a maturity of 5 years.

**INTEREST RATE SWAP**

US$6 MONTH LIBOR ON US$100 MILLION

| DERIVATIVES DEALER | ← ————————— → | COUNTERPARTY |

6.00% pa ON US$100 MILLION

**IS EQUIVALENT TO SYNTHETIC SECURITY POSITIONS**

SOLD FIXED RATE US$ BOND    US$100 MILLION FIXED RATE 6.00% pa BOND

US$6.00% pa

| DERIVATIVES DEALER | US$6 MONTH LIBOR |

US$100 MILLION FLOATING RATE BOND

BOUGHT FLOATING RATE US$ BOND

The valuation of the swap is predicated on the valuation of the two different securities. The two securities can be valued using traditional debt security valuation techniques based on present value concepts. The valuation of an interest rate swap is based on isolating the contracted cash flows and calculating the values of these contracted cash flows *at current market rates* (both interest rates and currency values).

The two synthetic components identified are then present-valued back to the valuation dates using current market zero coupon rates in the currency of the transaction to determine the value of the individual elements. The value of the interest rate swap is then determined by netting the values of the two elements of the transaction. The two sides are netted because the interest rate swap entails a combination of an asset or investment (the long US$ fixed rate position in the above example) and a liability or borrowing (the short US$ floating rate position in the above example).

Applying the above approach to an interest rate swap allows the valuation of the transaction to be stated as:

Present Value of Swap = Present Value of Fixed Rate Cash Flows
+ Present Value of Floating Rate Cash Flows

All present values are assessed using the original cash flows and the interest rates at the valuation date.

At the commencement date of the transaction, the present value of the swap is assumed to be equal to zero. This is because the present values of both sets of cash flows should be equal. This reflects the fact that the receipts and payments by the counterparty are economically equivalent at the start of the transaction. Where a swap is revalued at a later date, the present values of the two sets of cash flows may have changed. This will reflect changes in interest rates as a result of market movements. The valuation of the transaction at commencement can then be restated as follows:

Present Value of Fixed Rate Cash Flows + Present Value of Floating
Rate Cash Flows + Present Value Amount = 0

The present value amount is the actual valuation of the swap at the valuation date. The present value amount ensures the transaction is at market value at current market prices. This amount is equivalent to an amount that must be paid by or to the counterparty seeking to terminate the transaction to the new counterparty assuming the original cash flows revalued at current rates. All present values are assessed using the original cash flows and the interest rates prevailing at the valuation date.

Two factors of the basic valuation methodology require comment:

- The interest rate swap involves no investment at commencement and no final maturity payment as only coupon flows are swapped. This is not problematic as the party undertaking the swap simultaneously buys and sells the equivalent amount of a fixed rate and a floating rate security. This allows netting of the two cash flows both at commencement and at maturity, creating no net cash flow effect.

- The expected cash flows under the floating rate security are not certain as they are contingent on the level of future interest rates. The uncertainty of the floating rate cash flow stream is more difficult and can be resolved using different approaches. The simple explanation is that in an interest rate swap, unlike a true floating rate security there are two-way cash flows (fixed versus floating). This feature allows the swap market to value the relative attractiveness of a swap's floating index by adjusting the accompanying fixed rate. Consequently, the floating rate security may not require separate valuation. The value of the floating rate security is incorporated into the fixed cost quoted versus the floating payments.

Therefore, valuation questions for swaps focus on the hypothetical fixed rate security. An alternative way of looking at this is that it can be assumed that the floating rate component of a swap will tend to have a value close to par (its original value) at commencement or on any interest payment/re-pricing date, because of its re-pricing characteristic. In effect, the floating rate note component will always trade at par (100% of face value). This is also equivalent to using current forward interest rates to set up the actual expected cash flows of the floating rate security and discounting the cash flows back to commencement using zero coupon rates. This process would also yield a par value at commencement.

It is important that the above approach to pricing assumes no default or credit risk is present in the transaction. This means that in effect, each counterparty to the transaction (each of which is the *issuer of a bond*), is assumed free of default risk. This assumption is clearly unrealistic and creates difficulties in swap pricing[28].

## 4.2   Mechanics

The basic valuation procedure for an interest rate swap with a generic structure entails calculating the internal rate of return of the hypothetical fixed security cash flows. For analytical purposes, the flows from the perspective of the fixed rate payer are the proceeds received from the sale of the hypothetical fixed rate security versus an outflow of the fixed rate payments plus the notional principal amount at maturity. The proceeds in this context are not cash but instead are the value of the hypothetical floating rate security received in exchange. In a generic swap, the value of the floating rate security is taken to be par. For non-generic swaps, the basic procedure is similar but is adjusted. The internal rate of return (expressed as yield equivalent) of the hypothetical fixed security is quoted as the all-in cost versus the floating flows at the floating rate index flat.

The steps entailed in valuation are as follows:

- The cash flows of the two "securities" as specified in the swap contract are identified.
- The identified cash flows are discounted back to the valuation date (such as commencement date) using zero coupon rates.
- The swap rate is set at the rate that generates the cash flows that results in the net present value of the transaction equalling zero. In practice, in a generic swap that is transacted at current market rates, the prices of the exchanged "securities" are equal and thus no net cash payment is exchanged upon settlement.

---

[28]  This problem can be re-stated as the problem of determining the swap spread i.e. the spread above risk free bonds that swaps trade at. This issue is discussed in Chapter 11.

In non-generic swaps, the prices may not be equal. In such a case, the net of the two purchase prices would determine the cash payment upon settlement, or alternatively the adjustment to the swap rate.

- The final step in the process is to determine the internal rate of return (on a yield basis) of the analytical fixed flows.

The central element in valuing the identified elements (the synthetic security equivalents) is the concept of present value of the cash flows. Present value methodologies are generally accepted as the basis of valuation of a wide variety of financial market instruments including securities/bonds (of any maturity), currency and interest rate swaps, and other derivative contracts such as forward contracts. The essential element in such a present value calculation is the interest rate used to discount the future cash flows back to the valuation date. The rate used is the zero coupon rate in the relevant currency. Zero coupon rates are used to create and value swaps in the relevant currency. The rate for swaps, derived from the zero rates, is referred to as the swap rate and the term structure of swap rates is referred to as the swap yield curve. Zero coupon rates are generally not available directly and must be calculated from information about interest rates available in the market[29].

**Exhibit 10.12** sets out an example of the pricing of an interest rate swap using the zero coupon pricing methodology.

| Exhibit 10.12   Interest Rate Swap Pricing – Zero Coupon Rate Methodology |

**1.  Assumptions**
The following example sets out the pricing of a 5 year interest rate swap on $100,000,000. The swap has semi-annual cash flows. The swap is to be priced at commencement of the transaction. The derivative dealer will receive fixed in the transaction.

**2.  Cash Flows**
The swap cash flows using a hypothetical swap rate of 10% pa are set out in the Table below. Each fixed rate cash flow is accrued for the relevant interest rate period. The principal is included to equate the fixed rate swap flows into an equivalent long position in a fixed rate bond.

| Years | Days to Cash Flows | Swap (Coupon) Payments ($) | Swap (Coupon & Principal) Payments ($) |
|-------|--------------------|----------------------------|-----------------------------------------|
| 0.00  | 0                  |                            | (100,000,000)                           |
| 0.50  | 182                | 4,986,301                  | 4,986,301                               |

---

[29] Details of the rationale for the use of zero coupon rates and the methodology for their derivation is set out in Chapter 5.

| Years | Days to Cash Flows | Swap (Coupon) Payments ($) | Swap (Coupon & Principal) Payments ($) |
|---|---|---|---|
| 1.00 | 365 | 5,013,699 | 5,013,699 |
| 1.50 | 547 | 4,986,301 | 4,986,301 |
| 2.00 | 730 | 5,013,699 | 5,013,699 |
| 2.50 | 912 | 4,986,301 | 4,986,301 |
| 3.00 | 1095 | 5,013,699 | 5,013,699 |
| 3.50 | 1278 | 5,013,699 | 5,013,699 |
| 4.00 | 1461 | 5,013,699 | 5,013,699 |
| 4.50 | 1643 | 4,986,301 | 4,986,301 |
| 5.00 | 1826 | 5,013,699 | 105,013,699 |
| Total | | 50,027,397 | 50,027,397 |

### 3. Zero Coupon Rates
The zero coupon rates for the relevant maturity points are set out below:

| Years | Days to Cash Flows | Zero Coupon Rates (% pa Semi-annual) |
|---|---|---|
| 0.00 | 0 | |
| 0.50 | 182 | 5.75 |
| 1.00 | 365 | 5.80 |
| 1.50 | 547 | 5.90 |
| 2.00 | 730 | 6.01 |
| 2.50 | 912 | 6.01 |
| 3.00 | 1095 | 6.01 |
| 3.50 | 1278 | 6.16 |
| 4.00 | 1461 | 6.30 |
| 4.50 | 1643 | 6.33 |
| 5.00 | 1826 | 6.35 |

### 4. Swap Pricing
In order to price the swap, the swap cash flows are present valued back at the zero coupon rates to determine the net present value ("NPV") of the fixed rate transaction side of the transaction. This is set out below:

| Days to Cash Flows | Zero Coupon Rates (% pa Semi-annual) | Swap Payments ($) | Present Value of Swap Payments ($) |
|---|---|---|---|
| 0 | | (100,000,000) | (100,000,000) |
| 182 | 5.75 | 4,986,301 | 4,847,328 |
| 365 | 5.80 | 5,013,699 | 4,735,048 |
| 547 | 5.90 | 4,986,301 | 4,569,957 |
| 730 | 6.01 | 5,013,699 | 4,453,979 |
| 912 | 6.01 | 4,986,301 | 4,300,693 |

| 1095 | 6.01 | 5,013,699 | 4,197,651 |
| 1278 | 6.16 | 5,013,699 | 4,054,864 |
| 1461 | 6.30 | 5,013,699 | 3,911,206 |
| 1643 | 6.33 | 4,986,301 | 3,767,221 |
| 1826 | 6.35 | 105,013,699 | 76,803,592 |
| | | **Net Present Value** | 15,641,540 |

The NPV of the swap (at the assumed swap rate of 10.00% pa) is $15,641,540.

The swap price at commencement equates to the swap coupon that provides a NPV of zero when discounted back at the current zero coupon rates. This means that the NPV of the fixed rate side is zero, that equates to the assumed NPV of the floating rate side of zero (as noted above this is assumed to be par or zero NPV), giving the overall transaction a zero NPV.

The swap rate is determined using an iterative technique[30]. The solution is set out below:

| Days to Cash Flows | Zero Coupon Rates (% pa Semi-annual) | Swap Payments ($) | Present Value of Swap Payments ($) |
| --- | --- | --- | --- |
| 0 | | (100,000,000) | (100,000,000) |
| 182 | 5.75 | 3,151,369 | 3,063,537 |
| 365 | 5.80 | 3,168,684 | 2,992,576 |
| 547 | 5.90 | 3,151,369 | 2,888,237 |
| 730 | 6.01 | 3,168,684 | 2,814,939 |
| 912 | 6.01 | 3,151,369 | 2,718,061 |
| 1095 | 6.01 | 3,168,684 | 2,652,938 |
| 1278 | 6.16 | 3,168,684 | 2,562,696 |
| 1461 | 6.30 | 3,168,684 | 2,471,903 |
| 1643 | 6.33 | 3,151,369 | 2,380,904 |
| 1826 | 6.35 | 103,168,684 | 75,454,209 |
| | | **Net Present Value** | 0 |

The fixed rate swap payments are equivalent to a swap rate of 6.32% pa compounded semi-annually (in effect the internal rate of return of the swap cash flows).

## 5. Swap Pricing – Implications

The swap rate of 6.32% pa is the equivalent breakeven rate for the swap trader. It equates to the rate at which the swap, if transacted, would yield a zero net present value (no profit or loss) when revalued using the current zero coupon rates.

In practice, the dealer would adjust the rate for the dealer's costs and risk. In effect, the dealer may quote (based on the above information): 6.30/6.35% pa (the dealer is willing to receive fixed rates at 6.35% pa and pays fixed rates at 6.30% pa).

---

[30] This is done using the Solver function in Excel in this example.

Assuming the dealer transacts the swap where it receives fixed at 6.35% pa, the position is as follows:

| Days to Cash Flows | Zero Coupon Rates (% pa Semi-annual) | Swap Payments ($) | Present Value of Swap Payments ($) |
|---|---|---|---|
| 0 | | (100,000,000) | (100,000,000) |
| 182 | 5.75 | 3,166,301 | 3,078,053 |
| 365 | 5.80 | 3,183,699 | 3,006,756 |
| 547 | 5.90 | 3,166,301 | 2,901,923 |
| 730 | 6.01 | 3,183,699 | 2,828,277 |
| 912 | 6.01 | 3,166,301 | 2,730,940 |
| 1095 | 6.01 | 3,183,699 | 2,665,508 |
| 1278 | 6.16 | 3,183,699 | 2,574,839 |
| 1461 | 6.30 | 3,183,699 | 2,483,616 |
| 1643 | 6.33 | 3,166,301 | 2,392,185 |
| 1826 | 6.35 | 103,183,699 | 75,465,190 |
| | | **Net Present Value** | 127,287 |

The transaction NPV ($127,287) represents the profit to the dealer of the swap. It is the present value of the net earning that will accrue to the dealer where the swap is hedged or matched with an equal and exactly offsetting swap (that is, there is no market risk).

The dealer, where it pays fixed at 6.30% pa, would show a NPV on the transaction of $85,237.

# 5   Currency Swap Pricing – Forward Pricing[31]

## 5.1   Approach

The approach to pricing currency swaps follows a similar logic to that of pricing interest rate swaps. Currency swaps can either be decomposed into a portfolio of currency forward contracts or priced using a zero coupon methodology. The forward pricing methodology is examined in this Section. The zero coupon pricing methodology is outlined in the next Section.

The forward pricing approach to currency swap pricing entails the following steps:

- The currency swap is decomposed into a series of individual forward currency contracts.

---

[31]   See Hull, John (2000) Option Futures and Other Derivatives – Fourth Edition; Prentice-Hall Inc., Upper Saddle River, NJ at 140–141.

- The individual currency forwards are priced separately using the normal carry cost/interest differential approach[32].
- The portfolio of forwards making up the currency forwards is then priced.

## 5.2   Mechanics

The basic approach to pricing currency swaps using a decomposition into currency forward contracts is simple. **Exhibit 10.13** sets out an example of this approach. Several aspects of the approach should be noted:

- The methodology is suitable for fixed-to-fixed currency swaps. This is driven by the fact that the pricing of currency forwards requires that the interest rate in the two relevant currencies are known with certainty and fixed to the maturity of the forward contract. This means that where the currency swap is from fixed rate in one currency to floating rate in the second currency, or both rates are floating, an interest rate swap must be used to convert the fixed rate to floating rate in the relevant currency.
- The approach assumes that the currency forwards are either priced at fair value (free of arbitrage) or the forward rates used can be used to hedge the currency swap.

---

**Exhibit 10.13   Currency Swap – Pricing as Currency Forwards**

Assume that a fixed-to-fixed 5 year currency swap (US\$ to Yen) is to be priced. Assume that the interest rates and currency rates are as follows:

| Year | Interest Rates (% pa) | | Currency Rates |
| | US\$ | Yen | (US\$1 = Yen) |
|---|---|---|---|
| Spot | | | 120.00 |
| 1 | 6.00 | 2.00 | 115.47 |
| 2 | 6.00 | 2.00 | 111.11 |
| 3 | 6.00 | 2.00 | 106.92 |
| 4 | 6.00 | 2.00 | 102.89 |
| 5 | 6.00 | 2.00 | 99.00 |

Assuming that the US\$ side of the swap is fixed (at the US\$ interest rate for 5 years of 6.00% pa), the US\$/Yen spot and forward rates can be used to imply the yen cash flows are set out in the Table below. All cash flows are set out per US\$100.

---

[32]   See Chapter 6.

| Year | Currency Rates (US$1 = Yen) | Cash Flows | |
|---|---|---|---|
| | | US$ | FX |
| 0 | 120.00 | 100.00 | (12,000.00) |
| 1 | 115.47 | (6.00) | 692.83 |
| 2 | 111.11 | (6.00) | 666.69 |
| 3 | 106.92 | (6.00) | 641.53 |
| 4 | 102.89 | (6.00) | 617.32 |
| 5 | 99.00 | (106.00) | 10,494.42 |
| | **Total** | (30.00) | 1,112.79 |

The Yen side of the currency swap is given by the Yen cash flows in the above Table. The Yen currency swap rate is calculated as the internal rate of return of the yen cash flows of the US$ cash flows converted at the forward yen rates. This equates to a rate of 2.00% pa in Yen.

The full currency swap cash flows can be set out as follows:

| Year | Currency Swap Cash Flows | |
|---|---|---|
| | US$ | Yen |
| 0 | 100.00 | (12,000.00) |
| 1 | (6.00) | 240.00 |
| 2 | (6.00) | 240.00 |
| 3 | (6.00) | 240.00 |
| 4 | (6.00) | 240.00 |
| 5 | (106.00) | 12,240.00 |
| Total | (30.00) | 1,200.00 |

Please note that the currency swap results in slightly higher net cash flows in yen than the equivalent set of currency forwards. The differences in net cash flows are driven by the *timing* of the cash flows. In the case of the forwards, the yen received is available earlier than under the currency swaps. On a NPV basis, the two transactions are identical in value terms.

# 6   Currency Swap Pricing – Zero Coupon Pricing

## 6.1   Approach

The basic currency swap structure can be restated in equivalent security terms. The transaction can be deconstructed into equivalent hypothetical securities for the purposes of determining the market value of the transaction. The process of decomposition is set out **Exhibit 10.14.**

**Exhibit 10.14    Currency Swap – Decomposition into Security Positions**

**1. Paying Fixed Yen/ Receiving Floating US$**

Assume a currency swap where the derivative dealer enters into a swap where the dealer pays fixed rate at 5.00% pa on Yen 10,000 million against receipt of US$ LIBOR on US$100 million for 5 years (the spot exchange rate at transaction commencement is assumed to be US$1=Yen 100). The swap is decomposed as follows:

1. The component of the currency swap where the derivative dealer pays fixed rate Yen can be restated as a short position or sold Yen bond with a face value of Yen 10,000 million with a fixed coupon of 5.00% pa semi-annually in Yen with a maturity of 5 years.

2. The component of the currency swap where the derivative dealer receives floating rate is restated as a long position or bought US$ bond with a face value of US$100,000,000 paying a floating rate coupon semi-annually of US$6 month LIBOR with a maturity of 5 years.

CURRENCY SWAP

5.00% pa ON YEN
10,000 MILLION

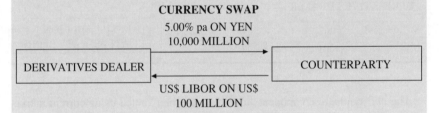

US$ LIBOR ON US$
100 MILLION

**IS EQUIVALENT TO SYNTHETIC SECURITY POSITIONS**

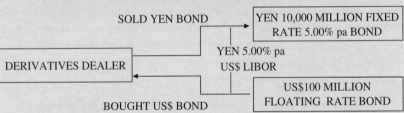

**2. Receiving Fixed Yen/ Paying Floating US$**

Assume currency swap where the derivative dealer enters into a swap where the dealer receives fixed rate at 5.00% pa on Yen 10,000 million against payment of US$ LIBOR on US$100 million for 5 years (the spot exchange rate at transaction commencement is assumed to be US$1 = Yen 100). The swap is decomposed as follows:

1. The component of the currency swap where the derivative dealer receives fixed rate Yen can be restated as a long position or bought Yen bond with a face value of Yen 10,000 million with a fixed coupon of 5.00% pa semi-annually in Yen with a maturity of 5 years.

2. The component of the currency swap where the derivative dealer pays floating rate is restated as a short position or sold US$ bond with a face value of US$100,000,000 paying a floating rate coupon semi-annually of US$6 month LIBOR with a maturity of 5 years.

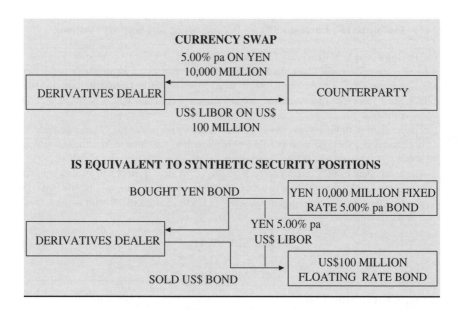

The two synthetic components identified are then valued using current market rates to determine the value of the individual elements. The value of the currency swap is then determined by netting the values of the two elements of the transaction. The two sides are netted because the currency swap entails a combination of an asset or investment (the long or short US$ position in the above example) and a liability or borrowing (the short or long Yen position in the above example).

Applying the above approach to a currency swap allows the valuation of the transaction to be stated as:

$$\text{Present Value of Swap} = \text{Present Value of Cash Flows in Currency 1} \\ + \text{Present Value of Cash Flows in Currency 2}$$

All present values are assessed using the agreed cash flows and the interest rates/spot currency exchange rates prevailing at the time the transaction is entered into.

At the commencement date of the transaction, the present value of the swap is generally assumed to be equal to zero. This is because the present values of both sets of cash flows should be equal. This reflects the fact that the receipts and payments by the counterparty are economically equivalent at the start of the transaction. Where a swap is revalued at a later date, the present values of the two sets of cash flows may have changed. This will reflect changes in either interest rates or in the spot foreign currency rate as a result of market movements. The valuation of the transaction at commencement can then be restated as follows:

Present Value of Cash Flows in Currency 1 + Present Value of Cash Flows in Currency 2 + Present Value Amount = 0

The present value amount is the actual valuation of the swap at the valuation date. This value ensures that the transaction is at market value at current market prices. This amount is equivalent to an amount that must be paid by or to the counterparty seeking to terminate the transaction to the new counterparty assuming the original cash flows revalued at current rates. All present values are assessed using the original cash flows, the interest rates and spot currency exchange rates prevailing at the valuation date.

In practice, the process of decomposition of a currency swap is undertaken in a slightly different manner. The approach is to decompose a fixed-to-floating currency swap into one interest rate swap and one cross currency swap (cross currency floating to floating or basis swap). In the case of a fixed-to-fixed currency swap, the approach is to decompose the transaction into two interest rate swaps and a cross currency basis swap. The approach is set out in **Exhibit 10.15** and **Exhibit 10.16**. The approach is predicated on the ability of the derivatives dealer to hedge the individual components in the respective markets.

The use of this approach does not alter the basic pricing logic. In practice, the currency swap is priced as a combination of the interest rate and currency swap elements. This requires the pricing of the cross currency basis swap and also the related concept of foreign exchange basis points.

**Exhibit 10.15    Fixed-to-Floating Currency Swap – Decomposition in Practice**

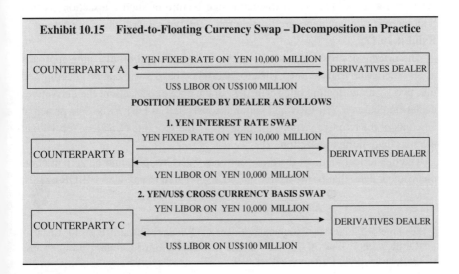

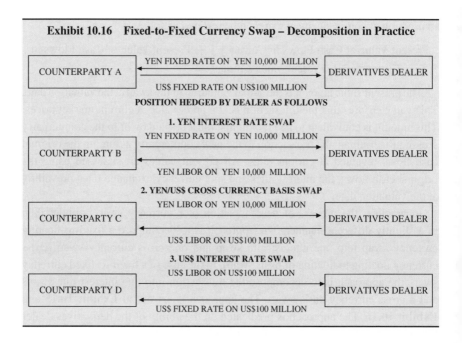

**Exhibit 10.16    Fixed-to-Fixed Currency Swap – Decomposition in Practice**

## 6.2    Pricing Cross Currency Basis Swap[33]

A cross currency basis swap is a floating to floating currency swap transaction. The cross currency basis swap is structurally identical to conventional currency swap transactions. The major distinguishing feature of such transactions is that both interest rate payments are floating rate. The typical cash flows are set out in **Exhibit 10.17**.

The pricing of cross currency basis swaps is predicated on the same approach as all other swap transactions. The cross currency basis swap can be decomposed into two separate floating rate securities. In the above transaction, the derivatives dealer purchases a Yen FRN and simultaneously sells a US$ FRN. The principal amounts of the two transactions are matched at the spot rate (US$1 = Yen 100) at the start date of the transaction.

The theoretical value of the cross currency basis swap should be zero at commencement date; that is, the dealer should be prepared to pay US$ LIBOR against

---

[33]  See Fruchard, Emmanuel, Zammouri, Caker and Willems, Edward "Basis for Change" (October 1995) Risk 70–75; Landis, Clark "Hedging Cross-Currency Basis Swaps" (25 January 1999) Derivatives Week 8–9.

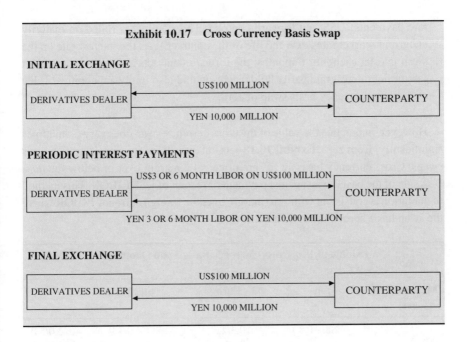

**Exhibit 10.17   Cross Currency Basis Swap**

INITIAL EXCHANGE

DERIVATIVES DEALER — US$100 MILLION → COUNTERPARTY
DERIVATIVES DEALER ← YEN 10,000 MILLION — COUNTERPARTY

PERIODIC INTEREST PAYMENTS

DERIVATIVES DEALER — US$3 OR 6 MONTH LIBOR ON US$100 MILLION → COUNTERPARTY
YEN 3 OR 6 MONTH LIBOR ON YEN 10,000 MILLION

FINAL EXCHANGE

DERIVATIVES DEALER — US$100 MILLION → COUNTERPARTY
DERIVATIVES DEALER ← YEN 10,000 MILLION — COUNTERPARTY

receipt of Yen LIBOR *plus or minus no margin*. The theoretical valuation can be justified in a number of ways:

- **FRN or security values** – the two FRNs should be valued at par or face value at the commencement of the transaction (using the logic set out above in relation to interest rate swaps). This will dictate that at commencement, the NPV of the purchase and sale of the two securities would be zero at the current spot exchange rate. This in turn dictates that the theoretical value of the cross currency basis swap should also be zero.

- **Forward interest rates** – the FRNs can be individually valued. This would entail using the forward rates implied in the relevant currencies and then using them to generate the actual cash flows of the FRNs. The cash flows would then be discounted back at the current zero coupon rates in the yield curve to determine the values of the securities. The securities would have zero NPV at commencement, implying a theoretical value of the cross currency basis swap of zero.

- **Currency forwards** – the cross currency basis swap can be equated to a series of currency forwards in the relevant currency pairing. This would mean that in the case of a US$/Yen cross currency basis swap, the transaction is equivalent to entering into a 3 or 6 month (depending upon the frequency of interest rate payments) US$/Yen forward contract. This contract is rolled on maturity at current market rates over the life of the contract[34]. As the interest rate on the swap is reset each 3 or 6 months, the forward contracts are exactly equivalent (assuming interest rate parity holds). This would also imply a theoretical value of the cross currency basis swap of zero.

However, in practice the value of the cross currency swap does vary (sometimes significantly) from zero. **Exhibit 10.18** sets out quotations for cross currency basis swaps. Cross currency basis swaps are priced at a margin over or below the *non-US$* side of the basis swap against payment or receipt of US$ LIBOR. This method of quotation is consistent with zero margin over the foreign currency LIBOR where the swap has a zero value at commencement.

| Exhibit 10.18 | Cross Currency Basis Swap Quotations | | | |
|---|---|---|---|---|
| **Maturity (years)** | **Yen** | **Euro** | **Sterling** | **A$** |
| 1 | −2.8/−0.8 | 0.3/2.3 | −1.8/0.3 | 3.0/5.0 |
| 3 | −4.0/−2.0 | −2.0/0.5 | −3.3/−1.3 | 5.5/8.5 |
| 5 | −7.8/−5.8 | −2.8/−0.8 | −4.0/−2.5 | 7.0/9.0 |
| 7 | −11/−9 | −2.8/−0.8 | −5.8/−2.8 | 8.0/11.0 |
| 10 | −16/−14 | −3.0/−0.5 | −7.0/−4.0 | 8.0/11.0 |

**Notes:**
All prices are in bps pa for paying and receiving the foreign currency floating rate (Yen LIBOR; Euro-ibor; GBP LIBOR; A$ BBR) against receipt or payment of US$ LIBOR flat.

The deviation from zero value is driven by a number of factors including:
- **Credit risk** – as with all swap valuation it is assumed that there is no credit or default risk in the transaction. In practice, counterparty credit risk is present in the fact that each security involved in the exchange is issued by a specific counterparty. Changes in credit quality (in particular deterioration of credit quality) has the effect changing the value of the two FRNs relative to the zero coupon swap curve, resulting in the cross currency basis swap having a non-zero value that is reflected in the margin on the cross currency basis swap.

---

[34]  The contract would ideally be structured as a par forward contract rather than at a discount or premium to the spot rate to assist in keeping the principal amounts in the two currencies constant over the life of the contract.

- **Market structure** – the pricing of the cross currency basis swap may reflect the underlying transaction flow. The cross currency basis swap is effectively a method for counterparties to acquire or shed foreign currency exposure. Therefore, the pricing in the market may reflect the underlying capital flows in the currency market in terms of either export or import of capital in the economy.
- **Transaction costs** – the zero cost hypothesis assumes no transaction costs and no dealer profit margin. Transaction costs would include the cost of hedging away any residual risk in the transaction. Incorporation of these costs would have the effect of moving the swap valuation away from zero and being priced at a margin to LIBOR in the foreign currency.
- **Capital costs** – the cross currency basis swap would result in the dealer incurring regulatory and economic capital costs for both market risk (mismatches) and credit risk (counterparty default). The pricing in of these capital costs would result in the swap being priced at a margin to LIBOR in the foreign currency.

In practice, credit risk and the market structure have the most significant impact on the pricing of cross currency basis swaps. **Exhibit 10.19** sets out the impact of credit risk and market structure factors using the US$/Yen basis swap market as a case study. **Exhibit 10.20** sets out an illustration of the transaction costs entailed in hedging a cross currency basis swap.

---

**Exhibit 10.19    Cross Currency Basis Swap – Pricing**

**1.   US$/Yen Basis Swap Market – Historical Structure**
The structure of the cross currency basis swap market has been driven historically by a number of factors:
- The Euro-yen bond market (and to a lesser extent the domestic Yen market) and the desire by issuers to swap the yen proceeds into other currencies via the US$.
- The ability of Japanese banks to access low cost dollar funding (based on their strong credit ratings).
- The role of Japan as a major exporter of capital that has underpinned the demand for foreign currency liabilities as Japanese corporations hedge their foreign currency exposure.

This dictated the market structure where dealers in Yen currency swaps had portfolios structured as follows:
- Paying fixed yen against new Euro yen versus receipt of US$ LIBOR.
- Receipt of fixed yen against payment of Yen LIBOR in interest rate swaps transacted with domestic Japanese banks or corporations seeking fixed rate Yen for asset liability management purposes.

• Cross currency basis swaps (paying US$ LIBOR and receiving Yen LIBOR) to offset the portfolio mismatches were transacted with Japanese banks and corporations swapping low cost US$ LIBOR funding (bond issues or short term commercial paper ("CP") issued in the US or Euro markets).

An additional factor was corporations generating US$ funding (off cheap yen funding provided by Japanese banks) to hedge foreign assets.

This market structure drove a yen basis swap pricing of US$ LIBOR versus Yen LIBOR minus 5–10 bps. The spread varied due to short term market conditions that altered supply and demand conditions.

This market structure is set out below.

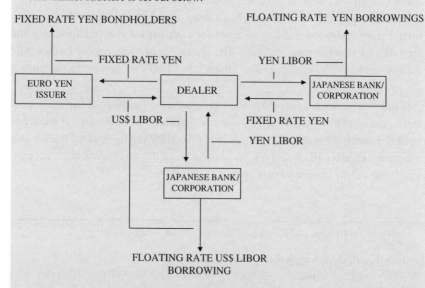

## 2. US$/Yen Basis Swap Market – Structure in 1990s

The market structure changed dramatically in the mid to late 1990s. The US$/yen basis widened with the swaps trading at US$ LIBOR versus Yen LIBOR minus 15–30 bps (the spread traded at minus 40–50 bps for a short period).

The reason for the change was primarily the change in the credit quality of the Japanese banks. The end of the "bubble" economy and the bad debt problems of Japanese banks led to the banks experiencing significant problems and being downgraded by the credit rating agencies. This was reflected in the emergence of the "Japanese Premium". This was evident in funding for Japanese banks. US$ LIBOR is calculated as an average of rates quoted by a number of banks (both non-Japanese and Japanese). The Japanese premium in US$ was at peak levels around 40–60 bps (that is, non-Japanese banks funded at US$ LIBOR flat against Japanese banks funding at US$ LIBOR plus 40–60 bps). The Japanese premium in Yen was at peak levels also around 40–60 bps (that is, non-Japanese banks funded at Yen LIBOR minus 30 bps against Japanese banks funding at Yen LIBOR plus 10–30 bps).

The presence of the Japanese banks affected the US$/Yen currency basis swap in several ways. The primary effect was that Japanese banks were only prepared to pay Yen at Yen LIBOR less substantial margins. This was to offset the higher cost of US$ funds when translated into Yen, as the banks' funding costs in US$ and Yen were significantly different. The cross currency basis swap margin tracked this difference consistently during the period[35].

The margins were reduced dramatically in the late 1990s. This was driven by the improvement in the credit quality of the Japanese banks (based on government support) and the attractive opportunity for Japanese and foreign corporations to generate Yen funding at attractive cost (in some cases at *negative* interest rates[36]).

---

**Exhibit 10.20    Cross Currency Basis Swap – Hedging Transaction Costs**

Cross currency basis swaps often result in cash flow mismatches that must be hedged, resulting in significant transaction costs. This can be illustrated with an example.

Assume Counterparty A can fund at US$ LIBOR plus 20 bps. The cross currency basis swap is trading at US$ LIBOR flat versus Yen LIBOR minus 15 bps. This results in a cash flow mismatch of 20 bps pa in US$ for A. If Counterparty B has funding at Yen LIBOR minus 15 bps, then B does not have any cash flow exposure but is exposed to changes in the pricing of the cross currency basis swap (the margin). The position is set out below.

CROSS CURRENCY BASIS SWAP

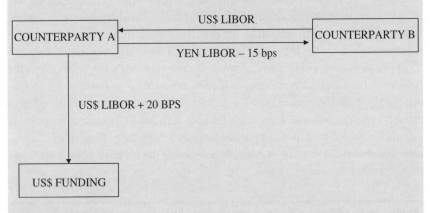

The cash flow exposure can be quantified as follows: swap modified duration x cash flow mismatch.

---

[35]  In effect, the US$/Yen basis was equal to the actual difference in LIBOR for non-Japanese and Japanese banks.

[36]  The cross currency basis swap margin was greater than the actual Yen LIBOR rate itself.

Assuming the swap has a 5 year maturity and a modified duration (4.26) the cash flow exposure in present value is 0.85% (4.26 × 0.20% pa). This equates to $850,000 in a $100 million swap.

This exposure will require the following hedges:
- Interest rate hedge on $200,000 pa for 5 years.
- Currency exposure of $850,000 that must be hedged with a spot foreign exchange transaction.

The cost of hedges will need to be incorporated in the pricing of the cross currency basis swap.

## 6.3   Foreign Exchange ("FX") Basis Points/Currency Conversion Factors

In the case of currency swaps, it may be necessary to calculate equivalencies between currencies. The requirement to match flows between currencies occurs usually in the context of spreads above or below the floating rate index in a particular currency. This requirement to make payments of spreads/margins above or below the relevant floating rate index effectively requires the party making or forgoing such payments to either borrow or lend the foreign currency. Consequently, the transaction pricing and the required adjustment require the borrowing and lending transactions to be encompassed in the pricing of the transaction. Pricing of the adjustments reflects the prevailing interest rates in the two currencies.

In practice, the spreads above or below the relevant index can be priced on the basis of either assumed borrowing or lending transactions in the relevant currencies, or alternatively as a string of forward foreign exchange contracts designed to convert exposure from one currency to another. **Exhibit 10.21** sets out an example calculating the FX basis point adjustment required using the present value of annuities. **Exhibit 10.22** sets out an example calculating the FX basis point adjustment required using currency forwards.

---

**Exhibit 10.21    Foreign Exchange Basis Points – Present Value of Annuities Method**

This technique seeks to equate the present value of x% pa in one currency payable periodically with y% pa in the second currency. This conversion is effected as follows:
1. The number of basis points being converted from one currency to the other is structured as an annuity stream for the relevant number of periods.
2. This annuity stream is then present valued at the prevailing interest rate applicable to the relevant maturity.

3. The present value equivalent of this annuity stream in one currency is then reconverted into an annuity in the second currency using the interest rate applicable to that currency for the relevant maturity.
4. The annuity amount generated as a result of this procedure equates to the equivalent number of basis points in the second currency.

Assume that it is necessary to convert 100 bps in Yen into the US$ equivalent for a 3 year transaction. Assume the following interest rates[37] are currently prevailing:

| Currency | Interest Rates (% pa) | Periods (Per Year) |
|---|---|---|
| Yen | 0.750 | 2 |
| US$ | 6.500 | 2 |

The present value of the yen annuity (50 bps per each semi-annual period) is calculated at Yen interest rates (0.75% pa or 0.375% per semi-annual period) over 3 years (6 semi-annual periods). The present value in Yen is 296.10 bps. The equivalent US$ annuity over 3 years (6 semi-annual periods) at US$ interest rates (6.50% pa or 3.25% pa per semi-annual period) is 55.11 bps each semi-annual period[38].

| Currency | Payments (bps) | Interest Rates (%) | Periods | Present Value (bps) |
|---|---|---|---|---|
| Yen | 50.00 | 0.375 | 6 | 296.10 |
| US$ | 55.11 | 3.250 | 6 | 296.10 |

This means that 100 bps in Yen is equal to 110.22 bps in US$.

---

**Exhibit 10.22    Foreign Exchange Basis Points – Currency Forward Method**

This technique seeks to convert the surplus or deficit in one currency to the other currency by hedging the relevant amounts at current currency forward rates. This conversion is effected as follows:
1. The number of basis points being converted from one currency to the other is structured as an annuity stream for the relevant number of periods. A notional principal is added at commencement and maturity for the purpose of the calculation.
2. The cash flows in the nominated currency are then converted into the second currency at the prevailing currency forward rates applicable to the relevant maturity.

---

[37] This example, for convenience, uses a single interest rate to discount the annuity cash flows. In practice, zero coupon rates for each maturity should be used.

[38] Please note that the spot exchange rate is irrelevant as the calculations are in bps on the notional principal in each currency at the market rate.

3. The internal rate of return of the cash flows in the converted currency is then computed.
4. The foreign exchange basis point is then derived from the internal rate of return as a net
   uniform series of cash flows on the notional principal in the second currency based on
   the prevailing spot rate.

Assume that it is necessary to convert 100 bps in Yen into the US$ equivalent for a 3 year
transaction. The calculations are set out in the Table below:

| Year | Currency Rates (US$1: Yen) | Cash Flows (Yen) | Cash Flows (US$)[39] |
|------|-----|-----|-----|
| Spot | 100.00 | 1,000,000 | 10,000 |
| 0.50 | 97.37 | (10,000) | (103) |
| 1.00 | 94.82 | (10,000) | (105) |
| 1.50 | 92.35 | (10,000) | (108) |
| 2.00 | 89.96 | (10,000) | (111) |
| 2.50 | 88.70 | (10,000) | (113) |
| 3.00 | 87.98 | (1,010,000) | (10,114) |

The internal rate of return for the US$ cash flows is 1.089% pa. This implies that 100 bps
in Yen is equivalent to 108.9 bps in US$.

## 6.4   Assembling Currency Swap Package

The separate identified elements of the cross currency swap are combined to determine the total swap price. **Exhibit 10.23** sets out an example of determining the
price of the cross currency swap.

## 7   Pricing Generic Versus Non-generic Swaps

The pricing and valuation methodology outlined to date is applicable to generic
swap structures. A generic swap structure refers to the underlying conventional
swap structure that forms the basis for all swap transactions. Characteristics
of a generic interest rate swap are summarised in **Exhibit 10.24**. The corresponding characteristics of the generic currency swap are summarised in **Exhibit
10.25**. Standard market prices such as those made available on Bloomberg,
Dow-Jones/Telerate, Reuters etc screens are usually for generic transactions.

---

[39]  Note that the principal cash flow in US$ at the final date is calculated at the spot exchange
rate but the annuity flow (Yen 10,000 in this example) is converted at the forward
rate.

### Exhibit 10.23    Currency Swap Pricing

Assume that a dealer is asked to price a US$/Yen cross currency swap where the dealer pays fixed yen against receipt of US$ LIBOR. The transaction is for 5 years on a notional principal of US$100 million (Yen 10,000 million at the current spot rate of US$1: Yen 100). The position is hedged as follows:

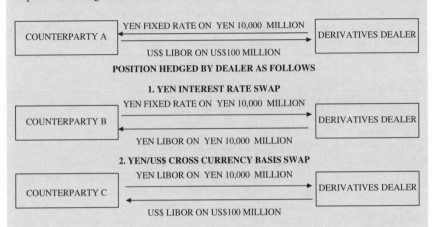

Assume the following prices of the components:
- Yen fixed to floating interest rate swap is trading at 3.00/3.03% pa for 5 years.
- US$/Yen cross currency basis swap is trading at US$ LIBOR against Yen LIBOR minus 13/15 bps.

The breakeven price of the combined position is Yen 2.85% pa against receipt of US$ LIBOR. This can be seen from the following diagram:

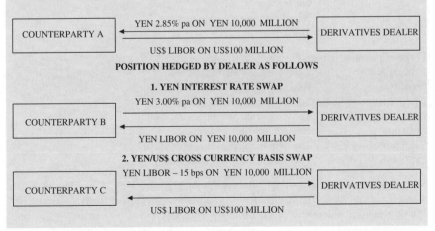

The dealer would adjust the breakeven price by its earning requirement (say, 5 bps pa). This would give a final price of Yen 2.80% pa against US$ LIBOR.

Assume that Counterparty A wishes to receive Yen at a rate of 3.10% pa to match the cash flows of its underlying fixed rate Yen funding being converted through the currency swap. This will require the extra Yen payments of 30 bps pa to be converted into US$ equivalent. This is done using the foreign exchange basis points or currency conversion factors. Assume 100 bps in Yen is currently valued at 110.2 bps in US$ using current interest rates.

This means that the final swap price the dealer pays is Yen 3.10% pa against receipt of US$ LIBOR plus a margin of 33.1 bps (calculated as 30 bps × 110.2/100).

---

**Exhibit 10.24    Characteristics of Generic Interest Rate Swap**

| Terms | Definition |
| --- | --- |
| Maturity | One to 30 years (up to 10–12 years in most currencies). |
| Effective date | Depending on market convention, up to five business days from trade date (typically 2 days). The effective date is such that the first fixed and first floating payment periods are full coupon periods (that is, no long or short first coupons). |
| Settlement date | Effective date. |
| All-in-cost | Depends on market convention, but usually the quarterly, semi-annual or annual equivalent of the internal rate of return of the fixed flows versus the floating index flat. |
| Premium or discount | None. |
| **Fixed payment** | |
| Fixed coupon | Current market rate. |
| Payment frequency | Either quarterly, semi-annually or annually depending on market convention. |
| Day count | Based on market convention. |
| Pricing date | Trade date. |
| **Floating payment** | |
| Floating index | Certain money market indices. |
| Spread | None. |
| Determination source | Some publicly quoted source. |
| Payment frequency | The term of the floating index itself. |
| Day count | Based on market convention. |
| Reset frequency | The term of the floating index itself. |
| First coupon | Current market rate for the index. |

Source: Adapted from Kopprasch, Robert W., Macfarlane, John, Ross, Daniel R. and Showers, Janet (1985) The Interest Rate Swap Market: Yield Mathematics, Terminology and Conventions; Salomon Brothers Inc., New York.

---

**Exhibit 10.25    Characteristics of Generic Currency Swap[40]**

| Terms | Definition |
|---|---|
| Maturity | One to 30 years (up to 10–12 years in most currencies). |
| Effective Date | Depending on market convention two to five business days from trade date (typically, 2 days). The effective date is such that the first fixed and floating payments are full coupon periods (that is, no long or short first coupons). |
| Settlement Date | Effective date. |
| Contractual Exchange Rate | Market exchange rate as between US$ and the relevant currency (or the two currencies if US$ is not involved) for value the effective date. |
| All-in-cost | Depends on market convention but usually quarterly, semi-annual or annual equivalent of the internal rate of return of the fixed flows in the relevant currency versus US$ three or six month LIBOR flat. |
| Premium or Discount | None. |
| **Fixed rates** | **Non-US$ currency** |
| Notional Principal | US$ notional principal × contractual exchange rate. |
| Fixed Coupon | Current market rate in the relevant currency. |
| Payment Frequency | Either quarterly, semi-annual or annual depending on market convention. |
| Day Count | Based on market convention. |
| Pricing Date | Trade date. |
| **Floating Payment** | **US$ currency** |
| Floating Index | US$ three or six month LIBOR. |
| Spread | None. |
| Determination Source | Some publicly quoted source (e.g. Reuters page LIBO). |
| Payment Frequency | The term of the floating rate index. |
| Day Count | Based on market convention (generally actual/360). |
| Reset Frequency | The term of the floating index itself. |
| First Coupon | Current market rate for the index. |

Source: Adapted from Balducci, Vince, Doraiswami, Johnson, Cal and Showers, Janet (September 1990) Currency Swaps: Corporate Applications and Pricing Methodology; Salomon Brothers Inc., New York.

---

The basic complexity of pricing swap transactions arises from the fact that swap transactions are seldom of a standard type. The most important variations cover

---

[40] Most currency swaps are quoted and transacted as a fixed rate swap (in a non-US$ currency) against US$ LIBOR and the terms set out here are for such a transaction.

changes in commencement dates, premiums or discounts to face value, spreads above or below the floating rate index, valuation of unwinds/reversals of interest rate/currency swaps and structured swaps transacted against bonds/securities. Price adjustments are usually necessary to accommodate these variations.

The valuation methodology in respect of non-generic swaps entails two specific and distinct phases:
- Valuation of a generic (or "plain vanilla") swap.
- Factoring in of the price/cost impact of variations from the generic structure.

The pricing mathematics of non-generic swaps encompasses the arithmetical and technical steps used to value individual swap transactions. In essence, the pricing mathematics starts with a given swap price (driven by the underlying pricing approach outlined) and translates it mathematically to an equivalent price for the specific swap being analysed. The arithmetical and technical procedures used are common to all financial transactions and are not necessarily peculiar to swaps. However, swap transactions give rise to particular complexities that are considered in detail in the final Section of this Chapter.

# 8 Pricing/Trading Non-generic Swaps

## 8.1 Pricing Delayed Start Swaps

A common variation on standard swap structures relates to the delay in the effective date of commencement of the swap[41]. This is generally driven by the need to match cash flows. **Exhibit 10.26** sets out the structure of such a transaction.

The delayed start swap equates economically to a *forward* on the interest rate swap that can be derived from the swap yield curve itself. There are several ways to price this transaction including:
- **Forward on swap rate** – the forward swap rate can be determined using normal forward interest rate determination models. This will typically be done in two possible ways:
  1. Calculate the forward swap rate using the rate to the commencement date of the swap and the rate to the actual swap maturity. For example, for a 5 year swap with a delayed start of 7 days, the calculation of the delayed start swap rate requires the 7 day swap rate and the 5 year 7 day swap rate (this would be interpolated). This can be done directly or by using zero coupon rates.

---

[41] A related transaction is the forward start swap, see Das, Satyajit (2004) Structured Products Volume 1; John Wiley & Sons (Asia), Singapore at Chapter 13.

2. Use the zero coupon rates coinciding with the dates on which the actual cash flows of the deferred swap cash flows take place. **Exhibit 10.27** sets out an example of this approach.

- **Adjust for cash flows resulting for delay** – this entails calculating the positive or negative accrual arising from the delay. This reflects the difference in interest between the fixed rate on the swap transaction and the interest rate applicable for the period between the normal commencement date and the delayed commencement date. The swap rate is then adjusted for the impact of this delay. **Exhibit 10.28** sets out the method for adjusting the swap rate for such a deferred start.

The prices derived using the different methodologies should, theoretically, be identical. However, the market may not be fully efficient and small differences may arise. In practice, the dealers will be concerned about the hedging mechanism available to hedge the actual transaction. This may dictate the specific pricing approach employed.

---

**Exhibit 10.26    Delayed Start Swap**

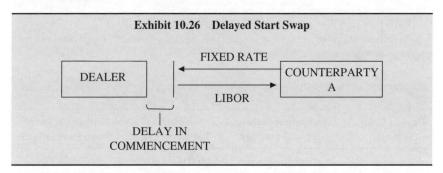

---

**Exhibit 10.27    Pricing Delayed Start Swap – Zero Coupon Methodology**

**1. Assumptions**

Assume the interest rate swap priced in **Exhibit 10.12**. The transaction is a 5 year interest rate swap on $100,000,000 with semi-annual cash flows. The derivative dealer will receive fixed in the transaction. Assume the swap commencement is to be delayed for a period of 1 month.

The original swap price, based on the prevailing zero coupon rates at commencement, is 6.32% pa. The solution is set out below:

| Days to Cash Flows | Zero Coupon Rates (% pa Semi-annual) | Swap Payments ($) | Present Value of Swap Payments ($) |
|---|---|---|---|
| 0 | | (100,000,000) | (100,000,000) |
| 182 | 5.75 | 3,151,369 | 3,063,537 |

| Days To Cash Flows | Zero Coupon Rates (% pa semi annual) | Swap Payments ($) | Present Value Of Swap Payments ($) |
|---|---|---|---|
| 365 | 5.80 | 3,168,684 | 2,992,576 |
| 547 | 5.90 | 3,151,369 | 2,888,237 |
| 730 | 6.01 | 3,168,684 | 2,814,939 |
| 912 | 6.01 | 3,151,369 | 2,718,061 |
| 1095 | 6.01 | 3,168,684 | 2,652,938 |
| 1278 | 6.16 | 3,168,684 | 2,562,696 |
| 1461 | 6.30 | 3,168,684 | 2,471,903 |
| 1643 | 6.33 | 3,151,369 | 2,380,904 |
| 1826 | 6.35 | 103,168,684 | 75,454,209 |
| | | **Net Present Value** | 0 |

## 2. Pricing the Delay in Commencement

The delay in commencement is priced as follows:
- The days to cash flow are re-specified to reflect the delay (31 days).
- The zero rates appropriate to the new cash flows dates are derived (through interpolation).
- The swap rate is then recalculated.

The results in the present case are summarised below:

| Days to Cash Flows | Zero Coupon Rates (% pa semi annual) | Swap Payments ($) | Present Value of Swap Payments ($) |
|---|---|---|---|
| 31 | 5.70 | (100,000,000) | (99,523,798) |
| 213 | 5.76 | 3,156,760 | 3,053,890 |
| 396 | 5.82 | 3,174,105 | 2,982,622 |
| 578 | 5.92 | 3,156,760 | 2,878,139 |
| 761 | 6.01 | 3,174,105 | 2,805,604 |
| 943 | 6.01 | 3,156,760 | 2,709,036 |
| 1126 | 6.03 | 3,174,105 | 2,642,204 |
| 1309 | 6.18 | 3,174,105 | 2,551,697 |
| 1492 | 6.31 | 3,174,105 | 2,462,703 |
| 1674 | 6.33 | 3,156,760 | 2,371,932 |
| 1857 | 6.35 | 103,174,105 | 75,065,973 |
| | | **Net Present Value** | 0 |

This equates to a swap rate of 6.33% pa for the delayed start swap (a difference of 1 bps to the spot start swap).

**Exhibit 10.28    Pricing Delayed Start Swap – Cash Flow Adjustment**

**1.  Assumptions**

Assume a dealer is asked to price a 5 year interest rate swap where the dealer receives fixed rate for a deferred start. The transaction date is 5 May 2002. The normal effective or commencement would be 7 May 2002. The price for the spot start swap is 9.00% pa annual. However, the counterparty wishes the swap to commence from 7 June (2002). This represents a delay of 31 days.

The pricing adjustment for the delay can be derived in two ways:
1. Adjusting for cash flows (the positive or negative accrual for the delay period).
2. Adjusting for the hedge cost.

**2.  Adjusting Cash Flows**

This assumes that the dealer enters into a normal (spot start) 5 year swap at the time of committing to the delayed start swap to hedge its exposure. This is set out below:

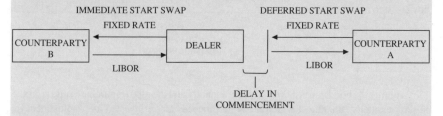

IMMEDIATE START SWAP        DEFERRED START SWAP

FIXED RATE        FIXED RATE

COUNTERPARTY B    DEALER    COUNTERPARTY A

LIBOR        LIBOR

DELAY IN COMMENCEMENT

This creates a cash flow mismatch that must be valued. Assuming the 6 month LIBOR rate is 7.25% pa semi-annually, the adjustment is as follows:

|  | % pa (Semi Annual Bond Equivalent Basis (365/365)) |
|---|---|
| Dealer pays | 8.81 |
| Dealer receives | 7.35 |

**Notes:**
1. 9.00% pa converted to semi-annual basis is equal to 8.81% pa
2. 7.25% pa semi-annually (money market 365/360 day basis) converted to 365/365 day basis.

This results in the dealer suffering a loss of 1.46% pa or 12.4 bps over 31 days (calculated as 1.46% pa × 31/365). This 12.4 bps is equivalent to 3.2 bps pa when amortised over five years (the term of the swap) at the swap rate (9.00% pa). The swap rate quoted is therefore 9.032% pa.

Please note that the hedge is imperfect. The maturity of the two swaps is mismatched by 31 days over the life of the transactions. This creates exposure to LIBOR resets over the life of the transactions that must be hedged. It also creates exposures to changes in interest rates as the maturity mismatch creates settlement date mismatch, requiring funding and re-investment of settlement cash flows.

### 3. Adjusting for the Hedge Cost

The approach outlined above assumes the delayed start swap is hedged with a normal commencement swap. In practice, an alternative means of hedging the swap would be to sell a 5 year government bond and re-invest the proceeds for the delay period. The short bond position would be closed and a 5 year swap entered into effective 7 June 2002 to hedge the delayed start swap. The change in value on the bond hedge would compensate for the movement in swap rates during the delay period. The process is summarised below:

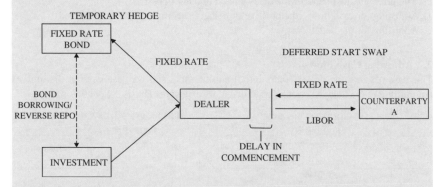

Assuming the bond rate is 8.00% pa semi-annually and the repo (repurchase) rate is 6.00% pa semi-annually (the rate at which the bond proceeds are re-invested after adjustment for the cost of borrowing the securities), the cost to the dealer is 2.00% pa or 17.0 bps over 31 days. This is equivalent to 4.4 bps pa over the life of the swap resulting in an adjusted swap price of 9.044% pa.

Please note that this hedge is also imperfect. Unlike the cash flow adjustment methods, there are no maturity and settlement date mismatches. However, the dealer is exposed to changes in the swap spread (the difference in the rates on the swap and the underlying government bond). In addition, where the bond borrowing must be renewed, there is exposure to changes in the cost of borrowing the security as well as the short term investment rate.

## 8.2   Pricing Swaps with Up-front Payments/Off Market Coupons

Another common variation to generic structures is off-market swaps (also referred to as premium or discount structures). Under these structures, the interest rate coupons and in the case of currency swaps, the currency rates utilised in the swap transaction, are varied from current market rates. This necessitates a payment at the commencement of the transaction by one counterparty to the other, compensating for the off-market coupon or notional principal amounts. The transactions are driven by desire to match cash flows on existing bonds or securities or the requirement for structured cash flows (for example, driven by cash flow or tax factors).

The off-market swaps are effectively economic equivalents of an *on market swap* (at current market rates) and a loan or borrowing transaction. The swaps are valued using two methods:

- **Matching cash flows** – where the cash flows of an offsetting swap (at normal market coupon) are compared to the off market swap cash flows, and the difference in cash flows is discounted using zero coupon rates.

- **Discounting swap cash flows** – where the cash flows of the off-market swap are discounted at current market zero coupon rates to derive the swap rate that equates to the required premium or discount (rather than the zero net present value usually used). **Exhibit 10.29** sets out an example of pricing an off-market interest rate swap.

The two methodologies outlined are equivalent and should be identical, provided that the same yield curves are used. In practice, the major issue is the valuation of the loan component of such transactions. Where the above two methodologies are used, the loan component is valued using the zero coupon rates or swap rates (effectively at LIBOR flat). This assumes that the credit or default risk on the loan is equivalent to that embedded in the swap curve[42]. This may not be consistent with the credit quality of the counterparty. **Exhibit 10.30** sets out a methodology for valuing these swap structure that incorporates the credit risk (through a risk margin over the swap rate) of the counterparty.

In the case of a currency swap, use of an off-market coupon in either currency would necessitate a similar adjustment to that used in the case of the interest rate swap. However, it is also feasible to vary the currency rate embedded in the swap transaction. In this particular case, it is feasible to either compensate the relevant counterparty for the off-market exchange rate through an up-front payment, or by altering the coupon flows on one or other payment side of the swap transaction.

The major issue in relation to off-market structures is the fact that such transactions are capable of being used to create *disguised* loans or investments. It is important that the loan component be specifically recognised and priced *as a loan or investment transaction*. In addition, it is important that the loan or investment component be incorporated in any credit risk analysis of the transaction, as the risk on an off-market swap will not be equivalent to that on a conventional swap[43].

---

[42] See discussion in Chapter 11.
[43] See discussion in Das, Satyajit (2004) Structured Products Volume 1; John Wiley & Sons (Asia), Singapore at Chapter 13.

**Exhibit 10.29    Pricing Swaps with Up-front Payments – Using Zero Coupon Rates**

**1.  Assumptions**

Assume the interest rate swap priced in **Exhibit 10.12**. The transaction is a 5 year interest rate swap on $100,000,000 with semi-annual cash flows. The derivative dealer will receive fixed in the transaction. Assume the counterparty wishes to receive a payment equal to $2,000,000 (2% of the face value) at the commencement of the transaction.

The original swap price, based on the prevailing zero coupon rates at commencement, is 6.32% pa. The solution is set out below:

| Days to Cash Flows | Zero Coupon Rates (% pa Semi-annual) | Swap Payments ($) | Present Value of Swap Payments ($) |
|---|---|---|---|
| 0 | | (100,000,000) | (100,000,000) |
| 182 | 5.75 | 3,151,369 | 3,063,537 |
| 365 | 5.80 | 3,168,684 | 2,992,576 |
| 547 | 5.90 | 3,151,369 | 2,888,237 |
| 730 | 6.01 | 3,168,684 | 2,814,939 |
| 912 | 6.01 | 3,151,369 | 2,718,061 |
| 1095 | 6.01 | 3,168,684 | 2,652,938 |
| 1278 | 6.16 | 3,168,684 | 2,562,696 |
| 1461 | 6.30 | 3,168,684 | 2,471,903 |
| 1643 | 6.33 | 3,151,369 | 2,380,904 |
| 1826 | 6.35 | 103,168,684 | 75,454,209 |
| | **Net Present Value** | | 0 |

**2.  Pricing the Up-front Payment**

The swap with the up-front payment is calculated by solving for the swap rate that has a net present value of $2,000,000.

The results in the present case are summarised below:

| Days to Cash Flows | Zero Coupon Rates (% pa Semi-annual) | Swap Payments ($) | Present Value of Swap Payments ($) |
|---|---|---|---|
| 0 | | (100,000,000) | (100,000,000) |
| 182 | 5.75 | 3,385,992 | 3,291,621 |
| 365 | 5.80 | 3,404,596 | 3,215,376 |
| 547 | 5.90 | 3,385,992 | 3,103,270 |
| 730 | 6.01 | 3,404,596 | 3,024,514 |
| 912 | 6.01 | 3,385,992 | 2,920,424 |
| 1095 | 6.01 | 3,404,596 | 2,850,452 |
| 1278 | 6.16 | 3,404,596 | 2,753,492 |
| 1461 | 6.30 | 3,404,596 | 2,655,939 |
| 1643 | 6.33 | 3,385,992 | 2,558,165 |
| 1826 | 6.35 | 103,404,596 | 75,626,747 |
| | **Net Present Value** | | 2,000,000 |

This equates to a swap rate of 6.79% pa for the swap with the up-front payment (a difference of 47 bps to the normal on market swap). The higher rate effectively compensates the dealer for the fact that the up-front payment of $2,000,000 must be recovered (together with interest costs) over the life of the transaction by way of a higher swap rate.

---

**Exhibit 10.30    Pricing Swaps with Up-front Payments – Incorporating Credit Risk**

**1.  Assumptions**
Assume the interest rate swap priced in **Exhibit 10.12**. The transaction is a 5 year interest rate swap on $100,000,000 with semi-annual cash flows. The derivative dealer will receive fixed in the transaction. Assume the counterparty wishes to receive a payment equal to $2,000,000 (2% of the face value) at the commencement of the transaction. The original swap price, based on the prevailing zero coupon rates at commencement, is 6.32% pa.

**2.  Pricing the Up-front Payment**
The swap with the up-front payment is calculated in two stages:
1. The price of the conventional swap (known to be 6.32% pa).
2. The annuity stream required to recover the principal and interest cost of a loan equivalent of $2,000,000 (2% of face value).

The second component may be priced as follows:
• Assume a loan value of 2.00% pa.
• The loan is to be repaid by way of 10 equal payments (semi-annual payments over 5 years).
• The interest rate on the loan is set at LIBOR plus 50 bps (equivalent to the swap rate of 6.32% pa plus 50 bps or 6.82% pa (6.71% pa semi-annual).
• This equates to annuity payments equal to 24 bps every semi-annual period or 48 bps pa.

This equates to a swap rate of 6.80% pa for the delayed start swap (a difference of 48 bps to the normal on market swap). The higher rate effectively compensates the dealer for the fact that the up-front payment of $2,000,000 must be recovered (together with interest costs incorporating the credit margin) over the life of the transaction by way of a higher swap rate.

---

# 8.3   Pricing Swap Terminations

## 8.3.1   Approach

Swap transactions may be terminated prior to maturity. Such early terminations may be required for a number of reasons including:
• Termination of the underlying business rationale (for example, the funding) to which the swap transaction related.
• Realisation of profit/minimisation of losses from the swap transaction.

Other reasons for determination of the termination value include:
* Establishing the mark-to-market valuation of the transaction. This is used for valuation of the position. It is also used to determine the counterparty credit risk of the transaction.
* Default by one counterparty necessitating determination of the liquidation value of the swap.

The approach to valuation in each case is identical. In this Section, the process of pricing swap terminations is set out.

## 8.3.2   Approaches to Unwinding Swap Positions

In order to terminate a swap, the counterparty enters into an economically equal but opposite position for the remaining life of the original transaction. This can be undertaken in several ways including:
* **Reverse swaps** – this would require the counterparty to enter into an equal but opposite transaction (a reverse swap) *with a counterparty other than the original dealer*. This reverse swap would, when combined with the first swap, result in the counterparty having no exposure under the original swap. No payment between the parties is required, at least where the reverse swap is transacted at the rates prevailing at the time of the termination. The economic value (if any) on the original transactions is reflected in the cash flows between the two transactions over the remaining life of the two transactions. **Exhibit 10.31** sets out the structure of a reverse swap.
* **Swap sale or assignment** – this would entail the counterparty assigning or selling its position in the existing swap to a new third party. The fair market value (cash payment) of the swap is the present value of the original contract that is paid to (by) the counterparty by (to) the dealer assuming the swap position. **Exhibit 10.32** sets out the structure of a swap sale or assignment.
* **Swap Cancellation** – this would require the counterparty to enter into an equal but opposite swap with the original counterparty. The swap reversing the original transaction is entered into on the *original swap terms* (dates and rates). This second swap will, when revalued at the *rates prevailing on the termination date,* have positive or negative value. This value will be paid between the two counterparties to equate the values and will equal the termination payment. **Exhibit 10.33** sets out the structure of a swap cancellation.

In economic terms, there should be no difference in valuation between the three alternatives. This is particularly the case where no counterparty credit risk is assumed to exist. In practice, the transactions have significant differences in

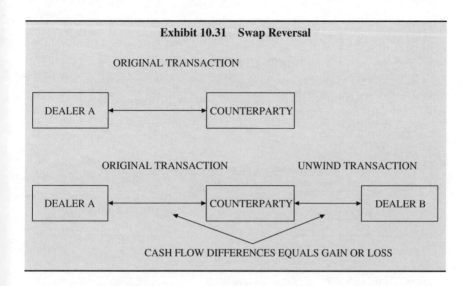

Exhibit 10.31 Swap Reversal

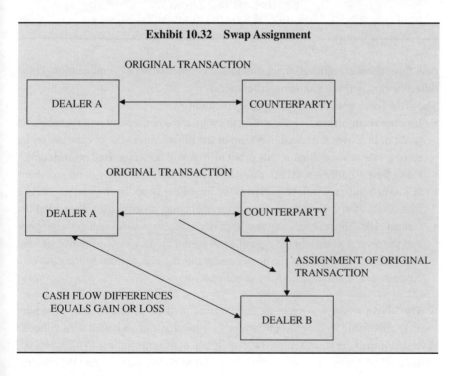

Exhibit 10.32 Swap Assignment

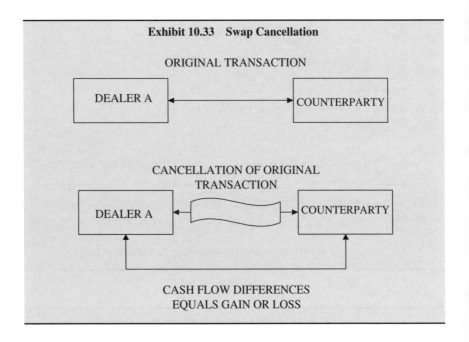

Exhibit 10.33    Swap Cancellation

cash flow, accounting/taxation treatment and counterparty risk implications. These differences may drive valuation differences.

The differences between the techniques include:

- **Income recognition** – under a reverse swap, the counterparty will recognise its profit or loss over the remaining term of the mirror contracts. In contrast, under a swap sale or cancellation, this profit or loss will be recognised immediately.
- **Cash flow** – under a reversal, there is no immediate cash flow, with any gains or losses being received or paid over the life of the swap. In contrast, there is an immediate cash receipt or payment triggered under a swap sale or cancellation.
- **Credit risk** – the reverse swap results in two credit exposures (under the original and the reverse swap). In the case of an assignment, the existing credit exposure continues to exist, but to the dealer assuming the transaction. In the cash of a cancellation, all credit exposure is eliminated.

The above examples relate to the reversal of interest rate swaps. A similar logic is applicable in the case of currency swaps that can be undertaken either as reversals/mirror currency swaps, swap assignment or cancellations. The difference in the case of currency swaps is that, in addition to any interest rate differential, there may be foreign exchange gains or losses in the original currency swap position that must be valued.

### 8.3.3    Pricing Interest Rate Swap Terminations

The value of an interest rate swap after commencement of the transaction reflects changes in interest rates in the particular currency. This will, in practice, be changes in the zero coupon rate or swap rates (derived using the zero coupon rates). The changes will reflect two separate factors:

- **General market rates** – as measured by movements in benchmark rates (such as the interest rates on government securities). This reflects the impact of broad macroeconomic factors.
- **Swap spreads** – the swap spread is the margin between the benchmark rate and the swap rate available in the market. This spread or margin reflects a range of factors including credit risk, the margin or spread charged by lenders, and supply and demand for swaps in the relevant currency or market at the time.

Applying this methodology, an interest rate swap of the type identified is usually valued in either of two ways:

- **Offsetting swap method** – this method assumes the original transaction cash flows are to be offset precisely by entering into an identical transaction, but in an opposite direction. The interest rates of the transaction are set at current market rates at the valuation dates. All payment dates and maturity dates are assumed to be the same as the remaining payment and maturity dates on the original transaction. The two sets of cash flows (fixed and floating rate) are then matched, and any net cash flows or differences are calculated. The differences are discounted at the zero coupon rates to determine the current value of the transaction[44].
- **Zero coupon method** – this method identifies both sets of cash flows (fixed and floating rate) of the original swap. Each set of cash flows is then discounted back at the zero coupon rates in the relevant currency. The present values are then netted to determine the current value of the transaction.

An example of how each method is used to determine the value of an interest rate swap is set out in **Exhibit 10.34** and **Exhibit 10.35**. In practice, both approaches are similar and should yield similar valuations provided there is a common set of interest rates (that is, consistent swap rates and the zero coupon rates are utilised).

---

[44] Please note this offsetting swap is a hypothetical transaction. It is not a transaction that is actually entered into. The transaction is used for the purposes of deriving the valuation.

**Exhibit 10.34    Pricing an Interest Rate Swap Termination – Offsetting Swap Method**

**1. Approach**

This method assumes the original transaction cash flows are to be offset precisely by entering into an identical transaction, but in an opposite direction. The interest rates are set at current market swap rates. All payment dates and maturity dates are assumed to be the same as the remaining payment and maturity dates on the original transaction. The two sets of cash flows are then matched, and any net cash flow or differences are calculated. The differences are discounted at the zero coupon rates to determine the current value of the transaction.

The structure of the transaction is set out in the diagram below:

**ORIGINAL INTEREST RATE SWAP**

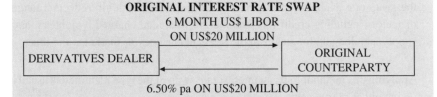

**OFFSETTING SWAP (DESIGNED TO ELIMINATE EXPOSURE UNDER ORIGINAL SWAP)**

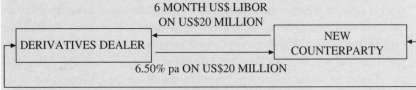

PAYMENT BETWEEN THE COUNTERPARTY (REFLECTING CURRENT VALUE)

**2. Assumptions**

The original transaction details together with the valuation details are summarised below:

| Notional Principal Amount ($) | 20,000,000 | |
|---|---|---|
| | Initial | Market |
| Fixed Rate (% pa semi-annual) | 6.50 | 7.10 |
| LIBOR (% pa semi-annual) | 6.00 | 6.25 |
| | Fixed | LIBOR |
| Days in Current Interest Rate Period | 184 | 184 |

Under the terms of the original transaction, the dealer pays fixed rates and receives floating rates.

The following details merit comment:

• The initial rates refer to the original payments and the market rates refer to the payments based on the current market rates as of the valuation date. In determining the market rates as of the valuation date, it is important to note that the fixed rate will be for a period to the maturity *of the original swap*. This will generally include a broken (stub) period at the start to align all the payments over the life of the transaction. The swap rate will generally need to be interpolated. Similarly, the floating rate will be for a shortened period, and an interpolated LIBOR rate will need to be used.

- The days in current interest rate period refers to the number of days in the current interest rate period running from the last payment date to the next payment date as per the original contract.

### 3. Pricing the Swap Termination

Using the information, the cash flows for both the original swap and the offsetting transaction can be generated. These cash flows are set out in the Tables below.

The following details merit comment:

- All cash flows are calculated either at the original rates or at current market rates.
- The accrual on the floating rate side of the transaction is based on a Money Market or LIBOR day count convention where all interest amounts are calculated on the basis of actual number of days/360. This is standard market convention for US$ LIBOR.
- The first period accrual on both the fixed rate side and the US$ floating rate side are as follows:
  - For the original transaction, using the days in the current period (the number of days in the current interest rate period running from the last payment date to the next payment date as per the original contract).
  - For the offsetting transaction, using the number of days from the valuation date to the next payment date (reflecting the shorter first interest period designed to match all future payment dates and final maturity exactly).
  - All future cash flows other than the nearest or next interest payment date on the US$ floating rate side are ignored, as these cash flows will exactly offset between the two transactions.

Fixed rate cash flows are as follows:

| Time to Cash Flow (days) | Annual Tenor (Years) | Fixed Rate (Original) ($) | Fixed Rate (Market) ($) | Fixed Rate Differences ($) |
|---|---|---|---|---|
| 0 | – | | | |
| 74 | 0.20 | 655,342 | (287,890) | 367,452 |
| 255 | 0.70 | 644,658 | (704,164) | (59,507) |
| 439 | 1.20 | 655,342 | (715,836) | (60,493) |
| 620 | 1.70 | 644,658 | (704,164) | (59,507) |
| 804 | 2.20 | 655,342 | (715,836) | (60,493) |
| 985 | 2.70 | 644,658 | (704,164) | (59,507) |
| 1169 | 3.20 | 655,342 | (715,836) | (60,493) |
| 1351 | 3.70 | 648,219 | (708,055) | (59,836) |
| 1535 | 4.21 | 655,342 | (715,836) | (60,493) |
| 1716 | 4.70 | 644,658 | (704,164) | (59,507) |
| | Total | 6,503,562 | (6,675,945) | (172,384) |

Floating rate cash flows are as follows:

| Time to Cash Flow (days) | Annual Tenor (Years) | Floating Rate (Original) ($) | Floating Rate (Market) ($) | Floating Rate Differences ($) |
|---|---|---|---|---|
| 0 | – | | | |
| 74 | 0.20 | (613,333) | 256,944 | (356,389) |
| 255 | 0.70 | | | |
| 439 | 1.20 | | | |
| 620 | 1.70 | | | |
| 804 | 2.20 | | | |
| 985 | 2.70 | | | |
| 1169 | 3.20 | | | |
| 1351 | 3.70 | | | |
| 1535 | 4.21 | | | |
| 1716 | 4.70 | | | |
| | Total | (613,333) | 256,944 | (356,389) |

The Table below sets out the net cash flow or cash flow differences discounted back at the current zero coupon rates to establish the current value of the transaction.

| Time to Cash Flows (Days) | Annual Tenor (Years) | Fixed Rates Differences ($) | LIBOR Differences ($) | Total Differences ($) | Zero Rates (% pa) | Discount Net Cash Flows |
|---|---|---|---|---|---|---|
| 0 | – | | | | | |
| 74 | 0.20 | 367,452 | (356,389) | 11,063 | 6.25 | 10,928 |
| 255 | 0.70 | (59,507) | | (59,507) | 6.30 | (57,020) |
| 439 | 1.20 | (60,493) | | (60,493) | 6.35 | (56,176) |
| 620 | 1.70 | (59,507) | | (59,507) | 6.38 | (53,572) |
| 804 | 2.20 | (60,493) | | (60,493) | 6.38 | (52,789) |
| 985 | 2.70 | (59,507) | | (59,507) | 6.65 | (50,016) |
| 1169 | 3.20 | (60,493) | | (60,493) | 6.72 | (49,118) |
| 1351 | 3.70 | (59,836) | | (59,836) | 7.00 | (46,580) |
| 1535 | 4.21 | (60,493) | | (60,493) | 7.10 | (45,334) |
| 1716 | 4.70 | (59,507) | | (59,507) | 7.30 | (42,727) |
| Total | | (172,384) | | (528,772) | | (442,405) |

The current value of the transaction is $442,405. This amount must be paid by the dealer upon termination of the swap.

---

**Exhibit 10.35    Pricing an Interest Rate Termination – Zero Coupon Method**

**1.  Approach**

This method identifies both sets of fixed and floating cash flows. Each set of cash flows is then discounted back at the zero coupon rates. The present values are then matched to determine the current value of the transaction.

## 2. Assumptions
Assume the same transaction as in **Exhibit 10.34**.

## 3. Pricing the Swap Termination
The Table below sets out the transaction cash flows that are then discounted back to the valuation date. Please note that both fixed and floating rate components are decomposed into security equivalents and the principal amount is included in the calculation.

| Time to Cash Flows (Days) | Annual Tenor (Years) | Fixed Rate (Original) ($) | LIBOR (Initial) ($) | Zero Rates (% pa) | Discounted Cash Flows – Fixed Rates | Discounted Cash Flows – LIBOR |
|---|---|---|---|---|---|---|
| 0 | – | | | | | |
| 74 | 0.20 | 655,342 | (20,613,333) | 6.25 | 647,337 | (20,361,525) |
| 255 | 0.70 | 644,658 | | 6.30 | 617,721 | |
| 439 | 1.20 | 655,342 | | 6.35 | 608,569 | |
| 620 | 1.70 | 644,658 | | 6.38 | 580,369 | |
| 804 | 2.20 | 655,342 | | 6.38 | 571,877 | |
| 985 | 2.70 | 644,658 | | 6.65 | 541,842 | |
| 1169 | 3.20 | 655,342 | | 6.72 | 532,114 | |
| 1351 | 3.70 | 648,219 | | 7.00 | 504,617 | |
| 1535 | 4.21 | 655,342 | | 7.10 | 491,122 | |
| 1716 | 4.70 | 20,644,658 | | 7.30 | 14,823,374 | |
| | | | | Total | 19,918,942 | (20,361,525) |

The value of the swap at the valuation date can be established in a number of ways:
* Taking the net present value of both sets of cash flows and then adding them to derive the swap valuation:

| | |
|---|---|
| Present Value of Fixed Rate Payments ($) | 19,918,942 |
| Present Value of Floating Rate Payments ($) | (20,361,525) |
| Value of Swap ($) | (442,584) |

* Calculating the value of each side by comparing the current value with the original face value to determine the value of the fixed rate and floating rate component of the transaction separately. The value of the swap being the sum of the two values:

| Component | Fixed Rate | Floating Rate |
|---|---|---|
| Original Value ($) | 20,000,000 | 20,000,000 |
| Current Value ($) | 19,918,942 | 20,361,525 |
| Net Value | (81,058) | (361,525) |

This implies a total value of the swap of $(442,584).

The current value of the transaction is $442,584. This amount must be paid by the dealer upon termination of the swap.

## 8.3.4   Pricing Currency Swap Terminations

The valuation of a termination of a cross currency swap is based on a similar approach to that used in the case of an interest rate swap. However, the value of a currency swap after commencement of the transaction reflects changes in both currency values and changes in interest rates in both currencies.

Currency swaps are usually valued in either of two ways (similar to the approaches used with interest rate swaps):

*   **Offsetting swap method** – this method assumes the original transaction cash flows are to be offset precisely by entering into an identical transaction, but in an opposite direction. The principal amounts and payments in both currencies of the transaction are set at current market rates at the valuation date. All payment dates and maturity dates are taken to be the same as the remaining payment and maturity dates on the original transaction. The two sets of cash flows are then matched and the net cash flows or differences are calculated. The differences are discounted at the zero coupon rates to determine the current value of the transaction[45].

*   **Zero coupon method** – this method identifies both sets of cash flows in the respective currencies of the original transaction. Each set of cash flows is then discounted back at the zero coupon rates in the relevant currency. The present values are then converted into one or other currency at the then spot currency exchange rate at the valuation date to determine the current value of the transaction.

An example of how each method is used to determine the value of a cross currency fixed to floating swap is set out in **Exhibit 10.36** and **Exhibit 10.37**. The approaches are similar and should yield similar valuations, provided there is a common set of interest rates (that is, consistent swap rates and zero coupon rates are utilised). Other types of cross currency swaps (fixed to fixed and fixed to floating) are also priced using a similar approach.

---

**Exhibit 10.36   Pricing a Cross Currency Swap Termination – Offsetting Swap Method**

**1.   Approach**
This method assumes the original transaction cash flows are to be offset precisely by entering into an identical transaction, but in an opposite direction. The interest rates and currency rates

---

[45]   Please note this offsetting swap is a hypothetical transaction. It is not a transaction that is actually entered into. The transaction is used for the purposes of deriving the valuation.

are set at current market swap rates. All payment dates and maturity dates are assumed to be the same as the remaining payment and maturity dates on the original transaction. The two sets of cash flows are then matched and any net cash flow or differences are calculated. The differences are discounted at the zero coupon rates to determine the current value of the transaction.

The structure of the transaction is set out in the diagram below:

**ORIGINAL CURRENCY SWAP**

**OFFSETTING SWAP (DESIGNED TO ELIMINATE EXPOSURE UNDER ORIGINAL CURRENCY SWAP)**

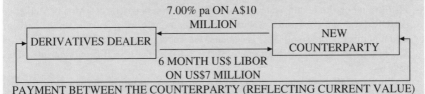

PAYMENT BETWEEN THE COUNTERPARTY (REFLECTING CURRENT VALUE)

## 2. Assumptions

The original transaction details, together with the valuation details, are summarised below:

| Currency | A$ | US$ | Currency Rate (A$1:US$) |
|---|---|---|---|
| Initial Amount | 10,000,000 | 7,000,000 | 0.7000 |
| Market Amount | 11,666,667 | 7,000,000 | 0.6000 |

| Interest Rates | Initial | Market |
|---|---|---|
| Fixed (% pa semi-annual) | 7.00 | 6.75 |
| LIBOR (% pa semi-annual) | 6.00 | 5.75 |
| | Fixed Rate | LIBOR |
| Days in Current Interest Rate Period | 184 | 184 |

Under the terms of the original transaction, the dealer pays fixed rates and receives floating rates.

The following details merit comment:

- The initial currency amounts are based on the original cash flows (initial and final exchange) of the currency swap. The market amounts are based on the cash flows (initial and final exchange) for a currency swap transacted as of valuation date. Please note that the LIBOR side notional principal (US$) is kept constant and the fixed rate side (A$) is allowed to fluctuate.

- The initial rates refer to the original payments, and the market rates refer to the payments based on the current market rates as of the valuation date. In determining the market rates as of the valuation date, it is important to note that the fixed rate will be for a period to the maturity *of the original swap*. This will generally include a broken (stub) period at the start to align all the payments over the life of the transaction. The swap rate will generally need to be interpolated. Similarly, the floating rate will be for a shortened period and an interpolated LIBOR rate will need to be used.
- The days in current interest rate period refers to the number of days in the current interest rate period running from the last payment date to the next payment date as per the original contract.

### 3. Pricing the Swap Termination

Using the information, the cash flows for both the original swap and the offsetting transaction can be generated. These cash flows are set out in the Tables below.

The following details merit comment:

- All cash flows are calculated either at the original rates or at current market rates.
- The cash flows for the offsetting swap are based on the *current* notional principal amounts.
- The accrual on the floating rate side of the transaction is based on a Money Market or LIBOR day count convention where all interest amounts are calculated on the basis of actual number of days/360. This is standard market convention for US$ LIBOR.
- The first period accrual on both the fixed rate side and the US$ floating rate side are as follows:
  - For the original transaction, using the days in the current period (the number of days in the current interest rate period running from the last payment date to the next payment date as per the original contract).
  - For the offsetting transaction, using the number of days from the valuation date to the next payment date (reflecting the shorter first interest period designed to match all future payment dates and final maturity exactly).
  - All future cash flows other than the nearest or next interest payment date on the US$ floating rate side are ignored as these cash flows will exactly offset as between the two transactions.

A$ fixed rate cash flows are as follows:

| Time to Cash Flows (Days) | Principal (Original) (A$) | Fixed Rate (Original) (A$) | Total Cash Flows (Original) (A$) | Principal (Market) (A$) | Fixed Rate (Market) (A$) | Total Cash Flows (Market) (A$) | Fixed Rates Differences (A$) |
|---|---|---|---|---|---|---|---|
| 74 | (352,877) | (352,877) | | 159,658 | 159,658 | (193,219) |
| 255 | (347,123) | (347,123) | | 390,514 | 390,514 | 43,390 |
| 439 | (352,877) | (352,877) | | 396,986 | 396,986 | 44,110 |
| 620 | (347,123) | (347,123) | | 390,514 | 390,514 | 43,390 |
| 804 | (352,877) | (352,877) | | 396,986 | 396,986 | 44,110 |
| 985 | (347,123) | (347,123) | | 390,514 | 390,514 | 43,390 |
| 1169 | (352,877) | (352,877) | | 396,986 | 396,986 | 44,110 |
| 1351 | (349,041) | (349,041) | | 392,671 | 392,671 | 43,630 |

| | | | | | | | |
|---|---|---|---|---|---|---|---|
| 1535 | | (352,877) | (352,877) | | 396,986 | 396,986 | 44,110 |
| 1716 | (10,000,000) | (347,123) | (10,347,123) | 11,666,667 | 390,514 | 12,057,180 | 1,710,057 |
| Total | | | | | 3,702,329 | | 1,867,078 |

US$ floating rate cash flows are as follows:

| Time to Cash Flows (Days) | Principal (Original) (US$) | LIBOR (Original) (US$) | Total Cash Flows (Original) (US$) | Principal (Market) (US$) | LIBOR (Market) (US$) | Total Cash Flows (Market) (US$) | LIBOR Differences (US$) |
|---|---|---|---|---|---|---|---|
| 74 | | 214,667 | 214,667 | | (82,736) | (82,736) | 131,931 |
| 255 | | | | | | | |
| 439 | | | | | | | |
| 620 | | | | | | | |
| 804 | | | | | | | |
| 985 | | | | | | | |
| 1169 | | | | | | | |
| 1351 | | | | | | | |
| 1535 | | | | | | | |
| 1716 | 7,000,000 | | 7,000,000 | (7,000,000) | | (7,000,000) | |
| Total | | | | | | | 131,931 |

The Table below sets out the net cash flow or cash flow differences discounted back at the current zero coupon rates to establish the current value of the transaction.

The A$ fixed rate position is as follows:

| Time to Cash Flows (Days) | Fixed Rate Differences (A$) | Zero Rates (% pa) | Discounted Net Cash Flows (A$) |
|---|---|---|---|
| 74 | (193,219) | 5.75 | (191,041) |
| 255 | 43,390 | 5.80 | 41,715 |
| 439 | 44,110 | 5.90 | 41,171 |
| 620 | 43,390 | 6.10 | 39,239 |
| 804 | 44,110 | 6.20 | 38,636 |
| 985 | 43,390 | 6.25 | 36,842 |
| 1169 | 44,110 | 6.40 | 36,161 |
| 1351 | 43,630 | 6.50 | 34,559 |
| 1535 | 44,110 | 6.70 | 33,581 |
| 1716 | 1,710,057 | 6.93 | 1,247,966 |
| Total | 1,867,078 | | 1,358,827 |

The US$ LIBOR position is as follows:

| Time to Cash Flows (Days) | LIBOR Differences (US$) | Zero Rates (% pa) | Discounted Net Cash Flows (US$) |
|---|---|---|---|
| 74 | 131,931 | 5.75 | 130,444 |
| 255 | | | |

| Time to Cash Flows (Days) | LIBOR Differences (US$) | Zero Rates (% pa) | Discounted Net Cash Flows (US$) |
|---|---|---|---|
| 439 | | | |
| 620 | | | |
| 804 | | | |
| 985 | | | |
| 1169 | | | |
| 1351 | | | |
| 1535 | | | |
| 1716 | | | |
| Total | 131,931 | | 130,444 |

The current value of the swap is based on converting the values in each currency to the other currency using the spot exchange rate applicable on the valuation date as follows:

| Currency | A$ | US$ |
|---|---|---|
| Value of A$ Fixed Rates | 1,358,827 | 815,296 |
| Value in US$ LIBOR | 217,406 | 130,444 |
| Total | 1,576,233 | 945,740 |

The current value of the transaction is US$945,740 (US$1,576,233). This amount must be paid to the dealer upon termination of the swap. The position incurs a loss on interest rates (A$ rates decline from original contract rates) but generates a currency gain (the A$ weakens from contract rates creating a gain on the A$ liability).

---

**Exhibit 10.37    Pricing a Currency Swap Termination – Zero Coupon Method**

**1. Approach**
This method identifies both sets of fixed and floating cash flows. Each set of cash flows is then discounted back at the zero coupon rates. The present values are then matched at the spot rate on the termination date to determine the current value of the transaction.

**2. Assumptions**
Assume the same transaction as in **Exhibit 10.36**.

**3. Pricing the Swap Termination**
The Table below sets out the transaction cash flows that are then discounted back to the valuation date. Please note that both fixed and floating rate components are decomposed into security equivalents and the principal amount is included in the calculation.

The A$ fixed rate position is as follows:

| Time to Cash Flows (Days) | Principal (Original) (A$) | Fixed Rate (Original) (A$) | Total Cash Flows (Original) (A$) (% pa) | Zero Rates | Discounted Net Cash Flows (A$) |
|---|---|---|---|---|---|
| 74 | | (352,877) | (352,877) | 5.75 | (348,900) |
| 255 | | (347,123) | (347,123) | 5.80 | (333,716) |
| 439 | | (352,877) | (352,877) | 5.90 | (329,367) |
| 620 | | (347,123) | (347,123) | 6.10 | (313,908) |
| 804 | | (352,877) | (352,877) | 6.20 | (309,085) |
| 985 | | (347,123) | (347,123) | 6.25 | (294,735) |
| 1169 | | (352,877) | (352,877) | 6.40 | (289,292) |
| 1351 | | (349,041) | (349,041) | 6.50 | (276,468) |
| 1535 | | (352,877) | (352,877) | 6.70 | (268,645) |
| 1716 | (10,000,000) | (347,123) | (10,347,123) | 6.93 | (7,551,127) |
| Total | | | | | (10,315,243) |

The US$ LIBOR position is as follows:

| Time to Cash Flows (Days) | Principal (Initial) (US$) | LIBOR (Initial) (US$) | Total Cash Flows (Initial) (US$) | Zero Rates (% pa) | Discount Net Cash Flows (A$) |
|---|---|---|---|---|---|
| 74 | 7,000,000 | 214,667 | 7,214,667 | 5.75 | 7,133,352 |
| 255 | | | | | |
| 439 | | | | | |
| 620 | | | | | |
| 804 | | | | | |
| 985 | | | | | |
| 1169 | | | | | |
| 1351 | | | | | |
| 1535 | | | | | |
| 1716 | | | | | |
| Total | | | | | 7,133,352 |

The value of the swap at the valuation date can be established by taking the present values in each currency (translated into the other currency at the spot rate at the valuation date) and taking the net of the two:

| Currency | A$ | US$ |
|---|---|---|
| Current Value | (10,315,243) | 7,133,352 |
| Foreign Currency Value | (6,189,146) | 11,888,921 |
| Total Value | 1,573,678 | 944,207 |

This implies a total value of the swap of US$944,207 (calculated as US$ value of the A$ fixed rates of US$6,189,146 against the US$ value of the LIBOR side of US$7,133,352). The equivalent value of the swap of A$1,573,678 (calculated as A$ value of the US$ LIBOR side of A$11,888,921 against the A$ value of the fixed rate side of A$10,315,243). This amount (either in US$ or A$) must be paid to the dealer upon termination of the swap.

## 8.4 Pricing Bond/Swap Packages

Swap transactions are frequently linked with securities issues as part of financing or investment transactions[46]. Such bond/swap packages entail a number of adjustments, encompassing many of the features identified above, to match the final cash flows of the bond/swap package to the exact requirements of the borrower. The typical adjustments include:

- Delayed commencement of the transaction.
- Up-front payments to reimburse issue fees and costs.
- Adjustment to cash flows to exactly match the cash flows of the underlying bond.

The structures fall into two categories: swaps transacted in the primary market against new issues and structured swaps transacted in the secondary market against existing bonds. **Exhibit 10.38** sets out an example of a bond issue with attached interest rate swap transaction. **Exhibit 10.39** sets out an example of a bond issue with currency swap attached. The examples detail the methodology for adjusting the market swap price to reflect the specific cash flow features dictated by the transaction. **Exhibit 10.40** and **Exhibit 10.41** set out examples of transacting a swap against an existing bond issue.

| Exhibit 10.38    Bond Issue Interest Rate Swap – Primary Market |
| --- |

Assume an issuer is to undertake a US$100 million fixed rate bond issue to be swapped via an interest rate swap into floating rate funding on the following terms:

**Bond Issue**

| | |
| --- | --- |
| Amount | US$100 million |
| Term | 5 years |
| Coupon | 8.00% pa annual |

---

[46] For a detailed discussion of the use of swaps in new issues, see Das, Satyajit (2004) Structured Products Volume 1; John Wiley & Sons (Asia), Singapore at Chapter 3; for a detailed discussion of the use of swaps in investments using asset swaps, see Das, Satyajit (2004) Structured Products Volume 1; John Wiley & Sons (Asia), Singapore at Chapter 4.

Issue price   100 or face value
Fees          1.875% flat
Expenses      US$125,000 or 0.125% flat[47]
Payment       In four weeks from launch
All-in cost   8.51% pa annual or 8.33% pa semi-annual

**Interest Rate Swap**
Structure     Issuer to receive fixed rate US$ and pay 6 month US$ LIBOR
Swap rate     8.78/8.85% pa semi-annual (based on Treasury + 78/85 versus six month
              LIBOR where the Treasury yield is 8.00% pa semi-annual).

Assume the swap structure requires reimbursement of fees and pricing adjustments to exactly match the swap cash flows. The reimbursement of fees and up-front costs of the issuer are dictated by:

• The desire to have a simple par borrowing.
• The need to avoid issuing at an effective discount (issue price less fees and expenses) to eliminate possible accounting and tax issues.
• The ability to accurately compare different borrowing structures in terms of margin relative to the floating rate index.

The exact structure of the swap, once adjusted, will be as follows:
• Swap counterparty pays ABC US$2 million at commencement of swap; that is, payment date.
• All cash flows will match the bond cash flows.

The swap rate set out above is the market swap rate for a generic or conventional swap transaction. The swap pricing will need to be adjusted to incorporate the specific structure of the swap.

The dealer will pay the following fixed rate versus 6 month LIBOR flat:

| Item | (% pa annual) |
|---|---|
| Swap rate | 8.96 |
| Amortisation of fee reimbursement | −0.51 |
| Adjustment for delay | +0.04 |
| Adjusted swap rate | 8.49 |

**Notes:**
1. The annualised equivalent of 8.78% pa semi-annual is 8.97% pa annual (a 19 bps gross up). However, the swap rate used is adjusted by 1 bp to reflect the added reinvestment risk to the counterparty.

---

[47] These are purely manager's expenses that are reimbursed by the borrower and do not include any costs of the borrower itself.

2. The swap rate is reduced by 0.51% pa to recover the 2.00% up-front payment (1.875% for fees and 0.125% for expenses) amortised over five years. The discount rate used is the swap rate (8.97% pa annual), but could be higher or lower, reflecting the cost of funding the payment to the dealer and the credit risk of the issuer.
3. The swap rate is increased by a 0.04% adjustment to cover the delayed start of 4 weeks. This represents the positive carry or earning on the hedged or offsetting swap with immediate start. This is calculated as earnings of 2.00% (based on short-term rates of 6.00% pa semi-annual versus bond rates of 8.00% pa semi-annual) over four weeks (around 15 bps) amortised over five years at the swap rate (8.97% pa annual).

The net result of the swap is that the dealer would pay 8.49% pa annual. However, the dealer is required to make annual payments of 8.00% pa annual to match the bond coupon and receives a spread under LIBOR. The swap dealer receives LIBOR minus a margin every six months.

The margin under LIBOR would be the floating rate equivalent of 49 bps. The 49 bps would require adjustment, unless the fixed rate and floating rate payments are calculated on the same day count basis and paid on the same frequency. In this example, both conditions are not met. The 49 bps annual bond basis would be adjusted by 3 bps to an equivalent spread of 46 bps semi-annual LIBOR or money market basis[48].

This means that the dealer would quote an adjusted swap price of:

- Payment of $2,000,000 (2% of face value) up-front to the issuer.
- Payment to the issuer of 8.00% pa annually on US$100 million.
- Receipt from the issuer of US$6 month LIBOR minus 46 bps on US$100 million.

A structural variation to improve swap pricing might be to reconfigure the bond to be issued at a premium. For example, the issue price could be 101 and the coupon 8.25% to yield a comparable return of 8.50% pa annual. This may allow the issuer to improve its sub-LIBOR margin where the funding cost of the fees significantly exceeds the swap rate.

---

### Exhibit 10.39    Bond Issue Cross Currency Swap – Primary Market

Assume the issuer undertakes an A$50 million fixed rate bond issue to be swapped into floating rate via a cross currency swap on the following terms:

**Bond Issue**
Amount      A$50 million
Term         5 years

---

[48] This is calculated as the swap rate (8.97% pa annual) minus the spread (49 bps annual) de-compounded into semi-annual equivalent (8.31% pa semi-annual) to derive the semi-annual spread (47 bps) by deducting the semi-annual swap rate (8.78% pa semi-annual) which is then converted to a LIBOR/money market basis to provide the final spread of 46 bps (47 bps × 360/365).

| Coupon | 14.00% pa |
|---|---|
| Issue price | 101.25% |
| Fees | 2% pa flat |
| Expenses | A$125,000 or 0.25% pa flat |
| Payment | In four weeks from launch |
| All-in cost | 14.29% pa annual or 13.82% pa semi-annual |

## Cross Currency Swap

| Structure | Issuer to receive fixed rate A$ and pay floating rate US$6 month LIBOR |
|---|---|
| Swap rate | 14.60/14.80% pa semi-annually |

Assume the swap structure requires reimbursement of fees and pricing adjustments to exactly match the swap cash flows. The swap can be structured in two separate ways.

## Structure 1

Under this structure, the swap dealer partially reimburses the issue fees up to par to issuer to provide it with proceeds of A$50 million.

The exact structure of the swap is as follows:

- At commencement, issuer will pay over issue proceeds of A$49.5 million to the dealer and in return, the issuer will receive US$34.65 million. This assumes an exchange rate of A$1 = US$0.70 (effectively the four week A$/US$ forward rate at the day the transaction is undertaken). The issuer will also receive US$0.35 million, being reimbursement of fees of 1.00% or A$0.5 million. Please note that the fee reimbursement is designed to create a par value issue for the issuer.
- Every year on the coupon payment date, the issuer will receive a payment of A$7 million representing 14.00% pa on A$50 million.
- Every six months, the issuer will pay 6 month US$ LIBOR minus a margin to the dealer.
- At maturity, issuer will receive A$50 million to make the principal repayment to the bondholders. The issuer will pay US$35 million to the swap dealer.

The swap rate set out above is the market swap rate for a generic or conventional swap transaction. The swap pricing will need to be adjusted to incorporate the specific structure of the swap.

The dealer will pay the following A$ fixed rate versus 6 month LIBOR flat:

| Item | (% pa annual) |
|---|---|
| Swap rate | 15.11 |
| Amortisation of fee reimbursement | −0.30 |
| Adjustment for delay | −0.05 |
| Adjusted swap rate | 14.76 |

**Notes:**
- The annualised equivalent of 14.60% pa semi-annual is 15.13% pa annual (a 53 bps gross up). However, the swap rate used is adjusted by 2 bps to reflect the added reinvestment risk to the counterparty.

- The swap rate is reduced by 0.30% pa to recover the 1.00% up-front payment amortised over five years. The discount rate used is the swap rate (15.25% pa annual) but could be higher or lower, reflecting the cost of funding the payment to the dealer and the credit risk of the issuer.
- The swap rate is decreased by a 0.05% adjustment to cover the delayed start of 4 weeks. This represents the negative carry or loss on the hedged or offsetting swap with immediate start. This is calculated as a loss of 2.00% (based on short-term rates of 16.00% pa semi-annual versus bond rates of 14.00% pa semi-annual) over four weeks (around 15 bps) amortised over five years at the swap rate (15.25% pa annual).

The net result of the swap is that the dealer would pay A$ 14.76% pa annual. However, the dealer is required to make annual payments of A$ 14.00% pa annual to match the bond coupon and receives a spread under US$ LIBOR. The swap dealer receives US$ LIBOR minus a margin every six months.

The margin under US$ LIBOR would be the US$ floating rate equivalent of A$ 76 bps. The 76 bps must be adjusted for:

- Currency conversion from A$ to US$.
- Compounding and day count adjustments.

The A$ 76 bps annual bond basis is equivalent to US$ 62 bps semi-annually. The 14 bps adjustment reflects the US$/A$ currency conversion factor. It reflects the notional need to borrow A$ to purchase a spot US$ investment which produces the necessary US$ flows to cover the periodic US$ shortfall over the life of the swap reflected in the sub-LIBOR US$ payments. The adjustment is calculated to equate the present value of off-yield curve margin in A$ at current A$ rates with an equivalent off-yield curve margin in US$ at current US$ rates. In this example, the equivalency is calculated on the basis of A$ interest rate of 15.25% pa annual and US$ interest rates 8.00% pa semi-annual for five years. The sub-LIBOR margin is then adjusted to a money market/LIBOR (360/365) day count basis to provide a final margin of 61 bps.

This means that the dealer would quote an adjusted swap price of:

- Initial exchange where issuer pays A$49.5 million and receives US$34.65 million.
- Payment of US$350,000 (1% of face value) up-front to the issuer.
- Payment to the issuer of A$7.00 million (A$14.00% pa annually on A$50 million).
- Receipt from the issuer of US$6 month LIBOR minus 61 bps on US$35 million.
- Final exchange where issuer receives A$50 million and pays US$35 million.

## Structure 2

This is identical to Structure 1 with the following major differences:

- In the initial exchange issuer pays over A$49.5 million and receives US$34.65 million only. There is no reimbursement of fees.
- Issuer receives A$7.0 million pa to cover the bond coupon.
- Issuer pays 6 month LIBOR minus a margin on US$34.65 million.
- In the final exchange, issuer repays US$34.65 million *but receives A$50 million.*

The swap pricing adjustments are slightly different. The dealer will pay the following A$ fixed rate versus 6 month LIBOR flat:

| Item | (% pa annual) |
|---|---|
| Swap rate | 15.11 |
| Adjustment for delay | −0.05 |
| Adjustment for A$ shortfall | −0.15 |
| Adjustment for lower A$ proceeds | −0.14 |
| Adjusted swap rate | 14.77 |

**Notes:**
- The reduction of 0.15% pa for the adjustment for the A$ shortfall represents the amortised effect (at 15.00% pa annual) of having notionally to invest A$ each year over the term of the swap to generate A$ at maturity to cover the extra A$ flow to issuer.
- The reduction of 0.14% pa for the lower A$ proceeds, represents an adjustment for the lower A$ proceeds received by the swap dealer, translates into a higher running coupon (calculated as A$7 million/A$49.5 million = 14.14% pa versus the coupon rate of 14.00% pa).

The base swap price of 14.77% pa annual is then adjusted (as set out above) to provide the issuer with sub-LIBOR margin equivalent of 62 bps pa (1 bps higher than that under the first structure).

---

**Exhibit 10.40   Bond Issue Cross Currency Swap – Secondary Market Example 1**

This example relates to a US$/A$ currency swap transacted against an existing issue. The issuer has an outstanding US$ issue that it now seeks to convert into an A$ liability in order to lock in the economic gains resulting from favourable movements in currency and interest rates since the liability was incurred.

A dealer arranges an A$ issue to specifically match the principal amount, maturity and interest payment dates of the outstanding US$ issue. The terms of the issuer's original issue are as follows:

| | |
|---|---|
| Amount (US$) | 50 million |
| Maturity | 5 years (remaining life of original 8 year issue) |
| Coupon (% pa annual) | 8.25 |

At the time of the original issue, the exchange rate was US$1 = A$1.50 (equivalent to A$75 million).

The dealer arranges an A$ issue for a counterparty willing to swap the A$ issue proceeds into US$ (by assuming the US$ liability under the existing issue). The terms of the new issue are as follows:

| | |
|---|---|
| Amount (A$) | 75 million |
| Maturity | 5 years |
| Coupon (% pa annual) | 12.50 |

| Issue Price | 100 or par value |
| Issue Fees & Expenses (%) | 2.125 |
| All in Cost (% pa annual) | 13.11 |

Assume that the counterparty has a US$ target rate of 10.00% pa annual (the market rate at the relevant time). However, under the swap agreement the counterparty will economically assume and service the original 8.25% US$50 million issue. Therefore, the counterparty will be required to compensate the issuer for the rate differential. In order to avoid any currency exposure, the compensation is in the form of an initial transfer payment.

Through its A$75 million borrowing, the counterparty obtains net proceeds of A$73,406,250. By converting these proceeds in the spot market at the time the issue is undertaken (US$1.00 = A$1.25), the dealer obtains US$58,725,000. However, the net present value of the US$ payment stream to be assumed, discounted at the counterparty's 10.00% pa target rate, is US$46,683,062. Therefore, the counterparty must pay the difference equal to A$15,052,423 (or US$12,041,938) to the company. This initial transfer payment effectively adjusts the counterparty's all-in US$ cost (to 10.00% pa) while lowering the issuer's A$ cost.

This initial transfer payment to the issuer represents the net present value of the following:
- **Interest rate gain** – being the difference between the current interest rate on US$ debt of the relevant maturity (10.00% pa) and the coupon on the existing US$ issue of 8.25% pa.
- **Exchange rate gain** – being the value of the borrowing in A$ reflecting the fact that the A$/US$ rate has moved from A$1.50 when the borrowing was undertaken to A$1.25.

The economics for each party is as follows:
- The all-in US$ cost to the issuer is determined by translating the US$ principal amount of the original issue into A$ at the spot rate, and adjusting this amount to reflect original issuance costs (A$73,406,250, assuming issuing costs of 2.125%). In addition, the issuer must take into account the initial transfer payment that it receives from the dealer (A$15,052,423) and the A$ payments it has agreed to make to cover the counterparty's A$ obligations of A$9,375,000 in years 1 through 4 and A$84,375,000 at maturity. The company would therefore effectively raise A$ at an all-in cost of 8.00% pa.
- The all-in US$ cost to the counterparty consists of the US$ proceeds of US$58,725,000 resulting from its own A$ issue, less the US$ transfer payment it makes to the company (US$12,041,938) and the US$ payments it has agreed to make to cover the issuer's US$ obligations of US$4,125,000 in years 1 through 4 and US$54,125,000 at maturity. The counterparty thus effectively raises US$ at an all-in cost of 10.00% pa.

---

**Exhibit 10.41    Bond Issue Cross Currency Swap – Secondary Market Example 2**

In July 1985, the Walt Disney Company ("WD") raised yen funding via an issue of European Currency Unit ("ECU")[49] denominated bonds swapped using a cross currency ECU/Yen swap into yen. The swap was transacted against an existing issue of a French utility.

---

[49]   The ECU was a precursor to the Euro.

The transaction was noteworthy in that it enabled WD, rated a weak A at the time of the issue, to raise funds at a rate that was superior to its credit rating and approached rates that were commanded by AAA borrowers[50].

The transaction represents an interesting example of a currency swap transacted against an existing issue, and some of the valuation issues that arise.

The detailed structure of the transaction was as follows:

- WD issued a ECU 80 million bond for a 10 year term with amortisation of principal after 5 years at a coupon of 9.125% pa.
- WD entered into a swap with the French utility whereby it economically assumed the payments on an existing yen liability.
- The swap was intermediated by Industrial Bank of Japan ("IBJ") to avoid exposing either WD or the French utility to counterparty risk on the swap other than to IBJ.

The terms of the ECU bond were as follows:

| | |
|---|---|
| Amount (ECU million) | 80.0 |
| Term (Years) | 10.0 |
| Coupon (% pa) | 9.125 |
| Issue Price | 100.25 |
| Fees (%) | 2.00 |
| Expenses (US$) | 75,000 |
| US$/ECU Exchange Rate | 0.7420 |

The cash flows of the ECU bond were as follows:

| Year | ECU Issue Cash Flows (ECU Million) |
|---|---|
| 0 | 78.499 |
| 1 | (7.300) |
| 2 | (7.300) |
| 3 | (7.300) |
| 4 | (7.300) |
| 5 | (7.300) |
| 6 | (23.300) |
| 7 | (21.840) |
| 8 | (20.380) |
| 9 | (18.920) |
| 10 | (17.460) |

The all in cost of the ECU issue to WD was 9.47% pa annual.

---

[50] See (5 September 1991) The Walt Disney Company's Yen Financing & Teaching Note; Harvard Business School, Cambridge ©1989 by the President and Fellows of Harvard College; see also Mason, Scott, Merton, Robert, Perhold, Andre and Tufano, Peter (1995) Cases in Financial Engineering: Applied Studies of Financial Innovation; Prentice-Hall, Upper Saddle River, New Jersey at 567–579.

The swap cash flows for WD were as follows:

| Year | ECU Receipts (ECU Million) | Yen Payments (Yen million) |
|------|---------------------------|----------------------------|
| 0    | (78.499)                  | 14,445.153                 |
| 0.5  |                           | (483.226)                  |
| 1    | 7.300                     | (483.226)                  |
| 1.5  |                           | (483.226)                  |
| 2    | 7.300                     | (483.226)                  |
| 2.5  |                           | (483.226)                  |
| 3    | 7.300                     | (483.226)                  |
| 3.5  |                           | (483.226)                  |
| 4    | 7.300                     | (483.226)                  |
| 4.5  |                           | (483.226)                  |
| 5    | 7.300                     | (1,808.141)                |
| 5.5  |                           | (1,764.650)                |
| 6    | 23.300                    | (1,721.160)                |
| 6.5  |                           | (1,677.670)                |
| 7    | 21.840                    | (1,634.179)                |
| 7.5  |                           | (1,590.689)                |
| 8    | 20.380                    | (1,547.199)                |
| 8.5  |                           | (1,503.708)                |
| 9    | 18.920                    | (1,460.218)                |
| 9.5  |                           | (1,416.728)                |
| 10   | 17.460                    | (1,520.450)                |

This equates to an all in cost in yen to WD of 7.01% pa annual. This compared to the alternative cost of funding to WD in yen of 7.75% pa. This equated to a saving of 74 bps pa[51].

The currency swap was transacted with a French utility against an existing yen issue. The economics for the French utility are interesting. The currency swap cash flows for the French utility are as follows:

| Year | ECU Payments (ECU Million) | Yen Receipts (Yen million) |
|------|---------------------------|----------------------------|
| 0    |                           |                            |
| 0.5  |                           | 483.226                    |
| 1    | (7.350)                   | 483.226                    |
| 1.5  |                           | 483.226                    |

---

[51] The source of this significant arbitrage cost saving is discussed in Chapter 11.

| 2 | (7.350) | 483.226 |
|---|---|---|
| 2.5 | | 483.226 |
| 3 | (7.350) | 483.226 |
| 3.5 | | 483.226 |
| 4 | (7.350) | 483.226 |
| 4.5 | | 483.226 |
| 5 | (7.350) | 1,808.141 |
| 5.5 | | 1,764.650 |
| 6 | (23.350) | 1,721.160 |
| 6.5 | | 1,677.670 |
| 7 | (21.880) | 1,634.179 |
| 7.5 | | 1,590.689 |
| 8 | (20.410) | 1,547.199 |
| 8.5 | | 1,503.708 |
| 9 | (18.940) | 1,460.218 |
| 9.5 | | 1,416.728 |
| 10 | (17.470) | 1,520.450 |

The small differences between the ECU cash flows paid by the French utility and received by WD represents the earning of IBJ on the swap. The Yen cash flows are identical between the two counterparties.

The effective cost to the French utility is interesting. In order to calculate the cost, it is necessary to assume an initial principal amount in ECU and/or Yen. The determination of the initial principal amount for the French utility is purely notional as the cash flows are not paid or received. This reflects the fact that the transaction creates no new funding for the counterparty, but changes the currency denomination of its existing yen liability.

The initial ECU principal can be set at ECU 80 million (the face value of the issue and the amount of principal that will need to be paid back). If this initial value is assumed, then the ECU cost to the French utility is 9.19% pa. This would be better than the cost of its existing ECU obligation for a similar maturity (around 9.37% pa).

However, this approach may be incorrect. The *correct* ECU initial notional principal would be equal to the present value of the Yen cash flows on the swap (discounted at the French utility's cost of funding in yen) converted to ECU at the spot rate. The present value of the Yen cash flows under the swap discounted at 6.83% pa annual (the yield on the French utility's outstanding yen obligations of similar maturity) is Yen 14,591.733 million. This is equal to ECU 79.296 million (translated as ECU1 = Yen 184.01 based on ECU/US$ exchange rate of 0.7420 and US$/Yen exchange rate of 248). If the initial ECU value is assumed to be ECU 79.296 million (rather than the ECU 80 million used in the previous case) then the ECU cost to the French utility is 9.35% pa. This is comparable to its current yen funding cost.

The example highlights the problems in determining the values of swaps transacted against existing issues.

# 9  Summary

Swap transactions are priced through a process where the transaction is decomposed into a series of individual forward contracts that are then priced. The price of the swap is given by the value of the portfolio of forwards. An alternative methodology is to use the zero coupon rates to price the swaps (based on the fact that the zero coupon rates effectively embed the current forward interest rate in the market).

In practice, short dated interest rate swaps are priced off forwards or (if available) short term interest rate futures rates in the market. The use of this approach requires an understanding of the non-convex nature of futures contracts and incorporation of an adjustment for the convexity bias. Longer dated interest rate swaps are decomposed into security or bond equivalents, and priced off the zero coupon rates to ensure that the transaction has a zero net present value at commencement.

The pricing of cross currency swaps is similar. Cross currency swaps may be priced as portfolios of forward currency contracts or using zero coupon methodology. In practice, currency swaps are generally decomposed into a portfolio of interest rate swaps and a cross currency basis swap that are then separately priced. This corresponds to how these transactions are traded and hedged in the market.

The basic methodology is used to price generic or conventional swaps. Non-generic swap structures are priced by adjusting the generic swap price for the cash flow differences between the generic swap and the relevant non-generic structure. This is done primarily using present value mathematics.

# 11
# Swap Spreads

## 1  Overview

The swap curve is a central element in the approach to pricing derivatives. The swap curve is used in combination with the short dated interest rate futures contracts to derive the zero coupon rates. The zero coupon swap rates are then used to price swaps directly. The zero coupon swap rates are also used to derive interest rate forwards and as the carry cost component of forward pricing in other asset classes.

In the pricing approach used to date, the swap rates have been assumed to be directly observable and available. However, the swap rates themselves (either as a concept or the manner of derivation) have not been examined. In this Chapter, the focus is on seeking to understand the nature of swap rates. This is done by seeking to understand the concept of the swap spread (that is, the positive or negative margin exhibited by swap rates relative to the underlying risk free government rates in the currency). This Chapter focuses on the concept and determination of swap spreads.

The structure of this Chapter is as follows:
- The concept of swap spreads is examined.
- The major determinants of swap spreads are considered.
- The general behaviour of swap spreads is analysed.
- The process of financial arbitrage that links the swap rates to underlying bond and money markets is outlined, including the drivers of financial arbitrage.
- The determinants and behaviour of swap rates in key currencies (US$, Euro and Yen) is discussed.

## 2  Swap Spreads – Concept

The swap spread is defined as the margin or spread between the prevailing market rate on an interest rate swap and an underlying risk free security (usually assumed to be a government bond) of the same or equivalent maturity. This spread can be both positive (swap rates greater than government bond rates) and negative (swap rates less than government bond rates).

In certain markets, generic interest rate swaps are directly quoted as a spread over the benchmark government bond[1]. For example, in US\$, historically, interest rate swaps have been quoted in this manner. Therefore a quote of 50 bps over for a 5 year interest rate swap implies a swap rate of the current 5 year US\$ Treasury bond rate plus 50 bps. In US\$, generic swap spreads are quoted for standard maturities (2, 3, 4, 5, 7, 10 and 30 years[2]). Other markets that follow this convention include C\$ and to a lesser extent, A\$.

In other markets, the interest rate swap is not quoted in spread terms. In these markets, the swap rate is quoted in absolute rate terms. The swap spread is implicit in the swap rate. It is derived by comparing the swap rate to the underlying benchmark government bond rate for the relevant maturity. In this sense, the swap spread is not directly traded but implied by swap trading generally.

The swap rate itself is the implied inter-bank funding rate. In US\$, it is the implied US\$ LIBOR rate (for say, 3 or 6 months) during the term of the swap. The position is similar in other currencies[3].

This reflects the fact that swaps can be decomposed into securities (bond) equivalent positions. In effect, swaps are self financed long or short positions in securities. For example, paying fixed in a swap is equivalent to short selling a bond and investing the proceeds in a floating rate security, and receiving fixed in a swap is equivalent to purchasing a bond and funding the bond by selling a floating rate security[4]. The two transactions must have equivalent value at the commencement of the transaction. This implies that the swap rate itself must be equal to the *average* expected funding or investment rate in the money markets over the life of the transaction. In the case of US\$, this will equate to the implied US\$ 3 or 6 month LIBOR rate over the swap term. The position will be similar in other currencies. For example, in yen this will equate to the implied average 3 or 6 month Yen LIBOR. In Euro, this equates to the implied average 3 or 6 month Euro-ibor. In Sterling this equates to the implied average 3 or 6 month Sterling LIBOR. In Swiss Franc this equates

---

[1] For a discussion of quotation conventions, see Chapter 3.

[2] The 4 and 7 year benchmark Treasury rate may be interpolated. In 2000, as a shortage of 30 year Treasury bonds emerged, 30 year swaps were quoted against the 10 year Treasury bond rate.

[3] See (5 February 1993) "Question From The Floor: Interest Rate Swap Spreads" in Derivatives Bulletin, Salomon Brothers Inc. US Derivatives Research, Fixed Income Derivatives, New York.

[4] For a detailed discussion, see Chapter 10.

to the implied average 3 or 6 month Swiss France LIBOR. In C$ this equates to the implied average 3 or 6 month C$ Bankers Acceptance rates. In A$ this equates to the implied average 3 or 6 month A$ Bank Bill Rate.

The swap spread can also be considered to be an expected differential to other money market rates. For example, in US$:

- The swap spread can be considered the expected average spread between 3 or 6 month LIBOR and the repo rates over the term of the swap. This reflects the fact that the swap and a purchase of the bond funded in the repo market or a sale of the bond funded by borrowing the security are similar economic transactions (using the security decomposition analogy).
- The swap spread can also be considered the equivalent of the expected spread between Treasury and LIBOR (Eurodollar) rates (known as the Treasury Eurodollar ("TED") spread). This is because the swap can be decomposed and hedged by trading in government securities funded in or proceeds invested at LIBOR.

These relationships are important in determining the swap spread and also influencing the behaviour of swap spreads. Similar relationships can be expected to exist in other currencies.

# 3   Swap Spreads – Determinants

## 3.1   Overview

There is no conclusive analysis that establishes the exact determinants of swap spreads[5]. However, observing the behaviour of swap spreads indicates that the spread is influenced by the following factors:

- **Credit risk** – swap spreads appear to track the credit spread of AA/A rated bonds. This reflects the fact that the process of replication/financial arbitrage allows swaps to be used to synthesise liabilities and assets, creating an immediate link to underlying bond and money markets.
- **Hedging costs/repo rates** – swap spreads are related to the hedging costs incurred by dealers. These costs are influenced by the movement of rates in the bond repo market. This reflects the fact that swaps (particularly medium to long maturity swaps) are traditionally hedged using physical government bonds or government bond futures.

---

[5]   See Evans, Ellen and Parente, Gloria M (1987) What Drives Interest Rate Swap Spreads; Salomon Brothers Inc Bond Market Research, New York.

- **Market or institutional structure** – swap spread behaviour is also affected by a number of other factors that relate to the structure of the underlying bond and capital market. These include factors such as market completeness (swaps may complete an incomplete market structure), liquidity/transaction costs of different types of instruments, and the structure of the market in terms of participants and their activity.

Each of these factors is considered below. Other short term factors that may drive swap spreads include:
- Temporary excess/oversupply or shortage/lack of supply of swap payers or receivers in a specific maturity or in a specific index.
- Dealer positions or structure of inventory that may lead to trading activity or lack of trading in a specific maturity or index.

These factors also drive the behaviour of, and changes in, swap spreads over time.

In practice, the link between the underlying bond/capital market and the swap market (effectively, the swap spread) is driven by several processes:
- The process of financial arbitrage in respect of both liabilities and assets.
- The repo rates and their impact on the funding of long bond positions and the capacity to borrow bonds for short selling.

**Exhibit 11.1** sets out the relationships between the various elements that determine swap spreads.

It is traditional in analysing swap spread behaviour to state that swap rates, and therefore swap spreads at the short end, are substantially driven by the short term interest rate futures contracts (for example, in US$ by the pricing of Euro-dollar futures contracts)[6]. While technically accurate, it begs the question as to the specific yield curve off which the forward/futures rates (in US$ the Eurodollar rates) are stripped. This circularity can only be resolved by linking the pricing of forward/futures on short term interest rates to the structure of swap spreads in general (that is, to the factors previously identified). In the short end of the maturity spectrum, bank funding costs (deposits and certificate of deposits ("CDs")) are an important factor in determining swap spreads.

---

[6] For example, see Evans, Ellen and Parente, Gloria M (1987) What Drives Interest Rate Swap Spreads; Salomon Brothers Inc Bond Market Research, New York; Sood, Arivinder, "The Long and Short of Interest Rate Swap Spreads" (April 1988) Risk 24–26.

Exhibit 11.1    Bond and Swap Spread Relationships

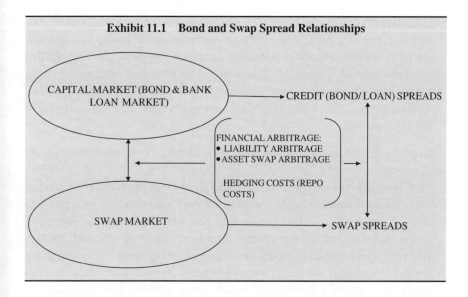

## 3.2   Swap Spread and Credit Risk

The link between swap spreads and underlying credit spreads is dictated by several factors:

- **Replication** – replication logic can be used to create synthetic assets or liabilities. For example, an issue of a fixed rate bond can be replicated by issuing a floating rate bond (or equivalent bank loan) and entering into a swap where the borrower pays fixed rates. Similarly, a floating rate borrowing can be replicated by issuing a fixed rate bond and entering into a swap where the borrower receives fixed rates. The fact that both transactions are economically equivalent (excluding any counterparty risk on the swap itself) the price of both transactions should be identical. In practice, because of the presence of counterparty risk in the transaction, the price of the swap should be close to but not necessarily the same as the equivalent direct transaction in the bond or loan markets. A similar logic operates in relation to assets. A purchase of a fixed rate bond and entry by the investor into a swap where it pays fixed is equivalent to a direct purchase of a floating rate asset. A purchase of a floating rate asset and entry by the investor into a swap where it receives fixed rate is equivalent to the purchase of a fixed rate asset. This dictates that the swap spreads must trade close to the credit spreads on the underlying fixed and floating rate investment assets available in the market. The failure of swap spreads to closely correspond to credit spreads on underlying bonds would allow arbitrage.

- **Counterparty risk** – the swap itself involves counterparty or performance risk on the transaction. An alternative way to express this relationship is to link it to the process of decomposition of the transaction into two separate securities that are simultaneously exchanged. The exchange entails both counterparties taking a risk on the other through the notional purchase of a security issued by the other. This means that the credit risk of the counterparty must also be manifested in the swap pricing.

In practice, the linkage occurs through a number of separate transmission mechanisms[7]:

- **New issue market** – fixed rate bond issues by high quality issuers (sovereigns, supra-national entities, banks and corporations) are frequently swapped into floating rate funding. The objective is to generate low cost funds (relative to other sources of floating rate funding)[8]. This means that if swap spreads are high relative to bond spreads (both relative to the underlying benchmark government bond rates) then this will trigger issuance of fixed rate bonds that will be swapped into floating rate via the swap. This will create downward pressure on swap spreads until they align the floating rate cost of funds in the direct (issuance of floating rate bonds or borrowing) and indirect market (fixed rate bonds swapped into floating rate). If the swap spread falls too far below the bond spread, then the absence of issuance will drive the lack of receiving interest in swaps, driving spreads higher, while lack of bond issuance will drive bond spreads lower until an equilibrium level is achieved. **Exhibit 11.2** sets out an example of how the process identified drives the level of swap spreads.

- **Asset swap market** – fixed and floating assets can be converted into alternative forms of investment via swaps[9]. This means that if swap rates are lower than bond spreads, then floating rate investors can purchase fixed rate bonds and pay fixed in a swap to create floating rate assets at spreads better than that available in direct floating rate assets. This drives swap (paying interest) and bond spreads (purchase of bonds) down as a result of the arbitrage activity. In contrast, high swap spreads relative to bond spreads encourage the creation of synthetic fixed rate bonds (purchase floating rate bonds and swap them into

---

[7]  See Evans, Ellen and Parente, Gloria M (1987) What Drives Interest Rate Swap Spreads; Salomon Brothers Inc Bond Market Research, New York; Sood, Arivinder, "The Long and Short of Interest Rate Swap Spreads" (April 1988) Risk 24–26.

[8]  This is often referred to as new issue arbitrage, see Das, Satyajit (2004) Structured Products Volume 1; John Wiley & Sons (Asia), Singapore at Chapter 3.

[9]  For discussion of assets swaps, see Das, Satyajit (2004) Structured Products Volume 1; John Wiley & Sons (Asia), Singapore at Chapter 4.

**Exhibit 11.2    Swap Spread – Relationship to Underlying Bond/Funding Spreads**

Assume a strong A/A+ or AA− borrower that enjoys good access to capital (bond and bank debt markets) as well as swap markets. Assume all borrowings and swaps are for 5 years. The Table below shows the behaviour of this borrower and its impact upon swap spreads.

| Current Position | Changed Position |
|---|---|
| Rates are as follows: | Changed rate structure is as follows: |
| • Borrowing costs: <br>  • Fixed rate bond issue at Treasury bond rate ("T") + 110 bps. <br>  • Floating rate (FRN or bank debt) at LIBOR + 25 bps. <br>• Swap rates: T + 80 (bid)/100 (offer) bps. | • Borrowing costs: <br>  • Fixed rate bond issue at Treasury bond rate ("T") + 160 bps. <br>  • Floating rate (FRN or bank debt) at LIBOR + 25 bps. <br>• Swap rates: T + 80 (bid)/100 (offer) bps. |
| | Bond spreads have increased while floating rate costs and swap rates have remained unchanged. |
| Borrower's funding cost is: <br>• Fixed rate: <br>  • Direct: borrow fixed rate at T + 110 bps. <br>  • Indirect: borrow floating at LIBOR + 25 bps and swap into fixed at T + 100 bps giving cost of T + 125 bps. <br>• Floating rate: <br>  • Direct: borrow floating rate at LIBOR + 25 bps. <br>  • Indirect: borrow fixed rate at T + 110 bps and swap into floating at T + 80 bps giving cost of LIBOR + 30 bps. | Borrower's changed funding cost is: <br>• Fixed rate: <br>  • Direct: borrow fixed rate at T + 160 bps. <br>  • Indirect: borrow floating at LIBOR + 25 bps and swap into fixed at T + 100 bps giving cost of T + 125 bps. <br>• Floating rate: <br>  • Direct: borrow floating rate at LIBOR + 25 bps. <br>  • Indirect: borrow fixed rate at T + 160 bps and swap into floating at T + 80 bps giving cost of LIBOR + 80 bps. |
| Therefore there are no arbitrage opportunities present. | There are clear arbitrage opportunities present. |
| Borrower's course of actions: <br>• If fixed rate funding is desired, then issue fixed rate bond. <br>• If floating rate funding is desired, then issue floating rate bond or borrow from bank. | Borrower's course of actions: <br>• If fixed rate funding is desired, then borrow floating rate debt and swap into fixed rate (cost saving of 35 bps). <br>• If floating rate funding is desired, then issue floating rate bond or borrow from bank. |

> The lack of alignment of bond and swap spreads in the changed position creates an incentive for all issuers (similar to the borrower) to use floating rate funding and swaps to raise any fixed rate funding requirements. This creates an increased demand for paying fixed in the swap, forcing swap spreads up. Bond spreads should fall as lack of fixed rate issuance creates a supply demand imbalance, forcing bond spreads to decline.
>
> Another way of exploiting the market position would be to issue floating rate debt, swap it into fixed rate (total cost T + 125 bps) and use the proceeds to buy the corporate bonds (T + 160 bps). This would lock in an arbitrage gain of 35 bps. This assumes that the credit risks are similar. This does not incorporate capital costs, costs associated with counterparty risks and usage of funding/balance sheet capacity.

fixed rates via paying fixed in a swap). This drives up both swap spreads (paying interest) and bonds (selling bonds to buy the synthetic assets) until equilibrium is achieved.

- **Spreads on other assets** – swap market participants such as banks and other financial institutions use swaps to create matching liabilities to fund fixed rate assets. This may include mortgages, loans etc. This means that swap spreads track credit spreads on assets that are to be funded[10].

This inter-relationship means that the swap spreads track *credit spreads on bonds*. In practice, they appear to track credit spreads on bank or financial institutions issues with credit ratings around AA to A[11]. In the short end of the swap curve, bank funding costs (deposits and CD costs) are an important factor in determining swap spreads. This relationship is evident most clearly in US$. However, a similar relationship is evident in other currencies. This is manifested by new issues being priced as a margin to US$ LIBOR or inter-bank rates in the relevant currency, and secondary market assets being priced as a margin to US$ LIBOR or inter-bank rates in the relevant currency[12].

---

[10] See Schumacher, Michael (27 February 1998) "Swap Spreads *Do* Matter" in Derivatives Bulletin, Salomon Brothers Inc. US Derivatives Research, Fixed Income Derivatives, New York; Schumacher, Michael (24 July 1998) "Swap Spreads *Still* Matter" in Derivatives Bulletin, Salomon Brothers Inc. US Derivatives Research, Fixed Income Derivatives, New York.

[11] See (12 February 1993) "Question From The Floor: Interest Rate Swap Spreads-Historical Perspective" in Derivatives Bulletin, Salomon Brothers Inc. US Derivatives Research, Fixed Income Derivatives, New York.

[12] For example, see Turpault, Christophe, Ober, Philippe and Muller, Erick "Swap Spreads" (September 1999) Euro Derivatives Supplement – Risk Magazine 8–11 at 11.

The strong correlation of swap spreads to that on bonds issued by banks/financial institutions is interesting. Possible explanations of this relationship include:

- The fact that swaps are effectively implied average inter-bank rates implies bank credit is creating the spread linkage.
- The role of banks in acting as intermediaries in the swap market results in the swap spreads exhibiting a close correspondence to bank credit spreads.
- The ability of banks to readily issue debt to take advantage of spread movements and arbitrage between funding sources results in a close correspondence between bank credit spreads and swap spreads.

## 3.3   Swap Spreads and Hedging Costs[13]

Swaps are hedged as follows[14]:

- Swaps with maturities for short maturities (up to 2 to 5 years depending upon the market) are hedged using short term interest rate futures contracts (where these are available). For example, US$ swaps are hedged out to 5 years and in some cases beyond using the Eurodollar futures contract.
- Swaps with longer maturities are hedged using government bonds or government bond futures contracts.

The impact of the hedging costs (in effect the bond repo market) on the swap spread is particularly significant in longer dated swaps.

This impact is driven by the process of hedging[15]. Where a swap dealer pays fixed rate, the position will typically be hedged (until an offsetting transaction can be found) by buying government bonds and financing the position. Similarly, where a swap dealer receives fixed rate, the position will typically be hedged (until an offsetting transaction can be found) by short selling government bonds and investing the proceeds until the hedge is unwound. The trading in bonds creates the linkage to the repo markets. Where the dealer buys the bond to hedge, it must be financed. Similarly, where the dealer sells the bond, it must be borrowed in the repo market[16]. **Exhibit 11.3** sets out the impact of repo costs on the swap spreads.

---

[13]   See Evans, Ellen and Parente, Gloria M (1987) What Drives Interest Rate Swap Spreads; Salomon Brothers Inc Bond Market Research, New York; Boughey, Simon "Spreading Interest" (December 1996) FOW 33–35.

[14]   See discussion in Chapter 10 and also Chapters 13 and 14.

[15]   For a discussion of swap hedging see Chapters 13 and 14.

[16]   In the US$ market, a product that replicated a swap through a repo has been available. This is the LIBOR financed Treasury repo. It is in effect a 3 month LIBOR financed

Where bond futures are used, the bond repo costs affect the pricing of the bond futures price. The swap spreads are affected indirectly by the cost of hedging through the bond futures price. The end effect is similar.

---

**Exhibit 11.3    Swap Spreads and Repo Costs**

**1.   Hedging a Fixed Rate Paying Position in a Swap**
Assume a swap dealer pays fixed rate, the position will typically be hedged (until an offsetting transaction can be found) by buying government bonds and financing the position. The bond will be financed in the repo market.
This means that the dealer's cash flows are as follows:

**Swap**
* Pay fixed rate at Treasury bond rate (T) plus the swap spread (S)
* Receive 3 or 6 month LIBOR.

**Hedge**
* Receive fixed rate on the bond (T) purchased as the hedge.
* Pay the repo rate to finance the bond.

This means that the dealer has net earnings or an expense based on the differential between the 3 or 6 month LIBOR rate and the repo rate. If there is shortage of a particular security that is much sought by bond borrowers (referred to as the bond going on "special" or trading tightly in the repo market) then the repo rates might be well below other market rates (such as LIBOR). If the repo rates are low then the dealer can repo the bonds at very low cost. This will favour dealers paying fixed rates under the swap and will put upward pressure on swap spreads. In effect, the dealer has higher earnings on the hedge that is used to pay higher rates under the swap.

**2.   Hedging a Fixed Rate Receiving Position in a Swap**
Assume a swap dealer receives fixed rate, the position will typically be hedged (until an offsetting transaction can be found) by short selling government bonds and investing the proceeds until the hedge is unwound. In order to short sell bonds, the dealer must borrow the security in the repo market.
This means that dealer's cash flows are as follows:

**Swap**
* Receive fixed rate at Treasury bond rate (T) plus the swap spread (S)
* Pay 3 or 6 month LIBOR.

**Hedge**
* Pay fixed rate on the bond (T) purchased as the hedge.
* Receive the repo rate on the proceeds of the bond sale less any borrowing fee (effectively the reverse repo rate).

---

rolling repo of a government bond. See Louis. J. C. "A New Alternative to Vanilla Swaps" (July-August 1997) Derivatives Strategy 12–13.

This means that the dealer has net earnings or an expense based on the differential between the 3 or 6 month LIBOR rate and the repo rate. If there is shortage of a particular security, that is, the bond is on "special" or trading tightly in the repo market, then the repo rates might be well below other market rates (such as LIBOR). In effect, the cost of borrowing the security is high. If the cost of borrowing the bonds is high, then the dealer can only borrow the bonds at high cost, reducing the earnings on the short sale proceeds. The dealer will increase swap spreads to compensate for the cost of the hedge.

## 3.4 Swap Spreads and Market Structure

Swap spread behaviour is also affected by a number of other factors that relate to the structure of the underlying bond and capital market. These include the following factors:

- **Market completeness** – in practice, markets are incomplete in that the range of instruments available in the market is limited and does not allow for a complete range of transactions to be undertaken. In this context, swaps may complete an incomplete market structure. For example, where there is no or a limited non-government bond market, swaps may operate as a surrogate fixed rate market. Similarly, where it is difficult to short sell securities or there is no active and liquid futures market in term securities, paying fixed in a swap may operate as a mechanism for hedging. These factors may make swaps trade at a lower or higher spread than that dictated by pure credit spreads or hedging costs.

- **Liquidity/transaction costs** – the different liquidity of different types of instruments in a market may dictate that swaps are used in preference to other instruments. For example, in Europe, the Euro swap market is very liquid and has low transaction costs relative to smaller European government bond markets. This has led to the use of swaps as a surrogate bond and benchmark rate. This may impact upon the swap spread.

- **Structure of the market** – differences in terms of participants and their activity in the capital markets will also affect the pricing of swap spreads. This may include regulatory factors that restrict or govern the market structure, controlling either participation in different market structures and also the use of instruments. This would also include economic bias in terms of the net export or import of capital in the market, or the bias between payers of fixed rates and receivers of fixed rate in the market. It may also include general credit conditions in the market, including the supply and demand for credit. These factors may be both short term or long term. These factors lead to supply and demand patterns in the market that may affect the determination of swap spreads.

# 4  Swap Spreads – Behaviour

The behaviour of and changes in swap spreads is driven by its primary determinants. Changes in swap spreads are influenced by a number of factors including:
- A change in credit conditions and credit spreads[17].
- Changes in the level of interest rates and shape of the yield curve.

Credit spreads in markets are generally subject to significant and often rapid changes[18]. The structure of spreads in markets is summarised in **Exhibit 11.4**.

|  | Exhibit 11.4 Market Credit Spread Structure | |
| --- | --- | --- |
| **Rates** | **Concept** | **Drivers** |
| Government bond rates (T) | Risk free benchmark rate | • Inflation<br>• Monetary policy<br>• Government borrowing requirement<br>• Credit quality of sovereign<br>• Macro-economic factors (fiscal policy; external account) |
| Swap rates (T plus swap spread) | Swap rates for paying and receiving fixed rate under a swap | • Credit spreads<br>• Bank credit (counterparty) risk<br>• Hedging (repo) costs<br>• Market structure factors<br>• General supply and demand for credit |
| Individual bond rates (swap rates plus/ minus asset swap spread) | Spread to swap rates for individual issuer's securities | • Credit quality of issuer<br>• Issuer specific factors<br>• Industry factors |

---

[17]  For discussions of behaviour of credit spreads generally, see Morrison, Randoph with Derham, Norman "Do Issuers Face a New Era in Credit Spreads?" Market Tactics, Global Wholesale Financial Services, National Bank 7–10; Clow, Robert "Spread Alert" (September 1999) Institutional Investor 29–32; Huang, Harry "Tie the Knot" (March 2000) Credit Risk Special Report – Risk S20–S22; Bevan, Andrew and Garzarelli, Francesco "Corporate Bond Spreads and the Business Cycle: Introducing GS-Spread" (March 2000) Journal of Fixed Income 8–18.

[18]  For a discussion of the drivers of credit risk and credit spreads, see Das, Satyajit (2004) Structured Products Volume 2; John Wiley & Sons (Asia), Singapore at Chapter 13.

The underlying government bond or equivalent[19] benchmark rate serves the following functions:

* It provides a spread to the best available credit in each market.
* It provides an indication of relative value of individual obligations.
* It functions as the optimal low cost hedging vehicle for interest rate risk.

Credit spreads *relative to the benchmark rate* appear to be driven by two separate sets of factors:

* **General or systematic market wide factors** – these are factors that drive the valuation of credit risk generally including:
  1. *Economic growth* – strong growth coincides with improved general corporate cash flows and improvements in credit risk. In contrast, recessions tend to increase general default risk and lower recovery rates.
  2. *Funding requirements* – the business cycle and net demand for funds by borrowers also affects the pricing of credit risk.
  3. *Asset volatility* – this refers to the underlying volatility of asset values. An increase in asset volatility levels (coupled with leverage) may increase the probability of default and hence credit risk.
  4. *Corporate leverage* – this refers to the general or average level of corporate debt. The higher the level of leverage, the greater the risk of default. This affects both credit risk and credit pricing.
* **Specific or unsystematic issuer specific factors** – these are factors that drive the valuation of credit risk of a specific issuer including:
  1. *Industry and issuer specific* – the structure of the industry and the position of an individual issuer within the industry drives the credit risk of the issuer in terms of default risk.
  2. *Corporate leverage* – this refers to the specific level of corporate debt of the issuer. The higher the level of leverage, the greater the risk of default. This affects both credit risk and credit pricing.

It is evident that the major drivers of credit spread changes are changes in general or market wide systematic factors, and changes in the underlying benchmark government bond market. This drives the general levels of credit spreads. Swap spreads represent the *generalised market credit spreads*. Consequently, these factors are the predominant drivers of swap spread changes[20].

---

[19] For example, in Germany, Pfandbriefe (bonds collateralised by government securities) are regarded as near risk free obligations.

[20] In early 2000, J. P. Morgan introduced the European Credit Spread Index ("ECSI"). The index was based on the price of credit default swaps (that are strongly correlated to the

This means that swap spread movements are driven by:
- General changes in credit spreads that are in turn driven by changes in general market credit conditions.
- Specific technical factors affecting the swap market itself.

The general market credit conditions influence credit spreads and therefore swap spreads as follows under normal market conditions[21]:
- During periods of strong economic growth, credit spreads should decrease as overall default risk diminishes and recovery rates improve.
- Credit spreads increase where there is a rise in funding requirements/contraction in supply (the financing gap), asset volatility (as measured by increase in equity volatility) and corporate leverage.

The relationship between credit and swap spreads to absolute levels of underlying rates is as follows:
- Credit spreads seem to increase with increases in absolute rates. This can be related to the increasing financing cost and its impact on default risk.
- Credit spreads have a more stable relationship with yield curve slope. Credit spreads tend to increase where the curve flattens. Credit spreads tend to decrease when the curve tends to become steeper. This is related to the relationship between the business cycle, economic growth and the interest rate cycle, and its impact on default risk generally. It is also affected by the market participant's desire to manage duration exposure as well as supply and demand of securities at different points in the yield curve.

---

spread to swaps of individual bonds or obligations – in effect, the asset swap spread). This was designed to isolate the pure credit risk elements. It was designed to eliminate the impact of cash market liquidity conditions as well as the swap spread. The *pure* credit spread was found to be relatively constant on a basket of 98 names. This is consistent with the fact that the major sources of credit spread volatility are the generalised market factors that affect the swap spread. See (11 February 2000) Introducing the J. P. Morgan European Credit Swap Index; J. P. Morgan, New York.

[21] See Bevan, Andrew and Garzarelli, Francesco "Corporate Bond Spreads and the Business Cycle: Introducing GS-Spread" (March 2000) Journal of Fixed Income 8–18. See also (12 February 1993) "Question from the Floor: Interest Rate Swap Spreads-Historical Perspective" in Derivatives Bulletin, Salomon Brothers Inc. US Derivatives Research, Fixed Income Derivatives, New York; Turpault, Christophe, Ober, Philippe and Muller, Erick "Swap Spreads" (September 1999) Euro Derivatives Supplement – Risk Magazine 8–11.

In periods of crisis, the behaviour of credit spreads and swap spreads appears to be affected by the following factors:

- **Flight to quality** – during periods of market turmoil (for example, the Asian crisis of 1997, the Russian/Long Term Capital Management crisis of 1998, the equity/corporate reporting crisis of 2001/2002), concerns about credit risk and liquidity drive massive investment re-allocation from non-government securities to government securities. This drives up non-government spreads and drives down government yields, increasing credit and swap spreads.

- **Increased bank and counterparty exposure** – the potential impact of market turmoil on default rates and bank credit quality means that bank credit is generally re-priced upwards. This has the impact of driving up credit spreads. The loss of capital (as a result of bad debt write-offs), as well as concern about increased default risk, drives credit spreads higher. The supply of funding decreases sharply. This decrease is exacerbated by the high gearing of the banks (around 10–12 times) that accelerates the contraction of credit supply. The second impact is that bank cost of funds itself rises, placing upward pressure on credit spreads as banks must recover higher funding costs.

In addition to the above general factors that affect credit markets overall, the swap market is affected by a number of factors that are specific to the market itself, including:

- **Bank credit risk** – as the swap market is based on inter-bank rates (for example, US$ LIBOR or Euro-ibor), a change in average bank credit quality will affect swap spreads. This will be so irrespective of whether general credit spreads move to the same extent.

- **Behaviour of market participants** –the structure of swap markets means that the supply and demand of payers and receivers in the swap market is driven by certain biases[22]. Typically, payers are lower rated entities (corporations) and financial institutions seeking to generate fixed rate funding, either to reduce interest rate risk or match assets and liabilities. Typical receivers of fixed rates are higher rated issuers of fixed rate bonds that are seeking floating rate funding. There will generally be mismatches between the payers and receivers that emerge from time to time that drive swap spreads. This is driven by lack of funding requirement, shape of the yield curve (the cost of paying fixed in a steep yield curve will deter paying interest) and expectations of future interest rates. **Exhibit 11.5** sets out an example of this type of behaviour and its impact on

---

[22] This market bias is driven by the structural arbitrage relationship in the bond and bank credit markets discussed in the next Section.

swap spreads. A secondary factor is the demand and supply for other derivatives (options on swaps, cap/floors). This reflects the use of swaps to hedge positions in these derivatives. This creates pressures on the swap spreads.

- **Use of swaps as a hedging tool** – swaps are used to hedge a wide variety of transactions. This includes the hedging of portfolios of investments in government bonds, non-government bonds, and also mortgage/asset backed securities. This is particularly important for instruments with credit risk driven by the fact that swap spreads are closely related to credit spreads generally. The increased use of swaps for credit hedging has become an increased factor in swap spread behaviour. For example, during 1997 to 2000, as credit risk increased in global markets, investors and banks sought to hedge their credit risk affected portfolios by paying fixed in swaps. This resulted in a sharp increase in swap spreads across currencies.
- **Impact of credit spread volatility** – increases in spread volatility force market participants to hedge the spread risk as the exposure to loss becomes unsustainable or requires too much capital to be committed in support of such activities. This means that increases in market volatility are generally associated

---

**Exhibit 11.5   Swap Spread Behaviour**

The following Table sets out the potential changes in supply and demand for paying/receiving interest in swaps driven by absolute levels of interest rates and expectations of future rates:

| Interest Rates | | Impact on Swap Spread | Key Drivers |
|---|---|---|---|
| Current level | High | Decreasing | Lack of paying interest as borrowers do not wish to lock in high absolute rates. |
| | Low | Increasing | High paying interest as borrowers wish to lock in low absolute rates. |
| Expectation | Increasing | Increasing | High paying interest as borrowers wish to lock in low absolute rates. |
| | Decreasing | Decreasing | Lack of paying interest as borrowers do not wish to lock in high absolute rates. |

with increases in credit spreads, as dealers and investors try to hedge positions forcing up spreads.

Swap spreads have also been affected in recent years by certain technical factors in the underlying government bond market itself. The primary factor is the reduction in supply of government bonds in certain markets including the USA, UK and Australia.

The reduction in supply of governments bonds generally leads to two effects:

* A sharp rally in the government bond benchmark rates while the swap rate remains relatively static, causing the swap spreads to increase. This phenomenon was observed in the US market in 1999/2000.
* The decreased supply and liquidity of government bonds makes it difficult to either use these bonds to hedge (either portfolios or derivatives), or increases the cost of hedging. This drives up swap spreads as the hedging costs increase.

In looking at the behaviour of swap spreads relative to credit spreads generally, a subsidiary issue is whether there are leads and lags in the changes in swap spreads and bond spreads. The position is not clear. There is empirical evidence that the movements in swap rates and bond rates are contemporaneous[23]. However, anecdotal evidence suggests that swap spread changes *lead* bond spread changes. This may reflect the fact that the swap market has superior liquidity in many currencies. This means that where there is a market *shock*, participants use swaps to hedge or take views, at least initially. The swap positions are then exchanged for positions in the underlying bonds over time[24].

# 5 Swap Spreads and Financial Arbitrage

## 5.1 Overview

Swap spreads are driven by credit spreads and hedging costs. The process of replication provides the essential linkage between the bond/bank market and the swap markets. The analysis demonstrates that swap spreads are related to credit spreads. However, it does not identify underlying biases in swap spreads that create systematic advantages for both fixed and floating rate borrowers.

---

[23] See Zucker, Jon "Does the Swap Market Lead or Lag the Bond Market?" (Summer 1992) Journal of International Securities Markets 121–124.

[24] This pattern of behaviour would be consistent with the use of equity index futures in hedging/adjusting portfolio positions.

Market participants can generate significant cost savings by combining an issue of securities with an interest rate or currency swap. This approach to swap spread determination is predicated on pricing such transactions as a means of financial arbitrage across different capital markets. The approach implies that mutual cost savings are achievable primarily because prices in various world capital markets are not consistent. Organisations can achieve lower borrowing costs by accessing particular markets with lower *relative* cost. The entity borrows in that market and swaps the exposure (both interest rate and currency) back into the preferred form of funding. This achieves a lower cost of funding than that attainable from directly accessing the relevant markets. The basic sources of swap arbitrage include financial arbitrage, tax/regulatory arbitrage, the existence of incomplete markets and the presence of transaction costs.

Financial economists have treated this potential and persistent arbitrage opportunity with some justifiable scepticism. The economists have argued that if there is an arbitrage opportunity, then entering into the swap to take advantage of that opportunity should ultimately eliminate the market mis-pricing[25]. The presence of arbitrage opportunities within capital markets contradicts the concept of market efficiency.

An efficient market, by definition, is one in which prices are set at levels where the resources traded in the market are allocated efficiently among the participants. This highly artificial construction of economic theory requires the satisfaction of a wide range of conditions:
- Costless availability of all relevant information to market participants.
- The price import of the information is unambiguous.
- The market structure and trading process allows transmission of the impact of information into the asset price/rate that implies the presence of many buyers and sellers.
- Transaction costs including market frictions such as taxes, regulation, or accounting impediments are absent.

In practice, the conditions are difficult to satisfy. The impact of taxation, regulation, differences between market structures, differences in the perceived price impact of information, differences in risk perception and differential valuation of risk between capital markets or even segments of capital markets, create anomalies or inefficiencies that allow arbitrage transactions to take place.

---

[25] For example, see Bicksler, James and Chen, Andrew H "An Economic Analysis of Interest Rate Swaps" (July 1986) Journal of Finance 645–655; Turnbull, Stuart M. "Swaps: A Zero Sum Game?" (Spring 1987) Financial Management 15–21.

Technically, arbitrage transactions are defined to mean one or more actions by market participants designed to exploit pricing inefficiencies or anomalies to earn profit from the inherent discrepancy in the pricing or valuation of assets between markets. In its simplest form, arbitrage would involve the simultaneous purchase and sale of an identical asset in different markets. Where identical assets are employed in the process of arbitrage, the transaction involves no risk. However, in practice, the type of arbitrage described here entails the simultaneous purchase and sale of *similar* although not identical financial assets.

In pure arbitrage, profits are possible because of inefficiencies or differences in alternative markets for the same asset. In the less restrictive form of arbitrage being considered here, profits are possible because of relative inefficiencies or differences in the pricing of *comparable* although not *identical* assets once adjustments are made for the relevant differences. The transactions entail profit opportunities arising from anomalies among markets for assets that are close substitutes for each other. This is made feasible by the fact that the underlying commodity used in the funding and investment transaction is money that is inherently fungible and virtual.

By definition, arbitrage transactions operate to eliminate their own incentive. Undertaking arbitrage transactions will inevitably move prices to eradicate the initial profit opportunity. However, where the profit opportunity is implied by market structure or externally imposed action (such as taxation or regulation), the act of seeking to take advantage of the arbitrage opportunity may not adjust market prices to eliminate the opportunity. The arbitrage opportunity will persist until the underlying market structure changes or the offending regulation is eliminated.

In this Section, the interaction of financial arbitrage and swap spreads is analysed. The basic relationship is consistent with the model of swap spreads outlined. This is because the arbitrage model relates swap spreads to the pricing of credit risk in markets. In the next Sections, the process of swap arbitrage and the key drivers of the arbitrage process are analysed.

## 5.2   Swap Arbitrage Process

### 5.2.1   Interest Rate and Currency Swap Arbitrage

Swap transactions may be predicated on the exchange by one party of a benefit that it enjoys in a particular market for a corresponding benefit available to another party in a different market. The economics of an interest rate swap arbitrage transaction are set out in **Exhibit 11.6**. The economics of a currency swap arbitrage transaction are set out in **Exhibit 11.7**.

### Exhibit 11.6   Interest Rate Swap Arbitrage

Assume that a major international bank (Borrower A) rated AAA/AA can issue fixed rate US$ debt for 5 years in the form of a Eurodollar bond issue at an interest cost of 10.50% pa. Borrower A pays LIBOR for its floating rate US$ funds for an equivalent 5 year maturity. In contrast, a lower rated (BBB/Baa) company (Borrower B) can issue 5 year fixed rate US$ debt at 12.00% pa. Borrower B can raise 5 year floating rate funds from Borrowers at LIBOR plus 0.75% pa.

The overall position is summarised below:

| Funding (5 year) | Borrower A | Borrower B | Cost Differential |
|---|---|---|---|
| Floating rate | LIBOR | LIBOR + 75 bps | 75 bps |
| Fixed rate | 10.50% pa | 12.00% pa | 150 bps |

The difference between the cost of funds for Borrower A and B is 0.75% pa in floating rate terms and 1.50% pa in fixed rate terms. This disparity between the fixed and floating rate markets provides the arbitrage that is the basis of all interest rate swaps. The discrepancy is exploited as set out below. Each party borrows from the market in which they get the best relative term (A in the fixed rate market and B in the floating rate market) and then exchange their interest obligations to convert into their preferred form of funding.

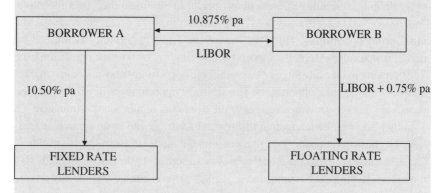

The net result of the transaction is as follows:

*   Borrower A has raised floating rate US$ funds at LIBOR minus 37.5 bps – a saving of 37.5 bps pa.
*   Borrower B has raised fixed rate US$ fund at 11.625% pa – a saving of 37.5 bps pa.

| Net Costs | Borrower A | Borrower B |
|---|---|---|
| Fixed rate – outflow | 10.50% pa | 10.875% pa |
| Fixed rate – inflow | 10.875% pa | |
| Floating rate – outflow | LIBOR | LIBOR + 75 bps pa |
| Floating rate – inflow | | LIBOR |

| Net Cost | LIBOR – 37.5 bps pa | 11.625% pa |
| Alternative Cost | LIBOR | 12.00% pa |
| Saving | 37.5 bps pa | 37.5 bps pa |

The split between counterparties is driven mainly on the basis of supply and demand, and on the basis of the cost of alternative available funding that is directly related to the credit standing of each party. In the above example, the arbitrage gains are split equally between the two parties. In addition, the transaction structure assumes no intermediation by a Borrower or financial institution. A more realistic transaction structure involving intermediation is depicted in the intermediated swap arbitrage structure illustrated below.

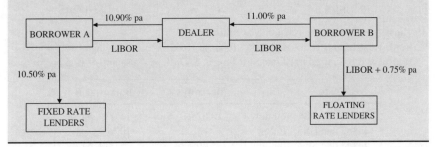

**Exhibit 11.7    Currency Swap Arbitrage**

Assume that a AAA/AA major multinational (Borrower A) has access to 5 year fixed rate Swiss francs (SFR) at 5.00% pa. Borrower A can also raise 5 year fixed rate US$ at 10.75% pa. In contrast, a company well known in the US$ domestic market but relatively unknown in the Swiss market (Borrower B) has access to 5 year fixed rate Swiss francs at 5.50% pa and 5 year fixed rate US$ at 11.00% pa.

The overall position is summarised below:

| Funding (5 year) | Borrower A | Borrower B | Cost Differential |
| --- | --- | --- | --- |
| Fixed rate SFR | 5.00% pa | 5.50% pa | 50 bps |
| Fixed rate US$ | 10.75% pa | 11.00% pa | 25 bps |

The discrepancy between the cost of funds clearly provides the basis of an arbitrage transaction. Where Borrower A is interested in raising US$ and conversely Borrower B is interested in raising SFR, the discrepancy can be exploited as set out below. Borrower A raises SFR and Borrower B raises US$ and they then exchange their principal and interest obligations to convert into their preferred form of funding.

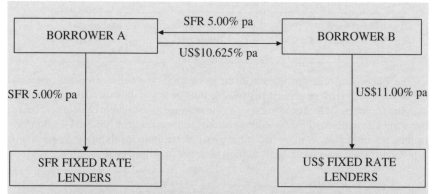

The net result of the transaction is as follows:
* Borrower A has raised fixed rate US$ funds at 10.625% pa – a saving of 12.5 bps pa.
* Borrower B has raised fixed rate SFR fund at 5.375% pa – a saving of 12.5 bps pa.

| Net Costs | Borrower A | Borrower B |
|---|---|---|
| Fixed rate US$ – outflow | 10.625% pa | 11.00% pa |
| Fixed rate US$ – inflow | | 10.625% pa |
| Fixed rate SFR – outflow | 5.00% pa | 5.00% pa |
| Fixed rate SFR – inflow | 5.00% pa | |
| Net Cost | 10.625% pa | 5.375% pa |
| Alternative Cost | 10.75% pa | 5.50% pa |
| Saving | 12.5 bps pa | 12.5 bps pa[26] |

## 5.2.2  Swap Arbitrage – General Methodology

The basic process of swap arbitrage can be generalised[27]. All swap transactions are predicated on the exchange by one party of a benefit that it enjoys in a particular market for a corresponding benefit available to another party in a different market. The economics and structuring of this process are usually undertaken in a series of discrete steps:
* Creating the cost/access matrix.
* Determining the comparative advantage of the respective parties.

---

[26] The real savings will be different as a result of the currency mismatch. B has a 37.5 bps pa shortfall in US$. This must be converted into equivalent basis points in SFR. The 37.5 bps in US$ would be equivalent to around 34.5 bps pa in SFR. This would equate to an all in cost to B of around 5.35% pa equivalent to a saving of around 15 bps pa.

[27] See Turnbull, Stuart M. "Swaps: A Zero Sum Game?" (Spring 1987) Financial Management 15–21.

- Structuring the swap.
- Pricing the swap arbitrage.

To facilitate the determination of swap arbitrages, it is initially necessary to construct a matrix of the relative cost and availability of access to certain markets of the different borrowers. Once this cost /access matrix is created, interest cost differentials between the parties can be determined, allowing identification of relative comparative advantage.

The process of identifying the relative comparative advantages between the two parties entails calculation of the differential cost of access to different markets. Structuring the swap arbitrage requires that the market in which each party has a comparative advantage be identified. Once this is completed, the swap can be structured on the basis that each party borrows in the market in which they enjoy a comparative advantage, and the swap is structured to exchange their interest obligations to convert their liabilities into their preferred form of funding.

The pricing of the arbitrage operates within the swap structure implied by the comparative advantage analysis. As the market in which each party will borrow is now known, it remains to calculate the swap price itself. The swap is calculated in two distinct parts:

- Maximum swap prices for each party are determined.
- Arbitrage gain is split between the parties.

Determining the outer limits of swap prices (the point of indifference) from both parties' perspective requires the identification of the cost of direct access into the preferred form of funding. The determination of this pricing limit or indifference point is important, as it provides the outer bounds of the swap price at any one time as the price at which each party can create its preferred form of funding indirectly at no cost advantage.

For example, using the data in our interest rate swap arbitrage example outlined above, Company B would not pay a fixed rate of more than 11.25% pa against the receipt of LIBOR. This is because having borrowed in the market in which it enjoys a comparative advantage (the floating rate market) at LIBOR plus 0.75% pa, and undertaking a swap as described at a rate of 11.25% pa, would give it an all-in fixed rate cost for 5 years of 12.00% pa. This is its direct cost of access to fixed rate funds for 5 years. At this pricing level, Company B is indifferent between direct and indirect access to fixed rate US$ funds. Similarly, using an identical methodology, the minimum swap pricing from the perspective of bank A could be determined as bank A receiving 10.50% pa against payment of LIBOR, as this would equate to its direct cost of floating rate funds.

The next part of the pricing phase is to then adjust the swap pricing on the basis of the split of the arbitrage gain implied. The arbitrage gain available for division between the parties to the swap is merely the differential cost of access to the two funding markets. In the interest rate swap example described above, the arbitrage profit is 75 bps pa, being the difference between the floating rate and fixed rate interest cost differentials.

**Exhibit 11.8** sets out the general methodology of swap arbitrage using an example.

---

**Exhibit 11.8    Currency Swap Arbitrage**

Assume the funding rates in the market are as follows:

| | Fixed Rate Funding (5 years) | Floating Rate Funding (3 years) |
|---|---|---|
| Government | B | LIBOR − 40 |
| AAA sovereign issuers | B + 20 | LIBOR − 20 |
| Supranational | B + 30 | LIBOR − 20 |
| Banks (AA or better) | B + 50 | LIBOR − 10 |
| Banks (A or better) | B + 90 | LIBOR + 5 |
| High quality corporate issuers | B + 120 | LIBOR + 20 |
| Lower quality corporate issuers | B + 250 | LIBOR + 75 |

**Note:**
1. B + 30 means the prevailing 5 year government bond rate + 30 bps pa.
2. LIBOR + 25 means 6 month US$ LIBOR + 25 bps pa.

The swap arbitrage can be structured in the following manner:
- Two likely swap counterparties are identified based on factors such as funding requirements. In this case they are the AAA Sovereign entity and the high quality corporate issuer.
- On the basis of the cost/access matrix outlined, it is possible to identify that the interest cost differential in the fixed rate market between the sovereign and corporate issuer is 100 bps pa in the fixed rate market, as against 40 bps pa in the floating rate market.
- The interest differentials imply that the sovereign entity enjoys a comparative advantage in the fixed rate market. The sovereign in fact enjoys an *absolute* cost advantage in both markets. The sovereign enjoys a *comparative* advantage in the fixed rate market in that its interest differential in the fixed rate market is greater than its interest differential in the floating rate market. In this bilateral arrangement, by implication, the corporate enjoys a *comparative* advantage in the floating rate market, that is, its absolute cost disadvantage is *lowest* in the floating rate market.
- Given the comparative cost structure, the arbitrage can be structured on the basis that:
  1. Sovereign borrows in the fixed rate funding market (the market in which it enjoys a comparative advantage).

2. Corporate issuer borrows in the floating rate funding market (the market in which it enjoys a comparative advantage).
3. A swap is arranged whereby the sovereign would receive fixed rate and pay floating rate while the corporate would undertake the reverse.

- The outer bound or point of indifference on the pricing equates to the level at which the two counterparties would be indifferent as to entering into the swap; that is, the swap price combined with the underlying funding equates to the cost of direct access to the respective markets. In this case, the outer bounds of the swap pricing are as follows:
  1. Sovereign issuer would receive fixed rate at no lower than B + 40, as this would generate floating rate funding at its direct cost of LIBOR − 20.
  2. Corporate issuer would not pay at a rate higher than B + 100 that equates to its direct cost of fixed rate funding.
- Within these outer boundaries, the arbitrage gain of 60 bps pa is apportioned. This 60 bps pa is the difference between the interest differential in the fixed rate funding market (100 bps) and the differential in the floating rate market (40 bps). Factors such as the relative bargaining powers of the two parties, supply and demand etc will influence the manner in which the arbitrage gain is shared between the parties. A possible swap pricing in this environment is set out below:

| | |
|---|---|
| Fixed side arbitrage: | 30 bps |
| Floating side arbitrage: | 20 bps |
| Cost of intermediation: | 10 bps |

This generates the likely swap pricing of: B + 70/80 bps pa

A possible transaction is set out below. Bank intermediation is assumed in this example.

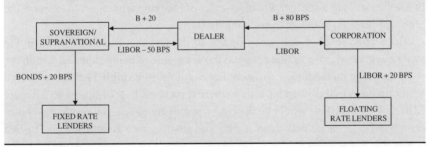

The analysis of the swap arbitrage highlights certain deficiencies in the general swap arbitrage methodology. These include:

- The analysis is predominantly bilateral rather than multi-lateral.
- The arbitrage analysis is mono-dimensional in that it is confined to a particular swap between two markets.
- Arbitrage as portrayed is confined to the liability side of the respective participants' activities. The analysis does not take into account the possibility of the

"reverse arbitrage", which allows the creation of higher yielding assets or assets not directly available, that is, an asset swap[28].

While swaps are bilateral transactions, the fact that there are more than two potential participants in the swap market at any given time means that the bilateral mode of analysis has shortcomings. In practice, swap markets gravitate to an arbitrage driven by the two most likely participants at a given point in time. The most likely participants at any given time are determined by a wide range of factors including:

• Attractiveness in absolute terms of the arbitrage.
• Asset liability management requirements of both counterparties that may be driven by fundamental business considerations (for example, finding requirements) as well as interest rate and currency expectations.
• Credit criteria that may limit the capacity of potential swap participants for transacting either directly or through a bank intermediary. In the latter case, the cost of intermediation may outweigh the benefits of the arbitrage.
• Investment objectives of fixed rate and floating rate investors across a wide range of currencies and their tolerance for particular credit risks as well as the state of their portfolios at a given point in time.

The major implication of a multi-lateral market is that the exploitation of the arbitrage inevitably means some change in the underlying cost/access matrix. This, in a sense, leads to a self-perpetuating series of evolving arbitrages. In essence, the arbitrage persists, but in an ever-changing form.

The second level of deficiency relates to the fact that each participant in the swap market may have options beyond those capable of being captured within the swap arbitrage methodology outlined. For example, in **Exhibit 11.8** the sovereign entity may not find a swap attractive where it receives B + 70 bps pa to generate LIBOR − 50 bps. This would be the case where it could issue *in another currency* on a fixed rate basis, and swap it first into floating rate at a lower rate to that achievable in the swap market in the first currency. Consequently, while arbitrage methodology may give indicative pricing within the context defined, the presence of other opportunities for funding arbitrages will to some extent determine the willingness of particular participants to transact at the levels implied.

The analysis also does not recognise the capacity for other market participants to enter into reverse arbitrages, creating higher yielding assets. This can be illustrated

---

[28]  See Das, Satyajit (2004) Structured Products Volume 1; John Wiley & Sons (Asia), Singapore at Chapter 4.

using the example in **Exhibit 11.8**. Assume that a comparable creditor to a sovereign entity is the intermediating bank. It is quoting a swap price of B + 70/80. This would allow an investor seeking sovereign assets to buy floating rate securities yielding LIBOR − 20 and swap them into fixed rate US$ assets yielding B + 50 by entering into a swap with the bank where it would pay LIBOR − 20 bps and receive B + 50 bps. Provided the additional credit risk in respect of the swap is less than 20 bps pa, the investor could create a higher yielding asset than that directly available in the form of fixed rate securities issued by the sovereign. This reverse arbitrage would impinge on the primary arbitrage process, as essentially it would create demand for sovereign floating rate assets but decrease demand for fixed rate securities issued by sovereigns. Moreover, it would also have the effect of changing the swap pricing, whereby the bank would gradually decrease the rate it is willing to pay from B + 70 to lower levels, thereby squeezing out the arbitrage for the sovereign.

This complex process of interaction is evident from the analysis of some of the deficiencies of the basic swap arbitrage methodology.

Financial economists have argued that the method of analysis identified may be fundamentally flawed. One argument is that the type of simple comparison is misleading, as a simple comparison of interest rates is insufficient if financial instruments differ in design and risk. Theoretically, this proposition must be correct. However, if the financial instruments are identical (that is the implicit assumption in the method of analysis outlined) it is not clear why a simple comparison is *not* sufficient[29].

In essence, the borrower must by definition determine whether or not it requires a fixed or floating rate liability or the currency of such a liability. That decision is totally separate from the swap arbitrage analysis being governed by factors such as interest and currency rate expectations, funding needs and asset liability matching requirements. Swap arbitrage merely assists in creating the required liability.

A relevant problem is the fact that it does not incorporate the credit exposure entailed in the swap itself. If a borrower uses a swap to create a synthetic liability, then it incurs credit exposures under both the borrowing and the swap, thereby utilising a scarce resource, namely access to credit. While this additional credit exposure is *not* encompassed by the methodology outlined, the presence of this

---

[29] For example, see Turnbull, Stuart M. "Swaps: A Zero Sum Game?" (Spring 1987) Financial Management 15–21. The paper gives the example of a comparison of issue of callable fixed rate debt against the issue of non-callable floating rate debt which is then swapped into fixed rate. This swap is, of course, inherently non-callable, although reversible at market rates.

additional risk merely dictates that there must be sufficient cost benefits in the swap to offset the credit exposure entailed[30]. In particular, it highlights that while swaps can be priced as a series of forward contracts, if the market traded swaps at that price there would be limited incentives for the existence of a viable swap market.

## 5.3  Sources of Swap Arbitrage

### 5.3.1  Overview

The arbitrage methodology used to derive swap rates is predicated on the relative comparative advantage of various participants in the capital market in accessing different sources of funding. In this model, swaps involve trading an advantage that a borrower or investor enjoys in one market for an equivalent advantage available to another company in a different market. The advantage that drives the underlying economics lies in one of two areas:
- (Post tax) cost of funding.
- Availability or access to funding.

The principle applies equally to all types of swaps and all swap markets irrespective of currency. Application of this theme allows asset and liability managers to separate decisions on the market in which to invest or borrow from decisions on the currency and interest rate basis of the investment or borrowing. In essence, the underlying arbitrage enables companies and investors to separate the source of liquidity from the management or the nature of the underlying asset or liability that is ultimately created.

The sources of the swap arbitrage can be classified into a number of separate categories:
- **Financial arbitrage** – in its purest form, this involves exploiting mutually inconsistent prices for securities of identical structural and issuer credit criteria in various world capital markets. This includes exploiting both structural credit mis-pricing in markets as well as short term volatility in credit valuation within markets.
- **Tax and regulatory arbitrage** – tax and regulatory arbitrage is predicated on the existence of restrictions on capital flows, or the pricing of capital flows that drives differential pricing, or differential access for different classes of participants in capital markets. This includes the impact of withholding tax, investment asset choice restrictions, taxation differentials and special subsidised funding sources.

---

[30] For a discussion of counterparty risk on the swap itself, see Das, Satyajit (2004) Risk Management; John Wiley & Sons (Aisa), Singapore at Chapter 5.

Two other sources of swap arbitrage are the role of swaps in completing incomplete market structure and the impact of the presence of transaction costs.

### 5.3.2 Credit Pricing Arbitrage

*Concept*
Credit arbitrage refers to market anomalies in the pricing of credit within and across markets. This is predicated on differences in credit spreads (or risk premiums) across capital markets (inter-market) or alternatively between different segments of a particular capital market (intra-market). Credit arbitrage is made possible by differences in the assessment of credit risk, capacity to assume credit risk and the resultant differences in credit spreads/risk premium. The examples outlined above of interest rate and currency swap arbitrage all rely on credit arbitrage. The differences in risk pricing reflect a number of different factors operating in the respective markets or market segments.

*Intra-Market Credit Pricing Arbitrage*
Intra-market credit pricing arbitrage is driven by a number of factors including:
• Differential credit risk assessment capabilities.
• Differential credit risk assumption capacity.
• Presence of agency and contracting costs.

In the case of intra-market credit arbitrage (such as the interest rate swap arbitrages described above), a major factor in the differential risk pricing is the fact that the suppliers of funds are different between the fixed and floating rate markets. The predominant suppliers of floating rate finance are banks and financial institutions. In contrast, the suppliers of fixed rate funding are direct rather than intermediated lenders such as institutional investors (insurance companies, pension funds and fund managers) and retail investors. The different lending groups have different capacities to assess and assume credit risk.

It is arguable that banks and financial institutions have a comparative advantage in credit risk assessment. These organisations operate sophisticated credit analysis systems and are able to analyse and accurately assess the credit risk of all borrowers. In particular, this allows them to assume credit risk in respect of lower rated borrowers more readily than direct investors.

This comparative advantage in credit risk assessment enjoyed by banks and financial institutions is certainly true in respect of retail investors who are not equipped to assess complex or difficult business organisations. However, capital markets have undergone significant changes in recent years, with a marked institutionalisation of investment. This has resulted in the concentration of investment decisions in professional money managers. These fund managers could easily perform the evaluation of credit and investment opportunities that traditionally have been functions in which the banks have enjoyed an advantage. In addition, the growth in the use of credit ratings (such as those provided by Moody's Investment Services, Standard & Poor's and Fitch-IBCA) have increased the availability of information related to credit risk of individual issuers. Consequently, while comparative capacities for credit risk assessment may explain the differential in risk pricing between banks/financial institutions and retail investors, the argument is less compelling in respect of institutional investors/fund managers.

Banks also enjoy the capacity to diversify their risk between different borrowers in terms of obligor, industry and geographic location. This allows banks to price risk premiums more competitively on a portfolio basis than investors that may not be able to diversify their portfolio as efficiently. This is driven by the size of portfolios, ability to access specific types of markets and transactions costs of trading. The diversification argument has explanatory power in respect of retail investor pricing of risk. However, large institutional fund managers should be able to achieve diversification at a level comparable to that of banks and financial institutions. In practice, fund managers can achieve a higher degree of diversification of portfolios than retail investors. However, investment restrictions and high transaction costs dictate that some portfolios do not attain the optimal level of diversification. This means that the diversification argument may explain in part the differential risk premiums between banks and institutional investors.

The discrepancy in risk premiums between the public and bank markets, particularly in respect of institutional investors, is also driven by the presence of agency and contracting costs[31]. Under this approach, it can be argued that banks and other financial institutions are able to more effectively monitor loans. This is driven by the relatively (larger) size of individual loans to individual borrowers, and the fact that borrowers usually deal with a relatively limited number of banks. In contrast, the monitoring costs faced by individual institutional investors with relatively smaller holdings of debt securities of an individual issuer are relatively higher and require costly contracting mechanisms such as trustees and trust deeds. The high monitoring cost faced by individual and institutional investors translates into a higher return required by such investors to provide loan funds to a firm of the stated risk profile relative to financial institutions. This may drive the differential in risk premiums.

Anecdotal evidence suggests that this argument is a factor in differential pricing. Typically, public securities issues are held in relatively small parcels (usually under

---

[31] For an introduction to these concepts, see Jensen, Michael C and Ruback, Richard S "Theory of the Firm: Managerial Behaviour, Agency Costs and Ownership Structure" (1976) Journal of Financial Economics vol 3 no 4 305–360.

US$10–25 million for an individual issuer). Bank loans provided by individual financial institutions to an individual borrower will usually be substantially larger than individual securities holdings.

The contracting and monitoring cost argument can also be extended to enforcement issues. For example, the absolute cost of enforcement of a particular creditor's claim is relatively fixed, and consequently translates into a higher percentage amount relative to a small individual investment in public securities relative to the percentage cost on a larger bank loan. Additional factors in this regard would include the fact that as individual borrowers may deal with a limited number of banks, as distinct from a large number of security holders, banks and financial institutions enjoy a significant advantage in managing and working out problem loans.

Underlying this enforcement problem is the fundamental nature of the contracting arrangements in intermediated and direct financing. In the case of intermediated financing, the bank or financial institution accepts a deposit. The bank undertakes to repay the deposit at maturity together with interest. The bank then in turn on-lends the funds to a borrower. Where the borrower gets into difficulties and is unable to repay the loan or to meet interest commitments, the bank's obligation to its depositors is quite separate from and in no way linked to the performance of the loan. This separation is achieved through interposition of the bank in the intermediation process. It provides the bank with some flexibility in the management of problem loans. This is particularly so with a diversified portfolio, where it is able to service its deposits, both interest and principal payments, without jeopardising its financial viability.

In contrast, an institutional investor has a different contractual arrangement with the beneficiaries of the funds under management. The fund manager acts in a fiduciary capacity, managing funds on behalf of individual investors. Under these contracting arrangements, a failure by a borrower to perform under its loan conditions (repayment of principal/interest or non-compliance with other loan conditions) will directly impact upon the investor. This is because the fund manager does not independently guarantee or ensure the payment of interest or principal, as does a bank in the intermediated finance case. This more direct relationship clearly limits the discretion of the fund manager in relation to rescheduling and restructuring problem loans. This different contractual relationship tends to bias fund managers toward placing a higher risk premium on less creditworthy borrowers than banks and financial institutions. This may also translate into differential recovery rates in the event of default between bank loans and bonds[32].

---

[32] For a discussion of differential recovery rates, see Das, Satyajit (2004) Structured Products Volume 2; John Wiley & Sons (Asia), Singapore at Chapter 13.

These factors have the following effects:

- Higher quality borrowers enjoy a comparative advantage in the public securities market, usually the fixed rate market. This reflects the fact that investors, for the reasons outlined, are willing to pay a high price (or sacrifice yield) to purchase the securities of these entities which have a low default risk.
- Lower quality or less creditworthy borrowers enjoy a comparative advantage in the floating rate market that is predominantly a bank or financial institution lending market. This is based on the fact that these institutions have certain advantages in dealing with lesser quality credits.

Both factors tend to create differential risk premiums that facilitate arbitrage.

*Inter-Market Credit Pricing Arbitrage*

Inter-market credit arbitrage is driven by different factors, including spread differences and name arbitrage factors.

Credit markets appear to display inter-market anomalies where the risk premium is significantly different between markets. In capital markets, a hierarchy of risk (expressed in terms of internal or public ratings) is established by security analysts or credit rating firms. The credit spread/risk premium should be directly related to the creditworthiness of issuers as ranked under this rating process in a more or less continuous scale of quality ratings.

For example, in one market a BBB rated credit may command a risk premium of say 100–200 bps pa greater than a higher quality AAA rated credit for term financing. However, in another capital market, the risk premium between a AAA and a BBB credit may be as low as 40–60 bps pa. This yield spread will vary significantly based on market conditions. The differences in risk premium may be related to the higher savings rates in particular countries, the liquidity levels in particular markets, the absolute yield levels in different currencies, or different financing practices. For example, in certain markets such as the Eurobond market, investors may be inclined to view a credit as either acceptable or unacceptable, and behave accordingly in investment decisions without a well defined attempt to differentiate between various degrees of creditworthiness.

This inter-market spread difference is often combined with investor focus on the name or reputation of a borrower as distinct from its strict creditworthiness. This phenomenon of name arbitrage is particularly significant in Europe and the Euromarkets. In these markets, a lower rated credit may enjoy superior access to funding at lower risk differentials than in its home market. This appears to be based on the company being a producer of a well known and accepted product that enjoys everyday use, and popularity and acceptance of the brand name. For example, companies such as Coca Cola, McDonalds, Walt Disney and IBM enjoy access to European capital markets at costs very favourable relative to their actual credit rating. This is particularly so in contrast to the relative cost of funding in their home markets (the United States) where the company's name and product association means far less than the credit rating of the firm's securities.

These factors allow certain categories of borrowers to obtain funds in certain markets at significantly lower risk premiums than would be available in their traditional domestic or home markets, generating the comparative advantages which can form the basis of swap arbitrage.

### 5.3.3 Credit Market Segmentation

Market segmentation exists within individual national capital markets as well as between various world capital markets. Market segmentation can take the form of restrictions on investment choice imposed by regulation or internal management policy. This is dealt with in the Section on tax and regulatory arbitrage.

Market segmentation exists at a number of levels. At the extreme, restrictions on cross-border capital flows create currency blockages that create attractive opportunities for participants who can circumvent capital flow restrictions by taking the opposite sides of desired transactions. For example, parallel and back-to-back loans, the precursors of interest rate and currency swaps, were largely an attempt to overcome government imposed currency restrictions on free cross-border capital flows[33]. This type of market segmentation creates problems of funding availability, encouraging arbitrage designed to exchange demand for a blocked currency for liquidity available in another capital market.

More typically, market segmentation reflects differing investor perceptions and preferences that manifest themselves in the form of risk pricing differentials similar to the spread differences. Market segmentation in this latter form appears to be predicated on administrative limitations on investment in certain instruments, or participation in different sectors of markets.

The international market for debt securities is subdivided into numerous national, regional and international sectors. The major distinctions in the international bond market are between international and domestic bond issues. Domestic bond issues are issues that are sold largely within the country of the borrower. In contrast, international bond issues are security issues that are sold largely outside the country of the borrower. International bond issues may be further subdivided into two types of issues – Eurobonds and foreign bonds. Eurobonds are international

---

[33] See Chapter 3.

bond issues underwritten by an international syndicate of banks and sold principally and at times exclusively in countries other than the country of currency in which the bonds are denominated. Foreign bonds, in contrast, are international bond issues underwritten by a syndicate of banks composed primarily of institutions from one country, distributed in the same way as domestic issues in that country and denominated in the currency of that country.

The distinctions between the various market segments, while accurate in theory, are considerably more difficult to determine in practice. The major difficulty arises as a result of the nature of the securities that typically enjoy considerable liquidity, as they can be freely bought and sold in an active secondary market. Consequently, one would expect that investors are able to purchase securities from different markets as and when their investment requirements dictate. This would lead to a breakdown in the strict categorisation proposed above. More importantly, it would lead to uniformity of pricing for comparable securities issued by the same borrower or same class of borrowers[34].

However, there is evidence to suggest that investors only participate in certain sectors of the respective markets world-wide for legal, liquidity and convenience reasons. In fact, there is evidence to suggest that a large proportion of the international bond market is not readily accessible or liquid enough for active international participation[35]. This lack of freedom for international fund flows implies a significant level of market segmentation and resultant pricing anomalies that facilitate arbitrage.

One example of this type of market segmentation motivated swap arbitrage is in the US$ market as between the Eurodollar and Yankee bond markets. The yield differential between Eurodollar and Yankee bond markets has varied significantly. However, there have been instances when yields of similarly structured Eurodollar and Yankee bonds issued by the same borrower differ by up to 20–30 bps pa in yield.

---

[34]  In the early 1990s, the emergence of global bond issuance structures was an attempt to create a truly global market for securities. This took the form of the issue of securities simultaneously in a number of markets combined with settlement, clearance and transfer mechanisms designed to facilitate trading in the securities on a global basis. Global bond issues were pioneered by the World Bank and used by a number of sovereign, supranational and corporate issuers. Issues were completed in US$, C$, A$, JPY and a few other currencies. See Lay, Kenneth G. and Wright, V. Jan "Taming the Dollar Market Machine: Reducing Friction in Distribution and Trading of Non-Treasury Bonds" (Autumn 1988) Journal of International Securities Markets 165–173.

[35]  See Marki, Frederick R V (1986) Size and Structure of World Bond Markets Special Report No 14 – Domestic and International Bond Markets (As of December 1985); Merrill Lynch Capital Markets, International Fixed Income Research Department, New York.

The divergent trading patterns create significant swap opportunities for market participants.

The pricing differences between the markets appear to be principally caused by the different credit perceptions and preferences of investors in the United States domestic and international market. These factors include:

- Different maturity and issuer preferences.
- Investor perceptions of credit quality of bond issuers.
- Currency factors and their relevance to the investment decision.

The differing investor perceptions and preferences can be seen in the fact that bonds offered by a variety of high quality sovereign issuers, irrespective of credit rating, have generally enjoyed a less favourable reception in the Yankee market[36] than in the Eurobond market. For example, debt issued by prime issuers such as the Kingdoms of Denmark, Sweden, Finland and the Government of New Zealand have traded at a significantly higher yield in the Yankee market than in the Eurobond market. In contrast, Canadian issuers have languished in the Eurobond market, but because of the proximity of the United States and Canada, have enjoyed an excellent reception in the United States domestic Yankee market.

The differential maturity preferences are evident in the fact that Eurodollar bonds with initial maturity over 20 years have fared relatively poorly in the international market. This reflects the fact that investors in the Eurodollar market have traditionally been composed of short to intermediate term security investors. This created significant pricing anomalies, with the World Bank's 30 year Eurodollar bonds at one stage yielding an average of 30 bps pa more than the 30 year Yankee bonds by the same borrower.

In addition, the Eurodollar bond market, in contrast to the Yankee market, demonstrates a high degree of sensitivity to the value of the US$. This appears to have contributed to wider spreads in the Eurodollar market relative to the domestic Yankee market. This differential partially reflects the fact that international (non-United States) investors in US$ view their investment as a currency as well as an interest rate play. Consequently, the investors will price the same credit risk differentially according to their expectations on the future direction of the US$ relative to other major currencies.

This analysis highlights how segmentation of markets creates differential risk pricing. This is turn creates opportunities for swap arbitrages of the type described. While the discussion above has been confined to the US$ market, similar considerations apply to a significant number of other markets where similar opportunities

---

[36]  The foreign bond sector of the United States domestic bond market.

are created by the different factors motivating investor participation in various segments of the international capital market.

### 5.3.4 Short Term Supply and Demand Factors

Short term supply and demand factors affecting an individual issuer's securities (in particular imbalances in the supply and demand conditions) create opportunities for arbitrage. The simplest type of supply and demand factor giving rise to financial arbitrage opportunities is market saturation or its reverse, the scarcity value of an issuer's securities.

An extreme case of supply and demand imbalance exists when a given capital market is unwilling to absorb any more debt of a given issuer. In this case, if the issuer still requires financing in the currency of that particular market, proxy borrowers who are acceptable to the saturated market must be sought. The borrower's financing objectives are met by exchanging the new obligations in the required currency for more easily saleable obligations in a currency where the market continues to have demand for the debt of the particular borrower.

Market saturation relates essentially to the relative elasticity or inelasticity of the demand curve for a particular issuer's securities. It is evident that the demand curve for a particular issuer's or risk class of securities, while relatively price insensitive when limited quantities of the issuer's securities are on issue, tends to become inelastic and highly price sensitive when a certain saturation point is reached. In that case, additional sales of securities by that particular issuer can only be achieved at significant increases in the risk differential or credit spread required to be paid to investors.

The issue of market saturation from the perspective of investors appears to relate to:
• Portfolio or credit diversification objectives of investors.
• Financing requirements of the particular issuer relative to the size of the particular capital market.

Investors on the whole seek to limit credit exposure within their investment portfolios to any particular issuer or class of issuer to a relatively small percentage of the total portfolio. This has the consequence of forcing issuers requiring substantial financing in a particular currency beyond the capacity of that particular sector or market to provide such financing. This requires the issuer to pay a penalty if it persists in seeking to raise funds from that particular market. In essence, at the margin, once saturation point has been reached, additional net investment in that issuer's securities will only grow in proportion to the total net growth in the funds available for investment, as investors are unwilling to increase their investment on a percentage basis.

Scarcity value considerations have the converse effect. Investors may be willing to purchase securities issued by *infrequent* issuers in that particular market or market sector at a much higher price (lower yield) than dictated by purely economic factors. This is on the basis of scarcity that allows the investor to achieve a greater degree of portfolio credit risk diversification.

This problem can be illustrated with reference to a number of supranational organisations that persist in a borrowing policy which dictates raising funds in particular currency markets. This particular category of borrowers (supranationals such as the World Bank and other development banks) are frequent borrowers in currencies such as US$, Euro, Swiss francs and Japanese Yen. In the case of the larger borrowers, the substantial size of their borrowing requirement places a heavy burden on the debt markets in these currencies. Consequently, these issuers need to pay a bigger penalty for frequent borrowings in these currencies. This problem has led to these issuers evolving a policy over time that dictates diversification of funding sources by issuing in a wide range of different currency markets. This allows the issuer to reach investors who would not invest in the borrower's usual funding currencies. The borrower's required currency is achieved by swapping the funds raised into the issuer's preferred currency and interest rate basis[37].

Short run supply demand imbalances (often referred to as market "windows") also create significant opportunities for swap arbitrage. Global debt markets operate on an opportunistic basis. Windows of attractive opportunities close and open as investor sentiment as to currency and interest rate outlook alters in the light of new available information. High levels of volatility in currency and interest rates, as well as improved global communications and information flows, mean that transactions are increasingly done on the basis of specific short-lived opportunities. These are predicated on investor demand that allows a particular security transaction because the market conditions are *right* and the investors are *there*.

In this type of market, rapidly changing investor demand for particular types of securities creates short-run supply imbalances that creates a premium on timing. For example, assume investor expectations in respect of a currency, say the A$,

---

[37] A number of institutions (primarily sovereign entities or major international banks) have also sought to diversify their funding base by issuing in a wide range of currencies. This allows them to reach investors other than in their traditional currencies on the basis that the funds raised are at an attractive relative rate, allowing swaps back into the desired currency at an attractive rate relative to direct market access. See discussion of new issue arbitrage in Das, Satyajit (2004) Structured Products Volume 1; John Wiley & Sons (Asia), Singapore at Chapter 3.

have improved dramatically in the light of market information. In this environment, investors will be seeking to purchase A$ securities for short-term capital gains as a result of currency fluctuations. This creates a short-term excess of demand over the supply of A$ securities, as the secondary market in A$ securities cannot meet the sudden upsurge in demand for investments. Under these circumstances, an opportunistic issuer may be able to take advantage of market sentiment to issue A$ securities at a relatively advantageous cost, fulfilling the supply gap in the market and creating a comparative cost advantage which may form the basis of a swap into its preferred currency.

A similar process would apply to an opportunistic issue of particular *types* of securities designed to capitalise on market opportunities. A number of the security structures described in other parts of the book were created as a result of market demand for a specific type of security with characteristics designed to provide the investor with a particular return profile linked to specific market conditions existing at the time of issue. Opportunistic issuers have frequently been able to take advantage of this demand for particular types of securities to create borrowings at relatively low cost, which have then been swapped into the borrower's preferred form of borrowing through a customised swap or derivative transaction.

### 5.3.5   Withholding Tax

The presence of withholding taxes creates a wedge between yields on domestic securities and those on comparable securities issued outside the domestic market, primarily in the Eurobond market. The creation of swap arbitrage opportunities as a result of the presence of withholding tax relates essentially to the differential treatment of different classes of transaction under withholding tax legislation. This can be best illustrated by an example involving the A$ market.

Under applicable regulations at the relevant time, an international (non-Australian) investor purchasing A$ securities issued in the domestic market is subject to a withholding tax of 10.00% on interest payments. For example, a European investor purchasing Australian government bonds yielding 13.00% pa would on each interest coupon date receive the equivalent of only 11.70% pa (being the 13.00% coupon reduced by the mandatory 10.00% withholding tax). The European investor may be able to recover this withholding tax by way of a tax credit in its own country. Consequently, at best, the investor will recover the withholding tax by way of adjustments to its domestic tax liability that will usually entail a delay and some loss in yield. At worst, the withholding tax will not be recoverable, resulting in a significant yield loss. For example, a tax exempt investor will not be in a position to recover the withholding.

Assume that the European investor can achieve its desired A$ investment objectives by purchasing A$ Eurobonds issued by a European issuer of high credit standing. The A$ Eurobond is free and clear of all withholding taxes, as essentially it does not involve a resident to non-resident transaction for Australian tax purposes, with fund flows taking place entirely outside Australia. Let us also assume that this Eurobond is priced at a yield *under* the equivalent Australian government bond rate of 13.00% pa, say 12.50% pa. The investor may be attracted to the Eurobond. This is because the Eurobond yield represents an effective yield pick up of 0.80% pa relative to the realised yield where the investor is unable to take advantage of the withholding tax. This is despite the Eurobond being priced at 50 bps *under* the government bond rate.

Under these circumstances, the A$ Eurobond issuer enjoys a comparative advantage in its access to A$ funding relative to domestic institutions. The issuer may, if not a direct user of A$, swap out of its A$ liability into another liability (floating rate US$) that is its preferred form of funding. The swap would be effected with a domestic Australian counterparty who would exchange its floating rate US$ liability for fixed rate A$. The domestic Australian swap counterparty's fixed rate debt would be trading at a margin above the Australian government bond rate. The issuer achieves a cost of funds under the bond rate that is a significant cost saving in fixed rate A$ terms for the swap counterparty.

The swap arbitrage related to withholding tax in our example is predicated on two important factors:

- The swap cash flows are free of withholding tax. In practice, swap payments are usually not subject to withholding tax, thereby satisfying the first condition.
- The Australian swap counterparty's underlying funding is free and clear of withholding tax.

The existence of withholding tax would have driven up swap rates/swap spreads as domestic counterparties sought to generate cheaper funding than that available directly in the domestic A$ market.

Another example of the impact of withholding tax on swap arbitrage opportunities is that which existed in the ECU market. Under then current tax regulations, the Italian government's Certificate Del Tresore in ECU ("CTE's") were subject to a 12.5% Italian withholding tax. Consequently, CTE's were issued at a gross yield above that of comparable ECU Eurobonds (up to 75–100 bps pa above comparable Eurobonds). However, many investors outside Italy were able to reclaim this withholding tax under tax credit arrangements between Italy and the investors countries. These circumstances created attractive tax arbitrage opportunities.

Investors, particularly those able to reclaim the Italian withholding tax, became aggressive buyers of CTEs. The CTE's were then swapped into attractive floating rate assets. This demand by investors seeking to undertake asset swap CTE investments forced up the fixed rate payable in the ECU swap market, particularly relative to prevailing ECU Eurobond yields, thereby providing issuing opportunities for borrowers who issued ECU Eurobonds and entered into a simultaneous swap to generate LIBOR related funding. **Exhibit 11.9** sets out this type of activity in the ECU swap market.

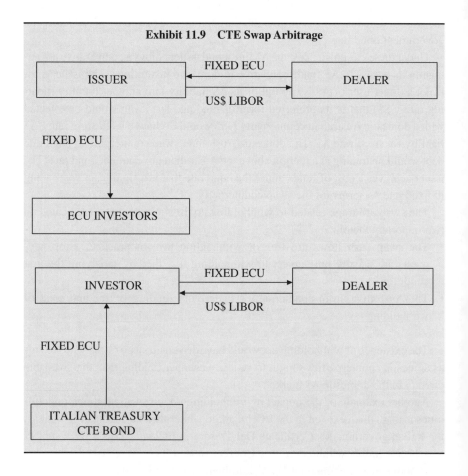

Exhibit 11.9    CTE Swap Arbitrage

As a consequence of the existence of this tax arbitrage, issues of CTE's by the Italian government were followed traditionally by issuing activity in the primary ECU Eurobond market. However, over time, the ECU swap market became more efficient at anticipating this type of arbitrage, somewhat reducing arbitrage opportunities available.

In summary, the presence of withholding tax impacts upon the pricing of capital flows across borders that may create significant differences in access and in the price of funding to different borrowers, facilitating swap structures designed to arbitrage the withholding tax.

### 5.3.6 Investment Asset Choice Restrictions

Restrictions on choice of investment assets usually limit a fund manager's investments in certain types of instruments. These are common in a variety of markets. The restrictions are usually imposed by regulatory authorities (both formally and informally), investors (in terms of the authorised investments/investment mandate) or by the fund itself based on prudential criteria. Restrictions usually operate on two levels:

- **Type of investment instrument** – for example, use of derivatives may be restricted.
- **Currency and issuer location restrictions** – for example, investment in foreign currency denominated investments or securities issued by foreign issuers may be subject to limitations.

Where such restrictions exist (particularly where imposed by regulatory authorities), fund managers often undertake transactions designed to circumvent the limitations on investment choice to better achieve the fund's overall investment objectives. To achieve these objectives, the fund may undertake complex transactions designed to *indirectly* achieve what cannot be done *directly*. In these circumstances, the fund will inevitably undertake the transaction at a pricing level significantly above the market price level as the transaction cannot be undertaken directly, resulting in arbitrage opportunities which can be exploited through swap structures. Structured notes and products are predicated at least in part on this factor[38].

Since the mid 1980s, the often Byzantine nature of Japanese investment restrictions has meant that Japanese investors have used a variety of structures to circumvent restrictions and broaden investment choice. Several examples of these are outlined below. However, it is important to note that similar asset choice restrictions also pervade other markets and create equally attractive arbitrage opportunities from time to time.

---

[38] See Das, Satyajit (2004) Structured Products Volume 1; John Wiley & Sons (Asia), Singapore at Chapter 4.

In the mid 1980s, Japanese investors sought to increase their exposure to foreign currency denominated securities. In particular, at that time, the high yields available on A$ securities made investment in A$ bonds particularly attractive. However, Japanese institutions were subject to a limitation that restricted investment in foreign currency securities to 10.00% of overall portfolios. At that time, the institutions' quota of foreign securities was close to or at the legal limit. It became apparent that the 10.00% rule was subject to a minor exception. Issues of foreign currency denominated securities *by a Japanese resident company* did not count, for some peculiar reason, as part of the 10.00% foreign security quota. This exemption, allied to the Japanese investor's appetite for A$ securities, led to issues by Japanese banks which were placed primarily with Japanese institutional investors. The issues were undertaken at substantially lower yields than the prevailing A$ government bond rates. The yield level accepted by investors reflected the fact that a comparison with domestic A$ interest rates was largely irrelevant, as under existing rules the investor could not invest in those instruments whereas they were able to purchase the A$ securities issued by the Japanese banks. The banks in turn converted their price advantage resulting from the demand for these A$ securities within Japan into low cost US$ funding. This was done by swapping with Australian domestic institutions, who in turn achieved cost effective fixed rate A$ at levels unobtainable in the domestic A$ or any market at that point in time.

Another example of tax and regulatory arbitrage circumventing investment asset choice restrictions involves dual currency bonds[39]. Under Japanese tax law, zero coupon bonds have historically received extremely favourable treatment. The difference between the purchase price and the face value of the bond was treated as a capital gain, and taxed at the favourable capital gains rate. However, the Ministry of Finance limited the amount a Japanese pension fund could invest in non-yen denominated bonds issued by foreign corporations. In response to these conditions, a number of issuers undertook issues of a zero coupon yen bond plus a dual currency bond with interest payments in yen and principal repayment in US$.

The Ministry of Finance ruled that the dual currency bonds qualified as a yen issue for purposes of pension fund investment restrictions, even though the dual currency bond had a US$ denominated zero coupon bond embedded within it. Effectively, the zero coupon yen bond, dual currency yen and US$ bond combined represented an investment in a normal coupon yen bond and an investment in a zero

---

[39] For a discussion of dual currency bonds, see Das, Satyajit (2004) Structured Products Volume 1; John Wiley & Sons (Asia), Singapore at Chapter 20.

coupon US$ bond. However, this particular structure allowed issuers to capitalise on the desire of Japanese investors to diversify their portfolios internationally within the regulations imposed by regulatory authorities.

The fact that this particular structure allowed the investors to achieve an exposure otherwise not available to them, led to a pricing level which was particularly advantageous to the issuer, who would usually swap the combined securities into a US$ exposure through a series of swap transactions. The cost achievable through that series of swaps was significantly better than that available from direct access to the US$ market.

Over time, a wide variety of issue structures combining derivative elements and asset classes (equity and commodity) with securities have appeared. The security structures have been designed to the specifications of investors (usually European, Japanese or Asian) who are unable to otherwise undertake the transactions. The fact that the direct alternative is not directly available to these institutions has meant that they are willing to pay above market prices to enter into these positions indirectly. This cost benefit has usually been translated by the issuer of the securities into cheaper cost funding in the borrower's desired currency and interest rate basis through a number of swap transactions.

### 5.3.7 Tax Differentials

Tax driven swap arbitrage usually focuses on the dissimilarity of taxation treatment across countries for similar financial instruments. Swap arbitrage involving withholding tax effects has already been discussed. The other two major categories of tax driven swap arbitrage are:

- Differential tax treatment of types of income in the hands of investors or conversely the different characterisations and treatments of interest expense from the perspective of the borrower or issuer of securities.
- Capital allowances (such as depreciation and one-off large capital investment or expenditure allowances) made available by national governments to stimulate capital investment. This is discussed in the later Section on subsidised funding sources.

Swap arbitrage predicated on differential treatment of revenue and/or expense focuses on the fact that investors seek to maximise *after tax* income while borrowers seek to minimise *after tax* costs of funding. Where a particular issuance format, either entailing a particular combination of cash flows or the location of the borrower or investor in a particular tax jurisdiction, is tax effective, there is a natural incentive for both borrowers and investors to gravitate towards the particular format. This is because it reduces after tax cost or increases after tax returns. The potential to enhance the economics of the transaction provides the essential arbitrage profit that can be allocated between the parties through a specially structured swap transaction.

This process can be best illustrated with an example. In the early 1980s, zero coupon securities emerged as an important financial instrument. Non-tax attributes of these securities such as reduction of reinvestment risk, call protection, price volatility and duration factors were important in the emergence of these debt instruments. However, it was tax factors which were instrumental in the upsurge of interest in zero coupon securities[40].

Zero coupon securities were particularly attractive for investors that were either not taxed or who were taxed at concessional rates of interest on the discount (that is, the difference between purchase price and face value which constitutes the economic return to the investor). In a number of jurisdictions, the difference between the investor's sale price and the purchase price of the discount security was treated as a non-taxable capital gain. In other jurisdictions, the discount was taxed at a concessional rate that was lower than the normal rate of taxation, or only taxed at maturity, allowing investors to achieve significant improvements in return on holdings of zero coupon securities relative to normal coupon securities. Investors, as a result of the tax factors, were willing to purchase zero coupon securities at prices that were substantially higher (implying lower yields) than conventional securities. The higher price willing to be paid reflected the willingness of investors to share part of the return benefit on an after tax basis with the issuer.

Allied to the tax factors was the preference for the investors who enjoyed tax benefits of zero coupon securities to purchase bearer securities (Eurobonds) that allow holders to preserve their anonymity. The absence of withholding tax also favoured Eurobond issues. The particular investors were also concerned that the issuers be of a higher credit quality. This was designed to satisfy not only their normal credit requirements but the additional credit risk given that the full return on the investment was deferred to maturity under the zero coupon structure.

In this environment, borrowers satisfying the identified requirements were able to access fixed rate funding on a zero coupon basis at significantly lower yield than through other sources. This cost advantage was used as the basis for swap arbitrages. In particular, the fact that the issuers may not have wanted to use the funding generated in the particular cash flow pattern of a zero coupon security

---

[40] For a discussion of zero coupon securities, see Das, Satyajit "Zero Coupon Securities" (1987 No. 1) Bulletin of Money, Banking and Finance 1–51.

necessitated the development of swap structures designed to convert this all-in cost advantage to a more acceptable or preferable form[41].

Other types of tax factors that have created opportunities for swap arbitrage include:

- Differential rates of income tax that create incentives for cross-border financial transactions conceived to defer or avoid income taxes.
- Treatment for tax purposes of hedging transactions of different types.
- Differential tax policies governing cross-border transfers.
- Differential foreign tax credit systems.

Often tax factors are combined with other conditions that together provide opportunities for swap arbitrage.

### 5.3.8 Subsidised Funding Sources

A major source of arbitrage opportunities derives from the fact that particular borrowers may enjoy preferential access to subsidised financing sources. Examples of such subsidised financing include:

- Export credit funding.
- Tax based financing structures, including leasing.

Most developed nations exporting large amounts of capital goods have established agencies to assist their exporters in financing sales overseas. The agencies, usually government departments or statutory bodies, typically provide low cost finance or interest subsidies as an inducement to foreign purchase of major items of capital investment. This type of export credit financing is clearly linked to the purchase of the underlying capital goods, but is usually also subject to significant restrictions as to the terms and conditions of the financing, in particular the currency and interest rate basis.

A purchaser of capital goods with access to export credit financing can therefore find itself in the position of having access to finance on preferential terms relative to the market, but in a currency or on an interest rate basis that differs from its preferred liability structure. In these circumstances, the potential arbitrage profit locked into its preferential funding sources can be mobilised through a swap structure to allow the borrower to achieve its desired mix of liabilities.

---

[41] These structures are discussed in detail in the section on accelerated and deferred cash flow swaps in Das, Satyajit (2004) Structured Products Volume 1; John Wiley & Sons (Asia), Singapore at Chapter 13.

Tax based financing opportunities, particularly in the area of leasing, function in a similar way. Government policies designed to stimulate capital investment usually provide for large capital investment allowances in the form of depreciation or immediate write-offs (investment tax credits). Potential users of equipment attracting such advantageous tax treatment, either directly through purchase or indirectly by some type of lease or hire arrangement, can usually structure financing arrangements designed to lower the all-in cost based on the available tax advantages. A limitation of this type of financing is that the tax advantage may dictate the financing being structured on a currency or interest rate basis other than the borrower's preferred liability structure. As in the case of export credits, this creates the opportunity for utilisation of swap arbitrage structures predicated on the tax-based financing arrangements generating a more attractive cost structure than normal financing arrangements.

### 5.3.9   Completion of Markets

The opportunity for swap arbitrage is also partially predicated on the incomplete nature of capital markets. In this regard, swaps contribute to the integration of financial markets by allowing market participants to fill gaps left by the unavailability of particular types of financial instruments. The use of swaps to overcome institutional market limitations is particularly apparent in smaller and less developed markets. For example, the institutional structure of these markets may not encompass a substantial long-term fixed rate corporate debt market. A factor underpinning the growth of swaps in such markets is that such transactions allow corporations to generate fixed rate liabilities under circumstances where such transactions are not directly available. This may impact upon the pricing of swaps in these markets.

### 5.3.10   Transaction Costs

The impact of transaction costs on arbitrage is more complex. Various types of transaction costs are identifiable, including the requirements for confidentiality, queuing restrictions and the opportunity to lock in gains or minimise losses on particular borrowings.

There are many reasons why a borrower may want to keep its fund raising behaviour in a particular market confidential. The requirement of confidentiality by particular borrowers may be motivated by such factors as the desire to avoid review by rating agencies or governmental bodies. Where confidentiality is an issue, the borrower's objectives can be accomplished by using proxy borrowers in the desired market that forms the basis of currency and/or interest rate swaps into the borrower's preferred form of liability. In these circumstances, the advantage of confidentiality means the borrower is willing to pay a premium for access in this particular form, which is the basis of the swap arbitrage.

Another form of transaction cost is the queuing procedure often applied by different national governments. The queue dictates the timing and order of access to particular capital markets. In essence, to control the flow of investment funds, financial authorities in many countries establish a quota of financing that is available to borrowers of particular types in each financing period. Borrowers apply for permission to borrow and if approved, are placed in a queue until their turn to borrow arrives. In certain circumstances, the queue can be extremely lengthy.

The existence of a queuing system creates problems in the sense that borrowers must be able to anticipate market conditions and their own financial requirements well in advance. Given the volatility of currency and interest rate markets, it is possible that even where the financial requirement has been anticipated in advance, the period between entering into the queue and being eligible to borrow may mean that market conditions have changed from those anticipated at the time the borrowing was contemplated. In these circumstances, borrowers can either accelerate or defer borrowings when in a queue by entering into a swap with another borrower. To accelerate its borrowing, the borrower would usually enter into a swap with a party that has currently arrived at the head of the queue. Where the borrower seeks to defer its borrowing in the particular currency or on the interest rate basis previously contemplated, the borrower (having reached the head of the queue) would undertake the borrowing transaction and swap out of the liability into a preferred interest rate or currency basis more in line with its expectations and requirements at the time of issue.

In these circumstances, the borrower in the queue may be willing to pay a premium to accelerate or defer its transaction, creating a natural arbitrage gain that can be the basis for swap transactions. A major factor underlying swaps predicated on queuing positions is that national regulatory authorities tend to take an unfavourable view of borrowers who, having positioned themselves in a queue, upon reaching the appropriate borrowing position do not undertake the originally contemplated transaction.

The desire of borrowers to lock in currency and interest rate gains, or alternatively to minimise losses from market movements, also creates the basis of swap arbitrage. Unless fully hedged, currency and interest rate transactions may result in accumulated gains or losses after their inception. Rather than run the risk that an unrealised gain will be dissipated or a book loss increased by subsequent changes in market conditions, organisations may undertake swaps to lock in the size of the gain or loss at its present level.

In this context, the use of swaps becomes relevant for a number of factors including:

- Alternative means of covering the exposures may not be available. For example, the borrowing may not be able to be repaid because of contractual agreements or penalties. The transaction costs create an incentive for the borrower in question to pay a premium to undertake the swap facilitating the swap arbitrage.
- Even where eligible to undertake the transaction by alternative means, market protocol may dictate that the borrower should not, in order to preserve its access to the particular sector, retire or otherwise restructure its borrowings. In these circumstances, an incentive exists for the borrower to once again pay a premium to achieve its objectives, thereby indirectly providing the arbitrage gain that can form the basis of swap transactions.

The potential dissipation of any gain or aggravation of any loss depending on the rate expectations of the organisation, and the likelihood of such an outcome eventuating, may be so great that the borrowers are once again willing to pay a substantial premium that can provide the source of arbitrage.

### 5.3.11 Arbitrage Sources – Comments

In considering the various sources of arbitrage, it is important to note that in a given market, several of the factors identified may coexist and combine to provide the basis of swap activity.

A persistent problem in seeking to explain the economics and pricing of swaps and swap spreads in terms of arbitrage is the problem of arbitrage erosion. In classical arbitrage, the very process of exploiting this type of opportunity would soon eliminate it. However, a careful analysis of the various sources of swap arbitrage suggests that a substantial number are structural in nature. This essentially means that growth in swap activity, while it may have the impact of reducing the scale of the arbitrage profit, does not of itself *eliminate* (as distinct from *reduce*) the arbitrage profit. In the case of tax and regulatory arbitrage, in particular, there is no reason for the arbitrage opportunity to disappear, at least until the relevant tax or regulatory provisions are altered.

In summary, while opportunities for classical financial arbitrage employing swaps may be eroded by competition, several of the sources of swap arbitrage profit are embedded in the very structure of modern capital markets and in particular, the imperfection of contracting arrangements and regulatory regimes, particularly between national markets.

# 6 Market Swap Spreads

## 6.1 Overview

In this Section, an analysis of swap spreads in different currency markets is set out[42]. The primary objective is to present the actual behaviour of swap spreads in practice. The major currency sectors analysed include: US$, Yen and Euro.

## 6.2 US$ Swap Spreads[43]

### 6.2.1 Overview

The US$ swap market is the largest single element of the global swap market. The market is sophisticated and structurally well developed. There is naturally no currency swap market in US$ as the US$ itself functions as the other side of almost all currency swaps.

The size of the market reflects a number of factors. The key factor is the size of the United States capital market, including the size of the market for United States Treasuries and a large corporate bond market both within the United States and in the international market. An additional factor contributing to the size of the US$ interest rate swap market is the fact that a large proportion of global financing flows continue to be denominated in US$.

The market has perhaps the best defined and most economically well defined spread and pricing structure. The US$ swap market can be broadly classified into two sectors:

- **Short term market** – under 3–5 years.
- **Medium to long term market** – over 3–5 years.

The distinction in the market is largely predicated on the factors driving activity, pricing and the method of hedging risk positions in these two segments.

---

[42] The author would like to thank Colin Keays (Deutsche Bank) for providing spread data on US$, Euro, Sterling and A$.

[43] See Das, Satyajit (1989) Swap Financing; Law Book Co, Sydney at Chapter 20; Das, Satyajit (1994) Swaps & Financial Derivatives – Second Edition; Law Book Co, Sydney/McGraw-Hill, Chicago at Chapter 23. See also Evans, Ellen and Parente, Gloria M (1987) What Drives Interest Rate Swap Spreads; Salomon Brothers Inc Bond Market Research, New York; Leibovitch, Richard "The US Dollar Swap Market" in Das, Satyajit (Editor) (1989) Global Swap Markets; IFR Publishing, London at Chapter 3; (12 February 1993) "Question from the Floor: Interest Rate

## 6.2.2    Market Structure – Short Term US$ Swaps

The short term sector functions as an extension of financial futures markets in US$ interest rates. The key participants in this short-term sector are a group of United States and non-United States banks that provide fixed rate US$, usually through their access to fixed rate Eurodollar deposits or to the fixed rate CD market in London and New York. They also act as payers of the fixed rate in US$ interest rate swaps. The activity in this area is largely driven by the structure of the bank's asset liability portfolio, and the primary motivation is either balance sheet management or speculative in nature.

The pricing in this segment of the market largely reflects the hedging practice where risk positions in the short swaps are usually managed by executing futures transactions in US$ interest rate futures (Eurodollar futures). Dealers in the short swaps traditionally use Eurodollar futures markets as the hedging vehicle for short-dated interest rate swaps. For example, a dealer entering into a swap where it receives fixed rate and pays floating rate for say two years will offset the risk on the swap by trading a series of sold or short Eurodollar futures positions, that is, a sold Eurodollar futures strip[44].

This segment of the market tends to be extremely volatile in price, reflecting its close proximity in maturity to the (potentially) volatile US$ money markets. The price volatility of financial futures based swaps requires a high level of execution skills to undertake transactions in markets susceptible to very quick and sharp movements. A particular characteristic of this section of the market is a very substantial level of speculative interest where dealers take positions on both absolute rate movements as well as spread movements between various indexes.

This type of speculative trading usually relates to the triangular relationship in this segment of the market between:

- Yield on the relevant United States Treasury note.
- Implied rate on the Eurodollars futures strip.
- Swap spread over the Treasury note.

Given any two of these variables, the remaining one is determinable. Traders trade the spread between the Eurodollar strip and corresponding United States Treasury note. The primary objective of this type of trading is to profit from a correct prediction of the change in the spreads of the Treasury note relative to

---

Swap Spreads-Historical Perspective" in Derivatives Bulletin, Salomon Brothers Inc. US Derivatives Research, Fixed Income Derivatives, New York.

[44] The use of strips of Eurodollar futures contracts to hedge interest rate swap positions is discussed in detail in Chapter 10.

the implied rate on the Eurodollar strip (in the argot of the market – "trading the TED (Treasury Eurodollar) spread"). For example, if a trader expects the TED to narrow, he or she would buy Eurodollar futures and sell Treasury notes. Conversely, if the trader expected the spread to widen, he or she would sell Eurodollar futures and buy Treasury notes. This type of activity requires participants to establish and unwind these positions rapidly to maximise profits. This activity greatly increases the liquidity in the futures markets and contributes to the depth and liquidity in these types of swaps.

In practice, the correlation between US$ interest rate swap and Eurodollar strip prices is high. Correlation is highest at the short end of the yield curve (up to 5 years). The relationship is reduced as maturity is increased due to a variety of factors, including decreased liquidity in the "back" Eurodollar months, increased futures execution risk and interest rate volatility.

One problem in using Eurodollar futures to hedge interest rate swap positions is that the PVBP of Eurodollars are fixed regardless of the level of absolute rates (the convexity bias). The PVBP of an equivalent swap will change according to the level of interest rates. Effectively, Eurodollars are non-convex whereas interest rate swaps are convex, creating the necessity to rebalance the Eurodollar futures hedge periodically, resulting in a loss of hedge efficiency[45].

### 6.2.3 Medium/Long-Term US$ Interest Rate Swaps

US$ swaps with maturity beyond 3–5 years are dominated by securities transactions, primarily the issuance of fixed rate bonds in the United States domestic and Eurodollar bond market. The debt markets and the US$ swap markets enjoy a symbiotic relationship with ever-increasing volumes of new debt issuance being predicated on the accompanying swap. Pricing in the longer term US$ interest rate swap market is almost exclusively related to the United States Treasury rates for comparable maturities. These are therefore quoted on a spread to Treasury basis.

US$ interest rate swaps not related to new issues are driven by trading and risk management activities. One rationale for activity in this market segment is that as interest rates fluctuate, a fixed rate payer or receiver may find that a substantial profit can be realised by reversing the original swap or cancelling the original swap in return for an up-front cash payment. Traders also use swaps as a surrogate interest rate instrument for the purposes of hedging existing positions and also trading. The fact that the swap spread tracks non-government spreads is a significant factor in their use for these purposes.

---

[45] See discussion in Chapter 10.

## 6.2.4   Pricing Relationships in US$ Interest Rate Swaps

The pricing structure in US$ interest rate swaps is well developed. This reflects a number of factors including:

- Mature nature of the underlying capital market.
- Defined structure of credit differentials (based on credit agency rating levels) that prevails in the US$ bond and securities markets.
- The availability of a wide variety of hedging tools, including the ability to short sell Treasury bonds (because of the large and liquid repo market) and the liquid market in government bond futures.
- Presence of a large number of dealers and market participants.

The pricing of short-term interest rate swaps is substantially driven by short-term interest rate futures market movements, reflecting activity in trading the TED spread. The major determinants of longer term US$ interest rate swap prices/spreads include:

- **Volume and type of fixed rate bond issuance in US$ bond market** – sovereign, international agency, corporate and financial institution debt issues are swapped into floating rate US$ LIBOR via the US$ interest rate swap market. Liability swaps linked to such new issues, particularly from higher quality issuers, are driven by the issuer's final objective of financing at margins relative to LIBOR. Increased volumes of issuance of high quality fixed US$ bond with the corresponding entry by the issuers into liability swaps typically create a large demand on US$ interest rate swap market makers to pay fixed rates, thereby inducing downward pressure on swap spreads. Periods of strong issuance of the US$ debt therefore impacts significantly on US$ swap prices.
- **Asset swap activity in the secondary market** – asset based swap transactions create demand for market makers to receive fixed rate in US$. The transactions arise from newly issued or seasoned bonds (lower rated (BBB or below)) that are placed on an asset swapped basis with banks or financial institutions. A high level of demand for asset swapped securities can therefore place downward pressure on US$ swap spreads.
- **Corporate bond spreads relative to US$ Treasury bonds** – the underlying arbitrage nature of the swap market dictates that the level of bond spreads relative to the corresponding US Treasury rates, and in turn the relationship to swap spreads, forces adjustments to US$ swap prices. Changes in spreads, particularly in the corporate/financial institution market, can lead to significant changes in swap spread levels. Such changes can be driven by a variety of factors. For example, high levels of corporate bond issuance to refinance high coupon fixed

rate debt or to take advantage of low absolute rate levels can change fixed rate bond spreads to US Treasuries and impact upon swap spreads.

• **Absolute interest rate levels and interest rate expectations** – the absolute level of interest rates as well as expectations of interest rates movement can influence swap spread levels.

Some additional factors which may influence US$ swap spread levels include spreads on long-term fixed rate bank liabilities as well as in the asset backed or mortgage backed securities markets. This reflects the fact that banks frequently fund on a long-term fixed rate basis that is then swapped into floating rate LIBOR in order to match their predominantly LIBOR based assets. Changes in the perceived credit standing of the bank sector generally can change the risk premiums on bank instruments, and in the process exert upwards or downwards pressure on US$ swap spreads. Changes in the level of spreads for asset and mortgage-backed instruments influences swap spreads because of their increased use as the basis for asset swaps where these securities are placed on a floating rate basis with a variety of investors. Changes in spread on mortgage backed securities also affect swap spreads because swaps are generally used to hedge such asset portfolios.

### 6.2.5 US$ Swap Spread Behaviour[46]

**Exhibit 11.10** sets out US$ swap spreads over time for different maturities.

The behaviour of US$ swap spreads has a number of key influences:

• Bond spreads for corporate borrowers in US$ public debt are a major factor in swap spread levels. Swap spreads seem to approximate the spreads over United States Treasuries on investment grade corporate securities, usually in a 20 to 30 bps range defined by AA and A rated spreads.

• Swap spreads also appear to be influenced by interest rate expectations. Swap spreads appear to move inversely to Treasury yields; they tend to widen when treasury yields fall and narrow when treasury yields increase.

The changing use of swaps and the evolving cast of participants, particularly the development of asset swaps, by influencing the supply and demand of fixed rate payers, has been a major determinant of swap spreads. Technical factors such as hedging costs have influenced spread changes over time.

---

[46] For example, see Pelletier, Steve "Spread Risk" (January 1999) Derivatives Strategy 52–54.

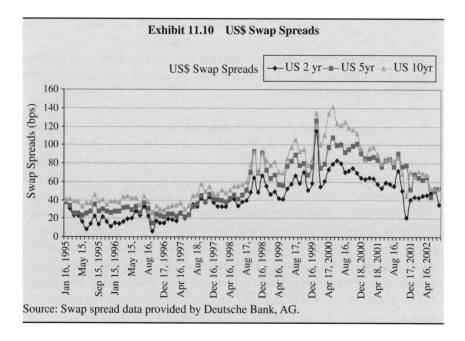

**Exhibit 11.10    US$ Swap Spreads**

Source: Swap spread data provided by Deutsche Bank, AG.

The US$ swap market has been characterised by a number of phases. Through the 1980s there was a very strong relationship between swap spreads and bond spreads. In the late 1980s and early 1990s, the relatively stable relationship that had previously existed between AA corporate bond spreads and swap spreads began to break down. Bond spreads increased in level as well as volatility. Major factors underlying this increase in spreads included:

- Increase in general credit risk as a result of macro factors (recession) and also micro factors (high degree of corporate leverage through leveraged buyouts and highly leveraged financing structures).
- Decrease in liquidity in the corporate bond market.
- Deterioration of bank credit quality resulting in margins relative to LIBOR on asset swaps increasing.
- Bank balance sheet constraints exacerbated by the BIS 1988 Accord[47] that favoured investments in instruments bearing less than 100% risk weightings.

As the spreads on bank paper increased, swap spreads lagged behind, influenced by the relative stability of sovereign bond credit spreads. The widening in the spread

---

[47]  See Das, Satyajit (2004) Risk Management; John Wiley & Sons (Asia), Singapore at Chapter 17.

differential minimised new issue arbitrage opportunities and therefore reduced the opportunities for liability swaps. In addition, the rising cost of funding for banks meant that traditional purchasers of asset swap securities were less aggressive in their purchase of these assets.

In the 1990s, US$ swap spreads in all maturities broadly decreased. This reflected a variety of factors. Bank lending became increasingly expensive. Lower rated borrowers forced swap spreads to an indifference level where their cost of fixed rate issuance versus their cost of funding on a floating rate from banks and swapping these funds into fixed rate were equal. As bank lending margins over LIBOR increased (as a result of BIS capital adequacy rules and higher bank cost of funds), there was downward pressure on swap spreads. Investors supported continuing high volumes of high credit quality new issuance in US$. This was driven by a shift away from bank deposits to bonds. This shift was driven, in part, by the impact of the deterioration in bank credit quality. This ensured that new issue spreads were relatively low. The combination of low new issue bond spreads and demand to receive fixed rate under swaps to create floating rate US$ funding kept swap spreads low.

In addition, the low absolute level of interest rates and the steep positive slope of the US$ yield curve through the early and mid 1990s also affected US$ swap spreads. The low absolute rates meant that investors sought non-government issues to generate higher yield through assumption of credit risk. This meant that all credit spreads (from high quality to low quality) decreased sharply. Swap spreads tracked this decline. The positive slope of the yield curve meant that borrowers swapping into fixed rate had a significant cost penalty. This meant that borrowers continued to borrow at the short end of the yield curve. They also did not wish to fix rates. This also placed downward pressure on swap spreads.

These conditions prevailed consistently throughout the 1990s. The only exception was in 1994 when the US Federal Reserve Board tightened interest rates. During this period, swap spreads were low and generally tracked bond spreads closely. Swap spreads were also not especially volatile.

The paradigm shifted again in 1997. The Asian crisis in 1997 and the Russian default and near collapse of Long Term Capital Management in 1998 affected spreads. The changes were driven by a number of factors including:

- The overall credit quality of borrowers declined. This was particularly true of those in lower credit ratings and those based in emerging countries.
- The credit quality of banks declined sharply as their credit portfolio quality deteriorated and bad debt losses rose sharply.
- Bond spreads increased rapidly as investors shifted to government securities in a flight to quality.

- The non-government bond market lost liquidity and investors and traders, unable to liquidate positions, used swaps (paying fixed rates) to hedge their portfolios.
- The demand for paying fixed in swaps required dealers to short bonds. As pressure grew, it became more difficult to borrow bonds and increased the cost of hedging.
- Increase in counterparty risk in derivatives meant that swap spreads increased to adjust availability of credit lines.

The combination of factors forced swap spreads to increase and also become very volatile.

The swap spreads recovered from the crisis levels but have remained high and even reached record levels. This new round of instability was driven by changes in the underlying government bond market[48]. The changes included:
- The reduction in supply of US Treasury government bonds (due to a fiscal surplus). The potential scarcity caused the yields on these bonds to fall sharply[49].
- The reduction in supply also resulted in a reduction in the ability to borrow Treasury bonds. This affected the ability to and cost of short selling, increasing swap spreads.

The market initially sought new benchmarks (primarily, US agency paper). However, concern about the lack of an *explicit* US government guarantee created problems in using these securities as a hedge and benchmark[50].

The problems in the government bond market and the continued high volumes of issuance in the non-government bond market have resulted in high swap spreads.

Another aspect of the behaviour of US$ swap spreads has been the uneven nature of movements in spreads across the yield curve. This has been particularly apparent for longer maturities. One factor has been the declining credit quality of financial institutions and the BIS capital adequacy requirements for swap transactions. These factors have limited the number of participants active in longer dated transactions. This has diminished liquidity in the longer end of the US$ swap market. This fact, combined with demand from special structured transactions (mortgage hedging,

---

[48]  See Boughey, Simon "The Irresistible Rise of US$ Swap Spreads" (September 1998) Derivatives Strategy 8–10.
[49]  See Youngdahl, John, Stone, Brad and Boesky, Hayley "Implications of a Disappearing Treasury Debt Market" (March 2001) Journal of Fixed Income 75–86.
[50]  See McNee, Alan "The Search for a New Benchmark" (March 2000) Risk 8; Mengle, David and Smithson, Charles "Swaps Become the New Benchmark" (April 2001) Risk 78–79.

aircraft lease and real estate transactions), has affected the term structure of swap spreads. In particular, the swap spread curve has been very steep beyond 10 years. The advent of collateralisation (to address the counterparty risk transactions) and the entry of a number of large well capitalised entities into the long end of the swap market, has begun to reduce the spread differences.

The use of swaps to hedge mortgage backed securities positions is an increasing factor in the behaviour of US$ swap spreads[51]. This is because of the increased use of swaps to hedge the negative convexity on mortgage backed and callable debt (particularly issued by the US agencies). The prepayment/call risk on these securities means that as interest rates fall, the risk of these securities being called/prepaid increases. This means that for every 1 bp decrease in yield, the price of these bonds increase *but by a decreasing amount*. This means that investors increasingly receive fixed rates (under interest rate swaps) to protect portfolio performance. This means that as interest rates fall, swap spreads tend to decrease, reflecting large receiving interest[52]. The reverse occurs when interest rates increase. A similar phenomenon is evident in some other markets such as the Euro.

## 6.3 Yen Swap Spreads[53]

### 6.3.1 Overview

The Yen swap market is a large and substantial market. The yen market enjoys many structural similarities with other major swap/derivative markets around the world. However, a major difference is that the arbitrage that drives swap transactions in yen tends to be more structural than the traditional forms of credit or other arbitrages that drive swaps in other markets. A key factor underlying this type of structural arbitrage is the regulatory framework governing the activities of financial institutions within Japan. For example, the historical classification of Japanese financial institutions between city banks and long-term credit banks has driven the

---

[51] See Wraith, John "The Dynamics of Swap Spreads" (September 2002) Risk – Risk Management for Investors Supplement – Sponsor's Statement.

[52] Between mid December 2001 and mid January 2002, it is estimated that convexity hedging accounted for an estimated US$60 billion in swap volume in the US$ market; see Wraith, John "The Dynamics of Swap Spreads" (September 2002) Risk – Risk Management for Investors Supplement – Sponsor's Statement.

[53] See Das, Satyajit (1989) Swap Financing; Law Book Co, Sydney at Chapter 21; Das, Satyajit (1994) Swaps & Financial Derivatives – Second Edition; Law Book Co, Sydney/ McGraw-Hill, Chicago at Chapter 24. See also Smout, Neil "The Yen Swap Market" in Das, Satyajit (Editor) (1989) Global Swap Markets; IFR Publishing, London at Chapter 11.

structure of the yen swap market. This creates artificial segmentation that leads to asset liability mismatches that drive yen swap transaction structures. Similarly, the regulation of interest rates and the complex inter-relationships between various interest rates within the Japanese market also drive the swap spread. Deregulation of the Japanese financial system has increasingly reduced the rigid structural barriers that have determined the framework of the yen swap market.

The principal participants in the Yen swap market include:

- International issuers of Euro-Yen bonds who use Yen currency swaps to convert Yen funding into floating rate US$ LIBOR based financing.
- Japanese financial institutions (primarily Japanese banks) that use swaps to both hedge their natural interest rate positions and for reasons of proprietary trading.
- Japanese corporations, insurance companies and other end users who either use swaps to convert foreign currency funding into Yen, or use Yen interest rate swaps to generate fixed rate funding or to assume trading positions on interest rates.
- Financial institutions active in trading in Yen swap and derivative products. Major market makers in Yen swaps are the larger Japanese banks that are active for internal asset-liability management reasons, proprietary trading and servicing client/end user demand. A number of foreign institutions maintain significant Yen swap portfolios, although a substantial proportion of these are related to new issue transactions in the Euro-Yen bond market. Securities houses are also active in the Yen swap market.

The Yen market has differentiated historically between the Yen/US$ currency swap market and the Yen interest rate swap market.

### 6.3.2    Structure of Yen/US$ Currency Swap Market[54]

Traditionally, there were two distinct and separate Yen/US$ swaps markets. Both markets were linked to either the Euro-Yen or the US$ bond markets. These markets were:

- Fixed yen versus floating rate US$ swap markets.
- Fixed yen versus fixed US$ market (the LTFX/currency forward market).

Traditionally, the two markets were not closely connected because of the different ways the swaps were constructed and the different pricing variables.

---

[54] The discussion of the structure of yen swaps draws on (1986) The Explosive Growth of the Yen/Dollar Swap Market; Nomura International Limited, London.

**Exhibit 11.11** sets out the typical structure of a fixed Yen/US$ LIBOR currency swap against a new issue.

---

**Exhibit 11.11    Structure of Yen / US$ LIBOR Currency Swap Market**

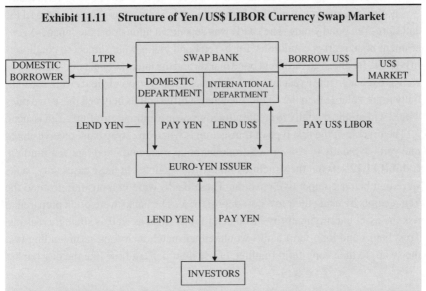

Source: (1986) The Explosive Growth of the Yen/Dollar Swap Market; Nomura International Limited, London.

---

The structure of the transactions was dictated by the participants. Pricing was closely linked to their ability to borrow long-term Yen funds. Pricing for fixed Yen/floating US$ LIBOR currency swaps were determined principally by the Yen long-term prime rate ("LTPR"). The LTPR is part of the regulated interest rate structure within Japan and is connected to the Japanese government bond coupon via the bank debenture rate. The rate the swap bank was willing to pay was typically a margin below LTPR (say 10–15 bps pa). The final rate depended upon expectations of future movements in the domestic Yen bond market and LTPR. Consequently, swap rates depended very heavily on current demand from borrowers that in turn depended upon market expectations.

There was a division between certain types of banks within the Japanese domestic market. City banks had access to short-term (up to 2 years) funds. This meant that they have historically concentrated on short-term lending. The long-term banks and trust banks, in contrast, had access to long-term debt primarily through the issue of bank debentures. The institutions specialised in providing long-term loans to industry. Therefore the long-term and trust banks predominated as payers of fixed rate Yen. However, as the markets deregulated, the city banks played a more active role as payers of fixed rate Yen in fixed Yen/floating US$ currency swaps in order to create fixed rate long-term Yen liabilities to match their domestic long-term loans.

The principal source of potential arbitrage was the differential between the LTPR and Euro-Yen bond yields. The LTPR was dependent upon domestic Japanese government bond market conditions. Euro-Yen bond yields were subject to conditions in both the Japanese government bond market and the international bond markets, as well as exchange rate expectations. Further, as Euro-Yen bond yields were substantially more volatile than the LTPR, the interest differentials between these two rates would widen substantially to create attractive swap arbitrages for Euro-Yen issuers.

The reverse of the first type of transaction is where the swap bank receives fixed rate yen – typically to convert a Eurodollar bond issue into fixed rate yen funding. **Exhibit 11.12** sets out the structure of these transactions. In these cases, city banks were in a better competitive position. These banks were in a position to fund the Yen receipts by using their low cost deposit base. The banks were often prepared to risk the asset liability maturity mismatch for historical as well as strategic reasons. Trust banks and long-term banks would either match their long-term lending (via the swap) to their long-term funding, or use their deposit base like the city banks.

**Exhibit 11.12　　Structure of Yen and US$ Swap for Eurodollar Issue**

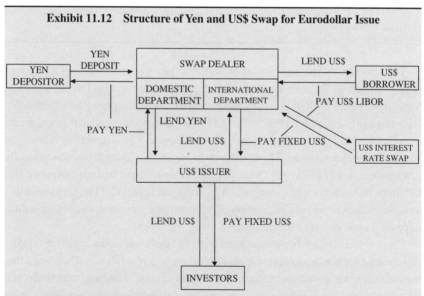

Source: (1986) The Explosive Growth of the Yen/Dollar Swap Market; Nomura International Limited, London.

There were a number of sources of arbitrage in these transactions. The swaps were often "harakiri" swaps (that is, the swaps were priced at off-market rates). It was often assumed by non-Japanese observers, including other financial institutions, that the swap bank was making a loss. In reality, the bank providing the hara-kiri swap was not making an actual loss but an "opportunity" loss (that is, it could have lent the funds at a higher rate). The banks' funding cost (via cheap deposits) was below the rate at which they were lending via the swap. An additional factor here was that the swap bank usually sought to time its entry into a swap to coincide with the large interest cost differential between the Japanese domestic and the Euro-Yen market. Typically this was at the time LTPR was expected to rise, and so Japanese corporations rushed to borrow from the banks. During these periods, what may have appeared to the observer as extraordinarily aggressive yen swap rates were primarily temporary imbalances in the supply and demand of fixed rate yen funding creating attractive swap opportunities. An additional more nebulous consideration was that the lending rate was determined by the bank. The Japanese banks may have been in a position to manipulate LTPR to essentially prevent large losses from their aggressive swap positions.

It is also clear that the so-called hara-kiri swaps were typically provided to obtain a coveted co-lead management position in a Eurodollar issue for a Japanese corporation and/or to maintain or improve relationships with its own clients. To an extent, the aggressive swap pricing is explainable on the basis of the aggressive competition between the Japanese banks and securities houses. The banks were seeking to establish a foothold in the London market, either as lead or co-lead managers for Eurobond issues. Simultaneously, the Japanese securities companies were also pricing swaps particularly aggressively as it provided them with the opportunities (via the Euro-Yen market) to establish relationships with prime non-Japanese borrowers.

A further element of arbitrage was that bonds issued by Japanese borrowers were exempt under Japanese regulations from inclusion in holdings of foreign securities by insurance companies and pension funds. As investors were in the process of rapidly expanding their US$ denominated portfolios, these bonds became particularly attractive. As demand for the bonds exceeded supply, Japanese issuers were able to borrow at substantially cheaper rates than non-Japanese borrowers in the Eurodollar market.

The combination of hara-kiri swaps with these bond issues produced very favourable terms for the issuers. The terms were more favourable than those available in the domestic market.

The historical pattern of involvement of various participants in the foreign exchange market largely determined the existence of this parallel market. The trust banks and long-term banks were more active in the long-dated foreign exchange markets, while the city banks concentrated more on the spot and short-dated forward markets. The trust banks and long-term banks used their long-dated foreign exchange dealing capabilities to develop their corporate relationships, both within and outside of Japan, and were therefore often prepared to offer attractive LTFX swaps if they were linked to public Eurobond transactions.

Changes in the financial structure of Japanese markets have assisted in the integration of the various market segments. However, the complex inter-relationship between the markets continues to be a major factor in the Yen market. In more recent times, a key driver of the Yen currency swap market has been the Yen/US$ cross currency basis swap. This market has been driven by credit factors. In particular, the deterioration of Japanese credit quality, especially of Japanese banks[55].

### 6.3.3    Structure of the Yen Interest Rate Swap Market

The Yen interest rate swap market evolved in the mid to late 1980's and has become an important component of the Japanese capital market. The growth in Yen interest rate swaps is predicated on the following factors:
* Structure of the banking system within Japan.
* Asset liability management requirements of Japanese corporations.
* Use of Yen interest rate swaps as a trading instrument to monetise interest rate views.

Central to the growth of Yen interest rate swaps historically was the tacit approval by the Ministry of Finance to these types of transactions. This was significant in that the transactions implicitly sanctioned the crossing of traditional banking divides within Japan. These types of transactions were utilised originally by the Japanese city banks as an entree into long-term lending. This was an area to which they had previously been denied access. The city banks used swaps as a means of generating synthetic fixed rate funding to match off their exposure on fixed rate lending to Japanese corporations. The long-term trust banks, at least in theory, provides the opposite side to these transactions as they were able to generate floating rate funding pricing off short-term interest rates to fund their growing short-term lending business.

The role of Yen interest rate swaps in bank asset liability management contributes to the fact that a high proportion of the activity is between financial institutions. However, Japanese corporations use Yen interest rate swaps. Liability management

---

[55]   See Chapter 10.

concerns predominate in attracting these participants into the Yen interest rate swap market.

The participation of non-financial institutions in Yen interest rate swaps was usually based on one of the following reasons:

- Fixed rate funding opportunities for companies with lower credit ratings. This is precisely the type of credit arbitrage that dominates many other swap markets.
- The use of interest rate swaps to unhinge high coupon Yen borrowings into floating rate liabilities to lower the absolute interest levels on outstanding loans. This particular type of transaction has been popular because of the reluctance of Japanese corporations to repay existing loans at high fixed interest rates. This reflects the complex relationship between lenders and borrowers in Japan. Against this background, by converting long-term fixed rate liabilities into floating rate through the swap market, Japanese corporations have sought to reduce their annual interest cost without having to risk falling out with their traditional house relationship bank.
- As liquidity has developed, corporations have sought to trade interest rates by entering into interest rate swaps. This is to take advantage of the differential between fixed and floating interest rates and also to seek to capitalise on interest rate movements. The fact that swaps are off-balance sheet transactions requiring no margin calls or cash payment has made this type of positioning activity increasingly popular.

The capacity to use Yen interest rate swaps to trade interest rates has also been important in allowing the market to develop. This was a major driving force in the late 1990s as low nominal rates and a steep yield curve encouraged aggressive trading of interest rate views. In addition, the flexibility of swaps in enabling short positions is an important factor that has driven activity.

### 6.3.4   Yen Swaps – Pricing Relationships

The Yen swap market trades as an absolute rate market, rather than a spread market. In practice, swap rates are not significantly correlated to the Japanese government bond ("JGB") market. This results in low correlation between Yen swap yields and the JGB yields.

This lack of correlation between JGB and swap yield reflects a variety of factors:

- The JGB market focuses on one benchmark bond, typically of 10 years maturity. JGBs of other maturity are not sufficiently liquid nor are their interest rate movements predictable enough to be used as a basis for swap pricing.

- The lack of continuous supply of government bonds has meant that no consistent yield curve exists over which swaps can be quoted, making relative valuation more difficult and creating inefficiencies in market pricing movements.
- Cash JGBs are sometimes subject to withholding tax for foreign entities, further limiting their use in hedging yen swaps.
- Structural restrictions mean that it is difficult to short sell JGBs except through the futures market.
- The JGB futures market is subject to limitations as well. The liquid JGB futures contract traded in Tokyo is subject to a transaction tax.

The structural difficulties mean that it is not, for all practical purposes, possible to use JGBs to hedge and price Yen swaps.

In practice, the spread between the 10 year JGBs and Yen interest rate swaps is one of a number of factors considered by traders who seek to take positions on the spread for proprietary trading purposes. In particular, because of foreign interest in Yen swaps, movements in Yen swap rates tend to anticipate changes in Yen JGB rates.

Yen swap rates show a strong correlation to Euro-Yen and LTPR rates. Yen swap rates are strongly correlated to Euro-Yen interest rates. Highly creditworthy Euro-Yen bonds and Yen swap rates trade at relatively consistent spread levels. The LTPR rate governs where long-term credit banks can issue 5 year debentures in the domestic Japanese retail market (a prime funding source for these banks). This relationship is evidenced by the degree of correlation between the LTPR and five year yen interest rate swap rates. The relationship between LTPR is closely monitored by Japanese banks active in Yen swaps who seek to arbitrage the markets.

Pricing for fixed Yen/fixed US$ swaps is determined principally by the interest rate differential between US Treasury bonds and JGBs. However, because the Yen/US$ currency forward market as at longer maturities is relatively illiquid, it is also dependent to a large extent on supply and demand. Because of lags between price and yield movements in the US Treasury market (that are relatively volatile) and movements in rates in the LTFX markets (that are relatively stable), it is possible to pick up attractive arbitrage opportunities. The source of the arbitrage, therefore, is the US$ and Yen interest differential implicit in the yen and US$ spot and forward rates and the yield on United States treasuries.

Increasingly, the Yen LIBOR/US$ LIBOR currency basis swap market rate is a very important component of the pricing of Yen/US$ currency swaps. Historically, this market has remained at a level of between $-3$ and $-10$ bps pa in favour of yen

LIBOR (the market pays more to receive yen LIBOR/pay US$ LIBOR). However, this relationship has become increasingly volatile[56].

In recent times (late 1990s), a number of other factors have emerged as significant drivers of Yen swap spreads. These factors reflect the problems inherent in the Japanese economy. The key factors include:

- The weakness of the Japanese banking system as a result of bad debts. This resulted in these institutions divesting assets, driving up credit spreads. It also adversely affected liquidity as counterparty limits to Japanese banks were reduced. This, combined with Japanese bank mergers, significantly affected pricing in the Yen swap market.
- The asset swap market in JGBs has allowed traders to purchase JGBs and swap them into a floating rate asset as Yen LIBOR plus a margin (1–2 bps pa). This was equal to around US$ LIBOR plus 15–20 bps pa for a AAA/Aaa credit rated asset. This reflected Yen swap spreads trading well below historical levels and the structure of the Yen/US$ currency basis swap markets.
- The development of a corporate bond market in Yen and interest by investors in lower credit rated assets affected Yen swap pricing.

The complex pricing inter-relationships in the Yen swap market creates significant difficulties in hedging risk positions. In practice, Yen swap market makers hedge their portfolio positions using a variety of instruments. Short-term interest rate swaps are hedged using the Euro-Yen short term interest rate futures contract. Longer-term swap positions are either hedged using the futures market in JGBs or through the use of curve hedging, where a swap in a particular maturity is hedged by undertaking an opposite swap in *another maturity* on a duration or PVBP consistent basis. The inefficiency of the hedge instruments available, in turn, contributes to the volatility of Japanese swap rates and spreads relative to the various benchmarks.

## 6.4 Euro Swap Market

### 6.4.1 Overview

The Euro swap market is quite unique. This reflects the fact that it is synthetic currency. The market commenced with monetary union between 11 member states in January 1999. The Euro market has a precursor in the European Currency

---

[56] See Chapter 10.

Unit ("ECU") market that existed in the late 1980s/early 1990s[57]. The Euro swap market has subsumed the swap markets in the individual constituent currencies, most notably, the swap markets in Deutschemark ("DEM"), French Franc ("FFR") and Italian Lira ("ITL")[58]. The market has also evolved, dynamically driven by a number of factors that are unique to its status as an artificial and synthetic currency.

In the Section, the structure and pricing dynamics of the Euro swap market are discussed. It is important to note that the market is still evolving and its behaviour is less established than that observed in other swap markets.

## 6.4.2   Euro Swaps Market Structure[59]

A fundamental driver of the Euro swap market is the impact that the creation of the Euro had on the underlying capital markets.

The implementation of the Euro has allowed the effective consolidation of 11 separate capital markets. The pre-existing capital markets (with some exceptions – Germany, France and Italy) were relatively small markets characterised by problems of differences in credit ratings, liquidity levels, regulatory structure, range of instruments traded, volatility and price transparency. The Euro consolidated these markets, integrating volume. This overcame problems of size, instrument range, volatility and price transparency. However, the problems of credit ratings and structure remain. If anything, the Euro market structure exaggerates these difficulties. These are manifested in terms of issues associated with pricing, relative value and pricing benchmarks.

However, notwithstanding these problems, the introduction of the Euro has given impetus to the development of an integrated large Euro denominated bond market[60].

---

[57] See Das, Satyajit (1989) Swap Financing; Law Book Co, Sydney at Chapter 22; Das, Satyajit (1994) Swaps & Financial Derivatives – Second Edition; Law Book Co, Sydney/ McGraw-Hill, Chicago at Chapter 25.

[58] See Das, Satyajit (1989) Swap Financing; Law Book Co, Sydney at Chapter 22; Das, Satyajit (1994) Swaps & Financial Derivatives – Second Edition; Law Book Co, Sydney/ McGraw-Hill, Chicago at Chapters 25 and 26.

[59] For example, see Simpkin, Guy "European Fixed Income Capital Markets: Benchmark Curves and Futures Contracts" in (1999) The Guide to Euro-Denominated Securities – Euromoney Supplement at 2–5.

[60] For example, following its introduction, the Euro denominated bond market has witnessed strong issuance volumes. The volumes have on occasion exceeded those in the US$ bond markets.

The principal problem in this regard is the issue regarding the existence of an underlying pricing benchmark[61]. In most markets, the underlying government bond curve provides the appropriate pricing benchmark. However, the structure of the Euro market means that there is no *one* government bond that the market can price off. In reality, this problem may be exaggerated. This is because the German government bonds (bunds) and French government bonds (OATs) function as a *de facto* Euro government bond market. However, this does not fully overcome the underlying problem.

This problem can be simply illustrated. For example, assume an Italian issuer is seeking to undertake a Euro denominated bond issue. The issue is underwritten by a US and Swiss banks. The issue is being placed in Germany, France and Benelux. In this situation, the issuer may look to its pricing relative to the Italian sovereign bonds (historically, this would have been its normal pricing benchmark). The investors will look at the issue pricing relative to their own sovereign benchmark. For example, a German investor may look at the spread to bunds; a French investor at the spread to OATs; a Dutch investor at the spread to Dutch government bonds; a Belgian investor at the spread to Belgian government bonds (OLOs) etc. The underwriters may look to the spread to bunds, interpolated Franco-German government curves or to the spread to swaps. The spreads to each benchmark rate will inevitably be different (although the differences may be small). The underwriters must look to reconcile the competing perspectives of the issuer and investor. *In this circumstance, the Euro swap curve itself has emerged as the pricing benchmark.*

The emerging central role of the Euro swap market reflects the confluence of a number of factors:

• It minimises the pricing discrepancies between the various sovereign and non-sovereign issues. The fact there is only *one* Euro swap rate provides benchmarking certainty. The pricing to Euro-ibor on an asset swap basis allows the consistent pricing of the credit risk using a single homogenous pricing basis.

• The size of the Euro swaps market is significantly greater than any individual government bond market. This means that its liquidity is greater, allowing it to act as a benchmark rate. The credit risk inherent in the swap is less problematic[62] as the Euro participant governments may in reality not have the ability to monetise their debt, thereby introducing default risk into government debt. This means

---

[61] See Webb, Andrew "Curve Balls" (February 1999) Futures & OTC World 19; Metcalfe, Richard "Shaping Up" (February 1999) Futures & OTC World 24–26; Shireff, David "Let a Thousand Yield Curves Bloom" (March 1999) Euromoney 29–31.

[62] The use of collateral may mitigate this risk in any case.

that the underlying government bond markets are themselves not risk free and exhibit a credit spectrum (in the spread to bunds or to the Euro swap rate).

- The use of a spread to a money market rate (Euro-ibor) is advantageous as it does not contain a term risk (inflation or political risk premium) and is a useful benchmark for bond market issuers seeking to convert fixed rate bonds into floating rate liabilities.
- The spread to Euro swap concept is useful for underwriters/bond traders as they finance bond positions (in both the primary and secondary markets) at money market rates (Euro-ibor) and hedge positions using offsetting Euro swap positions.

In reality, this role is not new. Prior to the introduction of the Euro, the DEM, FFR, ITL etc swap markets played a central role allowing credit instruments to be priced. However, prior to the Euro, individual bond and swap markets in a currency competed for the position as the pre-eminent pricing benchmark. For example, the DEM swap market and the bund market competed in terms of relative liquidity and transparency as a pricing indicator. In this environment, the government curve offered the advantage of the lowest credit risk, homogeneity within a currency, a wide range of instruments (futures contracts) and (sometimes) liquidity. However, the Euro shifts the capacity of *individual government bond markets* to provide these benefits. This has lead to the primacy of the Euro swaps market.

## 6.4.3  Euro Swaps – Pricing Relationships[63]

The pricing of Euro swaps is problematic. This reflects the fact that the approach in most markets is to price the swap *at a margin to the risk free government rate*. However, in the Euro market, the government bond rates of member countries a*re priced relative to the swap rate*. This reflects the fact that *all* securities are priced as to the margin relative to Euro-ibor. **Exhibit 11.13** sets out Euro swap spreads (relative to German Bunds) over time for different maturities.

In practice, the pricing of Euro swap appears to be driven by the following factors:

- **Credit markets** – the Euro swap rates appear to be heavily influenced by the volume of activity in the Euro denominated bond markets and the attendant demand and supply of payers and receivers of fixed rates in Euro. Euro swap

---

[63] See Engelhard, Fritz "Bund/Swap Spreads" (August 1999) German Supplement – Risk Magazine 4–5; Turpault, Christophe, Ober, Philippe and Muller, Erick "Swap Spreads" (September 1999) Euro Derivatives Supplement – Risk Magazine 8–11.

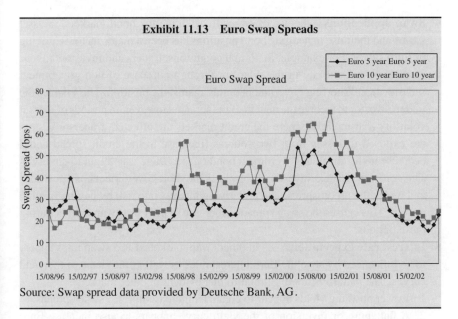

**Exhibit 11.13    Euro Swap Spreads**

Source: Swap spread data provided by Deutsche Bank, AG.

rates have generally tracked movements in credit spreads in the capital market. The Euro swap spread has tracked spreads on Euro denominated bonds issued by sovereigns and corporations and German Pfandbrief. However, single government bonds (in particular, bunds and OATs) still dominate in pricing influence (particularly, in a maturity where there is a liquid futures contract). Euro swap rates have also been affected by changes in the perceived credit quality of banks. For example, Euro swap spreads have increased during periods of uncertainty and crisis[64].

* **Hedging practices** – the Euro swap rates show strong correlation to the Euroibor futures strip at the short end of the maturity curve. The Euro swap rates also show strong correlation to the underlying bond and bond futures markets in bunds and OATs at the medium to long end of the yield curve. This reflects the use of these instruments to hedge swap positions. The trading liquidity in these instruments has led these to be the basic hedging instruments for Euro swaps. However, the underlying structure of these government bond markets has created pricing anomalies from time to time[65].

---

[64]  See Turpault, Christophe, Ober, Philippe and Muller, Erick "Swap Spreads" (September 1999) Euro Derivatives Supplement – Risk Magazine 8–11.

[65]  See Engelhard, Fritz "Bund/Swap Spreads" (August 1999) German Supplement – Risk Magazine 4–5.

- **Swap applications** – the use of swaps to arbitrage the bond markets, in asset swaps and their use in hedging bond positions has been a major factor in pricing of Euro swaps. For example, in normal conditions, traders and investors favour receiving the fixed rate in the swap (or through purchase of non-government securities) and shorting government bonds against the position. This enables the trader/investor to receive the benefit of the spread. However, in periods of market volatility (particularly, where the credit markets are affected, traders/investors are exposed to losses from two sources (increase in the credit spread and a decrease in the absolute government bond rates as there is a "flight to quality"). This forces the traders/investors to buy back the short government bond positions and hedge the credit spread and underlying interest rate risk by paying fixed in a swap. This causes the swap spread to increase in the Euro swap market during these periods.
- **Interest rate expectations** – as in other swap markets, Euro swap rates appear to be influenced by absolute Euro interest rates as well as the shape of the yield curves. The pattern is not dissimilar to that evident in other markets:
  1. Lower absolute yields appear to create an increase in Euro swap spreads.
  2. A flattening or inversion of the yield curve appears to also increase Euro swap spreads[66].

The use of bunds and OATs to hedge Euro swaps creates a complex inter-relationship between the government bond repo markets in Germany and France, the bond futures contracts in bunds and OATs and the Euro swap market.

The relationship between the repo markets and the Euro swap market is similar to that which exists in the US$ market. Increase in the cost of borrowing bonds for the purpose of short selling (a decrease in the repo rate), reflecting the relative scarcity of the relevant government bond, results in an increase in the Euro swap spread. However, peculiarities in the repo market make the impact on Euro swap spreads more complex. For example, 10 year bunds trade more expensively (lower yield) than OATs. This reflects their behaviour in the relevant repo markets. However, the bunds also tend not to trade on special (high borrowing costs/lower repo rates) relative to comparable US Treasury bonds. This reflects the structure of the German domestic markets. In the US$ market, there is no ready substitute for US Treasury securities with the possible exception of Agency paper. In contrast, the Pfandbrief market (in particular, the "jumbo" Pfandbrief issues)[67] are regarded

---

[66] See Turpault, Christophe, Ober, Philippe and Muller, Erick "Swap Spreads" (September 1999) Euro Derivatives Supplement – Risk Magazine 8–11.

[67] For a discussion of the Pfandbrief market, see Walker, Marcus "Germany's Secret Gamblers" (April 1999) Euromoney 22–28; von Baum, Werner "Structured Credit

as a close substitute for bunds by investors seeking liquid low cost and near government risk paper. This position existed prior to the implementation of the Euro. However, the position has accelerated since the advent of the Euro. This might in part explain the lower *absolute* spread structure in Euro relative to US$[68].

The structure of the futures markets in both bunds and OATs also affects Euro swap spread behaviour. Traders have favoured using the bund, Schatz and BOBL futures contracts traded on Eurex as the favoured hedging mechanism for swap positions. However, a bond futures contract is limited by the availability of the underlying cheapest to deliver ("CTD") bond. The bund contract has been vulnerable to short squeezes. This reflects the large trading volume relative to the outstanding CTD bonds[69]. This creates problems in pricing and hedging Euro swaps.

The behaviour of the Euro swap market is interesting when compared to the behaviour of the US$ swap market. The US$ swap market shows greater correlation to credit spreads (in particular, corporate debt) than the corresponding Euro swap market[70]. The use of swaps to hedge mortgage backed securities positions is an increasing factor in the behaviour of Euro swap spreads[71]. This is based on similar considerations to those that affect the US$ swap market[72].

## 6.5   Other Swap Markets

Swap markets in other currencies display similar characteristics to those identified in relation to the swap markets discussed. The major differences relate to the influence of individual factors and the presence of special factors driven by the structure of the capital market in the relevant currency. **Exhibit 11.14** sets out Sterling swap spreads over time for different maturities. **Exhibit 11.15** sets out A$ swap spreads over time for different maturities.

---

Products" (August 1999) Risk – Germany Supplement 16–17; Hagger, Euan "Tinkering with the Specialist Principle" (April 2000) Euromoney 60–69.

[68] See Engelhard, Fritz "Bund/Swap Spreads" (August 1999) German Supplement – Risk Magazine 4–5.

[69] A number of initiatives, including allowing delivery of a variety of government securities into a Euro bond futures contract, have been attempted.

[70] See Turpault, Christophe, Ober, Philippe and Muller, Erick "Swap Spreads" (September 1999) Euro Derivatives Supplement – Risk Magazine 8–11.

[71] See Linnebjerg, Peder "Euro Derivatives in the Nordic Markets" (September 2002) Risk – Nordic Risk Supplement – Sponsor's Statement.

[72] See Wraith, John "The Dynamics of Swap Spreads" (September 2002) Risk – Risk Management for Investors Supplement – Sponsor's Statement.

**Exhibit 11.14    Sterling Swap Spreads**

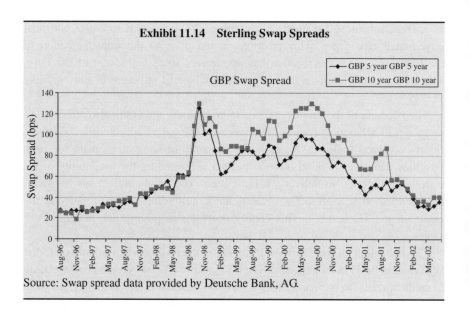

Source: Swap spread data provided by Deutsche Bank, AG.

**Exhibit 11.15    A$ Swap Spreads**

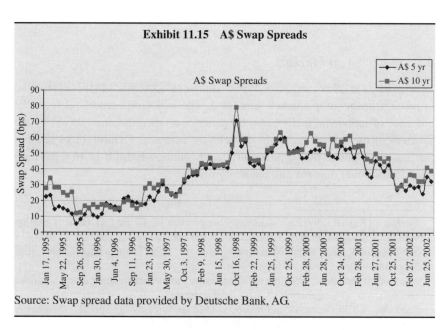

Source: Swap spread data provided by Deutsche Bank, AG.

# 7 Summary

Swap spreads reflect the margin or spread relative to the underlying government bond rate or equivalent benchmark rate. In practice, the swap spread is driven by general market credit spreads, hedging costs of the swap itself, interest rate expectations and the use of swaps in funding/risk management. Swap spreads exhibit a linkage to underlying bond spreads through a process of financial arbitrage between the credit markets and the swap markets. The capital markets appear to exhibit certain structural skews in credit pricing, segmentation and barriers to access, that enable swaps to be used to arbitrage credit pricing both within and across capital markets. These factors also drive the behaviour of swap spreads over time. Individual swap markets in different currencies exhibit distinctive behaviours within a broadly consistent framework. The behaviour of swap spreads and swap pricing also appears to shift over time.

# DERIVATIVES TRADING & PORTFOLIO MANAGEMENT

# 12
# Derivatives Trading and Portfolio Management

## 1 Overview

The discussion of derivatives pricing to date has focused on individual transactions. In reality, dealers trade and manage *portfolios of derivatives and cash instruments*. The principles underlying management of portfolios are similar to those underlying pricing and hedging of individual transactions. For example, the pricing models used are identical. However, the management of portfolios requires adoption of a process where the portfolio is reduced into a defined and clearly identifiable series of risk factors that are used to establish the risk of the portfolio and to trade in and manage/hedge the risks.

In this chapter, the overall process of derivative portfolio management is outlined. The major objective of this Chapter is to outline the approach to structuring the management of derivative portfolios. The next 4 chapters set out the detailed process of trading in and managing the individual risks in the portfolio. Chapter 13 sets out the trading/hedging of individual transactions such as interest rate and currency swaps. Chapter 14 sets out the process of trading/hedging the risk of interest rate portfolios. Chapter 15 sets out the process of using the Greek letters or alphabet to quantify the trading risk of option portfolios. Chapter 16 outlines the process of trading/hedging options by trading in the underlying asset (delta hedging or option replication).

The structure of this Chapter is as follows:

- Key drivers for the migration to *trading* or *market making* in derivatives are outlined.
- The risk framework for trading in derivatives is described.
- Integrated approaches to trading and risk management are identified.
- The process of risk decomposition of portfolios of derivative instruments is outlined.
- Implications of the proposed trading/risk management approach are considered.

The approach to risk management identified in this Chapter is similar to the approach used to determine the risk profile of a portfolio using Value-At-Risk ("VAR") techniques[1]. However, there are significant differences. In practice, there are two separate levels of risk management:

- **Trading risk management** – this is micro risk management at the level of individual traders and trading desks. This activity is focused on quantifying risk to changes in risk factors and implementing *specific* hedges. It also focuses on the ongoing management of risk and hedges, which seeks to continually manage the risk profile in line with expectations of changes in risk factors.
- **Firm wide risk management** – this is aggregate risk management at the level of the trading desk, business unit and the firm itself. This activity is focused on matching risk (measured in terms of large changes in risk factors) with capital to ensure the ability of the firm to absorb trading risk. It focuses on safeguarding the solvency of the firm.

The focus in this Chapter and the following Chapters is on trading risk management. The two approaches are complementary but distinct and separate.

## 2  Trading in Derivative Products

### 2.1  The Role of Derivatives Dealers

The development in swap and derivative markets, both in the range of products and the use of swaps and derivatives, has been driven by the emergence of dealers willing to trade in and make markets for the instruments. The earliest transactions were purely counterparty transactions where a commercial or investment bank structured a transaction on behalf of two (or more) counterparties with matched but mirror reverse requirements. However, as the market matured the major participants in the market moved to *dealing as principal* rather than only *acting as agents* structuring transactions on behalf of counterparties. This shift accelerated the creation of a market in swaps/derivatives as these institutions began to act as dealers routinely quoting two-way prices.

The change in emphasis from counterparty transactions to intermediated transactions, where financial institutions enter into derivative transactions as principals, took place on two separate levels:

- **Bank intermediation in a matched counterparty transaction** – this was used as a form of credit enhancement.

---

[1]  See Das, Satyajit (2004) Risk Management; John Wiley & Sons (Asia), Singapore at Chapter 2.

- **Principal trading without matching counterparty** – principal trading entailed market making; that is, willingness to enter into trades at a price. Market making was usually undertaken as part of positioning/arbitrage strategies, or on a fully hedged basis. This involved entry into a temporary unmatched derivative position until a counterparty could be located while hedging the risks entailed. Principal trading can but need not necessarily merge the market making function with the credit intermediation role.

Against this background it is possible to set out a hierarchy of derivative trading. Dealers can act in any of the following capacities:

- **Brokers** – arrange perfectly matched transactions acting solely as agents by introducing complementary partners to one another. Brokers collect an arrangement fee for their services.
- **Intermediated arrangers** – serve as principals to instantaneously priced and exactly matched counterparties. This technique merges the credit intermediary and broker functions. The intermediary bears no market risk but assumes credit risk (that is, if one counterparty to a matched transaction fails, then the principal must continue to service the other counterparty).
- **Dealers** – make continuous two-way markets and hedge open positions in the cash markets or other derivatives markets (such as exchange-traded futures/options markets). The positions are later matched with offsetting transactions and placed in the dealer's portfolio. The dealer merges a market making function with the credit intermediation role.
- **Arbitrage transactions** – involve a long or short derivative position versus an opposite position in another financial instrument, for example, the underlying asset or derivative contract. The motivation is to exploit inefficiencies between markets.

Virtually every major institution involved in the derivatives market participates in the swaps/derivative market as dealers. The analysis of swap/derivative market making and trading focuses primarily on this type of principal trading in these transactions without matching counterparties.

## 2.2   Derivative Trading/Market Making – Rationale

The emergence of trading/market making reflects a response to a number of developments in the derivative markets including:

- Increased range of applications of swap/derivative transactions.
- Increased desire for prompt execution on the part of users.

- Requirement of structural flexibility in swap/derivative transactions.
- Earnings potential from trading/market making in swaps and derivatives.
- Development of adequate hedging technology.
- Potential synergy of swap/derivative products with other activities (such as underwriting new issues, trading and sales/distribution of securities).

The cause and effect relationship in the emergence of market making is not easily discernible. The relationship is symbiotic. The development of dealers assisted in the actual further development of the derivative market. These developments, in turn, required participants who would act as dealers.

One of the major factors prompting the emergence of derivative dealers was the evolution of the interest rate and currency swap market. The swap market evolved from a market emphasising new issue arbitrage to a market focusing on trading and asset liability management. This increased emphasis on trading/asset liability management required the development of a relatively liquid swap market. The emergence of dealers providing two-way prices on transactions allows users of the market the requisite flexibility to reverse or unwind transactions at the current market rate.

Users of the derivatives market came increasingly to expect, demand and receive instantaneous pricing and transaction structures tailored to their needs. The original structure of the market, essentially a broker market predicated upon arranging matching counterparties, was not capable of meeting these demands. This is because the intermediary in question could not guarantee that it would be able to locate and instantaneously price a perfectly matched transaction with a counterparty. This resulted in the market becoming increasingly dominated by dealers.

The dealers provided both the required prompt execution and structural flexibility. The availability of intermediaries willing to commit to a trade without necessarily having a counterparty in position made possible a prompt execution capability. This eliminated the delay where it was necessary to have a precisely matched counterparty to complete a transaction. The dealers also provided structural flexibility. As structures grew more complex (usually to exploit identified trading/arbitrage opportunities or to meet complex hedging needs), the required derivative structures grew correspondingly more complex and varied from generic instrument structures. The existence of dealers who were willing, for a cost, to tailor the transaction to specifically match client requirements thus provided the basis for the further development of the derivatives market. An added impetus to the shift to principal trading or market making in derivative products is the increasing trend to multi-product combinations. Increasingly, engineered combinations of forwards, swaps and options are created in response to specific trading and hedging requirements. The highly individualised nature of the products being dealt with means that matching counterparties with exactly offsetting requirements would be extremely difficult, if not impossible, to locate. This necessitated an increasing role for dealers structuring, pricing and hedging such transactions.

The emergence of dealers also reflected the changing remuneration basis in the market. Originally, derivatives (in particular, swaps) were structured on the basis of arrangement fees and some ongoing "drip" income (in the form of an annuity being the difference between the cash flows on both sides of a matching trade). As the market developed and competition increased, the market rapidly evolved to a spread market with dealers earning the spread between the price/rate on one side of a transaction and the price/rate they received on the matching counterparty trade.

The change in the pricing of transactions became evident with the emergence of the first dealers. With the emergence of these dealers, other intermediaries not willing to act as dealers were placed in a position of significant competitive disadvantage. An organisation's policy not to trade derivatives resulted in two fundamental constraints in the organisation's operations. The intermediary effectively became a *price taker* (that is, buyers at the offered side of the market and sellers at the bid side of the market). The intermediaries were further disadvantaged as they were dependent on locating dealers who had to be persuaded to trade instantaneously and to match the specifications of their client.

The prerequisites for entering into transactions severely impacted on the non-dealer intermediary's price levels, price turnaround time etc. This naturally inhibited volume, and confined the intermediary's activities to delivering its client to another intermediary to get the order filled. An added problem in this type of operation was that it practically handed over the intermediary's client to a dealer, virtually inviting the client to go directly to the dealer for future transactions. The brokering fee earned in such transactions was significantly lower than one that could have been earned from entering into the transaction as a principal. In this situation, the non-dealer intermediary could book the transaction with the dealer as principal and then deal as principal with its clients. This would serve to disguise the identity of the ultimate derivative provider from its client. However, the intermediary would be required to mark up its price to cover risk and capital usage. This effectively would add a credit intermediation fee to the dealer's bid-offer price. This would mean that the actual price quote was above or below the actual dealer market price. The result was usually low volume and client dissatisfaction with the non-dealer intermediary's prices and turnaround time. Increasingly, many end users of the market refused to be brokered through, either directly or indirectly, to another dealer. Consequently, once a small group of dealers in derivative transactions emerged, it effectively forced other participants in the market to also commence market making in such transactions to avoid placing themselves at a competitive disadvantage.

The move to market making by intermediaries was also prompted by the potential to earn significant profits. This profit was primarily generated by changing the position of the intermediary from that of a *price taker* to a *price maker*. The basic profit strategy was for the dealer to opportunistically position and execute round lots trades (usually large transactions). These could be transacted at the most advantageous prices at the time of its choice. The dealer would subsequently re-offer or bid the opposite side of the transaction on a continuous basis in smaller parcels. This capacity to break down large positions into retail size and to distribute the smaller parcels, combined with the opportunity to trade at the time of the intermediary's choice, allows the intermediary to influence the market by letting the market come to it. This usually facilitates buying at the bid side of the market and selling at the offer side, greatly increasing the volume of profitable transaction put through its derivative book. For example, opportunities to buy swaps at the bid side tend to occur naturally through new securities issues. The position is then re-offered to market participants seeking to synthetically create fixed rate liabilities. This pattern of activity is largely true for a wide range of markets.

The profit potential from this type of activity can be viewed as earning the spread between the buy and sell side of the market supported by adequate hedging technology to manage the risks of booking open positions. Alternatively, the profit potential of the operation can be enhanced by operating the book, at least partially, on an unhedged basis to trade opportunistically to take advantage of price/rate, spread/basis and volatility movements.

The development of an adequate hedging technology was crucial in the emergence of derivative dealers. The hedging technology was based on recognition of the fact that the risks entailed in booking open derivatives positions were not substantially different to the risks entailed in the management of bank treasury or securities dealing operations. This allowed institutions to adapt existing technology to the management of derivative operations.

The emergence of dealers can also be traced to potential synergies arising from the natural linkages of derivative transactions with new issues of securities, trading and the sales of securities. Increasingly, intermediaries were attracted to act as dealers in view of the fact that a derivative trading capability (particularly in interest rate and currency swaps) was an essential complement to the new issue securities business. Alternatively, for institutions lacking a strong new issue business, such as commercial banks, derivatives represented an opportunity to further develop their new issue business. Intermediaries were also quick to realise that the ability to continuously make markets in derivatives of all sizes and maturities greatly enhanced their security trading, sales and distribution activities.

The impetus to develop principal trading or dealing capacities in derivative instruments was largely uniform. The factors identified were present in relation to each of the various types of instruments identified across all asset classes.

In part, development of dealing capabilities in derivative products should in reality be regarded as part of a broader move to an increased principal/proprietary trading approach by financial institutions *generally*. This tendency reflects an increased willingness by financial institutions to risk equity capital in order to:

* Generate a significant earnings stream.
* Facilitate servicing client product requirements.

This tendency to enhance and emphasise principal/proprietary trading approaches extends across all product groupings. At a macro level, this encompasses broad balance sheet asset liability mismatches and the resultant interest rate risk positions. At the micro level, this relates to positions assumed seeking to benefit from movements in financial market prices such as interest rates, currencies, commodity and equity market prices. Within each risk category, there may be different dimensions of exposure that are sought to be created. For example, interest rate risk specific exposures may be sought to be created to absolute or yield curve shape movements, spread movements between various indexes or changes in spreads between yield curves in different currencies. Exposure may also be sought to changes in the volatility of various financial market variables (primarily through trading options) or to the relationship between variables (correlation exposures).

A major element underpinning this increased emphasis on principal/proprietary trading is the increased pressure on earnings as a result of declining profitability from more traditional financial institution activities. This includes relatively low risk financial services products such as agency functions (arranging/broking transactions) or lending activities. Pressure on earnings and the need to build new substantial earnings streams has been assisted by developments in risk management technology. The developments in risk management technology typically allow more accurate identification, analysis, quantification and management of risks in trading. This has allowed financial institutions to better quantify risk-reward relationships in various types of activities, effectively increasing the potential for added earnings with an increase in overall organisational risk profile.

The relationship between the development of principal trading/market making in derivative products and the increased appetite for proprietary risk positions in these instruments is somewhat symbiotic. The entry by financial institutions into derivative products forced increased investment in risk analysis and risk management technology. This investment allowed a better understanding of the risk parameters within which financial institutions operate. In turn, this assists in the identification of proprietary trading opportunities. An added element that has encouraged entry by financial institutions into principal trading/market making in derivative instruments is that, at the very least, it assists the relevant financial institution *in its own risk management*. The technology acquired can, in the first instance, be applied to the internal risk management of the institution. At a secondary level, the capacity to trade in and at a given point in time to have positions in a variety of markets which are not perfectly correlated may in fact assist in the reduction of the overall risk profile of the institution and assist in its management.

## 3   Derivatives Trading – Risk Dimensions

The move to acting as a principal in derivatives transactions entails assuming a range of risk. In essence, the dealer earns a margin (the bid-offer spread) in return for the assumption of various types of risks.

The risks assumed include:

- **Market risk** – this covers exposure to changes in market prices and rates.
- **Credit risk** – this covers exposure to the default of or non-performance of the contract by the counterparty.
- **Liquidity risk** – this covers changes in trading conditions where the dealer is unable to enter into or has to incur unexpected losses in trading in the derivative or other instruments to hedge or offset the position assumed.
- **Operational risk** – this covers the exposure to losses arising from operational failures in operating and settlement of derivatives transactions (for example, processing errors, information technology/systems failures, legal or documentary problems, fraud etc).

The major focus in this Chapter is the market risk assumed in derivatives trading and operating a derivative portfolio[2]. Derivative trading is generally operated on the basis that the dealer can enter into a contract without a matching counterparty being available. In entering into unmatched transactions, the dealer incurs an exposure to movements in rates and/or price. The principal purpose of derivative portfolio

---

[2]   For a discussion of credit risk, liquidity risk and operational risk, see Das, Satyajit (2004) Risk Management; John Wiley & Sons (Asia), Singapore at Chapters 5, 8 and 10 respectively.

management is to preserve the value of the trades booked on the bid or offer side by hedging against the risk of loss from price/rate movements created by temporary open positions in the portfolio.

The generic types of market risks assumed in derivatives trading operations are set out in **Exhibit 12.1**. In general terms, they include price/rate (interest rates, spot currency, spot equity, spot commodity), spread risk and volatility risk.

### Exhibit 12.1   Derivatives Trading Market Risks

| | Interest Rates | | FX/Currency | | Equity/Equity Index | | Commodity | |
|---|---|---|---|---|---|---|---|---|
| **Types of Risks** | **Exchange Traded** | **OTC** | **Exchange Traded** | **OTC** | **Exchange Traded** | **OTC** | **Exchange Traded** | **OTC** |
| Interest rate | Interest rate futures<br>Options on interest rate futures | FRAs<br>Interest rate swaps<br>Caps/floors<br>Swaptions | Currency futures<br>Options on currency future | Currency forwards<br>Currency swaps<br>Currency options | Equity index futures<br>Equity index options | Equity forward<br>Equity swaps<br>Equity options<br>Equity Warrants<br>Convertible bonds | Commodity futures<br>Options on commodity Futures | Commodity forwards<br>Commodity swaps<br>Commodity options |
| Spread | | Interest rate swaps | | Currency swaps | | Convertible bonds | | |
| Interest rate volatility | Options on interest rate futures | Caps/floors<br>Swaptions | | | | | | |
| Currency | | | Currency futures | | | | | |
| Currency Volatility | | | Options on currency future | Currency options | | | | |
| Equity prices | | | | | Equity index futures | Equity forwards<br>Equity swaps<br>Convertible bonds | | |
| Equity volatility | | | | | Equity index options | Equity options<br>Equity warrants<br>Convertible bond | | |
| Commodity Price | | | | | | | Commodity futures | Commodity forwards<br>Commodity swaps |
| Commodity volatility | | | | | | | Options on commodity futures | Commodity options |

The types of market risks that must be managed by dealers in derivative products encompass two distinct categories of risk[3]:

- **Short-term risk** – this is the risk assumed where entry into a transaction is hedged temporarily with the intention of matching the transaction entered into with an offsetting position. The two transactions are only differentiated in terms of time of entry. A temporary hedge is constructed to protect against adverse movements in the relevant financial market variable to protect against changes in market prices during this interim period.

- **Portfolio risk** – this entails an ongoing series of risks assumed in managing a portfolio of offsetting *but not perfectly* matched transactions. The portfolio is generally immunised against movements in the relevant market factors. The process of matching is not undertaken on a transaction-by-transaction basis but rather on an aggregation concept. The aggregation of individual transactions into the portfolio necessarily creates a series of mismatches or portfolio risk positions that must be managed.

It is useful to differentiate between the *pre-closeout* period and the *post-closeout* period. The pre-closeout period is typically a relatively short period depending on the size and liquidity of the market during which the open position is maintained and hedged until it is closed out by an equal and opposite transaction (in practice, the degree of offset varies). The post-closeout period is the period until maturity of the two matched and offsetting transactions.

The risks between the pre and post-closeout period differ significantly. The primary risk in the pre-closeout period may be characterised as market risk; that is, the risk to movements in prices/rates or volatility. The post-closeout period is characterised principally by portfolio risk (where the transactions are not exactly matched). The differentiation between pre and post-closeout risk has become less relevant over time. This reflects the increased utilisation of a portfolio approach to the management of exposures incurred in transacting in these products. The move to a portfolio approach necessarily implies that the risk assumed as part of market making in these products alters from a short-term risk management to a portfolio risk management problem.

A significant component of derivatives trading risk is portfolio or mismatch risk. This refers to risk factors not precisely matched or imperfectly hedged. Mismatches usually occur from the dealer's attempt to accommodate customer

---

[3]  For a discussion of swap market making risks, see Lawton, William P. and Metcalf, Douglas "Portfolio Approach to Interest Rate Swap Management" in Antl, Boris (Editor) (1986) Swap Finance; Euromoney Publications Limited, London at Vol 2.

preferences. In practice, if a market maker insists on matching every transaction in all its aspects, compensation will have to be paid to the other counterparty as an incentive to accept the required structure that may be significantly different from its precise requirements. In addition to the reduction in margins, the institution must be willing to carry a large hedged inventory position for potentially longer periods while searching for the identical match, thereby incurring hedging and market risk. Inability to properly manage the mismatches within the portfolio has the potential to inflict substantial economic loss. It is incumbent on the dealer to measure and manage this mismatch risk. The management of mismatch risk is arguably the single most important aspect of derivative portfolio risk management.

The major areas of mismatch risk include:

- **Notional principal and maturity** – notional principal and maturity mismatches are particularly common where a portfolio may be hedged on a PVBP matched basis. In some markets, a common hedging strategy is to hedge a position of a particular maturity with duration weighted or volatility matched offsetting transactions in another maturity. For example, a 5-year swap may be hedged with an equivalent amount of 3-year swaps or the duration weighted equivalent of 1 and 10 year swaps. This is used where there are limitations on available hedging instruments (for example, the Japanese Yen market), and also where the hedging risk between the available interest rate instruments and swap rates is particularly significant.
- **Interest rate index** – a major area of mismatch relates to the index used to calculate the payments or derivative payoffs. A common example of this type of practice in the US$ market is to receive six month LIBOR while paying three month LIBOR, or to receive three month LIBOR while paying one month commercial paper rates.
- **Index reset dates and payment frequencies** – another major mismatch area is the reset dates. Even a 1 day mismatch on the rate index dates potentially exposes the principal to large daily changes in the index. As the size of a portfolio increases, diversification may reduce the significance of small reset date mismatches as the gains and losses may tend to offset each other. However, due to trading patterns in most markets, some structural mismatches persist.
- **Payment dates** – payment dates represent another important area of potential mismatch. A payment date mismatch results from either payment cycle mismatches (annual to semi-annual) or different payment dates when the cycle is the same (semi-annual to semi-annual). There are two risks with payment mismatches. The first risk is a credit exposure for the payment amount. For example, the semi-annual payer has credit exposure to the annual payer for the

entire semi-annual payment for six months. In addition to any credit risk, there is the reinvestment risk incurred in mismatching payments. At the time of the transaction, the assumption is made that the semi-annual coupon received will be reinvested at an assumed reinvestment rate. If the coupon is reinvested at a lower reinvestment rate than the assumed rate, then the semi-annual receiver suffers a loss.

- **Cash flow mismatches** – derivative portfolios may exhibit significant cash flow mismatches. Portfolio mismatches essentially create portfolio cash surpluses or deficits that must be invested or borrowed, creating exposures to interest rate movements. This exposure is not only to the absolute interest rate movements but also to yield curve shape.
- **Volatility skew/term structure positions** – option portfolios will generally exhibit volatility smile/skew and/or term structure positions even where the portfolio is substantially matched. This reflects mismatches resulting from different option strikes and maturities created in meeting client requirements.

# 4 Derivative Portfolio Risk Management

## 4.1 Overview

The management of risk within derivative product portfolios has been increasingly oriented towards aggregating risk management functions into an integrated framework. Under this approach, the risk of *all* derivative products is managed within an overall integrated conceptual framework. This is in line with a trend to manage financial risk within banks/financial institutions on a consistent basis.

The major impetus for this move towards integration of portfolio risk management reflects the following factors:
- Need for consistency of valuation approaches to ensure pricing consistency and comparability between various products.
- Potential improvements in pricing and hedging efficiency through an integrated approach. This greater hedging and pricing efficiency is usually attributed to the following factors:
  1. Structured transactions involving combinations of various individual products do not need to be separately priced by several trading risk management units within an institution. This avoids transfer pricing and a series of bid-offer spreads that would inflate the price of the whole structure.
  2. Presence of offsetting exposures within portfolios of individual products that can be effectively reduced to the net exposure of the aggregated portfolios. This minimises the number of *external* hedging transactions required.

- An integrated approach to risk management facilitates a total understanding of the exposures within the swap and derivative product portfolio.
- The fact that an integrated approach to risk management is theoretically more correct.

The integrated framework for risk management also overcomes obvious disadvantages of an approach that emphasises independent hedging of individual transactions or product portfolios. This includes its superiority in modelling and valuing complex transactions (transactions combining various product elements) and the greater correspondence between practice and the reality of how portfolios are increasingly managed.

The BIS Market Risk Guidelines[4] that require capital to be held against trading portfolios has created additional impetus for implementing portfolio-based risk management approaches. This reflects the fact that the guidelines are predicated on an integrated approach to risk management.

## 4.2 Modern Portfolio Theory

A number of constructs of modern portfolio theory underpin integrated approaches to risk management of derivative portfolios. Modern portfolio theory ("MPT") has its origins in the work of Harry Markowitz. In a famous article published in 1952, Markowitz drew attention to the common practice of portfolio diversification and exactly showed the capacity for an investor to reduce the risk of a portfolio return by choosing equity stocks that did not move exactly together[5].

Under MPT, risk is defined as a variability of asset return as measured by standard statistical measures of dispersion such as variance and standard deviation. MPT demonstrates that risk is best judged in a portfolio context, and that diversification reduces the risk of the overall portfolio, at least where returns on the assets within the portfolio are not perfectly correlated. MPT dictates diversification reduces risk only when the correlation is less than one, with the greatest diversification benefit coming when the returns on the two assets are negatively correlated. However, as long as there is less than perfect correlation, diversification yields benefits.

Central to MPT is the classification of risk into two distinct categories:

- **Systematic risk** – which can be equated to market risk and cannot be reduced by diversification (for example, generic interest rate risk – Treasury or equivalent government bond rates).

---

[4] See Das, Satyajit (2004) Risk Management; John Wiley & Sons (Asia), Singapore at Chapter 18.
[5] Markowitz, H. M. "Portfolio Selection" (March 1952) Journal of Finance 77.

- **Unsystematic risk** – which represents unique risk aspects associated with the particular asset that can be reduced substantially through diversification (for example, swap spread or credit spread risk).

Implications of the findings of MPT for the management of derivative portfolios include:

- Exposures to similar market factors should be aggregated and managed on an integrated basis.
- Risk factors have to be identified, and if possible, separated into systematic and unsystematic risk dimensions with unsystematic risk dimensions being reduced through diversification practices.
- The covariance, that is, the correlation relationship between risk factors, has to be determined. For example, interest rate risk, particularly yield curve risk, can be regarded as a covariance risk related to correlation in movements in interest rates at various points of the term structure. Similarly, the correlation relationship between movements in various currencies and/or movements in interest rates against currencies should be determined to establish a risk profile of the portfolio.
- The portfolio of derivative and underlying assets should be managed on a *net* basis, with the net aggregated exposure position being hedged.

## 4.3   Integrated Risk Management Approaches

Traditional approaches to derivative risk management have generally focused on a series of separate product portfolios that are managed independently. Some integration may be encompassed with similar products. For example, interest rate products may be managed within one portfolio[6].

Under this model, derivative products in interest rates, currency, equity and commodity products are structured, priced, traded, hedged and managed *separately*. This may even extend to *individual products within an asset class*. Within each product grouping, distinct risk management constructs are used to price and manage risk. For example, interest rate portfolios may be hedged in terms of constructs such as modified duration or PVBP/DVO1. Equity portfolios may be hedged in terms of equity index contract equivalents.

---

[6]   For example, see Babbs, Dr Simon "Measuring Market Risks on Interest Rate Derivatives Portfolios" and Lawrence, Dr Colin "A Portfolio Approach to Risk Management" (conference papers presented at *Financial Risk Measurement and Management of Derivatives*, IIR Conference London, 28–29 April 1992).

The traditional approach can be illustrated using the example of interest rate risk management. An early approach to measurement and management of interest rate risk was gap analysis. This technique, which derived from traditional bank asset liability management practices, required construction of cash flow "ladders" by either due date or rate re-fixing date (whichever was earlier). Within the cash flow ladders, receipts and payments within (arbitrary) time periods are summed to give total net position for a given time period. Impact of interest rate changes as reflected under various yield curve scenarios are then used to simulate the interest rate risk of the portfolio. The major weakness of this type of approach was that specific exposures were often hidden within the arbitrary time bands, and it could not provide information such as the actual impact of the immediate 1 bps rise in a specific rate.

Gap analysis was supplanted in the early 1980s by duration analysis techniques that were originally used in bond portfolio management. Duration facilitated the measurement represented by changes in net present value of a given portfolio of instruments for a rise or fall in interest rates. The duration techniques were subject to the weakness that they generally depended on parallel shifts in the yield curve that, as an empirical fact, was not justified. A further difficulty was duration techniques did not exclude risky hedges, for example, hedging 10 year bond positions with 30 day discount securities. Duration analysis of interest rate risk was complemented by convexity analysis (that is, duration changes with yields). Use of convexity to complement duration measures was useful but did not assist in overcoming some of the deficiencies identified.

A major problem with these traditional approaches to interest rate risk management was the difficulty in incorporating non-linear or asymmetric risk instruments such as options within this framework. The separate risk management approach with respect to other asset classes had similar shortcomings.

A fundamental problem with the traditional approach is the inability to consolidate risk. For example, an institution may incur interest rate risk in several of its operations. Interest rate risk is evident most obviously in its balance sheet, securities investments/trading and interest rate derivatives. However, interest rate risk is also incurred in derivatives trading in all other assets. This is because forward/futures transactions and options on currency, equity and commodity all have embedded interest rate risk (effectively, the embedded carry cost of the forward). Under the traditional approach to risk management, it is not obvious how the interest rate risk is to be consolidated and managed. At best, it is aggregated on an ad hoc basis and managed as a series of separate interest rate risks. This tends to lead to significant over trading in hedging risk. This results in inefficient and expensive risk management.

The deficiencies identified in traditional approaches to risk management led to dealers examining more integrated approaches to risk management of swap/derivative portfolios. Central to this concept are the following concepts:

- **Product versus portfolio risk** – the individual product positions are consolidated into portfolios. This allows offsetting positions to be consolidated to show *net* risk. This is irrespective of where the risk originates.
- **Product versus asset risk** – the consolidated positions are risk mapped to separate and aggregate individual risk elements. The primary risk elements are interest rates (usually government and non-government (swap) rates), spot currency, spot equity and spot commodity positions. This is irrespective of the precise origin of the risk. For example, *all interest rate risk* (from all the areas identified above) is consolidated into yield curves in the relevant currencies.

This approach effectively amalgamates all risk into the following categories:

- **Interest rate risk** – this is represented as at least 2 yield curves (zero coupon rates) per currency (government and swap). Under this approach, all cash flows within each portfolio are partitioned by their dates into time periods (referred to as vertex points, "buckets" or "vectors").
- **Spot asset risk** – this is the equivalent of the spot positions in currency transactions, equity securities and commodities.
- **Option risks** – this is the exposure to volatility (vega) and option hedging risk (gamma) in options on the respective assets.

**Exhibit 12.2** sets out the risk elements in major derivative transactions. The risk portfolio as derived by this mapping process is then analysed to determine its sensitivity to identified risk factors. This entails the use of the Greek alphabet of risk to quantify the risk of the positions to enable hedging. **Exhibit 12.3** sets out the key risk management constructs within this approach[7].

The principal measurement technique used is the delta of the positions. This is equivalent to the price sensitivity of the positions. For example, this is equivalent in interest rates to the modified duration and PVBP/DVO1. Using this approach, within interest rate portfolios the cash flows identified in each currency are allocated to appropriate time vectors. They are discounted using zero coupon rates. The yield curve is then shocked by 1 bps pa to measure the exposure to *individual* market interest rates at any point in the yield curve. This allows analysis of portfolio risk to parallel and non-parallel shifts in the yield curve. The risk can then be hedged

---

[7] For a detailed discussion of the Greek alphabet of risk see Chapter 15.

if desired. The delta/PVBP can be utilised in all other assets. The spot position derived from the risk mapping process is shocked (in terms of price movements) to derive the risk of price changes. This provides an estimate of the risk that can then be hedged.

The basic framework can be adapted quite readily to options. Delta/PVBP simply expresses the sensitivities of the value of the underlying position or instrument to changes in market prices/rates. The delta/PVBP of an option is simply the change in the value of the option (the premium) for a specified change in market prices/rates. In addition to its delta/PVBP, the option portfolio is analysed for its gamma risk as noted above. In essence, non-option positions have relatively stable PVBP's, that is, as prices/rates move, such positions exhibit negligible gamma. In contrast, option instruments have unstable PVBP's; that is, these positions exhibit high gamma exposure. This makes hedging such exposures more difficult. An additional risk factor incorporated in relation to option products is a measure of volatility exposure (measured by vega)[8].

The financial market variables identified will be significantly correlated. For example, yield curve movements between currencies, movements in different parts of the yield curve in the same currency, and movements in different foreign exchange rates will all exhibit some degree of correlation. Increasingly, portfolios are managed to take advantage of the correlation relationships to diversify risk, reduce risk, or facilitate the creation of surrogate hedges to manage existing risk exposures. The correlation exposure can be specifically created through instrument design. Many exotic option structures specifically enable correlation exposures to be traded[9]. Correlation introduces an additional risk dimension relating to the non-stability or change of the relationships. This reflects the fact that changes in the correlation or relationships will impact upon the efficiency of the various hedges used.

The key issues in derivative portfolio risk management in practice are the identification of risk factors affecting portfolio value, the management of these risks, and pricing to cover the cost of hedging/risk management. Individual dealers exhibit significant differences in their approach to the management of their derivative portfolios. Some institutions regard derivatives trading as a client focused function to support sales of risk management products or securities sales and distribution. Other institutions treat derivatives as part of their overall treasury

---

[8]  For a detailed discussion of gamma risk see Chapters 15 and 16.
[9]  See Das, Satyajit (2004) Structured Products Volume 1; John Wiley & Sons (Asia), Singapore at Chapters 5, 7 to 11 (inclusive).

activity. The majority of institutions initially operated their derivative activities as an identifiable and separate profit centre. In recent times, most dealers have consolidated derivative activities with trading in the relevant asset. Depending on the framework used, derivative portfolios are operated in slightly different ways.

| Exhibit 12.2 Risk Mapping – Overview | | | | |
|---|---|---|---|---|
| **Instrument** | **Asset Risk** | **Asset Volatility** | **Interest Rate** | **Interest Rate Volatility** |
| ***Interest Rates*** | | | | |
| Futures on short term rates | | | Swap rates | |
| Futures on government bonds | Bond prices | | Repo rates | |
| Options on futures on short term rates | | | Swap rates | Swap rate volatility |
| Options on futures on government bonds | Bond prices | Bond price volatility | Repo rates | |
| Bond forwards | Bond prices | | Repo rates | |
| Bond options | Bond prices | Bond price volatility | Repo rates | |
| FRAs | | | Swap rates | |
| Interest rate swaps | | | Swap rates | |
| Caps/floors | | | Swap rates | Swap rate volatility |
| ***Currencies*** | | | | |
| Currency futures | Spot currency | | Swap rates | |
| Option on currency futures | Spot currency | Spot currency volatility | Swap rates | |
| Currency forwards | Spot currency | | Swap rates | |
| Currency swaps | Spot currency | | Swap rates | |
| Currency options | Spot currency | Spot currency volatility | Swap rates | |
| ***Equities*** | | | | |
| Equity index futures | Spot equities in index | | Swap rates | |
| Equity index options | Spot equities in index | Volatility of index equities | Swap rates | |
| Equity forwards | Spot equity | | Swap rates | |
| Equity swaps | Spot equity | | Swap rates | |
| Equity options/ warrants | Spot equity | Spot equity volatility | Swap rates | |

| *Commodities*[10] | | | |
|---|---|---|---|
| Commodity futures | Spot commodity | | Swap rates |
| Commodity options | Spot commodity | Spot commodity volatility | Swap rates |
| Commodity index futures | Spot commodities in index | | Swap rates |
| Commodity index options | Spot commodities in index | Volatility on index commodities | Swap rates |
| Commodity forwards | Spot commodity | | Swap rates |
| Commodity swaps | Spot commodity | | Swap rates |
| Commodity options (caps; floors) | Spot commodity | Spot commodity volatility | Swap rates |

#### Exhibit 12.3   Generalised Risk Measures

| Risk Measure | Concept for General Risk |
|---|---|
| Delta ($\Delta$) | Measures exposure to price change of underlying asset; equivalent to Present Value of Basis Point or Dollar Value of 1 Basis Point |
| Gamma ($\gamma$) | Measures exposure to change in delta; equivalent to measure of convexity |
| Vega ($\kappa$) | Measures exposure to changes in volatility (only applicable to options) |
| Theta ($\tau$) | Measures exposure to or change in value arising from the effluxion of time; analogous to carry income or expense. |
| Rho ($\rho$) | Measures exposure to changes in the discount rate(s) applicable. |

There are differences between dealers in the extent of risk taking in individual derivative trading operations. For example, some institutions explicitly trade or position derivatives to take advantage of anticipated movements in financial market prices/rates. Other dealers restrict their activities to trading portfolios on a substantially hedged basis within specified risk limits. In general, derivative portfolios are operated on a partial or fully hedged basis. Limit structures allow a certain degree of positioning activity to be undertaken. This generally

---

[10] Please note that this analysis of risk ignores exposure to changes in convenience yield; see Chapter 6.

places an emphasis on trading basis and spread relationships, yield curve shapes and hedge risk relationships, rather than positioning for absolute directional price/rate movements. In considering the use of derivatives for the purpose of positioning, it is important to note that derivatives trading offers inefficient positioning opportunities. Other markets (such as futures markets) may provide greater liquidity in opening/closing positioning trades, lower transaction costs, limited credit risk and greater capital efficiency. These markets may also allow traders to more efficiently capture anticipated movements in the relevant price/rate.

In general, derivative trading is operated on a hedged basis with dealers substituting hedging (basis) risk for absolute price/rate risk. The hedging risk derives from the fact that portfolio hedging is based on matching risk positions with surrogate instruments as a proxy for transactions being hedged. This exposes the dealer to a risk of gain or loss from the imperfect correlation in the movement of the hedge value as against the underlying transaction sought to be hedged.

# 5   Risk Decomposition[11]

## 5.1   Risk Decomposition – Concept

The process of trading/risk management requires the reduction of instruments to pure asset and interest rate risk. This is referred to as risk decomposition. This process is also referred to as risk mapping[12], cash flow mapping, and cash flow shredding[13].

The process of risk decomposition entails the process by which individual transactions and products are reduced into cash flows and mapped to the relevant risk factors to enable the measure of market risk. **Exhibit 12.4** sets out the basic model of risk decomposition used for financial instruments. The process consists of a number of distinct and separate steps:

• Similar products and transactions are aggregated to establish net positions in each instrument.

---

[11] For a discussion on risk decomposition/risk mapping, see (1996) RiskMetrics[TM] Technical Document – 4th Edition; J.P. Morgan, New York at Chapter 6.

[12] The term used by JP Morgan in RiskMetrics[TM].

[13] The process of risk decomposition as described in this Chapter is used to reduce instruments to risk equivalents for the purpose of risk measurement and hedging. The same process is used to separate out risks for the purpose of deriving risk estimates such as value at risk (VAR). This is discussed in Das, Satyajit (2004) Risk Management; John Wiley & Sons (Asia), Singapore at Chapter 2.

**Exhibit 12.4 Risk Decomposition Model**

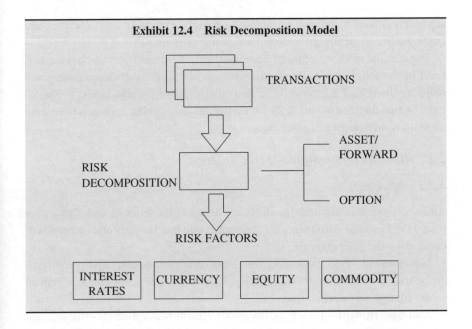

- The cash flows of each transaction are identified. The products or transactions are then decomposed into the following components:
  1. The asset class (debt/interest rates, currency, equity or commodities)[14].
  2. The instrument itself – asset/forward (linear price risk) and option (non-linear price risk).
- The transactions are then restated in terms of the relevant risk factors.

The process of decomposing the position within the asset class into the various instruments (asset or derivative) is designed to facilitate a second order reallocation of the cash flows and risks. For example, a forward on an asset can be decomposed into an asset risk and an interest rate risk, reflecting the exposure to changes in the cost of the forward through the carry cost.

The key building block of the risk decomposition is the individual cash flows. Each instrument/product is mapped to individual cash flows. Each cash flow is then

---

[14] It is increasingly feasible to add credit as a separate asset class, particularly with the advent of credit derivatives; see Das, Satyajit (2004) Structured Products Volume 2; John Wiley & Sons (Asia), Singapore at Chapters 11 to 14 (inclusive); Das, Satyajit (Editor) (2000) Credit Derivatives & Credit Linked Notes – Second Edition; John Wiley & Sons, Singapore.

separately defined by reference to amount, timing (the payment date), currency and credit quality (typically, government and non-government).

The specific methodologies of decomposing risk factors by asset class are outlined in the following Sections. In each case, the process of decomposing and mapping the risk of asset and linear derivatives (forward transactions) is considered. Option transactions are dealt with separately as a similar approach is used for all options, irrespective of asset class.

## 5.2 Risk Decomposition – Fixed Interest

### 5.2.1 Approach

All fixed income instruments/products are defined as a series of cash flows over time. Fixed income instruments are segmented into two fundamental categories of credit risk. The categories are:

- **Government** – this is basically government securities and derivatives on government securities in the relevant currency. These are valued against the government or risk free zero coupon rates.
- **Non-government** – this is basically all other instruments/products in the relevant securities. These are assumed to be subject to credit or default risk. These cash flows are valued against the zero coupon swap rates.

Within each category, the mapped cash flows of the fixed income instruments/products are stated in terms of:

- Amount.
- Timing (the payment date).

The basic approach requires each individual cash flow to be treated as a separate zero coupon bond. The zero coupon bond is then valued using the relevant zero coupon rate (the government or risk free zero rate for government securities or the zero coupon swap rates for all other instruments). If the bond has any embedded optionality (for example, callable or putable bonds) then the option element is isolated and treated consistently with the treatment of other options[15].

In a large portfolio, the number of individual cash flows, and the time at which the payment is made or received, is very large. It may be daily over a period of 10 or more years. This creates problems of risk management in both the measurement of risk and the hedging of the risks (because of the limited number of hedging

---

[15] For example, see Chapter 1; see also the discussion of callable/putable bonds in Das, Satyajit (2004) Structured Products Volume 1; John Wiley & Sons (Asia), Singapore at Chapter 16.

---

**Exhibit 12.5 Risk Decomposition – Cash Flow Maturity Vertices**

| Developed Currency Markets (US$; Yen; Euro) | Less Developed Markets |
|---|---|
| Overnight | Overnight |
| 7 days | 7 days |
| 1 month | 1 month |
| 3 months | 3 months |
| 6 months | 6 months |
| 12 months | 12 months |
| 2 years | 2 years |
| 3 years | 3 years |
| 4 years | 5 years |
| 5 years | 7 years |
| 7 years | 10 years |
| 10 years | 10+ years |
| 15 years | |
| 20 years | |
| 30 years | |

---

instruments available). In practice, the problem is overcome by using a limited number of maturity points or vertices. This simplifies the process of risk management by simplifying the time structure of cash flows. The advantage of this approach is that the pre-specified vertices are fixed and hold for all instruments/products. **Exhibit 12.5** sets out the typical maturity points used.

The major issue with the risk decomposition of fixed interest instruments is the allocation of cash flows to specific maturity points or vertices. The problem arises because of the limited number of maturity points usually used.

The cash flows mapping process requires each cash flow to be cash flow mapped (that is split) to the two closest vertices. This will always be the case except where the cash flow timing coincides with a fixed maturity vertex. The cash flow allocation process is usually designed to satisfy certain conditions including[16]:

- **Preservation of value** – this is done by ensuring that the present value of the cash flows after allocation is the same as the market present value of the original cash flow.

- **Preservation of sign** – the allocated cash flows have the same direction (inflow or outflow) as the original cash flows.

---

[16] See (1996) RiskMetrics™ Technical Document – 4th Edition; J.P. Morgan, New York at 117–121.

- **Preservation of risk** – the market risk of the allocated cash flows (as measured by, for example, historical volatility) is equivalent to the market risk of the original cash flows. There are a number of feasible approaches to ensuring risk preservation. For example, one approach is to use the modified duration/PVBP. Under this approach, the modified duration/PVBP of the original cash flow and the allocated cash flows are equated. An alternative approach is based on the variance of financial returns[17].

The algorithms for allocating cash flows to individual maturity points are potentially complex. **Exhibit 12.6** sets out the algorithm presented as part of the RiskMetrics™ approach.

---

**Exhibit 12.6    RiskMetrics™ Cash Flow Mapping/Allocation Approach**

The process of converting actual cash flows to allocated cash flows is illustrated with an example of allocating a 6 year cash flow to the 5 and 7 year maturity vertices. The process entails the following steps:

**Step 1** – Calculate the actual cash flow's interpolated yield and the 6 year cash flow's original present value as follows:
- The 6 year zero coupon yield is interpolated as:

$$y_6 = ay_5 + (1 - a)y_7$$

Where
  $y_6$ = interpolated zero coupon yield for 6 year maturity
  $y_5$ = zero coupon yield for 5 year maturity
  $y_7$ = zero coupon yield for 7 year maturity
  $a$  = linear weighting co-efficient[18] $(0 \leq a \leq 1)$
- The 6 year cash flow is then discounted by $y_6$ to derive the present value $(P_6)$.

**Step 2** – Calculate the standard deviation of the price return on the actual cash flow as follows:

$$\sigma_6 = a\sigma_5 + (1 - a)\sigma_7$$

---

[17]   This approach is used in (1996) RiskMetrics™ Technical Document – 4th Edition; J.P. Morgan, New York at 117–121.

[18]   a = 0.50 in this example. However, if the timing of the actual cash flow is not equidistant between the 2 maturity vertices, the calculation is:
- a = the number of days from actual cash flow date to the relevant vertex/the number of days between the two maturity vertices.
- the greater of the two values (a and $(1 - a)$) is used to weight the closer maturity vertex.

Where

$\sigma_6$ = interpolated standard deviation of 6 year maturity
$\sigma_5$ = standard deviation of 5 year maturity
$\sigma_7$ = standard deviation of 7 year maturity[19]
a   = linear weighting co-efficient[20] ($0 \le a \le 1$) [this is the same as calculated in Step 1]

**Step 3** – Compute the allocation coefficient for the actual cash flow ($\alpha$ and $(1 - \alpha)$) from the following equation:

$$\text{Variance}(r_{6\text{yr}}) = \text{Variance}[\alpha r_{5\text{yr}} + (1 - \alpha)r_{7\text{yr}})$$

$$\sigma_6^2 = \alpha^2 \sigma_5^2 + 2\alpha(1 - \alpha)\rho_{5,7}\sigma_5\sigma_7 + (1 - \alpha)^2 \sigma_7^2$$

Where

$$\rho_{5,7} = \text{correlation between the 5 and 7 year returns}$$

This equation can be re-stated in quadratic form as follows:

$$a\alpha^2 + b\alpha + c = 0$$

Where

$$a = \sigma_5^2 + \sigma_7^2 - 2\rho_{5,7}\sigma_5\sigma_7$$

$$b = 2\rho_{5,7}\sigma_5\sigma_7 - 2\sigma_7^2$$

$$c = \sigma_7^2 - \sigma_6^2$$

The solution to a is given by:

$$\alpha = [-b \pm \sqrt{(b^2 - 4ac)}]/2a$$

**Step 4** – Distribute the actual cash flow into the 2 maturity vertices with $\alpha$ is allocated to the 5 year maturity vertex and $(1 - \alpha)$ to the 7 year maturity vertex.

Source: (1996) RiskMetrics[TM] Technical Document – 4th Edition; J.P. Morgan, New York at 119–120.

---

[19]  The standard deviation in RiskMetrics[TM] is taken directly from the VAR statistic.
[20]  a = 0.50 in this example. However, if the timing of the actual cash flow is not equidistant between the 2 maturity vertices, the calculation is:
  • a = the number of days from actual cash flow date to the relevant vertex/the number of days between the two maturity vertices.
  • the greater of the two values (a and $(1 - a)$) is used to weight the closer maturity vertex.

## 5.2.2 Risk Decomposition of Fixed Interest Products

*Overview*
Fixed interest products can be separated into two categories:
- **Bonds or securities** – for example, fixed rate bonds/notes and floating rate bonds/notes ("FRNs").
- **Fixed income derivatives** – for example, futures on short term interest rates or bonds, bond forwards, FRAs and interest rate swaps.

*Risk Decomposition of Bonds/FRNs*
Bonds are risk mapped as a series of cash flows to the appropriate maturity vertices. This entails taking a bond and separating it into a series of zero coupon bonds. The zero coupon bonds correspond to each coupon and the final principal (inclusive of the final coupon) payable under the bond. For example, a 3 year bond is represented as 3 zero coupon bonds – 2 zero coupon bonds corresponding to the annual coupon on the bond and the final zero coupon bond corresponding to the final payment (principal and coupon) under the bond. **Exhibit 12.7** sets out an example of the process of allocating the cash flows of a fixed interest bond to a set of maturity points.

A FRN entails a bond where interest consists of a series of floating rate principal payments (based on a margin relative to some underlying benchmark money market rate e.g. LIBOR). At the time of evaluation of the risk of a FRN, only the current coupon is known (it has been fixed). All future interest payments are unknown.

In order to determine the risk, it would be necessary to generate all the future cash flows using the implied forward interest rates. Once the forecast cash flows are generated, the projected cash flows could be discounted to commencement using the current zero coupon rates. However, as the forward rates are generated off the same zero curve used to discount the cash flows, the present value of the FRN value can be simplified. The present value of the FRN is equal to the cash flow equivalent of the face value/nominal amount of the FRN, plus the known interest payment due at the first interest payment date discounted back to the valuation date at the applicable zero coupon rate for that maturity. This is equivalent to a short dated zero coupon bond where the face value is the nominal amount plus the first coupon[21]. The FRN is then risk mapped as a zero coupon bond at the relevant interest rate payment date. The approach is identical to that used for a fixed rate bond.

---

[21] For a proof, see (1996) RiskMetrics™ Technical Document – 4th Edition; J.P. Morgan, New York at 109–111.

**Exhibit 12.7    Risk Decomposition – Bond Cash Flow Allocation**

Assume the following bond:

| | |
|---|---|
| Principal | $1,000,000 |
| Coupon | 7.50% pa (annual) |
| Maturity | 27 August 2012 |
| Settlement Date | 15 November 2002 |

The bond cash flows are set out below:

| Date | Flow ($) | Term (Years) |
|---|---|---|
| 27 August 2003 | 75,000 | 0.78 |
| 27 August 2004 | 75,000 | 1.78 |
| 27 August 2005 | 75,000 | 2.78 |
| 27 August 2006 | 75,000 | 3.78 |
| 27 August 2007 | 75,000 | 4.78 |
| 27 August 2008 | 75,000 | 5.79 |
| 27 August 2009 | 75,000 | 6.79 |
| 27 August 2010 | 75,000 | 7.79 |
| 27 August 2011 | 75,000 | 8.79 |
| 27 August 2012 | 1,075,000 | 9.79 |

The bond cash flows are to be allocated to the following 9 maturity vertices:

| 1 month | 1 year | 2 years | 3 years | 4 years | 5 years | 7 years | 10 years | 15 years |
|---|---|---|---|---|---|---|---|---|

The current yield levels and yield/price volatility are summarised below:

| Maturity Vertices | 1 month | 1 year | 2 years | 3 years | 4 years | 5 years | 7 years | 10 years | 15 years |
|---|---|---|---|---|---|---|---|---|---|
| Current yield (%) | 8.25 | 7.04 | 7.28 | 7.39 | 7.54 | 7.63 | 7.79 | 7.92 | 8.15 |
| Yield volatility (%) | 7.00 | 3.16 | 2.10 | 1.74 | 1.63 | 1.50 | 1.37 | 1.36 | 1.29 |
| Price volatility (%) | 0.04 | 0.21 | 0.29 | 0.36 | 0.46 | 0.53 | 0.70 | 1.00 | 1.46 |

Using the approach outlined in **Exhibit 12.6**, the cash flows are discounted back to the commencement of the transaction using the current zero coupon rates as follows:

| Date | Flow ($) | Term (Years) | (Interpolated) Yield (% pa) | Present Value ($) |
|---|---|---|---|---|
| 27 August 2003 | 75,000 | 0.78 | 7.33 | 70,941 |
| 27 August 2004 | 75,000 | 1.78 | 7.22 | 66,227 |
| 27 August 2005 | 75,000 | 2.78 | 7.37 | 61,538 |

| Date | Flow ($) | Term (Years) | (Interpolated) Yield (% pa) | Present Value ($) |
|---|---|---|---|---|
| 27 August 2006 | 75,000 | 3.78 | 7.50 | 57,037 |
| 27 August 2007 | 75,000 | 4.78 | 7.61 | 52,812 |
| 27 August 2008 | 75,000 | 5.79 | 7.69 | 48,844 |
| 27 August 2009 | 75,000 | 6.79 | 7.78 | 45,118 |
| 27 August 2010 | 75,000 | 7.79 | 7.83 | 41,713 |
| 27 August 2011 | 75,000 | 8.79 | 7.87 | 38,557 |
| 27 August 2012 | 1,075,000 | 9.79 | 7.91 | 510,350 |

The cash flows are now allocated to individual vertices based on the allocation methodology outlined in **Exhibit 12.6** as follows[22]:

| Term (Years) | Present Value ($) | Modified Duration | Price Volatility | 1 month | 1 year | 2 years | 3 years | 4 years | 5 years | 7 years | 10 years |
|---|---|---|---|---|---|---|---|---|---|---|---|
| 0.78 | 70,941 | 0.73 | 0.22 | 0 | 70,941 | | | | | | |
| 1.78 | 66,227 | 1.66 | 0.28 | | 3,098 | 63,129 | | | | | |
| 2.78 | 61,538 | 2.59 | 0.35 | | | 9,155 | 52,383 | | | | |
| 3.78 | 57,037 | 3.52 | 0.44 | | | | 11,220 | 45,816 | | | |
| 4.78 | 52,812 | 4.45 | 0.52 | | | | | 10,227 | 42,584 | | |
| 5.79 | 48,844 | 5.37 | 0.60 | | | | | | 26,988 | 21,855 | |
| 6.79 | 45,118 | 6.30 | 0.68 | | | | | | 4,100 | 41,018 | |
| 7.79 | 41,713 | 7.22 | 0.77 | | | | | | | 30,803 | 10,909 |
| 8.79 | 38,557 | 8.15 | 0.87 | | | | | | | 15,589 | 22,968 |
| 9.79 | 510,350 | 9.07 | 0.97 | | | | | | | 35,649 | 474,700 |
| | | | Total | 0 | 74,039 | 72,285 | 63,603 | 56,044 | 73,673 | 144,915 | 508,578 |

For example, assuming the 3 conditions noted in **Exhibit 12.6**, the allocation of the cash flow as at 1.78 years is based on $\alpha$ and $(1 - \alpha)$ of $\alpha = 0.0468$ and $(1 - \alpha) = 0.9532$. This process is repeated for each of the cash flows.

The original or actual bond is therefore represented by a series of zero coupon bonds as follows

| Maturity Vertices | 1 month | 1 year | 2 years | 3 years | 4 years | 5 years | 7 years | 10 years |
|---|---|---|---|---|---|---|---|---|
| Present Value of Cash Flow ($) | 0 | 74,039 | 72,285 | 63,603 | 56,044 | 73,673 | 144,915 | 508,578 |

The synthetic cash flows have the same present value and market risk as the actual bond.

Source: The above calculations are based using the diskette and spreadsheet supplied with (1996) RiskMetrics™ Technical Document – 4th Edition; J.P. Morgan, New York at 134–135.

---

[22] Please note there may be small rounding errors in the calculations.

*Risk Decomposition of Fixed Interest Derivatives*

The approach to linear fixed income derivatives is very similar. The fundamental technique requires restating the derivative in terms of a combination of underlying fixed interest transactions at different maturities. This approach is usually applied as follows:

- **Futures contracts** – are treated as a borrowing (investment) at one maturity and an offsetting investment (borrowing) at a different (more distant) maturity. The first maturity will usually coincide with the settlement date of the futures contract, while the second date will relate to final maturity of the security underlying the futures contract. In the case of a futures contract where the underlying is a short term interest rate, the contract is risk mapped as a borrowing (deposit) to the futures contract expiry date and a deposit (borrowing) to the maturity date of the underlying deposit (loan). In the case of a futures contract on a bond, the contract is risk mapped as a long (short) position in the underlying cheapest-to-deliver bond and a borrowing (deposit) to futures expiry date. Where the contract is not deliverable, the underlying bond is taken to be the notional bond on which the contract is based.

- **Forward Rate Agreements ("FRAs")** – are treated exactly the same as futures contracts on short term interest rates described above for the purposes of risk mapping. **Exhibit 12.8** sets out an example of the risk decomposition of a FRA.

- **Bond Forwards** – are treated exactly the same as futures contracts on bonds described above for the purposes of risk mapping.

- **Interest Rate Swaps** – are decomposed into two separate fixed interest transactions. The fixed leg is treated as a position in a fixed rate bond. The floating rate flows are treated as a position in a FRN. A position where the entity is receiving (paying) fixed/paying (receiving) floating rates is risk mapped as a long (short) position in a bond (coupon equal to the swap rate and maturity equal to swap maturity) and a short (long) position in a FRN (coupon equal to the swap floating rate index). The two bonds are then risk mapped as separate transactions as individual bonds for the purposes of risk analysis and hedging.

---

**Exhibit 12.8    Risk Decomposition – FRA**

Assume the following FRA contract:

| Contract | 6 × 12 FRA |
| --- | --- |
| Position | Sold FRA (forward investment or deposit) |
| Notional Principal | $1,000,000 |
| FRA Rate | 7.24% pa |

The above transaction is based on the following market rates:

6 month        6.39% pa
12 month       6.93% pa

The transaction is risk mapped as the following money market transactions:
- 6 month zero coupon borrowing at 6.39% pa. This would entail borrowing future value of $1,000,000 (the notional principal of the FRA) to generate $969,121 in present value terms.
- 12 month zero coupon deposit at 6.93% pa. This would entail depositing $969,121 (the amount borrowed) to provide a future value (principal plus interest) of $1,036,282.
- The combined transaction results in a cash outflow of $1,000,000 after 6 months and an inflow of $1,036,282 at 1 year. The difference represents the earnings at the FRA rate of 7.24% pa.

The transaction cash flows are set out below:

| Maturity Vertices | Maturity (days) | Cash Flow ($) | Rate (% pa) | Present Value ($) |
|---|---|---|---|---|
| 6 month | 182 | −1,000,000 | 6.39% | 969,121 |
| 1 year | 365 | 1,036,282 | 6.93% | −969,121 |
| | | | Total | 0 |

The transaction exactly replicates the cash flows under the FRA.

The FRA is mapped for risk purposes as a 6 month borrowing (present value of $969,121) and a 12 month deposit (present value $969,121) in the relevant maturity vertices. Where the FRA cash flows do not correspond to a nominated vertex, the cash flow allocation methodology is used to map the cash flow to an appropriate vertex.

Source: (1996) RiskMetrics™ Technical Document – 4th Edition; J.P. Morgan, New York at 136–137.

The credit risk of the underlying instrument will determine the underlying market rate of the derivatives. Government bond rates are used for futures contracts on government bonds and bond forwards. Swap rate factors will generally be used to calculate the risk of futures on short term interest rates, FRAs and interest rate swaps.

## 5.3   Risk Decomposition – Currency

### 5.3.1   Approach

Currency positions are decomposed for risk measurement in terms of the cash flows in the relevant currencies. All currency positions are translated and risk measured in terms of a base functional currency presumed to be the home currency of the relevant entity. The basic approach is to identify the currency positions in terms of the inflow and outflow in the relevant currency pairings (amount and the two relevant currencies) at the relevant maturity point. All currency derivatives are decomposed into a spot position in the relevant currencies and interest rate positions in the underlying currencies.

### 5.3.2 Risk Decomposition – Currency Instruments

Spot positions are stated as the cash flows receivable and payable in the relevant currencies.

Currency derivatives are decomposed as follows:

- **Currency forwards or futures** – are treated as cash inflows and outflows at a forward maturity date. The position is then decomposed into separate currency and interest rate positions as follows:
  1. *Spot currency position* – calculated by discounting the cash flows back to the spot date using the zero coupon swap rates for the relevant maturity.
  2. *Interest rate positions* – these are the underlying long (deposit/investment) and short (borrowing) positions in the relevant interest rates in each currency.

**Exhibit 12.9** sets out an example of the risk decomposition of a currency forward.

---

**Exhibit 12.9    Risk Decomposition – Currency Forward**

Assume the following currency forward contract:

| | |
|---|---|
| Contract | Purchase Yen/sell US$ forward |
| Amount | Yen 100 million |
| Maturity | 1 year |
| Forward Rate | US$1 = Yen 106.38 |

The currency forward has the following cash flows:

| | |
|---|---|
| Yen | Receive Yen 100,000,000 |
| US$ | Pay US$939,982 |

The market prices and rates are as follows as of the date of entry into the transaction:

| | |
|---|---|
| Spot Rate | US$1 = Yen 110.00 |
| Yen zero coupon 1 year swap rate | 3.00% pa |
| US$ zero coupon 1 year swap rate | 6.50% pa |

The cash flows of the forward can be replicated with the following transactions:
- Borrow US$882,613 for 1 year at a rate of 6.50% pa requiring repayment at maturity of US$939,982.

- Convert the US$882,613 into Yen at the spot rate (US$1 = Yen 110) to generate Yen 97,087,379.
- Invest Yen 97,087,379 for 1 year at a rate of 3.00% pa creating a cash inflow at maturity of Yen 100,000,000.

The combined transactions exactly replicate the cash flows of the Yen/US$ forward. The resulting exposure is summarised in the Table below:

| | Maturity Vertex | Cash Flows (in local currency) | Market Value of Cash Flows (in local currency) |
|---|---|---|---|
| Yen/US$ Spot Exposure | Spot | | US$ (882,613) |
| Yen | 1 year | Yen 100,000,000 | Yen 97,087,379 |
| US$ | 1 year | −US$ (939,982) | US$ (882,613) |

The currency forward is mapped for risk management purposes as follows:
- **Currency spot position** – this will depend upon the base or functional currency of the entity:
    1. *For a US$ functional currency dealer* – a long Yen 97,087,379 (in current market value terms).
    2. *For a Yen functional currency dealer* – a short US$882,613 (in current market value terms).
    3. *For a non-US$ or Yen functional currency dealer* – a long Yen 97,087,379 and a short US$882,613 (in current market value terms).
- **Interest rate positions** – this will be as follows:
    1. *US$ interest rates* – a 1 year US$ borrowing equal to US$882,613 (in current market value terms).
    2. *Yen interest rates* – a 1 year Yen deposit equal to Yen 97,087,379 (in current market value terms).
    Where the cash flows do not correspond to a nominated vertex, the cash flow allocation methodology is used to map the cash flow to an appropriate vertex.

Source: The above calculations are based using the diskette and spreadsheet supplied with (1996) RiskMetrics™ Technical Document – 4th Edition; J.P. Morgan, New York at 143.

- **Currency swaps** – are treated as two separate fixed interest transactions in the respective currencies. The fixed interest bond or security is decomposed into the separate interest rate risk factors in the individual currency. The currency exposure is then incorporated when each fixed interest bond is translated into the base reporting currency. Where one leg of the currency swap is on a floating rate basis, the approach utilised is identical to that used for the floating rate component of an interest rate swap. For example, a cross currency swap where the counterparty pays fixed rate Yen and receives floating rate 6 month US$ LIBOR is restated as a short position in a fixed rate yen bond (coupon equal to the yen fixed swap rate and maturity equal to the swap maturity) and a US$ FRN (paying US$6 month LIBOR and maturity equal to the swap maturity). The two bonds are then treated in a manner identical to that for fixed and floating rate bonds generally. The bond flows are mapped to the relevant maturity vertices in each currency using the risk decomposition process outlined previously.

## 5.4 Risk Decomposition – Equity

### 5.4.1 Approach

The risk decomposition of equity transactions will depend on whether it represents a well diversified portfolio of equities that approximates the market index, or positions in individual equity securities with a large component of firm specific risk.

The categorisation is related to the risk factors that are applicable. Where the equity positions approximate the risk of the market index, the transaction may be represented by the position (amount and currency) in the equity index. Where the position does not approximate the market index, there are two choices for identifying the risk of the position:

- The individual position is re-stated as an *index equivalent* position adjusted for stock specific risk using the beta of the individual stock. The use of stock beta introduces the problem of basis or correlation risk as between the price changes of the individual stock and the changes in the index.
- The individual position is regarded as a specific risk factor and the position is mapped to a stock equivalent position.

The decision between index and specific stocks as the underlying risk factors is driven by the nature of the trading operations. Where trading is focused on equity index based products, index specific risk factors are more appropriate. Where trading is focused on individual equity stocks, stock specific risk factors are more appropriate. The critical determinant of choice is the accuracy with which the underlying price risk is captured and hedged.

### 5.4.2 Risk Decomposition – Equity Products[23]

Irrespective of the risk factors to be used, the decomposition of the position embodies the following approach. Each equity position is restated in terms of the market value of the security (amount and currency) at the specific maturity point.

---

[23] For a discussion of equity product structures, see Das, Satyajit (2004) Structured Products Volume 2; John Wiley & Sons (Asia), Singapore at Chapters 1 to 6 (inclusive).

Spot equity positions are stated as positions in the equity security or equity index. Equity derivatives are also decomposed in a similar manner:

- **Equity forwards or futures** – are treated as a position in the equity as at a forward maturity date. The position is then decomposed into separate equity and interest rate positions:

  1. *Spot equity position* – calculated by discounting the transaction cash flows back to the spot date using the swap rates for the relevant maturity. Where the contract involves an equity index forward/futures and the positions are to be stated in stock specific risk factors, the position is mapped to each of the individual stocks in the position based on the index composition.

  2. *Interest rates* – the forward equity position is assumed to be funded by a borrowing, or the proceeds of a short position are assumed to be invested at the relevant zero coupon swap rate through to the maturity date of the contract.

- **Equity swaps** – are treated as two separate transactions:

  1. *Equity* – the equity exposure is mapped as a series of forwards on the index or the individual stock.

  2. *Interest rates* – this is represented as a floating rate bond. The interest rate exposure on the floating rate leg is calculated using an identical approach to that used for the floating rate component of an interest rate swap.

The process of restating the forward equity position by discounting the future cash flows back to the spot dates requires assumptions to be made regarding the expected dividend income cash flows payable on the security or the portfolio.

## 5.5 Risk Decomposition – Commodity Products[24]

Commodity positions are decomposed in a manner analogous to that applicable to equities.

Spot positions are stated as positions in the commodity, the risk of which is determined by the application of the volatility of the specific commodity or a similar or related commodity.

Commodity derivatives are also decomposed in a similar manner:

- **Commodity forwards or futures** – are treated as a position in the commodity at a forward maturity date. The position is then decomposed into separate spot commodity positions (calculated by discounting the transaction cash flows back to the spot date using the swap rates for the relevant maturity) and long or short

---

[24] For a discussion of commodity product structures, see Das, Satyajit (2004) Structured Products Volume 2; John Wiley & Sons (Asia), Singapore at Chapters 7 to 10 (inclusive).

positions in the relevant interest rates in each currency. **Exhibit 12.10** sets out an example of the risk decomposition of a commodity forward position.

- **Commodity swaps** – are treated as a series of forward contracts on the commodity that are decomposed[25].

The process of restating the forward commodity position by discounting the future cash flows back to the spot dates requires assumptions to be made regarding the convenience yield on the commodity. In order to avoid this problem, commodity spot and forward contracts are often mapped to the *near month futures contract* in the relevant commodity[26].

---

**Exhibit 12.10   Risk Decomposition – Commodity Forward/Futures Contract**

Assume the following commodity futures position:

| | |
|---|---|
| Contract | West Texas Intermediate ("WTI") oil future contract |
| Amount | 1 million barrels |
| Futures price | US$18.30 |

The position is equivalent to a long position in 1 million barrels of WTI on a notional amount equivalent to US$18,300,000.
The US$ zero coupon swap rate for 6 months is 5.813% pa.
The position is decomposed into the following positions:
- **Spot WTI position** – this is equivalent to US$17,783,133 (calculated as US$18,300,000/ [1 + .05813 × .5]).
- **US$ interest rate position** – this is equivalent to borrowing US$17,783,133 for 6 months at 5.813% pa. Where the cash flows do not correspond to a nominated vertex, the cash flow allocation methodology is used to map the cash flow to an appropriate vertex.

Source: (1996) RiskMetrics™ Technical Document – 4th Edition; J.P. Morgan, New York at 145.

---

[25] For the purpose of risk management, an alternative approach is available. This approach is generally not used for trading risk management. The swap can be treated as a position in a fixed interest bond (represented by the fixed cash flows to be paid or received calculated as the amount commodity purchased or sold at the agreed forward price) and an opposite position in a floating rate bond (where the cash flows are based on a floating commodity price usually based on the near month futures contract price). The fixed leg can be treated as a fixed interest security, while the risk of the floating is analogous to the floating rate note component of the interest rate swap where only the first cash flow is known with a price exposure on the near contract. This approach is discussed in Das, Satyajit (2004) Risk Management; John Wiley & Sons (Asia), Singapore at Chapter 2.

[26] For a discussion of this aspect of decomposition of commodity positions, see Das, Satyajit (2004) Risk Management; John Wiley & Sons (Asia), Singapore at Chapter 2.

## 5.6   Risk Decomposition – Options

The approach outlined is used with non-option instruments (asset and forward/swap positions). These instruments have linear price characteristic. This means that there is a relatively constant relationship between the value of the instrument and the underlying asset price or rate. The rate of change in the value of the instrument for given changes in the underlying price/rate is equivalent to the delta. Where the instrument value/price or rate relationship is non-linear, the rate of change of the value of the instrument is not constant. It generally varies with the starting level of price/rate. This is equivalent to convexity or gamma[27]. Where an instrument exhibits convexity/gamma, its delta is variable and unstable. The major non-linear instruments are options. Options have convex, non-linear payoffs.

The measurement of risk of options or portfolios containing options presents difficulties. This difficulty arises from a number of sources:

- The price movements of options are non-linear; that is, for a given change in the asset price the price change of the option is not constant. This potential acceleration or de-acceleration of the market risk (which is equivalent to the gamma risk of an option) creates difficulties in modelling the exposure of options.
- The impact of changes in volatility on the price of options (the option's vega risk).
- The impact of time decay on the price of the option (the option's theta risk)[28].

There are several possible approaches to the calculation of risk for options. These approaches are used consistently across asset classes. The approaches include:

- The delta method.
- Simulation approaches.

In practice for risk management, the delta method is used[29]. The delta based method entails the risk decomposition of the option position using the following steps:

- The option delta is calculated using an appropriate option pricing model.
- The delta is used to determine a position in the asset equivalent to the option.
- The asset position is then included in the appropriate asset class as the relevant risk position.

This methodology is applied consistently with options across all asset classes.

---

[27] For a detailed discussion of the Greek alphabet of risk see Chapter 15.

[28] See discussion in Chapter 15 of option risks.

[29] Simulation methods and more advanced delta methods (delta+ or delta/gamma methodologies) are used to measure the VAR of options/portfolios containing options; see Das, Satyajit (2004) Risk Management; John Wiley & Sons (Asia), Singapore at Chapter 2.

The approach requires the embedded asset price risk to be managed as an asset price risk. The option risk (convexity/gamma, volatility etc) is isolated and managed separately.

# 6 Integrated Portfolio Management – Implications

The process of risk decomposition described reduces the risk of all traded products/instruments into a series of distinct risks including:

- **Spot positions** – these are in currencies, equities and commodities.
- **Interest rate positions** – these are in each currency across pre-specified maturity vertices in either government or non-government (swap) interest rates.

The mapped positions then form the basis of risk management and hedging.

The process as identified has significant implications for both risk management/trading and the structure/operation of derivative trading businesses.

The approach to integrated risk management was driven by several objectives. A major objective was the need to integrate portfolios for the calculation of risk in VAR terms to allow market risk capital to be derived[30]. An additional objective was the need to improve the efficiency and hedging of derivatives trading operations.

In practice, the two objectives are independent. In most institutions, the integration of risk management/trading is primarily driven by the need to quantify the market risk for capital purposes. This is done in practice as an overlay on the existing trading architecture. This means that existing businesses continue to be operated as previously around asset classes and (in some cases) individual products. Information from these businesses is integrated for the purpose of establishing the total market risk of the businesses.

The degree of integration for trading and hedging is more limited. In reality, most dealers have integrated their trading risk management to varying degrees. The lack of integration is driven by:

- **Systems problems** – the presence of legacy systems often restricts the capacity to move to a fully integrated trading risk management model.
- **Organisation and regulatory issues** – the historical structure of businesses, organisational models and often the need to conduct businesses within particular corporate structures dictated by regulations, also inhibits full integration.

---

[30] This is particularly the case under the internal model (VAR) approach; see Das, Satyajit (2004) Risk Management; John Wiley & Sons (Asia), Singapore at Chapters 2 and 18.

In practice, the current business model consists of integrating *certain* businesses. Typically, fixed interest/interest rate and currency businesses are integrated to some lesser or greater degree[31]. However, equity and commodity businesses are frequently conducted separately. Within the integrated fixed interest/currency business, the degree of *internal* integration is also variable. While most dealers have some degree of integration, the businesses may still be operated along product lines. Limited integration may be achieved by individual desks/business units transferring risks to other units through a system of internal trades. For example, the currency derivative desk or the equity derivative desk may hedge their interest rate risk internally with the institution's interest rate traders. The problem of this approach is the lack of efficiency in risk management, hedging and the possibility of higher hedging/trading costs.

The true potential of integrated risk management derives from several sources. The first benefit derives from improvement in risk management methodology, the concurrent increase in hedging efficiency and lower hedging costs. Significant benefits are also available from the potential to completely re-structure the process of creation and delivery of financial products. This is evident from a consideration of the current structure of most dealers/trading institutions.

**Exhibit 12.11** sets out the typical structure of a dealer/trading operations. The organisational diagram shows the operation as being built around individual asset classes (interest rates, currency, equity, commodity)[32]. The internal organisation of interest rate products is highlighted. Within interest rates, the businesses will typically be organised around individual or related products. The internal organisation of the businesses in the other asset classes will be very similar.

The principal features of this organisation include:
- Each product or set of products will be organised linearly around a trading and sales/distribution team. The sales group will originate transactions that are priced and hedged by the traders. Structuring functions will typically be located within the sales team, trading team, a separate team or shared between sales and trading teams.
- The back office/operations and other support functions will typically be dedicated units aligned to each product/set or products or shared between multiple units.
- Risk measurement is bifurcated. *Trading risk management* is undertaken on a product/set of products basis (consistent with the business organisation). This entails business units hedging their own risks with some limited internal hedging.

---

[31]   This is often undertaken by creating a debt capital markets business.
[32]   Not all institutions will be active in all asset classes.

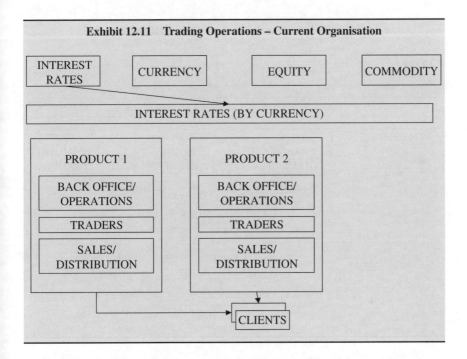

**Exhibit 12.11    Trading Operations – Current Organisation**

*Firm wide risk management* is undertaken as an *overlay function*. Risk information from individual businesses is collected and integrated for regulatory and economic capital and risk management.

- The focus is product based. Client marketing is also based primarily around products. A single client may be covered by *multiple* sales groups responsible for marketing different products. This means that often similar risk management problems may be dealt with by different product groups within the same organisation. This may result in proposals for overlapping/competing product solutions for any particular financial problem.

There is an inherent difficulty in marketing cross product transactions or cross asset products under this structure. This often leads to the creation of structured product groups or special/strategic risk solutions units. The mandate of these units is to often deal with non-standard products that cross product or asset market boundaries. The experience with these groups is mixed.

**Exhibit 12.12** sets out a potential re-structure of dealer/trading operations. The principal differences between this structure and the traditional structures are:

- Trading organised around asset classes with no product specialisation.

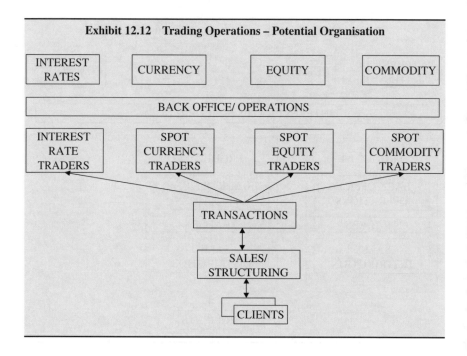

Exhibit 12.12   Trading Operations – Potential Organisation

- Unified sales and structuring force covering multiple products/asset classes.
- A unified back office/operations and support functions.

Under this approach, the sales/structuring function interfaces with clients. The marketing approach is built around client focused risk solutions. Products (ranging from conventional to more complex financial products) are *manufactured* by the sales/structuring teams. This is done by assembling the different assets (interest rates, currency, equity, commodity) and risk elements (spot price, yield curves, credit spreads/risk, volatility and correlation) into a specific product offering. Once the transaction is completed, the risk elements are decomposed and distributed to the different trading units that are responsible for the risk management and hedging.

The principal driver of this approach is an integrated approach to trading risk management. In this approach, the traders are responsible for management of the specific risk element in the relevant asset class, irrespective of where the risk was generated or the specific product that created the risk. However, traders may not price *individual products*. These are *assembled/constructed by the sales/structuring teams* from price elements provided by traders. This is consistent with the process of risk mapping and integrated risk management. Under this approach, there is a greater degree of correspondence between trading and firm wide risk management.

Within this structure, both trading and sales/structuring units can be structured around specific specialisation. For example, interest rate traders may be specialised by currency, part of the yield curve, credit quality or volatility/option trading. In a similar manner, sales/structuring units can be organised around client groups (industry or product requirements) or product requirements (commodity/standard products versus complex/structured products).

The implementation of this approach to dealing/trading operations has significant potential benefits. These include greater efficiency in risk management and ability to distribute products more effectively to clients (in particular, higher value structured products and risk solutions). A major element of this approach is the improved client focus of marketing and improved client penetration. Additional benefits include the ability to significantly reduce the overheads/staffing costs of dealing and trading operations.

The ability to realise these potential benefits requires the significant challenges to be overcome including:

- Re-engineering the trading and sales functions including re-training/re-skilling a significant portion of the personnel involved in these activities.
- Systems changes required to support the new trading/sales paradigm.
- Overcoming entrenched and ossified organisational arrangements and cultural/political barriers to change.

It is inevitable that the organisation paradigm of trading/dealing operations will shift over time closer to that described in **Exhibit 12.12**. A major factor in this process will be the impact of electronic financial markets in trading assets and derivatives[33].

# 7   Summary

Dealers in banks and financial institutions trade and manage *portfolios of derivatives and cash instruments*. The management of portfolios requires adoption of a process where the portfolio is reduced into a defined and clearly identifiable series of risk factors that are used to establish the risk of the portfolio and to trade in and manage/hedge the risks. The approaches are based on and relate closely to the methodologies used to price individual derivative transactions.

The requirement for portfolio management is driven by the role played by dealers in derivatives where transactions are entered into on an unmatched basis. This

---

[33] See Das, Satyajit (2004) Structured Products Volume 2; John Wiley & Sons (Asia), Singapore at Chapter 20.

requires the trader to hedge its risk exposure using surrogate instruments, pending entry into an offsetting transaction at a time of the dealer's choice.

The approach to structuring the management of derivative portfolios uses a process of integrated trading and risk management. This is driven by the process of risk decomposition or mapping. This requires portfolios of derivative instruments to be mapped into risk factors. Individual positions are mapped to equivalent spot positions (currency, equity, commodity), interest positions (yield curves defined by specific maturity points or vertices in each currency and differentiated as to credit risk – government or swap) and option risk (volatility and gamma/convexity). The risk factors enable both quantification of risk and hedging as required.

The approach to risk management identified is similar to the approach used to determine the risk profile of a portfolio using VAR techniques[34]. However, there are significant differences between trading risk management (quantifying risk to changes in risk factors and implementing *specific* hedges) and firm wide risk management (focused on matching risk with capital to ensure the ability of the firm to absorb market risk).

The integrated approach to derivatives trading and portfolio management is powerful. It has significant benefits in increased efficiency of risk management, lower hedging costs and improvements in the capability to structure and trade complex financial products. The integrated approach to risk management also has the potential to influence the organisational structure of dealer/trading operations in terms of improving client focused marketing, and also the capability to structure higher value added risk management solutions/financial products to clients.

---

[34] See Das, Satyajit (2004) Risk Management; John Wiley & Sons (Asia), Singapore at Chapter 2.

# 13
# Hedging Interest Rate
# Risk – Individual Instruments

## 1  Overview

The approach to derivatives trading and risk management focuses on a portfolio approach. Central to this process is the adoption of an integrated approach to risk management. This approach results in individual positions within the portfolio being mapped or decomposed primarily into positions in spot assets (currency, equity, commodity), yield curves (government or swap curves defined by specific maturity vertices in each currency) and (in the case of options) volatility of assets/interest rates[1].

Within this portfolio approach, risk management is focused on the management of exposures to individual risk factors through specific hedges. The hedging approach varies between the type of assets. Exposures to currency, equity and commodity (after risk mapping) are exposures to changes in spot prices. Exposure to interest rates is exposure to the risk of changes in zero rates in the relevant yield curve. The only additional risk is to asset/rate volatility in option transactions.

In hedging the identified risks, the degree of complexity in implementing specific hedges varies between the category of exposure. Spot exposures to changes in the price of the underlying currency, equity and commodity positions are relatively easy to hedge. These are hedged by taking the opposite spot positions. Long (short) positions are hedged undertaking offsetting short (long) positions. The major difficulty is in hedging interest rate risk. The major difficulties in hedging the interest rate risk include:

- **Yield curve risk** – interest rate exposure entails exposure to changes in a series of separate zero coupon rates. The changes in the separate zero rates are not

---

[1]  This ignores hedging risk (gamma or convexity) which is primarily applicable where options are hedged dynamically by trading in the underlying assets; see Chapter 16.

perfectly correlated (that is, non-parallel yield curve movements). This entails exposure to correlation risks.

- **Time decay** – the impact of interest rate changes on valuation is time dependent. The change in the time remaining to maturity (as a result of time decay) will change the value of the position *irrespective of any change in rates*. This entails exposure to change in time (remaining maturity) that is not present in other assets (currency, equity, commodity). This is because debt instruments have fixed maturity. In contrast, other assets have no fixed maturity and are perpetual in nature.

Interest rate risk may be hedged in two potential ways. Under the first approach, interest rate risk *in individual transactions* is specifically hedged as transactions are completed *on a transaction by transaction basis*. Under the second approach, the interest rate exposure is hedged *on a portfolio basis*. In this Chapter and the following Chapter, the process of hedging interest rate risk is considered. In this Chapter, the process of specific hedging of individual transactions is examined. Chapter 14 examines the hedging of interest rates on a portfolio basis.

The structure of this Chapter is as follows:

- The basic approach to hedging interest rate risk in individual transactions is considered.
- Examples of hedging a range of transactions (interest rate swaps, FRAs, currency swaps, currency forwards) are described.
- Issues in relation to hedging in this manner are considered.

## 2   Hedging Individual Instruments – Approach

The preferred method of controlling exposure to market risks on any derivative transaction is to match it by entering into an offsetting transaction. Where derivative transactions are matched in this way, if inflows match outflows apart from spreads taken by the dealer as income, then the dealer should theoretically be fully hedged against market risks. Mismatches lessen the effectiveness of the hedge created by matching out the two offsetting transactions.

Under current market conditions, dealers do not precisely match each transaction as it is booked. The structure of and competitive pressures in the derivative market dictate that most dealers enter into each transaction independently; that is, most dealers are ready to commit themselves to one leg of a transaction before the offsetting leg has been arranged. This activity is undertaken on the assumption that the matching derivative transaction can be completed without an adverse change in the market during the interim period.

The market risk entailed in booking open interest rate positions can be approached in two different ways:

- It is possible to open positions to speculate on spread and interest rate movements.
- The position is booked and hedged against market risk, pending arrangement of the matching part to the transaction.

In practice, dealers use a variety of interest rate risk management techniques to hedge (at least partially) against the risk of market movements in the period between the entry into the first derivative and the entry into the offsetting transaction. In essence, dealers do not seek to use their derivative activities to take positions in interest rate or currency markets, but operate their portfolios on a risk averse/risk controlled basis.

A number of approaches to interest rate portfolio risk management exist. These include:

- **Hedging approach** – entailing individual hedges for each transaction undertaken.
- **Portfolio approach** – based on the practice of hedging entire portfolios.

The hedging approach described in detail in this Chapter represents the original approach to interest rate portfolio risk management. It is predicated on a number of factors including:

- Risk management entails hedging of *temporary* risk positions.
- An offsetting transaction is the best hedge for another transaction. Hence any hedge is necessarily of a transient nature.

**Exhibit 13.1** sets out this model of hedging and risk management.

Under this approach the primary hedging mechanism is to re-state risk positions into equivalent instruments (generally this will be some debt instrument). The position is then hedged by taking offsetting positions in these instruments. This approach is illustrated with a number of examples of hedging specific types of transactions in the next Section of this Chapter.

However, over time the relative inflexibility of the hedging approach has emerged. This has become evident as the market has evolved with the development of non-generic structures creating large portfolios of transactions with complex mismatches. This has necessitated the adoption of portfolio management approaches. The portfolio management approaches are considered in Chapter 14.

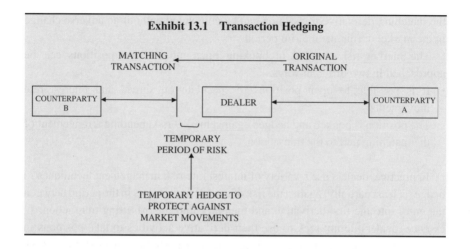

**Exhibit 13.1    Transaction Hedging**

# 3   Hedging Interest Rate Risk in Individual Transactions

## 3.1   Hedging Interest Rate Swaps

Where interest rate swap transactions are booked without a matching counter-party transaction, hedging is based on the fact that the exposure underlying unmatched swaps is directly analogous to cash market positions in debt instruments. Consequently, transactions involving physical/cash debt instruments or financial futures on the relevant debt instrument are used to offset the market risk assumed until the swap is matched with an offsetting transaction.

An interest rate swap transaction in any currency corresponds to positions in debt instruments. Given the cash market equivalent positions, it is possible to hedge the market risk by trading in the cash instrument. This effectively entails reversing the cash market position to provide a hedge against fluctuations in the value of the swap. **Exhibit 13.2** sets out the equivalent positions of an interest rate swap and the required hedges.

For example, assume a dealer commits to a 5 year swap with a corporation when the yield on 5 year bonds is 8.00% pa. Under the terms of the swap, the dealer pays bonds plus 40 bps pa in return for receiving 6 month US$ LIBOR. The dealer, not having a matching counterparty, hedges the swap temporarily by buying 5-year Treasury bonds. Subsequently, a few days later the dealer matches out its original swap exposure by entering into a matching offsetting swap. In the pre-closeout period, between the original swap and the matching swap, the spread on swaps has remained constant at bonds plus 40 bps (bid) and bonds plus 50 bps (offer). However, the yield on 5-year bonds has fallen to 7.50% pa. This effectively means

| Exhibit 13.2    Interest Rate Swaps – Equivalent Debt Positions and Hedges | | |
| --- | --- | --- |
| Interest Rate Swap Position | Equivalent to | Hedge |
| Receive fixed rate/pay floating rate | Long fixed rate bonds/short floating rate bonds | Short fixed rate bonds/purchase floating rate bonds. |
| Pay fixed rate/receive floating rate | Short fixed rate bonds/long floating rate bonds | Purchase fixed rate bonds/short floating rate bonds. |

that in *absolute rate* terms the dealer is paying 8.40% pa (8.00% pa plus 40 bps pa) and receiving 8.00% pa (7.50% pa plus 50 bps pa) on the fixed rate side of the swaps. It is assumed in this case that the floating rate sides (that is, the payment and receipt of floating rate LIBOR) are matched.

In terms of the matched swap positions, the bank loses 40 bps pa on the notional principal at every payment date. However, this periodic loss is offset by the gain on the holdings of bonds. The bonds bought to hedge the swap position would have increased in price when government bond rates fell from 8.00% pa to 7.50% pa. This gain is realised when the dealer sells the bonds at the time it enters into the matching swap transaction to close out its exposure. Once the value of the profit on the government bonds is factored into the transaction, the dealer will earn approximately 10 bps pa, representing the spread between the bid and offer rates on the matched swap positions.

In the reverse situation, where the dealer had received a fixed rate under the swap, it would have hedged by selling bonds and buying back those bonds when the offsetting swap was arranged. Under this transaction, the fall in rates would have resulted in a gain on the swap offset by a loss on the short bond position.

The basic technology described forms the basis of all swap portfolio risk management. **Exhibit 13.3** sets out the basic hedging strategy used for individual interest rate swaps. **Exhibit 13.4** sets out an example of this type of hedge for interest rate swap transaction.

## 3.2   Hedging FRAs

### 3.2.1   Approach

The basic approach to managing interest rate risk incurred in a FRA transaction is similar to that used with interest rate swaps. The transaction is risk mapped into equivalent transactions – generally borrowing and deposits to different maturities.

## Exhibit 13.3    Hedging Interest Rate Swaps

### 1.  Hedging a Fixed Rate Receiver Position

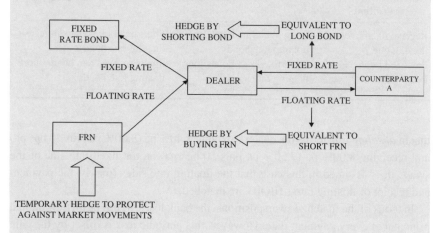

### 2.  Hedging a Fixed Rate Payer Position

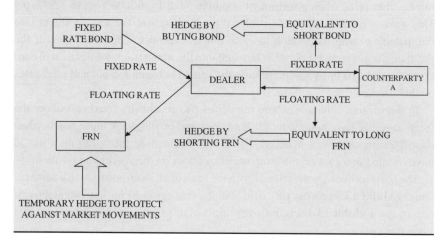

## Exhibit 13.4    Interest Rate Swap Hedge

### 1.  Initial Transaction

At 3 January 2001, a dealer enters into a 3 year interest rate swap commencing 5 January 2001 where the dealer pays fixed rate US$ at Treasury bonds plus 45 bps for 3 years against receipt of 6 month US$ LIBOR.

Swap terms are as follows:

| | |
|---|---|
| Amount | US$100 million |
| Start date | 5 January 2001 |
| Maturity | 5 January 2004 |
| Swap fixed rate | 7.45% pa semi-annual (calculated as bonds plus 45 bps pa where bonds are trading at 7.00% pa) |

The initial 6 month LIBOR leg is set at 5.00% pa.

The transaction is not matched and the dealer hedges the transaction, pending locating an offsetting counterparty.

## 2. Hedge

Assume the 3 year swap market is pricing the 7.50% November 2003 Treasury note, although the bond maturity is less than 3 years. The 7.50% November 2003 is trading at 7.00% pa. Short-term overnight rates/repo rates are 4.50% pa.

The dealer hedges through the purchase of 7.50% November 2003. The hedge amount is US$103.5 m, reflecting weighting of the hedge due to different price volatility of the swap and bond arising from different maturities. In effect, the dealer calculates a PVBP match to effect the hedge.

The hedge ratio is calculated as:

$$N = \text{PVBP of Swap/PVBP of bond} = 0.0266/0.0257 = 1.035$$

Where

$N$ = hedge ratio

PVBP of swap = PVBP of swap as 7.00% pa coupon bond equivalent maturing 5 January 2004

PVBP of bond = PVBP of 7.50% 15 November 2003 bond

Please note the following points in respect of matching the PVBP/price volatility of the swap and bond used as a hedge:

*   The swap is stated as a bond equivalent to a 7.00% pa coupon 3 year bond (that is, 7.45% (the swap rate) minus 45 bps (swap spread)). This reflects the fact that the hedge (using the Treasury Note) will only insulate the dealer against movements in the underlying bond rate *but not the spread*. This is a matter for individual dealers. Some may prefer to *include* the spread component, requiring the swap to be restated with the *swap rate* as the coupon equivalent. This would result in small differences in the hedge ratio.
*   The hedge does not adjust for convexity.

The details of the hedge are as follows:

| | |
|---|---|
| Amount | US$103.5 million |
| Yield | 7.00% pa |
| Price | 101.263 or US$104,806,707 |
| Accrued interest | 1.057 m or US$1,093,612 |
| Total price | 102.319 or US$105,900,319 |

### 3.  Offsetting Transaction

The open (hedged) swap is matched off on 19 January 2001. The dealer receives fixed rate US$ versus 6 month LIBOR at bond plus 55 bps pa. The terms of the matching swap are as follows:

| | |
|---|---|
| Amount | US$100 million |
| Start date | 19 January 2001 |
| Maturity | 5 January 2004 (with a short first interest period) |
| Swap fixed rate | 7.20% pa semi-annual (calculated as bonds plus 55 bps pa where bonds are trading at 6.65% pa) |

The swap is two weeks shorter than 3 years to enable the two swaps to be exactly matched as to final maturity and cash flows/payment dates.

The initial LIBOR leg is set at 4.80% pa. This is for LIBOR through to 5 July 2001 (effectively LIBOR for 5 month 2 weeks (167 days)). This would be calculated on an interpolated basis.

### 4.  Closure of Hedge

As the matching swap is entered into, the dealer sells its bond position. Assume that the 7.50% November 2003 is trading at 6.65% pa. The proceeds of closing out the bond position are as follows:

| | |
|---|---|
| Amount | US$103.5 million |
| Yield | 6.65% pa |
| Price | 102.140 or US$105,714,386 |
| Accrued interest | 1.347 or US$1,393,819 |
| Total price | 103.486 or US$107,108,205 |

### 5.  Matched Swap Position – Earnings

The result of the transactions is two sets of cash flows:
* Hedge gains (losses).
* Cash flows on the matched swaps.

The hedge gains (losses) on the fixed rate hedge are as follows:

| | |
|---|---|
| Cash profit on hedge | US$907,679[2] |
| Interest income | US$300,207[3] |
| Funding cost | US$(182,787)[4] |
| Net | US$1,025,099 |

---

[2]  US$105,714,386 – US$104,806,707.
[3]  US$1,393,819 – US$1,093,612.
[4]  4.50% pa on US$105,900,319 for 14 days.

The swap cash flows are as follows:
- At first payment date (on 5 July 2001):
  **Fixed rate side**

| | |
|---|---|
| Fixed rate amount received | US$3,294,247[5] |
| Fixed rate amount paid | US$3,694,384[6] |
| Net (fixed side) | US$(400,137) |

  **Floating rate side**

| | |
|---|---|
| Floating rate amount received | US$2,513,889[7] |
| Floating rate amount paid | US$2,226,667[8] |
| Net (floating side) | US$287,222 |
| **Total difference** | US$(112,915) |

- All other settlement dates:
  **Fixed rate side**

| | |
|---|---|
| Fixed rate amount received | US$ 3,600,000[9] |
| Fixed rate amount paid | US$(3,725,000)[10] |
| Net | US$(125,000) |

- All floating rate flows are assumed to match after the first period as they reprice on identical dates.

The transaction produces the following cash flows overall:
- Hedge profit of US$1,025,099.
- Net difference at first settlement of US$(112,915).
- Net difference at each subsequent settlement date of US$(125,000).

Assuming that the hedge profit is reinvested at the swap rate (7.20% pa), the transaction yields a present value profit of US$371,520 which is equivalent to US$69,952 every 6 months or 13.9 bps pa. This compares to a bid-offer spread of 10 bps pa. The discrepancy reflects hedging errors (primarily the failure to adjust for convexity), the carry on the hedge and also the shift in the short-term US$ LIBOR rates.

In practice, the hedging error would be sought to be minimised by dynamically managing the hedge. This would entail adjusting the amount of the hedge as bond yields changed to ensure the PVBP of the hedge and the swap was maintained. This would adjust for the convexity of the position. In addition, the specific interest rate risks on the LIBOR set and the hedge carry could be hedged separately. However, the hedging of these risks would result in the dealer incurring transaction costs in hedging.

---

[5] 7.20% on US$100 million for 167 days (19 January 2001 to 5 July 2001).
[6] 7.45% on US$100 million for 181 days (5 January 2001 to 5 July 2001).
[7] 5.00% on US$100 million for 181 days (5 January 2001 to 5 July 2001 – based on 360 day year).
[8] 4.80% on US$100 million for 167 days (19 January 2001 to 5 July 2001 – based on 360 day year).
[9] 7.20% on US$100 million for 6 months.
[10] 7.45% on US$100 million for 6 months.

The interest rate risk is then stated as the risk of these equivalent transactions. The interest rate risk is then hedged by taking offsetting positions in the equivalent transactions.

Within this framework, there are two basic approaches to managing interest rate exposures under FRA transactions:

- Cash market transactions involving borrowing and lending to different maturities.
- Offsetting the exposure through interest rate futures (on short term interest rate indexes) transactions.

The risk management approaches closely reflect the pricing methodology for interest rate forwards/FRAs[11].

## 3.2.2   Hedging FRAs in Cash Markets

FRA transactions can be hedged by a dealer through the creation of mismatched borrowing and lending transactions on its own balance sheet. For example, the dealer providing a FRA to hedge a drawdown on a loan for a client can hedge its risk through two cash transactions. In order to hedge its risk, the dealer borrows for a maturity coinciding with the maturity of the FRA contract, but invests for a shorter period which is the commencement date of the FRA. The mismatched investment and borrowing transaction is engineered to cover the risk under the FRA transaction created. In contrast, the dealer would borrow for a short period and invest for a longer period to create a FRA position for an investor seeking to lock in rates on a future investment. **Exhibit 13.5** sets out an example of a FRA hedge utilising borrowing and lending transactions.

This type of hedging technique uses the dealer's balance sheet. The balance sheet utilisation can be justified where the dealer would have undertaken the borrowing or lending transaction in any case. This may have been as part of their general asset liability management activities. The dealer restructures either the borrowing or investment decision to encompass the FRA transaction. However, where the FRA position cannot be engineered as part of its general treasury activities, it must be priced to earn a profit that compensates the dealer for balance sheet utilisation.

Another alternative may be to offset the risk exposure under a FRA against a mismatch in the dealer's overall interest rate portfolio. For example, where the dealer is matching an immediate start swap against a deferred or forward swap, it

---

[11]   See Chapter 6.

---

**Exhibit 13.5     FRA Hedge Utilising Borrowing and Lending Transactions**

Assume the FRA transaction set out in **Exhibit 12.8**. The details of the transaction are summarised below:

| | |
|---|---|
| Contract | 6 × 12 FRA |
| Position | Dealer buys the FRA (forward investment or deposit) from the counterparty |
| Notional Principal | $1,000,000 |
| FRA Rate | 7.24% pa |

The above transaction is based on the following market rates:

| | |
|---|---|
| 6 month | 6.39% pa |
| 12 month | 6.93% pa |

The transaction is risk mapped as the following money market transactions:
* 6 month zero coupon borrowing at 6.39% pa. This would entail borrowing future value of $1,000,000 (the notional principal of the FRA) to generate $969,121 in present value terms.
* 12 month zero coupon deposit at 6.93% pa. This would entail depositing $969,121 (the amount borrowed) to provide a future value (principal plus interest) of $1,036,282.
* The combined transaction results in a cash outflow of $1,000,000 after 6 months and an inflow of $1,036,282 at 1 year. The difference represents the earnings at the FRA rate of 7.24% pa.

To hedge the interest rate risk of the FRA, the dealer enters into two offsetting transactions:
* Lend $1,000,000 cash for 6 months at 6.39% pa (net proceeds $969,121).
* Borrow $1,036,282 cash for 12 months at 6.93% pa (net proceeds $969,121).

The hedge transactions replicate a bought FRA offsetting the original position entered into by the dealer.

---

may be possible to characterise the deferral period or delayed start as a string of FRA contracts to effectively match out the risk positions within the swap portfolio.

### 3.2.3   Hedging by Utilising Futures

As an alternative to hedging in the cash market, FRAs can be hedged by using futures contracts on short-term interest rates. In effect, the dealer offsets the position in the FRA with an offsetting position in the futures contract (effectively a forward contract in the exchange-traded market). The basic hedge structure using futures entails the dealer selling futures to hedge against the price risk of writing/selling a FRA designed to protect a borrower. Conversely, the dealer buys futures to hedge

---

**Exhibit 13.6    FRA Hedge Utilising Futures**

Assume a borrower approaches a dealer seeking to purchase a FRA to hedge a US$ loan drawdown for 90 days only, drawing down in early December 2001. Assume it is *now* mid September and December Eurodollar futures are quoted as:

**Sale    Bid    Offer**
88.95    88.94    88.95

The dealer will sell contracts to hedge its FRA position. The dealer will look to the bid price (the buyer) of 88.94. The dealer quotes a price of 88.94 plus a margin of 0.02% pa which means a quote of 11.08% pa to the client.

In early December, the client draws down its loan and settles the FRA with the dealer at the agreed yield rate of 11.08% pa. At the same time, the dealer closes out the futures position by buying contracts at or about the same yield that the borrower's loan is re-priced.

If the client is an investor, then the dealer would buy the contract (88.95) and deduct its margin (0.02% pa). The quoted rate would be 11.03% pa.

---

where it buys a FRA to protect investment yields. **Exhibit 13.6** sets out an example of using futures to hedge a FRA transaction.

In **Exhibit 13.6**, the structure of the FRA coincides perfectly with the specification of the futures contract and the contract dates (the commencement date of the FRA and futures contract is the same). In this case, the futures contract can be used as a perfect substitute for the FRA. This allows an efficient hedge to be created. However, in practice, the terms of the FRA will depart significantly from the specifications of the futures contract used to hedge the FRA. This will require considerable structuring of the hedging process.

The objective of using futures to hedge a FRA position is to construct positions in the futures market that offset the dealer's position in the FRA. This requires that the dollar price change for a given movement in interest rates is identical but opposite in direction on the hedge. However, the efficiency of the hedge will be affected by the changing relationship between the value of the security being hedged and the price at which the corresponding futures contract trades. The difference between the cash and futures price is referred to as the "basis". Using futures to hedge FRAs essentially entails substituting basis risk for absolute market risk on changes in interest rates.

Using futures to hedge FRA positions therefore requires considerable structuring of the hedge including:

• **Adjusting and anticipating basis fluctuations** – hedge management requires determination of possible gains and losses due to basis fluctuation. The effect of basis changes on the efficiency of the hedge can be viewed as the basis either increasing in value (strengthening) or decreasing in value (weakening). A short hedger who buys the basis will have a net gain as the basis strengthens (that is, the basis becomes increasingly more positive or less negative). A long hedger will have a net gain as the basis has weakened (that is, where the basis has become increasingly more negative or less positive).

- **Determining the appropriate hedge ratios** – where basis changes occur, the net profit or loss on the futures positions will not exactly offset the gain or loss in the cash position. This will effectively create a cash flow mismatch with resulting economic gains or losses between the settlement on the FRA contract and the settlement on the futures contract. Consequently, when dealers are using futures to hedge FRAs, they adjust the hedge for the anticipated changes in basis by slightly over or under-hedging. The hedge ratio (the number of futures contracts required to hedge the FRA position) is determined to ensure that the hedge performs as expected. The hedge ratio is determined to equate the price changes of the FRA and the futures contract. The price changes are not always of the same magnitude because of differences in terms/specifications of the FRA and the futures contract. The hedge ratio represents the principal face value of the futures contract held relative to the principal face value of the FRA position. There are a number of techniques for calculating the hedge ratio. These are discussed in relation to hedging interest rate swaps with futures contracts[12]. In the case of FRAs, basis point equivalency (PVBP Matching)) is commonly used to make the necessary hedge adjustments.

- **Selecting the appropriate contract and delivery month** – a critical decision for the dealer using futures to hedge FRAs is to select the contract to be utilised to effect the hedge and the delivery month in which the hedge will be placed. Selection of the contract is usually based on the correlation between movements in the price of the relevant futures contract and the price of the FRA. For example, Eurodollar futures will be used to hedge LIBOR based FRAs. The selection of contract month is more problematic. FRAs written to meet client requirements rarely exactly match the traded futures delivery dates. The selection of the delivery month to be used generally depends on the time horizon over which the hedge must be held, the liquidity of the particular delivery month and the pricing of contracts across delivery months (the basis relationship between contract dates). A variety of hedging strategies is used. These range from placing the hedge in the nearest liquid contract month to the relevant FRA, to using a

---

[12]   See Chapter 10.

**Exhibit 13.7    Currency Swaps – Equivalent Debt Positions and Hedges**

| Currency Swap Position | Equivalent to | Hedge |
|---|---|---|
| Receive fixed rate A$/pay US$ floating rate | Long fixed rate A$ bonds/ short US$ floating rate bonds | Short fixed rate A$ bonds/ purchase floating rate US$ bonds |
| Pay A$ fixed rate/receive US$ floating rate | Short fixed rate A$ bonds/ long US$ floating rate bonds | Purchase fixed rate A$ bonds/short floating rate US$ bonds |

Notes: The relevant amounts in each currency are determined by the total notional principal amount of the swap and the spot currency rates between the US$ and A$ at the time of entry into the currency swap.

basket of delivery months and contracts appropriately weighted to effect the hedge. Special hedging techniques (stack hedging, structured arbitrage and strip hedging) may also be utilised[13].

## 3.3   Hedging Currency Swaps

The basic technique of hedging currency swaps is similar to that used with interest rate swaps. The major difference lies in the fact that two interest rates and the spot currency exchange rate must be hedged in open currency swap positions. **Exhibit 13.7** sets out the basic hedging concepts in a conventional fixed-to-floating rate currency swap transaction, the equivalent analogous cash market positions in the relevant currencies and the required hedge. The hedging of a cross-currency fixed-to-fixed or floating-to-floating swap is similar, with either fixed rate or floating rate securities in both currencies being bought and sold to hedge the currency risk positions booked. The major difference in hedging currency swaps arises from the requirement to hedge interest rates in both currencies and the currency risk. **Exhibit 13.8** sets out an example of hedging a currency swap.

## 3.4   Hedging Currency Forwards

Currency forwards are hedged similarly to currency swaps. The transaction is risk mapped into equivalent transactions – generally a spot currency position and two

---

[13]  These techniques are discussed in relation to hedging interest rate swaps with future contracts; see Chapter 10.

| Exhibit 13.8    Currency Swap Hedge |
|---|

**1. Initial Transaction**

Assume a dealer enters into the following 5-year A$ fixed/US$ LIBOR currency swap commencing 8 March 2001:

- At commencement, based on a spot exchange rate of US$0.70/A$1.00, the dealer will receive A$49,500,000 from the swap counterparty. In return, the dealer will pay US$34,650,000. The dealer will also pay US$350,000 (being reimbursement of fees on the underlying bond issue of 1.00% or A$500,000).
- Over the life of the swap:
  1. Every six months, the dealer will receive 6 month LIBOR less 55 bps upon US$35,000,000. The initial 6 month US$ LIBOR is set at 8.00% pa.
  2. Every year on the coupon payment date, the dealer will make a payment of A$7 million, representing 14.00% pa on A$50,000,000.
- At maturity, the dealer will pay its counterparty A$50,000,000 and the dealer will receive US$35,000,000 from the swap counterparty.

**2. Hedge**

Assume that the swap is priced off the A$ 13.00% August 2006 government bond. The dealer is quoting bonds plus 60/80 bps pa versus six month LIBOR. The current bond yield is 14.00% pa semi-annual. Therefore, the corresponding all-in swap rate is 14.60/14.80% pa semi-annual[14].

Other market interest rates are assumed as follows:

| A$ overnight rate | 16.00% pa |
|---|---|
| US$ overnight rate | 7.00% pa |
| US$5 year rate | 10.00% pa semi-annual |

The swap is initially hedged by buying the A$13.00% August 2006 government bond. The bond is funded by borrowing US$ on an overnight basis.

The details of the hedge are as follows:

- The dealer buys A$48,342,581 face value[15] of the 13.00% August 2006 bonds on the following terms:

| Amount | A$48,342,581 |
|---|---|
| Yield | 14.00% pa semi-annual |
| Price | 96.255 or A$46,532,175 |
| Accrued interest | 0.754 or A$364,573 |
| Total price | A$46,896,748 |

- The dealer borrows US$35,000,000 on an overnight basis.

---

[14] The actual swap price reflects specific adjustments described in more detail in Chapter 10 (see **Exhibit 10.37**).

[15] The amount of bonds purchased is based on a PVBP match. The hedge ratio is 0.967. In practice, the hedge amount would be rounded up or down to a round lot or marketable amount for convenience.

On a cash flow basis, the dealer's position in A$ is:

| | |
|---|---|
| Receipts from swap exchange | +A$49,500,000 |
| Payment for bond | −A$46,896,748 |
| Net | +A$2,603,252 |

This balance is invested in the overnight cash market.
  On a cash flow basis, the dealer's position in US$ is:

| | |
|---|---|
| US$ borrowing | +US$35,000,000 |
| Payment under swap exchange | −US$35,000,000 |
| Net | −US$0 |

As a separate matter, the sub-LIBOR margin has to be hedged. This hedge requirement derives from the off market structure of the swap where the dealer structures the cash flows to match the counterparty's requirement. The hedge is separate from the pricing FX basis points/currency conversion factor adjustment, although it follows the same logic[16]. This hedge operates as follows:

* The dealer has an A$ cash flow surplus of A$340,000 annually (68 bps)[17] and a US$ shortfall of US$97,587 semi-annually (55 bps on US$35,000,000).
* The dealer borrows the present value (discounted at 15.25% pa annual) of the A$ surplus equivalent to A$1,133,019.
* The A$ borrowing proceeds are exchanged in the spot market for US$793,113 (at US$0.70/A$1.00) and the US$ are invested at an average rate of 8.00% pa semi-annual.
* Every 6 months, the US$ investment matures to produce a US$ cash flow which offsets the US$ shortfall under the swap structure. The A$ surplus is allocated annually to reduce the A$ borrowing. Under this structure, the A$ borrowing and the US$ investment declines over the life of the transaction[18].

### 3. Offsetting Transaction

The open (but hedged) currency swap position is closed off for value at 15 March 2001, with the dealer receiving fixed A$/paying 6 month LIBOR at the original offer spread of bond plus 80 bps. The precise terms of the offsetting transaction are:

| | |
|---|---|
| Amount | A$50,000,000 |
| Maturity | 8 March 2006 (with a short first interest period) |
| Swap fixed rate | 14.00% pa semi-annual (14.49% pa annual) based on bond plus 80 bps where bonds are 13.20% pa. |

As at 15 March 2001, the spot exchange rate is US$0.6940/A$1.00.

---

[16] See Chapter 10.

[17] This is the difference between the adjusted A$ swap rate payable by the dealer and the actual A$ payment made by the dealer under the swap.

[18] Please note in practice, precise actual borrowing and lending transactions may not be executed to hedge the margin exposure. The exposure may be absorbed into the institution's overall treasury currency position.

The offsetting currency swap has the following cash flows:
- On 15 March 2001, the dealer will pay A$50,000,000 and receive US$34,700,000.
- Over the life of the swap:
  1. Every six months, the dealer will pay 6 month LIBOR on US$34,700,000. The initial LIBOR leg is set at 4.80% pa. This is for LIBOR through to 8 September 2001 (effectively LIBOR for 5 month 3 weeks (177 days)). This would be calculated on an interpolated basis.
  2. Every year, on 8 March 2002 through to 8 March 2006, the dealer will receive the equivalent of 14.49% pa on A$50,000,000.
- On 8 March 2006, the initial exchange will be reversed.

The offsetting currency swap is shorter than 5 years to enable the two swaps to be exactly matched as to final maturity and cash flows/payment dates.

## 4. Closure of Hedge
When the offsetting swap is entered into, the dealer will unwind its hedges as follows:
- The dealer sells its A$48,342,581 face value of the 13.00% August 2006 on the following terms:

| | |
|---|---|
| Amount | A$48,342,581 |
| Yield | 13.20% pa |
| Price | 99.215 or A$47,963,311 |
| Accrued interest | 1.006 or A$486,097 |
| Total price | A$48,449,408 |

- The dealer repays its US$35,000,000 borrowing with interest.

## 5. Matched Swap Position – Earnings
The result of the transactions is two sets of cash flows:
- Hedge gains (losses).
- Cash flows on the matched swaps.

The dealer's overall cash position in A$ is:

| | |
|---|---|
| Payment under closeout swap | −A$50,000,000 |
| Sale of bond | +A$48,449,408 |
| Proceeds of maturing cash surplus | +A$2,611,240[19] |
| Net | +A$1,060,648 |

The dealer's overall position in US$ is:

| | |
|---|---|
| Receipts from swap exchange | +US$34,700,000 |
| Repayment of US$ borrowings | −US$35,046,986[20] |
| Net | −US$346,986 |

---

[19] A$2,603,252 (principal) plus A$7,988 (interest at 16.00% pa for 7 days).
[20] US$35,000,000 (principal) plus US$46,986 (interest at 7.00% pa for 7 days).

At current exchange rates, this creates a cash surplus (hedge gains) of A$560,668 after offsetting the A$499,980 shortfall (US$346,986 at US$0.6940/A$1.00).

The actual matched swap positions will produce the following cash flows:

- **Fixed rate A$**

  *On first settlement date (on 8 March 2001)*

| | |
|---|---|
| Fixed amount received | A$7,106,055[21] |
| Fixed amount paid | A$(7,000,000)[22] |
| Repayment of A$ borrowing | A$(340,000)[23] |
| Net | A$(233,945) |

  *On subsequent settlement dates*

| | |
|---|---|
| Fixed amount received | A$7,245,000[24] |
| Fixed amount paid | A$(7,000,000)[25] |
| Repayment of A$ borrowing | A$(340,000)[26] |
| Net | A$(95,000) |

- **Floating rate US$**

  *On first settlement date (on 8 September 2001)*

| | |
|---|---|
| Floating amount received | US$1,332,722[27] |
| Floating amount paid | US$(1,364,867)[28] |
| Maturing US$ investment | US$97,784[29] |
| Net | US$65,639 |

  *On subsequent settlement dates*

| | |
|---|---|
| Floating amount received | US$(LIBOR −55bps on US$35,000,000) |
| Floating amount paid | US$(LIBOR on US$34,700,000) |
| Maturing US$ investment | US$97,784[30] |
| Net | US$(LIBOR on US$300,000) |

The transaction overall produces the following cash flows:

- Hedge profit of A$560,668.
- Net difference on the fixed A$ payments of:
  A$(233,945) on the first settlement
  A$(95,000) on subsequent settlements.

---

[21]  14.49% pa on A$50,000,000 for 358 days (15 March 2001 to 8 March 2002).

[22]  14.00% pa on A$50,000,000 for 365 days (8 March 2001 to 8 March 2002).

[23]  Repayment of A$340,000 pa on borrowing to hedge sub-LIBOR margins.

[24]  14.49% pa on A$50,000,000 for 365 days.

[25]  14.00% pa on A$50,000,000 for 365 days.

[26]  Repayment of A$340,000 pa on borrowing to hedge sub-LIBOR margins.

[27]  7.45% pa (LIBOR − 55 bps) on US$35,000,000 for 184 days (8 March 2001 to 8 September 2001) (based on 360 days).

[28]  8.00% pa (LIBOR) on A$34,700,000 for 177 days (15 March 2001 to 8 September 2001) (based on 360 days).

[29]  Maturing US$ investment to hedge sub-LIBOR margin.

[30]  Maturing US$ investment to hedge sub-LIBOR margin.

- Net difference on the floating rate US$ payment of:
  US$65,639 on the first settlement;
  US$12,000 on subsequent settlements (assuming LIBOR of 8.00% pa).

  The overall transaction profit can be determined as follows:
- Discount back the A$ loss at the appropriate rate (15.25% pa annual) giving a current value of approximately A$437,128.
- Discount each of the US$ profits at the appropriate rate, say 8.00% semi-annual giving a current value of approximately US$148,907 (at US$0.6940/A$1.00 equivalent to A$214,563).
- The total profit is A$338,103. The profit amortised (at 15.25% pa annual) yields a profit margin of approximately 20.3 bps pa. The profit margin is slightly different from the original bid/offer spread due to hedging inefficiencies.

interest rate positions (borrowing and deposits in different currencies to the same maturity). The currency spot risk and interest rate risk is then stated as the risk of these equivalent transactions. The currency and interest rate risk is then hedged by taking offsetting positions in the equivalent transactions.

Currency forwards are generally segmented by maturity into two categories:
- **Short dated** – generally currency forwards with maturities of 12 months or less.
- **Long dated (LTFX transactions)** – generally currency forwards with maturities of greater than 12 months.

Short dated currency forwards are hedged using spot transactions and cash borrowing/deposit transactions to the maturity of the forward. **Exhibit 13.9** sets out an example of hedging short dated currency forwards.

Long dated currency forward transactions are usually hedged in one of two ways:
- Fixed-to-fixed zero coupon currency swaps.
- Outright forward contracts.

Long dated contracts are functionally identical to zero coupon fixed-to-fixed currency swaps[31]. One approach to pricing and managing the risks inherent in booking these positions is to incorporate these transactions into the overall cross currency swap portfolio. Long dated forward contracts are incorporated in swap portfolios

---

[31] See Chapters 3 and 10.

---

**Exhibit 13.9    Short Dated Currency Forward Hedge**

Assume the currency forward transaction set out in **Exhibit 12.9**. The details of the transaction are summarised below:

Contract        Purchase Yen/sell US$ forward
Amount          Yen 100 million
Maturity        1 year
Forward Rate    US$1 = Yen 106.38

The currency forward has the following cash flows:

Yen     Receive Yen 100,000,000
US$     Pay US$939,982

The market prices and rates as of the date of entry into the transaction are as follows:

Spot Rate                             US$1 = Yen 110.00
Yen zero coupon 1 year swap rate      3.00% pa
US$ zero coupon 1 year swap rate      6.50% pa

The cash flows of the forward are equivalent to the following transactions:
- Borrow US$882,613 for 1 year at a rate of 6.50% pa requiring repayment at maturity of US$939,982.
- Convert the US$882,613 into Yen at the spot rate (US$1 = Yen 110) to generate Yen 97,087,379.
- Invest Yen 97,087,379 for 1 year at a rate of 3.00% pa creating a cash inflow at maturity of Yen 100,000,000.

To hedge the risk of the currency forward, the dealer enters into the following offsetting transactions:
- Borrow Yen 97,087,379 for 1 year at a rate of 3.00% pa, creating a cash outflow at maturity of Yen 100,000,000.
- Convert the Yen 97,087,379 into US$ at the spot rate (US$1 = Yen 110) to generate US$882,613.
- Invest US$882,613 for 1 year at a rate of 6.50% pa, creating a cash inflow at maturity of US$939,982.

The hedge transactions replicate a sold Yen/bought US$ 1 year currency forward, offsetting the original position entered into by the dealer.

---

operated on a portfolio basis as single period single cash flows. **Exhibit 13.10** sets out an example of using swaps to hedge a currency forward position.

The structuring of a long dated forward hedge entails multiple steps. Standard currency swaps are based on a fixed rate in the foreign currency against a floating

---

**Exhibit 13.10    Long Dated Currency Forward Hedge**

Assume the following market rates:

**Currency Rate**

| Maturity (years) | A$1 = US$ |
|---|---|
| Spot | 0.7000 |
| 1 | 0.6567 |
| 2 | 0.6161 |
| 3 | 0.5779 |
| 4 | 0.5422 |
| 5 | 0.5086 |

**Interest Rate Swap Rates**[32]

| A$ | 14.75/14.70% pa annual |
|---|---|
| US$ | 7.68/7.65% pa annual |

Assume the dealer is asked to enter into a 5 year purchase A$/sell US$ currency forward. The position is equivalent to a purchase of a 5 year zero coupon A$ bond and a sold 5 year zero coupon US$ bond.

The dealer would hedge the position as follows:
- The spot currency position is hedged by selling A$/buying US$ spot.
- The interest rate positions are hedged by:
  1. Entering into A$ swap where the dealer pays A$ fixed at 14.75% pa.
  2. Entering into US$ swap where the dealer receives US$ fixed at 7.65% pa.

The floating rate legs of the swap are offset by cash interest positions in the respective currencies that would earn money market rates in both currencies. In practice, this could be replicated by rolling short dated forwards (for example, if the swaps are transacted against 3 month benchmark rates, then the dealer may adjust the currency spot position into a 3 month forward position that is rolled quarterly).

The two swaps produce the following net cash flows (all cash flows are worked off A$100 and its equivalent in US$):

| Notional Principal | US$ Swap (US$) 70.00 | A$ Swap (A$) (100.00) |
|---|---|---|
| **Maturity (Years)** | | |
| 1 | 5.36 | −14.75 |
| 2 | 5.36 | −14.75 |
| 3 | 5.36 | −14.75 |
| 4 | 5.36 | −14.75 |
| 5 | 75.36 | −114.75 |

---

[32] For convenience, a flat term structure of interest rates is assumed. However, the conclusions derived are applicable, irrespective of the shape of the yield curve in either currency.

The hedged position can be demonstrated by a simple process. Assume the A$ swap flows are now covered using the currency forward market:

| Notional Principal | US$ Swap (US$) 70.00 | A$ Swap (A$) (100.00) | Currency Rates (A$ = US$) | A$ Swap Flows Covered to US$ (US$) |
|---|---|---|---|---|
| **Maturity (Years)** | | | | |
| 1 | 5.36 | −14.75 | 0.6567 | −9.69 |
| 2 | 5.36 | −14.75 | 0.6161 | −9.09 |
| 3 | 5.36 | −14.75 | 0.5779 | −8.52 |
| 4 | 5.36 | −14.75 | 0.5422 | −8.00 |
| 5 | 75.36 | −114.75 | 0.5086 | −58.37 |

This produces the following net US$ position:

| Maturity (Years) | US$ Swap (US$) | A$ Swap Flows Covered to US$ (US$) | Net Position (US$) | Discount Factors (at US$ Swap Rate) | PV of Net Position (US$) |
|---|---|---|---|---|---|
| 1 | 5.36 | −9.69 | −4.33 | 0.93 | −4.02 |
| 2 | 5.36 | −9.09 | −3.73 | 0.86 | −3.22 |
| 3 | 5.36 | −8.52 | −3.17 | 0.80 | −2.54 |
| 4 | 5.36 | −8.00 | −2.64 | 0.74 | −1.97 |
| 5 | 75.36 | −58.37 | 16.99 | 0.69 | 11.75 |
| | | | | **Total** | **0** |

The net cash flow position is zero, highlighting the capacity to construct the 5 year forward at the current interest rate parity currency forward rate through the hedges outlined.

If the forwards are mispriced (that is, trade away from interest rate parity) then this allows the dealer to construct a profitable arbitrage position. Assume the currency forwards are as follows:

| Maturity (years) | A$1 = US$ |
|---|---|
| Spot | 0.7000 |
| 1 | 0.6412 |
| 2 | 0.6018 |
| 3 | 0.5649 |
| 4 | 0.5326 |
| 5 | 0.5067 |

Assume all other factors are as above. The A$ swap flows are now covered using the (new) currency forward market rates:

| Notional Principal | US$ Swap (US$) | A$ Swap (A$) | Currency Rates (A$ = US$) | A$ Swap Flows Covered to US$ (US$) |
|---|---|---|---|---|
| | 70.00 | (100.00) | | |
| **Maturity (Years)** | | | | |
| 1 | 5.36 | −14.75 | 0.6412 | −9.458 |
| 2 | 5.36 | −14.75 | 0.6018 | −8.877 |
| 3 | 5.36 | −14.75 | 0.5649 | −8.332 |
| 4 | 5.36 | −14.75 | 0.5326 | −7.856 |
| 5 | 75.36 | −114.75 | 0.5067 | −58.144 |

This produces the following net US$ position:

| Maturity (Years) | US$ Swap (US$) | A$ Swap Flows Covered to US$ (US$) | Net Position (US$) | Discount Factors (at US$ Swap Rate) | PV of Net Position (US$) |
|---|---|---|---|---|---|
| 1 | 5.36 | −9.69 | −4.10 | 0.93 | −3.81 |
| 2 | 5.36 | −9.09 | −3.52 | 0.86 | −3.04 |
| 3 | 5.36 | −8.52 | −2.98 | 0.80 | −2.39 |
| 4 | 5.36 | −8.00 | −2.50 | 0.74 | −1.86 |
| 5 | 75.36 | −58.37 | 17.21 | 0.69 | 11.91 |
| | | Total | 4.11 | | 0.81 |

The net cash flow position shows a surplus of US$4.11 per US$70 (A$100). Assuming a US$ cost of funding the US$ deficit equal to 7.65% pa, the transaction yields a net present value of US$0.81 per US$70. This would attract trading interest to ensure that interest rate parity was enforced.

In the analysis above, the dealer assumes the interest rate risk on the funding or re-investment of cash flows – effectively to the zero coupon rate curve. This risk can be covered by structuring the A$ and US$ interest rate swaps as zero coupon swaps where the interest payments are paid in a single lump sum amount (including compound interest on the payments) at maturity[33].

rate in US$. The first step is therefore to combine a typical currency swap with an interest rate swap in US$ that results in known flows in both US$ and the relevant currency. The currency swap structure entails an exchange of principal at both the beginning and end of the swap at the current swap rate at the outset of the transaction.

---

[33] See discussion of zero coupon swap structures in Das, Satyajit (2004) Structured Products Volume 1; John Wiley & Sons (Asia), Singapore at Chapter 13.

It also creates a series of cash flows in which the interest differentials between the two currencies are spread over the life of the swap as differentials in the value of the interest flows being exchanged. The interest flows can be characterised as a series of currency contracts with implied forward currency exchange rates. This allows the currency swap to be divided into a series of forward-to-forward contracts. By treating each settlement separately, a number of currency forward contracts can be created by fixing the foreign currency cash flows in one of the swap currencies for an equivalent amount of the other currency calculated at the current currency forward rates. The hedge will generally create either a funding or investment requirement for the dealer.

The alternative hedging technology for long dated currency forwards treats these transactions similarly to short dated currency forward transactions. This approach entails hedging the spot currency risk and the interest rate risk with positions with borrowings and deposits in the respective currencies. It results in significant potential capital/balance sheet costs as the borrowing and deposit need to be booked for a substantial duration.

This means that in practice, most dealers hedge long dated currency forward positions using the swap approach. Where the position is hedged in cash, the currency exposure is usually hedged using spot currency positions. The interest rate risk may be left unhedged. This is on the basis that the exposure to the forward points is acceptable. Where long dated currency forward trades are hedged in this way, the dealers will seek to adjust the spread to protect against minor movements in interest rate differentials and consequently, the forward points. A variation on this technique is to use forwards mismatched as to maturity to hedge long dated currency forward positions. The dealer may not match the offsetting currency forward contract as to the exact cash flow maturity. For example, a bank may sell US$ forward/buy Yen for value in 5 years and match the position with an offsetting purchase of US$ forward/sell Yen for value in 1 years time. The mismatch in value dates represents a gap that is managed within position limits until a counterparty can be found or the transaction squared in a different way. The gap mismatches in maturity may be managed through interest rate hedges separately.

## 4   Hedging Efficiency

The unifying principle underlying the risk management approach outlined is the objective of the dealer to maximise earnings on a risk adjusted basis. This can be restated as:

$$PV \text{ (net)} = PV \text{ (cash inflows)} - PV \text{ (cash outflows)}$$

Where

PV signifies the present value of the relevant cash flows at the appropriate rate

The application of this type of approach to conventional trading activities such as trading in securities is relatively straightforward. This is because the market value of the securities usually implies their true economic value. However, in the case of derivatives, it is necessary to establish the economic value for inflows and outflows of both fixed and floating rates of interest at dates in the future.

This is undertaken in practice by equating the fixed rate cash flows under derivatives to a fixed rate debt security or bond. The floating rate flows are equated to short-dated debt securities. In managing the risk of a transaction the dealer substitutes hedging risk for the market risk of an open position. The basic presumption is that by buying or selling securities of the appropriate maturity, the interest rate risk on the cash flows can be offset. Hedging risk arises because hedging of positions is difficult as there is no single perfect hedging instrument other than a directly matching, but offsetting, transaction.

Fixed rate flows are usually hedged by using fixed rate debt securities of the appropriate maturity (or equivalent futures contracts). It is customary to use government bonds in the relevant currency. This reflects the pricing behaviour in most markets where swaps trade at a spread (often volatile) relative to the fixed rate government bond yields[34]. The efficiency of the hedge is determined by the correlation between price movements of the hedge instrument and the swap pricing benchmark instrument. The lower the correlation between the two, the greater the hedging or basis risk. Where a security with differential pricing characteristics to the swap pricing benchmark is utilised, this additional hedging or basis risk must be managed. Risk management on the floating rate side entails the purchase or sale of instruments (physical securities or futures) which replicate the price behaviour of the floating rate index.

Interest rate risk management substitutes hedging risk for market risk. The strategy of using hedging techniques to immunise portfolio value from changes in market rates is never perfect. Limitations in the hedging mechanisms, and imperfections and illiquidity in the relevant markets, generally impact upon the efficiency of the hedge. However, the hedging methodology usually used allows quantification of the residual risk after hedging, and permits a high degree of control over the risks incurred.

---

[34] See discussion in Chapter 11.

The factors that affect the efficiency of the hedging process include:

- **Changes in the shape of the yield curve** – non-parallel movements of the yield curve usually affect hedge efficiency. Where such changes in the shape of the yield curve occur, equality of the price change between the transaction and the hedge cannot be assured.
- **Basis movements** – additional loss of hedge efficiency occurs where movements in the hedge instrument are imperfectly correlated with the price changes in the underlying transaction. In particular, variables such as the swap spread itself cannot be hedged, unlike the benchmark price or rate. This intrinsically precludes an efficient hedging strategy.
- **Reinvestment and funding assumptions** – the hedging technology developed requires assumptions on reinvestment rates and funding rates – effectively, exposure to the current zero coupon rates. To the extent that the zero rates cannot be effectively hedged, the hedge efficiency may be reduced.
- **Hedge carry costs** – this covers the fact that hedges will entail either a carry cost or generate investment income. This loss or gain on the hedge must be factored into the overall transaction. This may require assumptions about reinvestment rates, or alternatively, funding costs. In addition, there may be costs of shorting securities (the cost of borrowing the bond to maintain a hedge in a short position).
- **Hedge transaction costs** – this represents costs incurred in establishing and then unwinding or adjusting the hedge.

The process of risk management includes risk control measures. This usually takes the form of daily re-valuations of both the transactions/portfolios. In addition, projected risk is also determined (using worst case or adverse scenarios)[35]. The total risk is controlled by limit systems. In this regard, the derivative hedging system is part of the formal risk control/limit and administration processes allowing the financial risk of such transactions to be estimated and managed.

# 5 Choice of Hedging Instrument – Cash Instruments or Futures Contracts

In choosing hedging instruments, the principal consideration is to seek a security or instrument that has a relatively high correlation between the hedge instrument and the benchmark pricing instrument. This is to eliminate, as far as possible, hedging or basis risk.

---

[35] See discussion of VAR in Das, Satyajit (2004) Risk Management; John Wiley & Sons (Asia), Singapore at Chapter 2.

The choice of hedging instrument is as follows:

- **Cash market instruments** – usually physical securities such as government bonds or floating rate securities.
- **Futures contracts** – typically futures on short term interest rates or a government bond.

The two instruments have different characteristics, including:

- **Balance sheet impact** – use of cash market instruments is usually reflected directly on the balance sheet. In contrast, futures contracts are usually off-balance sheet.
- **Transaction costs** – the relative transaction costs of trading in cash instruments and futures contracts may affect the choice of hedging instruments. In general, futures contracts have lower trading transaction costs.
- **Liquidity considerations** – differences in liquidity between the physical and futures markets may dictate one or other would be preferred.
- **Institutional considerations and flexibility** – the greater institutional flexibility of futures markets, in particular the ability to short sell, may be relevant.
- **Carry cost** – in the case of futures contracts, the carry cost is built into the actual futures price. The discount or premium relative to the spot cash security price reflects the positive or negative carry. In the case of a physical security, the carry cost will usually reflect the difference between the coupon accrual on the security and the interest cost of funding the position. This will result in actual cash surpluses or deficits. There may also be slight differences in funding costs/investment returns.
- **Hedge structuring** – in practice, a hedge involving both physical securities as well as futures would necessitate hedge structuring to match out the relative volatility of the swap and the hedging instrument. However, where futures are used as the hedge, there is an additional risk of rolling over the futures contract. This occurs where the dealer is required to close out a futures contract at the futures settlement date in order to maintain a hedge. This creates a potential exposure to the rollover cost. This means that hedge efficiency is reduced at the point of rollover.

In practice, the swap market tends to favour the use of futures in hedging positions. This approach means that the dealer incurs basis risk and (potential) rollover risk. However, futures are favoured because of the off balance sheet structure, lower transaction costs, greater liquidity and ease of short selling.

There are, in effect, different segments of the market. The choice of hedging instrument differs significantly between the segments. The interest

rate market, for example in US$, Euro and Yen, can be separated into two segments:
- **Short term interest rates** – this is usually between 1 and 5 years in maturity
- **Long term interest rates** – this is usually beyond 1 to 5 years in maturity.

The short term segment is traditionally hedged using strips of futures on short term interest rates (such as the Eurodollar contract or its equivalent)[36]. This entails the purchase or sale of a series of futures contracts to hedge the position. The futures trades are subsequently reversed where a matching transaction is entered. However, in some cases, the position may be left open for the full maturity of the transaction. In contrast, swaps of longer maturity are traditionally hedged using futures on government bonds or cash securities (usually government bonds). The hedges are temporary, with the hedge being unwound when an offsetting position is traded.

A key issue in using futures or cash securities to hedge positions is to optimise the correlation between the hedge and the position being hedged. A number of identifiable problems exist in relation to using futures contracts as a hedge against interest rate risk positions:
- **Limited types of futures contracts available** – this difficulty relates to the fact that futures contracts are typically only available on limited and highly specific types of securities. In most currencies, there are few relevant futures contracts of sufficient liquidity available for use as a hedge for swap risk positions. This means that the use of futures contracts as a hedge creates exposure to changes in the yield curve shape. This exposure to the yield curve shape is most significant where the hedge is to be maintained for a significant duration. Futures contracts on government bond rates usually provide an accurate short term surrogate in the short-term but the efficacy usually decreases with the time and inevitable changes in the shape of the yield curve.
- **Cash-futures pricing relationship** – the exposure to yield curve shape also exists through the cash-futures pricing relationship. The pricing of futures contracts reflects the cost of carry (interest rate differential) between the time of entry into the futures/forward contract and the expiry of delivery date of the contract. Where a futures contract is used as a hedge, changes in short term interest rates that will change the pricing of the futures contract may reduce the correlation between movements in the price of the futures contract relative to the position being hedged. This effectively represents the impact of changes in

---

[36] For a discussion of pricing interest rate swaps of interest rate futures contracts; see Chapter 10.

the yield curve shape. Changes in short-term rates may change the path of convergence between the cash and futures markets that may also cause deterioration in the efficiency of the hedged transaction.

- **Non-convex nature of futures contracts** – the convexity problem relates to the fact that the present value of a basis point ("PVBP") for some futures contracts is usually fixed, regardless of the level of absolute rates. The PVBP of most positions depends on the level of rates as well as the time to maturity. Consequently, where futures are used to hedge positions, the amount of futures contracts used will only be appropriate for the swap rate at the time the trade is done. As absolute yields change and the period to maturity of the swap changes, the PVBP relationship between the futures contract and the hedged position will change. Consequently, the number of contracts and the hedge will need to be constantly adjusted causing further slippage in hedge efficiency[37].

# 6 Swap Futures Contracts

The concept of an interest rate swap futures contract has been actively discussed since the middle 1980s[38]. A swap futures contract is a contract with delivery effected by entry into an interest rate swap contract on the delivery date of the futures contract. The swap futures contract is priced at the fixed rate that market participants expected to prevail in the swap market on the delivery date, based on the current market swap yield curve. For example, a futures contract maturing in December 2001 off a 5-year interest rate swap would be priced at the *forward* 5-year swap rate that is expected to prevail on the relevant delivery date as embodied in the current swap yield curve.

In theory, major users of a swap futures contract would be swap dealers and to a more limited extent, end users of the swap market. For the dealers, the major advantage would be the ability to hedge swap spread risk and some improvements in the cost of hedging. Major advantages in relation to hedging cost would be the capacity to use the swap futures contracts in preference to physical securities,

---

[37] For a discussion of convexity issues in pricing interest rate swaps of interest rate futures contracts; see Chapter 10.

[38] See Dew, James Kurt "The Case for Interest Rate Swap Futures" (Winter 1987) Journal of International Securities Markets 149–155. See also Rombach, Ed "Zen and the Art of Trading the Convexity Bias" (December 1995) Financial Derivatives & Risk Management Issue 4 17–22; Simpkin, Guy "European Fixed Income Capital Markets: Benchmark Curves and Futures Contracts" in (1999) The Guide to Euro-Denominated Securities – Euromoney Supplement at 2–5.

thereby avoiding balance sheet utilisation costs. The interest rate swap futures would provide a means to hedge swap spread risk, and also in the case of options on the futures contracts, the spread volatility component option on swap products that is currently difficult to manage. An additional advantage is that under current capital adequacy guidelines, futures contracts are zero risk weighted for capital purposes[39]. This may in some cases improve the cost of hedging where the futures contracts are used in preference to holding physical non-government securities.

An additional benefit that might be applicable to weaker swap market participants would be that the implied financing or investment rates would be priced at the margin, and therefore would be the same for most market participants. For the end user, the swap futures contract would allow creation of forward swaps by trading in the futures, rather than directly transacting forward swaps with financial institutions.

The significant theoretical potential of swap futures contracts has created an impetus for a number of futures and options exchanges to consider introducing such a contract. One initiative was from the Chicago Board of Trade ("CBOT") which introduced a US$ interest rate swap futures contract. The contracts covered 3 and 5 year swap futures and futures options.

The contract competed to a substantive degree against the Chicago Mercantile Exchange ("CME") 3 month Eurodollar futures contract. The Eurodollar futures contract is traditionally used to hedge short dated US$ interest rate swaps. Strips of Eurodollar futures contracts have been traded as the offsetting component to interest rate swaps transacted by financial institutions with relevant counterparties[40]. The CME Eurodollar contracts traded out to 10 years. This theoretically allows dealers to hedge interest rate position out to 10 years.

The CBOT swap futures contract was designed to offer some significant advantages over the CME Eurodollar futures contract including:

- Reduction in commissions reflecting the reduced number of contracts needing to be transacted.
- Lack of liquidity in the CME Eurodollar contracts beyond 3 years at the time.

In a parallel development, the Financial Instrument Exchange ("FINEX"), a division of the New York Cotton Exchange, originally introduced 2 year and 5 year

---

[39] See Das, Satyajit (2004) Risk Management; John Wiley & Sons (Asia), Singapore at Chapter 17.
[40] For a discussion of pricing interest rate swaps off interest rate futures contracts; see Chapter 10.

treasury notes futures contracts to specifically assist interest rate portfolio managers (such as swap portfolio managers). FINEX also offered an exchange for physical ("EFP") mechanism from swaps to five year or two year interest rate futures or vice versa. However, neither initiative was successful and the swap futures contracts were discontinued. CBOT subsequently re-launched swap futures products in 2001[41].

More recently, LIFFE launched a Euro futures contract based on swap rates. The Swapnote® contracts are structured as a cash settled bond futures contract with a single notional bond in the deliverable basket. Each contract has a series of notional cash flows, comprising a fixed coupon and a principal repayment. The contract is cash settled, based on a price calculated by discounting the notional cash flows using a swap curve constructed from the ISDA benchmark Euro-ibor swap rate fixings. The Swapnote® contracts initially covered 2, 5 and 10 years. In addition, there was an options contract on the 10 year Swapnote® contract. The contracts have had limited success[42].

Given the obvious advantages and benefits of a swap futures contract, it is surprising that the efforts to introduce such a facility have not encountered more success. The major factors against an increased role for interest rate swap futures appear to include:

- Lack of liquidity in these contracts that reflects the lack of institutional support for the concept which would create the necessary liquidity to provide the basis for future growth.
- Suspicion regarding the accuracy of cash/futures convergence in these products, and some concern about the mechanism for setting closing rates that some market participants fear is open to manipulation.
- The non-convex nature of the interest rate swap futures contracts which requires constant adjustment of the hedge position to reduce hedge slippage.

# 7 Financing Hedge Positions

Hedges entail the use of either cash securities or futures on the cash securities. Where cash securities are utilised, the purchase of bonds to hedge open risk

---

[41] See Polyn, Gallagher "Make or Break New Swap Contracts" (November 2001) Risk 9.

[42] See Simpkin, Guy "European Fixed Income Capital Markets: Benchmark Curves and Futures Contracts" in (1999) The Guide to Euro-Denominated Securities – Euromoney Supplement at 2–5; Butler, Ross "Swaps are Popular, Exchanges are Not" (January 2002) FOW 28–29; Hoppe, Stephanie "Swap Futures – Reaching New Heights" (March 2002) FOW 47–49.

positions requires the holdings of securities to be financed. Conversely, short selling of securities to hedge a portfolio necessitates borrowing the necessary physical securities to short sell, and investing the proceeds of the sale.

The financing or investment requirements required by the management of the hedge portfolio can be undertaken in the short-term cash/money market. This entails borrowing/investing on an overnight or short-term basis to offset the liquidity requirements of the hedge portfolio. The alternative is to use the bond repurchase market that performs a similar function[43].

The market used to manage the liquidity requirements of the hedge portfolio varies significantly between currencies. In US$, for example, the bond repurchase market is predominantly used. This reflects the highly developed nature of the US$ bond repurchase market. In other currencies, the cash market may be used, reflecting the absence of well developed bond repurchase markets. However, increasingly, repurchase markets in a variety of currencies have developed rapidly.

The use of short-term financing investment markets to manage the liquidity requirements of hedges creates a variety of problems. The markets are predominantly variable rate markets with interest rates fixed for short periods (overnight to one/two weeks). This creates exposures to interest rate movements in relation to hedging activities designed to insulate portfolios from interest rate exposures by purchasing and selling securities. Assumptions are made in respect of the cost of financing hedge positions or investing the proceeds of short sales of securities. In reality, some slippage may occur in relation to cost of financing a hedge or investing proceeds of a short securities position. This arises from a combination of uncertainty as to the time period for which the hedge is required, and the inability to lock in interest rates/securities borrowing for the required period.

Given that the assumed earnings or cost must be factored into the pricing of transactions at the time of entry into the transaction, the uncertain outcome regarding these costs or income creates an extra dimension of risk in managing hedges. The financing or reinvestment exposure is in addition to financing or reinvestment exposure in respect of interest rate movement that affects the portfolio as a whole on an ongoing basis.

## 8   Summary

Risk management entails decomposition of portfolios of positions through risk mapping into a series of spot and yield curve positions (for asset and forward

---

[43]   For a discussion of bond repurchase markets, see Chapter 6.

positions). The positions are then hedged. The hedging process entails offsetting the spot exposure with an equal but opposite position in the spot market. The hedging of the interest rate risk is more complex. This is driven by the exposure to yield curve shape changes and also the impact of time decay on the value of positions. Interest rate risk is, in practice, hedged in one of two ways. The first entails transactional hedging (described in this Chapter). The second entails portfolio hedging (described in Chapter 14).

Transactional hedging requires each transaction to be risk mapped into equivalent cash security positions. The positions are then offset by opposite positions in either cash instruments, or futures contracts on the cash instruments. This approach can be used to establish hedges for the risks in conventional instruments (FRAs, currency forwards, interest rate and currency forwards).

Implementation of the transactional hedging approach requires the ability to match the price changes in the position and the price changes in the hedging instrument using a process of matching the price sensitivity. Market considerations require dealers to use a variety of techniques to both optimise and control the risk of these specific hedges.

# 14
# Hedging Interest Rate Risk – Portfolios

## 1 Overview

Interest rate risk may be hedged in two ways. Under the first approach, interest rate risk *in individual transactions* is specifically hedged as transactions are completed *on a transaction by transaction basis*. Under the second approach, the interest rate exposure is hedged on a portfolio basis.

The transaction hedging approach entails the following steps:

• When a position is entered into, the corresponding hedge (usually consisting of debt instruments or futures contracts) is established.

• When a matching transaction is arranged, the hedge is unwound to coincide with the entry into the matching or offsetting transaction.

The transaction hedging approach requires the original transaction to be matched relatively closely by the offsetting transaction in terms of notional principal, interest rate levels (adjusted for hedge profits and losses), final maturity and payments dates. Under this approach, for example, a 5 year interest rate swap is matched *with another 5 year swap (or similar transaction)*. The transaction hedging approach is predicated on matching transactions (this approach was outlined in Chapter 13).

The transaction hedging approach is relatively simple. However, it is relatively inflexible and does not accommodate non-generic swap transactions within the framework. The portfolio approach to interest rate portfolio management evolved to overcome some of the difficulties associated with the transaction hedging approach. The approach entails hedging the *entire* portfolio of transactions *on an aggregated basis*. The relative inflexibility of the transaction hedging approach, its focus on individual transactions and the problem of hedge transaction costs (*as each transaction has to be hedged*), means that almost all dealer interest rate portfolios are now managed under some sort of portfolio approach to hedging. The portfolio approach to interest rate risk management is discussed in this Chapter.

Portfolio approaches model the existing portfolio of transactions by aggregating the individual cash flows. Portfolio value is determined by calculating the net present value of the cash flows within the portfolio. Present value of the portfolios is calculated using discount factors based on zero coupon interest rates based on the existing swap yield curve[1]. The net present value (the profit of the portfolio) is then hedged to preserve portfolio value. As new positions are added, the impact of the marginal transaction on the overall portfolio is calculated. Appropriate adjustments to portfolio hedges are implemented to continue to preserve the value of the portfolio.

The portfolio approach to interest rate management has itself evolved over time. The earliest portfolio approaches were based on a duration based hedging approach. Under this approach, the net duration of the cash flows in the portfolio is calculated. Hedges are implemented to offset the duration of the portfolio. Duration in this context functions as a measure of the interest rate risk within the portfolio required to be managed.

The duration based approach requires a number of assumptions that in practice are difficult to justify[2]. This created an impetus to new approaches to portfolio management including the generalised cash flow approach. Under the generalised cash flow approach, portfolio risk is measured in terms of the change in portfolio value as a result of movements in interest rates at specified yield curve points and over time. The risk is hedged using a regression based minimum variance hedging methodology that seeks to address the problems of basis risk in interest rate risk management.

The portfolio approach has the advantage of being flexible as well as reducing transaction costs. The portfolio approach's emphasis on *cash flows* rather than transactions is also advantageous in that it accords with the evolution of the derivatives business itself. Derivative activity is increasingly focused on managing and transmuting characteristics of streams of cash flows. A central element in the portfolio approach is that it allows the portfolio manager to determine the risk of the portfolio, and then establish the impact of adding various hedge instruments or new transactions to the existing portfolio in terms of profit and loss and risk characteristics. This allows a greater degree of precision in the measurement of the risk that the portfolio carries, the risk to be hedged and also facilitates more accurate pricing of new transactions.

---

[1]   For discussion of the derivation of the zero coupon swap curve, see Chapter 5.
[2]   For a discussion of duration, see Chapter 5.

In this Chapter, portfolio hedging techniques (duration based approaches and generalised cash flow approaches) are described. The structure of this Chapter is as follows:

- The portfolio approach is outlined.
- Duration based portfolio hedging is discussed.
- Generalised cash flow approaches are described.
- The inter-relationship between different approaches to interest rate risk management is considered.

In examining portfolio hedging techniques, it is important to note that to some extent the valuation technology used to measure value of a portfolio is objective specific. In this regard, one aspect of valuation is the valuation of transaction portfolios in the context of a purchase of the portfolio by a dealer. Specific issues relating to the valuation of portfolios for the purpose of purchase are considered in Appendix A to this chapter.

## 2 Portfolio Hedging

The key feature of the portfolio approach to hedging interest rate transactions is the treatment of the transactions as a portfolio of *fungible* cash flows. The basic principles underlying the implementation of the portfolio approach are consistent with the integrated portfolio management approach[3].

The key measure of portfolio value utilising this approach is identical to that applicable under the basic hedging approach:

Present value (net) = present value (asset inflows)

− present value (liability outflows)

Present value in this context signifies the discounted value of the cash inflows and outflows within the portfolio, using the relevant discount factors or zero coupon rates. The portfolio manager's objective is to maintain and increase the net present value of the portfolio.

The application of the portfolio approach necessitates the following steps:

- **Aggregation of cash flows** – all known transaction cash flows (irrespective of origin) are included in the portfolio. Cash inflows and outflows are typically aggregated into points of time ("time buckets", "time vectors" or "maturity points").
- **Valuation of portfolio cash flows** – the value of the portfolio is then determined by discounting the cash flows using zero coupon or spot yield rates.

---

[3] See Chapter 12.

- **Determination of portfolio risk** – portfolio risk is determined by measuring the change in portfolio value for changes in the zero coupon interest rates. Portfolio value is measured for parallel yield curve movements as well as non-parallel yield curve movement (that is, changes in the shape of the yield curve). Additional sensitivities such as to changes in spread relationships (swap spreads) may be measured to estimate portfolio risk. This risk measured is the *marginal* risk position of the portfolio. The portfolio approach is predicated on the analysis of the risk position *of the portfolio in aggregate*. The theory underlying this approach is that various cash flows within the portfolio at least partially offset *other* cash flows within the portfolio, effectively creating offsets and internal hedges. The marginal risk measured provides an indication of the aggregated risk of the portfolio, that is, a summation of the net positive and negative changes in value in individual cash flows.
- **Hedging of portfolio risk** – the basic hedge strategy is:

  Change in value of hedge $=$ (negative) change in value of portfolio.

This implies that the portfolio manager will buy or sell interest rate instruments that create the *opposite* exposure in the hedge portfolio to that measured in the portfolio. The consequence of the hedge strategy is to preserve the value of the portfolio by ensuring that the changes in value of the portfolio are offset by equal but opposite changes in value in the hedge. A variety of instruments can be used to hedge portfolio risk. These include cash/physical securities, futures on physical securities and other derivatives (including swaps)[4].

# 3   Duration Hedging Approach

## 3.1   *Approach*

One approach to interest rate portfolio management entails hedging the interest rate risk using duration techniques[5]. The utility of duration[6] as a measure of interest rate risk derives from the following factors:
- The modified duration of a stream of cash flows provides a representation of the percentage price change corresponding to a given change in yield (in effect the interest rate risk).

---

[4]   The issues relating to the use of one or other type of hedging instrument are not significantly different between the transaction hedging and portfolio approach to risk management.

[5]   For a discussion of duration, see Chapter 5.

[6]   The duration used throughout this Section is modified duration based on zero coupon interest rates.

- Duration is additive; that is, the duration of a set of assets or liabilities is equal to the weighted average of the duration of each component asset and liability (the weights being equal to the proportion that each asset or liability represents of the total asset or liability portfolio).
- Instruments, streams of cash flows or portfolios with equivalent duration can be regarded as equivalent in risk terms. This implies that instruments or portfolios with the same duration will experience similar changes in value for a given change in interest rates (provided the assumptions underlying the concept of duration are satisfied).

These features allow duration concepts to be used in portfolio management. The duration approach to portfolio management is implemented as follows:

- Aggregate portfolio cash flows are determined.
- Duration of the cash inflows and cash outflows is determined separately.
- Net duration of the portfolio is determined.

The net portfolio duration represents the interest rate risk profile of the portfolio. In order to insulate the portfolio from the risk of changes in value as a result of interest rate movements, a hedge portfolio is constructed through the purchase and sale of physical securities, futures contracts or other swap/derivative products. The hedge portfolio is created with the specific objective of having the *same* duration as the net duration of the portfolio. The sole exception is that the hedge is structured to change value in an opposite direction to the underlying portfolio for a given movement in interest rates. **Exhibit 14.1** sets out an example of using duration concepts to hedge an interest rate portfolio.

---

**Exhibit 14.1 Duration-Based Hedge**

**1. Portfolio Structure**

Assume the following portfolio of interest rate swaps[7] entered into with identical commencement dates:

- Pay fixed at 10.00% pa annual/receive 6 month LIBOR on notional principal of $100 million for 1 year.
- Receive fixed at 10.20% pa annual/pay 6 month LIBOR on notional principal of $50 million for 1 year.
- Receive fixed at 10.20% pa semi-annual/pay 6 month LIBOR on notional principal of $50 million for 1 year.

---

[7] In this example, interest rate swaps are used to illustrate the concept of a duration based hedge. The approach is identical, irrespective of the source of the underlying interest rate risk.

The structure of the portfolio together with its discounted value (at current zero coupon discount rates) is summarised below:

| Maturity (days) | Cash Flow ($) | Zero Coupon Rate (% pa semi-annual) | Present Value ($) |
|---|---|---|---|
| 182 | 2,550,000 | 5.00 | 2,487,973 |
| 366 | 52,550,000 | | |
| | 55,100,000 | | |
| | (110,000,000) | | |
| Net | (2,350,000) | 10.00 | (2,130,950) |
| **Total** | 200,000 | | 357,024 |

The floating rate (6 month LIBOR) is ignored as the cash flows are perfectly matched as to amount and re-pricing dates.

## 2. Portfolio Interest Sensitivity

The modified duration of the portfolio is then calculated using zero coupon rates as follows:

| | Receipts | Payments | Net |
|---|---|---|---|
| **Modified Duration** | 0.9406 | 0.9524 | −0.0118 |

## 3. Hedging Interest Rate Risk

Utilising the modified duration measure (calculated using zero coupon yields), hedging of the portfolio requires a transaction with a positive modified duration of 0.0118 to offset the negative modified duration of the portfolio of the same amount.

Assume the following bond is to be used to hedge the position:

| | |
|---|---|
| Coupon | 0% pa |
| Maturity | 1 year |
| Yield to Maturity | 10% pa semi-annual |
| Modified Duration | 0.9524 |

In order to hedge the portfolio risk, it would be necessary to purchase $1,238,975 of one year bonds (calculated as $100,000,000 \times 0.0118/0.9524$).

## 4. Hedge Performance

Assume yields rise uniformly across the yield curve by 1 bps pa. The value of the portfolio will alter as set out below:

| Maturity (days) | Cash Flow ($) | Zero Coupon Rate (% pa semi-annual) | Present Value ($) | Delta or PVBP ($) |
|---|---|---|---|---|
| 182 | 2,550,000 | 5.01 | 2,487,852 | (121) |
| 366 | (2,350,000) | 10.01 | (2,130,746) | 203 |
| **Total** | 200,000 | | 357,106 | 82 |

The change in value of the portfolio and hedge is as follows:

|  | At Original Rates | After Rates Change | Change |
|---|---|---|---|
| **Value of Portfolio ($)** | 357,024 | 357,106 | 82 |
| **Value of Hedge ($)** | 1,123,787 | 1,123,680 | (107) |
| **Net ($)** |  |  | (25) |

The change in the value of the portfolio and hedge offset, although not exactly. The impact of the hedge reduces the potential volatility of the value of the portfolio.

The hedge error arises from the weakness of duration as a measure of interest rate risk. The portfolio is duration matched but not cash flow matched. This means that the change in value in the underlying portfolio is influenced by changes in rates at both points of the yield curve. The hedge is only affected by changes in the 1 year zero interest rates. This creates the hedge mismatch. The steep slope of the yield curve exacerbates this hedge error.

Management of a duration hedge will require periodic re-balancing. This reflects the fact that the duration of the portfolio will alter over time; reflecting changes in interest rates, changes in the shape of the yield curve and the passage of time. This is the effect of convexity. Adjustment of the hedge is further complicated by the fact that changes in the duration of the underlying portfolio will not necessarily be the same as the change in the duration of the hedge. This will require the hedge portfolio to be re-balanced. This process of re-balancing will incur trading and transaction costs, which will decrease the efficiency of the hedge.

## 3.2   Duration Based Hedging – Issues

The major benefits of using duration to manage the interest rate risk profile of a portfolio include:
- Reduction in portfolio basis risk.
- Overcoming the lack of availability of hedge instruments.
- Lower transaction costs of hedging.

The major issues relating to the use of the duration hedging approach relates to problems in duration itself as a measure of interest rate risk. Duration calculations make a number of assumptions including:
- Duration measures only hold for *small* changes in interest rates.
- Duration assumes a flat term structure of interest rates.
- Duration assumes parallel yield curve shifts.

The change in price in the underlying portfolio and the hedge instruments for a given change in interest rates is non-linear. This reflects the convexity of the interest rate function. Convexity measures the curvature of price plotted against yield. In essence, convexity is a measure of how much an instrument or portfolio's price-yield curve deviates from a straight line. The fact that duration only holds for very small changes in interest rates necessitates frequent re-balancing or adjustment of the hedge as interest rates change. One advantage of the generalised cash flow approaches described in the following Section is that they can be used to create convexity adjusted hedges.

Yield curve shape changes are also problematic. Duration based hedging approaches assume perfect substitutability across the yield curve. This implies a capacity to hedge any portion of the yield curve with another portion of the yield curve. In practice, attempting to hedge a portfolio of cash flows with a few instruments creates the probability of severe mismatches of cash flows and cash flow timing. This may create significant residual risk to non-parallel changes in the yield curve. Multi factor duration models have been developed and are used to seek to overcome this problem.

Two alternative ways to deal with the yield curve problem are:
- Partitioning the portfolio into maturity bands.
- Using co-variance across various points of the yield curve.

Under the partitioning approach, the duration of the portfolio is calculated both for the portfolio as a whole, and for specific maturity blocks within the portfolio. Using this partitioning approach, the specific risk component in each portion of the yield curve is determined. An appropriate mixture of hedge instruments representative of the yield curve as a whole is used to minimise the portfolio risk to yield curve changes.

An alternative method of handling changes in the term structure of interest rates is to consider the cash flow at each of the relevant points in the portfolio as zero coupon securities, and to assess their individual price volatility. Simultaneously, the correlation between rates at different maturities on the yield curve is determined (in essence, a parallel yield curve movement assumes that movements between various points of the yield curve are perfectly correlated). Given known correlation between various maturity points in the yield curve based on historical data, a covariance matrix of price volatility can be established. Using this approach, the volatility of a portfolio of cash flows can be measured, incorporating likely relationships across the term structure of interest rates. This approach can be refined by adjusting the amount of any hedge instrument used to incorporate the correlation of the hedge with the estimated risk of yield curve shape changes within the portfolio as a whole.

In using duration as a means of measuring the interest rate risk within a swap portfolio, it is useful to classify market interest rate movements into two types:

- **Systematic movements** – that is, consistent with statistically determined relationships.
- **Non-systematic movements** – that is, residual interest rate movement.

It should be noted that duration hedge matching immunises the portfolio from systematic movements in interest rates. For duration hedge matching to be efficient, it is necessary to assume that non-systematic movements in market interest rates are random or are normally distributed. These are assumptions that in practice are difficult to realise.

# 4 Generalised Cash Flow Hedging Approach[8]

## 4.1 Approach

The generalised cash flow hedging approach to portfolio management is an extension of the portfolio approach. It seeks to overcome some of the difficulties identified with duration based approaches.

The key features of the generalised cash flow approach include:

- It is predicated on a complete aggregated portfolio approach and is not based on matching up or offsetting particular cash flows or transactions.
- It focuses on identifying specific risk characteristics of portfolio (measured as portfolio delta, gamma and theta)[9].
- It uses a regression based minimum variance hedging methodology.

The aggregation or portfolio approach underlying generalised cash flow techniques is similar to that applicable to duration based hedging approaches. The focus on specific risk characteristics of the portfolio seeks to overcome difficulties with using duration as a measure of interest rate sensitivity of portfolios.

---

[8] See Luedecke, Bernd P. "Measuring, Displaying and Hedging the Market Risk on a Swap" in Das, Satyajit (Editor) (1991) Global Swaps Market; IFR Publishing, London at Chapter 30. The concept is also similar to the concept of key rate duration or risk point methodology, see Dattatreya, Ravi "A Practical approach to Asset/Liability Management" in Fabbozzi, Frank J. and Konishi, Atsuo (Editors) (1991) Asset/Liability Management; Probus Publishing, Chicago; Ho, Thomas S.Y. "Key Rate Duration: Measures of Interest Rate Risk" (September 1992) Journal of Fixed Income 29–44.

[9] These terms have a similar meaning to that used in relation to options; see discussion in Chapters 12 and 15.

In particular, it seeks to address the issues relating to convexity. Similarly, the regression based minimum variance hedging methodology seeks to overcome some of the problems of non-parallel yield curve shift and basis risk entailed in hedging.

The generalised cash flow approach is sometimes referred to as the present value of a basis point ("PVBP") or delta approach. This reflects the fact that the delta of an instrument or cash flow (the value impact of changes in the underlying asset price) can be estimated using PVBP (rather than calculating the partial derivative of the instrument value function).

## 4.2 Utilising Generalised Cash Flow Hedging Approach

### 4.2.1 Overview

In practice, using the generalised cash flow approach entails a number of specific steps:

- As with duration based hedging approaches, portfolio cash flows are aggregated in accordance with the principles outlined previously.
- It is necessary then to identify the value functions of individual instruments and inputs such as financial market variables (interest rates), time and contractual features of specific instruments.
- The portfolio cash flows are valued by discounting back both cash inflows and outflows using zero coupon rates.
- The risk profile of the portfolio is measured calculating portfolio sensitivity to movements in interest rates. This risk profile is measured using delta, gamma and theta concepts.
- The portfolio management objective under the generalised cash flow approach is to preserve or increase portfolio present value. Hedging strategies are developed to protect portfolio present value. The objective in undertaking hedging transactions is to create a portfolio of transactions that will exhibit equal and opposite changes in value to that of the underlying portfolio itself for specified changes in interest rates. Typical hedge instruments used under the generalised cash flow approach are identical to those used in the case of transaction hedging and duration based hedging. The only major difference in hedging practice is to determine hedging coefficients which are designed to protect the portfolio and improve hedging efficiency through the capture of the impact of non-parallel shifts in the yield curve.

Key aspects of the generalised cash flow approach and its implementation are considered below.

## 4.2.2 Portfolio Risk Measures – Value Function Basis

The value function of any instrument is merely the mathematical technique used to value that instrument. The value function is the formula or algorithm that gives a dollar value of the instrument. For example, in the case of a bond it would be the normal bond price formula. Value functions for derivative products vary in complexity. The value function for interest rate derivatives is more complex. This reflects the fact that such transactions involve two components, being the simultaneous purchase and sale of two securities.

The inputs into the valuation function include:
- Interest rates, including the complete yield curve for the relevant security.
- Time.
- Specific contractual features of the instrument including face value, coupon rates, settlement practices etc.

Inputs into the value function (other than time) are determined by market forces. Two features of the inputs should be noted:
- Time represents a special input as it is only capable of progressing in a single direction.
- The contractual features of instruments do not necessarily change significantly. However, certain instruments such as interest rate swaps will have a specific contractual feature (such as the floating rate level) which must be reset periodically.

## 4.2.3 Delta – Gamma Risk

In the context of option pricing and risk measurement, the concept of delta is used to signify the sensitivity of the price of the option to changes in the price of the underlying asset. Under the generalised cash flow approach, delta is similarly used as a risk measure to facilitate monitoring the effect of changes in interest rates.

Delta in this context is defined as the change in value function resulting from a one basis point rise in an interest rate at a specific point on the yield curve. Mathematically, delta is the partial derivative of the instrument value function with respect to interest rates. A feature of delta is that changes in delta provide a measure of the convexity of the instrument price movements. This overcomes one of the major difficulties with using duration to measure interest rate risk.

The major significance of delta as a risk measurement construct is that it provides information about specific profits or losses to the portfolio for specific interest rate movements *at a given point in the yield curve*. The key characteristics of delta are

as follows:
- Zero delta signifies the portfolio is immune to interest rate movements; that is, it neither profits nor loses value as a result in movements in interest rates.
- Cash inflows have a negative delta while cash outflows have a positive delta. This is because long positions in the relevant security or cash inflows decrease in value as interest rates rise, or increase in value as interest rates fall. Conversely, short/sold positions in securities or cash outflows increase in value as interest rates rise, and decrease in value as interest rates fall.

The delta of any portfolio of cash flows is dynamic and is characterised by the following:
- Delta values change with changes in maturity (as a result of time decay).
- Delta values change with absolute levels of interest rates as well as changes in the shape of the yield curve.

In practice, the delta of any portfolio can be estimated by calculating the PVBP of the relevant cash flows.

In using delta, it should be noted that any portfolio has *multiple* deltas. The multiple deltas correspond to each point in the yield curve specified. This signifies that the value of the portfolio changes as a result of changes in interest rates *at each of the specific maturity points in the yield curve*. This effectively provides a profile of the risk within the portfolio to changes in the shape of the yield curve.

Gamma measures the *change in delta* for a given change in the underlying asset price for any instrument. Mathematically, gamma is the second partial derivative of the instrument value function with respect to interest rates. Gamma measures the degree to which portfolio delta will change. A large gamma of a portfolio indicates the potential for a portfolio delta to change rapidly when the relevant interest rate changes. In essence, gamma is a measure of how much risk or exposure the portfolio is subject to from a sudden and possibly discontinuous move in interest rates.

The concept of gamma risk is important in the risk management of options. The gamma of non-option instruments is relatively low. This reflects the fact that the delta of an asset or forward does not change significantly, at least for small movements in interest rates. In contrast, for option portfolios, gamma can be significant.

The significance of gamma within the generalised cash flow hedging approach to portfolio management is that of hedge efficiency. The portfolio may be immunised from interest rate risk by achieving delta neutrality. Delta neutrality, in this context, is usually achieved by creating a hedge portfolio that offsets the interest rate risk characteristics of the portfolio. Under these conditions, gamma measures the fact that for a given change in interest rates, the portfolio delta may change prior to the hedge being re-balanced to neutralise portfolio risk. In this sense, it measures the potential inefficiency or slippage of the hedge itself.

### 4.2.4   Theta/Time Decay Risk

Time decay will alter the value of the portfolio. The concept of changes in the value of an instrument as a result of the passage of time is well understood in the context of option pricing. Theta is the measure of time decay. Theta is defined as the change in value function as a result of the effluxion of time, assuming no change in interest rates. Mathematically, theta is the partial derivative of the instrument value function with respect to time. Theta is analogous to the portfolio's carry cost or a daily portfolio accrual.

Future cash inflows have positive thetas. Future cash outflows have negative thetas. This reflects the fact that the passage of time increases the value of cash inflows because of the declining time to maturity. Cash outflows have negative thetas, representing increasing present value of cash outflows as time to maturity decreases.

Theta is a function of:
- Slope of the yield curve (that is, changes in zero coupon discount rates).
- Time to maturity.

The slope effect on theta is particularly important[10]. Changes in the slope of the yield curve can alter portfolio theta/cash flow characteristics. Cash inflows can have negative thetas while outflows can have positive thetas as the shape of the yield curve changes.

Under normal circumstances, a future cash outflow will have a negative theta and a future cash inflow will have a positive theta. This reflects the fact that as time decays, the present value of both assets and liabilities increase. However, if the zero coupon yield curve is sufficiently negative, future cash outflows may exhibit positive theta and (vice versa) future cash inflows show negative theta. This will happen when a yield curve or a section of the yield curve rotates or flexes. This reflects the fact that the increase (decrease) in value of the relevant cash inflow (outflow) as a result of the passage of time is offset and exceeded by the higher discount rate applicable for the shorter maturity. While the sign of future cash flows in this situation may not have altered, the behaviour over time of the present value of those cash flows may change.

---

[10]   See Luedecke, Bernd "Weather Eye on Theta" (May 1991) Risk 35–38.

## 4.2.5    Generalised Cash Flow Approaches – In Practice

In practice, using the generalised cash flow approach to portfolio management necessitates a number of distinct steps:
- Determination of the portfolio delta, gamma and theta risk measures.
- Identifying portfolio risk from the measured portfolio risk characteristics.
- Establishment of hedges or addition of new transactions to reduce portfolio risk.

Portfolio delta and gamma are calculated consistent with the methodology outlined above. Deltas are calculated for each cash flow within the portfolio. The deltas are then summed to produce a delta profile for the entire portfolio. The global delta profile will provide information to the portfolio risk manager at two distinct levels:
- The total portfolio delta will show the overall sensitivity of the portfolio to a 1 bps increase in interest rates across the yield curve (effectively, a parallel yield curve shift). This information will be the summation of the deltas of all cash flows within the portfolio for changes in value corresponding to simultaneous and uniform changes in the relevant interest rates.
- Delta profiles are also available for movements in interest rates *at a specific point in the yield curve*. This is calculated by determining the change in value of the net cash flow for an increase of 1 bps in interest rates at that specific maturity point in the yield curve. This allows a precise measurement of the impact on portfolio value of movements at particular points of the yield curve. This provides information on the impact of non-parallel yield curve shifts within the portfolio.

This approach to portfolio delta measurement and analysis highlights the significant advantages of this approach to portfolio risk management including:
- The global portfolio delta allows the risk manager to analyse the overall portfolio risk (in effect, to absolute interest rate changes or parallel yield curve shifts).
- The calculation of delta individually for each cash flow at a maturity point within the portfolio allows analysis of yield curve risk. This facilitates the capacity to analyse and provide information on portfolio risk derived from non-parallel yield curve shifts. In fact, this type of analysis identifies the precise risk in the portfolio for *a given change in any one of the relevant interest rates used in valuing the portfolio*. The calculation of delta at each point in the yield curve facilitates analysis of every type of yield curve movement, including specific dangers in each individual point in the yield curve.
- This approach displays the specific risk characteristics of the portfolio to interest rate movements. This makes it feasible to use the portfolio delta analysis as the

basis for determining specific hedging strategies required to neutralise portfolio risk.

**Exhibit 14.2** sets out an example of the global delta profile of a portfolio using hypothetical data.

---

**Exhibit 14.2   Portfolio Global Delta Profile**

Assume an interest rate portfolio with the following cash flows over 12 years bucketed into 24 maturity vertices at 6 month intervals:

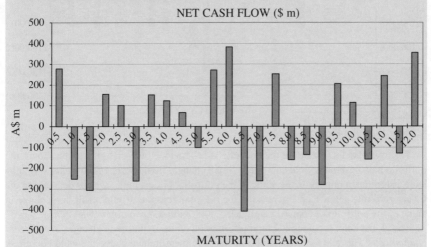

The portfolio is revalued using the following zero coupon swap rates:

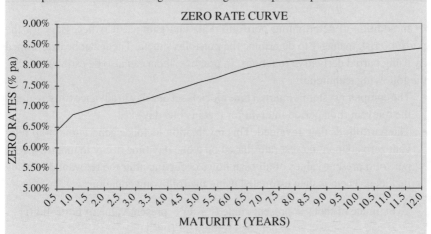

The delta (PVBP) of the overall portfolio and *at each maturity vertex* (for an increase in zero rates) is set out in the graph below:

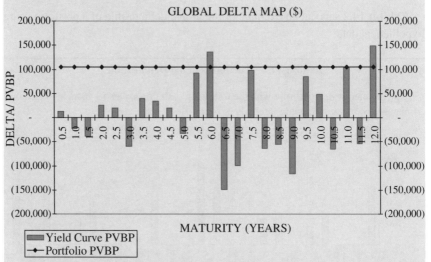

GLOBAL DELTA MAP ($)

MATURITY (YEARS)

Yield Curve PVBP
Portfolio PVBP

The overall delta (PVBP) of the portfolio is $104,868. However, as the graph shows, the portfolio has substantial yield curve risk. Small changes in *the shape of the yield curve* may have a significant impact on the value of the portfolio. For example, a 1 bps decrease in the 6 year zero rate and a 1 bps increase in the 6.5 year zero rate would result in a change in value of the portfolio of approximately $285,000 (*3 times the total portfolio delta*).

The global delta provides essential information on the exposure to changes *in each zero coupon rate*. This allows the portfolio manager to measure and hedge the yield curve risk in the portfolio (both parallel shifts and shape changes).

In addition to determining portfolio delta and gamma, it is necessary for the portfolio risk manager to determine the portfolio's theta. Theta can be determined by using partial derivative functions. In practice, theta can also be estimated using the following technique:

- The computer system's internal time clock is set one day in advance (this assumes the relevant time period interval for theta is one day).
- The portfolio is then revalued. This revaluation includes generation of all relevant zero coupon interest rates based on a one day time decay in maturity, with portfolio present values of all cash flows occurring after the relevant day being included. Theta is then estimated using the following equation:

$$\text{Estimate of theta} = \text{present value } (t + 1) - \text{present value of portfolio } (t) + \text{net cash settlement } (t + 1)$$

Where

t = today

t + 1 = tomorrow

Net cash settlement (t + 1) = the net cash flow settlements on existing transactions taking place tomorrow.

Management of a portfolio theta risk requires an understanding of the two components of portfolio theta – namely the slope effect and the simpler time effect. Dynamic variations in the slope of the yield curve, particularly at the point in time at which the zero coupon yield curve switches from being positively sloped to negatively sloped (or vice versa), can lead to significant changes in portfolio value. In order to hedge the portfolio against risk of changes as a result of time decay, the portfolio manager will need to add hedges or new transactions to the portfolio to offset the portfolio's theta characteristics.

For example, portfolios can occasionally be characterised by very large negative thetas with the consequent loss of portfolio value, often at a very rapid rate. Under these circumstances, the portfolio manager may seek to preserve portfolio values by entering into new transactions with *positive theta*. The new transactions themselves may well have *negative present value*; that is, they may be loss making transactions. However, such transactions may help minimise the portfolio's overall theta and preserve the *total* value of the portfolio[11].

Identification of the risk characteristics of the portfolio is only at a *specific point in time*. This reflects the fact that the risk characteristics of the portfolio are dynamic in nature. In this context, interaction of delta and theta is clearly pivotal. Portfolio risk management will, in practice, almost certainly require some trade-offs between the two.

In summary, the portfolio risk characteristics determined from the type of analysis discussed will be as follows:

- **Portfolio delta** – provides information on the *specific* interest rate movements that will affect portfolio value.
- **Portfolio gamma** – will identify specific interest rate movements that will affect the portfolio delta.
- **Portfolio theta** – measures the impact of time decay on the portfolio.

Once the portfolio risk characteristics have been determined, the portfolio risk manager will add hedges or new transactions to minimise the portfolio risk.

---

[11]  See Luedecke, Bernd "Weather Eye on Theta" (May 1991) Risk 35–38.

Where new transactions are proposed, the transactions will be assessed according not only to their individual present value or profit potential, but in accordance with their potential impact on the existing portfolio risk profile. The interaction between the existing portfolio and the new transaction will be reflected in the pricing of the transaction. For example, from a portfolio perspective, a relatively low value transaction may be able to be priced extremely attractively as it may impact positively on the value of the portfolio as a whole.

**Exhibit 14.3** sets out a simplified example of using the generalised cash flow approach to measuring and managing interest rate portfolio risk.

---

### Exhibit 14.3   Generalised Cash Flow Hedge

**1.  Portfolio Structure**
Assume the same portfolio of transactions as in **Exhibit 14.1**. The structure of the portfolio, together with its discounted value (using zero coupon rates), is summarised below:

| Maturity (days) | Cash Flow ($) | Zero Coupon Rate (% pa semi-annual) | Present Value ($) |
|---|---|---|---|
| 182 | 2,550,000 | 5.00 | 2,487,973 |
| 366 | (2,350,000) | 10.00 | −2,130,950 |
| **Total** | 200,000 | | 357,024 |

**2.  Portfolio Risk**
The interest rate sensitivity of the portfolio is measured by the portfolio delta for each point along the yield curve (PVBP for a 1 bps pa increase in the zero coupon rate). The change in portfolio value is set out below:

| Maturity (days) | Cash Flow ($) | Zero Coupon Rate (% pa semi-annual) | Present Value ($) | Delta or PVBP ($) |
|---|---|---|---|---|
| 182 | 2,550,000 | 5.01 | 2,487,852 | −121 |
| 366 | (2,350,000) | 10.01 | −2,130,746 | 203 |
| **Total** | 200,000 | | 357,106 | 82 |

The analysis indicates that the portfolio will increase in value by $82 for a 1 bps pa increase in zero coupon rates in each point in the yield curve (a parallel yield curve shift). This indicates that the portfolio will experience losses where zero coupon rates decrease across the yield curve.

The sensitivity of the portfolio to the shape of the yield curve can be measured by "toggling" the zero rates to alternatively steepen and flatten the yield curve.

The change in portfolio values for a 1 bps pa steepening in the yield curve is set out below:

| Maturity (days) | Cash Flow ($) | Zero Coupon Rate (% pa semi-annual) | Present Value ($) | Delta or PVBP ($) |
|---|---|---|---|---|
| 182 | 2,550,000 | 5.00 | 2,487,852 | 0 |
| 366 | (2,350,000) | 10.01 | −2,130,746 | 203 |
| **Total** | 200,000 | | 357,106 | 203 |

The change in portfolio values for a 1 bps pa flattening in the yield curve is set out below:

| Maturity (days) | Cash Flow ($) | Zero Coupon Rate (% pa semi-annual) | Present Value ($) | Delta or PVBP ($) |
|---|---|---|---|---|
| 182 | 2,550,000 | 5.01 | 2,487,852 | −121 |
| 366 | (2,350,000) | 10.00 | −2,130,746 | 0 |
| **Total** | 200,000 | | 357,106 | −121 |

The analysis indicates that the portfolio gains (loses) value from a steeper (flatter) yield curve.

The sensitivity of the portfolio to time decay is measured by re-setting the valuation timing one day forward. The change in portfolio values is set out below[12]:

| Maturity (days) | Cash Flow ($) | Zero Coupon Rate (% pa semi-annual) | Present Value ($) | Delta or PVBP ($) |
|---|---|---|---|---|
| 181 | 2,550,000 | 5.00 | 2,488,310 | 337 |
| 365 | (2,350,000) | 10.00 | −2,131,519 | −570 |
| **Total** | 200,000 | | 356,791 | −233 |

The analysis indicates that the portfolio loses significant value with the passage of time ($85,332 over the year).

## 3. Portfolio Hedging

The risk profile of the existing portfolio reflects the structure of deferred cash outflows and earlier cash inflows. This gives the portfolio the following risk profile (on a *ceteris paribus* basis):

- Portfolio value increases (decreases) for a rise (fall) in rates.
- Portfolio value increases (decreases) for a steeper (flatter) yield curve.

---

[12] Note that the net cash flow settlements in the portfolio would normally be included in the calculation of theta. In this case, there are no cash flows on the relevant day and they are therefore ignored.

- Portfolio value decreases with time as the effect of discounting on the future cash outflows decreases.

The hedge strategy adopted would be structured to offset the impact of the factors identified above. The analysis indicates that the portfolio should be hedged for a parallel 1bps pa yield curve rise by:
- Borrowing in 6 months.
- Investing in 12 months.

Assume that the following hedge instruments are available:
- Zero coupon cash deposits for 6 months[13]:
  Delta/PVBP (per $1 million at 5.00% pa) = US$47.59
  Theta (per $1 million for 1 day time decay) = US$130.76
- Zero coupon cash deposit for 1 year[14]:
  Delta/PVBP (per $1 million at 10.00% pa) = US$86.38
  Theta (per $1 million for 1 day time decay) = US$243.19

A number of hedge strategies can be posited:
- Hedge with the 6 or 12 month deposit.
- Hedge using *both* the 6 and 12 month deposit.

The use of both the 6 month and 12 month deposit is desirable as it replicates the zero coupon rates in the yield curve to which the portfolio is exposed.
The hedge would take the following structure:
- Borrow $2,542,551 in 6 months (take a deposit).
- Invest $2,350,081 in 12 months (make a deposit).

For a 1 bps pa uniform rise in interest rates, the portfolio will increase in value by $82. The hedge portfolio will change in value as follows:
- 6 month cash deposit – $121
- 12 month cash deposit – $(203)
- Net movement in hedge portfolio – $(82)

The composite hedge will provide protection against changes in the shape of the yield curve, as individual components of the hedge will offset changes in portfolio value at each maturity vertex.
The hedge has *net* time value of $239 per day that will offset the time decay of the portfolio.
As an alternative to the hedges using cash instruments, a hedge could be structured using a derivative. Borrowing 6 month cash and lending 12 month cash is equivalent to a bought $6 \times 12$ interest rate forward (sold $6 \times 12$ FRA). This means that the portfolio could be hedged by either buying, say 2 futures contracts (near month and the next contract), or selling the FRA.

---

[13] Based on 5% pa semi-annual yield, 182 day run and actual/actual day count.
[14] Based on 10% pa semi-annual yield, 366 day run and actual/actual day count.

## 4.3 Hedging Methodology

The hedging methodology implied by the generalised cash flow approach to portfolio management is that the risk measured by delta and theta is offset by entering into transactions with equal but exactly opposite delta and theta. This approach is the same as that applicable under either the transaction hedging approach or duration based hedging approaches. However, an interesting feature of the generalised cash flow approach is its capacity to incorporate a regression-based minimum variance hedging methodology. This is designed to overcome some of the difficulties of hedging portfolios.

The approach to global delta measurement effectively provides a detailed mechanism to hedging the overall portfolio of cash flows. The present value of the existing portfolio depends on the interest rates defined in the zero coupon yield curve. A hedge for the portfolio devoid of basis or yield curve risk is constructed by holding a mixture of instruments with different maturities. In essence, the hedge is constructed by using debt instruments *that are valued off an identical set of interest rates as the portfolio itself*. Under this approach, the portfolio manager must trade in instruments that replicate the zero coupon rates in the yield curve. This is to create a relatively risk free hedge to immunise the portfolio's risk characteristics.

Major difficulties with this approach include high transaction costs. This is because a wide variety of instruments will need to be traded (in theory, instruments corresponding to each maturity vertex would be needed). In addition, this hedging approach may use significant balance sheet capacity.

In practice, the problems can be overcome to an extent by the approach of partitioning the yield curve into bands/defined maturity vertices and trading in selected instruments. This provides the required hedging with lower transaction costs but (hopefully minimal) loss of hedge efficiency. In practice, traders minimise the number of hedging instruments used. In addition, for balance sheet reasons, traders prefer to use futures contracts in preference to cash debt instruments. Where this approach is favoured, the generalised cash flow approach to portfolio management can be extended to encompass a regression based minimum variance hedging methodology. This methodology is quite similar to the covariance approach described above in the connection of duration based hedging approaches.

The problem of hedging under these conditions is the lack of perfect correlation (either positive or negative) between changes in the interest rate of the instruments being hedged, and changes in the interest rate *of the hedging instrument*. Basis risk is the absence of a perfect linear relationship between movements in interest rates as between different instruments. This deficiency can be overcome by determining the correlation between each of the individual interest rates in the zero coupon yield curve and the hedging instruments that are to be used. The objective is to exploit the correlation that exists to derive the correct number of hedging contracts to maximise hedge efficiency and minimise basis risk.

This approach entails implementing the following steps:

*   Historical data (usually daily) on every rate used to value the portfolio is collected and organised into time series matrixes.
*   Historical data on the relevant hedging instruments is also similarly collated into time series matrixes.
*   Daily changes (that is, today's value minus yesterday's value) in each time series are determined.
*   Simple (ordinary least squares) regressions for each of the variables constructed are performed. Regressions performed include simple single explanatory variable regressions, as well as possible combinations of two explanatory variables, and multiple explanatory variable regressions[15].

The regressions performed need to be undertaken regularly. Some traders perform the regressions daily, reflecting the fact that one day's additional information has been added to the information set. This re-computation is designed to counter the fact that the relationship between the various rates varies over time. Frequent re-computation re-estimating the relationships whenever a new observation is available is designed to counteract this problem of changing correlation. In practice, depending on the size of the time series, each additional day's information will have minimal impact on regression results. Consequently, some traders perform these re-computations at less frequent intervals (say, monthly or weekly).

The technique outlined above allows construction of several linear basis relationships relating changes in the value of the hedging instrument to changes in each of the rates to be hedged. The portfolio manager then reviews the model equation and generally selects the most highly correlated hedging instruments to hedge individual interest rates. The hedging coefficients implied are then used to determine the number of hedge instruments required to hedge identified risk positions at each maturity vertex in the yield curve.

The approach to hedge management has a number of advantages:

*   The technology is extremely flexible. The trader can exercise his or her discretion in choosing both the most accurate and best correlated model equation to establish and maintain the hedge. A particular feature in this context is that the re-estimation of the relationships allows the trader to adopt the best hedging instrument *at any given point in time.*

---

[15]   Please note that there should be no constant term intercept in any of these regressions.

- The trader can minimise transaction costs by choosing between hedge instruments with similar correlation properties, but different transaction costs and balance sheet utilisation considerations.
- The hedging approach is perfectly consistent with the overall objective of managing the total risk profile of the portfolio *at the margin*. Hedges are constructed on the basis of the highest degree of efficiency available to manage the residual risk of the portfolio.
- The hedging approach provides a consistent and accurate method for pricing *new* transactions off the cost of the hedge. Based on available hedging coefficients, zero coupon rates can be predicted to relatively high degrees of tolerance. In fact, this is a useful check upon and affirmation of the basic methodology, as it allows frequent re-calibration of the basic methodology.

The major difficulty with this particular technology is that relationships that exist between various interest rates may not be stable over time. However, the linear relationships derived by the regression procedure have a certain minimum residual variance property. This means that tomorrow's relationships are accurately reflected in the sample from which the regressions have been computed (a necessary assumption common to most statistical analysis). Using any other set of coefficients would add more variability to the value of the combined position than the minimum variance technique outlined. In practice, traders will typically "trade" the hedge by maintaining delta neutrality by taking positions in respect of anticipated movements in the hedging coefficients. In effect, an advantage of the generalised cash flow hedging approach is that such a positioning approach to hedge management is not precluded. The availability of model implied hedging coefficients allows quantification of the degree of additional risk assumed in trading the hedge.

# 5  Risk Management Approaches – Comparison

The three methods of managing swap portfolios identified (the transaction hedging approach, the duration based hedging approach and the generalised cash flow approach) have significant differences and correspondingly, different advantages and disadvantages.

The transaction hedging approach requires close matching of the offsetting swaps in terms of maturity, interest rate levels (after adjustment for hedge profits and losses) as well as notional principal amounts. The advantage of the transaction hedging approach is that it is relatively low risk. Individual positions are identified, and profitability determined for each transaction, as basically the transaction cash flows and the hedge flows are capable of being determined objectively. The main disadvantage with the basic hedging approach is its relative inflexibility, making it difficult to undertake complex or non-generic transaction structures. An additional disadvantage is the higher transaction costs, as each transaction is separately hedged.

The transaction hedging approach is particularly relevant and useful in the context of transactions that are booked by traders on an assignment basis. Under these transactions, the dealer would commit to one part of the matching pair of transactions, with the intention of assigning the position to or entering into an offsetting transaction with the eventual counterparty when this counterparty was located. In the interim pre-closeout period, the dealer would maintain an individual hedge that would be unwound at the time of the assignment/matching transaction. Consequently, the transaction hedging approach is likely to be favoured by dealers who prefer to operate on an assignment basis (either assigning transaction or exactly matching trades). In practice, this approach would be rare.

The duration based portfolio hedging approach has the advantage that it is predicated on a pure cash flow approach. The major advantage of the duration based portfolio approach is that it gives the trader the flexibility of transacting non-generic or complex structures. This reflects the fact that the portfolio-based approach does not focus on an individual transaction. The focus is on a stream of cash flows. This means that each new cash flow booked in the portfolio can be aggregated with other cash flows, and the residual risk managed. This means that the trader is not concerned about matching equal but opposite transactions. This allows the trader to incur greater mismatches, and to manage the risks of these mismatches. Duration based hedging approaches also have the advantage of improving risk management practices and minimising transaction costs through the practice of hedging marginal risk positions only. The improvement in management of portfolio risk is achieved only at the expense of assuming the risk of the assumptions underlying duration itself as a measure of interest rate risk.

However, with any portfolio based approach, the profitability of individual transactions is considerably more difficult to establish. Profitability can only be meaningfully calculated on the basis of overall portfolio performance rather than for individual components of the portfolio. Profitability on an individual transaction is based on the marginal contribution of individual transactions to portfolio earnings.

The generalised cash flow hedging approach combines elements of the duration based approach with pure statistically based risk management techniques. It shares some of the same advantages and disadvantages as the duration based hedging approach. A major advantage of the generalised cash flow approach is its flexibility. In addition, it allows hedging to be undertaken within a unified risk management framework and facilitates continuous dynamic hedging of portfolio risk.

A common criticism of the generalised cash flow approach is the assumption of higher levels of basis risk relative to other techniques for portfolio management. In reality this is not correct. All techniques of hedging essentially require the substitution of outright risk to movements in financial market variables for basis risk. The generalised cash flow approach relies on the assumption that the experience of the recent past is a reasonable basis for predicting future relationships between interest rates. A similar problem exists in relation to other hedging techniques. For example, duration based measures of interest rate risk only hold for small movements in interest rates. Where transaction hedging approaches are used, portfolio risk is matched by purchasing or selling relevant hedge instruments. The amount of the hedge is determined based on a hedge ratio calculated by equating the PVBP movements in the portfolio and the hedge instrument. This approach assumes that the PVBP of the two instruments move identically (that is, there is no convexity). In practice, this is only infrequently the case.

The generalised cash flow hedging approach has a significant advantage in that it is based on modelling the relationship between multiple time series of financial market variables. This is in marked contrast to most available hedging techniques that typically concentrate on a single time series. The difference in approach is, from a statistical view point, the substitution of multivariate time series analysis for univariate time series analysis.

The problem of determination of individual versus aggregate profitability also exists in the case of generalised cash flow approaches. A significant feature of duration based and generalised cash flow hedging approaches is the tendency to show a significantly different perspective of risk and profitability of the portfolio. An advantage in this regard is that it enables the sensitivity of the portfolio to be tested to changes in pricing and portfolio structure.

# 6 Performance Measurement

In a portfolio context, the measurement of performance of the portfolio requires a specific approach. Performance measurement in this context can be defined as the decomposition of total portfolio returns over a given period of time into components of the return.

Traditionally, the basic concept underlying measurement of earnings has been traditional accounting accrual concepts. This would entail accruing interest components of transactions and bringing earnings to account within an accrual accounting framework.

Duration based and generalised cash flow hedging approaches to portfolio management effectively preclude application of such techniques for portfolio performance measurement and analysis. Performance measurement under these approaches is based on a mark-to-market approach.

This requires a return over a given period to be defined as the net change in the present value in all portfolio assets and liabilities. This can be expressed as:

$$R(t1 - t0) = [\text{PV of Cash Inflows (t1)} - \text{PV of Cash Inflows (t0)}]$$
$$- [\text{PV of cash Inflows (t1)} - \text{PV of Cash Outflows (t0)}]$$
$$+ \text{Net Cash Inflows (Outflows) (t1)}$$

Where:

$R(t1 - t0)$ = return over period from time t0 to t1

PV of Cash Inflows (t1) = present value of all portfolio inflows at time t1

PV of Cash Inflows (t0) = present value of all portfolio inflows at time t0

PV of Cash Outflows (t1) = present value of all portfolio outflows at time t1

PV of Cash Outflows (t0) = present value of all portfolio outflows at time t0

Net Cash Inflows (Outflows) (t1) = net cash settlement (inflows or outflows)
at t1

An example of using this type of present valuing concept to measure portfolio earnings is set out in **Exhibit 14.4**. As will be evident from a review of the basic approach, the passage of time and the addition of transactions to the portfolio increasingly complicate the problem of obtaining an accurate present value estimate of portfolio earnings. Detailed analysis of changes in portfolio value is made more difficult. This difficulty is further complicated as additional instruments are added to the portfolio.

---

**Exhibit 14.4    Swap Portfolio Earnings and Performance Measurement**[16]

**1.   Example 1 – Matched Interest Rate Swaps**

Assume a portfolio of two matched interest rate swaps as follows:
* $1,000,000 notional principal 1 year swap where the dealer receives fixed at 10.00% pa semi-annual and pays 6 month LIBOR (Swap 1).

---

[16]   See Lawton, William P "Swap Portfolio Attribution and Analysis" in Boris, Antl (Ed) (1988) Euromoney Swap Finance Service Update II; Euromoney Publications, London at Chapter 5.

- $1,000,000 notional principal 1 year swap where it pays fixed at 9.00% pa semi-annual and receives 6 month LIBOR (Swap 2).

Initial 6 month LIBOR for both transactions is set at 8.00% pa.
The portfolio cash flows are summarised below:

| | Swap 1 | | Swap 2 | |
|---|---|---|---|---|
| **Time to Maturity (days)** | **Fixed Rate ($) (at 10.00% pa)** | **Floating Rate ($) (at 5.00% pa)** | **Fixed Rate ($) (at 9.00% pa)** | **Floating Rate ($) (at 5.00% pa)** |
| 183 | 50,137 | (40,667) | (45,123) | 40,667 |
| 365 | 49,863 | | (44,877) | |

The net cash flows of the portfolio are as follows:

| Time to Maturity (days) | Net Cash Flows ($) |
|---|---|
| 183 | 5,014 |
| 365 | 4,986 |

In order to estimate the portfolio earnings over a period of 7 days, the portfolio value is measured at the current date and after 7 days:

| Time to Maturity (days) | Zero Coupon Rate (% pa) | Net Cash Flows ($) | Present Values of Net Cash Flows ($) |
|---|---|---|---|
| 183 | 8.00 | 5,014 | 4,824 |
| 365 | 10.00 | 4,986 | 4,533 |
| | **Total** | 10,000 | 9,357 |

| Time to Maturity (days) | Zero Coupon Rate (% pa) | Net Cash Flows ($) | Present Values of Net Cash Flows ($) |
|---|---|---|---|
| 176 | 8.00 | 5,014 | 4,831 |
| 358 | 10.00 | 4,986 | 4,541 |
| | **Total** | 10,000 | 9,372 |

Initially, the present value of the portfolio is $9,357 (the income on the transactions). The present value of the portfolio after 7 days is $9,372. This means that the increase in the portfolio value over the 7 days is $15 (this equates to the actual income attributable to this period).

## 2. Example 2 – Unmatched Interest Rate Swap with Portfolio Hedges

Assume the following variation on the above portfolio:

- Swap 1 is entered into.
- The swap is hedged with the short sale of $1,000,000 face value of 9.00% pa annual coupon 1 year bonds trading at 9.00% pa. The proceeds of the short sale are invested at 7.00% pa on an overnight basis through the repo market. The first 6 month LIBOR rate is set at 8.00% pa semi-annual.
- Swap 2 is dealt in 7 days but for a notional principal of $500,000. As rates have moved, the fixed rate payable on the swap is now 9.00% pa semi-annual. The first 6 month LIBOR rate is set at 8.00% pa semi-annual.
- At the time Swap 2 is entered into, 50% of the hedge is closed at a yield of 8% pa. The hedge results in a loss of $4,630.

The portfolio cash flows are summarised below. The cash flows from the two swaps are as follows:

| Time to Maturity (days) | Swap 1 | | Swap 2 | | Net Cash Flows ($) |
| | Fixed Rate ($) (at 10.00% pa) | Floating Rate ($) (at 8.00% pa) | Fixed Rate ($) (at 9.00% pa) | Floating Rate ($) (at 8.00% pa) | |
| --- | --- | --- | --- | --- | --- |
| 0 | | | | | |
| 7 | | | | | |
| 183 | 50,137 | (40,667) | | | 9,470 |
| 190 | | | (22,562) | 20,333 | (2,228) |
| 365 | 49,863 | | | | 49,863 |
| 372 | | | (22,438) | | (22,438) |
| | | | | Total | 34,667 |

The hedge cash flows are as follows:

| Time to Maturity (days) | Closed Hedge ($500,000) | | | Open Hedge ($500,000) | | Net Cash Flows ($) |
| | Fixed Rate ($) (at 9.00% pa) | Investment ($) (at 7.00% pa) | Hedge Gains & Losses ($) | Fixed Rate ($) (at 9.00% pa) | Investment ($) (at 7.00% pa) | |
| --- | --- | --- | --- | --- | --- | --- |
| 0 | 500,000 | (500,000) | | 500,000 | (500,000) | – |
| 7 | (500,863) | 500,671 | (4,630) | | | (4,822) |
| 183 | | | | (22,562) | 17,548 | (5,014) |
| 190 | | | | | | – |
| 365 | | | | (22,438) | 17,452 | (4,986) |
| 372 | | | | (863) | 671 | (192) |
| | | | | | Total | (15,014) |

The portfolio cash flows (inclusive of the hedge) are as follows:

| Time to Maturity (days) | Portfolio Cash Flows ($) | Hedge Cash Flows ($) | Net Cash Flows ($) |
|---|---|---|---|
| 0 | | | |
| 7 | | (4,822) | (4,822) |
| 183 | 9,470 | (5,014) | 4,457 |
| 190 | (2,228) | – | (2,228) |
| 365 | 49,863 | (4,986) | 44,877 |
| 372 | (22,438) | (192) | (22,630) |
| **Total** | 34,667 | (15,014) | 19,653 |

In order to estimate the portfolio earnings over a period of 7 days (between spot plus 7 days and spot plus 14 days), the portfolio value is measured at those two dates. The results are set out below.

The value of the portfolio at spot plus 7 days is:

| Time to Maturity (days) | Zero Coupon Rate (% pa) | Net Cash Flows ($) | Present Values of Net Cash Flows ($) |
|---|---|---|---|
| 0 | | (4,821) | (4,821) |
| 176 | 8.00 | 4,457 | 4,294 |
| 183 | 8.04 | (2,228) | (2,144) |
| 358 | 9.00 | 44,877 | 41,239 |
| 365 | 9.05 | (22,630) | (20,752) |
| **Total** | | 19,654 | 17,817 |

The value of the portfolio at spot plus 14 days is:

| Time to Maturity (days) | Zero Coupon Rate (% pa) | Net Cash Flows ($) | Present Values of Net Cash Flows ($) |
|---|---|---|---|
| 169 | 8.00 | 4,457 | 4,301 |
| 176 | 8.04 | (2,228) | (2,147) |
| 351 | 9.00 | 44,877 | 41,308 |
| 358 | 9.05 | (22,630) | (20,787) |
| **Total** | | 24,475 | 22,675 |

The value must be adjusted for the realised loss on the portfolio of $4,822 (loss on the bond and the associated funding cost/investment return). This reduces the portfolio present value to $17,853.

The present value of the portfolio at spot plus 7 days is $17,817 (the income on the transactions). The present value of the portfolio after an additional 7 days is $17,853. This means that the increase in the portfolio value over the 7 days is $36 (this equates to the actual income attributable to this period).

# 7 Summary

Interest rate risk may be hedged on a portfolio basis. Portfolio approaches model the existing portfolio of transactions by aggregating the individual fixed and floating rate cash flows. Portfolio value is determined by calculating the net present value of the cash flows within the portfolio. Present value of the portfolios is calculated using discount factors based on zero coupon interest rates based on the existing yield curve. The net present value (the profit of the portfolio) is then hedged to preserve portfolio value. As new positions are added, the impact of the marginal transaction on the overall portfolio is calculated, with appropriate adjustments to portfolio hedges being implemented to continue to preserve the value of the portfolio. The portfolio approach to interest rate management can be implemented using duration based hedging approach or the (preferred) general cash flow hedging approach.

The portfolio approach has the advantage of being flexible and reducing transaction costs. A central element in the portfolio approach is that it allows the portfolio manager to determine the risk of the portfolio, and then establish the impact of adding various hedge instruments or new transactions to the existing portfolio in terms of profit and loss and risk characteristics. This allows a greater degree of precision in the risk that the portfolio carries, and the risk to be hedged, and also facilitates more accurate pricing of new transactions.

Portfolio hedging techniques alter the valuation technology used to measure value of a portfolio. Portfolio values are based on mark-to-market changes in the portfolio rather than accrual approaches.

# Appendix A: Valuation of Interest Rate Portfolio for the Purpose of Purchase[17]

## A.1. Background

A feature of the global derivative market is the reassessment of individual institutions' participation in swap and derivative activities. Based on this reassessment, a number of institutions have reduced their involvement in derivative activities generally, or in particular sectors of this market.

Where an institution decides to exit a particular segment or all of its derivative activities, it has two alternatives. Under the first alternative, new business in the relevant products is not transacted but the existing portfolio continues to be maintained and managed to realise its value. The second approach entails sale of the entire portfolio or the relevant part thereof to other derivative market participants to realise its value. While both techniques increasingly coexist for the reasons identified below, sales of portfolios of swap and derivative products have become more prevalent.

The practice of sale and corresponding purchase of derivative portfolios creates specific valuation problems. The general principles determining valuation of interest rate transactions and portfolios of products are still applicable. However, a number of additional factors are relevant and are considered in this Appendix.

## A.2. Portfolio Sales – Advantages

The major impetus for disposing of derivative portfolios as a set of continuing obligations is the potential benefits to both the seller and purchaser.

From the seller's perspective, the sale of the portfolio can reduce ongoing costs of running down the portfolio. The ongoing costs include costs of maintaining the book as well as costs of systems, settlement and administration. A portfolio may include transactions with remaining maturities of (up to) 10 or more years. This means that ongoing costs are significant. Major problems in terms of ongoing cost where a portfolio is to be "run down" is the fixed nature of a variety of costs, and the loss of economies of scale and scope as the portfolio contracts in size.

A related problem is that of managing the ongoing market risk of the portfolio. All portfolios have ongoing risk dimensions that require management. Where the

---

[17] See Coleman, Malcolm "Purchasing an Interest Rate Portfolio" in Das, Satyajit (Editor) (1991) Global Swaps Market; IFR Publishing, London at Chapter 33.

portfolio is to be maintained, a significant problem that often emerges is that value may be difficult to preserve without the capacity to add transactions to the existing portfolio. In this connection, the portfolio may require high levels of hedging to allow the existing value of the portfolio to be preserved.

A significant additional factor requiring consideration is the ongoing credit risk of the portfolio. Where the portfolio is sold, the existing transactions are typically novated to the purchaser. The credit risk on counterparties is assumed by the purchaser. Where the portfolio is to be maintained and run down, the credit risk of the portfolio continues to be assumed by the original counterparty, requiring commitment of capital to the transactions.

A significant but intangible and unquantifiable difficulty with running down a swap portfolio is the problem of attracting and maintaining quality staff to undertake such activities.

The difficulties typically lead most institutions seeking to exit their derivative businesses, in part or in its entirety, to decide on a sale of the portfolio to realise a sum certain to equal to, at least, an approximation of the present value of the portfolio.

From the perspective of the purchaser, the primary commercial or economic value is the potential income stream from the portfolio. In addition, the purchase may enable a growing operation to rapidly expand its portfolio, gaining market share and achieving the benefits of developing the appropriate critical mass. This has the advantage of greater efficiency in pricing and hedging. This potential advantage of achieving critical mass through purchase can, on occasion, dictate that an entrant to a particular market segment will pay a higher price for the portfolio compared to the intrinsic value of the portfolio or the value that would be paid by other potential buyers. Purchase of portfolios may also allow a purchaser to gain exposure to a client base that is significantly different to its existing market. This may allow further development of the purchaser's derivatives business.

## A.3. Valuation Issues

The valuation of a portfolio from the perspective of purchase entails two distinct steps:

- Valuation of the present value of the cash flows (and hedging instruments) within the portfolio.
- Value placed on the portfolio based on the purchaser's estimation of the risks of the portfolio including credit risk, market risk and the ongoing cost of running the portfolio.

The first phase of valuation is relatively straightforward. In effect, the "mark-to-market" value of the portfolio is determined. The valuation is undertaken on a portfolio basis. Portfolio cash flows are revalued at mid price (between the bid and offer) on the relevant zero coupon yield curves. Major causes of discrepancy in valuation between sellers and buyers as well as different purchasers include disagreements about the actual curve to be used for revaluation.

In estimating the value of the portfolio, all hedges maintained in the portfolio (such as physical securities as well as futures contracts) have to be valued. Hedges within the portfolio are usually valued at the normal liquidation value of the instruments at a given point in time.

In practice, portfolios are typically purchased inclusive of the hedges. The main benefit is that outright risk is minimised during the purchase and sale process. In practice, once the transaction is agreed and completed, the portfolio is incorporated within the purchaser's existing portfolio. At that time, the hedge portfolio, including the hedges purchased, is adjusted.

An issue that is often debated in the context of valuation of the hedge portfolio is the appropriateness of pricing hedge instruments at mid rate. This valuation may favour the purchaser or the seller. In practice, if the purchaser wished to purchase the portfolio *without the hedges*, then the seller would be forced to liquidate the hedge portfolio at the bid or offer side of the market (as appropriate). This potential benefit must be weighed against the risk assumed in the process of completing the purchase and sale transaction.

The overall value of the portfolio as determined must then be adjusted for the market risk and credit risk of the portfolio. The adjustment for market risk is necessarily subjective. A part of the assessment of the portfolio risk would be to seek to analyse the marginal impact of incorporating the purchased portfolio into the purchaser's existing portfolio and its impact on risk and earnings.

The adjustment for credit risk can also be complex in practice. The purchaser will generally classify the counterparties into two classes:
- Acceptable credit risks.
- Unacceptable credit risks.

Acceptable credit risks do not represent any problem and specific contracts are novated as described below. Where the credit risk of a counterparty is considered unacceptable, the purchaser will pursue one or other of the following courses of action:
- Seek a guarantee/counter indemnity from the seller (if it is of an acceptable credit standing) in respect of unacceptable counterparties.

- Seek some form of credit enhancement in respect of the specific counterparty, through third party guarantees, letters of credit or collateralisation provisions[18].
- Agree with the seller that the contract with the unacceptable counterparties be terminated, with resulting cash payments or receipts reflecting the market value of the transaction. This can be undertaken prior to the sale or immediately after the sale. In the latter case, agreement from the counterparty is usually sought before the purchase is consummated.

Attempts to deal with unacceptable counterparty credit exposure by pricing for the risk is rare. This reflects the difficulty of determining an appropriate price adjustment for the added credit risk.

Adjustments for ongoing maintenance costs are also subjective. In reality, given that one of the motivating factors for purchase of such product portfolios is the economies of scale and scope, subjective estimates must be made of the ongoing cost of management of the portfolio. The present value of the expenses is deducted from the portfolio's pure economic value. Added costs are particularly significant where the portfolio being purchased entails currencies or geographical locations not currently serviced by the purchaser.

The adjustment for market and credit risk, as well as ongoing costs generally, is built into the premium or discount relative to the pure economic value of the portfolio. This premium and discount can, in practice, vary quite significantly between institutions.

## A.4. Mechanical Issues

A number of mechanical issues in relation to the purchase and sale of swap and derivative portfolios require consideration. These include:

- Documentation issues.
- Negotiating points.
- Process and timing factors.

The sale of derivative portfolios is usually structured as a novation of existing contracts from the seller to the purchaser. The old contract between the counterparty and the seller is terminated and a new contract between the counterparty and the purchaser created.

The purchaser effectively inherits any defects in the documentation, necessitating detailed and thorough review of all derivative documentation. In certain cases,

---

[18]   See Das, Satyajit (2004) Risk Management; John Wiley & Sons (Asia), Singapore at Chapter 6.

this may necessitate implementing new revised documentation with the existing counterparty. This must be agreed to between the potential purchaser and the counterparty prior to the transaction being completed. The use of standard contracts (such as the ISDA Master Swap Agreement) is helpful. Where such contracts are used, there is a greater degree of documentary consistency. This greatly reduces the time frame needed to review the seller's documentation.

Sellers are typically required to give a number of warranties regarding the derivative portfolio, including:
- Accuracy of all transactions as disclosed to the purchaser.
- No transactions have been amended.
- No events of default on any derivative transactions within the portfolio have occurred.

Purchasers will also insist that the seller agree to assist in the event that there is a dispute regarding a specific transaction with an existing counterparty.

The seller and purchaser will usually agree on an adjustment to the price in the event that a counterparty specifically refuses to novate its contract. In this regard, there are two possible approaches. Under the first approach, all counterparties are approached prior to the transaction being completed, requesting their agreement. This approach entails entering into heads of agreement followed by a period in which appropriate consents are sought. The sale is completed upon receipt of appropriate consents. Alternatively, the transaction can be closed, with novation with the counterparty to be concluded subsequently. This requires agreement between the parties regarding adjustments to the sale price based on pre-agreed criteria in the event that counterparties refuse to undertake the novation.

The negotiation of the sale or purchase of derivatives portfolio is complex. Typically, where an institution decides to sell all or part of its derivative portfolio, it will seek to negotiate with interested purchasers on either a bilateral basis or through a tender process. Where the institution itself is not experienced in the derivative markets, it may retain the services of a financial institution with established expertise in derivative products to assist in the process of sale. The advising institution should be precluded from bidding from the portfolio to avoid conflicts of interest.

Potential purchasers of a portfolio will typically include:
- Institutions with strong relationships with the seller.
- Institutions seeking to expand their derivative portfolios in the relevant market sector.
- Established institutions with significant market position in the relevant products and market who may benefit by purchasing a portfolio to reinforce those dominant market positions.

Dealers with existing exposure to the market may also find a purchase an inexpensive mechanism for offsetting existing market exposures of positions.

Typically, a list of potential buyers is established. Bilateral negotiations are undertaken with potential purchasers. Tender documents are prepared and circulated to the potential purchasers. Information provided includes the relevant details of the portfolio including the hedging instruments maintained. Details about counterparties are not normally disclosed at this stage.

Potential purchasers are requested to submit their preliminary bids for the portfolio at a given point in time. In seeking to maximise the benefit of the sale, sellers will typically focus on a number of factors. The purchaser must have an acceptable credit rating, strong systems and administration. The purchaser should be regarded in the market place as a professional institution with a commitment to the particular product. In particular, the presence of a strong credit rating will assist in maximising the likelihood that existing counterparties will agree to novate existing agreements.

A counterparty with which the seller has a large number of existing transactions may be prepared to pay a premium for the purchase. This is because the purchaser's credit exposure would be reduced as a result of the purchase. This is because transactions within the portfolio are terminated through the process of purchase. It would effectively result in an unwinding of a portion of the combined portfolio.

Once indicative bids have been received for the portfolio, irrespective of whether a tender process or a bilateral negotiation approach has been adopted, the seller and potential purchaser would enter into negotiations. At this particular stage, the seller of the portfolio may provide details of counterparties in the portfolio to the potential purchaser. This enables the evaluation of the credit risk of the counterparties to be undertaken following this round of negotiations.

Timing and process of the sale can be quite critical. Where the portfolio has substantive mismatches, purchasers may prefer to bid and receive information on the result of a tendering process during market trading hours. This is so that any appropriate hedging action can be implemented. Where a portfolio is relatively well matched and has minimal market risk positions, the transaction is closed at the end of the business day. In the case of a purchase of a very large derivative portfolio, the transaction may be completed at the close of business at the end of the week. This gives additional time to transfer transactions and incorporate the portfolio into the purchaser's existing portfolio, ensuring the transfer is rapidly completed.

Where significant discrepancies in portfolio valuation between the purchaser and the seller are identified, a process of due diligence may be undertaken. This entails a process where the purchaser and the seller go through the portfolio and check each individual swap revaluation to reconcile the differences.

# 15
# Measuring Option Price Sensitivities – The Greek Alphabet of Risk[1]

## 1 Overview

Within an integrated framework of portfolio management[2], transactions are segregated into symmetric/linear instruments (asset and forwards) and asymmetric/non-linear instruments (options). The risks of both types of transactions are stated in terms of the Greek alphabet of risk. This enables traders to quantify the risk of the positions to enable risk management/hedging. The Greek alphabet of risk is associated with option trading. However, the Greek alphabet of risk can be used in the context of any financial risk and instruments.

---

[1]  For a general discussion of the Greek letters, see Briys, Eric Bellalah, Mondher, Mai, Huu Minh and De Varenne, Francois (1998) Options, Futures and Exotic Derivatives: Theory, Application and Practice; John Wiley & Sons, Chichester at Chapter 6; Hull, John (2000) Option Futures and Other Derivatives – Fourth Edition; Prentice-Hall Inc., Upper Saddle River, NJ at Chapter 13; Wilmott, Peter (1998) Derivatives: The Theory and Practice of Financial Engineering; John Wiley & Sons, Chichester at Chapter 7. See also Cox, J. and Rubinstein, M (1985) Options Markets; Prentice-Hall, Inc; Brown, Stephen J. "Estimating Volatility" in Figlewiski, Stephen, Silber, William L., and Subrahmanyam, Marti G. (1990) Financial Options; Business One Irwin: Homewood, Illinois at 516–537; Tompkins, Robert (1994) Options Explained[2]; MacMillan Press, England at Chapter 3; Chance, Don M. "Translating The Greek; The Real Meaning of Call Option Derivatives" (July-August 1994) Financial Analyst's Journal 43–49; Chriss, Neil A. (1997) Black-Scholes and Beyond: Option Pricing Models; Irwin Professional Publishing, Chicago. For a perspective of the Greek letters used in practice by traders, see Taleb, Nassim (1997) Dynamic Hedging; John Wiley & Sons, New York at Chapter 6, 7, 8 and 11.

[2]  See Chapter 12.

In this Chapter, the techniques of quantifying the sensitivity of option prices using the Greek alphabet of risk is described. The structure of the Chapter is as follows:

- An overview of option price sensitivities and risk measures including potential uses of these risk measures is considered.
- Each of the individual risk elements – delta ($\Delta$), gamma ($\gamma$), vega ($\kappa$)[3], theta ($\theta$) and rho ($\rho$) – are separately described including their function, significance and behaviour.
- Other risk factors – such as lambda ($\lambda$), speed, charm, colour, fugit etc – are also identified. In addition, newer risk measures – vomma, vanna etc – are examined.
- The use of the risk measurement framework to cover risk generally (as distinct from risk in relation to option transactions) is outlined.

## 2  Option Price Sensitivities & Risks – Overview[4]

The fair value of an option is a function of five parameters – the price of the asset (S), the option strike price (K), the time to option expiry (T), the risk free or discount rate (Rf) and the volatility of the asset returns ($\sigma$). Changes in any of the variables directly impact upon the price of the relevant option[5]. In practice, precise and quantitative estimates can be obtained of the *directional* as well as *quantum* effect of changes in the option pricing input parameters. The sensitivities of the option premium are represented by a number of Greek letters (following the notation conventions of mathematics) that are used to quantify and estimate the risk of options.

The sensitivities and risks of option transactions with references to changes in option pricing parameters are based on mathematical option pricing models. The models provide a means of valuing option contracts. In addition, the models provide a wealth of additional data with respect to the various formula variables. For example, delta is the derivative of the option premium with respect to asset price. It provides investors, portfolio managers or market makers with the exact hedge

---

[3]  Vega is not a Greek letter and in practice the Greek letter kappa ($\kappa$) is used to denote the sensitivity of the option premium to changes in volatility. However, the term vega is used in the text to denote this sensitivity. Other Greek letters used to denote this sensitivity include epsilon ($\varepsilon$) and lambda ($\lambda$).

[4]  The discussion in this Chapter is focused on conventional options. The application of Greek letters to exotic or non-standard option structures is complex. This is discussed in relation to exotic options; see Das, Satyajit (2004) Structured Products Volume 2; John Wiley & Sons (Asia), Singapore at Chapters 5 and 7 to 11 (inclusive).

[5]  See discussion in Chapter 7.

ratio required to hedge their portfolio position in options or in the underlying assets. The derivatives allow market participants to identify the short-term sensitivity of option premiums to changes in the underlying security price, volatility, time to expiration etc. In mathematical terms, the sensitivities are partial derivatives of the premium with respect to these parameters.

**Exhibit 15.1** summarises the key partial derivatives in relation to a European option on a non-income paying asset. **Exhibit 15.2** sets out the actual mathematical partial derivatives for a European option on a non-income paying asset.

The major applications of these measures of risk include:

- Measurement of the risk of options to changes in individual market parameters such as the asset price.
- Facilitating the replication of asset by synthetically creating the option's economic payoffs by trading in the underlying asset[6].
- Using the sensitivity and behaviour of the option to hedge positions or enable the creation of more efficient strategies.

| Exhibit 15.1   Option Risk Measures – The Greek Alphabet | |
|---|---|
| **Option Derivative** | **Concept** |
| Delta ($\Delta$) | Delta is the derivative of the option pricing formula with reference to the asset price (S). It measures the estimated change in the option premium for a change in S. |
| Gamma ($\gamma$) | Gamma is the second derivative of the option pricing formula with reference to the asset price (S). It measures the estimated change in the delta of the option for a change in S. |
| Vega ($\kappa$) | Vega is the derivative of the option pricing formula with reference to the volatility of the asset returns ($\sigma$). It measures the estimated change in the option premium for a change in $\sigma$. |
| Theta ($\theta$) | Theta is the derivative of the option pricing formula with reference to the time to option expiry (T). It measures the estimated change in the option premium for a change in T. |
| Rho ($\rho$) | Rho is the derivative of the option pricing formula with reference to the risk free rate (Rf). It measures the estimated change in the option premium for a change in Rf. |

---

[6]   See discussion in Chapter 16.

| Exhibit 15.2 | Option Derivatives – European Options on a Non-Income Producing Asset |
| --- | --- |

| Option Derivative | Partial Derivative |
| --- | --- |
| Delta – Call | $\Delta = N(d1)$ |
| Delta – Put | $\Delta = N(-d1)$ |
| Gamma – Call & Put | $\gamma = N(d1)/S \cdot \sigma\sqrt{T}$ |
| Vega – Call & Put | $\kappa = S \cdot \sqrt{T} \cdot N(d1)$ |
| Theta – Call | $\tau = (S \cdot \sigma \cdot N(d1)/2\sqrt{T}) - Rf \cdot K \cdot e^{-Rf \cdot T}N(d2)$ |
| Theta – Put | $\tau = (S \cdot \sigma \cdot N(d1)/2\sqrt{T}) - Rf \cdot K \cdot e^{-Rf \cdot T}N(-d2)$ |
| Rho – Call | $\rho = K \cdot T \cdot e^{-Rf \cdot T}N(d2)$ |
| Rho – Put | $\rho = K \cdot T \cdot e^{-Rf \cdot T}N(-d2)$ |

In the following Sections, the analysis of the risk measures is illustrated using a series of examples based on a consistent set of inputs. The example used, that of a European option on a non-income paying asset, is set out in **Exhibit 15.3**.

| Exhibit 15.3 | Option Risk Measures – Example | |
| --- | --- | --- |

| Pricing Inputs | | |
| --- | --- | --- |
| Underlying Asset Price (S) ($) | 100.00 | |
| Strike Price (K) ($) | 100.00 | |
| Trade Date | 1 January 2001 | |
| Expiry Date | 1 July 2001 | |
| Volatility ($\sigma$) (% pa) | 20.00 | |
| Risk Free/Discount Rate (Rf) (%) | 10.00 | |
| European (0)/American (1) Exercise | 0 | |
| Income on Asset (y) (% pa) | 0.00 | |
| **Model Outputs** | **Call** | **Put** |
| Option Premium | 8.23 | 3.39 |
| Delta | 0.6637 | −0.3363 |
| Gamma | 0.0259 | 0.0259 |
| Vega | 0.26 | 0.26 |
| Theta (pa) | 10.99 | 1.48 |
| Theta (Per Day) | 0.030 | 0.004 |
| Rho | 0.2883 | −0.1836 |

**Exhibit 15.4   Option Delta**

| Pricing Inputs | | |
|---|---|---|
| Underlying Asset Price (S) ($) | 100.10 | |
| Strike Price (K) ($) | 100.00 | |
| Trade Date | 1 January 2001 | |
| Expiry Date | 1 July 2001 | |
| Volatility ($\sigma$) (% pa) | 20.00 | |
| Risk Free/Discount Rate (Rf) (%) | 10.00 | |
| European (0)/American (1) Exercise | 0 | |
| Income on Asset (y) (% pa) | 0.00 | |
| **Model Outputs** | **Call** | **Put** |
| Option Premium | 8.30 | 3.36 |
| Delta | 0.6663 | −0.3337 |
| Gamma | 0.0258 | 0.0258 |
| Vega | 0.26 | 0.26 |
| Theta (pa) | 11.01 | 1.49 |
| Theta (Per Day) | 0.030 | 0.004 |
| Rho | 0.2896 | −0.1823 |

# 3   Delta

## 3.1   Concept

Delta is the first derivative of the option pricing formula with respect to the asset price. The delta measures the expected change in the value of the option for a given change in the asset price. The expected price change is given by:

Change in the asset price times Delta = Expected Change in Option premium

In **Exhibit 15.3**, the deltas are as follows:

Call option: 0.6637

Put option: (0.3363)

This implies that for a small change of $0.10 in the asset price, the option value will change by:

Call option: 0.6637 times $0.10 = $0.07

Put option: (0.3363) times $0.10 = $(0.03)

**Exhibit 15.4** shows the result of the change in terms of its impact on the premium that is consistent with the predicted changes. Note the change in delta itself.

## 3.2 Behaviour

The delta of an option is characterised by the following pattern of behaviour:

- The delta of a call (put) option is positive (negative), reflecting the direction of change of the option value for a given increase in the asset price.
- The option delta is between 0 and 1 for a call option and 0 and −1 for a put option. The delta of the asset is always 1. A long position has a delta of +1. A short position has a delta of −1.
- Deep out-of-the-money options have deltas close to 0 because they are not very responsive to changes in the underlying asset price. Deep in-the-money options have deltas close to +1 or −1 because they move in step with the underlying price. At-the-money options tend to have deltas close to 0.5.
- The higher the delta, the closer the option price changes are to the changes in the asset price. Consequently, the gains and losses on the option are similar to that on a position in the underlying asset.

**Exhibit 15.5** sets out a delta surface to illustrate the behaviour of the delta for the option depicted in **Exhibit 15.3**.

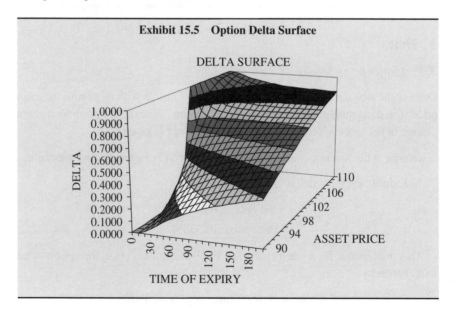

**Exhibit 15.5    Option Delta Surface**

In utilising delta, it is important to recognise that it only holds for small movements in the asset price. This can be illustrated by comparing the expected change in the option premium and the *actual change* in the option premium (using full revaluation). **Exhibit 15.6** sets out the comparison of actual changes in the option premium against the predicted change in the option premium using delta.

| | Exhibit 15.6 | Delta Performance | |
|---|---|---|---|
| **Change in Asset Price ($)** | **Estimated Change in Call Option Premium Using Commencing Delta ($)** | **Actual Change in Call Option Premium ($)** | **Difference ($)** |
| +20 | +13.27 | +16.92 | 3.65 |
| +10 | +6.64 | +7.74 | 1.10 |
| +5 | +3.32 | +3.62 | 0.30 |
| +1 | +0.66 | +0.68 | 0.02 |
| +0.10 | +0.07 | +0.07 | 0 |
| −0.10 | −0.07 | −0.06 | 0.01 |
| −1 | −0.66 | −0.65 | 0.01 |
| −5 | −3.32 | −2.97 | 0.35 |
| −10 | −6.64 | −5.21 | 1.43 |
| −20 | −13.27 | −7.59 | 5.68 |
| **Change in Asset Price ($)** | **Estimated Change in Put Option Premium Using Commencing Delta ($)** | **Actual Change in Put Option Premium ($)** | **Difference ($)** |
| +20 | −6.73 | −3.08 | 3.65 |
| +10 | −3.36 | −2.26 | 1.10 |
| +5 | −1.68 | −1.38 | 0.30 |
| +1 | −0.34 | −0.32 | 0.02 |
| +0.10 | −0.03 | −0.03 | 0 |
| −0.10 | +0.03 | +0.03 | 0.01 |
| −1 | +0.34 | +0.35 | 0.01 |
| −5 | +1.68 | +2.03 | 0.35 |
| −10 | +3.36 | +4.79 | 1.43 |
| −20 | +6.73 | +12.42 | 5.69 |

Notes: The calculations are based on the data in **Exhibit 15.3**.

For other than relatively small changes in the asset price, the delta predicted changes in the option premium over or underestimate the actual change in the option premium. This reflects the fact that the option delta is in effect the slope of the curve that plots the change in the option premium for given changes in asset price. **Exhibit 15.7** shows the curve relating changes in option premium to changes in asset price. The graph illustrates the curvilinear relationship. The slope of the curve changes with respect to the underlying asset price. As the asset price moves by large increments (or jumps) and larger portions of the curve are covered, the delta estimate becomes increasingly inaccurate as a predictor of option price movements. This is effectively because delta itself changes. This change is measured by gamma.

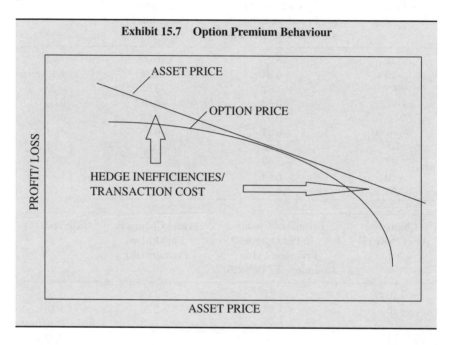

**Exhibit 15.7    Option Premium Behaviour**

A feature of option deltas is the fact they are additive; that is, the delta of a portfolio of options is the sum of the face value weighted deltas of the options contained within the portfolio. This relationship can be stated as:

$$\Delta_p = \sum_{n=1}^{n} W_n \cdot \Delta_n$$

Where

$\Delta_p$ = the portfolio delta

$\Delta_n$ = the delta of the n th option in the portfolio

$W_n$ = the weight for the n th option calculated as the face value of the option divided by the total face value of options in the portfolio

The additive nature of delta greatly facilitates the management of a portfolio of options.

## 3.3 Application

Delta is the most important measure of option price sensitivity. It conveys a wide range of information, including the asset content of the option and the probability of the option being exercised.

The delta of an option is often referred to as its *equivalent asset position*. This reflects the fact that a holding of delta amount of the asset (a long (short) position of .6637 (−0.3363) in the asset) will allow the option to be replicated. This means that the delta hedge provides an economic result in terms of gains or losses for small movements in the asset price that are identical to purchases of the option itself.

The delta of an option also gives the probability of the option being exercised. The higher the delta (for a call option), the greater the chance of the option being exercised. This provides important information in terms of enabling the risk of the option to be assessed.

The properties of the option delta are intrinsic to the application and pricing and trading of options. The asset content implicit in delta allows the assessment and comparison of option strategies. An important aspect of this process is the ability to use the delta equivalence to compare positions between the *asset* and the *option*.

This equivalence has an important implication for replication of options that is central to the trading of options[7]. The fact that delta provides the asset content as well as the probability of the option being exercised, allows the option to be replicated by maintaining and dynamically adjusting a portfolio consisting of the asset and cash. This asset portfolio will, under certain conditions, give the same economic payoffs as the option being replicated. This relationship is central to the derivation of the option value[8].

## 3.4 In Practice

Delta has a number of practical limitations[9]. The major weaknesses of delta include:
* Delta as noted above only holds for small changes in the asset price. This is a direct result of the basic derivation of option pricing models within a continuous time framework. In practice, traders are unlikely to be able to hedge continuously

---

[7] This process is referred to as delta hedging. It forms the basis of all trading and risk management of options; see detailed discussion in Chapter 16.

[8] Black-Scholes and other option pricing approaches, such as the binomial models, are predicated on the concept of this replicating portfolio which is free of risk which allows derivation of the option price, as the combined portfolios should only yield the risk free rate of interest.

[9] See Taleb, Nassim (1997) Dynamic Hedging; John Wiley & Sons, New York at 112–114; Chapter 7.

in a world where the asset price moves by relatively small increments[10]. Delta can provide misleading information on changes in value for large or discontinuous price changes (price gaps or jumps).

- Delta is sensitive to changes in volatility. This is very important for options with different strikes (out-of and in-the-money options) because of the implied volatility smile/skew. It is also important for any option in the case of large price changes. Such large changes may be accompanied by substantial shifts in implied volatility.
- Delta of a portfolio of options (combining long and short option positions) can be theoretically calculated. However, in practice, the delta loses significance as a risk measure for a portfolio. This is because different options may have different sensitivity to *other risk factors* (for example, volatility changes or large discontinuous price changes).
- Delta of cash flows that have been bucketed into specified maturity vertices may also be misleading. This reflects the fact that the delta does not reflect the basis risk between the maturity vertices.

In practice, traders supplement traditional model based delta measures with a number of additional risk measures including:
- Scenario analysis using *estimated* shifts in the asset price to generate the expected changes in the option value. This allows the trader to adjust the increment based on the trader's estimate of future volatility.
- Use of gamma to supplement the delta as it provides an indication of the stability of delta. Some traders also use the sensitivity of gamma to changes in spot prices. This provides an indication of the stability of gamma.
- Use of the sensitivity of delta to changes in volatility. This provides an indication of potential changes in delta to changes in volatility that may accompany large changes in asset prices.

The traditional delta measure generated indicates the amount of cash asset needed to hedge the option. In practice, traders will generally hedge the position with *a forward or futures contract on the asset*. This requires an adjustment to the delta used in hedges. This is because the differences between the two (asset delta and forward delta) may be significant. The difference is driven by the sensitivity of the forward price to interest rates, the income term on the asset, and time remaining to maturity. Traders generally transform the delta of the spot asset into the delta of the forward by discounting the forward exposure.

---

[10] For a discussion of the impact of this on option replication, see Chapter 16.

# 4 Gamma

## 4.1 Concept

Gamma is the second derivative of the option premium (delta is the first derivative) with respect to the underlying security price. It indicates the change in delta for a given change in the underlying price; that is, the change in the price delta given the unit change in the underlying price. The expected price change is given by:

Change in the asset price times Gamma = Expected Change in Option Delta

In **Exhibit 15.3**, the gamma is as follows:

Call option: 0.0259

Put option: 0.0259

This implies that for a small change of say, $1.00 in the asset price, the option value will change by:

Call option: 0.0259 times $1.00 = 0.0259

Put option: 0.0259 times $1.00 = 0.0259

**Exhibit 15.8** shows the result of the change in terms of its impact on the premium that is consistent with the predicted changes. The slight mis-estimation reflects the curvature of the option premium with respect to asset price that gives gamma a certain curvature. Note the change in gamma itself is consistent with the curvature of gamma.

## 4.2 Behaviour

The gamma of an option is characterised by the following pattern of behaviour:
- A low gamma indicates that the option delta changes slowly for a given change in the underlying asset price. A high gamma indicates that the option delta is sensitive to changes in the price of the underlying asset.
- Deep out-of-the-money or in-the-money options have gamma close to zero because these options are not very responsive to changes in the underlying asset price.
- At-the-money options, particularly where the time to maturity is relatively short, have the highest gamma. This reflects the fact the option is equally likely to be exercised or expire unexercised, and the resulting option delta will go to either +1 or −1 (in the case of exercise) or 0 (in the case of non-exercise). **Exhibit 15.9** sets out the change in gamma for changes in remaining maturity.

- Assets have minimal gamma. For most assets, the gamma is zero. The only exception to this is fixed interest securities that have some gamma because of the convex nature of price changes for given changes in interest rates.

**Exhibit 15.10** sets out a gamma surface that illustrates the behaviour of the gamma for the option depicted in **Exhibit 15.3**.

| Exhibit 15.8   Option Gamma | | |
|---|---|---|
| **Pricing Inputs** | | |
| Underlying Asset Price (S) ($) | 101.00 | |
| Strike Price (K) ($) | 100.00 | |
| Trade Date | 1 January 2001 | |
| Expiry Date | 1 July 2001 | |
| Volatility ($\sigma$) (% pa) | 20.00 | |
| Risk Free/Discount Rate (Rf) (%) | 10.00 | |
| European (0)/American (1) Exercise | 0 | |
| Income on Asset (y) (% pa) | 0.00 | |
| **Model Outputs** | **Call** | **Put** |
| Option Premium | 8.91 | 3.07 |
| Delta | 0.6891 | −0.3109 |
| Gamma | 0.0248 | 0.0248 |
| Vega | 0.25 | 0.25 |
| Theta (pa) | 11.14 | 1.62 |
| Theta (Per Day) | 0.031 | 0.004 |
| Rho | 0.3009 | −0.1710 |

| Exhibit 15.9   Option Gamma –Changes in Option Maturity | | | | |
|---|---|---|---|---|
| Assume the option set out in **Exhibit 15.3**. The Table below sets out the gamma of the option where the maturity is varied: | | | | |
| **Pricing Inputs** | | | | |
| Underlying Asset Price ($) | 100.00 | | | |
| Strike Price ($) | 100.00 | | | |
| Valuation Date | 1 January 2001 | 1 March 2001 | 1 June 2001 | 30 June 2001 |
| Expiry Date | 1 July 2001 | | | |
| Volatility (% pa) | 20.00 | | | |
| Risk Free/Discount Rate (%) | 10.00 | | | |
| Option Exercise | European | | | |
| Income on Asset (% pa) | 0.00 | | | |

| Model Outputs | Call | Call | Call | Call |
|---|---|---|---|---|
| Option Premium | 8.23 | 6.37 | 2.71 | 0.43 |
| Delta | 0.6637 | 0.6357 | 0.5683 | 0.5125 |
| Gamma | 0.0259 | 0.0325 | 0.0686 | 0.3809 |
| | Put | Put | Put | Put |
| Option Premium | 3.39 | 3.08 | 1.89 | 0.40 |
| Delta | −0.3363 | −0.3643 | −0.4317 | −0.4875 |
| Gamma | 0.0259 | 0.0325 | 0.0686 | 0.3809 |

The gamma increases as the time remaining to maturity becomes very short. This reflects the fact that the asset price is trading exactly at the strike price. This means that the option will be exercised or not exercised, depending upon a relatively small movement in the asset price. This means that option delta will go to 1/−1 or 0. This drives the very high gamma.

If the asset price moves slightly up or down, then the gamma falls appreciably, as set out below:

| Pricing Inputs | | | |
|---|---|---|---|
| Underlying Asset Price ($) | 100.00 | 98.00 | 102.00 |
| Strike Price ($) | 100.00 | | |
| Valuation Date | 30 June 2001 | | |
| Expiry Date | 1 July 2001 | | |
| Volatility (% pa) | 20.00 | | |
| Risk Free/Discount Rate (%) | 10.00 | | |
| Option Exercise | European | | |
| Income on Asset (% pa) | 0.00 | | |
| **Model Outputs** | **Call** | **Call** | **Call** |
| Option Premium | 0.43 | 0.01 | 2.04 |
| Delta | 0.5125 | 0.0288 | 0.9728 |
| Gamma | 0.3809 | 0.0641 | 0.0588 |
| | **Put** | **Put** | **Put** |
| Option Premium | 0.40 | 1.98 | 0.01 |
| Delta | −0.4875 | −0.9712 | −0.0272 |
| Gamma | 0.3809 | 0.0641 | 0.0588 |

## 4.3 Application

Gamma can be best regarded as a measure of the convexity of the option and the resultant hedging risk of replicating the option with a position in the asset through delta hedging. It is a measure of hedging risk. It provides information about the sensitivity of the asset equivalent position of the option for given changes in asset prices. It provides a measure of the convexity of the option position.

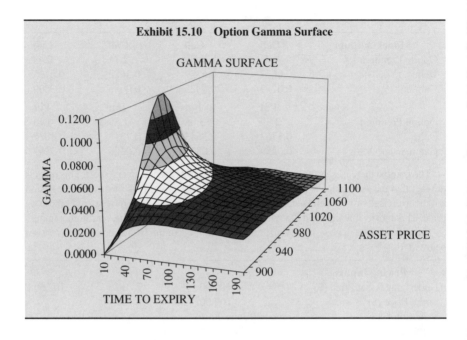

**Exhibit 15.10    Option Gamma Surface**

## 4.4   In Practice

Gamma has a number of practical limitations[11]. The major weaknesses of gamma include:

- Gamma only measures the change in delta for a move in the asset price at current levels. Even where *model gamma* (the model generated risk measure) is low, a large change in the asset price will result in a large change in the delta of the option. Gamma does not measure this risk to large discontinuous price moves and jumps.
- Gamma assumes volatility is constant. It does not capture the potential impact of changes in volatility where the asset moves. Traditional measures of gamma do not incorporate the impact of the volatility smile/skew.
- Portfolio gamma, where gamma in two different maturities is added, can be misleading. This is because the rate of change in the gamma of individual positions may vary. In addition, the cash forward basis will change at different rates, resulting in a misleading gamma measure.

---

[11]   See Taleb, Nassim (1997) Dynamic Hedging; John Wiley & Sons, New York at 112–114; Chapter 8.

In practice, traders supplement traditional model based gamma measures with a number of additional risk measures including:
- Scenario analysis using *estimated* shifts in the asset price to generate the expected changes in the option's delta. This is done for separate increases and decreases in the asset price. This allows the trader to adjust the increment based on the trader's estimate of future volatility and also incorporate the impact of the volatility smile or skew.
- Use shadow gamma to measure the sensitivity of volatility (both changes in volatility level and skew shape). Shadow gamma may be defined as the change in delta taking into account *estimated* changes in spot prices and volatility. Shadow gamma is usually augmented by taking into account changes in interest rate (carry cost) changes. This is to ensure the changes in the forward price are fully incorporated.
- Some traders also use the sensitivity of gamma to changes in spot prices. This provides an indication of the stability of gamma.

## 5 Vega

### 5.1 Concept

Vega is the first derivative of the option premium with respect to the volatility. Vega measures the expected change in the value of the option for a given change in the volatility parameter. The expected price change is given by:

Change in the volatility times Vega = Expected Change in Option premium

In **Exhibit 15.3**, the vega is as follows:

Call option: 0.26

Put option: 0.26

This implies that for a small change of say, 1.00% pa in volatility, the option value will change by:

Call option: 0.26 times 1.00 = $0.26

Put option: 0.26 times 1.00 = $0.26

**Exhibit 15.11** shows the result of the change in terms of its impact on the premium that is consistent with the predicted changes. Note the sensitivity of delta and gamma to changes in volatility.

| Exhibit 15.11   Option Vega | | |
|---|---|---|
| **Pricing Inputs** | | |
| Underlying Asset Price (S) ($) | 100.00 | |
| Strike Price (K) ($) | 100.00 | |
| Trade Date | 1 January 2001 | |
| Expiry Date | 1 July 2001 | |
| Volatility ($\sigma$) (% pa) | 21.00 | |
| Risk Free/Discount Rate (Rf) (%) | 10.00 | |
| European (0)/American (1) Exercise | 0 | |
| Income on Asset (y) (% pa) | 0.00 | |
| **Model Outputs** | **Call** | **Put** |
| Option Premium | 8.49 | 3.65 |
| Delta | 0.6588 | −0.3412 |
| Gamma | 0.0248 | 0.0248 |
| Vega | 0.26 | 0.26 |
| Theta (pa) | 11.21 | 1.69 |
| Theta (Per Day) | 0.031 | 0.005 |
| Rho | 0.2846 | −0.1873 |

## 5.2   Behaviour

The vega of an option is characterised by the following pattern of behaviour:

- A low vega indicates that the option premium changes slowly for a given change in volatility. A high vega indicates that the option premium is sensitive to changes in volatility.
- At-the-money options, particularly where the time to maturity is long, have the highest vega.
- Deep out-of-the-money or in-the-money options have lower vega because they are not very responsive to changes in volatility. This reflects the fact that these options either have values dominated by the intrinsic value of the option, or have low absolute values.
- Assets have zero vega. This reflects the fact that volatility is not a parameter relevant to pricing of *assets*.

**Exhibit 15.12** sets out a vega surface that illustrates the behaviour of the vega for the option depicted in **Exhibit 15.3**.

**Exhibit 15.12    Option Vega Surface**

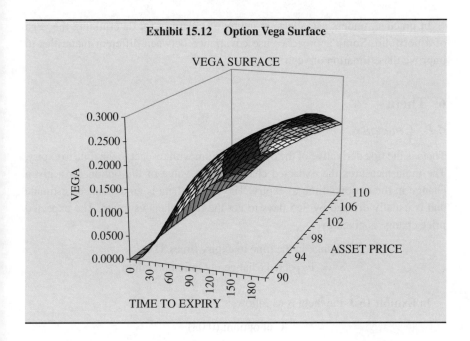

VEGA SURFACE

5.3   *Application*

Vega measures the sensitivity to changes in volatility of a single option or a portfolio. In this regard, it measures the exposure or risk to volatility changes present in the position under consideration.

5.4   *In Practice*

Vega has a number of practical limitations[12]. The major weakness of vega is that it is potentially misleading in a portfolio of options containing time spreads (long and short option positions at different maturities). This is because the different options should be valued using different volatility, reflecting the term structure of volatility. In addition, the rate of change of the option value for changes in volatility is time dependent.

---

[12]   See Taleb, Nassim (1997) Dynamic Hedging; John Wiley & Sons, New York at 112–114; Chapter 9.

In practice, traders use a term structure of volatility for determining the vega of a portfolio. Some approaches use covariance between different maturities to improve the estimation of vega.

# 6  Theta

## 6.1  Concept

Theta is the first derivative of the option premium with respect to the time to expiry. The theta measures the expected change in the value of the option for a given change in the option's time to expiry. The option theta is an annualised estimate and is usually divided by 365 days to get the daily theta estimate. The expected price change is given by:

Change in the time to expiry times Theta
= Expected Change in Option premium

In **Exhibit 15.3**, the theta is as follows:

Call option: (0.03)

Put option: (0.004)

This implies that for a small change of, say 10 days in time to expiry, the option value will change by:

Call option: (0.03) times 10 = $(0.30)

Put option: (0.004) times 10 = $(0.04)

**Exhibit 15.13** shows the result of the change in terms of its impact on the premium that is consistent with the predicted changes. Note the sensitivity of delta, gamma and vega to the change in remaining time to expiry.

## 6.2  Behaviour

The theta of an option is characterised by the following pattern of behaviour:
- The theta is negative, reflecting the loss of value as the time to expiry diminishes. This fall in value accrues to the seller as a gain that is offset by the loss suffered by the purchaser.
- A high theta indicates that the value of the option declines rapidly with a change in remaining maturity. A low theta indicates that the value of the option is less sensitive to a change in remaining maturity.

| Exhibit 15.13 Option Theta | | |
|---|---|---|
| **Pricing Inputs** | | |
| Underlying Asset Price (S) ($) | 100.10 | |
| Strike Price (K) ($) | 100.00 | |
| Trade Date | 11 January 2001 | |
| Expiry Date | 1 July 2001 | |
| Volatility ($\sigma$) (% pa) | 20.00 | |
| Risk Free/Discount Rate (Rf) (%) | 10.00 | |
| European (0)/American (1) Exercise | 0 | |
| Income on Asset (y) (% pa) | 0.00 | |
| **Model Outputs** | **Call** | **Put** |
| Option Premium | 7.93 | 3.35 |
| Delta | 0.6593 | −0.3407 |
| Gamma | 0.0268 | 0.0268 |
| Vega | 0.25 | 0.25 |
| Theta (pa) | 11.16 | 1.62 |
| Theta (Per Day) | 0.031 | 0.004 |
| Rho | 0.2718 | −0.1753 |

- The highest theta is for an at-the-money option with a short time to expiry.
- The theta of an option, typically for a deep in or out-of-the-money option, is lower than for a corresponding at-the-money option.

Assets will generally have thetas. The source of theta will vary. For example, options on debt instruments will exhibit a theta consistent with the accrual of interest income or expense on the instrument. Similarly, the impact of dividends or commodity convenience yields will be reflected in the asset thetas for equities/equity indexes or commodities/commodity indexes. The changes in futures prices, reflecting changes in the carry cost as a result of changes in the time to delivery/settlement, will provide futures/forward contracts with theta.

**Exhibit 15.14** sets out a theta surface that illustrates the behaviour of the theta for the option depicted in **Exhibit 15.3**.

## 6.3 Application

Theta measures the sensitivity to changes in the time to expiry of a single option or a portfolio. In this regard, it measures the exposure or risk present in a position over the passage of time.

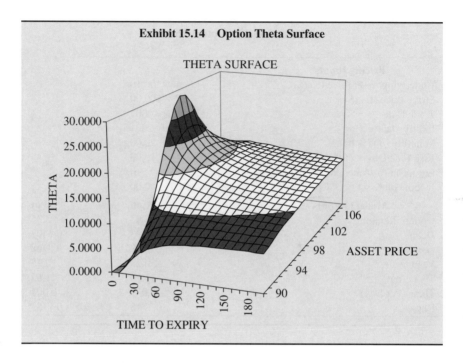

**Exhibit 15.14    Option Theta Surface**

## 6.4   In Practice

Theta has a number of practical limitations[13]. The major weakness of theta is that it is potentially misleading as it assumes constant volatility. Change in remaining time to expiry may result in a change of applicable volatility, reflecting the term structure of volatility. It does not take into account the impact of changes in asset prices and changes in volatility (whether or not linked to changes in asset prices).

In practice, traders use a term structure of volatility for determining the theta of a portfolio. Some approaches use the concept of shadow theta to accelerate time decay where asset prices are stable and reduce it where asset prices are volatile. In effect, this uses a scenario/simulation approach to measuring theta.

## 7   Rho

### 7.1   Concept

Rho is the first derivative of the option premium with respect to the risk free interest or discount rate. Rho measures the expected change in the value of the option for a

---

[13]   See Taleb, Nassim (1997) Dynamic Hedging; John Wiley & Sons, New York at 112–114; Chapter 10.

given change in the risk free interest rate. The expected price change is given by:

Change in the risk free rate times Rho = Expected Change in Option premium

In **Exhibit 15.3**, the rho is as follows:

Call option: 0.29

Put option: (0.18)

This implies that for a small change of, say 1% pa in the risk free rate, the option value will change by:

Call option: 0.29 times 1.00 = $0.29

Put option: (0.18) times 1.00 = $(0.18)

**Exhibit 15.15** shows the result of the change in terms of its impact on the premium that is consistent with the predicted changes. Note the changes in delta, gamma, vega and theta. The change is driven by the change in the forward price of the asset as a result of the change in the carry cost.

| Exhibit 15.15 Option Rho | | |
|---|---|---|
| **Pricing Inputs** | | |
| Underlying Asset Price (S) ($) | 100.00 | |
| Strike Price (K) ($) | 100.00 | |
| Trade Date | 1 January 2001 | |
| Expiry Date | 1 July 2001 | |
| Volatility ($\sigma$) (% pa) | 20.00 | |
| Risk Free/Discount Rate (Rf) (%) | 11.00 | |
| European (0)/American (1) Exercise | 0 | |
| Income on Asset (y) (% pa) | 0.00 | |
| **Model Outputs** | **Call** | **Put** |
| Option Premium | 8.52 | 3.21 |
| Delta | 0.6764 | −0.3236 |
| Gamma | 0.0255 | 0.0255 |
| Vega | 0.25 | 0.25 |
| Theta (pa) | 11.60 | 1.19 |
| Theta (Per Day) | 0.03179 | 0.00326 |
| Rho | 0.2932 | −0.1764 |

## 7.2 Behaviour

The rho of an option is characterised by the following pattern of behaviour:
- A high rho indicates sensitivity to changes in interest rates. A low rho indicates relative lack of sensitivity to changes in interest rates.
- The rho for a call (put) is positive (negative), reflecting the directional impact of an increase in interest rates on the value of the option.
- The rho decreases with time to maturity, reflecting the diminished impact of the discounting of the exercise price.
- Deep in-the-money options show a higher rho. This reflects the fact that the value of these options is dominated by intrinsic value. In effect, they are "funding" trades. This accounts directly for the higher interest rate sensitivity.

**Exhibit 15.16** sets out a rho surface that illustrates the behaviour of the rho for the option depicted in **Exhibit 15.3**.

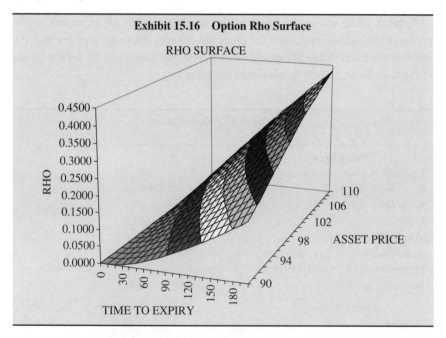

**Exhibit 15.16   Option Rho Surface**

## 7.3 Application

Rho measures the sensitivity to changes in the risk free interest rate of a single option or a portfolio. In this regard, it measures the exposure or risk present in a position resulting from changes in the discount rate.

Most option positions will display *two* rhos. The first rho is that described – the sensitivity to the risk free or discount rate. The second is the sensitivity of an option value to changes in the income on the asset. This rho (also referred to sometimes as phi ($\phi$)) measures the sensitivity of the option premium to changes in coupon, foreign interest rate or coupon/interest rates).

## 7.4   In Practice

Theta suffers from the weakness that a parallel yield curve shift is assumed. In practice, traders adjust for this weakness by using an interest rate term structure model[14].

# 8   Interaction of Risk Measures

**Exhibit 15.17** summarises the option sensitivities for underlying asset (that does not pay any income) and option positions.

| Exhibit 15.17 | Greek Letter Sensitivities – Summary | | | |
| --- | --- | --- | --- | --- |
| **Asset or Option Position** | **Delta** | **Gamma** | **Theta** | **Vega** |
| Purchased Asset | Positive | Not applicable | Not applicable | Not applicable |
| Sold Asset | Negative | Not applicable | Not applicable | Not applicable |
| Purchased Call | Positive | Positive | Negative | Positive |
| Sold Call | Negative | Negative | Positive | Negative |
| Purchased Put | Negative | Positive | Negative | Positive |
| Sold Put | Positive | Negative | Positive | Negative |

The analysis of the individual risk measures to date has been undertaken on a separate basis. In practice, there is substantial interaction between the risk measures. The most significant interactions include:

- The relationship between delta, gamma, vega and theta.
- The impact of time on the Greek letters.

Delta and gamma are both affected by changes in volatility. The pattern of interaction is as follows:

- Increases in volatility result in higher deltas for out and at-the-money options. Increases in volatility reduce the delta for in-the-money options. This pattern

---

[14]   See Taleb, Nassim (1997) Dynamic Hedging; John Wiley & Sons, New York at 112–114; Chapter 10.

reflects the fact that delta is, in one sense, a measure of the probability of exercise of the option. The increase in volatility increases or decreases the probability of exercise for out and at-the-money options and in-the-money options respectively.

• Gamma generally decreases with an increase in volatility and vice versa. The change in gamma for a change in volatility is greatest for an at-the-money option while the change in gamma is much lower for changes in volatility for in and out-of-the-money options.

The relationship between delta and volatility is set out in the delta-volatility surface in **Exhibit 15.18**. The relationship between gamma and volatility is set out in the gamma-volatility surface in **Exhibit 15.19**.

The implication of this relationship is that where the delta of an option or portfolio is used to hedge or replicate the underlying option, changes in volatility can significantly erode the efficiency of the hedge.

The relationship between gamma and theta is more complex. Where theta is large and positive, the corresponding gamma of the option also tends to be large

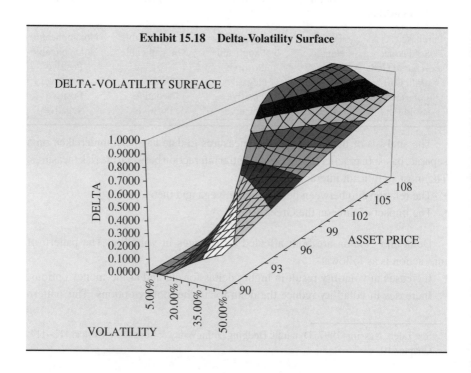

**Exhibit 15.18    Delta-Volatility Surface**

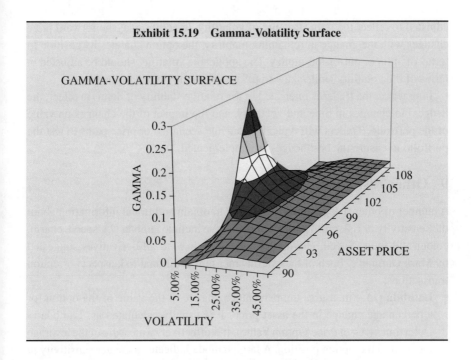

Exhibit 15.19    Gamma-Volatility Surface

and negative[15]. This means that the gamma of a portfolio under certain conditions offsets the theta of that portfolio.

The impact of time on the Greek letters and their behaviour is important. This is often termed the "bleed"[16]. The bleed captures the change in delta and gamma for a change in remaining time to maturity[17]. The impact of the bleed is that it pushes all options either further into or out-of-the-money, depending on whether they are in the money or out-of-the-money. This reflects the change in the forward price of the asset. In practice, the importance of the bleed is that it will change the value of positions and require re-hedging or re-balancing of the hedge. This will be the case even if there is no change in any other pricing variable.

The measurement of the bleed is typically done with changes in volatility. In effect, as the remaining time to expiry is reduced, the applicable volatility is

---

[15]  For a formal mathematical proof of this, see Hull, John (2000) Option Futures and Other Derivatives – Fourth Edition; Prentice-Hall Inc., Upper Saddle River, NJ at 326.

[16]  See Taleb, Nassim (1997) Dynamic Hedging; John Wiley & Sons, New York at Chapter 11.

[17]  This is the risk measure – charm and colour; see discussion later in this Chapter.

adjusted to reflect the term structure of volatility. In addition, as the forward price changes with the change in remaining maturity, the option changes its position in terms of at, in or out-of-the-money. The applicable volatility should be adjusted in terms of the volatility smile/skew to fully capture the impact of the bleed.

In practice, the trader is interested in the relative stability of delta (in effect, the hedges) to changes in time and volatility, and the impact of the changes on value of the portfolio. Traders will typically generate scenarios or price paths to test the portfolio to ensure the best hedges are implemented.

# 9 Other Risk Measures

A number of other risk parameters are used to obtain additional information about the sensitivity or risk profile of an option. These include lambda ($\lambda$), speed, charm, colour and fugit. Speed, charm, colour and fugit were all derivatives suggested by Mark Garman[18]. Each of these terms measure additional risk aspects of option transactions:

- **Lambda** ($\lambda$) – measures the percentage change in the value of the option for a percentage change in the asset price. It is usually calculated as: Lambda = Delta times (Asset Price/Option Value). It is effectively a measure of the leverage inherent in the option position. A large lambda indicates a greater sensitivity *in proportional terms* to movements in the asset price.
- **Speed** – is the measure of the change in gamma for a given change in the asset price[19].
- **Charm** – is the measure of the change in delta for a given change in time to expiry.
- **Colour** – is the measure of the change in gamma for a given change in time to expiry.
- **Fugit** – is the expected value of the time to exercise of an American option[20]. It is usually calculated using an iterative procedure within a binomial option pricing framework[21].

Each of these measures has significance for traders seeking to manage a portfolio of options.

---

[18] See Garman, Mark "Charm School" (July-August 1992) Risk 53–54.
[19] This is effectively the third derivative of the option premium with respect to the asset price.
[20] See Garman, Mark "Semper Tempus Fugit" (May 1989) Risk 34–35; "Semper Tempus Fugit" in (1992) From Black Scholes to Black Holes; Risk Publication, London at 89–91.
[21] This is often also called omega. Fugit/omega does not incorporate the impact of the volatility smile or skew on time to early exercise.

The increased trading of exotic options[22] has exposed some of the weaknesses of traditional option risk measures. That has led to the use of additional ways of measuring the risk of options, both standard options, and exotic or non-standard options. These include[23]:

- **Vomma** – this is the change in vega for a change in implied volatility.
- **Vanna** – this is the change in vega for a change in spot rate.

These supplement a generalised group of risk measures that calculate the impact of a change in asset price on various option risk measures such as volatility[24].

The additional measures are designed to attempt to overcome weaknesses in vega (particularly important for exotic options). They are also attempts to capture the changes in volatility for a change in spot price and also the impact of the volatility smile/skew.

## 10 Extensions for Options on Different Assets

In the above analyses, the focus has been on a European option with non-income paying asset. The same approach can be extended to cover options on different underlying assets. The options covered include:

- American options.
- Options where the underlying asset pays continuous income.
- Options on a forward or futures contract.
- Option on a currency.

The risk measures for a European option on a commodity or equity are identical to that for either an option where the underlying asset pays continuous income, or an option on a currency. The commodity payout or convenience yield or equity dividend yield is substituted for either the income or foreign interest rate.

## 11 Summary

The derivatives of the valuation formula for options provide a quantifiable measure of the value sensitivity and risk of the option to changes in one or more of the

---

22 See Das, Satyajit (2004) Structured Products Volume 1; John Wiley & Sons (Asia), Singapore at Chapters 5 and 7 to 11 (inclusive).
23 See Owens, Tim "Vomma, Vomma, Hey!" (May 1998) Futures & OTC World 24–25; Webb, Andrew "The Sensitivity of Vega" (November 1999) Derivatives Strategy 16–24.
24 See Taleb, Nassim (1997) Dynamic Hedging; John Wiley & Sons, New York at Chapter 11.

underlying factors that determine the price of the option. These risk measures are central to the management of the risk of options, hedging options and using options to manage risk in asset portfolios.

In recent times, the derivative measures of risk have been used more generically to capture and present the risk of *all instruments*. This encompasses *assets and forwards* as well as options. This reflects the fact that the risk or value sensitivities of all instruments are capable of being measured, expressed, and communicated easily using this general vocabulary of risk. **Exhibit 15.20** sets out this generalised language of risk that is increasingly utilised.

**Exhibit 15.20    Generalised Risk Measures**

| Risk Measure | Concept for Options | Concept for General Risk |
|---|---|---|
| Delta ($\Delta$) | Delta is the derivative of the option pricing formula with reference to the asset price (S). It measures the estimated change in the option premium for a change in S. | Measures exposure to price change of underlying asset; equivalent to present value of basis point or dollar value of 1 basis point |
| Gamma ($\gamma$) | Gamma is the second derivative of the option pricing formula with reference to the asset price (S). It measures the estimated change in the delta of the option for a change in S. | Measures exposure to change in delta; equivalent to measure of convexity |
| Vega ($\kappa$) | Vega is the derivative of the option pricing formula with reference to the volatility of the asset returns ($\sigma$). It measures the estimated change in the option premium for a change in $\sigma$. | Measures exposure to changes in volatility (only applicable to options) |
| Theta ($\theta$) | Theta is the derivative of the option pricing formula with reference to the time to option expiry (T). It measures the estimated change in the option premium for a change in T. | Measures exposure to or change in value arising from the passage of time; analogous to carry income or expense. |
| Rho ($\rho$) | Rho is the derivative of the option pricing formula with reference to the risk free rate (Rf). It measures | Measures exposure to changes in the discount rate(s) applicable. |

| | the estimated change in the option premium for a change in Rf. | |
|---|---|---|
| Phi ($\phi$) | Phi is the derivative of the option pricing formula with reference to the income on the asset (y). It measures the estimated change in the option premium for a change in the asset income (foreign interest rate, coupon/interest rate, dividend and convenience yields) | Measures exposure to changes in income on the asset. |

# 16
# Delta Hedging/Management of Option Portfolios[1]

## 1 Introduction

The process of risk management of derivative transactions focuses on portfolios. The discussion to date has focused on the risk management of symmetric/linear portfolios (assets/forwards). This requires the portfolio to be mapped into spot asset risks and interest rate positions. The mapped positions are then hedged as required by trading in spot assets or by trading in debt instruments.

Option positions are treated in a similar manner. The option position is mapped in terms of its delta to measure its risk. The management of option portfolios is different. The difference is driven by the asymmetric/non-linear nature of options. Options are hedged by trading in the underlying asset. The intention is to match the delta of the option with the delta of the asset. This means that the return profile of an option cannot be replicated or hedged in a static manner. While other portfolios require some level of dynamic management, risk management of options requires a greater degree of hedge management than other portfolios. This form of

---

[1] The literature of practical option portfolio risk management is limited. The major title is Taleb, Nassim (1997) Dynamic Hedging; John Wiley & Sons, New York at Chapters 3, 13, 14, 15 and 16. See also Briys, Eric, Bellalah, Mondher, Mai, Huu Minh and De Varenne, Francois (1998) Options, Futures and Exotic Derivatives: Theory, Application and Practice; John Wiley & Sons, Chichester at Chapter 6; Hull, John (2000) Option Futures and Other Derivatives – Fourth Edition; Prentice-Hall Inc., Upper Saddle River, NJ at Chapter 13; Cox, J. and Rubinstein, M (1985) Options Markets; Prentice-Hall, Inc; Tompkins, Robert (1994) Options Explained[2]; MacMillan Press, England at Chapter 11 and 14. See also Silber, William L. "Marketmaking in Options: Principles and Implications" in Figlewiski, Stephen, Silber, William L., and Subrahmanyam, Marti G. (1990) Financial Options; Business One Irwin, Homewood, Illinois at 485–516.

dynamic risk management is referred to as delta hedging. Delta hedging is based on using the Greek alphabet of risk to measure and then manage the risk of the position.

Delta hedging refers to the replication or synthesis of the economic return profile of an option transaction by a process of trading in the underlying asset. The capacity to replicate the option using the underlying asset is implicit in the inherent nature of delta that provides a measure of the asset content of the option. The concept is also referred to as option replication, synthetic options or dynamic hedging.

The synthetic replication of an option is used for a number of purposes including:

- Option dealers may enter into transactions with clients where the dealer either sells or buys options. The dealer must offset the market risk of the transaction. The dealer can offset the client position with an offsetting option transaction (either on an exchange or over-the-counter). Where it is not possible to offset the exposure in this way, the dealer may hold and hedge the position either till maturity, or more often, until an offsetting transaction can be entered into. In the period between the initial transaction and the offsetting transaction, the option dealer delta hedges the position to reduce any exposure to movements in the price of the underlying asset.
- Traders may need to synthesise options where, such options are not readily available or traded, or, it is more cost effective to create such options rather than purchasing the options.
- The creation of structured investment products such as capital protected funds or portfolio insurance products requires either the creation or purchase of options. In these situations, the fund/asset manager may prefer to synthesise the option for reasons of cost or customisation[2].

In this Chapter, the process of delta hedging and risk management of option portfolios is examined. The structure of the Chapter is as follows:

- The process of delta hedging is described with a series of examples of increasing complexity.
- The cost of hedging and synthetically creating the option is discussed.
- The risk and risk management of trading and hedging options are analysed.
- Newer approaches to option risk management (such as static option replication) are outlined.
- Issues in managing option portfolios in different asset classes are examined.

---

[2]   The use of synthetic option technology in portfolio insurance applications is discussed in Das, Satyajit (2004) Structured Products Volume 2; John Wiley & Sons (Asia), Singapore at Chapter 5.

## 2 Delta Hedging

### 2.1 Concept

The concept of using a position in the underlying asset to replicate the economic profile of an option is central to both the *pricing* and *valuation* of an option, and the trading and hedging of these instruments.

Delta is the partial derivative of the option valuation formula with respect to asset price. It provides a measure of the change in the option premium for a small change in the asset price. This allows the construction of a portfolio (consisting of the asset and the option) that is protected from small changes in the asset price. For example, a short call position may be hedged with a long position in the asset. The amount of asset held would be equivalent to delta times the face value of the option[3].

For small changes in the asset price, the change in the value of the asset portfolio would offset the equal and opposite changes in the value of the option portfolio. The portfolio would, economically, be a risk free portfolio. This means to avoid arbitrage, the portfolio would only return the risk free rate of interest on the investment in the portfolio. This basic insight is used in all option pricing models such as Black-Scholes-Merton and the binomial pricing approaches to derive the fair value of the option[4]. **Exhibit 16.1** sets out the risk free fully hedged portfolio positions possible.

Implicit in this approach is the capacity for the final payoff of the option to be replicated by trading in the asset underlying the option. This creates an instantaneous hedge against small movements in asset price. This approach can then be extended by dynamically adjusting the hedge. This requires alteration of the holding of the asset and the amount of the borrowing/lending as asset prices change over time, to replicate the option until maturity. The approach allows the synthetic creation of an option by holding delta weight of the asset underlying the option and adjusting the holding of the asset in accordance with changes in the delta of the option[5]. This process is referred to as delta hedging.

---

[3]  Alternatively, the position could be constructed as for each unit of asset held, it would be necessary to sell 1/delta of the call option on the asset.

[4]  See Chapter 7.

[5]  For an introduction to delta hedging, see Rubinstein, Mark and Leland, Hayne E. "Replicating Options with Positions in Stock and Cash" (July-August 1981) Financial Analyst Journal 63–72; Asay, Charles and Edelsburg, Charles "Can a Dynamic Strategy Replicate the Returns of an Option" (1986) Journal of Futures Markets 63–70.

**Exhibit 16.1    Risk Free Hedge Positions**

| Position | Hedge |
|----------|-------|
| Long position in calls | Short $\Delta$ assets for each call held |
| Short position in calls | Long $\Delta$ assets for each call sold |
| Long position in puts | Long $\Delta$ assets for each put held |
| Short position in puts | Short $\Delta$ assets for each put sold |

Delta ($\Delta$) refers to the sensitivity of the option premium to changes in the asset price[6].

## 2.2    Delta Hedging – Simple Example

Delta hedging entails the creation of a synthetic option by using a portfolio consisting of two instruments:

- The asset into which the option can be exercised (cash market instrument or futures/forwards on the underlying asset).
- A risk-free asset, usually cash or high quality securities.

The key to creating a synthetic option is to determine the proportion of cash and asset to maintain in the portfolio. This proportion is adjusted through time in a specific way to replicate the price behaviour of an option. In practice, such a portfolio can be created and managed to give approximately the same premium and outcome as a traded option on the underlying asset.

The intuition for synthetic options derives from the fact that, for example, the price behaviour of a call option is similar to that of a portfolio with combined positions involving holding the underlying asset and cash. Although the price of a call option and the price of the underlying asset change in the same direction, the effect on the price of the call option of a given change in the asset price depends on the current price level of the asset. This is because the number of units of the asset held in the replicating portfolio must be sufficient to equate to the slope of the call option price curve at that particular price level, or the particular option's delta.

**Exhibit 16.2** sets out a simple example of a delta hedge to replicate a call option. The portfolio of short call options and the offsetting portfolio of delta amount of the asset are insulated from small changes in asset price. The change in the value of the options for a given movement in the asset price is substantially offset by the

---

[6]    See discussion in Chapter 15.

equal but opposite change in the value of the asset. The example focuses on a short call position. An identical logic can be used in relation to all option positions. For example, the technique for replicating put options is similar. It entails maintaining a portfolio (where the put option is sold), consisting of cash and a short position in the underlying asset, that is adjusted as the price of the asset changes.

---

**Exhibit 16.2    Delta Hedge – Simple Example**

Assume a call option on a non-income producing asset where the asset is trading at $100. The call option is on the following terms:

Strike price    = $100
Time to expiry = 0.50
Risk free rate  = 10% pa
Volatility     = 20% pa

The call option premium (using Black Scholes) is $8.26. The option delta is 0.6641. Using this information, two portfolios can be constructed:
1. A short position in the options, say 100 options (each on 1 unit of the asset).
2. A long position in 66.41 units of the asset (calculated as delta times the face value of the options or 0.6641 times 100).

The changes in value of the two portfolios, for small changes in the asset price, are set out below:

**Increase In Asset Price (from $100 to $100.10)**

| Initial Portfolio | | | Final Portfolio | | | |
|---|---|---|---|---|---|---|
| **Portfolio 1 = Option** | | | | | | |
| **Asset Price = $100** | | | | **Asset Price = $100.10** | | |
| Amount ($) | Value ($ per Option) | Portfolio Value ($) | Amount ($) | Value ($ per Option) | Portfolio Value ($) | Change In Portfolio Value ($) |
| 100 | 8.26 | 826 | 100 | 8.33 | 833 | −7 |
| **Portfolio 2 = Assets** | | | | | | |
| **Asset Price = $100** | | | | **Asset Price = $100.10** | | |
| Amount ($) | Value ($ per Unit) | Portfolio Value ($) | Amount ($) | Value ($ per Unit) | Portfolio Value ($) | Change In Portfolio Value ($) |
| 66.41 | 100 | 6641 | 66.41 | 100.10 | 6648 | 7 |
| | | | | **Change In Overall Portfolio Value ($)** | | 0 |

| Decrease in Asset Price (from $100 to $99.90) | | | | | | |
|---|---|---|---|---|---|---|
| **Initial Portfolio** | | | **Final Portfolio** | | | |
| **Portfolio 1 = Option** | | | | | | |
| **Asset Price = $100** | | | **Asset Price = $99.90** | | | |
| Amount ($) | Value ($ per Option) | Portfolio Value ($) | Amount ($) | Value ($ per Option) | Portfolio Value ($) | Change in Portfolio Value ($) |
| 100 | 8.26 | 826 | 100 | 8.20 | 820 | 6 |
| **Portfolio 2 = Assets** | | | | | | |
| **Asset Price = $100** | | | **Asset Price = $100.10** | | | |
| Amount ($) | Value ($ per unit) | Portfolio Value ($) | Amount ($) | Value ($ per unit) | Portfolio Value ($) | Change in Portfolio Value ($) |
| 66.41 | 100 | 6641 | 66.41 | 99.90 | 6635 | −6 |
| | | | **Change in Overall Portfolio Value ($)** | | | 0 |

The replicating portfolio must be adjusted as the asset price changes. Changes in the asset price trigger changes in the delta of the option. This will usually entail, in the case of a call option, selling assets as the asset price falls, and buying assets as the asset price rises. If the asset price declines, then the option delta falls. The holding of the assets is sold, with the proceeds being used to partially repay the borrowings used to finance the position. If the asset price at maturity is below the strike price, then the replication portfolio should end up with no holding of the asset at maturity and no corresponding borrowing. This portfolio would have a value of zero. This corresponds to the value of the option at maturity. If the asset price increases, then the option delta increases. The holding of the assets is increased with borrowing being undertaken (for the value of the asset less the premium received) to finance the position. If the asset price at maturity is above the strike price, then the option will be exercised. The replication portfolio should equal the units of asset underlying the option, financed by borrowing equal to the strike price.

Prior to expiry of the option, the replicating portfolio is generally never fully invested when the asset price increases nor fully dis-invested when the asset price falls. The process of portfolio adjustment will increase or reduce the initial investment. Theoretically, by the expiration of the option, the cumulative depreciation should approximately equal the initial theoretical value of the option.

From a theoretical position, the process of delta hedging entails the final option payoff being replicated by the position in the stock financed by borrowings and the option premium received. A model such as Black-Scholes can be reduced for a call option to the following relationship:

Option Premium = Delta times Asset − Amount of Borrowing

This can be given more formally as[7]:

$$P_{ce} = S \cdot N(d1) - K \, e^{-Rf \cdot T} \cdot N(d2)$$

The asset holding is dictated by the delta, or sensitivity to asset price changes of the option. The amount of borrowings is equivalent to the present value of the exercise price of the option, adjusted for the probability that the call option expires in-the-money at maturity. The rationale in a risk neutral and arbitrage free world is that the expected amount due for repayment to the lender is equivalent to this amount.

Two aspects of the replication process should be noted:
- The replication portfolio is inherently self financing.
- The replication portfolio must be dynamically managed, reflecting changes in the factors affecting the option price, leading to changes in the relative holding of the asset and the amount of borrowings.

The concept of creating synthetic options permits option dealers to replicate not only call options, but any option position. Using replicating portfolios, the dealer can, where it has created a risk position by writing options, cover the open positions by creating synthetic options to hedge the existing exposure.

## 2.3   Costs of Replication

The process of replication is not free of cost. The major costs include:
- **Financing of the asset position/investment of the proceeds of a short sale** – the financing cost element is self explanatory. The holding of assets required to hedge a short call option or a long put option will require financing, with the resulting interest expense being incurred. In contrast, a long call or short put option will require short selling the asset, releasing cash that can be invested to earn interest (less any cost of borrowing the asset). In certain assets (such as commodities), there will be additional costs such as physical holding costs (storage, insurance, location/transport and wastage[8]).

---

[7]   The notation used is that in Chapter 7.
[8]   See discussion in Chapter 6.

- **Trading costs** – trading costs cover a variety of items:
  1. *Transaction costs of trading* – this includes the bid-offer spread, commissions and other trading costs. This means that in actual markets, each transaction undertaken as part of the hedge results in a cost to the dealer.
  2. *Gains or losses on trading* – the process of replication requires the dealer (for a call option) to buy high/sell low in the process of dynamic hedge management. This reflects the changes in delta where the holding of assets must be increased as the price goes up, and decreased as the price of the asset falls. For a put option, a similar process is applicable. The short position in the asset must be increased as the price decreases, and decreased as the price increases, resulting in the same pattern of selling low buying high. This pattern of trading inherently creates losses that, together with other costs, make up the cost of replicating the option.
- **Hedge inefficiencies** – loss of hedge efficiency covers the following items, including:
  1. *Delta slippage* – it may not be possible to maintain a delta neutral position under all circumstances. This may be the result of:
     - Use of *periodic re-balancing* rather than *continuous re-balancing*.
     - Incorporation of transaction and trading costs.
     - Discontinuous prices movements that introduce lags in adjustment of the delta hedge.

     The failure to maintain perfect delta neutrality creates exposures to the movement in the *price of the underlying asset*, resulting in gains and losses.
  2. *Re-balancing costs* – this reflects the impact of periodically re-balancing the portfolio. This creates the delta slippage as price movements *between hedge adjustments* are not fully hedged. All delta hedging is a compromise between increased frequency of re-balancing the hedge (that incurs additional trading costs) and less frequent re-balancing (that reduces efficiency of the hedge and exposes the portfolio to gains/losses from changes in the asset price).

In perfect frictionless capital markets, the cost of the delta hedge should exactly equal the theoretical premium of the option. In practice, the factors identified make this unlikely.

## 2.4 Delta Hedging – Issues

In most situations, the value of an option behaves in a manner that is similar to a portfolio consisting of short or long positions in the asset, and cash borrowings or investments. This allows the process of replication.

However, delta hedging, in practice, suffers from a number of difficulties including:

- **Market structure issues** – this includes the ability to borrow/finance or lend the asset. The process of option replication assumes that, where the delta hedge requires holding a position in the asset, it is possible to finance the asset position. Similarly, where the delta hedge requires a short sale of the asset, it is assumed that it is feasible to effect the short sale and it is possible to borrow the asset to implement the short sale. These conditions may not be able to be met in every market.

- **Impact of transaction costs** – the requirement to trade in the underlying asset results in the dealer incurs trading costs. The trading costs are related to the frequency of re-balancing of the hedge. The more frequent the re-balancing, the more accurately the replicating portfolio tracks the underlying option being hedged. The frequency of trading obviously affects the cost by way of increased transaction costs. A related problem is the inability to accurately predict the *level* of transaction costs *in advance*. The position in the asset must be adjusted periodically as the option delta changes. The delta changes are unknown, being a function of the path of asset prices (in effect, path dependent). This means that the exact number or quantum of hedge adjustments is not known in advance, and therefore the transaction costs are not known in advance. **Exhibit 16.3** sets out the trade-off between the frequency of re-hedging and the transaction costs.

- **Pattern of changes in the asset price** – the ability to replicate the value changes in the option through trading in the asset will only be possible for small changes in the asset price, and where the asset price changes are continuous. A large discrete change in the asset price (a discontinuous movement or gap) will significantly impair the effectiveness of the hedge. This reflects the fact that in the event of a discontinuity or gap, the change in the asset position cannot be undertaken sufficiently quickly. The price of the option will adjust immediately. The hedge cost will lag the change in the asset price, creating hedging errors that will create a divergence in the value of the hedge relative to the option. This reflects the fact that the change in the asset price will result in a change in the option's delta. However, the delta of the asset does not change. This means that unless the hedge adjustment can be done instantaneously, the option will be under or over hedged. **Exhibit 16.4** sets out the problem of over and under hedging under delta hedging schemes.

- **Constant volatility and interest rates** – theoretical models of delta hedging assume that the volatility of asset price changes and the interest rate are both

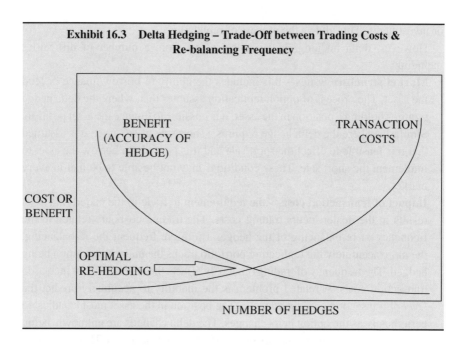

**Exhibit 16.3    Delta Hedging – Trade-Off between Trading Costs & Re-balancing Frequency**

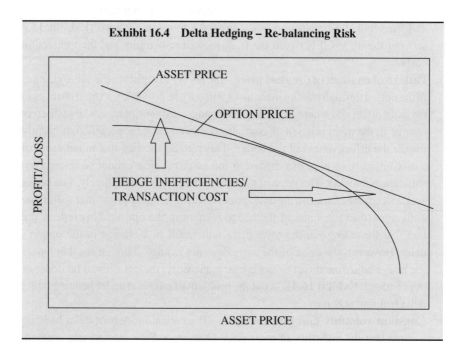

**Exhibit 16.4    Delta Hedging – Re-balancing Risk**

constant over the life of the option. In practice, both variables are uncertain. Changes in each of these terms will impact on the efficiency of the hedge. For example, a change in volatility levels may not be accompanied by a change in the price of the asset. In these circumstances, the value of the option will change, but will not be accompanied by a corresponding change in the value of the asset position. Changes in volatility will also alter the option delta, resulting in changes in the required hedge and impacting on the cost of replicating the option. Changes in interest rates will affect the process of delta hedging in a number of ways. Rate changes alter the forward price of the asset, and hence the value of the option. In addition, it affects the cost of the hedge as it will increase the cost of holding the asset and reduce the cost of shorting.

- **Use of forwards or futures contracts on the asset** – the major rationale for the use of forwards or futures on assets to replicate the option is the off-balance sheet nature of these instruments, and the accompanying efficiencies in the use of capital. However, the use of forwards or futures introduces additional risk factors into the hedging process[9]. The use of forward/futures contracts assumes the fair value pricing of these contracts; that is, the forward price is arbitrage free. In reality, the forward contract may be priced away from fair value, thereby introducing additional errors in the hedging process. The changes in the cash-futures basis (effectively, the cost of carry) may result in higher hedging costs. Similarly, where the forward or futures contract used is of a different maturity to that of the option, the introduced maturity mismatch creates an exposure to changes in the shape of the yield curve. This reflects the fact that changes in short term rates will affect the forward/futures contract value differently from the impact of longer term rates on the value of the underlying option.

## 2.5   Delta Hedging – More Complex Examples

### 2.5.1   Examples

**Exhibit 16.5** and **Exhibit 16.6** describe the concept of using option replication techniques with a series of more complex examples. The examples are designed to highlight some of the risks and difficulties in seeking to replicate options through trading in the underlying assets.

---

[9]   See Kat, Harry M. "Delta Hedging of S & P 500 Options: Cash Versus Futures Market Execution" (Spring 1996) Journal of Derivatives 6–25.

### Exhibit 16.5    Delta Hedge of a Call Option – More Complex Example

**1. Assumptions**

Assume the dealer sells the following call option:

| | |
|---|---|
| Asset Price ($) | 100.00 |
| Strike Price ($) | 100.00 |
| Time to Expiry (days) | 28 |
| Volatility (% pa) | 20.00 |
| Interest Rate (% pa) | 10.00 |

The underlying asset is taken to be a forward contract. The volatility used is the implied volatility at the time of entry into the transaction. The option premium is $2.19 per unit of asset.

The option is on 10,000 units of the asset. This equates to a total strike price of $1,000,000. This is equivalent to a total option premium of $21,927.

The option is to be hedged by trading in the underlying asset. The dealer purchases $\Delta$ units of the asset to hedge the sold call option position. The hedge is to be re-balanced once every week[10].

**2. Option Hedge**

The option hedge is set out in the Table below. The asset price is assumed to fluctuate over time. At the end of each week, the hedge is adjusted by buying or selling assets to equate the asset holding to the delta of the option. The cost of the option is calculated as the interest cost of funding the asset, and the losses on adjustment of the hedge.

| Number of Assets | | | 10,000 | 10,000 | 10,000 | 10,000 | 10,000 |
|---|---|---|---|---|---|---|---|
| Time to Expiry (Days) | | | 28 | 21 | 14 | 7 | 0 |
| Asset Price ($) | | | 100.00 | 101.50 | 99.00 | 100.50 | 102.50 |
| Volatility (Current) (% pa) | | | 20.00 | 20.00 | 20.00 | 20.00 | 20.00 |
| Interest Rate (Current) (% pa) | | | 10.00 | 10.00 | 10.00 | 10.00 | 10.00 |
| Option Premium ($) | | | 2.19 | 2.75 | 1.10 | 1.37 | 2.50 |
| Delta | | | 0.5071 | 0.6273 | 0.4048 | 0.5758 | 1.0000 |
| **Delta Hedge** Hedge Required (asset units) | | | 5,071 | 6,273 | 4,048 | 5,758 | 10,000 |
| **Hedge Transactions** | **Amount** | **Price ($)** | | | | | |
| Purchase Assets | 5,071 | 100.00 | 507,143 | | | | |

---

[10] In practice, the hedge would be re-balanced more frequently. The less frequent re-balancing is used for convenience in this example.

| Purchase Assets | 1,202 | 101.50 | 121,980 | | | | |
| Sell Assets | −2,225 | 99.00 | | | | | |
| Purchase Assets | 1,710 | 100.50 | | | 171,860 | | |
| Purchase Assets | 4,242 | 102.50 | | | | | 434,829 |
| **Value of Hedge Portfolio** | | | | | | | |
| Number of Assets | | | 5,071 | 6,273 | 4,048 | 5,758 | 10,000 |
| Average Value of Assets ($) | | | 100.00 | 100.29 | 100.29 | 100.35 | 101.26 |
| Total ($) | | | 507,143 | 629,123 | 405,936 | 577,795 | 1,012,624 |
| Hedge Adjustment Loss ($) | | | | | (2,865) | | (12,624) |
| Interest Cost ($) | | | | (973) | (1,207) | (779) | (1,108) |
| Cumulative Cost ($) | | | | (973) | (5,044) | (5,823) | (19,554) |

In the above case, the call option expires in the money and is exercised. The dealer is required to deliver the assets to the purchaser of the option. In the case where the asset price at option expiry is below the strike price, the option would not be exercised. Any holding of the asset would be liquidated at maturity, as the option delta would go to zero.

## 3. Hedge Performance
The performance of the hedge is summarised below:

| | |
| --- | --- |
| Premium Receipt ($) | 21,927 |
| Interest on Premium ($) | 168 |
| Hedge Costs ($) | (19,554) |
| Net ($) | 2,541 |

The hedging costs are made up of:

| | |
| --- | --- |
| Hedge Cost ($) | (15,489) |
| Funding Costs ($) | (4,066) |
| Total ($) | (19,554) |

---

**Exhibit 16.6   Delta Hedge of a Put Option – Complex Example**

## 1. Assumptions
Assume the dealer sells the following put option:

| | |
| --- | --- |
| Asset Price ($) | 100.00 |
| Strike Price ($) | 100.00 |
| Time to Expiry (Days) | 28 |

| Volatility (% pa) | 20.00 |
| Interest Rate (% pa) | 10.00 |

The volatility used is the implied volatility at the time of entry into the transaction. The option premium is $2.19 per unit of asset.

The underlying asset is taken to be a forward contract. The option is on 10,000 units of the asset. This equates to a total strike price of $1,000,000. This is equivalent to a total option premium of $21,927.

The option is to be hedged by trading in the underlying asset. The dealer purchases Δ units of the asset to hedge the sold put option position. The hedge is to be re-balanced once every week[11].

## 2.  Option Hedge

The option hedge is set out in the Table below. The asset price is assumed to fluctuate over time. At the end of each week, the hedge is adjusted by buying or selling assets to equate the asset holding to the delta of the option. The cost of the option is calculated as the interest income on the proceeds of the short sales of the asset, and the losses on adjustment of the hedge.

| Number of Assets | | | 10,000 | 10,000 | 10,000 | 10,000 | 10,000 |
|---|---|---|---|---|---|---|---|
| Time to Expiry (Days) | | | 28 | 21 | 14 | 7 | 0 |
| Asset Price ($) | | | 100.00 | 98.00 | 97.00 | 100.50 | 97.00 |
| Volatility (Current) (% pa) | | | 20.00 | 20.00 | 20.00 | 20.00 | 20.00 |
| Interest Rate (Current) (% pa) | | | 10.00 | 10.00 | 10.00 | 10.00 | 10.00 |
| Option Premium ($) | | | 2.19 | 3.04 | 3.47 | 0.87 | 3.00 |
| Delta | | | (0.4852) | (0.6506) | (0.7728) | (0.4223) | (1.0000) |
| **Delta Hedge** | | | | | | | |
| Hedge Required (asset units) | | | −4,852 | −6,506 | −7,728 | −4,223 | −10,000 |
| **Hedge Transactions**[12] | **Amount** | **Price ($)** | | | | | |
| Sell Assets | −4,852 | 100.00 | (485,215) | | | | |
| Sell Assets | −1,654 | 98.00 | | (162,092) | | | |
| Sell Assets | −1,222 | 97.00 | | | (118,536) | | |
| Purchase Assets | 3,505 | 100.50 | | | | | |
| Sell Assets | −5,777 | 97.00 | | | | | (560,362) |

---

[11]  In practice, the hedge would be re-balanced more frequently. The less frequent re-balancing is used for convenience in this example.

[12]  The negative refers to the cash received from the hedge (a negative borrowing).

| Value of Hedge Portfolio | | | | | | |
|---|---|---|---|---|---|---|
| Number of Assets | | | −4,852 | −6,506 | −7,728 | −4,223 | −10,000 |
| Average Value of Assets ($) | | | 100.00 | 99.49 | 99.10 | 99.10 | 97.89 |
| Total ($) | | | (485,215) | (647,307) | (765,843) | (418,496) | (978,858) |
| Hedge Adjustment Loss ($) | | | | | | (4,916) | (21,142) |
| Interest income ($) | | | | 931 | 1,241 | 1,469 | 803 |
| Cumulative Cost ($) | | | | 931 | 2,172 | (1,275) | (21,614) |

In the above case, the put option expires in the money and is exercised. The dealer is required to purchase the assets from the purchaser of the put option. The dealer then sells the assets into the short position acquired. In the case where the asset price at option expiry is above the strike price, the option would not be exercised. Any short position in the asset would be re-purchased at maturity as the option delta would go to zero.

**3. Hedge Performance**

The performance of the hedge is summarised below:

| | |
|---|---|
| Premium Receipt ($) | 21,927 |
| Interest on Premium ($) | 168 |
| Hedge Costs ($) | (21,614) |
| Net ($) | 481 |

The hedging cost is made up of:

| | |
|---|---|
| Hedge Cost ($) | (26,057) |
| Interest income ($) | 4,443 |
| Total ($) | (21,614) |

## 2.5.2 Delta Hedge Performance

In the following discussion, the focus is on the replication of the call option that expires in-the-money (set out in **Exhibit 16.5**). However, the issues in all other cases are similar.

The hedge profit and loss on the call option shows a net gain of $2,541. The gain is calculated as the premium receipt, interest on premium and the hedging cost, incorporating trading losses and the cost of financing the asset positions.

If the option replication position had been consistent with the theory, then the net hedge profit and loss should have been zero. The cost of synthesising the option should have been exactly equal to the option premium. In reality, this will rarely be the case. The difference reflects the following factors:

- *Actual experienced* volatility of asset price changes relative to the *implied* volatility used to price the option.
- Inefficiencies in the hedge process.

In this case, the actual experienced volatility of asset price changes was approximately 18.02% pa. This compares to the volatility of 20.00% pa used to price the option. **Exhibit 16.7** sets out the performance of the hedge portfolio where the actual experienced volatility is used to price the option. The net hedge profit and loss is zero. **Exhibit 16.8** sets out the performance of the hedge where the actual volatility experienced during the term to option expiry is higher than the implied volatility (actual 21.31% pa versus implied 20.00% pa). The hedge performance, in this instance, locks in a loss[13].

The second factor that may affect the hedge profit and loss is the inefficiency in the hedging process. This is caused by a number of factors, including the frequency of re-balancing, the presence of discontinuities or gaps in the asset price path, or non-constant volatility and/or interest rates. In this Section, the impact of re-balancing errors is considered. The other factors are considered in subsequent sections.

The frequency of re-balancing will influence the efficiency of the hedge. As the objective of the hedge is to maintain delta neutrality, each time the asset price changes, the delta of the option will also change. This requires re-balancing of the hedge. The presence of transaction costs dictates that the hedge only be readjusted *periodically*. This is designed to minimise the transaction costs while maintaining delta matching to an acceptable degree. The process of periodic rather than continuous re-balancing necessarily means that the trader will have small exposures to the *asset price changes*. This creates gains and losses from the directional exposure to asset prices, and causes the performance of the hedge to vary from the theoretical option premium.

---

[13] The fact that the actual cost of creating the option synthetically is driven by the *actual experienced volatility* means that end users of options should replicate options where the implied volatility in the market is above the *expected volatility*. This would allow the option user to create the option more cheaply than purchasing it from a dealer. However, the process of hedging/replicating contains significant risks that must be considered. This rationale drives option users to replicate options through delta hedging under certain circumstances.

The impact of the two factors (actual versus implied volatility, and the re-balancing or hedging error) cannot be separated easily (at least on an ex-ante basis). The combination of the two generates the deviation of the hedge cost from the theoretical price of the option.

---

**Exhibit 16.7 Call Option Delta Hedge – Actual Volatility Equal to Implied Volatility**

Assume all the facts set out in **Exhibit 16.5**, except that the option is priced with an implied volatility of 18.02% pa. The option hedge is set out in the Table below.

Changed volatility input

| | Amount | Price ($) | | | | | |
|---|---|---|---|---|---|---|---|
| Number of Assets | | | 10,000 | 10,000 | 10,000 | 10,000 | 10,000 |
| Time to Expiry (Days) | | | 28 | 21 | 14 | 7 | 0 |
| Asset Price ($) | | | 100.00 | 101.50 | 99.00 | 100.50 | 102.50 |
| Volatility (Current) (% pa) | | | 18.02 | 18.02 | 18.02 | 18.02 | 18.02 |
| Interest Rate (Current) (% pa) | | | 10.00 | 10.00 | 10.00 | 10.00 | 10.00 |
| Option Premium ($) | | | 1.98 | 2.57 | 0.95 | 1.27 | 2.50 |
| Delta | | | 0.5061 | 0.6391 | 0.3932 | 0.5830 | 1.0000 |
| **Delta Hedge** | | | | | | | |
| Hedge Required (asset units) | | | 5,061 | 6,391 | 3,932 | 5,830 | 10,000 |
| **Hedge Transactions** | | | | | | | |
| Purchase Assets | 5,061 | 100.00 | 506,058 | | | | |
| Purchase Assets | 1,331 | 101.50 | | 135,087 | | | |
| Sell Assets | −2,460 | 99.00 | | | | | |
| Purchase Assets | 1,898 | 100.50 | | | | 190,725 | |
| Purchase Assets | 4,170 | 102.50 | | | | | 427,471 |
| **Value of Hedge Portfolio** | | | | | | | |
| Number of Assets | | | 5,061 | 6,391 | 3,932 | 5,830 | 10,000 |
| Average Value of Assets ($) | | | 100.00 | 100.31 | 100.31 | 100.37 | 101.26 |
| Total ($) | | | 506,058 | 641,145 | 394,407 | 585,132 | 1,012,603 |
| Hedge Adjustment Loss ($) | | | | | (3,228) | | (12,603) |
| Interest Cost ($) | | | | (971) | (1,230) | (756) | (1,122) |
| Cumulative Cost ($) | | | | (971) | (5,428) | (6,184) | (19,910) |

The performance of the hedge is summarised below:

| Premium Receipt ($) | 19,758 |
|---|---|
| Interest on Premium ($) | 152 |
| Hedge Costs ($) | (19,910) |
| Net ($) | 0 |

The hedging cost is made up of:

| Hedge Cost ($) | (15,831) |
|---|---|
| Funding Costs ($) | (4,079) |
| Total ($) | (19,910) |

**Exhibit 16.8    Call Option Delta Hedge – Actual Volatility Exceeds Implied Volatility**

Assume all the facts set out in **Exhibit 16.5**, except that the actual price experienced over the option life equates to actual volatility of 21.31% pa versus the implied volatility assumed of 20.00% pa. The option hedge is set out in the Table below.

Changed asset price

| | | | | | | Changed asset price | | |
|---|---|---|---|---|---|---|---|---|
| Number of Assets | | | 10,000 | 10,000 | 10,000 | 10,000 | 10,000 |
| Time to Expiry (Days) | | | 28 | 21 | 14 | 7 | 0 |
| Asset Price ($) | | | 100.00 | 101.50 | 98.00 | 100.50 | 102.50 |
| Volatility (Current) (% pa) | | | 20.00 | 20.00 | 20.00 | 20.00 | 20.00 |
| Interest Rate (Current) (% pa) | | | 10.00 | 10.00 | 10.00 | 10.00 | 10.00 |
| Option Premium ($) | | | 2.19 | 2.75 | 0.75 | 1.37 | 2.50 |
| Delta | | | 0.5071 | 0.6273 | 0.3087 | 0.5758 | 1.0000 |
| **Delta Hedge** | | | | | | | |
| Hedge Required (asset units) | | | 5,071 | 6,273 | 3,087 | 5,758 | 10,000 |
| **Hedge Transactions** | **Amount** | **Price ($)** | | | | | |
| Purchase Assets | 5,071 | 100.00 | 507,143 | | | | |
| Purchase Assets | 1,202 | 101.50 | | 121,980 | | | |
| Sell Assets | −3,186 | 98.00 | | | | | |
| Purchase Assets | 2,671 | 100.50 | | | | 268,419 | |
| Purchase Assets | 4,242 | 102.50 | | | | | 434,829 |

| Value of Hedge Portfolio | | | | | | |
|---|---|---|---|---|---|---|
| Number of Assets | | 5,071 | 6,273 | 3,087 | 5,758 | 10,000 |
| Average Value of Assets ($) | | 100.00 | 100.29 | 100.29 | 100.39 | 101.28 |
| Total ($) | | 507,143 | 629,123 | 309,580 | 577,999 | 1,012,828 |
| Hedge Adjustment Loss ($) | | | | (7,288) | | (12,828) |
| Interest Cost ($) | | | (973) | (1,207) | (594) | (1,108) |
| Cumulative Cost ($) | | | (973) | (9,467) | (10,061) | (23,998) |

The performance of the hedge is summarised below:

| Premium Receipt ($) | 21,927 |
|---|---|
| Interest on Premium ($) | 168 |
| Hedge Costs ($) | (23,998) |
| Net ($) | (1,902) |

The hedging cost is made up of:

| Hedge Cost ($) | (20,116) |
|---|---|
| Funding Costs ($) | (3,881) |
| Total ($) | (23,998) |

## 2.5.3 Discontinuous Price Changes/Jumps

The discussion of hedge performance to date assumes that asset price changes are relatively small and continuous. In practice, this condition is unlikely to be met. The presence of discontinuous price changes results in additional hedge inefficiency.

Delta hedging requires changes in asset price (that drive changes in delta) to be matched by adjustments in the hedge. If the change in the asset price is large, in particular a discontinuity or sharp jump, then the lag in adjusting the hedge will necessarily mean a divergence between the replication costs and the theoretical value of the option. In effect, the delta hedge does not cover the gamma risk of the strategy.

This process can be illustrated with an example. **Exhibit 16.9** sets out an example of a hedge under conditions where the asset price jumps sharply (in a classic whipsaw).

The impact of large price jumps is distinct and separate from the impact of higher *actual experienced volatility*. This is because the process of delta hedging is sensitive to *both* the level of *actual* volatility and the *price paths*. In effect, where an option is dynamically hedged, all options are *path dependent*. Discontinuous price changes and price jumps reflect the impact of the different price paths. **Exhibit 16.10** sets out a number of different price paths with the *same* actual realised volatility. In practice, the price paths will create different hedge gains and losses for an option hedged in the underlying asset. This reflects the difficulty of adjusting hedges in discontinuous markets.

---

**Exhibit 16.9    Call Option Delta Hedge – Impact of Large Price Jumps**

Assume the following out-of-the-money call option on an equity index:

| | |
|---|---:|
| Underlying Asset Price (Equity Index Value) | 10,000.0 |
| Strike Price (Equity Index Value) | 15,000.0 |
| Trade Date | 1 November 2001 |
| Expiry Date | 1 November 2004 |
| Time to Expiry (Years) | 3 |
| Volatility (% pa) | 15.00 |
| Risk Free Rate (% pa) | 8.00 |
| Type of Option | Call |
| Exercise | European |
| Dividends (% pa) | 2.50 |

The current value of the option and its delta is set out below:

| | |
|---|---:|
| Option Premium (Index Points) | 259.61 |
| Option Premium (%) | 2.60 |
| Delta (%) | 19.79 |

The dealer hedges the position by trading in index futures or the stocks underlying the index.
    Assume the asset market experiences a series of large price moves (a whipsaw or spike) as follows[14]:

| 1 November 2001 | 2 November 2001 | 3 November 2001 |
|:---:|:---:|:---:|
| 10,000 | 8,000 | 10,000 |

---

[14]    This type of price movement (while very large) was observed in the emerging market crisis in Asia in 1997 and 1998. In addition, similar movements have been observed in gold and equity markets (in particular, technology stocks) over recent years.

The change in value of the option and its delta is as follows:

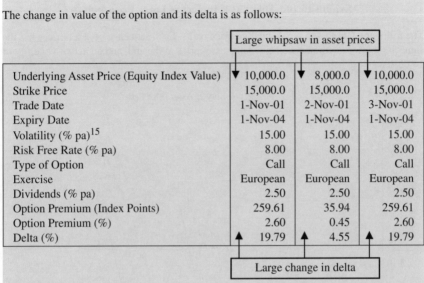

| | Large whipsaw in asset prices | | |
|---|---|---|---|
| Underlying Asset Price (Equity Index Value) | ▼ 10,000.0 | ▼ 8,000.0 | ▼ 10,000.0 |
| Strike Price | 15,000.0 | 15,000.0 | 15,000.0 |
| Trade Date | 1-Nov-01 | 2-Nov-01 | 3-Nov-01 |
| Expiry Date | 1-Nov-04 | 1-Nov-04 | 1-Nov-04 |
| Volatility (% pa)[15] | 15.00 | 15.00 | 15.00 |
| Risk Free Rate (% pa) | 8.00 | 8.00 | 8.00 |
| Type of Option | Call | Call | Call |
| Exercise | European | European | European |
| Dividends (% pa) | 2.50 | 2.50 | 2.50 |
| Option Premium (Index Points) | 259.61 | 35.94 | 259.61 |
| Option Premium (%) | 2.60 | 0.45 | 2.60 |
| Delta (%) | ▲ 19.79 | ▲ 4.55 | ▲ 19.79 |
| | Large change in delta | | |

The impact of the large price "spike" on the dealer will be that the hedge will be adjusted *after the two large price changes*. The effect of this hedge adjustment is that the dealer sells at the bottom and buys back the delta position at the top of the market. The loss on this single hedge adjustment is 305.8 index points (the price changes in the index (2,000) times the change in delta (19.79 − 4.55 = 15.24). *The loss on this single hedge adjustment is larger than the premium received.*

## 2.5.4 Non-constant Volatility

The theoretical assumptions that volatility and interest rates remain constant are unlikely to be realised in practice. In this context, the volatility relevant is *implied volatility*. Changes in volatility will affect the hedging process in two separate ways:
- Changes in implied volatility will impact upon the value of the option, but not the value of the asset position.
- Changes in volatility will alter the option delta and will thereby affect the costs of the hedge.

---

[15] The volatility has not been adjusted. In practice, volatility may also have adjusted significantly as a result of the large price move.

---

**Exhibit 16.10   Volatility – Impact of Large Price Jumps**

The following Graph sets out 4 separate price paths. Each sequence of asset prices has the same asset price at commencement, same asset price at the end, and an actual volatility of 14.05% pa.

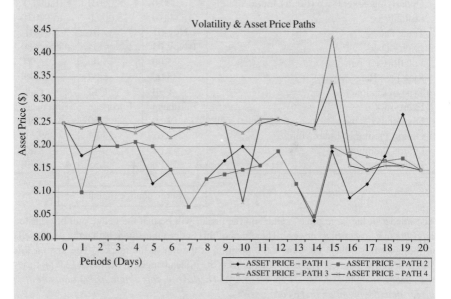

As is evident, some of the paths (Path 3 and Path 4) are characterised by large discontinuous jumps as well as very small price changes.

---

**Exhibit 16.11** sets out the impact of volatility changes. There are the following specific changes:

- The value of the option changes as a result of the changes in implied volatility levels. The impact of the change is only *unrealised gains or losses* where the option is marked-to-market. *There is no realised or cash impact of the change in volatility unless the option is sold or repurchased (that is, the current market volatility is paid or received).* Where the option position is hedged with a dynamically managed position in the asset, changes in *implied* volatility have *no direct cash impact* on the cost of replicating the option, other than through the impact on the option deltas.

- The change in *implied* volatility impacts on the option deltas. An increase (decrease) in volatility decreases (increases) the option delta. **Exhibit 16.11** sets out this effect[16]. The altered position in the asset affects the hedging costs.

It is this second effect on hedging that is critical for the dealer. For the hedge to be accurate, the dealer must satisfy several conditions, including:

- The dealer must price the option using an implied volatility that is at least the same as *the actual volatility to be experienced* over the term of the option.
- The dealer where the option is being delta hedged must use the *actual volatility to be experienced* to calculate the deltas to be used as a hedge. This may be different to the *implied volatility* observable in the market.
- Price change must be reasonably continuous; that is, there must be no large discontinuous price changes/jumps. This requires the dealer to anticipate the asset price path to a certain degree.

---

**Exhibit 16.11   Call Option Delta Hedge – Impact of Changes in Implied Volatility**

Assume all the facts set out in **Exhibit 16.5**, except that implied volatility increases from the original level (20% pa) to 25% pa, or decreases to 15% pa. In each case, the change occurs after 1 week and the volatility remains at the higher or lower level for the remainder of the life of the option.

The option hedge where implied volatility is higher (25% pa) is set out in the Table below.

| | | Increase in implied volatility | | | |
|---|---|---|---|---|---|
| Number of Assets | | 10,000 | 10,000 | 10,000 | 10,000 | 10,000 |
| Time to Expiry (Days) | | 28 | 21 | 14 | 7 | 0 |
| Asset Price ($) | | 100.00 | 101.50 | 99.00 | 100.50 | 102.50 |
| Volatility (Current) (% pa) | | 20.00 | 25.00 | 25.00 | 25.00 | 25.00 |
| Interest Rate (Current) (% pa) | | 10.00 | 10.00 | 10.00 | 10.00 | 10.00 |
| Option Premium ($) | | 2.19 | 3.22 | 1.48 | 1.65 | 2.50 |
| Delta | | 0.5071 | 0.6061 | 0.4266 | 0.5630 | 1.0000 |
| **Delta Hedge** Hedge Required (asset units) | | 5,071 | 6,061 | 4,266 | 5,630 | 10,000 |

---

[16] Compare the deltas with changed implied volatility to those at the original volatility level (see **Exhibit 16.5**). Also see discussion in Chapter 15.

| Hedge Transactions | Amount | Price ($) | | | | | |
|---|---|---|---|---|---|---|---|
| Purchase Assets | 5,071 | 100.00 | 507,143 | | | | |
| Purchase Assets | 990 | 101.50 | | 100,441 | | | |
| Sell Assets | −1,795 | 99.00 | | | | | |
| Purchase Assets | 1,364 | 100.50 | | | | 137,073 | |
| Purchase Assets | 4,370 | 102.50 | | | | | 447,906 |
| **Value of Hedge Portfolio** | | | | | | | |
| Number of Assets | | | 5,071 | 6,061 | 4,266 | 5,630 | 10,000 |
| Average Value of Assets ($) | | | 100.00 | 100.24 | 100.24 | 100.31 | 101.27 |
| Total ($) | | | 507,143 | 607,584 | 427,672 | 564,745 | 1,012,651 |
| Hedge Adjustment Loss ($) | | | | | (2,234) | | (12,651) |
| Interest Cost ($) | | | | (973) | (1,165) | (820) | (1,083) |
| Cumulative Cost ($) | | | | (973) | (4,372) | (5,192) | (18,927) |

The performance of the hedge is summarised below:

| | |
|---|---|
| Premium Receipt ($) | 21,927 |
| Interest on Premium ($) | 168 |
| Hedge Costs ($) | (18,927) |
| Net ($) | 3,169 |

The hedging cost is made up of:

| | |
|---|---|
| Hedge Cost ($) | (14,886) |
| Funding Costs ($) | (4,041) |
| Total ($) | (18,927) |

The option hedge where implied volatility is lower (15% pa) is set out in the Table below.

| | | Decrease in implied volatility | | | | |
|---|---|---|---|---|---|---|
| Number of Assets | | 10,000 | 10,000 | 10,000 | 10,000 | 10,000 |
| Time to Expiry (Days) | | 28 | 21 | 14 | 7 | 0 |
| Asset Price ($) | | 100.00 | 101.50 | 99.00 | 100.50 | 102.50 |
| Volatility (Current) (% pa) | | 20.00 | 15.00 | 15.00 | 15.00 | 15.00 |

| Interest Rate (Current) (% pa) | | | 10.00 | 10.00 | 10.00 | 10.00 | 10.00 |
|---|---|---|---|---|---|---|---|
| Option Premium ($) | | | 2.19 | 2.30 | 0.73 | 1.10 | 2.50 |
| Delta | | | 0.5071 | 0.6632 | 0.3702 | 0.5977 | 1.0000 |
| **Delta Hedge** | | | | | | | |
| Hedge Required (asset units) | | | 5,071 | 6,632 | 3,702 | 5,977 | 10,000 |
| **Hedge Transactions** | **Amount** | **Price ($)** | | | | | |
| Purchase Assets | 5,071 | 100.00 | 507,143 | | | | |
| Purchase Assets | 1,561 | 101.50 | | 158,428 | | | |
| Sell Assets | −2,930 | 99.00 | | | | | |
| Purchase Assets | 2,275 | 100.50 | | | | 228,635 | |
| Purchase Assets | 4,023 | 102.50 | | | | | 412,309 |
| **Value of Hedge Portfolio** | | | | | | | |
| Number of Assets | | | 5,071 | 6,632 | 3,702 | 5,977 | 10,000 |
| Average Value of Assets ($) | | | 100.00 | 100.35 | 100.35 | 100.41 | 101.25 |
| Total ($) | | | 507,143 | 665,571 | 371,557 | 600,192 | 1,012,501 |
| Hedge Adjustment Loss ($) | | | | | (3,964) | | (12,501) |
| Interest Cost ($) | | | | (973) | (1,276) | (713) | (1,151) |
| Cumulative Cost ($) | | | | (973) | (6,213) | (6,926) | (20,578) |

The performance of the hedge is summarised below:

| Premium Receipt ($) | 21,927 |
|---|---|
| Interest on Premium ($) | 168 |
| Hedge Costs ($) | (20,578) |
| Net ($) | 1,518 |

The hedging cost is made up of:

| Hedge Cost ($) | (16,465) |
|---|---|
| Funding Costs ($) | (4,113) |
| Total ($) | (20,578) |

In effect, errors in volatility estimation will affect the price of the option and the delta hedge performance.

### 2.5.5 Non-constant Interest Rates

The change in interest rates impacts on the cost of replication in the following ways:
• The first is its impact on the option delta (through the impact on the forward price).
• The second and more significant impact is by way of higher funding costs in financing the asset holding, or higher investment returns on the proceeds of the short sale.

**Exhibit 16.12** sets out an example of the impact of interest rate changes on the process of replication for an increase and decrease in interest rates[17].

---

**Exhibit 16.12    Call Option Delta Hedge – Impact of Changes in Interest Rates**

Assume all the facts set out in **Exhibit 16.5**, except that the interest rate increases from the original level (10% pa) to 15% pa, or decreases to 5% pa. In each case the change occurs after 1 week and the volatility remains at the higher or lower level for the remainder of the life of the option.

The option hedge where the interest rate is higher (15% pa) is set out in the Table below.

| | | Increase in interest rate | | | |
|---|---|---|---|---|---|
| Number of Assets | | 10,000 | 10,000 | 10,000 | 10,000 | 10,000 |
| Time to Expiry (Days) | | 28 | 21 | 14 | 7 | 0 |
| Asset Price ($) | | 100.00 | 101.50 | 99.00 | 100.50 | 102.50 |
| Volatility (Current) (% pa) | | 20.00 | 20.00 | 20.00 | 20.00 | 20.00 |
| Interest Rate (Current) (% pa) | | 10.00 | 15.00 | 15.00 | 15.00 | 15.00 |
| Option Premium ($) | | 2.19 | 2.75 | 1.10 | 1.37 | 2.50 |
| Delta | | 0.5071 | 0.6255 | 0.4040 | 0.5752 | 1.0000 |
| **Delta Hedge** Hedge Required (asset units) | | 5,071 | 6,255 | 4,040 | 5,752 | 10,000 |

---

[17]  In this case, there is no impact on the forward price as the option is assumed to be on the forward.

| Hedge Transactions | Amount | Price ($) | | | | | |
|---|---|---|---|---|---|---|---|
| Purchase Assets | 5,071 | 100.00 | 507,143 | | | | |
| Purchase Assets | 1,184 | 101.50 | | 120,151 | | | |
| Sell Assets | −2,215 | 99.00 | | | | | |
| Purchase Assets | 1,712 | 100.50 | | | | 172,084 | |
| Purchase Assets | 4,248 | 102.50 | | | | | 435,394 |
| **Value of Hedge Portfolio** | | | | | | | |
| Number of Assets | | | 5,071 | 6,255 | 4,040 | 5,752 | 10,000 |
| Average Value of Assets ($) | | | 100.00 | 100.28 | 100.28 | 100.35 | 101.26 |
| Total ($) | | | 507,143 | 627,294 | 405,144 | 577,228 | 1,012,622 |
| Hedge Adjustment Loss ($) | | | | | (2,844) | | (12,622) |
| Interest Cost ($) | | | | (1,459) | (1,805) | (1,165) | (1,661) |
| Cumulative Cost ($) | | | | (1,459) | (6,107) | (7,273) | (21,556) |

The performance of the hedge is summarised below:

| | |
|---|---|
| Premium Receipt ($) | 21,927 |
| Interest on Premium ($) | 168 |
| Hedge Costs ($) | (21,556) |
| Net ($) | 540 |

The hedging cost is made up of:

| | |
|---|---|
| Hedge Cost ($) | (15,466) |
| Funding Costs ($) | (6,089) |
| Total ($) | (21,556) |

The option hedge where the interest rate is lower (5% pa) is set out in the Table below.

| | | Interest rate is lower | | | | |
|---|---|---|---|---|---|---|
| Number of Assets | | 10,000 | 10,000 | 10,000 | 10,000 | 10,000 |
| Time to Expiry (Days) | | 28 | 21 | 14 | 7 | 0 |
| Asset Price ($) | | 100.00 | 101.50 | 99.00 | 100.50 | 102.50 |
| Volatility (Current) (% pa) | | 20.00 | 20.00 | 20.00 | 20.00 | 20.00 |
| Interest Rate (Current) (% pa) | | 10.00 | 5.00 | 5.00 | 5.00 | 5.00 |

| | Amount | Price ($) | | | | | |
|---|---|---|---|---|---|---|---|
| Option Premium ($) | | | 2.19 | 2.76 | 1.10 | 1.37 | 2.50 |
| Delta | | | 0.5071 | 0.6291 | 0.4055 | 0.5763 | 1.0000 |
| **Delta Hedge** | | | | | | | |
| Hedge Required (asset units) | | | 5,071 | 6,291 | 4,055 | 5,763 | 10,000 |
| **Hedge Transactions** | | | | | | | |
| Purchase Assets | 5,071 | 100.00 | 507,143 | | | | |
| Purchase Assets | 1,220 | 101.50 | | 123,814 | | | |
| Sell Assets | −2,236 | 99.00 | | | | | |
| Purchase Assets | 1,708 | 100.50 | | | | 171,634 | |
| Purchase Assets | 4,237 | 102.50 | | | | | 434,262 |
| **Value of Hedge Portfolio** | | | | | | | |
| Number of Assets | | | 5,071 | 6,291 | 4,055 | 5,763 | 10,000 |
| Average Value of Assets ($) | | | 100.00 | 100.29 | 100.29 | 100.35 | 101.26 |
| Total ($) | | | 507,143 | 630,957 | 406,729 | 578,363 | 1,012,625 |
| Hedge Adjustment Loss ($) | | | | | | (2,886) | (12,625) |
| Interest Cost ($) | | | | (486) | (605) | (390) | (555) |
| Cumulative Cost ($) | | | | (486) | (3,977) | (4,367) | (17,547) |

The performance of the hedge is summarised below:

| | |
|---|---|
| Premium Receipt ($) | 1,927 |
| Interest on Premium ($) | 168 |
| Hedge Costs ($) | (17,547) |
| Net ($) | 4,548 |

The hedging cost is made up of:

| | |
|---|---|
| Funding Cost ($) | (15,511) |
| Hedge Costs ($) | (2,036) |
| Total ($) | (17,547) |

# 3 Option Risk Management[18]

## 3.1 Overview

The use of delta hedging to dynamically replicate option positions entails significant risks that require management. In practice, the risks are expressed, measured and managed using the sensitivities of options as depicted by the Greek alphabet of risk[19]. The major risk dimensions include:

- Delta/gamma (and speed) or exposure to asset price or changes in delta.
- Vega/kappa or volatility risk.
- Theta or time decay risk.
- Rho or interest rate risk.
- Rho with reference to the asset income (phi) or asset income risk.

In addition, the risk impact of time (the "bleed" as manifested through charm and colour) is important in the risk management of option portfolios.

The Greek letters provide a measure of the behaviour of option value as market conditions change. This allows evaluation and management of the risk for an individual option, or more realistically in practice, within an option portfolio. In practice, it is important to differentiate between *model based* risk measures and risk created from large movements in asset price or interaction between risks.

The basic premise of option risk management in a dynamic hedging framework is to minimise or eliminate all risk exposures within the portfolio. This is based around changing the asset position as the delta changes as a result of movements in the asset price or time. It also requires hedging of the other risks (gamma, vega and rho) as markets move or the time to expiry reduces[20].

In this Section, the risk management process for options is examined.

---

[18] For a discussion of option risk management, see Taleb, Nassim (1997) Dynamic Hedging; John Wiley & Sons, New York at Chapters 3, 13, 14, 15 and 16.

[19] See discussion in Chapter 15.

[20] See Rutherford, Janette, Sher, Answer, and Fitzgerald, Desmond "Building Blocks" (July-August 1989) Risk 42–43; Westminister Equity "Building Confidence" (April 1990) Risk 33–36; "The Dangers of Neutrality" (November 1991) Risk 48–49; Leong, Kenneth "Solving Mystery" (December 1990-January 1991) Risk 68–71; Gupta, Ajay "On Neutral Ground" (July 1997) Risk 37–41 Margrabe, William "Delta Hedging Problems & Solutions" (March 1998) Derivatives Strategy 42–44; Rubinstein, Mark "The Real World Pitfalls of Portfolio Insurance" (September 1999) Derivatives Strategy 52–55.

## 3.2 Delta-Gamma Risk

The delta for derivative securities can be defined as the change of its price with respect to the price of the underlying asset. Delta, as a construct, emerges quite clearly from the Black-Scholes-Merton option pricing approach. It implies the possibility of establishing an instantaneous risk free portfolio, consisting of a position in the derivative security and a position in the underlying asset.

The option's delta is essential to managing its risk within a hedge portfolio. The option is hedged by purchasing or selling delta units of the underlying asset. The risk management function (at least for small price changes) is determined by delta neutrality. Where the overall portfolio of options and hedges has a delta of zero, the portfolio is assumed to be protected for changes in value from both price increases and decreases.

The concept of delta also enables one option to be hedged *with another option* on the same underlying asset by creating delta neutral positions. Each option is affected by movements in the price of the underlying asset. Where the options are held in the right proportion (to neutralise delta), the changes in value of the option offset minimising the risk of the portfolio.

By definition, the delta of the underlying asset is always 1.0. In practice, delta hedging generally uses a futures or forward contract on the underlying asset rather than the asset itself. The delta of the forward/futures contract is not exactly 1.0 but is relatively stable[21]. The principles of delta hedging are equally applicable where a futures/forward position in the underlying asset is used, provided the correct forward delta is utilised. The futures or forward contract used as the hedge does not necessarily have to have the same maturity as the derivative security. However, the use of futures or forward contracts introduces the issues of fair value pricing of the forward/futures contracts.

Deltas have the property of additivity. The delta of a portfolio of options and other derivative securities on an asset is the sum of the deltas of the individual options and other assets in the portfolio. This facilitates the use of delta to summarise the price sensitivity of even a very complex portfolio of assets and derivative products.

Delta only holds for very small changes in the asset price. Therefore any movement in the asset price outside a small range leads to a reduction in hedge efficiency. This change in the asset price exposes the portfolio to gap/jump risk, or gamma risk.

Gamma is the change in delta as the underlying asset price changes. As changes in delta produce exposure in a portfolio, the level of gamma can be used to quantify

---

[21]   See discussion in Chapter 15.

the risk of an option portfolio. The gamma of an option is not stationary, but changes as the asset price changes. Gamma is highest when the option is at-the-money with a short time to expiry.

The basic problem of delta hedging is that while the delta of an option varies substantially through its life, the delta of the underlying asset is stable. Consequently, in theory, continual re-hedging is required to keep the portfolio perfectly delta neutral. This problem is sought to be averted by a technique known as gamma hedging, where the intermediary seeks to match the rate at which the deltas themselves vary with changes in asset prices[22].

The concept of gamma neutral hedging recognises that adjusting the portfolio to delta neutrality after each asset price change does not give adequate protection to a portfolio. A gamma hedge is a hedge strategy that attempts to reduce the exposure of the portfolio by reducing total portfolio gamma. A portfolio that is fully hedged will have both a zero delta and a zero gamma. The only means of creating a zero gamma position is to match each option with the offsetting position in that option series. Consequently, gamma is minimised by changing the composition of the option component of the portfolio. Changing the underlying asset side of the portfolio has no impact on gamma.

The notion of delta and gamma neutrality can be stated more precisely. A delta neutral option or book of options hedged with offsetting positions in the underlying asset is one where the value is unaffected by (small) changes in the price of that underlying asset. A gamma neutral option portfolio is one that remains delta neutral as the price of the underlying asset changes.

In practice, gamma indicates the extent of portfolio re-balancing that will be needed for a delta neutral position. A large gamma position indicates that a portfolio will require substantial re-hedging when the asset price alters. In essence, gamma is a measure of the risk exposure of a hedge position that will emerge when the price of the underlying asset changes, particularly where it changes rapidly, in a discontinuous manner or the hedge cannot be adjusted instantaneously. This is particularly the case where there is a jump or large discontinuous change in asset price. The use of gamma to measure and manage the hedge risk is an acknowledgement of the fact that the hedge position in the underlying asset cannot be adjusted continuously as required by theoretical delta hedging.

Gamma risk can be reduced by purchasing options. An alternative measure of managing the gamma exposure on a portfolio is to restructure the portfolio

---

[22] See Frye, Jon "Greek Alphabet Soup: A Recipe for Success" (March 1988) Risk 26–29.

configuration of options to replicate synthetic positions in the underlying asset itself. This entails creating purchased/sold positions in the relevant series of call and put options to offset purchased or sold position equivalents in the underlying asset. This portfolio, by definition, has limited gamma exposure.

In extreme situations, the gamma risk of a portfolio of options or a single option is similar to the risk on a spot position in the asset. **Exhibit 16.13** sets out an example of this type of position.

In summary, delta hedging is only tractable in continuous time markets that are unlikely to be found in practice. The ability to re-hedge accurately is the major problem for the dealer. This problem is complicated by the fact that the Greek letters may not adequately reveal risks under certain conditions. This is the result of the impact of the following factors including:

- Large asset price changes (particularly jumps) will require a large adjustment in the hedge, resulting in hedge losses. This may or may not be detected by *model gamma*.
- Delta is dependent upon the dealer's estimate of the *actual* volatility to be experienced over the term of the option. Inaccurate estimates of volatility will result in inaccurate hedging. This problem is compounded by the fact that large changes in asset price may be accompanied by changes in volatility.
- The performance of the hedge is *path dependent*. The realised volatility *and* the actual price path are critical determinants of the efficiency of the hedge. A sequence of large "choppy" price changes (whipsaws) can lead to significant problems for the dealer in hedging option portfolios.

---

**Exhibit 16.13    Gamma Risk On Short Dated Option**[23]

Assume a dealer has a short position in the following currency option:

| | |
|---|---|
| Amount: | US$1,000 million |
| Type: | A$ put /US$ call |
| Term to Expiry: | (Original term) 6 months |
| Strike Price: | A$1: US$0.7210 |

The option currently has 1 day to go until expiry. The spot exchange rate is A$1: US$0.7330. The option is out-of-the-money. The option has no value. The option's delta is close to 0. The dealer does not hold any hedge position as the option is expected to expire unexercised. In the event that the dealer needed to hedge, it would be necessary to sell A$/buy US$ to offset the underlying risk of the position.

---

[23] The example is hypothetical but based on an actual event.

On the day the option is due to be exercised (at 3:00 PM Tokyo time), the following events unfolded. At Sydney open, a hedge fund aggressively sold A$'s. The hedge fund used the illiquidity of the Sydney market open to simultaneously sell directly to market-makers and through brokers. The hedge fund sold in large amounts and forced the A$/US$ exchange rate down to around A$1:US$0.7220. As a result of follow through selling by other traders, the A$/US$ exchange rate settled by mid-morning around A$1: US$0.7208/0.7215.

The exchange rate is now trading around the strike of the option. The option now clearly has value and the delta of the option is now close to 0.50, reflecting the possibility of exercise.

The dealer was unable to hedge as the exchange rate fell suddenly as a result of the selling onslaught (the market gapped). The dealer is completely unhedged. The magnitude of risk carried by the dealer can be seen by the fact that if the option is exercised, each 0.0001 (1 FX point) will result in a loss to the dealer of around US$139,000(A$192,000). This ignores the premium received. By any measure, the risk is very substantial. It is probable that the dealer has breached its limits as a result of the large spot move.

The resolution of this particular trading problem offers an insight into the relationship between gamma and spot risk in these circumstances. In effect, the dealer is now long A$/short US$ *in spot terms*. The position can be hedged by selling A$/buying US$. The *theoretical* or *model* delta is irrelevant to the risk analysis. In effect, the dealer must decide whether the option is going to be exercised (spot below US$0.7210) or not exercised (spot above US$0.7210). If the option is going to be exercised then the dealer should buy US$1,000 million of US$/sell the equivalent A$. This would exactly cover the option cash flows. If the option is not exercised, then the dealer should not hedge.

In reality, the following events unfolded through the day. The dealer did not hedge to match the option's delta. The option dealer and the spot A$/US$ trader monitored the position closely. They formed the view that the hedge fund had traded opportunistically to exploit the illiquidity of the market. They also formed the view that the hedge fund had taken a short term, not a structural, position. The position was also in-the-money. The dealer formed the view that the hedge fund would look to reverse the position opportunistically to take profits.

The dealer executed the following strategy. In the Sydney afternoon, when the Tokyo market was coming back from lunch, the dealers initiated a modest amount of tactical buying through both brokers and the direct inter-bank dealer lines. This had the effect of changing the A$/US$ trading range to around A$1: US$0.7235/0.7242. This was followed by a sudden and sustained bout of buying (in part to provide the impression of a large buy order). The A$ market predictably gapped up. As the market gapped up, the hedge fund, concerned at the possible loss of its substantial profits on the trade, bought back its original short A$ position (possibly as a result of a stop loss). This had the effect of underpinning the rise in the A$. The dealer sold the A$'s purchased in their trading operation into the market as the hedge fund sought to reverse the position.

The currency ended the day at A$1: US$0.7308/0.7315. In other words, the currency was little changed from its previous day's close or morning open. The option was not exercised.

## 3.3 Volatility Risk

Option values are particularly sensitive to changes in the volatility of the underlying asset. This is referred to as vega or volatility risk.

Volatility risk is a particularly important factor in option portfolio management. This reflects the fact that portfolio management is, in part, an exercise in management of volatility positions. Dealers converse in terms of being short (net short options) or long (net bought options) volatility. The underlying premise is that the dealer's task is to attempt to position the portfolio volatility exposure to seek to profit from changes in volatility level within pre-specified limits.

An important aspect of managing volatility risk is that it can only be neutralised by taking positions in the same or a difference series of options. Volatility is not a determinant of value of the underlying asset, and consequently cannot be neutralised through positions in the asset market itself.

## 3.4 Theta Risk

The option theta measures the rate of change in the value of the portfolio with respect to time where all other value parameters are held constant. In effect, theta measures the rate of time decay for the options or the degree to which it loses its inherent value as a "wasting asset". Theta measures the cost of holding an option, and conversely, the reward of selling an option.

Management of theta is particularly important and the interactions with gamma and vega risks constitute a major component of option portfolio management.

## 3.5 Interest Rate Risk/Asset Income Risk

Rho measures option portfolio risk with respect to changes in the interest rate. The time value for a call option comes partly from the interest that can be earned investing the strike price from the present until the expiration date. Conversely, the purchaser of put options loses interest while waiting until option maturity to receive the strike price. Consequently, changes in interest rates will have an impact on the value of the option. This will depend upon the relationship between the current asset price and the option strike. In-the-money options will generally have a larger interest rate exposure than out-of-the-money options. In practice, the rho or interest rate risk of the portfolio can be managed using positions in the underlying interest rate market based on traditional interest rate risk management techniques[24].

The rho (phi) with reference to asset income is also important. Changes in asset income can have significant impact upon the value of options (through changes in the underlying forward price[25]). Changes in asset income are more difficult to hedge.

---

[24]  See Chapters 13 and 14. In practice, the interest rate exposure is usually amalgamated with and treated as part of the overall interest rate risk of the dealer.

[25]  See for example the discussion on dividend rate changes in Chapters 6 and 7.

## 3.6  Risk Interactions

The individual risk dimensions identified are substantively interrelated. This necessitates a constant process of trade-offs between the various risk dimensions in the management of an option portfolio. In this Section, some key aspects of the trade-offs entailed in option portfolio management are examined.

For the dealer, offsetting the price risk of the portfolio of options by delta based purchases and sales of the underlying asset reduces the risk of the delta neutral portfolio. The value of the portfolio is insulated from the effects of small price changes in the underlying assets. However, such a position still exposes the dealer to significant risks. Delta neutral positions entailing a net purchase of options will have a negative theta; that is, the option position will decline in value over time reflecting the nature of the option as a wasting asset. The value of the option evolves towards its intrinsic value as expiration approaches. In contrast, a delta neutral position that entails sold options will gain in value as expiration approaches.

Interaction of delta and theta in this context may dictate that dealers prefer delta neutral positions that are net sold options to enable them to earn the erosion in the value of the option; that is, benefit from the option portfolio theta. Structuring a portfolio to benefit from theta entails the dealer assuming gamma and vega risk. A portfolio that is delta neutral and short options will require the dealer to rebalance the hedge. This requires, in the case of a sold call, buying when the price of the underlying asset increases and selling the underlying asset where the price falls. Similarly, the portfolio is exposed to increases in value from falls in actual volatility, but loses value from increases in actual volatility.

To an extent, some of these risks are offsetting. For example, theta and gamma tend, at least to some degree, to offset the other. A net purchased option portfolio that is delta neutral simultaneously loses value because of time decay or theta with the passage of time, but improves in value as a result of the movement in price because of the position's gamma risk. Conversely, a delta neutral position entailing a net sold position in options increases in value because of theta each day, but generally decreases in value when the market moves up and down because of the portfolio's gamma risk.

However, the risks are not necessarily entirely offsetting. Theta erosion in option values occurs relatively smoothly over the period to expiration. In contrast, the gains and losses from gamma re-balancing can be large and discontinuous. This reflects the fact that larger gains and losses from gamma occur when there is a sharp change in the price of the underlying asset. This prevents the dealer from adjusting or re-balancing the delta hedge appropriately.

In addition, in a large portfolio, the change in the behaviour of individual risk measures is far from predictable or even. For example, the change in gamma, theta and vega can be different for an up move and a down move. In addition, the risks can change differently, depending upon the magnitude of the asset price move or the specific price path being experienced. For example, a dealer long gamma (that is long options) will prefer to see large price moves around the strike of the options held (at-the-money) than similar magnitude moves a long way away from the strike (out-of-the money). This is because the gamma benefit to the dealer's portfolio will be different. These factors are complicated in the context of a large option portfolio.

## 3.7   Delta Hedging – In Practice

The interaction of these risks forces dealers to generally seek to generate earnings/value from an option portfolio by one or other of the following strategies:
- Operate the portfolio on the basis that portfolio value/earnings derive from the bid-offer spread on purchasing and selling options. By implication, the dealer would, under this strategy, seek to balance the portfolio by purchasing some options and selling others in contrast to being a net purchaser or seller of options.
- Maintain delta neutral/net long or short options portfolio positions, where it is anticipated that the underlying price movements will not be discontinuous (that is, the portfolio has low gamma risk) and volatility of the underlying assets is not expected to change substantially (that is, low vega risk).
- Managing the option portfolio as a volatility risk management function where the dealer seeks to benefit from changes in volatility levels in the underlying asset.

The first approach is relatively straightforward. It is predicated on the notion that dealers view delta hedging in the underlying asset or option replication techniques as a *temporary* substitute for an offsetting option transaction. In effect, the portfolio manager plans to earn the bid-offer spread without worrying about the erosion in value of the option portfolio or the management of the complex gamma and vega risks entailed. The dealer assumes mismatches (either in strike or maturity), but will generally minimise the net long or short position in the option portfolio.

The matching approach often entails what are effectively option spreads[26]. The dealer will buy a quantity of options (with certain strikes and expiry dates) and

---

[26] This is often called neutral spreading. For a discussion of spreading as a form of option risk management, see Smith, A.L.H. (1986) Trading Financial Options; Butterworths, London at Chapters 6, 7, 9, 10 and 11; Taleb, Nassim (1997) Dynamic Hedging; John Wiley & Sons, New York at 258–260.

sell an offsetting (in a delta sense) quantity of other options (with *different* strikes and expiry dates). This will take the form of time or calendar spreads (expiry mismatches) or strike spreads (call and put spreads; back spreads; butterfly spreads[27]). The dealer seeks to capture value from identifying cheaper options and using these to hedge the sold options rather than taking hedging risks.

The matching approach has a number of advantages including:

- The lack of large net positions means that the dealer can reduce the variance of the option portfolio. The strategy has a low level of risk, and will generally have a closely matched book in terms of delta, gamma and vega risks.
- There is limited exposure to the risks of large asset price jumps, shifts in asset volatility and unexpected price paths.
- There is also little exposure to the problems in option valuation and volatility estimation.
- The dealer has limited exposure to liquidity of the market as there is no requirement to specifically match individual options. The focus is on matching the overall risk characteristics of the option portfolio.

The second and third approaches are more trading oriented and are inherently more risky. The approaches entail taking hedging risks (gamma, speed, charm and colour) and volatility risks (vega). The approaches have all the problems identified above.

There are similarities in the two approaches. Both approaches essentially take views on volatility and price movements over time. The approaches seek to generate profits according to the dealer's capacity to anticipate price volatility changes for the underlying asset market without taking a large market risk. The major problem for any option dealer is that the volatility of the underlying asset, as it is used to calculate option values, has a significant level of uncertainty associated with its estimation. Consequently, the expected or true volatility of the asset can change over the life of the option, resulting in changes in portfolio valuation. There are various levels of volatility trading that seek to capture value from different types of changes in volatility[28].

The approaches outlined above are not mutually exclusive. In practice, this dictates that dealers may seek to balance the portfolio to earn the bid-offer spread (in volatility terms) whilst managing the portfolio to be delta, gamma, theta and

---

[27] See Das, Satyajit (2004) Structured Products Volume 1; John Wiley & Sons (Asia), Singapore at Chapter 1.

[28] For a discussion of volatility trading, see Smith, A.L.H. (1986) Trading Financial Options; Butterworths, London at Chapter 8; Taleb, Nassim (1997) Dynamic Hedging; John Wiley & Sons, New York at 260–270.

vega neutral. This is particularly the case where prices or volatility levels in the underlying asset are subject to uncertainty or are experiencing rapid and sudden changes. In contrast, in a market where volatility is "trending"' in one or other direction or the asset price is relatively stable, the dealer may take portfolio positions. The positions are designed to facilitate increases in portfolio value in the event of the anticipated change in portfolio volatility occurring or from the benefit of accruing time value from selling options. Such positions regarding changes in volatility can be both for outright movements in volatility for a particular asset, or positions for changes in the implied pattern of volatility (smile/skew or term structure).

The positioning approach to option portfolios requires additional risk measures. A common approach used is that of strike concentration or expiration pin risk[29].

The concept of pin or strike risk is designed to measure the concentration within the portfolio at specific strike levels in specific time periods. This entails identifying the outstanding volume of options with specific strikes with given times to expiry. **Exhibit 16.14** sets out a typical form of such an analysis.

The primary objectives of this analysis include the following:

- The need to identify large strike concentrations that may give rise to large hedging problems (gamma) in the event of either the asset price trading around the strike close to expiration, or a large price change.
- The ability to anticipate potential hedging requirements in advance. This enables the dealer to decide upon a hedge management strategy in advance in an effort to reduce the overall risk exposure. For example, an anticipated gamma problem can be reduced or eliminated prior to it occurring. The occurrence of a large gamma problem very close to maturity is difficult to hedge[30] in practice.
- The approach overcomes some of the problems of traditional Greek risk measures and the deficiency of option valuation models.

The major driver of this approach to risk management includes:

- The tendency of option strikes to become concentrated around certain critical technical or market boundary levels.
- The behaviour of the asset price can become very volatile around these levels, creating difficulties in managing option positions.

The expiration pin or strike concentration report is typically used by dealers to review the portfolio and scale back/adjust positions consistent with their

---

[29] For example, see Taleb, Nassim (1997) Dynamic Hedging; John Wiley & Sons, New York at Chapter 13.

[30] See the discussion in **Exhibit 16.13**.

expectations/risk tolerances or limits. This is done by trading in options to adjust the portfolio gamma and vega risk.

An additional risk measure used is scenario analysis or simulation methodologies. This is designed to test the risk of the portfolio for specified changes in the asset price as well as the behaviour of dynamic hedges of the portfolio under different price paths[31].

---

**Exhibit 16.14   Strike Concentration/Expiration Pin Report**

The strike concentration/expiration pin report would be structured as follows:

| Time Buckets (business days) | 0 to 2 | 2–5 | 5–10 | 10–20 | 20–40 |
|---|---|---|---|---|---|
| **Option Strikes** | | | | | |
| >110 | | | | | |
| 108 to 110 | | | | | |
| 106 to 108 | | | | | |
| 104 to 106 | | | | | |
| 102 to 104 | | | | | |
| 100 to 102 | | | | | |
| 100 (Current Spot) | | | | | |
| 98 to 100 | | | | | |
| 96 to 98 | | | | | |
| 94 to 96 | | | | | |
| 92 to 94 | | | | | |
| 90 to 92 | | | | | |
| <90 | | | | | |

The selection of the time buckets and the specific strike buckets are based on the relevant market. The dealer/risk manager would select ones that are appropriate to the market structure and conditions.

In each cell, the face value of open option positions would be inserted. The degree of detail varies but would include the following:

• Face value amount of option within the strike and maturity bucket.
• Volume of puts and calls.
• Sign of the position (long or short).

Additional information may be presented, such as the current delta and gamma, as well as the delta and gamma if the asset price moves up or down by a specified level (say, 5 or 10%).

---

[31]  This is identical to stress testing, see Das, Satyajit (2004) Risk Management; John Wiley & Sons (Asia), Singapore at Chapter 3.

## 3.8 Delta Hedging – Experience

The risk of using delta hedging techniques to replicate options can be assessed from the practice of portfolio insurance[32]. This is a practice where asset managers create capital guaranteed (at a pre-agreed level) investments. This is done in several ways, including:

- Holding the asset and dynamically creating a put option on the asset to establish a minimum investment value.
- Investing in cash and trading in the asset to synthesise a call option on the asset to create exposure to increases in the asset price. The minimum portfolio value is represented by the total portfolio value adjusted for the cost of replicating the portfolio (effectively, the option premium).

This practice performed poorly in the equity market crash in 1987[33].

Similarly, delta hedges of option positions in currency, interest rate and commodity markets performed below expectation in the ERM crises in 1992, the bond market collapse in 1994, the Gulf War, the sharp fall in copper prices in 1996 following the disclosure of the Sumitomo copper trading losses and the Asia monetary crisis/Russian default/LTCM failure in 1997/1998[34]. There were also problems in delta hedging of equity options during the LTCM crises of 1997/1998 and the equity market corrections in 2000/2001.

In each case, the failure of the dynamic hedge to efficiently replicate the option position being hedged can be attributed to a combination of the following factors:

- Sharp and discontinuous jumps in asset prices made it difficult to maintain delta neutrality, creating exposure to the *asset price movements*.
- Sharp and unanticipated changes in volatility also affected hedge performance.
- Change in liquidity conditions in the underlying asset markets and the increase in transaction cost that led to rises in the cost of the hedge over that anticipated.

The use of futures contracts to replicate the option due to significant savings in transaction costs may have exacerbated the problems, as the pricing of the futures

---

[32] See Das, Satyajit (2004) Structured Products Volume 2; John Wiley & Sons (Asia), Singapore at Chapter 5.

[33] See Taylor, Jon and Smith, Matthew "Option Replication" (December 1987) Intermarket 16–55; Fitzgerald, Desmond and Rutherford, Janette "Variations on a Theme" (June 1988) Risk 30–31.

[34] For a perspective on practical issues in option hedging see Kryzak, Krystna "Gamma Raison" (May 1990) Risk 21–27; Cookson, Richard "Models of Imperfection" (October 1992) Risk 55–61; Cookson, Richard and Chew, Lilian "Things Fall Apart" (October 1992) Risk 44–53; Chew, Lilian (1996) Managing Derivatives Risk; John Wiley & Sons, Chichester at Chapter 6.

contracts in these stressful conditions may have deviated from fair value, creating further hedge slippage.

# 4 Option Replication – Developments

The risk of replicating options dynamically has led dealers/risk managers and researchers to experiment with different strategies to improve the efficiency of the hedge. The major areas of development include:
- Separate hedging of short versus long dated options.
- Transaction cost incorporated strategies.
- Static option replication techniques.

The distinction between hedging short versus long dated options is driven by the different risk characteristics. For short dated options, the typical option sensitivities (delta, gamma, vega, theta, and rho) may not provide accurate risk measures. This reflects the more significant impact of sharp movements in asset price and volatility in these options. This has led to the development of approaches to option portfolio management that segment the portfolio by remaining time to maturity. A typical segmentation would be short (under 30 days), medium (up to 6–12 months) and long (beyond 12 months).

Within this segmented framework, the principal, albeit not the sole focus, is as follows:
- For short options, gamma risk management is important.
- For medium to longer dated options, vega risk management is important.

This segmentation also has implications for the process of replication and the underlying instrument used. The risk of volatility changes for longer dated options favours the use of *options* rather than the asset to replicate these positions. This is discussed below in the context of static option replication.

The presence of transaction costs impacts on the cost of the hedge, leading to a trade off between frequency of re-hedging and the transaction costs incurred. The impact of transaction costs is that the trader must, of necessity, select a hedging strategy incorporating a discrete hedging algorithm. This has implications for the valuation of the option. A number of models have emerged that provide hedging strategies for the replication of options incorporating transaction costs. The models are based on placing boundaries on the risk of replication measured by the variance of the hedge portfolio. Alternative approaches use utility functions that relate both the risk and return[35].

---

[35] For discussion on different strategies for optimising the cost of hedging options see Wilmott, Paul (1998) Derivatives: The Theory and Practice of Financial Engineering;

Static portfolio replication entails the use of *options* rather than trading in the underlying asset to replicate the option. The major rationale for this type of replication is that it avoids the risk of under performance of the hedge where the asset price moves are discontinuous/large or where there are shifts in volatility levels. The major application of static portfolio replication is in relation to longer dated or more complex options (including exotic options[36]).

The basic approach is to model the option payoff (using an option pricing model) at maturity using different asset prices and volatility. The model payoff is then replicated by a portfolio of options (with different expiry and strike prices). The technique usually involves the use of some form of optimisation technique such as multiple regression to generate the portfolio of options which best replicates the option sought to be synthesised[37].

# 5 Delta Hedging – Different Asset Classes

## 5.1 Adapting Delta Hedging to Other Assets

The concept of delta hedging has been developed within a generic framework. In practice, the approach is used in relation to individual assets. In this Section, the adaptation of the generic framework to specific types of assets is considered.

The primary issue in adapting the generic approach is the instrument to be used to effect the hedge. **Exhibit 16.15** sets out a summary of options and the types of hedges generally used by dealers.

Forwards/futures are used frequently by dealers to hedge option positions. The delta of the forward/futures contract is not identical to that of the asset, and the hedge needs to be adjusted for this fact.

---

John Wiley & Sons, Chichester at Chapter 21. See also Whalley, Elizabeth, and Wilmott, Paul "Counting the Cost" (October 1993) Risk 59–66; Whalley, Elizabeth, and Wilmott, Paul "Hedge with an Edge" (October 1994) Risk 82–85.

[36] Static hedging of options is examined in the context of exotic options, see Das, Satyajit (2004) Structured Products Volume 1; John Wiley & Sons (Asia), Singapore at Chapters 5 and 7 to 11 (inclusive).

[37] For a discussion of static hedging see Hull, John (2000) Option Futures and Other Derivatives – Fourth Edition; Prentice-Hall Inc., Upper Saddle River, NJ at 487–489; Wilmott, Paul (1998) Derivatives: The Theory and Practice of Financial Engineering; John Wiley & Sons, Chichester at Chapter 30. See also Frye, Jon "Static Portfolio Replication" (November 1988) Risk; Choie, Kenneth S. and Novomestky, Frederick "Replication of Long Term with Short Term Options" (Winter 1989) Journal of Portfolio Management 17–19; Derman, Emanuel, Ergener, Deniz and Kani, Iraj "Forever Hedged" (September 1994) Risk 139–145.

| Exhibit 16.15    Delta Hedging – Options on Different Assets | |
| --- | --- |
| **Asset Class/Instrument** | **Hedging Instrument** |
| *Interest Rates/Debt* | |
| Options on futures on short term rates | Short term interest rate futures contract |
| Options on futures on government bonds | Bond futures contract |
| Bond options | Bonds or bond forwards/bond futures contracts |
| Caps/floors | FRAs, interest rate swaps or short term interest rate futures contracts |
| Options on Interest Rate Swaps/Swaptions | (Forward starting) Interest rate swaps |
| *Currencies* | |
| Option on currency futures | Currency futures |
| Currency options | Spot currency or currency forwards/futures |
| *Equities* | |
| Equity index options | Equity index futures contracts or equity index swaps |
| Equity options/warrants | Spot equities or equity swaps |
| *Commodities* | |
| Commodity options | Spot commodity or commodity forwards/futures |
| Commodity index options | Commodity index futures |
| Commodity options (caps; floors) | Spot commodity, commodity swaps or commodity forwards/futures |

The most complex form of hedging relates to the management of cap/floor portfolios. This reflects the fact that the instruments are a *series of options*. This special issue related to hedging caps/floors is discussed in the next Section.

## 5.2   Hedging Cap/Floor Portfolios[38]

The complexity of hedging cap/floor portfolios derives from the fact that the instrument consists of a series of separate options *all having the same strike price*. Caps/floors are typically hedged in a number of ways:
• By trading in options on short term interest rate futures contracts.

---

[38] See Miron, Paul and Swannell, Philip (1991) Pricing and Hedging Swaps; Euromoney Books, London at Chapter 10; Flavell, Richard (2002) Swaps and Other Derivatives; John Wiley & Sons, Chichester at Chapters 7.

- Using futures contracts on short term interest rates (for example, the Eurodollar contract) or options on the futures contracts. FRAs are used less frequently.
- Using interest rate swaps because the interest rate swap replicates the strip of underlying forward interest rates that drive the value of caps/floors.

Dealers trading in caps/floors may use options on short term interest rates to hedge risk positions in the cap/floor portfolios. The OTC option (that is, the cap or floor) is designed to suit the needs of the user. This results in contract sizes, exercise prices and expiration dates that may not correspond to the limited ranges of values that characterise the futures options market. This means that construction of the hedge requires determination of a traded option position which best approximates the cap or floor position over time.

In designing the exchange-traded hedge for the cap or floor position, the following factors are relevant:
- Where the dealer in the cap or floor is likely to trade the option before expiration, the hedge in the exchange-traded market must be equivalent and opposite to the OTC option position. This is to ensure matching movements continuously in the fair price of the OTC option in the period before expiration.
- In the event that the OTC option is likely to be held till expiry, then the dealer may construct a hedge to immunise the portfolio from an *increase* in the intrinsic value of the option that exceeds the original fair price.

In practice, it is difficult to identify the two specific classes of options, resulting in sellers designing the hedge as an equivalent, opposite and offsetting position for the cap or floor that is created.

In designing the hedge, a number of specific factors need to be considered:
- **Size mismatches** – the size mismatch relates to the fact the size of the option on the futures contract is fixed, and only multiples of the exchange-traded option can be used. This can result in size mismatches between the hedge and the cap or floor option.
- **Strike price mismatches** – strike price mismatches result from the fact that the exchange-traded option strike prices may not correspond to the prices of the cap or floor being hedged. Such an exercise price mismatch can be handled using a mixture of options from either side of the cap or floor strike price to produce the combined position that behaves similarly to the option being hedged. The objective is to produce a weighted average exercise price approximating the cap or floor option exercise price. In practice, such a hedge will be imperfect. This results from the fact that the price of the cap or floor is, as a theoretical matter, not simply a linear combination of the option premiums on either side.

• **Expiry date mismatches** – expiry date mismatches reflect the fact that the maturity of the cap and floor being hedged may not be capable of being matched by the corresponding expiry date of the exchange-traded options, which are fixed. The difficulty that this mismatch gives rise to is that if an exchange-traded option with an expiry date longer than the expiration date of the cap or floor is used, the time value of the traded option is greater than that of the cap or floor. This difference will be lost if a major change in the underlying asset price occurs and the option expires out-of-the-money.

Where exchange-traded options are used to hedge cap and floor positions, simple linear interpolation/extrapolation produces effective hedge positions only within specific profit and loss boundaries. In the event that volatility of the underlying asset market changes significantly, interaction of volatility and time to maturity may greatly affect the efficiency of the hedge.

Where the caps or floors are dynamically hedged, the issues are different. Where futures contracts on short term interest rate futures are used, the dealer will determine the delta of each caplet or floorlet. The delta of each caplet or floorlet is then matched by taking a long or short position in the underlying futures contract. Where futures contracts are used, it is necessary to adjust for the following factors:

• The convexity of the futures contract.
• Any potential mis-pricing of the futures contracts.
• The impact of funding margin calls on the futures position.
• The potential mismatches identified above in relation to using options on futures contracts to hedge.

Where interest rate swaps are used, the dealer determines the delta of the total options (that is, the combined delta of the individual caplets or floorlets). The delta of the cap/floor is then matched by taking an offsetting position in an interest rate swap with an equivalent delta.

There are a number of special considerations in managing the risk of cap/floor portfolios[39], mostly due to the fact that the cap or floor consists of a series of options.

Caps and floors are usually modelled as a strip of European options on the relevant floating rate index. Each option has an expiry date corresponding to the

---

[39] See discussion on the risks of delta hedging in Conde, Cristobal "Risk Management Techniques for Writers of Caps and Floors" in (1986) Interest Rate Caps, Floors and Collars; Proceeding of conference organised by Institute for International Research at 10 St. James Square, London SW1.

settlement frequency and strike prices corresponding to the interest rate cap or floor level under the agreement. As the cap or floor level is set at a single interest rate, then the distant periods typically are either deep in-the-money or out-of-the-money, depending on the shape of the yield curve.

In certain circumstances, this allows the distant periods to be hedged at nearly a one to one hedge ratio or delta of 1. This would entail matching this component with an interest rate swap. This is because the low gamma of that section of the commitment should, in theory, require infrequent re-balancing of the hedge. In these circumstances, the short term portion of the cap is hedged separately. This type of approach requires complex modelling techniques that split the transactions into various constituent elements that are analysed and hedged separately. The separation of the various elements of these agreements is important, as typically each element reflects significant differences in market conditions and/or rate expectations. For example, once a cap is decomposed, it can be hedged using portfolio hedging techniques such as a strip of delta hedges or option gamma matching techniques.

A special problem relating to long-term caps and floors is that the long maturities extend well beyond the usual hedging tools used to manage delta hedge portfolios in debt options, such as futures contracts that are only available for periods generally up to 2 to 5 years in most currencies. In these circumstances, it is common to construct hedges that combine standard option hedging strategies with interest rate swap transactions. This can be seen from the following example.

Assume a flat yield curve at 8.00% pa. A 5 year cap on 6 month US$ LIBOR is equivalent to a purchase of a 5 year floor plus a position in an interest rate swap (paying fixed/receive floating) with a fixed semi-annual coupon of 8.00% pa, where both the cap and the floor are struck at the swap rate and if the fixed rate is paid on the same basis as the floating rate. For all changes in rates, it can be shown that the positions will generate equivalent cash flows. For rates above the cap level, say 10.00% pa, the holder of the cap will be paid the difference between LIBOR and 8.00% pa; that is, 2.00% pa. The floor and the swap combination generate the same cash flow. Since rates are above 8.00% pa, the floor by itself generates no income, while the swap entitles the holder to the difference between the 8.00% pa fixed outflow and the 10.00% pa floating index which gives a net payment of 2.00% pa. For rates below the cap level, say 6.00%, the cap holder receives no payment. The floor generates a positive cash flow equal to the difference between 8.00% pa and the index level, that is 2.00% pa. This covers the shortfall on the interest rate swap between the fixed payment outflow of 8.00% pa and the floating payment received, 6.00% pa. At exactly 8.00% pa, none of the transactions generate cash flows. Since the two positions are equivalent, the cost of the two portfolios should be the same. Thus, the cost of the cap will be the same as the cost of the interest rate swap plus the cost of the floor. Since an at-the-market swap is a par swap, no payment would pass between the two parties, and the cost of the floor would equal the cost of the gap[40].

Delta or gamma neutral hedging does not completely eliminate risk. The risks in the context of hedging cap/floor portfolios include:

- **Volatility risk** – option positions hedged through delta hedging are susceptible to losses on changes in the volatility of the market. The volatility risk is eliminated only by hedging caps/floors with other options. The general problems of volatility are complicated by the fact that the value and hedging of the cap is affected by shifts in the volatility of each of the forwards underlying the individual caplets and floorlets. This is compounded by the fact that some of the caplets and floorlets are deeply in or out-of-the-money. This means that the hedge is affected by the term structure and skew of volatility.

- **Interest rate shifts** – as interest rates move, different instruments in the portfolio will be affected differently. Shifts through time and non-parallel yield curve shifts are particularly problematic as they require modelling the behaviour of forward-forward rates through time, based on the underlying yield curve. Assumptions must be made in relation to the basis relationship between instruments exhibiting different yield curves, as well as the shape of various yield curves. This has led to the use of term structure models to price and hedge interest rate caps/floors[41].

- **Jump or "gap" risk** – a major problem relates to the fact that the delta hedge requires constant re-balancing, which is not practically feasible. Where periodic re-balancing is used, the portfolio is adjusted after asset prices have moved, which means that the wrong proportion of asset is held in the portfolio. This problem is accentuated where asset prices jump or gap significantly, as the change in value of the hedge position is different from that which would be achieved with an option. This problem is complicated where the position is whipsawed. As re-balancing of the hedge is undertaken after the initial move in asset prices, any immediate reversal in the asset price, after adjustment of the hedge, can lead to the option grantor sustaining losses as a result of holding the wrong number of contracts. Interest rates are mean reverting or subject to boundaries that tend to complicate the behaviour of the hedge. This is particularly at the short end of the yield curve, where the impact of changes in monetary policy can have the effect of driving jumpy discontinuous changes in interest rates.

---

[40] This analysis is effectively an application of put-call parity.
[41] See Chapter 8.

- **Settlement policies** – different settlement policies between the option granted and the hedge instruments have to be accounted for in the computation of the hedged risk position for those instruments.
- **Transaction costs** – trading incurs transaction costs. In volatile markets, the transaction costs can become very large, as bid-offer spreads widen and markets become thin. Even if volatility remains fairly stable, strict delta hedging can be more costly than expected if a market becomes choppy. Delta hedging also requires the writer to monitor the position to continually adjust hedge positions, an approach that can be quite costly. This is exacerbated in the case of caps/floors hedged with interest rate swaps because of the higher transaction costs. In addition, the higher counterparty credit risk may create higher trading costs.

# 6   Summary

The potential to replicate options through trading in the underlying asset is inherent in the approach to valuation of options. By trading in the asset and either financing the investment or investing the proceeds of a short sale and adjusting the asset position as asset prices, volatility, interest rates and time to maturity changes, it is theoretically possible to replicate the economic profile of an option. However, the process of delta hedging is only accurate for small movements in asset. In particular, sharp and discontinuous changes in asset prices, changes in volatility or changes in interest rates may expose the trader to the risk of the asset hedge underperforming the option sought to be replicated. This dictates the use of sophisticated risk control mechanisms to monitor and manage the risk of the replicating portfolio to maintain the accuracy of the hedge and to match its performance to that of the option.

# Index

# The Swaps & Financial Derivatives Library

*The Swap & Financial Derivatives Library* is a unique, authoritative and comprehensive 4 volume reference work for practitioners on derivatives. It brings together all aspects of derivative instruments within a cohesive and integrated framework covering:

- **Derivative Instruments and Pricing** – including derivative instruments (exchange-traded markets and over-the-counter markets), pricing, valuation and trading/hedging of derivatives.
- **Risk Management** – including market risk, credit risk, liquidity risk, model risk, operational risk as well as documentation, accounting, taxation and regulatory aspects of derivatives.
- **Structured products** – including synthetic asset structures (asset swaps), exotic options, interest rate/ currency products, equity products, commodity (energy, metals and agricultural) products, credit derivatives and new derivative markets (insurance, weather, inflation/ macro-economic indicators, property and emissions).

The *Library* is organised into individual volumes:

> **Derivative Products & Pricing**
> **Risk Management**
> **Structured Products: Exotic Options, Interest Rates; Currency**
> **Structured Products: Equity, Commodity, Credit; New Markets**

Each volume is a standalone work. The reader can acquire and use an individual volume or any combination of the 4 separate volumes based on their requirements.

The organisation of each volume is as follows:

> **Derivative Products & Pricing**

> **Role and Function of Derivatives**
1. Financial Derivatives Building Blocks - Forward & Option Contracts
> **Derivative Instruments**
2. Exchange-Traded Products - Futures & Options On Futures Contracts
3. Over-The-Counter Products - FRAs, Interest
   Rate Swaps, Caps/ Floors, Currency Forwards, Currency Swaps, Currency Options
> **Pricing & Valuing Derivative Instruments**
4. Derivatives Pricing Framework
5. Interest Rates & Yield Curves
6. Pricing Forward & Futures Contracts
7. Option Pricing
8. Interest Rate Options Pricing
9. Estimating Volatility & Correlation
10. Pricing Interest Rate & Currency Swaps
11. Swap Spreads
> **Derivative Trading & Portfolio Management**
12. Derivatives Trading & Portfolio Management
13. Hedging Interest Rate Risk - Individual Instruments
14. Hedging Interest Rate Risk - Portfolios
15. Measuring Option Price Sensitivities - The Greek Alphabet Of Risk
16. Delta Hedging/Management Of Option Portfolios

> **Risk Management**

> **Risk Management Principles**
1. Framework For Risk Management
> **Market Risk**
2. Market Risk Measurement - Value At Risk Models
3. Stress Testing
4. Portfolio Valuation/Mark-To-Market
> **Credit Risk**
5. Derivative Credit Risk: Measurement
6. Derivative Credit Exposure: Management & Credit Enhancement
7. Derivative Product Companies
> **Other Risks**
8. Liquidity Risk
9. Model Risk
10. Operational Risks
> **Organisation of Risk Management**
11. Risk Management Function
12. Risk Adjusted Performance Management

**Operational Aspects**
13. Operational, Systems &Technology Issues
**Legal/ Documentary, Accounting & Tax Aspects of Derivatives**
14. Legal Issues & Documentation
15. Accounting Issues
16. Taxation Aspects of Swaps and Financial Derivatives
**Regulatory Aspects of Derivatives**
17. Credit Risk: Regulatory Framework Appendix: Basle II
18. Market Risk: Regulatory Framework Appendix: Basle I996

**Structured Products Volume 1**

**Applications of Derivatives**
1. Applications of Derivative Instruments
2. Applications Of Forwards/Futures, Swaps & Options
3. New Issue Arbitrage
**Synthetic Assets**
4. Synthetic Assets - Asset Swaps, Structured Notes, Repackaging And Structured Investment Vehicles
**Exotic Options**
5. Exotic Options
6. Packaged Forwards & Options
7. Path Dependent Options
8. Time Dependent Options
9. Limit Dependent Options
10. Pay-off Modified Options
11. MultiFactor Options
12. Volatility Products
**Interest Rate & FX Structures**
13. Non Generic Swap Structures
14. Basis Swaps
15. Options On Swaps/ Swaptions
16. Callable Bonds
17. Constant Maturity Products
18. Index Amortising Products
19. Interest Rate Linked Notes
20. Currency Linked Notes

**Structured Products Volume 2**

**Equity Linked Structures**
1. Equity Derivatives - Equity Futures, Equity Options/ Warrants & Equity Swaps
2. Convertible Securities
3. Structured Convertible Securities
4. Equity Linked Notes
5. Equity Derivatives - Investor Applications
6. Equity Capital Management - Corporate Finance Applications Of Equity Derivatives
**Commodity Linked Structures**
7. Commodity Derivatives - Commodity Futures/Options, Commodity Swaps And Commodity Linked Notes
8. Commodity Derivatives - Energy (Oil, Natural Gas And Electricity) Markets
9. Commodity Derivatives - Metal Markets
10. Commodity Derivatives - Agricultural And Other Markets
**Credit Derivatives**
11. Credit Derivative Products
12. Credit Linked Notes/ Collateralised Debt Obligations
13. Credit Derivatives/ Default Risk - Pricing And Modelling
14. Credit Derivatives - Applications/ Markets
**New Markets**
15. Inflation Indexed Notes And Derivatives
16. Alternative Risk Transfer/ Insurance Derivatives
17. Weather Derivatives
18. New Markets - Property; Bandwidth; Macro-Economic & Environmental Derivatives
19. Tax And Structured Derivatives Transactions
**Evolution Of Derivatives Markets**
20. Electronic Markets And Derivatives Trading
21. Financial Derivatives - Evolution And Prospects

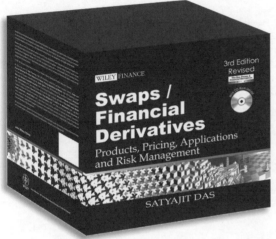